BUILDI TEACHERS

SECOND EDITION

A Constructivist Approach to Introducing Education

David Jerner Martin
Kennesaw State University

Kimberly S. Loomis
Kennesaw State University

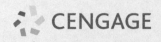
CENGAGE

Australia • Brazil • Canada • Mexico • Singapore • United Kingdom • United States

CENGAGE

Building Teachers: A Constructivist Approach to Introducing Education, **Second Edition**
David Jerner Martin and Kimberly S. Loomis

Editor-in-Chief: Linda Ganster

Executive Editor: Mark Kerr

Managing Development Editor: Lisa Mafrici

Editorial Assistant: Greta Lindquist

Media Editor: Elizabeth Momb

Brand Manager: Melissa Larmon

Senior Market Development Manager: Kara Kindstrom

Content Project Manager: Samen Iqbal

Art Director: Jennifer Wahi

Manufacturing Planner: Doug Bertke

Rights Acquisitions Specialist: Don Schlotman

Production Service: Jill Traut, MPS Limited

Text and Photo Researcher: Sarah Evertson

Copy Editor: Heather McElwain

Designer: Diane Beasley

Cover Image: shutterstock/16186921

Compositor: MPS Limited

For product information and technology assistance, contact us at
Cengage Customer & Sales Support, 1-800-354-9706.

For permission to use material from this text or product,
submit all requests online at **www.cengage.com/permissions**.
Further permissions questions can be e-mailed to
permissionrequest@cengage.com.

Library of Congress Control Number: 2012939241

Student Edition:
ISBN-13: 978-1-133-94301-3
ISBN-10: 1-133-94301-2

Loose-leaf Edition:
ISBN-13: 978-1-133-94306-8
ISBN-10: 1-133-94306-3

Cengage
200 Pier 4 Boulevard
Boston, MA 02210
USA

Cengage is a leading provider of customized learning solutions with office locations around the globe, including Singapore, the United Kingdom, Australia, Mexico, Brazil, and Japan. Locate your local office at **www.cengage.com/global**.

To learn more about Cengage platforms and services, register or access your online learning solution, or purchase materials for your course, visit **www.cengage.com**.

Printed in the United States of America
3 4 5 6 7 8 25 24 23 22 21

This work is dedicated to

Marilyn Kern Loomis and the memory of A. Reeve Loomis, Jr.

The memory of Mary Lou Martin

And all the teachers, professors, colleagues, and students who have taught us

Brief Contents

Contents

2 Your Philosophy of Education   34

White Cross Productions/Getty Images

PART II   STUDENT   67

White Cross Productions/Getty Images

4 The Student and the Teacher: Acknowledging Unique Perspectives 93

5 ## The Student and the Teacher: Acknowledging Unique Abilities 126

White Cross Productions/Getty Images

PART III   SCHOOL   157

6   Purposes of Schools   158

White Cross Productions/Getty Images

7 Structure of Schools   182

White Cross Productions/Getty Images

White Cross Productions/Getty Images

PART IV SOCIETY

253

10 Historical Perspectives 254

White Cross Productions/Getty Images

11 School Governance and Finance   291

White Cross Productions/Getty Images

White Cross Productions/Getty Images

12 Social Issues and the School's Response 319

White Cross Productions/Getty Images

14 Education Reform: Standards and Accountability 365

White Cross Productions/Getty Images

PART V   BUILDING A TEACHER   395

15 Your Motives for Teaching 396

White Cross Productions/Getty Images

Features

CONTROVERSIES IN EDUCATION

TECHNOLOGY & EDUCATION

Preface

Welcome to the second edition of *Building Teachers: A Constructivist Approach to Introducing Education*. Being a teacher in today's society is difficult. Students have heard or read about many of the challenges facing teachers, such as accountability, standardized testing, integrating technology effectively into teaching, engaging and motivating *all* students to learn, addressing diversity including students with special needs, managing the classroom, and working with parents and the community, among others. Those of us who have been in education for any length of time know, however, that the rewards of teaching can make meeting those challenges head-on very worthwhile. How can this book help you and your teacher education students begin their preparation? Certainly, there is a lot they already know about education. But, there is also a lot that they don't know and, of course there is a lot that they don't even realize that they don't know. This book is a great place for them to start their program. It is packed with individual inquiries, descriptions of best practices, and some of the suggested solutions to today's challenges. The material we present is entirely research-based and has been shown to be effective.

The Constructivist Approach

This book is constructivist in nature. It is markedly different from other introduction to education textbooks. From the ground up, we designed it around a constructivist framework that reflects our sincere belief that people learn best when they are able to construct their own knowledge and understandings of any given topic. Its purpose is to encourage students who are interested in becoming teachers to construct basic understandings of what it means to be a teacher. We wrote it to help instructors and students actually implement the constructivist approach. This means that the book is interactive in nature and inductive in approach.

We begin each chapter by asking students to explore what they already know about the topic at hand, and we encourage them to build on that knowledge by investigating additional information from the research, the media, government agencies, professional societies, psychologists, philosophers, other teachers, and many other sources. We then ask students to construct new understandings by combining the new information with their existing information.

We included all the topics normally found in an introduction to education course, although they might not be in the same order as in a traditional textbook. The information and issues are current, complex, and important for anyone thinking about a career in education to consider.

Organization of the Text

The overall organization of the text can be represented by a set of concentric circles in which the *Self* is in the center, and the *Student, School,* and *Society* occupy larger circles that encompass the inner ones (see the inside front cover). Thus, students begin with an exploration of what they already know about education (*Self*). Then, as they progress onward through the material (and outward through the concentric circles), they consider the *Student,* the *Schools,* and *Society,* while recalling the context of their earlier explorations. The lines between those concentric circles blur as students build personal and powerful understandings of the complex relationship between the rewards and challenges of teaching.

Because this textbook may be different from others in the students' experience, To the Student provides a short introduction designed to familiarize readers with the nature of the book, how to use it to develop their own understandings, and how to use its various features.

Part I deals with the *Self*—the individual student and his or her beliefs and informed opinions about education. In Chapter 1, students examine the characteristics of excellent teachers and exemplary teaching. In Chapter 2, students consider the conclusions they developed in Chapter 1, together with research findings, contemporary thinking about education, and philosophies and psychologies to develop their own philosophy of education that will provide a personal and flexible framework to guide them through the rest of the text.

Part II extends the explorations beyond the Self to the *Student* in the classroom. It asks readers to think about how students are alike, how they are different, and how these characteristics factor into the complex relationships teachers have with students. In Chapter 3, readers explore ways in which students are alike, their common needs, and general motivational factors. Chapter 4 asks readers to explore the unique perspectives of the students they will be teaching, such as cultural, language, and religious diversity; socioeconomic status; gender; and sexual orientation. In Chapter 5, they explore the unique abilities of students in such areas as learning disabilities, intelligence, and learning styles and preferences.

Part III helps students extend their awareness of the Self and Students to the context of the *School*. In Chapter 6, they examine purposes of schools, and in Chapter 7, they look at how the purpose of a school is reflected in its structure. Chapter 8 guides the exploration of what schools expect of students and what students expect of schools, including an investigation of behavior management techniques. Chapter 9 focuses on what schools expect of teachers and what teachers expect of schools.

Part IV further broadens students' understandings by looking at education in the context of our *Society*. Chapter 10 deals with the historical foundations of education in the United States. In Chapter 11, students explore broad concepts of governance and finance. In Chapter 12, they consider additional social issues to which schools feel they should respond, and Chapter 13 guides students through an exploration of the legal and ethical issues to which schools, teachers, and students are accountable. In Chapter 14, they consider contemporary trends and issues in accountability, curriculum standards, and educational reform.

Part V (Chapter 15) returns students to their thinking about what makes excellent teachers and exemplary teaching and asks them to examine their motives for wanting—or not wanting—to be a teacher.

Distinctive Features of this Text

Because this book is written with a constructivist orientation, it actively engages students by encouraging intellectual interaction. Students consider what they already know about the topics, explore additional and new information, and then construct new understandings.

Unique Interactive Features

Several special features promote student interaction and are highlighted in textboxes throughout the chapters.

Building Blocks

The *Building Block* features comprise the basic tools of learning and serve as inquiry activities for student explorations. Some Building Blocks ask students to reflect on existing knowledge, some ask them to reflect on contemporary problems and issues, and some ask them to put together new knowledge with their existing knowledge and describe and give reasons for their conclusions. The Building Blocks can be used in several ways—as assignments before reading the textual material, as short beginning-of-class activities, as springboards for class discussions, as homework assignments, as tools for assessment, and so on. The Building Blocks are intended to foster the constructivist nature of the book; student responses to the Building Blocks are one of the better ways of seeing how they are constructing information. For the most part, the Building Blocks do not presuppose any "right" or "wrong" answers; they are intended to enable students to express and examine their own thinking. Some ask students to compare their conclusions with those of the authors. Hopefully there will be a degree of congruence.

TeachSource Videos

New! This feature includes a set of award-winning *Video Cases* that allow your students to go on virtual field observations in the context of the current discussion. The videos provide students with a chance to hear from real educators in real classroom settings. The Video Cases and other engaging video clips provided on the Education CourseMate website offer critical-thinking questions and give students ample opportunities for reflection and discussion.

From the Field

Students hear from award-winning teachers in the *From the Field* features (formerly called "From the Teacher"). These first-person testimonies from teachers across the United States are personal accounts of rewarding experiences and challenges from the field.

Controversies in Education

New! Controversies in Education features present opposing perspectives on current issues and encourage students to consider the various sides of each story. Examples include controversies surrounding bilingual education and the inclusion of Gay-Straight Alliances on middle school and high school campuses.

Technology & Education

Technology & Education features describe specific kinds of technology that are used in education, along with their applications to teaching and learning. Examples include the use of mobile devices for teaching and learning and the use of online resources in instruction.

Biography

Biography features detail professional and personal information about prominent individuals in the education field and provide insight into how these people influenced schooling in the United States.

Integrated Themes: Diversity, Technology, and More

The topics students explore in this book are interdependent. To this end, you will find that we have integrated important themes throughout several chapters instead of treating them as independent topics. For example, material on **diversity, social** issues, and **current trends** in education are addressed not only in specific chapters, but also in the context of several other chapters. The No Child Left Behind and Race to the Top legislation is addressed throughout the text and gives students the opportunity to explore their effects on education in the United States today in a variety of contexts.

The material on **technology** is infused throughout the text, and individual elements of technology are addressed contextually where they are most meaningful.

Correlation to Standards

This textbook supports the InTASC (Interstate New Teacher Assessment and Support Consortium) standards. **Chapter Objectives** are correlated with the standards; and in the **Deconstructing the Standards** features at the end of each chapter, students are asked to analyze ways in which their investigations helped them apply the standards. Students are also asked to locate and consider their own state standards for educators in the context of what they have learned from their inquiries. Specific correlations between the InTASC standards and the contents of this textbook are provided inside the back cover.

Additional Learning Aids

There are several additional learning aids at the beginning, throughout, and at the end of every chapter. These aids include:

- *New*—Chapter Objectives at the beginning of each chapter are correlated to the related **InTASC Standards**.
- **Open-ended questions** integrated throughout the chapter encourage readers to pause and consider their ideas.

- *New*—**Key Terms** are defined in the margins where they appear in the chapters, and a full **Glossary** is also included in the back of the book.
- *New*—**Web Searches** are features in the margins that ask students to put their web searching skills in action to find additional information and websites on current topics and issues.
- Many Internet sites are suggested and can be accessed through direct links on the Education CourseMate website.
- **End-of-chapter** elements include the following:
  - **A Summary** of key chapter concepts
  - A list of **Key Terms and Concepts** for quick review
  - The **Construct and Apply** feature asks students to draw on the conclusions that they have made throughout the chapter and apply them to new and different situations.
  - The **Deconstructing the Standards** features ask students to analyze how the topics and activities in the chapter address the InTASC Standards with which the chapter objectives are correlated, and extend this analysis into the readers' state standards.
  - The **Your Portfolio** feature contains suggestions for artifacts that can be included in the students' learning portfolio.

New Topic Coverage in the Second Edition

In addition to general updates and refinements, we have introduced many new topics, have expanded other topics, and have deleted topics that seem less important now than they used to be. Key changes include:

Chapter 1

- New material on the new Council for the Accreditation of Educator Preparation

Chapter 2

- New material on homework

Chapter 3

- New material on bullying
- Increased emphasis on motivation

Chapter 4

- New comprehensive section on cultural diversity and multiculturalism
- Expanded section on English language learners, especially teaching subject matter to ELLs
- New material on socioeconomic status and achievement
- Increased material on gender and sexual orientation

Chapter 5

- New section on Response to Intervention (RTI)
- Expanded section on ADHD
- New section on autism

- Additional material on existential intelligence
- New sections on co-teaching and differentiated instruction

Chapter 6

- New material on No Child Left Behind, Blueprint for Reform, waivers, and other federal government initiatives
- Revised section on education management organizations (EMOs)
- New section on online learning and virtual schools together with supportive technologies

Chapter 7

- New material on the current thinking about class size

Chapter 8

- New material on physical safety in schools
- New and comprehensive section on bullying, cyberbullying, and anti-bullying measures
- New material on sexual harassment and sexual orientation

Chapter 9

- Expanded section on teacher certification to include virtual forms of teacher preparation for certification and Teach for America
- New material on teacher merit-based salary administration
- Expanded section on mentoring to include online professional development opportunities

Chapter 10

- Expanded material on Asian Americans

Chapter 11

- New section on the digital divide to reflect current technological trends
- New section on school choice and the voucher system

Chapter 12

- Entire chapter rewritten to reflect current social issues of concern to schools, especially family structures, unemployment, school dropouts, after-school programs, nutrition, childhood obesity, drugs and alcohol, gangs, sexual behavior, service learning, immigration, parent incarceration, and homelessness

Chapter 13

- Updated to include recent court rulings

Chapter 14

- New section on curriculum and instruction reform
- New section on the Common Core Standards
- Expanded treatment of differentiated instruction and interdisciplinary approaches

Chapter 15

- New material on teacher attitude
- New material on teaching as a profession

Accompanying Teaching and Learning Resources

We have developed several new ancillary support items to go with *Building Teachers* that can support and enhance the text experience and an instructor's presentation of the course. From planning to presentation to testing, materials are available to provide students with an engaging and relevant exposure to the broad scope of topics in education.

Education CourseMate Website

Cengage Learning's Education CourseMate brings course concepts to life with interactive learning, study, and exam preparation tools that support the printed textbook. Course-Mate includes an integrated eBook, glossaries, flash cards, quizzes, TeachSource videos, a downloadable field observation guide, and more—as well as Engagement Tracker, a first-of-its-kind tool that monitors student engagement in the course. The accompanying instructor website, available through login.cengage.com, offers access to password-protected resources such as an electronic version of the instructor's manual, test bank files, and PowerPoint® slides. CourseMate can be bundled with the student text. Contact your Cengage sales representative for information on getting access to CourseMate.

Online Instructor's Manual with Test Bank

The instructor's resource manual contains resources created by David Martin and Kimberly Loomis and designed to streamline and maximize the effectiveness of your course preparation. It includes a variety of resources to aid instructors in preparing and presenting text material in a manner that meets their personal preferences and course needs. It presents chapter-by-chapter suggestions and resources to enhance and facilitate learning. The manual includes an introduction, chapter outlines/objectives, chapter strategies, supplementary readings, and a test bank including multiple-choice, matching, and essay questions for those instructors who wish to use more traditional assessment methods.

Online PowerPoint Slides

These vibrant, Microsoft PowerPoint lecture slides for each chapter assist you with your lecture, by providing concept coverage using images, figures, and tables directly from the textbook!

ExamView

Available for download from the instructor website, ExamView® testing software includes all the test items from the printed Test Bank in electronic format, enabling you to create customized tests in print or online.

Field Experience Companion

Available for download from the instructor website, the Field Experience Companion is ideal for use in courses with a required field component. This activities workbook—created specifically for use with *Building Teachers*—contains suggestions for several exercises that are related to the application of the material in the chapter. The workbook also gives students a means by which they can more easily correlate what they've learned in the text and your course to the observations and hands-on activities they accomplish during their field experiences.

WebTutor

Jump-start your course with customizable, rich, text-specific content within your Course Management System. Whether you want to Web-enable your class or put an entire course online, WebTutor™ delivers. WebTutor offers a wide array of resources including access to the eBook, glossaries, flash cards, quizzes, TeachSource videos, and more.

Acknowledgments

This work would not have been possible without the support and help of a great many people. We are especially grateful to the following:

- Lisa Mafrici, managing development editor, who patiently offered strong ideas, gentle guidance, and a tremendous amount of help in every aspect of this work. Also a special thanks to the entire editorial and production staff at Cengage Learning for their insightful and strong collaboration in pulling together this work.
- Dr. Lynn Stallings, who helped with the material on mathematics and who provided great support and encouragement through the whole process of writing this book.
- All the instructors of the introduction to education course at Kennesaw State University, especially the course coordinator, Professor Beth Marks, who provided suggestions for content, organization, and editing.
- Dr. Linda Webb, who wrote Chapter 13, "Teachers, Students, and the Law" for the first edition.
- Dr. Bryan Gillis, who helped with the material on the language arts.
- Dr. Guichun Zong, who helped with the material on social studies.
- All the many professional colleagues who have supported our work through the years.
- The students in our introduction to education classes who have shown us what works and what doesn't; we have used many of their ideas and vignettes in this book.

We would also like to acknowledge all of the professors who reviewed *Building Teachers* and provided invaluable feedback and suggestions at various stages in the writing and revising. We thank the following reviewers of the second edition:

Elizabeth Dorman, Regis University

Virginia Garland, University of New Hampshire

Linda Harvest, Essex County College

Leanna Manna, Villa Maria College

Beth Marks, Kennesaw State University

Raja Nasr, Marymount University

Barbara Stern, James Madison University

Janet Stramel, Fort Hays State University

Renee Sturm, Medaille College

Curtis Visca, Saddleback College

Colleen Wilson, Jacksonville University

In addition, we thank the numerous reviewers of the first edition of this text:

Harvey Alvy, Eastern Washington University

Lloyd Anderson, Bismarck State College

Patricia Bason, Elon University

John J. Bertalan, Hillsborough Community College

Robert E. Bleicher, California State University–Channel Islands

John Bruno, Florida State University

Ted Bulling, Jr., Nebraska Wesleyan University

Susan Carson, Grand Valley State University

Margaret Denny, Louisiana State University

Elizabeth D. Dore, Radford University

John A. Ellis, Valparaiso University

Steven R. Greenberg, Bridgewater State College

Susan Allen Gulledge, University of North Carolina, Chapel Hill

Gwendolyn Guy, East Carolina University

Ann S. Hernandez, University of Saint Francis

Charles Howell, Minnesota State University, Moorhead

Edward Janak, University of Wyoming

Robert Leahy, Stetson University

William Patrick Leedom, Shawnee State University

Delinda Dent Lybrand, Eastern Kentucky University

Helena Mariella-Walrond, Bethune-Cookman College

Wendy L. McCarty, University of Nebraska, Kearney

Anthony P. Murphy, College of St. Catherine

Raja T. Nasr, Marymount University

Terry Nourie, Illinois State University

Melvin J. Pedras, University of Idaho

Rachel G. Ragland, Lake Forest College

Dutchie S. Riggsby, Columbus State University

Rochelle P. Ripple, Columbus State University

Richard F. Rodriguez, Western New Mexico University

Robert Shearer, Miami University

Rosemary Traoré, Florida State University

Cara Livingstone Turner, University of Charleston

Alexander Urbiel, Ramapo University

Laura M. Wendling, California State University–San Marcos

Carol S. Whelan, Tulane University

Ginger Williams, Oglethorpe University

Henry S. Williams, Sr., Central Washington University

Carlisle E. Womack, Bainbridge College

We also wish to extend a note of thanks to the following individuals who served as specialist reviewers for specific chapters of the manuscript:

Richard M. Gargiulo, University of Alabama, Birmingham

Paul Gorski, Hamline University

Gerald Gutek, Loyola University

Leslie S. Kaplan, Newport News Public Schools

William Owings, Old Dominion University

DAVID JERNER MARTIN

KIMBERLY S. LOOMIS

To The Student

SERIOUSLY. READ THIS FIRST. Welcome to your textbook. This textbook is different from others you have read. Most textbooks *tell* you the information you are supposed to learn, but this one asks you to come to your own conclusions. To be sure, this book offers a great deal of information about education, but our primary goal is for you to use this information to build your own ideas rather than to simply memorize the ideas of others.

This text is written from a *constructivist* viewpoint, which means you will be asked to *construct* your own conceptualizations about education by combining the information presented in the text with your own prior experiences. Because no two people have the same prior experiences, we expect each individual will construct something different.

Most textbooks assume readers have limited or no knowledge about the topics presented. However, we know you already have a great deal of information about education. You amassed this information through being a student yourself, through discussions with family members or friends who work in the field of education, through watching public portrayals of education in movies and TV shows, through hearing or reading about education in the news, and through Internet search engine headlines, online videos, and blogs, as well as many other sources.

The way people learn is by attaching new information to the information they already have, thereby building their own personal conceptualizations. Accordingly, we have written a book that enables you to do just that. It encourages you to recall the information you already know about teaching and schools, and it then introduces new ideas and helps you put the two together. Learning in this manner is consistent with a learning theory called *constructivism*.

If people learn best in a constructivist environment, then it makes sense that teachers should teach using constructivist-based methods. Because you are *learning* about *teaching*, we believe the organization of this textbook should be especially conducive to learning, *and* it should model the best way of teaching. Your venture into this method of learning consists of three main steps:

1. You will use your prior knowledge and experiences to help establish your familiarity with the material presented.
2. You will obtain new information and experiences from the text, your class work, your fieldwork, and other sources.
3. You will draw your own personal conclusions by combining your prior knowledge with the new information and experiences. These conclusions will likely be different from the conclusions of others because each person has different prior experiences.

By using this text, you will approach this course in a manner similar to the way you will approach the act of teaching. It is our conviction that you will become a better teacher as a result of using this book because you will be learning the basic material about education in a way that parallels the best way of teaching.

This textbook has several unique features that will help you in your constructions. Here are a few examples:

- Building Blocks are the meat of this book. They will help you:
  - Recall what you already know
  - Develop new information
  - Think and draw conclusions
  - Stimulate informal and formal reflection
  - Summarize topics

Here is an example:

BUILDING BLOCK What Do You Expect from a Textbook?

1. Why do you suppose your instructor requires you to purchase a textbook?
2. What do you expect from a textbook?
3. How can a textbook engage you as a learner?
4. Based on what you have read so far, how do you think this textbook will address the expectations that you and your instructor have?
5. How does this textbook use Building Blocks to engage learners?

■ **From the Field** features are essays written by experienced teachers, new teachers, and student teachers about their experiences as teachers. Here is an example:

FROM THE FIELD

From a Student

I have just now finished reading Chapter 1 of our new textbook, and I wanted to make a few comments. First of all, reading this chapter has in some way put a greater desire in me to teach, and not only to teach but also to be the best teacher there is! The section that lists the basic conditions of teaching was very interesting, and I found the five "beliefs" very helpful as well. Something I am really enjoying about this book is that the authors have taken many quotes and ideas from other people, enabling the reader to think about multiple ideas and methods of teaching. When I was in school, I remember the teachers always had quotes all over the room. You have provided some really thought-provoking quotes in this book that one day may be seen on the walls of my classroom. The Building Blocks are a really interesting and unique aspect of this book and one I haven't seen in this form in any other book I have read. I really like the idea of the Building Blocks, and I believe they challenge the reader to think!

Rebecca, a teacher education student
who used a prior edition of Building Teachers

■ **Biographies** are included as appropriate so you can tell the background of some of our more prominent educators. Here are two examples:

BIOGRAPHY

Courtesy of Kimberly Loomis

Kimberly S. Loomis is a professor of science education in the Department of Secondary and Middle Grades Education at Kennesaw State University. She has taught science and education courses at the middle grades through college levels for 25 years. Many of her presentations and publications focus on inquiry teaching strategies, and are grounded in constructivist learning theory. Currently, her work is focused on using inquiry teaching in the field of wolf education and in exploring the effective use of informal science education centers and national parks by science learners and teachers.

BIOGRAPHY

Courtesy of Dave Martin

David Jerner Martin is a retired professor of science education in the Department of Elementary and Early Childhood Education at Kennesaw State University, where he taught education and science education for 21 years. Prior to his university work, he taught science and mathematics for 18 years at the elementary, middle grades, and high school levels. He is author of *Elementary Science Methods: A Constructivist Approach*, currently in its sixth edition, and *Constructing Early Childhood Science*. He has made numerous presentations fostering process-oriented constructivist inquiry science teaching and has consulted on this topic both at home and abroad.

- **Controversies in Education** address current topics in education that are controversial and present several sides of each issue for you to grapple with as you form your own opinion.
- **TeachSource Video** features are short video clips relevant to topics addressed in each chapter. Teachers, administrators, students, and others involved in education provide their opinions and insights, and demonstrate their skills in these informative virtual field experiences to provide a context for the application of your learning and to provoke further thought and exploration.
- **Technology and Education** features address the growing use of technology to assist teachers in teaching and managing classrooms. These features will help you find ways to use technology to support learning.
- **Web Resources** challenge you to use your web-surfing skills to find more information about important topics.

You will find that issues related to diversity in education are purposely <u>not</u> set apart as separate *features* in this text. Instead, these issues are featured as integral parts of the topics addressed in each chapter.

This text and its supporting ancillary materials are arranged in a manner that encourages you to interact with the material presented rather than memorize its content. By using this textbook, you will begin to *build* your knowledge about teaching and learning in a way that parallels the most effective way of teaching—the constructivist way. Enjoy your explorations.

David Jerner Martin
Kimberly S. Loomis

PART

I Self

pedagogy The art and science of teaching.

THIS TEXTBOOK DEALS with pedagogy, which is the art and science of teaching. Part I of this book deals with your *self*. You already know a lot about effective teaching. In the two chapters that make up Part I, you will look at yourself as a prospective teacher. You will investigate the characteristics of excellent teachers and effective teaching, comparing your beliefs with the beliefs of others and the results of research, and you will use these comparisons to augment and refine your existing ideas of what it means to be an excellent teacher. In addition, you will examine your philosophical and psychological convictions about high-quality teaching, and you will compare your beliefs with the major philosophies and psychologies that form the foundation for education. Using these comparisons, you will continue to augment and refine your personal ideas of what it means to be an excellent teacher.

The primary goal of Part I is to help you construct personal and valid conceptualizations about the role of teachers.

CHAPTER 1

Teaching Excellence and You

SCHOOLS ARE WONDERFULLY rich and exciting. Students walk in the footsteps of great thinkers, explore the natural world, master and expand numerous aspects of literacy, experience the joys and inspirations of the arts, and participate in many other enriching activities.

How does this happen? Through a good teacher.

You have decided that you might want to be a teacher, and you probably believe you will be a good one. But considering the tremendous amount of information and experiences—often conflicting—to which you have been exposed, you may be asking yourself, "Just what is good teaching, anyway?"

Research shows that the teacher is the most important factor in the classroom (DuFour and Marzano, 2011). In fact, in their seminal study of the records of over three million students in elementary grades in Tennessee, Sanders and Rivers (1996) found that not only is the teacher the single most dominant factor affecting student achievement, but that the effects of both very effective and ineffective teachers remained with the students for at least two years, regardless of the effectiveness of the teachers the student has later. In fact, according to David Imig, past president and chief executive officer of the American Association of Colleges for

Teacher Education, the quality of the teacher is 20 times more important in student learning than any other factor (2002). A high-quality teacher is more important to student learning than class size, funding, academic specialty, the school building or campus, the makeup of the student population, or anything else.

The purpose of this chapter is to help you identify qualities of teaching excellence that effective teachers possess. You will begin by examining these factors from the perspective of your own familiarity with education. Everyone has had experiences with schools—as students, employees, volunteers, parents, concerned citizens, and as just plain members of society. From your experiences, you have acquired much knowledge and many feelings about excellence in teaching. You will then examine public portrayals of education, as in movies, television shows, newspaper and magazine articles, and information found on the Internet—both old and new—and you will explore relationships between these portrayals and your own thoughts and feelings about teaching and education. Finally, you will compare all this with research, expert opinion, and the positions of professional education societies to refine your personal conceptualizations of excellent teachers and effective teaching.

This chapter invites you to participate in several activities designed to help you bring your current thinking to the surface. You will be amazed at how much you already know about good teaching!

In this chapter, you will use a constructivist approach—combining what you already know with new information, to reach your own conclusions about what constitutes effective teachers and teaching. The constructivist perspective suggests that learning occurs best when you question your own preconceived ideas. This happens through exposure to experiences you must reconcile with the understandings you already have. This chapter **sets the stage** for you to identify your current understandings of excellent teachers and effective teaching and begin to question, enlarge, and refine these understandings in light of new experiences. These experiences include listening to others; watching movies and television newscasts and programs; reading newspapers and magazines; checking out material on the Internet; studying the work of researchers, educational experts, and psychologists; and familiarizing yourself with current standards for high-quality teachers. At the end of the chapter, you will put all this information together as you reconsider and refine your ideas about what it means to be an excellent teacher.

Chapter Objectives

As a result of your explorations in this chapter, you will be able to:

1. Describe your beliefs about excellence in teaching.
   InTASC Standard #9: Professional Learning and Ethical Practice

2. Investigate others' beliefs about excellence in teaching.
   InTASC Standard #8: Instructional Strategies; Standard #9: Professional Learning and Ethical Practice

3. Examine the results of research on excellent teachers and effective teaching.
   InTASC Standard #8: Instructional Strategies; Standard #9: Professional Learning and Ethical Practice

4. Reflect on educational experts' theories about excellence in teaching.
   InTASC Standard #8: Instructional Strategies; Standard #9: Professional Learning and Ethical Practice

5. Survey the standards for excellence in teaching established by professional educational organizations.
   InTASC Standard #9: Professional Learning and Ethical Practice

6. Formulate your conclusions about characteristics of excellent teaching.
   InTASC Standard #9: Professional Learning and Ethical Practice

Characteristics of Excellent Teachers and Effective Teaching: Your Beliefs

Everyone has favorite teachers. Your experience as a student has given you invaluable insight into factors that characterize excellent teachers and effective teaching. In fact, you may have decided to consider teaching because you were affected by a particular teacher. To begin, look at your beliefs about the characteristics of excellent teachers and effective teaching.

BUILDING BLOCK 1.1

Your Favorite Teachers

Think back to your precollege years (elementary school, middle school, junior high, or high school) or your previous college experience:

- Who were your favorite teachers? Why?
- In whose classes did you learn the most? What did these teachers do to help you learn?
- Were your favorite teachers also the teachers in whose classes you learned the most? (You may have identified the same person in your answers to both questions, or you may have identified different individuals.)
- Which characteristics on your list relate to personality?
- Which characteristics on your list relate to the teaching itself?

Now look at the opposite side:

- Who were your least favorite teachers? Why?
- In whose classes did you learn the least? Why?
- Were your least favorite teachers also the teachers in whose classes you learned the least?
- Which characteristics on your list relate to personality?
- Which characteristics on your list relate to the teaching itself?

Save this list; you will use it again later.

You probably ended up with a fairly long list of your favorite teachers' attributes. Note that you have been considering two separate but related notions: personality characteristics and teaching characteristics. Students in introductory education classes similar to yours have come up with many characteristics they identify with excellent teachers and effective teaching. Figure 1.1 shows the words these students used to identify *personality* characteristics.

According to a survey conducted by *eSchool News* (2011), an online education newsletter, the five most prevalent things students say they want from education are the following:

1. Real-world application and relevancy
2. Choice
3. Innovation
4. Teacher mentors
5. Interactive technology

Note how these are similar to the characteristics of excellent teaching, which you have already explored.

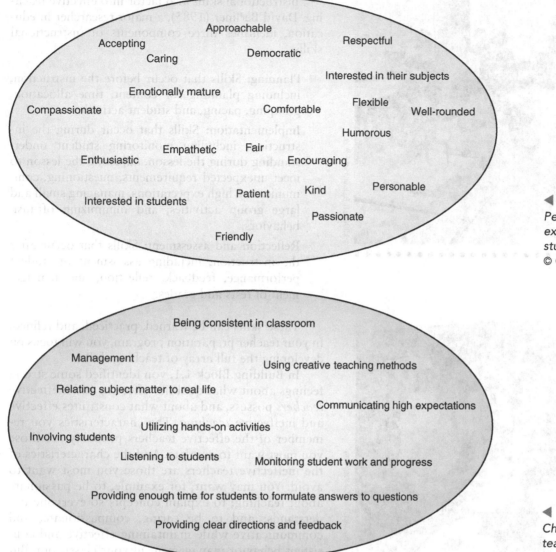

Accepting
Approachable
Caring
Democratic
Respectful
Interested in their subjects
Emotionally mature
Flexible
Compassionate
Comfortable
Well-rounded
Humorous
Empathetic
Fair
Enthusiastic
Encouraging
Interested in students
Patient
Kind
Personable
Passionate
Friendly

◀ **Figure 1.1**
Personality characteristics of excellent teachers identified by students.
© Cengage Learning 2014

Being consistent in classroom
Management
Using creative teaching methods
Relating subject matter to real life
Communicating high expectations
Utilizing hands-on activities
Involving students
Listening to students
Monitoring student work and progress
Providing enough time for students to formulate answers to questions
Providing clear directions and feedback

◀ **Figure 1.2**
Characteristics of effective teaching identified by students.
© Cengage Learning 2014

Figure 1.2 shows the characteristics of *effective teaching* that these students described. What can you conclude about the characteristics of excellent teachers and effective teaching? It seems clear that several characteristics identify excellent teachers and effective teaching, and that different students identify different characteristics. Some of these characteristics reflect the teacher's personality and some reflect the teacher's instructional skill.

Personality plays a large role in teaching. Perhaps someone who knows you well has told you, "You'd be a good teacher!" Has this person ever seen you teach in a classroom? Probably not. What made this person think you would be a good teacher? It must be something about your personality. Maybe you have had experience working with young people. Some people seem to attract small children; others seem able to establish an immediate rapport with young adults. Maybe you are a "good explainer" and have found that others understand ideas better thanks to something you said or demonstrated. People who possess this connection with children and young adults have not necessarily had actual teaching experience. Yet something about their personalities enables them to establish the kind of relationship that is foundational in creating a learning environment.

What are the characteristics of an excellent teacher?

Instructional skills also factor into effective teaching. David Berliner (1985), a major researcher in education, identifies three components of instructional skills:

- **Planning:** Skills that occur before the instruction, including planning for content, time allocation, grouping, pacing, and student activities.
- **Implementation:** Skills that occur during the instruction, including monitoring student understanding during the lesson, adjusting the lesson to meet unexpected requirements, questioning, communicating high expectations, managing small and large group activities, and minimizing off-task behaviors.
- **Reflection and assessment:** Skills that occur after the instruction, including assessment of student performance, feedback, reflection, and management of tests and grades.

These skills can be learned, practiced, and refined. In your teacher preparation program, you will focus on developing the full array of teaching skills.

In Building Block 1.1, you identified some strong feelings about what qualities effective and ineffective *teachers* possess, and about what constitutes effective and ineffective *teaching*. The characteristics you remember of the effective teachers probably are those you most want to emulate. And the characteristics of the ineffective teachers are those you most want to avoid. You may want, for example, to be passionate about teaching; to explain concepts so everyone understands; and to be caring, compassionate, and communicative while maintaining effective and consistent behavior management in your classroom. But under *no* circumstances do you ever want to belittle or humiliate students or have ineffective behavior management in your classroom.

Engaging, knowledgeable, and positive teachers make learning enjoyable for students.

Characteristics of Excellent Teachers and Effective Teaching: Outsider Perspectives

You have looked at the qualities of excellent teachers and effective teaching through your experiences as a student. Those experiences have given you invaluable insights into factors that characterize excellent teachers and effective teaching. Your thoughts about teaching and education also may be influenced by other experiences you have had. Let us look at teacher excellence and teaching effectiveness from the perspective of a parent, a teacher's aide, a school volunteer, a company executive, or local business owner who might hire graduates from the local school system, or a concerned, taxpaying citizen.

Outsider Perspectives

Think of teachers from the viewpoint of an outsider. You might want to imagine that you are a specific outsider such as a parent, or you might want to consider your own parents when they were in school.

- Taking the outsider's viewpoint, list the characteristics about teachers you would consider to be effective.
- Taking the outsider's viewpoint, list the characteristics about the teachers you consider to be the least effective.
- Did you identify new characteristics or any characteristics different from the ones you cited in Building Block 1.1?
- What concerns influenced your perspective in this Building Block?

Save your list; you will use it again later.

Are the characteristics of quality teaching you identified from the perspective of an outsider the same as those you identified from the perspective of a student? In all probability, there were differences. As students, we value certain characteristics of teachers; as parents or other outsiders, we may find we value other attributes. For example, as a student, you may put very high value on mutual respect between teacher and student and on classroom order. As a parent, however, you may place higher priority on attributes such as communication with the home and student performance on achievement tests.

As you have seen, there are different ways of looking at what constitutes quality in teaching. Perspective is influenced by the stakes someone has in education. A student's perspective is likely to be different from a parent's; the stakes are different. Can you see how they are different?

Components of Excellence in Teaching

We have been discussing two aspects of effective teaching: attributes of excellent *teachers* (personality) and attributes of effective *teaching* (instructional skill). We can construct a Venn diagram showing these two categories in two overlapping circles (see Figure 1.3). One circle is labeled *Personality Characteristics* and contains the personality traits that you indicated are associated with excellent teachers. For example, the attributes of *caring, fair,* and *friendly* would be listed in this circle. The other circle is labeled *Instructional Skills* and contains the instructional abilities that you indicated are associated with effective teaching, such as providing clear directions and utilizing hands-on materials.

Many attributes we associate with excellence in teaching are functions of both personality and instructional skill; these attributes occupy the area of intersection of the two circles, which is labeled *Excellence in Teaching*. For example, teachers whose lessons are clear and understandable know how to teach the concepts in the lessons, and also act in an understanding and encouraging way while they teach the lessons. Teachers who succeed in engaging students in their learning also are accepting and empathetic. Teachers whose students have a sincere desire to learn also are fair, reliable, and often humorous.

It is important to realize that you do *not* have to possess all the personality characteristics that have been identified to be an effective teacher. However, if any are identified that you feel might help you become a more effective teacher, by all means try to

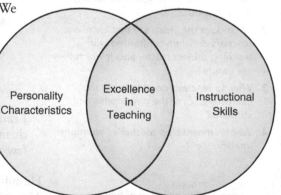

▲ **Figure 1.3**
Venn diagram showing attributes of personality and instructional skill.
© Cengage Learning 2014

empathetic Having understanding of or participating in someone else's feelings or ideas.

assimilate them. For example, if you learned that effective teachers exhibit a sense of humor, you might try to kid around or joke with your students a bit more.

This Venn diagram in Figure 1.3 may be used to show how the art of teaching and the science of teaching come together to form excellence. The art of teaching often is considered a function of personality, and the science of teaching often is considered a function of instructional skill. When both are effective, we have excellence in teaching.

Characteristics of Excellent Teachers and Effective Teaching: Views from Teachers

TeachSource Video

View the *TeachSource Video Case,* "Teaching as a Profession: What Defines Effective Teaching?" In this video, you'll see vivid examples of the various dimensions of teaching excellence—from developing command of one's subject matter and drawing upon one's own emotional intelligence, to setting up an effective learning environment. Throughout the video, you'll hear from educators themselves, those who, in the words of student teacher Caitlin Hollister, "love what they do and take on challenges." Also be sure to watch the Bonus Videos. After watching this video, answer the following questions:

1. How are the characteristics of excellent teachers described by the educators in this video like those you have already learned about?
2. What does the video say that excellent teachers do when confronted with teaching subject matter about which they are unsure?
3. Why do teachers need to know the characteristics of the development of students?
4. What is meant by a teacher's "emotional intelligence"?

pedagogical content knowledge The knowledge of how to teach the content to others and the ability to develop higher-order thinking skills in learners.

Some of the best information about the desirable characteristics of teachers comes from teachers themselves. Throughout this textbook, we include "From the Field" features, in which experienced, novice, and preservice teachers from across the United States describe their thoughts about various topics from the point of view of the classroom teacher. Many of the experienced teachers have been named Teacher of the Year in their respective states as testimony to their excellence, and many others have received the prestigious Teacher of Honor award from Kappa Delta Pi, the international honor society in education. You can read what one Teacher of the Year has to say about effective teachers and teaching in the From the Field feature on the next page.

Linda Darling-Hammond, a noted educator at Stanford University, wrote that the personality characteristics we have been discussing could be thought of as *teacher qualities* (2009). She lists the following qualities as being among those that research has identified as contributing to teacher effectiveness:

1. Strong intelligence and verbal skills that enable teachers to organize and explain information
2. Strong content knowledge
3. Strong pedagogical content knowledge, which is the knowledge of how to teach the content to others, and the ability to develop higher higher-order thinking skills in learners
4. An understanding of *who* is being taught to accommodate and support special needs in learning and language
5. The ability to adapt instruction and the learning environment in response to the needs of learners

To examine teacher perceptions of qualities of excellent teachers, *Educational Leadership* (2010/2011) asked educators to respond to a questionnaire asking them to state what they believe is the main quality of excellence in teaching. A few examples follow:

- Humility in an age of hubris—*Sonia Nieto, professor emerita, University of Massachusetts*
- Excitement about learning—*Joseph Semadeni, fifth-grade teacher, Wyoming*
- Making meaning—*Johanna Mustacchi, media library teacher, New York*
- Reflecting on how you teach—*Pete Hall, elementary school principal, Washington*
- Willingness to grow—*Deidra Grode, codirector/principal K–12, New Jersey*
- Designing good questions—*Terrence Clark, superintendent, New York State*

Being an Effective Teacher
Linda Winburn

In a world of rapidly shrinking education budgets and ever-increasing concerns about new government mandates, my philosophy behind what I do every day in the classroom does not change—teach all children! Albert Einstein said what is so applicable in my classroom: "It is the supreme art of the teacher to awaken joy in creative expression and knowledge." This thinking drives me to inspire young minds and empower them to seek creative expression and knowledge in a student-centered, engaging classroom. I believe that I, as a teacher, must recognize and develop the potential in all students through challenging and stimulating material that is directly related to their lives. I build on their previous learning accomplishments and tackle their challenges. I tell my students that the quotation "the more you know, the more you want to grow" will ring true for them for a lifetime. Students should be challenged to immerse themselves in a world of learning that will take them to the highest levels of expectations, greatest wisdom, and lifelong striving. The curriculum meets the academic, social, and physical needs of students, while challenging them to discover their inherent curiosities in a world that is constantly changing.

I know that I must actively involve parents as co-teachers in the classroom by providing varied opportunities for them to engage in my classroom as curriculum presenters, field study chaperones, writing coaches, mock trial attorney coaches, and service project supporters. As teachers, we must understand that parents are their child's first teachers. We must see our students through the eyes of the parents and build relationships with families. Meeting students and families on their playing fields of life bridges the world of school to the world of family and community and unites us as scholars in a quest for a common goal—lifelong learning in an ever-changing, global world, while maximizing each child's potential.

I know students must learn to think critically and then develop conclusions that will result in more questions and a quest for more answers. "The one real object of education is to have a man in the condition of continually asking questions" (Bishop Creighton). This happens when teachers challenge students' thinking and then offer a safe environment for inquiry. I do this best when I open myself to building relationships with my students—sharing my own challenges and celebrations and allowing them to share theirs. It happens when I welcome students with a smile and personal comment into a classroom filled with warm, glowing lamps, framed prints, and rugs; when I sit among them in a group discussion listening and questioning; and when I learn along with my students and admit that we can research the answer together. It happens, too, as I understand that no two students learn the same way, and I vary my teaching style and differentiate learning.

I know that teachers must respect students and seek to understand their complex world of emotional highs and lows. If a teacher backs a child into a corner, that child will come out fighting. I rely on the philosophy in my classroom that I used with my own four children—give children choices, but make sure that all the choices are good ones. I know this works; I have not written a discipline notice in my classroom in years. My students understand that they have control of their learning and behavior.

I know my personal teaching style and philosophy. Both were acknowledged by a student teacher who said to me, "I've never seen so much learning in such a creative classroom. Students are actively participating by researching, questioning, discussing, and moving from activity to activity, and even actively involved in teacher instruction." This style reflects my philosophy about awakening the joy in creative expression and knowledge. It is not one that came easily or overnight.

Teachers must constantly research new strategies to facilitate learning and bring the curriculum to life. We must be willing to recognize that students' explorations and investigations may lead a lesson in another direction—we must celebrate their insights. We must adopt a philosophy of teaching that says we can make a difference in our students' lives—one child at a time. We do this as we facilitate a classroom that leads students to understand the challenges of a constantly changing world and as we lead them to discover for themselves new and deeper truths with real problems that are relevant to the past, present, and future.

2005 South Carolina Teacher of the Year
Summit Parkway Middle School
Richland School District Two
Columbia, South Carolina

Courtesy of Linda Winburn

Characteristics of Excellent Teachers and Effective Teaching: The Media

You have examined teaching from your personal experience as a student and from experiences that you may have had in other roles. But there is still more information to consider in thinking about excellence in teaching.

Let us look at the issue of effective teaching from the perspective of the media.

Lou Ann Johnson (center) with former students

Jaime Escalante

Teachers in Films

Movies sometimes portray fictional conceptualizations of teachers and teaching based on true stories. Although intended for entertainment, these movies present some insight into society's general views of what teachers do, and they may depict examples of both effective and ineffective teaching. For example, *Dangerous Minds* (Smith, 1995), based on fact, stars Michelle Pfeiffer as Lou Ann Johnson, an ex-Marine who wants to become a high school English teacher. Her first class comprises supposed troublemakers who seem to have more important things to take care of than learning poetry. To gain control and the ability to teach, Ms. Johnson uses unconventional techniques, such as teaching karate and reciting Bob Dylan lyrics, as she tries to associate school with her students' lives. This film shows many characteristics of excellence in teaching, such as relating subject matter to real life; involving students and listening to them; and being caring, accepting, compassionate, and mature.

Stand and Deliver (Menendez, 1988) is the true story of Jaime Escalante, a tough high school mathematics teacher who motivates his classes of potential losers to amazing achievements. Mr. Escalante believes in his students; holds extremely high expectations; and exhibits great enthusiasm, interest, and passion for his subject—all qualities of an excellent teacher.

Movies about Teachers

Do you remember watching movies that deal with teaching? The movies you remember may not be documentaries or dramas; they could be comedies. What specific characteristics of effective teaching can you recall? It is well known that Hollywood often skews reality. What do these movies tell the public about teachers and teaching? Based on the understandings of teaching you have developed so far, do you believe that the teaching characteristics portrayed are realistic?

Use your favorite search engine to find the official website of *Waiting for "Superman"* where you can read a very interesting discussion of excellence in teaching.

You might enjoy watching one or more movies that portray teachers. A few examples include *Waiting for "Superman"* (documentary, 2010); *The School of Rock* (PG13, 2003); *The Emperor's Club* (PG13, 2002); *October Sky* (PG, 1999); *Good Morning, Miss Toliver* (TV documentary, 1994, available through the Public Broadcasting System, PBS); *Kindergarten Cop* (PG13, 1990); *Lean on Me* (PG13, 1989); *Fast Times at Ridgemont High* (R, 1982); *Ferris Bueller's Day Off* (PG13, 1986); and *To Sir, with Love* (unrated, 1967).

While you are watching these movies, ask yourself questions such as the following, which are based on the material you have been studying so far:

- How is the teaching done?
- What are the movie teacher's most effective characteristics?
- What are the teacher's least effective characteristics?
- What are the most and the least effective lessons?
- What makes them so?

View the ABC News video, "Freedom Writers: Teachers Can Inspire Students to Learn and Achieve." This video offers an interview with Erin Gruwell, the teacher who inspired the movie *Freedom Writers*. This story is about a high school English teacher who taught the art of writing to students whom others had written off. In the video, Erin speaks about the transformation her students made as a result of becoming "diarists" of their own experiences.

After watching this video, answer the following questions:

1. How would you describe Ms. Gruwell's effectiveness as a teacher?
2. Where do you think the students in Ms. Gruwell's class got their ideas about effective teachers and teaching?
3. Describe the aspects of Ms. Gruwell's personality and instructional strategies that made her teaching excellent.
4. How are the aspects you listed in #3 like those you have already determined are characteristics of excellent teachers and effective teaching?

Teachers on TV and in the News

The information you get from journalists may play a role in forming your opinions about the characteristics of effective teaching. You get this information from television shows, TV newscasts and news programs, newspapers, magazines, radio, and the Internet. Television is an important source of information. Education is often the topic of news programs, both locally and nationally. These reports can focus on everything from providing recognition for the accomplishments of a particular teacher, student, or school to investigations of school board members and activities, budget expenditures, and inappropriate behavior of teachers.

Other times you may see weekly programs about schools that are dramas or comedies. School shows from the past include a popular teacher-focused television show called *Boston Public*. This show offered a fictional, behind-the-scenes look at the professional and personal lives of teachers and administrators at a midsize, urban high school. In 2009, a TV series called *Glee* first premiered. It told the story of a high school Spanish teacher who took over the school's failing glee club. Throughout the seasons of the show, the glee club members, labeled as losers by the other students in the school, learn to accept themselves for their various talents and attributes. The show also addresses many social issues that impact schools and teaching such as bullying and sexuality, and it portrays some very good and very bad teachers. *Friday Night Lights* was started in 2006, and centers around the trials and tribulations of small-town Texas football players, as well as their friends, families, coaching staff, and school.

Other classic TV shows include *Saved by the Bell* (1989–1993), *The White Shadow* (1978–1981), *Welcome Back, Kotter* (1975–1979), and *Room 222* (1969–1974).

Have you seen any of these classic TV shows about teachers and teaching? You can find episodes or clips on YouTube simply by searching for them. How do these shows present education in relation to how we see it being presented by shows that are currently on TV?

Student Reactions to the Portrayal of Teachers in Films

The following are reactions from students in introductory education classes, written in response to the films *Dead Poets Society* and *Mr. Holland's Opus*. *Dead Poets Society* (1989) stars Robin Williams as Mr. Keating, a literature teacher who pushes his students to be involved, to think, and to use their minds. His teaching style is unconventional and opposes the traditional lecture method with its requirements for accurate recitation. One student said the following about *Dead Poets Society*:

> When I become a teacher, I would like to mimic some of Mr. Keating's teaching styles. I like the idea of his unconventional methods of teaching. He was always able to maintain the interest of the class. Lessons were taught in an interesting and fun way. I liked the idea of eliminating the parts of the curriculum that seem to be irrelevant to real life. I think Mr. Keating had good intentions. He knew how to get the students to learn and want to participate. However, I think he seemed to want to be more their peer than their teacher. Like Mr. Keating, when I teach I want to be unafraid, bold, and ambitious.

Mr. Holland's Opus (1995) stars Richard Dreyfuss as Mr. Holland, a music teacher who has been trying all year to teach his music students to appreciate the classics, with little success. In an attempt to relate the material to his students' lives, he begins a lesson by playing what the students think are excerpts from a popular song. All the students can name the song and the artist. They are surprised, however, when Mr. Holland reveals that the piece was actually written by a classical composer and then used by the popular band. Following this, the students are eager to learn more.

College students wrote the following reactions to Mr. Holland and his qualities as a teacher:

> At the beginning of the movie, Mr. Holland personified many of those qualities that are not wanted in a teacher. He had poor lecture skills, taught straight out of the book, was not enthusiastic, and did not want to be in the classroom. As he learned the tricks of the trade, he began to incorporate many interesting techniques into his teaching. He involved the students, included real-life scenarios, was creative, and was very passionate about his profession. His transformation from one of the worst teachers to one of the greatest teachers shows that while he didn't have the qualities of a good teacher in the beginning, he still had the heart—and that is what made him a good teacher. I hope my future students will see me as a vital part of their lives and as someone who cares and makes a difference.

Network and local TV stations frequently report on teachers and school activities and sometimes present opposing sides of controversial issues, such as the growing controversy over the benefits of the Head Start program discussed on National Public Radio (Jones, 2005).

Print material also is a very important source of information about education. Newspapers and popular magazines regularly report on educational issues and offer pros and cons related to education, such as the controversy surrounding the use of standardized test scores in making high-stakes education decisions (see Controversies in Education, page 22).

You will have many opportunities to think through educational issues during this course. Be sure to keep up with the current news and opinions about education given by the media. For each, ask yourself, "Is this news story realistic? Does this item really portray education as we know it?"

Characteristics of Excellent Teachers and Effective Teaching: The Experts

You have looked at effective and ineffective teachers and teaching from several viewpoints: your own beliefs, outsiders, teachers, and the media. You have also heard ideas from students in your class and you have read ideas generated by students in other classes and by practicing educators. You have identified what you believe are the most important attributes of effective teachers and teaching and of ineffective teachers and teaching, thereby becoming conscious of your thoughts about what constitutes good and bad teaching. How do your thoughts compare with those of the experts?

Sometimes it's interesting to come across a quote you can strongly identify with because it is consistent with your beliefs. Several quotations written by individuals who are not necessarily classroom teachers but who are deeply involved with education follow. How strongly do you agree or disagree with each?

That type of scholarship which is bent on remembering things in order to answer people's questions does not qualify one to be a teacher.

—Confucius

The teacher's job is limited to offering the materials, and it suffices if she demonstrates their use; after that, she leaves the child with his work. Our goal is not so much the imparting of knowledge as the unveiling and developing of spiritual energy.

—Maria Montessori

The man who can make hard things easy is the educator.

—Ralph Waldo Emerson

I have one rule—attention. They give me theirs and I give them mine.

—Sister Evangelist, RSM, teacher in Montana

I had learned to respect the intelligence, integrity, creativity, and capacity for deep thought and hard work latent somewhere in every child; they had learned that I differed from them only in years and experience, and that I, an ordinary human being, loved and respected them. I expected payment in kind.

—Sybil Marshall, on 18 years as a teacher
in a one-room schoolhouse in rural England

You cannot teach a man anything; you can only help him find it within himself.

—Galileo

A child must feel the flush of victory and the heart-sinking of disappointment before he takes with a will to the tasks distasteful to him and resolves to dance his way through a dull routine of textbooks.

—Helen Keller

A teacher must believe in the value and interest of his subject as a doctor believes in health.

—Gilbert Highet, The Art of Teaching

> Teaching is an instinctual art, mindful of potential, craving of realization, a pausing, seamless process.
>
> —A. Bartlett Giamatti, president, Yale University, 1978–1986, and president, National Baseball League, 1986–1989

> Much that passes for education is not education at all but ritual.
>
> —David P. Gardner, president, University of Utah, 1973–1983

> We don't receive wisdom; we discover it for ourselves after a journey that no one can take for us or spare us.
>
> —Marcel Proust

Search the Internet for additional quotes about education and/or about your content area. Use your favorite search engine and search for terms such as "Education Quotes" or "(Content Area) Quotes," inserting your content area in the parentheses, to see what you can find.

The extent to which you agree or disagree with these statements may be an indicator of how you are constructing your ideas about effective teaching. All these quotations are from outstanding educators. Were any of them particularly meaningful to you? There are literally thousands of memorable quotations on education by outstanding individuals. Consider starting a collection of meaningful quotations to read when you want inspiration or when the going gets tough.

Many prominent educators have suggested basic qualities of effective teaching. Gurney Chambers, former dean of the College of Education at Western Carolina University, identified five fundamental traits common to what he called "great teachers" (Chambers, 2000):

1. Great teachers are empathetic and see things from the students' perspectives.
2. Great teachers are energetic.
3. Great teachers have high expectations.
4. Great teachers are concerned with the whole child.
5. Great teachers perceive the hidden curriculum (the learning that goes on but that is not part of the daily course of study) in the classroom.

hidden curriculum What children learn in school that is not content related, but rather a part of being in a school. The hidden curriculum includes the procedures and routines of school functions.

Parker Palmer, the founder and senior partner of the Center for Courage & Renewal, an organization that oversees the "Courage to Teach" program for K–12 educators, reinforces the observation that excellent teachers demonstrate a variety of personality traits and classroom skills. Additionally, Palmer says excellent teachers show that they value academic and personal relationships with their students, whereas poor teachers seem disconnected from their students and seem to work at keeping the academic material disconnected with the result that students can neither establish relationships with the information nor take ownership of it (Palmer, 1998).

Characteristics of Excellent Teachers and Effective Teaching: The Research

Many experts in education have conducted extensive research into the subject of excellent teachers and excellence in teaching. We refer to educational research throughout this textbook. Educational research takes many forms and serves many functions, but its primary purpose is to inform educators on issues of best practice. As a student preparing to enter the field of education, you are advised to study the referenced material, question the usefulness of its results to classroom practice, and determine whether you accept its conclusions. Questioning is the key to intelligent consumption of research. When you question, you become a proactive consumer of research. Ask yourself questions such as those that follow as you review research reports:

- What is the purpose of the research?
- Who is the intended audience?
- What methodology did the researchers use?
- Does the analysis seem valid?
- Is the research useful to teachers?

Research Involving Perceptions

A great deal of educational research has focused on characteristics of quality teaching from the perspectives of different groups of people. From the accounts that follow, try to gain an idea of some of the commonalities and some of the differences in thinking among different groups about the characteristics of excellence in teaching. Pay particular attention to the differences among ethnic groups.

Perceptions of Teacher Excellence by Students

A considerable amount of the research has dealt with the perceptions students have of their teachers. In 2009, the Bill and Melinda Gates Foundation funded a massive research project called the Measures of Effective Teaching (MET) Project to measure several aspects of effective teaching. The study included surveying almost 30,000 students about their perceptions of their teachers' effectiveness. The survey asked students to agree or disagree with statements that described the teacher and the teaching in the classroom; the descriptions were classified into seven categories of characteristics of the teacher and teaching (Bill and Melinda Gates Foundation, 2010). They are:

perceptions Mental images of what one experiences.

1. Caring about students (providing encouragement and support during learning)
2. Controlling behavior (encouraging cooperation and collaboration among peers)
3. Clarifying lessons (helping students realize that they can learn the skills and information successfully)
4. Challenging students (emphasizing effort and perseverance)
5. Captivating (making lessons relevant and interesting to students)
6. Conferring with students (respecting students' contributions to the lesson)
7. Consolidating knowledge (relating and connecting ideas for learning)

The power of student perceptions was represented in the initial findings of the MET Project, which covered just math and English language arts teachers in grades four through eight. The study found that:

Student perceptions of a given teacher's strengths and weaknesses are consistent across the different groups of students they teach. Moreover, students seem to know effective teaching when they experience it: student perceptions in one class are related to the achievement gains in other classes taught by the same teacher. Most important are students' perception of a teacher's ability to control a classroom and to challenge students with rigorous work. (Bill and Melinda Gates Foundation, 2010, p. 9)

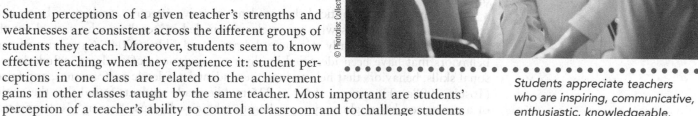

Students appreciate teachers who are inspiring, communicative, enthusiastic, knowledgeable, and caring.

Excellent teachers have a sense of humor.

Minor, Onwuegbuzie, and Witcher (2000) asked students in introductory education classes to identify the characteristics of excellent teachers. The authors grouped the characteristics students identified into seven basic categories:

- Student-centeredness
- Effective classroom and behavior management
- Competent instruction
- Ethics
- Enthusiasm about teaching
- Knowledge of subject
- Personableness

Young, Whitley, and Helton (1998) examined characteristics of effective teachers perceived by students at different levels of maturity: high school, college freshmen, and college seniors. These researchers found that the two most important indicators of teacher effectiveness according to these students are how knowledgeable the teacher is and how much the students learn. They also identified humor in the classroom, the ability to inspire students, effective parent–teacher communications, and friendliness as important attributes.

Perceptions of Teaching Excellence by Teachers

Some educational research has involved practicing teachers. In one study, Norton (1997) found that first-year teachers described effective teachers in the following ways:

- Caring
- Committed
- Highly creative
- Reflective
- Having a "strong internal locus of control" (believing in one's own abilities)

locus of control A characteristic that describes whether an individual attributes responsibility for failure or success to internal or external factors.

socioeconomic Involving both social and economic factors.

ethnicity Affiliation with a group that has general customs, language, and social views and based on common racial, national, tribal, religious, linguistic, or cultural origin or background.

Perceptions of Teacher Excellence in Diverse Populations

Other educational research has focused on the perceptions of people of different nationality, affiliation, socioeconomic group, and ethnicity. For example, McDermott and Rothenberg (2000) studied the perceptions of effective teachers in a high-poverty urban neighborhood. They found that exemplary urban teachers are those who build respectful and trusting relationships with students and their families. Students felt that effective teachers are those who show respect, provide comfort, provide personal connections, exhibit humor, and use a variety of learning techniques. Parents felt that effective teachers are those who have positive relationships with the children and good communication with the parents.

You have probably noticed that students perceive effective teachers as being caring teachers. Indeed, students who are in classrooms led by teachers who care about them perform better academically (Crosnoe, Johnson, and Elder, 2004). Categories of caring behaviors that have been identified by diverse populations of students include interpersonal skills, behaviors that help to increase students' academic performance, and fairness (Tosolt, 2008a). However, a study of 825 middle-grade students found that the qualities of a caring teacher might vary according to ethnicity. Because "caring" is demonstrated primarily by communication, students have different definitions of behaviors that indicate caring based on their culture and language. The implication is that even though teachers may think they are doing their best to form caring relationships with their students, some minority students may not interpret the teachers' behaviors as such because their behaviors do not conform with the students' ideas of caring. Teachers must be familiar with students' lives at home, must talk to their students about what the students need in a relationship, and must be willing to exhibit behaviors in the classroom that meet those needs (Tosolt, 2008b).

Research Involving Teacher–Student Relationships

Roorda, Koomen, Spilt, and Oort (2011) studied the research that dealt with positive and negative associations between teachers and students and the effects these relationships have on both the engagement and the achievement of students. They found that the effects of both positive and negative relationships on student engagement were medium to large, but that the effect on student achievement was small. They also found that the effects in the higher grades were the strongest, but that the effects of negative relationships were strongest in elementary school.

Research Involving Student Achievement

As mentioned previously, students believe that one of the characteristics of effective teachers is that they care about their students, and that students who are in classrooms led by teachers who care about them tend to perform better. Research on effective teachers and teaching often is tied to student achievement. This means that one of the major measures of a teacher's excellence is how well his or her students achieve. See the following Controversies in Education section to examine some issues related to judging teacher effectiveness by student performance.

As you have reviewed the collection of information presented by prominent educators and the research, you have seen that excellence in teaching is characterized by a myriad of factors, many of which you have already identified. These factors seem to center on instructional skill and the teacher's relationship with students.

Characteristics of Excellent Teachers and Effective Teaching: Psychologists

What do psychologists say about effective teachers? Educational psychologists are psychologists whose primary interest is in the area of education. Some educational psychologists work with students in schools, some work with school accountability and administrative programs, and some specialize in research. We will focus our attention on the psychologists who specialize in research. More detail about major psychologies of learning is given in Chapter 2.

© Craig Ferre Photography/Courtesy William Glasser Institute

Glasser and the Quality School

William Glasser (pictured here) is one of the pioneer educational psychologists of the United States. Trained as a psychiatrist, he became interested in education in the 1960s and 1970s. He developed the "Quality School" approach in which he holds that all human beings have

William Glasser

Test Scores and Measures of Teacher Excellence

There is a great deal of controversy regarding how teaching effectiveness can be measured for purposes of merit pay or job retention. The methods for evaluating teachers vary from state to state and sometimes even from school system to school system within the same state. During a time of economic uncertainty, such issues become increasingly important as many teachers must be "let go." How do principals decide who to keep? How do principals decide who should get the highest merit pay increases? And, for that matter, should there be a merit system of pay increases for teachers at all? Or should all teachers receive the same increase every year because they aren't responsible for which students are in their classes?

An obvious source of data for determining teacher effectiveness lies in student achievement. But what data should be used? Standardized test scores? Class performance? Both? If standardized test scores are used, we must ask how well these scores indicate student achievement and whether this achievement can be linked directly to the teacher or if other factors affect it. Darling-Hammond (2009) outlines several reasons why standardized test scores alone may not be a good indicator of teacher effectiveness. For one, the population of students assigned to any one teacher may differ greatly from the population assigned to another teacher. A teacher may have several students whose performance on standardized tests is impacted by their home life; they may have difficult family situations, be homeless, or experience other circumstances that contribute to poor attendance or distractibility while learning in the classroom or taking a test. A teacher may have students in the class who have other challenges related to learning and test taking such as special education or language needs.

In addition, standardized test scores don't allow for other influences on student performance that exist at the school: Students have other teachers who may motivate them to acquire some skills that are typically learned in a different teacher's course. For example, a science teacher may apply the skills learned in a math course, and the student, seeing this application, may gain a deeper understanding of the math skill in science class rather than when he learned it in math class. A student writing a research paper for her history teacher may refine and develop the skills originally learned in her English class. Yet, these distinctions are not represented in the scores for math or English on the standardized tests.

Teachers also have varying levels of access to instructional resources such as textbooks, computers and other technology, laboratory equipment, and manipulatives. Certainly a teacher who has access to and uses such resources may design and implement more effective instruction than one who does not, and therefore may be evaluated as being more effective.

Using data from student achievement in class may also provide information on teacher effectiveness. To judge teachers' impact on student achievement, some schools or school systems require teachers to collect data from pretests and posttests over units of instruction. Student gains from pretest to posttest is considered to be a good representation of the teacher's effectiveness. Additionally, the pretest–posttest gains data may be a better measure of teacher effectiveness than scores on achievement tests because the teacher may be able to control the instruction for the previously mentioned special circumstances that affect student performance. Also, while presenting this data from student class performance to administrators, teachers may reflect on it and their own performance and provide evidence of improving their performance over time through modifying instruction and materials.

Many school systems use a combination of student achievement and teacher performance assessments to judge the effectiveness of teachers. During the school year, an administrator from the school may visit a teacher's classroom to observe and evaluate the instruction. A formal evaluation instrument that has been adopted for use by the school system or the state usually guides the administrator in this observation and evaluation. These instruments have been developed by experts and have been informed by research on effective teachers and teaching.

So, as you have seen, many sources of information may be used to evaluate the effectiveness of a teacher; the most commonly used data are scores on standardized achievement tests, pretest–posttest gains, and teacher observations. Please note that, even though there are problems with using student achievement on standardized tests as a measure of teacher effectiveness, usually, the general public only has access to these test scores. Therefore, the general public uses only these test scores to form their opinions about the effectiveness of teachers and schools.

WHAT DO YOU THINK?

1. *What criteria do your local school systems use to evaluate teacher effectiveness?*
2. *If you can, obtain a copy of any evaluation instruments that are used. How do the criteria on these instruments compare with the characteristics of effective teachers and teaching that you already identified? In your opinion, can this instrument really identify teachers of excellence?*
3. *To what extent do you believe that scores on standardized achievement tests are indicative of excellence in teaching? Why?*

five basic needs: love, power, freedom, fun, and survival. In Glasser's approach, the basic premise of quality education is that "we will work hard for those we care for (*love*), for those we respect and who respect us (*power*), for those who allow us to think and act for ourselves (*freedom*), for those with whom we laugh (*fun*), and for those who help us make our lives secure (*survival*)" (Glasser, 1993, p. 30). He identifies six basic conditions under which quality teaching is done in school:

1. There must be a warm, supportive classroom environment.
2. Students should be asked to do only meaningful work.
3. Students are always asked to do the best they can do.
4. Students are asked to evaluate their own work and improve it.
5. Quality work is always good.
6. Quality work is never destructive. (Glasser, 1993, pp. 22–25)

Glasser believes that good teachers are those who design lessons and create learning environments that are relevant and satisfying to students.

The Quality School

Look again at the six conditions of the Quality School outlined by Glasser. How do these conditions compare with the characteristics of effective teaching you have listed?

BUILDING BLOCK

1.4

Combs and Perceptual Psychology

Arthur Combs (1993) investigated what makes people good "helpers" (including teachers, counselors, clergy, nurses, and therapists). Combs (pictured here) concluded that what makes an effective helper is *not* knowledge and *not* methodology. Rather, the effectiveness of a helping professional is a result primarily of that individual's *beliefs* (or perceptions). Teachers and other helping professionals behave in terms of their beliefs. Combs identified five areas of beliefs:

Courtesy of The Field Psych Trust

Arthur Combs

Beliefs about the kind of data to which we should be tuned: Good helpers tune into data concerned with *people* questions; poor helpers tune into data concerned with *things* questions.

Beliefs about what people are like: Good helpers believe people are *able*; poor helpers *doubt* that people are able.

Beliefs about self (self-concept): Good helpers see the self in essentially positive ways and are self-actualizing; poor helpers see the self in essentially negative ways.

Beliefs about purpose (what is truly important): Good helpers see their purpose to be essentially a *freeing* behavior; poor helpers see their purpose to be essentially a *controlling* behavior.

Beliefs about methods: Good helpers utilize *self-revealing* methods; poor helpers utilize *self-concealing* methods.

Beliefs are innate and are integrated into one's personality. They are based on the life experiences that occur from earliest childhood onward. We cling to our beliefs because they are deeply rooted in our experience. Beliefs drive people's actions. Combs tells the story of a little boy who was lost in the halls of his elementary school on the first day of school. The principal saw the boy and escorted him to his classroom. The teacher, who was in the middle of a lesson, stopped and went to greet the boy, who was worried about being late. She showed she believed that this boy was important when she said, "Welcome! I am so glad you are here!" rather than scolding him for being late.

If a teacher believes a particular student is a troublemaker, the teacher unconsciously will interpret some of the student's behaviors as disruptive and will act accordingly. Similarly, if you, the teacher, believe that each student can learn, you will act differently from the teacher who believes there will always be one or two students each year who simply do not have what it takes to achieve.

BUILDING BLOCK
1.5

My Beliefs

Consider the following questions carefully and purposefully:

- What do you believe about students? Do you believe all students are capable and can learn?
- What do you believe about yourself as a teacher?
- How do your beliefs compare with those Combs identified as integral to effective teachers?

Good teachers examine their beliefs and change them in light of new evidence. Is this difficult? Yes. It is possible? Most assuredly. Because teachers' beliefs are so crucial to professional behavior, we ask you to examine your beliefs on a number of issues and factors throughout this textbook.

The quotations that follow about the power of beliefs seem appropriate:

Whatever one believes to be true either is true or becomes true in one's mind.
—John C. Lilly
U.S. physician, neuroscientist, and philosopher

The real difficulty in changing the course of any enterprise lies not in developing new ideas but in escaping from the old ones.
—John Maynard Keynes
British economist

There is a principle which is a bar against all information, which is proof against all arguments, and which cannot fail to keep a man in everlasting ignorance—that principle is contempt prior to investigation.
—Herbert Spencer
English philosopher

Perhaps the most important single cause of a person's success or failure educationally has to do with the question of what he believes about himself.
—Arthur Combs
U.S. educational psychologist

Characteristics of Excellent Teachers and Effective Teaching: The Federal Government

Even the federal government has become involved in the discussion of the characteristics of effective teachers and teaching. On January 8, 2002, President George W. Bush signed into law the No Child Left Behind Act of 2001 (NCLB). This act is the most recent reauthorization of the Elementary and Secondary Education Act (ESEA), originally signed into law by President Lyndon B. Johnson in 1965. NCLB increases the federal role in K–12 education and aims to close the achievement gap between disadvantaged and minority students and their peers. The act is based on four basic principles (U.S. Department of Education, 2002):

1. Stronger accountability for results
2. More choices for parents and students
3. Increased flexibility and local control
4. Emphasis on teaching methods that have been proved to work

The act specifically addresses the quality of U.S. teachers and aims to increase the academic achievement of all students by enhancing the quality of their teachers. High-quality teachers are defined as those who demonstrate subject-matter knowledge and skills in basic subject areas, and are licensed by the state in which they teach, hold at least a bachelor's degree, and demonstrate competence in core academic subjects.

NCLB was scheduled for reauthorization by Congress in 2007. However, President Barack Obama and Secretary of Education Arne Duncan have new and different ideas about the way the federal government should support education. Consequently, the reauthorization of ESEA has been postponed, and the Race to the Top strategy, funded by the American Recovery and Reinvestment Act of 2009, has been used as an interim measure. Race to the Top emphasizes four areas:

- Decisions about teaching children based on data
- Talent(s)
- Turning around chronically low-performing schools
- Tailoring the teaching to the needs of the community

Moving forward, President Obama presented a more comprehensive plan in March 2010 (U.S. Department of Education, 2010), which he calls the Blueprint for Reform. The Blueprint "builds on significant reforms already made in response to the Race to the Top" (ibid., p. 3), and introduces major changes with the goal of the United States becoming "the most educated country in the world" (Richardson, 2009, p. 24).

The *Blueprint for Reform* emphasizes four areas:

1. Improving teacher and principal effectiveness to ensure that every person has a great teacher and every school has a great leader
2. Providing information to families to help them evaluate and improve their schools, and to educators to help them improve their students' learning
3. Implementing college- and career-ready standards, and developing assessments aligned with those standards
4. Improving student learning and achievement in the lowest-performing schools in the United States by providing intensive support and effective interventions

Of particular note is the intent of the administration to shift the focus of the standardized tests to measuring the growth of each student regardless of the performance level at which he or she starts.

There are concerns with this new proposal. The National Education Association and the American Federation of Teachers feel that the Blueprint signals an increase in federal control and that, although it provides teachers with more responsibility, it provides no additional authority. In addition, the professional organizations see a continued reliance on standardized tests which, as we have seen, are intrinsically unreliable measures of achievement.

Most recently, President Obama has announced a plan that offers flexibility from the key provisions of NCLB in exchange for firm commitments to reforms that boost student achievement (U.S. Department of Education, 2011). As of this writing, forty-four states, the District of Columbia, and Puerto Rico have signaled their intent to seek ESEA flexibility. Nineteen states have been approved (U.S. Department of Education, 2011, 2012). Meanwhile, Congress continues to work on a reauthorization of the Elementary and Secondary Education Act and No Child Left Behind to craft a bill that does the desired job of promoting academic achievement of *all* children and also receives the nods of the major professional organizations. When the revised version is passed, its major provisions will be posted on this textbook's website.

You should bear in mind that the reauthorization of ESEA has *not* been passed and has *not* been signed into law. And when the new law is passed, it will take some time for the details to reach the level of the school districts. Meanwhile, most states still are accountable to the provisions of No Child Left Behind.

We will leave our discussion of federal involvement in education at that for now, but you will investigate many of the provisions, criticisms, and consequences of federal legislation throughout this book, this course, and throughout your teacher education program.

Characteristics of Excellent Teachers and Effective Teaching: Professional Standards

You have done a great deal of work constructing your understanding of what effective teaching is. Now, let us look at statements from professional organizations within the teaching profession itself. After all, it is those in the teaching profession who set the professional standards. Over the past decade, education professionals have worked to build a quality system to assure that every child is taught by a caring and competent teacher. Several important groups have established standards for quality teaching and the preparation of high-quality teachers. These groups include the National Council for Accreditation of Teacher Education (NCATE), the Teacher Education Accreditation Council (TEAC), the Interstate New Teacher Assessment and Support Consortium (InTASC), the National Board for Professional Teaching Standards (NBPTS), and individual state licensing agencies. (Note that NCATE and TEAC merged in 2012 to form the Council for the Accreditation of Educator Preparation – CAEP.) These groups are staffed by educators and obtain extensive input from other educators in shaping their standards. They all have one interest in mind—to staff every classroom with high-quality teachers.

Let us look at the standards of these national organizations. As you examine the standards, compare them with the ideas you constructed about the characteristics and attributes of excellent teachers and excellent teaching. Are they similar?

National Council for Accreditation of Teacher Education (NCATE)

accreditation The formal, official approval signifying that the requirements of excellence described in professional standards developed by professionals in a particular discipline have been met.

NCATE has been one of the primary bodies responsible for accrediting teacher preparation institutions. Accreditation means that an institution has met all formal official requirements of excellence described in the professional standards developed by the professionals in that discipline. Institutions accredited by NCATE have met rigorous,

NCATE-established standards for the preparation of teachers. In many states, teacher preparation institutions are required to be accredited by NCATE in order for their graduates to be eligible for teaching certification in that state. The Teacher Education Accreditation Council (TEAC) also accredits teacher preparation institutions, and the American Association of Colleges for Teacher Education (AACTE) is developing standards for the preparation of teachers. However, NCATE has been the largest and most well-known accreditation body.

NCATE is a coalition of 33 national associations that represent all aspects of the education profession. Its mission is to help establish high-quality teacher, specialist, and administrator preparation (National Council for the Accreditation of Teacher Education, 2002, p. 1). In 2011, 656 teacher preparation institutions were accredited and 70 more were candidates for accreditation by NCATE. Twenty-five states had adopted the NCATE standards as their state teacher education unit standards as of 2009. Institutions are reviewed every seven years for compliance with the standards. Reviews are made by committees of professors from other NCATE-accredited teacher preparation institutions, who are trained by NCATE, and are assembled as a team to review a specific institution.

NCATE requires teacher preparation institutions to meet the criteria inherent in six broad standards. The standards, in effect as of 2008, were developed by professionals in the field of teacher education and deal with the following:

1. Candidate knowledge, skills, and dispositions
2. Assessment system and unit evaluation
3. Field experience and clinical practice
4. Diversity
5. Faculty qualifications, performance, and development
6. Unit governance and resources

Standard 1 identifies standards for effective teacher candidates. This standard describes basic characteristics of excellent teachers.

NCATE Standard for Effective Teacher Candidates

1. *Content knowledge.* Teacher candidates know the subject matter that they plan to teach and can explain important principles and concepts delineated in professional, state, and institutional standards.
2. *Pedagogical content knowledge.* Teacher candidates have a broad knowledge of instructional strategies that draws upon content and pedagogical knowledge and skills delineated in professional, state, and institutional standards to help all students learn. They facilitate student learning of the subject matter through presentation of the content in clear and meaningful ways and through the integration of technology.
3. *Professional and pedagogical knowledge and skills.* Teacher candidates can apply their professional and pedagogical knowledge and skills delineated in professional, state, and institutional standards to facilitate learning. They consider the school, family, and community contexts in which they work and the prior experience of students to develop meaningful learning experiences.
4. *Student learning.* Teacher candidates focus on student learning. Teacher candidates assess and analyze student learning, make appropriate adjustments to instruction, and monitor student progress. They are able to develop and implement meaningful learning experiences for students based on their developmental levels and prior experience.
5. *Professional dispositions.* Candidates are familiar with the professional dispositions delineated in professional, state, and institutional standards. Candidates demonstrate classroom behaviors that are consistent with the ideal of fairness and the belief that all students can learn. Their work with students, families, colleagues, and communities reflects these professional dispositions.
   (National Council for the Accreditation of Teacher Education, 2010)

The Teacher Education Accreditation Council (TEAC)

An alternative to NCATE, the Teacher Education Accreditation Council (TEAC) is a major accrediting agency that has accredited teacher preparation programs in over 100 schools and colleges of education. TEAC was founded in 1997, to foster preparation of competent, caring, and qualified professional educators. TEAC requires the teacher preparation program being considered for accreditation or continuing accreditation to present evidence to justify its case that it prepares professional educators who are competent, caring, and qualified.

The Council for the Accreditation of Education Preparation (CAEP)

In late 2010, NCATE and TEAC announced plans to merge with each other to form a new accrediting body, the Council for the Accreditation of Education Preparation (CAEP). The initial standards developed for accreditation by CAEP are comprised of a blend of the NCATE and TEAC standards. The goals of CAEP are to raise the performance of candidates as practitioners in our nation's P–12 schools and to raise standards for evidence that supports claims of quality by combining the best of both NCATE and TEAC, thereby raising the stature of the entire profession. It is anticipated that CAEP will begin reviewing teacher education programs for accreditation in 2013 (NCATE News and Press Releases, 2012).

Interstate New Teacher Assessment and Support Consortium (InTASC)

InTASC is a group of educators representing state education agencies, higher education institutions, and national educational organizations. Formed within the Council of Chief State School Officers, InTASC has developed a "set of model core teaching standards that outline what teachers should know and be able to do to ensure that every K–12 student reaches the goal of being ready for college or the workforce in today's world" (InTASC, 2011). In 2011, this group presented an updated set of standards that replaces the standards published in 1992 (Council of Chief State School Officers, 2010). These standards were designed to be compatible with the certification standards of the National Board for Professional Teaching Standards (presented in the next section) and are used by many institutions as benchmarks for effective teacher preparation programs. Indeed, many institutions show how their programs are aligned with the InTASC standards. We have grounded this text in the 2011 InTASC standards.

The standards are provided on the inside back cover of this book for your reference. This is the time for you to study the standards carefully so you will be familiar with the way this textbook and the InTASC standards are integrated. Note especially that the Chapter Objectives listed at the beginning of each chapter are correlated to the appropriate InTASC standard so you are aware of how the standard is addressed. Additionally, the end of each chapter contains a section called "Deconstructing the Standards," which asks you to put in writing the ways you have become familiar with the intent of each of the referenced standards.

National Board for Professional Teaching Standards (NBPTS)

Teachers can acquire certification at the national level after they have been certified at the state level and have taught for at least three years. National certification, recognized in all states, shows that a teacher has demonstrated characteristics and competence of the highest order. National certification is a long and demanding process administered by NBPTS.

It requires passing six exercises of thirty minutes each, administered in an examination setting, and receiving passing scores on a series of portfolios demonstrating the candidate's teaching of certain lessons, reflections on the planning and results of the lessons, proposed changes, interpretations of the instructional activity in terms of sound instructional practice, and describing the teacher's impact of accomplishments outside the classroom with families, the community, and/or colleagues. Review of these materials is carried out by groups of teachers and other education professionals who have been trained in the rubrics used to assess the materials.

The NBPTS consists of classroom teachers and public school administrators. Its mission is to advance the quality of teaching and learning through the following activities:

- Maintaining high and rigorous standards for what accomplished teachers should know and be able to do
- Providing a national voluntary system certifying teachers who meet these standards
- Advocating related education reforms to integrate national board certification in American education and to capitalize on the expertise of national board–certified teachers (National Board for Professional Teaching Standards, 1999)

NBPTS identifies five core propositions that describe the knowledge, skills, and dispositions that characterize accomplished teaching.

The Five Core Propositions of the National Board for Professional Teaching Standards

- Teachers are committed to students and their learning.
- Teachers know the subjects they teach and how to teach those subjects to students.
- Teachers are responsible for managing and monitoring student learning.
- Teachers think systematically about their practice and learn from experience.
- Teachers are members of National Board for Professional Teaching Standards learning communities.

State Certification Requirements

Each state has its own set of certification requirements. Find your state's education preparation and certification requirements; these requirements have great influence on the nature and content of your teacher preparation program. Compare these requirements to the competencies and dispositions you will be required to demonstrate as you progress through your program. You will satisfy some of these requirements in this course. You will satisfy others in future courses. You will satisfy still others in your field experiences.

Assessment of Your Field Experiences

BUILDING BLOCK
1.6

As teacher candidates progress through their programs, they will be assigned to several field experiences. The teaching and professional behavior they exhibit during their field experiences and student teaching are evaluated using criteria that correlate with standards developed by state and national accreditation agencies:

- What competencies are you expected to demonstrate in your field experiences?
- How do these competencies compare with the professional standards?

Putting It All Together

From your explorations in this chapter, you can see that many characteristics contribute to excellence in teachers and teaching. You have investigated these characteristics from numerous sources: yourselves as students, outsiders, the media, research, expert educators, psychologists, the federal and state governments, and professional education organizations. Now it is time for you to summarize all this material. In so doing, you will continue to construct your own ideas as to what constitutes a good teacher and good teaching.

Your conclusions are entirely your own, formed on the basis of your personal experiences and previous knowledge, as well as the new information to which you have been exposed in class and by reading this chapter. There are no right or wrong responses to this activity. However, there are valid conclusions. You can validate your conclusions by reflecting on the progression of your thinking as you read through this chapter and participate in the suggested activities. Perhaps your ideas about effective teaching have been reinforced. Perhaps you have integrated some new ideas into your original understanding. Perhaps your original understanding has undergone radical revisions. Whatever the case, you are now ready to draw some definite conclusions.

This is the first of many situations you will encounter in this book where there are no right or wrong answers. In this case, there simply is no consensus on the attributes all excellent teachers possess. What is important is that you have brought your own experiences and ideas together with those of others and constructed your own understanding.

BUILDING BLOCK 1.7

Putting It All Together: Attributes of Effective Teachers

Combine the material you developed in the Building Blocks of this chapter with the new information you explored.

- List the most important attributes you now believe characterize excellence in teaching.
- Explain why you selected these attributes and why you believe they are important.
- Compare these attributes with those you selected in the earlier activities. Which attributes do you still believe to be important? Which do you believe less important than you originally thought? Which have you added?
- Keep the work you do in this Building Block; you will use it again in later chapters.

How have you seen teachers use technology effectively? How have you seen teachers use technology ineffectively? If you consider the pervasiveness of technology in today's society, it should not surprise you that effective teachers know how to integrate technologies into classroom instruction and management.

In this chapter, you have identified some characteristics of effective teachers. How can technology contribute to effective teaching? Remember that merely using technology does not make teaching effective. The *teacher* makes the technology effective. When a teacher directs students to a flashy website or has them create a fancy electronic slide show, these assignments do not necessarily enhance the lesson. The use of technology in instruction must be guided by the teacher's professional knowledge and skills to the end of enhancing the instruction.

Teachers should not separate technology from other instructional tools, such as textbooks and manipulatives, as if it were an effective tool in and of itself. Technology does not automatically engage students, nor does it automatically improve learning. Teachers must determine where and how the use of technology would be most appropriate in any given lesson, based on learning objectives, state standards, and students' needs. As a teacher, you must apply what you know about students and how they learn when making decisions about *when*, *how*, or even *if* you should use technology in your teaching.

Effective teachers possess strong content-area knowledge, efficient organizational skills, and a repertoire of teaching methods and activities that keep learners engaged. How can technology help teachers express these characteristics in their teaching?

Teachers can use technology to present instruction, keep students active, produce instructional materials, and manage classroom records and information. Following is a list of some of the ways teachers can use technology to enhance their teaching effectiveness:

- Television programs and DVDs for students to view educational programs
- YouTube for students to view clips of demonstrations, events, or educational programs
- Online animations (such as those found in BrainPop) to present short content information cartoons and to assess student learning
- Electronic slide shows with color, graphics, sound, video, and animation to present content
- Content-area software on CD-ROMs for students to use independently or in groups
- Content-related Internet sites projected for the class or viewed on individual computers
- Teacher-made websites and blogs to post interesting content information, calendars, syllabi, and events
- Word-processing and publishing programs to create neat and colorful handouts, signs, and bulletin boards
- Assistive and adaptive technologies for students with special needs

- Response system technology ("clickers") for on-the-fly assessments of student learning
- Interactive whiteboards (such as Smart Boards) to present information interactively for students
- E-mail to communicate with parents and students
- Electronic spreadsheets or databases to keep track of grades, attendance, and other data
- Podcasts to provide additional content information for interested students
- Applications that allow teachers to design and create online multimedia interactive posters

Of course, the list is not exhaustive and is constantly changing! You will read more about these technologies throughout this text, and we will ask you to carefully consider their use in teaching.

Technology can help teachers add to their professional knowledge when it serves as a resource for content information and provides teaching ideas. As you already know, the Internet is a vast source of content information and instructional ideas. You can find almost anything by searching on the Internet. Many teachers share their lessons, classroom management, and discipline plans by posting these online. It is necessary, however, to evaluate all Internet-accessible information in terms of credibility, accuracy, and applicability for use in your classroom. You must verify the credibility of all web-based content information. The best way is to check the site author's credentials. Is the author an individual, an organization, or a company? If the author is an individual, what are his or her credentials regarding the content? Is the author (whether an individual or an organization) biased in any way that might affect the presentation, inclusion, or exclusion of content on the site?

Similarly, classroom management ideas are frequently posted online. But, not all classroom management or discipline plans posted on the Internet are good. How will you know if a particular plan is good? Some website owners review information before they post it. In all cases, however, you must use your knowledge and skills in your content area and pedagogy to evaluate what you find, judging its appropriateness for use in your classroom.

Technology also can help teachers be more productive. Teachers can use word-processing applications to create handouts, quizzes, and tests. Teachers may use a database program to manage student records, a spreadsheet program to calculate student grades, and e-mail to communicate with students and parents. When used together with the student record database, a word-processing program can generate personalized letters asking parents to volunteer, informing them of classroom events, or sharing good news; this is especially useful for large classes like those frequently encountered in high school.

The use of technology can contribute to teacher effectiveness by helping teachers increase professional knowledge, present information, and increase productivity.

How does using available technologies contribute to excellence in teaching?

■ SUMMARY

You have explored a great deal of information about excellent teachers and effective teaching in this chapter, and this is just the beginning of your introduction to education.

- You already have your own very good conceptualizations about excellent teachers and effective teaching.
- Other ideas about excellent teachers and effective teaching come from other students, outsiders, the media, researchers, exemplary educators, psychologists, professional organizations, and governmental agencies. The ideas from these sources are probably very consistent with your own ideas.
- Common characteristics of excellent teachers include having interpersonal skills (including knowing the students *personally*), being empathetic, helping to increase student achievement, having high expectations for all learners, being consistent and fair, and caring about students. Effective teachers must also have strong content knowledge, pedagogical content knowledge, and verbal skills.
- Common components of effective teaching include managing the classroom well so that it is supportive, keeping students active and busy and making the lesson relevant to students. Effective teaching encourages students to use higher-order thinking skills and is responsive to the needs of students.

■ Key Terms and Concepts

Accreditation, 26	Locus of control, 20	Perceptions, 19
Empathetic, 11	Pedagogical content	Socioeconomic, 20
Ethnicity, 20	knowledge, 12	
Hidden curriculum, 18	Pedagogy, 5	

■ Construct and Apply

1. List the characteristics of excellent teachers and effective teaching that are common to all the groups you investigated.
2. What do you think is the ultimate measure of a teacher's effectiveness? Explain your response.
3. To what extent do you believe an individual's personality characteristics can be learned and refined?
4. Which characteristics of an effective teacher would you like to develop within yourself? What kinds of experiences could help you develop these characteristics?
5. Discuss how Venn diagrams are used in education, such as locating the commonalities between two scientific theories, elements of literature, and so on.
6. Which skills do you expect to learn as you participate in your teacher preparation program?
7. Where and how do you expect to gain experience in developing these skills?

■ Deconstructing the Standards

1. Recall the InTASC Standards associated with the objectives for this chapter:

   InTASC Standard #8: Instructional Strategies reads, "The teacher understands and uses a variety of instructional strategies to encourage learners to develop deep understanding of content areas and their connections, and to build skills to apply knowledge in meaningful ways."

   InTASC Standard #9: Professional Learning and Ethical Practice reads, "The teacher engages in ongoing professional learning and uses evidence to continually evaluate his/her practice, particularly the effects of his/her choices and actions on others (learners, families, other professionals, and the community), and adapts practice to meet the needs of each learner."

   a. What part(s) of these standards does this chapter address?
   b. How will the concepts in this chapter help you apply these standards as a teacher?

2. Use your favorite search engine to find your state's standards for certification. When you find it, bookmark the site. You will refer to it often as you progress through this book.

   a. How are your conclusions about effective teachers and teaching represented in your state certification standards?

   b. How do the InTASC Standards compare to your state's certification standards regarding effective teaching?

   c. Do you believe the degree of representation concerning effective teaching is adequate in your state certification standards? Why or why not?

Your Portfolio

During your teacher preparation program, you will be asked to demonstrate your achievement of certain competencies. Many education departments ask students to demonstrate their competencies through *portfolios*. A portfolio demonstrates the student's mastery of various concepts and skills. It is not a scrapbook; it is a record of the student's achievements. The portfolio can be "pen and paper," but it is more likely to be electronic now; an electronic portfolio is known as an "e-portfolio."

In this chapter, you have considered numerous factors dealing with qualities of excellent teachers and teaching. Begin to develop your portfolio by selecting two or three pieces of evidence that show your mastery of this topic and putting them in your portfolio. This evidence may come from work done in class, work done out of class, summaries of class discussions, or field experience assignments.

Also include a copy of the requirements for the teacher preparation program you plan to pursue and a copy of your state's requirements for the certification you plan to seek.

Keep your portfolio in a safe place, and be ready to add to it throughout this course. If you are using an e-portfolio, be sure to save it frequently after each new addition.

Education CourseMate Resources

Check out this text's Education CourseMate website (at www.cengagebrain.com) for more information about effective teacher qualities, interactive study tools, and useful resources. You will find the TeachSource videos, a guide for doing field experiences, glossary flashcards, activities, tutorial quizzes, direct links to the websites mentioned in the chapter, and more.

Your Philosophy of Education

IN CHAPTER 1, you looked at qualities of effective teachers and effective teaching. You examined these attributes from several perspectives: your own thoughts and feelings, the ideas of classmates and other preservice teachers, the media, the Internet, educational research, educational psychologists, and professional associations. After considering this new information and using it to augment your own initial ideas, you developed a list of the most important attributes you believe characterize effective teachers.

Your work in Chapter 1 may have left you with the impression that all teachers should have the same qualities and should teach in the same way if they are to achieve excellence. Nothing could be further from the truth.

Doubtless, there are areas where your thoughts about teaching excellence are decidedly different from those of others, even though you may agree in principle on the qualities that characterize effective teachers. These thoughts are based in large measure on your beliefs and predispositions.

Your beliefs and predispositions about teaching and education have a profound impact on how you teach and what you teach, just as your beliefs and predispositions about living have a profound impact on how you live your life. As human beings, we carry beliefs from tradition, experience, education, religion, and socialization, and we revise and refine them through experience. Over time, these beliefs become stronger as we find they serve us well and prove to be true for us. These beliefs ultimately become our philosophy of life.

The same can be said about teaching. You have current beliefs which you are beginning to think about and which you are beginning to modify in response to new experiences and your explorations of new information. What you know and come to believe about education will become stronger through the experiences you will have in your teacher preparation program. Over time, you will learn more and more about education and will revise and refine your beliefs as a result of your experiences. These beliefs will form the basis of your ever-evolving philosophy of education.

There are many different philosophies in education that motivate the approaches excellent teachers exhibit. In this chapter, you will consider several prominent philosophies that guide U.S. education and find where your current beliefs fit. You will examine your own philosophical beliefs, compare them with these basic philosophies of education, study the applications of these philosophies in schools, investigate prominent psychologies that seek to explain the mechanism of learning, and put all this together as you develop your own tentative philosophy of education that will guide your inquiries through the rest of this course.

Chapter Objectives

As a result of your explorations in this chapter, you will be able to:

1. Explore the nature of philosophy by examining the main branches of philosophy.
   InTASC Standard #9: Professional Learning and Ethical Practice

2. Relate the main branches of philosophy to educational issues and educational philosophy.
   InTASC Standard #9: Professional Learning and Ethical Practice

3. Investigate the schools of philosophic thought in education and examine your thoughts about each.
   InTASC Standard #9: Professional Learning and Ethical Practice

4. Describe the primary characteristics of humanist, behaviorist, information processing, and constructivist educational psychologies.
   InTASC Standard #2: Learning Differences

5. Develop your personal preliminary philosophy of education.
   InTASC Standard #9: Professional Learning and Ethical Practice

The Nature of Philosophy

Let us eavesdrop on a conversation between two students who have just finished their explorations in Chapter 1 of this text:

> *"Sure," says one, "I agree that teachers should be respectful, listen to the kids, and show a sense of humor. But, that doesn't mean I am going to let them run my classroom. I am the authority, and I am going to run it my way."*
>
> *The other preservice teacher responds, "I agree that teachers should show respect to students, should listen to students, and should have a sense of humor. But if they are to learn anything at all, they have to have a say-so about what goes on in the classroom."*

Here are two people with the same thoughts about the qualities of effective teachers but opposite thoughts about how to run the classroom. One believes teachers must have total control of the classroom if students are to learn; the other believes teachers must allow students to have an input into what goes on in the classroom if they are to learn.

These two people differ fundamentally in their beliefs about the most effective practices in the classroom. They have different views about human beings and human nature, and they have different beliefs and concepts about how people learn, especially in schools. In short, they have different philosophies of education.

What Is Philosophy?

The word *philosophy* comes from two Greek words *philos*, which means "love," and *sophy*, which means "wisdom." Literally speaking, then, *philosophy* means "love of wisdom." In common use, *philosophy* refers to the general beliefs, concepts, and attitudes possessed by an individual or group. You have a philosophy of life that consists of a set of general beliefs, concepts, and attitudes about life, and you probably have a philosophy of education in which you have a set of general beliefs, concepts, and attitudes about education.

Throughout history, people have struggled to find answers to fundamental questions such as:

- What is real?
- What do we know?
- How do we know what we know?
- What is of value?
- What is logical?
- What is beautiful?
- What is right? What is wrong?

There are many complex and elusive questions about life, education, and other areas of our existence that are similar to these questions. There are also many different, complex, and elusive answers to these questions. The study of these kinds of questions is the substance of philosophy.

Branches of Philosophy

To facilitate the studies of these kinds of questions, philosophy has been arranged into several branches, each addressing different, but related, questions. The chief branches are metaphysics, epistemology, axiology, and logic (see Figure 2.1).

Metaphysics

Metaphysics is the branch of philosophy that addresses questions of reality. Metaphysics is concerned with such philosophical questions as:

- What is reality?
- Are people basically good or bad?
- What is the nature of the world in which we live?
- What is the nature of being and of reality? (a branch of metaphysics called ontology)
- What is the origin and what is the structure of the universe? (a branch of metaphysics called cosmology)
- What or who is God? What are the relations among God, humankind, and the universe? (a branch of metaphysics called theology)

metaphysics The branch of philosophy concerned with questions of reality.

epistemology The study of knowledge.

axiology The branch of philosophy concerned with values.

logic The branch of philosophy concerned with reasoning.

ontology The branch of metaphysics concerned with the nature of being and reality.

cosmology The branch of metaphysics in philosophy concerned with the origin and structure of the universe.

theology The branch of metaphysics in philosophy concerned with God and the relations among God, mankind, and the universe.

Branch of Philosophy		Chief Topic	Questions Related to Education
Metaphysics	Ontology	Reality	• What is knowledge? • Are students basically capable people or incapable people? • How does our view of knowledge determine what should be taught?
	Cosmology	The Universe	• How orderly should my classroom be? • Should the curriculum be structured or determined by students? • Should I teach the theory of evolution or creationism? • What texts should I use as authoritative?
	Theology	God	• Is it possible to motivate all students to want to learn? • Is a student's ability to learn innate or acquired? • Should all people have the same access to education?
Epistemology		Knowledge	• Should teachers lecture, ask questions, provide experiences, or encourage activities to enable students to learn? • How do scientists do science?
Axiology		Values Ethics Aesthetics	• Are students basically good or bad? • How should I treat students? • How should students treat others and me? • Should my behavior management system be punitive or encouraging? • What different understandings of "beautiful" might there be in my classroom? • What values should be taught in character education? • What is the importance of art education and music education in schools?
Logic		Reasoning	• Should I use deductive or inductive reasoning in my lessons? • How can I understand the ways my students are reasoning?

◄ **Figure 2.1**
Branches of philosophy and representative educational questions associated with each.
© Cengage Learning 2014

In classrooms, teachers invoke metaphysical issues regularly when they make decisions about what they should teach on any particular day, how they should organize the classroom to facilitate maximum learning, and what motivational strategies they should use. Several metaphysical questions related to educational situations are shown in Figure 2.1.

Epistemology

Epistemology is the study of knowledge and how we come to know. This branch of philosophy seeks to answer several basic questions, such as:

■ What is knowledge?
■ What is truth?
■ Where did knowledge originate?

- How do we come to know?
- How do we learn?

As you can imagine, much of your teacher preparation program will deal with epistemological topics. For educators, epistemology (the nature of knowledge and learning) and its cousin, *pedagogy* (the art and science of teaching), are the primary areas of concern. Figure 2.1 also shows a few education-related questions that deal with epistemological ideas.

Axiology

Axiology is the branch of philosophy that deals with values. Axiology seeks to answer such questions as:

- What is of value?
- What values are essential?
- What is morality? Is morality defined by our actions or our thoughts? (a branch of axiology called *ethics*)
- What is beauty? (a branch of axiology called *aesthetics*)
- What is beautiful?

Axiology addresses our thinking about what teacher-student interactions should be and how teachers should behave toward students. As you will learn, according to Abraham Maslow, axiology also addresses one of the basic needs of human beings—the need for aesthetic satisfaction. Figure 2.1 shows a few education-related questions dealing with axiological concerns.

Logic

Logic is the branch of philosophy that deals with reasoning. There are two basic types of reasoning: deductive reasoning and inductive reasoning. In *deductive* reasoning, thinking proceeds from the most general concepts to the most specific examples. In *inductive* reasoning, thinking proceeds from the most specific examples to the most general concepts; generalizations are derived from the specific examples (see Figure 2.2).

deductive reasoning The type of reasoning that proceeds from the most general to the most specific.

inductive reasoning The type of reasoning that proceeds from the most specific to the most general.

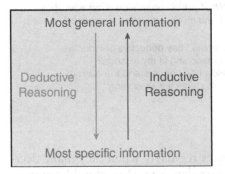

Figure 2.2 ▶
Deductive versus inductive reasoning.
© Cengage Learning 2014

As you may have observed, this entire text uses an inductive approach. The following sets illustrate deductive and inductive reasoning:

Deductive reasoning	Inductive reasoning
All humans are mortal	I am mortal.
I am human.	You are mortal.
Therefore I am mortal.	We are humans. Therefore humans are mortal.

A famous puzzle in deductive logic, "Who Owns the Zebra?," was published by *Life* magazine in 1962. You can access this puzzle through the direct link available on the Education CourseMate web site.

Figure 2.1 shows a few education-related questions dealing with concerns of logic.

Educational Philosophy

Whereas general philosophy seeks to answer questions about metaphysics, epistemology, axiology, and logic, educational philosophies extend to questions about the general beliefs, concepts, and attitudes people have about education. You have already looked at some general philosophical questions as they apply to education. In this chapter, we narrow our focus to six basic questions:

- What should be taught?
- Who should decide what should be taught?
- Why should this material be taught?
- How should this material be taught?
- What should the teacher's role be?
- What should the student's role be?

There are many possible answers to these questions based on various factors. The answers differ according to the person considering the questions and what that person's culture, ethnicity, experiences, and beliefs are. The answers differ from one historical time period to another, from region to region, and among different kinds of schools, such as public, private, parochial, charter schools, and home schools. The answers change as the cultural makeup of our country becomes increasingly diversified.

What are *your* responses to these questions? You probably have some initial thoughts and ideas based on your beliefs and past experiences. These thoughts represent the beginnings of your philosophy of education.

To help you move toward finding your own personal niche in the world of educational philosophy, let us start with an examination of your personal beliefs about what is important and what is not important in education.

Characteristics of Educational Philosophies

BUILDING BLOCK
2.1

Study the statements in each of the following groups and circle the numbers of the statements with which you agree. Then consider the questions that follow. (This activity can also be found on the CourseMate website so you can print it out or take the inventory electronically.)

GROUP I

1. The most important knowledge for students to learn in school are the profound truths discovered and developed in the past.
2. Above all, schools should develop students' abilities to think deeply, analytically, and creatively.
3. Drill and acquisition of factual knowledge are very important components of the learning environment.
4. There is certain basic information that everyone must know.

5. When it comes to knowledge, the teacher is the most authoritative person in the classroom.
6. Students should study great works that have been validated by society over time.
7. Students should focus primarily on learning the knowledge and insights their teachers impart.
8. The teacher should be a strong authority figure in the classroom.
9. Ideal teachers present knowledge to students and interpret it for them to ensure that they understand it correctly.
10. The curriculum in a given grade or subject should be the same for everyone.

GROUP II

1. The student is the receiver of knowledge.
2. The curriculum of schools should center on the basic subjects of reading, writing, history, mathematics, and science.
3. Students should not be promoted from one grade to the next until they have mastered certain key material.
4. Recitation and demonstration of acquired knowledge are essential components of learning.
5. The curriculum of a school should consist primarily of the skills and subjects that are essential for all students to know.
6. Schools should reflect the social and economic needs of the society they serve.
7. Lecture-discussion is the most effective teaching technique.
8. Memorization, drill, and practice are the keys to learning skills.
9. Teaching by subject area is the most effective approach.
10. Effective classrooms are quiet and orderly.

GROUP III

1. Schools should prepare students for analyzing and solving the types of problems they will face outside the classroom.
2. New material is best taught through facilitating students in their own investigations.
3. Teachers must stress the relevance of what students are learning to their lives outside, as well as inside, the classroom.
4. Many students learn best by engaging in real-world activities rather than by reading.
5. Art lessons should focus primarily on individual expression and creativity.
6. Students should be active participants in the learning process.
7. The curriculum of a school should be built around the personal experiences and needs of students.
8. Teachers should be seen as facilitators of learning.
9. Students should have substantial input into the curriculum being studied.
10. Classrooms should have areas for large group discussion and small group inquiries.

GROUP IV

1. Students should be permitted to determine their own rules in the educational process.
2. Schools should offer students choices in what to study and when classes are held.
3. Ideal teachers are constant questioners.
4. Effective learning can be unstructured, informal, and open.
5. The purpose of the school is to help students understand and define themselves and find the meaning of their existence.

6. It is more important for a student to develop a positive self-concept than to learn specific subject matter.
7. Students should be permitted to determine their own curriculum.
8. The ideal teacher helps students identify their most effective methods of study.
9. The furniture in the classroom should be movable by both students and teachers to meet multiple and flexible purposes.
10. Teachers function as facilitators and resource persons rather than as instructors.

GROUP V

1. Schools should foster change through orderly means when dealing with controversial issues.
2. Schools must place more emphasis on teaching about the concerns of minorities and women.
3. The United States must become more cooperative economically with countries such as Japan, China, and Mexico, and schools have an obligation to provide the education students need to facilitate such change.
4. Schools should plan substantial social interactions in their curriculum.
5. The primary aim of schools is to prepare students to accomplish social reform.
6. Education should focus on injustices and inequities in society and ways of solving these difficulties.
7. Teachers should be committed to achieving a new social order.
8. Students should learn to identify problems and situations that affect society.
9. Students should focus on community building in their classes rather than obedience of the teacher's directions.
10. Community service and involvement with community projects are essential components of education.

Each group represents a particular philosophy of education—a set of beliefs, concepts, and attitudes about what should happen in schools. Different philosophies contend that education ought to be handled in ways that are markedly different from the contentions of other philosophies.

The five philosophies of education discussed in this chapter are the primary sets of educational beliefs that govern education in the United States. Although many other philosophies of education exist and many philosophies originate from non-European roots, the five presented here represent the mainstream of thinking about education in the United States.

▪ Is there a group in which you agreed with all or most statements? Which one?

▪ Is there a group in which you disagreed with all or most statements? Which one?

▪ In which group or groups did you agree with some of the statements and disagree with others?

▪ If you had to select only one group that represents your beliefs about education, which would it be? What is its name?

In this Building Block, Group I contains statements with which *perennialists* strongly agree. Group II contains statements with which *essentialists* strongly agree. Group III contains statements with which *progressivists* strongly agree. Group IV contains statements with which *existentialists* strongly agree. Group V contains statements with which social *reconstructionists* strongly agree.

From this activity, you can identify one or more labels for your philosophic thoughts.

The Power of Beliefs in Education: Homework

As you can imagine, each of the philosophies shown in Building Block 2.1 have different convictions about homework. Some educators stress the importance of children doing homework to acquire mastery. Some stress doing homework as a means to solve problems generated by classroom discussions. Homework has become part of the fabric of U.S. education and is given from kindergarten through the senior year of high school. Homework assignments are meant to be completed outside of class—at home, at a different nonschool venue, or during study halls or free time at school, and sometimes even during after-school supervised times. Homework as traditionally viewed consists of answering specific questions or reading particular material that relates to that day's studies or helps prepare students for the next day's studies. Most schools and many individual classrooms or middle grades and high school classes also have homework policies. These policies are often posted online. In writing for the website *About.com: Teaching*, Meador (n.d.) provides an example of homework policies that says schools believe "the purpose of homework should be to practice, reinforce, or apply acquired skills and knowledge." The College Board (2012) states that homework has several purposes: reinforcement of what has been learned during the day; building study habits that are essential in college; preparing for classes; and getting a sense of progress.

It is nearly universally agreed (among students) that doing homework is a painful and undesirable task. Homework has been made somewhat less painful through the use of telephone help lines, online tutoring, studying together with peers, parental assistance, and, yes, even the Internet. Mendicino, Razzy, and Heffernan (2009) found that, in a class of fifth graders, students learned significantly more math from web-based homework assignments than from traditional homework assignments.

Because the primary purpose cited for giving homework is to increase achievement, let us take a look at the research. Cooper, Robinson, and Paul (2006) reviewed the research done about homework between 1987 and 2003; they found that the research generally showed that homework had a positive effect on achievement, and that this effect was stronger in middle school and high school than in elementary school. In his introductory article to a special issue of the *Journal of Advanced Academics*, Benbenutty (2011) writes, "Homework is an important and an effective educational supplement" (p. 185), and that "Research has established that homework has a positive effect on learning, particularly at the middle and secondary school levels" (p. 186). Baker and LeTendre (2005) report that some 70 percent of U.S. teachers use homework

assignments to calculate grades (compared with 20 percent in Canada, 14 percent in Japan, and 9 percent in Singapore). However, Vatterott (2011) found that grading homework did not increase achievement; in fact, there was a negative correlation between grading homework and increased achievement.

On the other hand, there is a growing revolt against homework. Perhaps the most outspoken author on this subject is Alfie Kohn. He has argued for many years that homework has a negative impact, or, at best, no value. He cites Harris Cooper, the nation's foremost researcher of topics dealing with homework (and whose summary of research you just read from the article by Cooper, Robinson, and Patall, 2006). According to Kohn, Cooper says, "There is no evidence that any amount of homework improves the academic performance of elementary students" (Cooper, Robinson, & Patall 2006, as cited in Kohn, 2006, p. 13), and he makes the point that results of research can be (and often are) slanted to support the bias of the consumer of the research. So, for example, the statement that doing homework has "little or no effect" can be interpreted to mean that there *is* an effect, and therefore homework works because the word *little* is included in the statement. A large body of research concludes that homework relates to little or no increase in achievement.

Thus, it appears that the homework issue is a conundrum, with people on both sides of the issue citing research and personal experience to bolster their arguments. Besides, as you saw in Chapter 1, families and the community have great influences on what happens in school, and the vast majority of parents want their children to bring homework home. What to do? *The New York Times* reports that schools and school districts across the nation are rethinking their homework policies, suggesting alternatives, and reducing the homework requirements, especially in elementary schools (Hu, 2011). But this reform is just beginning. With time, we will see more and more alternatives to the current homework situation being implemented in schools.

WHAT DO YOU THINK?

1. *What are some reasons why teachers should give homework?*
2. *What are some reasons why teachers should not give homework?*
3. *What are some alternatives to traditional homework assignments?*
4. *When you are a teacher, will you give homework? Or not? Explain your response.*

Schools of Philosophic Thought

Let us examine the five philosophies presented in Building Block 2.1 in a bit more detail. While you are doing this, compare the inventory you took with the discussions of each philosophy. Ask yourself where you agree and where you disagree. In this manner, you can interpret your initial thoughts about educational philosophies, and you can judge whether you are satisfied with the label(s) you gave yourself, or whether any labels are appropriate.

Exploring Educational Philosophies

BUILDING BLOCK

2.2

In this Building Block, you will become better acquainted with the major philosophies of education. Answer the six questions we raised earlier for each philosophy shown in the following table. Use your exploration of philosophies in Building Block 2.1 and your current understandings of what should occur in schools to help you in your thinking.

What are the root words for the terms *perennialism, essentialism, progressivism, existentialism,* and *social reconstructionism?*

Based on the root words for each of the five philosophies, what inferences can you make about the following questions?

Use your favorite search engine to explore the websites of several schools. Do they post homework policies? See if they have online or any other kind of resources for help with homework available.

	Perennialism	Essentialism	Progressivism	Existentialism	Social Reconstructionism
What should be taught?					
Who should decide what is taught?					
Why should this material be taught?					
How should this material be taught?					
What should the teacher's role be?					
What should the student's role be?					

Perennialism

As you probably have surmised, the root word of *perennialism* is "perennial." The philosophy of perennialism advances the idea that the focus of education should be the universal truths conveyed through the classic and profound thoughts and works that have lasted through the centuries and have recurred in each generation. Like a perennial plant that returns year after year, these thoughts and works are everlasting. They have withstood the test of time and are as important and relevant today as they were when first conceived. The enduring wisdom of the past is a guide to the present.

Examples of these classic materials include works of great literature, findings of great scientists, and timeless concepts of history. High school students study Shakespeare's plays, Homer's *Iliad*, Melville's *Moby Dick*, Newton's laws of motion, Einstein's theories, and other works that have become part of today's classic repertoire. Students take courses that focus on the traditional subjects of reading, writing, language, mathematics, science, history, and the arts. Elementary and middle school students prepare for more advanced work by studying basic subjects from the perspective of the classic tradition in a tightly controlled and well-disciplined atmosphere. Perennialists believe the emphasis of school should be the mastery of content and the development of reasoning skills in the arts and sciences, and that thoughtful consideration of the classical works is the way to achieve these goals.

Perennialists believe that truth does not depend on time or place but rather is the same for all people. They believe the same curriculum should be required of all students. Their reasoning is twofold: (1) Because the goal of school is to teach the truth, and the truth is the same for everyone, the curriculum must be the same. (2) Because people are born equal and have the same opportunities, to give some students a curriculum that is different from that of others is to treat them differently and is a form of discrimination.

Use your favorite search engine to find out more about the philosophy of Paideia and Mortimer Adler.

Who decides what should be taught? Society at large makes these decisions because it is society that has validated the importance of these works over time and has continued to hold these classics in high esteem. Many individuals have assembled canons of material they believe should be taught. Noteworthy is Mortimer Adler, whose 1982 work *The Paideia Proposal* describes a system of education based on the classics. His book has led to the development of an innovative school model called the Paideia (pronounced py-DAY-ah) program. The Paideia Group has worked with several hundred schools in all grade levels throughout the United States since its inception. Teachers use three basic methods of teaching: (1) didactic teaching in which the teacher lectures (10 percent to 15 percent of the time); (2) Socratic seminars[1] in which the teacher uses directed questioning to help students arrive at desirable answers (15 percent to 20 percent of the time); and (3) coaching in which the teacher coaches students in the academic subjects (60 percent to 70 percent of the time) (Brandt and Voke, 2002; National Paideia Center, 2011). The outcomes of these three types of instruction are knowledge acquisition, achievement in mathematics and language skills, and an increase in understanding of basic ideas (National Paideia Center, 2011).

In the 1930s, Adler and Robert Maynard Hutchins, then president of the University of Chicago, organized the classics into a set of more than 400 works titled *Great Books of the Western World* (1952), which they believed would enable students to become independent and critical thinkers. They held that people can discover the truths through their senses and their reasoning—that they do not

© Image State/Alamy

Of the five philosophies of education—perennialism, essentialism, existentialism, progressivism, or social reconstructionism—which is demonstrated in this elementary classroom?

[1]The Socratic method is patterned after the way the Greek philosopher Socrates taught. He believed people were born with all the information they need in life and that all people were born with the same basic information. Through skillful question-and-discussion sessions with students, he would be able to get his students to bring this hidden information to the surface.

construct truths because they are already in existence. The *Great Books of the Western World* represent the fruit of these discoveries made by other people; as students read and discuss them, they, too, can encounter the great truths of the universe.

Of course, because perennialists believe the primary goal of school is for students to learn what others have created and to use this knowledge in their own lives, teachers are expected to present this material to the students. There is little or no room for students to venture into tangents of their own interest; the curriculum must be covered. A teacher's role is to impart knowledge. To do this, teachers hold seminars, engage students in Socratic discussions, foster directed readings of great books, explain principles and concepts, and lecture as effectively as possible, presenting dynamic lessons with all the interest-grabbing devices available. The work is demanding, and the classroom is disciplined.

The student's role is to discuss, examine, and reexamine the information presented by the teacher with the ultimate goal of learning the content.

BUILDING BLOCK
2.3

Your Thoughts about Perennialism

- Review the statements associated with perennialism (Group I) in Building Block 2.1. What key words in these statements describe the perennialist philosophy of education?

- How did the inferences you made about perennialism in Building Block 2.2 compare with the textbook's description of this educational philosophy?

- What do you think are the strengths of perennialism as applied to education?

- What do you think are the weaknesses of perennialism as applied to education?

Essentialism

The philosophy of essentialism takes its name from the word *essential*. Essentialists believe there are certain basic or essential knowledge, skills, and understandings students should master. Essentialists assert that, over time, society has found that certain skills, such as reading, writing, calculating, and computer skills, are needed for people to function effectively. Accordingly, certain subjects, such as the language arts, mathematics,

Mortimer Jerome Adler (1902–2001) was born in New York City, the son of an immigrant jewelry salesman. He dropped out of school at the age of 14 to become a copy boy for a New York newspaper, but, hoping to become a journalist, he took courses in writing at Columbia University. While there, he became intensely interested in philosophy. He completed his course work but did not graduate because he had not completed the physical education requirement. He later earned his PhD at Columbia. Adler served as a professor of psychology at Columbia during the 1920s, and

he taught at the University of Chicago during the 1930s. At the University of Chicago, he advocated the adoption of the classics as a main part of the curriculum, although the rest of the faculty disagreed.

Adler believed in providing the same liberal education without electives or vocational classes for all people. He believed education should teach people (1) to think critically, (2) to use their leisure time well, (3) to earn their living ethically, and (4) to be responsible citizens in a democracy. He believed that people should become lifelong learners.

Mortimer Adler is best known in the education community for his devotion to the adoption of the classics as the mainstream of education, the Paideia schools, and his insistence that students read key works of Western literature and philosophy.

science, history, and computer training, are essential for people to gain the knowledge and skills they need. According to the essentialist viewpoint, this knowledge and these skills will always be needed. Thus, we can say that society at large decides in general what these essentials are. Businesses, banks, manufacturers, retailers, and others provide input to the institutions of education, detailing the strengths and weaknesses they see in high school graduates. The educators, in turn, use this input to help them develop programs of study that will prepare students to enter the workforce. Because most of the people who provide input into the educational system are concerned with students mastering the basic skills of reading, writing, and basic mathematics (the "three Rs"), the programs developed naturally reflect these concerns. Thus, essentialism can be termed the "back-to-basics" approach to education.

Essentialism has been the guiding philosophy of education in the United States for a very long time. (You will consider this again in Chapter 10, when you investigate the history of U.S. education.) The Soviet launching of Sputnik in October 1957 rekindled this thinking. The United States felt deeply humiliated by the Soviet success. Our scientists had been working on launching a U.S. spacecraft for a number of years in order to be first in the race to space. When the Soviets beat the United States, citizens asked, "How did this happen? How did the United States, with all its technological capabilities, all its talent, and all its money, not achieve the goal of being first in space?" As so often happens, education took much of the blame.

Two opposing views addressed the seeming weaknesses in American education. One advocated an increased emphasis on education in science, mathematics, and technology and an increase in inquiry teaching strategies. This thrust was strengthened by the Woods Hole Conference of 1959, chaired by Jerome Bruner and attended by scientists, mathematicians, psychologists, and technology specialists (Bruner, 1965). The conference affirmed the increasing momentum in science, mathematics, and technology education; it also called for studying less material but studying it in greater depth and requiring students to inquire and figure things out for themselves.

The other view was a growing concern that U.S. students were not mastering the basic material of reading, writing, mathematics, science, and other areas. This concern was later highlighted in *A Nation at Risk,* the 1983 report of the President's Commission on Excellence in Education (National Commission on Excellence in Education, 1983). The report essentially said that U.S. children were at risk for lagging behind other nations in achievement of basic subjects and that we had better teach our children to read, write, and do mathematics—and we had better do it *now*. In 1998, the Center for Education Reform reaffirmed these findings in *A Nation Still at Risk*. These are the same concerns as those that underlay the No Child Left Behind Act of 2001 (*The No Child Left Behind Executive Summary,* 2001). This wide support for a back-to-basics curriculum and the emphasis on basic subjects has eclipsed the recommendations made at the Woods Hole Conference.

You can access the full text and executive summary of *A Nation at Risk* through a direct link on the Education CourseMate website.

In essentialist education, students receive instruction in the basic subjects of reading, writing, mathematics, science, history, foreign language, and technology. Unlike perennialism, which emphasizes a canon of great works and classics, essentialism emphasizes fundamental knowledge and skills that business and political leaders believe members of today's society need to know to be productive in the workplace.

Teachers transmit this essential knowledge and expect students to learn it. Teachers are considered repositories of knowledge to be transmitted. This means educators develop and employ a sequence of topics in each subject, progressing from less complex to more complex material through successive grade levels. It also means using lecture and recitation, discussion, drill and practice (sometimes called "drill and kill"), and a variety of teaching and learning materials to ensure that students learn the content. For example, a middle grades social studies teacher might give a lecture on why large cities are located where they are, using maps and videos as aids, rather than having students investigate the phenomenon for themselves by engaging in map exploration activities.

The role of the students is to learn the content and skills being taught and to demonstrate their mastery of them on achievement tests, often in the form of standardized tests that are used to make local, regional, statewide, and national comparisons.

E. D. Hirsch, Jr., has written extensively on what should be included in essentialist education. His works include *Cultural Literacy: What Every American Needs to Know* (Turtleback Books, 1988), *The New Dictionary of Cultural Literacy: What Every American Needs to Know* (Houghton Mifflin, 1987), and *The New First Dictionary of Cultural Literacy: What Your Child Needs to Know* (Turtleback Books, 2004). In addition, he has published several volumes in his *Core Knowledge Series* that deal with what children in elementary grades should know (Hirsch, 1994–1999). Hirsch's work could be considered perennialist in nature except for its emphasis on science, which reflects his essentialist viewpoint.

 Use your favorite Internet search engine to find out more about the Core Knowledge Foundation that E. D. Hirsch, Jr. established.

BIOGRAPHY

E. D. Hirsch, Jr. (b. 1928) is a prominent figure in the theories underlying essentialist education. He holds degrees from Cornell and Yale, and he retired as the university professor of education and humanities at the University of Virginia. He is founder and chairman of the Core Knowledge Foundation, a nonprofit organization dedicated to the establishment of a curriculum of Core Knowledge, a sequenced body of knowledge recommended by the foundation to be taught in preschool through eighth grade. The foundation is a major source of research, theory, and practical lessons and assessments for all recommended subjects in pre-K–8 schools. Although his Core Knowledge schools operate nationwide, critics have challenged Hirsch's essentialist theories, contending that students who use the Core Knowledge curriculum are taught what to think rather than *how* to think and that the perspective is Eurocentric, giving only minor attention to non-Eurocentric influences.

Your Thoughts about Essentialism

BUILDING BLOCK 2.4

- Review the statements associated with essentialism (Group II) in Building Block 2.1. What key words in these statements describe the essentialist philosophy of education?

- How did the inferences you made about essentialism in Building Block 2.2 compare with the description of this educational philosophy?

- What do you think are the strengths of essentialism as applied to education?

- What do you think are the weaknesses of essentialism as applied to education?

Progressivism

The educational philosophy of progressivism takes its name from the word *progressive*. The dictionary defines *progressive* as "making use of or interested in new ideas, findings, or opportunities" and "… an educational theory marked by emphasis on the individual child, informality of classroom procedure, and encouragement of self-expression" (Merriam-Webster, 2012). Thus, the philosophy of progressivism espouses the idea that the focus of education should be students rather than content and that whatever is taught should be meaningful. To progressivists, the purpose of education is to prepare students to be lifelong learners in an ever-changing society.

One of the key figures in the progressivist movement was John Dewey. Dewey's writings and his work at the Laboratory School at the University of Chicago, where he tested and refined his educational ideas, have produced tremendous innovations in U.S. education. To Dewey, the traditional school where students sat in rows and passively received information imparted by the teacher was ineffective. He argued that if students are to learn, they must be involved with real problems and meaningful questions, must solve problems according to a scientific method, must be free to develop their own theories and their own conceptualizations, and must be encouraged to test their conclusions in real situations. The progressivist movement focused on several basic principles:[2]

1. Students should be free to develop naturally.
2. Student interest should guide the teaching.
3. The teacher should be a guide, not a taskmaster.
4. Student development should involve the *whole* student, and should include physical, mental, moral, and social growth.
5. Schools should attend to the physical development of students.
6. There should be school–home cooperation to meet the needs of students realistically.

Progressivists focus the curriculum on the needs of students. These needs include academic, social, and physical needs and are fueled by the interests of the students. Therefore, the material to be studied is determined jointly among the school, the teacher, and the students. Learning is considered a natural response to curiosity and the need to solve problems. In the progressivist school, teachers expose students to many new developments in science, technology, literature, and the arts to show that knowledge is constantly changing. Progressivists believe that students should study great ideas and thoughts of the past, but they also believe knowledge is changing and the job of students is to learn *how* to learn so that they can cope successfully with new challenges in life and discover what truths are relevant to the present.

Of prime importance is the idea that knowledge that is true in the present may not be true in the future. Costa (2007) estimates that by the year 2020, the amount of knowledge in the world will double every 73 days. Considering that 2020 is not that far off, what do you think of that proposal? Not only is knowledge expected to grow exponentially, but new knowledge will replace old knowledge and old knowledge will become obsolete.

Progressivist teachers engage students in inquiries that the students themselves develop. Students learn from one another in addition to the teacher, so the progressivist classroom fosters social learning by having students work in cooperative groups. Progressivist teachers are facilitators, resource people, and co-inquirers. The primary role of students is to develop new and deeper understandings continuously through their own investigation. Thus, in an elementary education progressivist mathematics class dealing with place value, we see children in small groups using various kinds of manipulatives to develop their own understandings of place value and helping one another clarify their ideas. The teacher facilitates these activities but does not lecture.

Which philosophy of education encourages active, hands-on learning, like using mathematics manipulatives in a math lesson?

© Richard Hutchings/PhotoEdit Inc.

[2]From "The Principles of Education," stated by the Progressive Education Association in 1924; cited in Tyack, 1967, pp. 347–48.

© Hulton Archives/Getty Images

John Dewey (1859–1952) was born on a farm near Burlington, Vermont. He was arguably the most influential U.S. educator in the 20th century. He graduated from the University of Vermont, and after three years of teaching, earned his doctorate at Johns Hopkins University. Dewey taught philosophy at the University of Michigan and the University of Minnesota before becoming chair of the Department of Philosophy, Psychology, and Pedagogy at the University of Chicago. He developed the university's Laboratory School in 1896, and directed it for the next seven years, pioneering experimental efforts and translating their results into practice. Because of disagreements with the university over the Laboratory School, Dewey left in 1904, to become a professor of philosophy at Columbia University.

In addition to his contributions in the areas of philosophy, psychology, politics, and social thought, Dewey was instrumental in developing modern education theory. His was a prominent voice in educational philosophy, with an emphasis on progressivism.

He rejected authoritarian teaching methods and advocated the importance of experiential education— learning by doing. He also stressed the importance of the development of the person.

Dewey's ideas were adopted by the "progressivist education" movement, but they frequently were distorted, with the result that, contrary to Dewey's intentions, subject-matter education was often neglected in favor of classroom entertainment or vocational education.

To some of Dewey's admirers, he was the greatest educator who ever lived. On the other hand, many attribute the "ills" of U.S. education to the influence of his ideas. Whatever one believes about John Dewey, there is no mistaking the fact that he taught generations of students to examine ideas carefully and objectively before deciding on their own conclusions or course of action. Several of Dewey's quotes are apropos:

- "Anyone who has begun to think places some portion of the world in jeopardy."
- "Education is not preparation for life; education is life itself."
- "Every great advance in science has issued from a new audacity of the imagination."

Your Thoughts about Progressivism

BUILDING BLOCK
2.5

- Review the statements associated with progressivism (Group III) in Building Block 2.1. What key words in these statements describe the progressivist philosophy of education?

- How did the inferences you made about progressivism in Building Block 2.2 compare with the description of this educational philosophy?

- What do you think are the strengths of progressivism as applied to education?

- What do you think are the weaknesses of progressivism as applied to education?

Existentialism

Existentialism focuses on the *existence* of the individual. Existentialists emphasize that people are responsible for defining themselves. To exist is to choose, and the choices people make define who they are. According to the existentialist point of view, people have two choices: They can either define themselves, or they can choose to be defined by others. The existentialist believes the only "truth" is the "truth" determined by the individual. Individuals determine for themselves what is meant by such terms as *right, wrong, beautiful, ugly, true, false,* and the like. Existentialists truly believe that "beauty is in the eye of the beholder." Existentialists believe that, whereas the great thinkers of the past had their own ways of thinking about life and the natural world, their thoughts were uniquely theirs, and today's students need to find their own ways of thinking and develop their own conclusions.

In the existentialist classroom, students determine what they need to study, guided, of course, by the teacher. The idea is for students to come to their own understandings. Because every student is different, no single set of learning outcomes is appropriate for

BIOGRAPHY

Jean-Paul Sartre (1905–1980), a leader of existentialism, was born in Paris. After earning his doctorate, he taught philosophy in French high schools until he was drafted into the army at the start of World War II. He was captured by the Germans, but escaped and became a leader in the resistance movement.

The philosophy of existentialism became very popular in Europe after the war. According to existentialism, we first exist and then we define ourselves through the choices we make. Sartre believed man's responsibility is vested in man, himself. People are entitled to be human with dignity, and a human is a human only when he or she is entirely free and accepts responsibility for this freedom. Sartre's basic premise was that life has no meaning or purpose except for the personal goals each person sets. This philosophy captured the attention of post–World War II Europeans who were yearning for freedom, and it is embraced today by people who believe they have the freedom to take responsibility for their own actions.

Although Sartre was principally a novelist, essayist, and playwright (he won the Nobel Prize in Literature in 1964), his works captured the essence of his philosophy and have become the underpinnings of today's application of existentialism to education.

all students. Teachers and the school lay out the topics that are considered appropriate for the students to study at each grade level, and the students make their own meaningful choices.

The teacher is a facilitator, working with each student to help him or her find appropriate materials and the best methods of study. The teacher is also a resource—one of many resources that also include other students, books, great works, contemporary works, the Internet and other technological resources, television programs, newspapers and magazines, and other people.

In the existentialist classroom, students do many different things and study many different topics at the same time. For example, in a science class, a group of three or four students might be dissecting a frog, using models, manuals, and drawings to guide their work; another group might be watching a video on the human circulatory system (using headphones); and yet another group might be recording the observations they had previously made of the night sky in chart form. The teacher moves from group to group, working to facilitate the investigations, probing for understandings, and challenging students' conclusions.

The role of the student is to pursue his or her investigations of the chosen topic until the desired learning and understandings have taken place.

BUILDING BLOCK 2.6 Your Thoughts about Existentialism

- Review the statements associated with existentialism (Group IV) in Building Block 2.1. Which key words in these statements describe the existentialist philosophy of education?
- How did the inferences you made about existentialism in Building Block 2.2 compare with the description of this educational philosophy?
- What do you think are the strengths of existentialism as applied to education?
- What do you think are the weaknesses of existentialism as applied to education?

Social Reconstructionism

Social reconstructionism is particularly germane in today's shrinking world. As its name suggests, the social reconstructionist philosophy of education asserts that society needs to be changed (reconstructed) and that schools are the ideal instrument to foster such changes. Social reconstructionists believe that world crises require the use of education to facilitate the development of a new social order, one that is truly democratic in nature. Schools are seen as agents of the reformation of society rather than as transmitters of knowledge.

To this end, teachers help their students understand the validity and urgency of social problems. The determination of which of the many important and controversial social problems should be studied is made through democratic consensus of the students under the leadership of the teacher. There is an abundance of social problems at the local, national, and global levels that can be the focus of the curriculum. Examples include violence, hunger, poverty, terrorism, inflation, inequality, racism, sexism, homophobia, acquired immunodeficiency syndrome (AIDS), pollution, homelessness, substance abuse, bullying, and many others. In social reconstructionism, the students select the social priorities to be studied and decide on the educational objectives to be attained from the study. The curriculum integrates all the traditional subjects into single thematic interdisciplinary units. The students and teacher work together to uncover, solve, and propose solutions to the selected problems. The teacher helps students explore the problems, suggests alternative perspectives, and facilitates student analysis and conclusion formation. Throughout the study, the teacher models the democratic process. Teaching methodologies include simulation, role playing, group work, internships, work–study programs, and other forms of cooperation with the community and its resources.

Similar to their role in the existentialist classroom, students in a social reconstructionist class engage in many different activities to study the agreed-upon topic, such as researching through the Internet, reading case histories, analyzing multiple aspects of the topic, formulating predictions, proposing and justifying workable revisions and solutions, and taking action to implement these solutions.

Examples of actual social-reconstructionist projects include nationwide literacy programs, and providing potable water sources in Africa. You may have had the opportunity to experience a social reconstruction curriculum during your freshman year at your college or university. Often institutions of higher education design first-year experiences for entering students to include not only orientations to college life and tips on time management and study habits, but also the chance to participate in a service learning activity that may promote social change. According to the National Service Learning Clearinghouse, service learning "integrates meaningful community service with instruction and reflection to enrich the learning experience, teach civic responsibility, and strengthen communities" (National Service Learning Clearinghouse, 2011). The National Resource Center for the First-Year Experience and Students in Transition conducted a national survey of first-year programs. A survey of 1,019 institutions found that 40.3 percent of the responding institutions with first-year programs reported that their first-year experience included a service learning component (National Resource Center for the First-Year Experience and Students in Transition, 2009). Such service learning activities include both a chance to provide service to the community, and an agenda to promote social change. College students in first-year seminars may organize and participate in many national initiatives as part of a service learning activity that serves to promote social change. One example is Take Back the Night (TBN). TBN is an initiative that involves organizing peaceful marches in an effort to end violence against women and children. Another national example is the Day of Silence, sponsored by the Gay, Lesbian, and Straight Education Network (GLSEN), which encourages people to participate in a day of silence to advocate for the quashing of bullying and harassment of gay, lesbian, bisexual, and transgendered students in schools. In yet another example, the organization called Dogs Deserve Better works to promote legislation that would make chaining dogs outside illegal. Their website offers ideas on how individuals can get involved in hopes of promoting change.

Social reconstructionist service learning projects do not have to be focused on national movements. There are also plenty of opportunities locally for students to become involved. Notice that the examples provided here are not only appropriate for college students, but students in grades K–12 can also organize events to support social change.

service learning A teaching strategy that engages students in meaningful service to their communities through integration of community issues and the school curriculum.

Learn more about these national organizations by finding their websites on the Internet. Use your favorite browser to locate other opportunities to promote social change. Consider acting on what you find!

BIOGRAPHY

Paulo Freire (1921–1997) was a Brazilian educator who, although educated in law, became interested in education after he had children. He worked in literacy campaigns with the poor in Brazil to help them overcome their sense of powerlessness and empower themselves. Because he challenged the ruling elite, he was exiled from Brazil during a military coup in 1964. He taught at Harvard University from 1969 until 1979, when he was able to return to Brazil. In 1988, he assumed the position of minister of education for the City of São Paulo, a large city that contains two-thirds of Brazil's schools.

Freire is considered among the most influential educational thinkers in the late 20th century. He has been a major figure in progressive education, especially as it relates to empowering poor and oppressed adults. In his *Pedagogy of the Oppressed*, a significant and highly popular education book, he discussed his belief that education must involve dialogue and mutual understanding and must nurture respect between student and teacher, stressing that this was the key to the liberation of the oppressed. According to Freire, education is a two-way exchange of beliefs, thoughts, and ideas, unlike the traditional system of schooling, which he called a "banking approach" in which the teacher makes deposits of information into the students. He believed that true knowledge can result only from experiences in which students inquire into unknown phenomena and thereby establish their need for further knowledge. He believed that teachers must be sensitive to their students' viewpoints and lifestyles.

According to Freire, students must be viewed as being in charge of their own education and destinies. Once they arrive at this point, they can find their own ideas and then begin to "reconstruct" society on the basis of their new and validated conclusions.

A social reconstructionist curriculum helps students become involved and successful in school by promoting civic engagement and social skills (Furco and Root, 2010). As you can infer, social reconstructionist principles are important in helping guide schools, teachers, and students toward a multicultural emphasis.

Social reconstructionism is a very influential and powerful philosophy, especially when its goals of social reform are combined with other philosophies such as progressivism and existentialism. Critics of social reconstructionism are concerned with its singularity of purpose (the formation of a utopian democratic world society) and the indoctrination of students into this purpose. However, the new world order of the 21st century may well need the type of impact that can be given by students whose education is provided in a social reconstructionist environment.

BUILDING BLOCK 2.7

Your Thoughts about Social Reconstructionism

- Review the statements associated with social reconstructionism (Group V) in Building Block 2.1. What key words in these statements describe the social reconstructionist philosophy of education?
- How did the inferences you made about social reconstructionism in Building Block 2.2 compare with the description of this educational philosophy?
- What do you think are the strengths of social reconstructionism as applied to education?
- What do you think are the weaknesses of social reconstructionism as applied to education?

The Eclectic Approach

Many people find they agree with some of the statements and premises of several of the philosophies but disagree with other parts.

One Teacher's Philosophies
Kathy Heavers

Come observe my classroom. Students have assigned seats. They receive a list of upcoming assignments once every three weeks. On the board are posted the assignments due the previous class meeting, the assignments due that day, and the assignments due during the next week. Papers to be handed back are in the center of each table, and materials we will be using during the class period are stacked neatly in a pile at the edge of the table. I determine the curriculum. The first 45 minutes are mine to present information, take questions, and facilitate teacher-directed activities; the last 45 minutes constitute student work time. Sounds pretty structured doesn't it? *Perennialism perhaps?*

Take a closer look. The students are seated at hexagonal tables scattered throughout the room, not desks in a straight row. If seats weren't assigned, students would sit at the same table, in the same chair, usually by a friend, all semester long. Instead, I change the seating arrangements every four weeks so that students will have sat at each table and with every person in the class by the end of the semester. Most likely they will have met classmates they never knew before (and I still have control over seating arrangements if there are conflicts). *Is it looking more like progressivism?*

Students have a three-week list of assignments so that they can see what is coming up, have time to think about their approach to the assignments, budget their time, and work ahead should they choose. If they were absent, the board reminds them of what was due the day they missed. Today's assignments tell everyone what will be covered that day, and the upcoming assignments allow them to work ahead should they finish the work due that day. Students budget their own time and have total control over what they accomplish. *Students have total control? Is this existentialism?*

As soon as the students are seated at their tables, they look through the corrected papers and take theirs, so corrected work is retrieved by each student before the tardy bell rings; no time is wasted distributing handouts to the class because they are already at the individual tables. Organization is modeled, and one by one, students begin to pick up on that mode of operation. *One by one? Progressivism or existentialism?*

Although I determine the curriculum, it is based on what postsecondary school admissions and scholarship committees require. Each student determines his or her approach to the assignments. I assign a personal essay for use with school or scholarship applications, but each student begins by listing his or her three most outstanding character traits. The student then asks two acquaintances to list what they consider to be his or her three most outstanding traits. Each student then chooses on which of the nine traits he or she will focus and how he or she will develop the essay. *Is this progressivism with an emphasis on the individual child and encouragement of self-expression, or is it existentialism where the truth is determined by the individual and the thoughts uniquely their own?*

Students finish their personal essay and go on to a goals essay, which can also be used with school and scholarship applications. After individual exploration and listening to essays developed by former students, each student outlines his or her career goal, education goal (two-year, four-year, vocational, technical, military, or apprenticeship), major, and choice of school(s), as *no single set of curricular outcomes is appropriate for all students*. Carefully, the students craft their goals essay. Teacher and peer evaluations result in several drafts before the final copy is submitted. Acceptance to a postsecondary school and funding are the desired outcomes. *Individual students, individual traits, individual goals. Teacher facilitates investigation, working with each student to probe for understanding and determine approach. Existentialism?*

So what philosophy most closely approximates not only my beliefs about education but my practices as well? At the beginning of my career, as a traditional English teacher, it was *perennialism*. I addressed the rigorous curriculum others determined and imparted the knowledge, dealing mostly with the classics. We covered the material primarily through lecture and direct questioning, with some self-expression periodically as a motivator.

I moved on to *essentialism* in a class called Skills Lab. Students worked to improve reading, listening, study, and critical thinking skills, all essential for success, not only in school but also in the real world. My approach was one of *progressivism*. I prepared students to be lifelong learners. I pretested each student to determine ability level and then engaged that student in hands-on activities on that level. Although the class began with teacher-directed activities, these were followed by individual students working their way through "stations" focusing on the goals of the class. There were 24 students, each working on his or her own ability level at a station, improving personal skills in that area. *Individuality ... informality of classroom procedure ... meaningful ... student-focused ... teacher as facilitator ... progressivism.*

And now, although there are aspects of progressivism in my Senior Seminar class, I have moved on again, to *existentialism*. Why all this movement over the years? The subject matter demanded it. The needs of the students determined it. And my change in philosophy influenced it. Education is not a static field; my years of experience have prompted me to grow and change ... shift and adjust ... to the benefit of the students and to the renewed interest of the teacher.

2005 Colorado Teacher of the Year
Montrose High School
Montrose County School District
Montrose, Colorado

Courtesy of Kathy Heavers

If you embrace some of the tenets of two or more philosophies, you are said to be **eclectic** in your philosophical thoughts about education. Eclecticism is an approach in which you select and use what you consider to be the most appropriate portions of several different philosophies. For example, you may believe students should learn classic and other timeless concepts (perennialism) as well as the basics (essentialism), but also that students should accomplish their studies through investigating, inquiring, and discovering on their own (progressivism). Or, you may believe in using group work to help students increase their academic knowledge (progressivism) and in encouraging students to make responsible choices about what to study (existentialism), but also insist that their choices include topics that have an impact on society and social issues (social reconstructionism).

BUILDING BLOCK 2.8

Reexamining Your Philosophical Beliefs about Education

Take a few minutes to reexamine your philosophical tenets in education as revealed by your initial thoughts in Building Blocks 2.1 and 2.2, and refined by your studies in this chapter. Then, write your answers to the following questions:

1. What do you believe should be taught? To which of the philosophies is this the closest?
2. Who do you believe should decide what should be taught? To which of the philosophies is this the closest?
3. Why do you believe this material should be taught? To which of the philosophies is this the closest?
4. How do you believe this material should be taught? To which of the philosophies is this the closest?
5. What do you think the teacher's role should be? To which of the philosophies is this the closest?
6. What do you think the student's role should be? To which of the philosophies is this the closest?

▶❚❚ **TeachSource** Video

View the TeachSource Video Case, "Philosophical Foundations of American Education: Four Philosophies in Action," to see a demonstration of three of the educational philosophies you've been learning about in this chapter, plus an additional one, and the implications of each for classroom practices. You'll also observe how various teachers draw upon these philosophies to shape various aspects of their teaching—everything from the arrangement of desks, to the selection of texts and the role of the teacher. Be sure to watch all four segments and the bonus videos. After watching the videos, answer the following questions:

1. What are the educational philosophies you saw in the first three videos? What are the defining characteristics of each?

2. The last video shows *critical theory* in which you may have identified similarities with existentialism and social reconstructionism. What characteristics did you recognize that would make you think of existentialism? What characteristics would make you think of social reconstructionism?

A Continuum of Schools of Philosophic Thought

The five major philosophies of education you have explored can be placed on a continuum, with the highest amount of curriculum direction provided by teachers, educators, and society on the left and the highest amount of curriculum direction provided by students on the right (see Figure 2.3).

On the left (no political analogy implied) of Figure 2.3 is the perennialist philosophy in which society at large, through numerous citizen and political task forces, has established certain basic classics and truths that should be transmitted to students; this curriculum preserves the liberal arts tradition. Then comes essentialism, in which the educators have determined the basic subjects and skills all students must know and be able to do based on society's determination of basic subjects and skills.

Next is progressivism, in which the teacher and the students jointly decide what is important to learn—basic classics and truths, basic skills, and current and changing topics. This is followed by social reconstructionism, in which classes of students decide what to learn based on a democratic decision of which of the many societal ills should receive their attention. On the right is existentialism, in which students decide what to learn based primarily on their perceived needs and interests.

Other philosophies, such as idealism, realism, experimentalism, and critical theory, impact education, but we have focused in this chapter on the philosophies we believe are basic to education.

Perennialism	Essentialism	Progressivism	Social Reconstructionism	Existentialism
Curriculum determined by society	Curriculum determined by society and teachers	Curriculum jointly determined by teachers and students	Curriculum determined democratically by teachers and students	Curriculum determined by students

◀ **Figure 2.3**
Educational philosophy continuum.
© Cengage Learning 2014

School Philosophy and Mission Statements

Most schools formalize their educational philosophies in written mission statements. A mission statement gives the school's basic purpose and goals and often provides insight into its prevailing educational philosophy.

Portions of actual mission statements of a few schools are given here. As you read them, try to identify their primary educational philosophies. What aspects of the mission statement lead you to that specific philosophy?

Mission Statement of a Public Elementary School:

The mission of our school is to offer all students an opportunity to achieve their greatest potential by providing the highest quality of learning. We believe that with the guidance of our staff, the involvement of parents, and the encouragement of the community, all students can learn and master basic academic skills. Our mission is to provide each child with a superior education and necessary skills to lead them in becoming self-sufficient, productive citizens in our ever-changing world.

Mission Statement of a Public Middle School:

Our mission is to provide a unique learning experience for all students which will be academically challenging, interdisciplinary in nature, and which will reflect the values of the local community and of society as a whole. Students will be enabled to develop individually while being given the means to recognize their own self-worth, and to achieve their role as knowledgeable and responsible members of the society of the future.

Mission Statement of a Public High School:

The mission of our school is to provide each student with a safe learning environment and an equitable opportunity to develop competencies necessary to become a productive member of society.

Mission Statement of a Private School:

We believe that a child learns best within an environment which supports each individual's unique process of development. We emphasize cognitive and physical development along with global awareness and peaceful conflict resolution. The teacher functions as a "guide" to help students carry out many different kinds of research following their interests, and develop their curiosity and a love of learning. Our priorities are for students to make intelligent choices, focus and concentrate, and engage in caring and purposeful interaction with the environment and with others.

Use your favorite search engine to find mission statements of schools in your area. Are they consistent with what you think about education? Would you want to teach at these schools? Why or why not?

Philosophic Perspectives of Non-Eurocentric Cultures

The educational philosophies we have discussed so far are steeped in European philosophical traditions. These philosophies are the driving force behind U.S. education. Using this Eurocentric view, you have examined what you think is important in education and how those thoughts inform the beginnings of your philosophy of education.

An important aspect of the philosophy of education of effective teachers is an awareness of their students' diversity.

However, as you have seen, our philosophy of education is strongly influenced by who we are and what our beliefs are. Tradition and culture are very important factors in the formation of our beliefs. Many teachers grew up in non-Eurocentric cultures, and many received their education in countries other than the United States. Cultural diversity among students is the norm in the classroom, and groups that used to be considered the minority are rapidly becoming the majority in many school districts. Thus, the cultural heritages of the teacher and students in a classroom are very likely to be different from each other. This means your philosophy of education could be in conflict with the philosophical beliefs of your students and their families. As a teacher, you must be aware and respectful of the values of your students, their families, and the community, even if these values differ from your own convictions. Activities and teaching methodologies that are inconsistent with the value structures of any particular culture represented in your classroom may limit motivation and may precipitate conflict between what the student experiences at school and at home. You must recognize and deal with these differences to avoid misunderstandings that can interfere with your effectiveness as a teacher. In Chapter 4, you will explore in more detail cultural diversity and how it affects teaching.

Theories of Educational Psychology

This investigation into educational thought would not be complete without a look at the basic and pervasive psychologies of education. Whereas one's educational philosophy focuses on the now-familiar questions of what should be taught, how it should be taught, and what teachers and the students should do in the teaching/learning process, educational psychologies deal with ways in which the mind actually behaves while it is learning—that is, how learning occurs. As you will see, educational psychologies exert strong influences on teaching and philosophical practices, and teaching and philosophical practices exert strong influences on educational psychologies. They help provide structures for teaching methodologies, curriculum selection, and assessment procedures. You will examine educational psychologies in detail as you progress through your teacher preparation program.

As with philosophies, there are no right or wrong psychologies. During this discussion, you will examine your *own* thoughts and form your *own* conclusions. In so doing, you are forming the platform on which you will construct your personal conceptualization of excellence in teaching. And, as you have seen, excellent teachers have many different qualities.

There are many psychologies—many ways of explaining how people learn and what motivates them to behave the way they do. In this section, we focus on four psychologies that have different understandings of the human mind and therefore different applications in school. *Humanism* focuses on the need for personalization to achieve meaningful learning. *Behaviorism* explains learning in terms of external factors and stimulation. *Information processing* explains learning through analysis of how the brain processes new and stored information. *Constructivism* holds that learning occurs by attaching new experiences to existing knowledge in meaningful ways.

BUILDING BLOCK
2.9

Let us examine these four theoretical approaches to learning.

Humanism

The psychology of humanism emphasizes people's intrinsic capacities for personal growth and their abilities and desires to control their own destinies. Humanists believe people are capable of learning through their own efforts. You became somewhat familiar with humanist principles in Chapter 1, when you looked at the work of William Glasser and Arthur Combs.

Humanism was formalized as a psychology in the 1960s. Humanists believe it is necessary for teachers to understand the perceptions of individual students—to find how things seem from the students' point of view. Humanists see two basic components of learning: (1) the acquisition of information and (2) the individual's personalization and internalization of that information. According to humanists, teachers not only must know their subjects and see that the material is properly organized and presented but also must help students make personal meaning out of the material.

Humanism is well represented by the work of Glasser and Combs and also by the work of Abraham Maslow and Carl Rogers. Maslow developed a hierarchical theory of human motivation that asserts that people become self-actualized to accomplish higher motives after they have fulfilled certain basic needs. (You will investigate Maslow's hierarchy in Chapter 3.) Rogers developed the "person-centered" approach to psychology that says if we approach a person with empathy, genuineness, and non-possessive warmth, we can enable that person to grow and develop maximally (Rowan, 2001). He believed that people have a natural desire to learn and that learning must be meaningful, self-initiated, and free from threat. To Rogers, the teacher is a facilitator of learning, acting as a guide and providing students with the needed resources.

Rather than focusing exclusively on the material to be taught, humanist educators also focus on the people who are doing the learning. They focus on people's feelings, interests, likes, dislikes, abilities, and other personal qualities. Humanist educators believe learning is an "inside job"—that people learn through their own intrinsic efforts. This contrasts with other approaches that focus on pouring the information into the student without particular regard for the individual. Humanist educators believe teachers are not essential as a condition for learning; students can learn through their own internal efforts. They believe teachers cannot "teach" something to an entire class of students and expect every student will learn it. Humanist teachers adopt a position of "facilitator" to help students find and implement their most effective ways of learning.

humanism The psychological approach that stresses people's capacity and desire for personal growth.

Behaviorism

behaviorism The psychological approach that explains behavior by examining external experiences.

classical conditioning A form of learning in which an organism learns to associate a stimulus with a nonrelated response.

operant conditioning An approach to learning in which the consequences of a behavior produce changes in the likelihood that the behavior will occur again.

Behaviorism is a psychology that contends that learning is shaped by the environment. According to behaviorists, the behavior of an individual is formed more by the actions and reactions of other people than by the individual's own free will. The psychology of behaviorism arose in the late 1940s, and was based on the work of the Russian physiologist Ivan Pavlov, who developed the concept of classical conditioning through his research with dogs. In Pavlov's scheme, dogs can be conditioned to salivate in response to the ringing of bells, even though the bell ringing has nothing to do with actually receiving food.

B. F. Skinner (1904–1990) extended the work of Pavlov to develop his operant conditioning theory. According to Skinner, a person's behavior is a function of its consequences; that is, it is what happens *afterward*, not before, that influences behavior. This has come to be known as behaviorism. To visualize this theory, imagine a student who takes an algebra test. The teacher announces that a candy bar will be given to every student who earns a perfect score. A student gets a perfect score on the first test, gets the candy bar, and, according to behavioral theory, studies hard for the next test because of the expected reward. As another example, suppose you begin a conversation with your neighbor during class. The instructor stops the class and reprimands you. According to behavioral theory, you will not talk with your neighbor again because you want to avoid similar consequences in the future. It is the reprimand that has shaped your future behavior. The basic principle is that the consequences of any behavior will cause an increase, decrease, or no change in the likelihood of that behavior occurring again.

The psychology of behaviorism has wide use in the classroom. As you can imagine, numerous classroom and behavior management strategies, such as the rules-rewards-punishment approach, are grounded in behaviorism. (You will investigate methods of classroom management in Chapter 8.) Many instructional strategies are behaviorist in nature. Programmed instruction was one of the earliest educational applications of behaviorism; this has given way to computer programs, interactive CD-ROMs, computer-based tutorial programs, and other computer-assisted instruction applications. Behaviorist teachers tend to favor drill, repetition, and reward-based teaching methodologies.

programmed instruction A teaching strategy in which students work their way through small chunks of information. At the end of each part, students are tested over the material. Correct answers earn praise as a reward and the student progresses on to additional information. Incorrect answers result in remediation.

Much debate surrounds the efficacy of using a behavioral approach in motivation. Certainly there are times when rewards and punishments foster students' attainment of desired goals. We all are behaviorists to some extent. Who, for example, has not wondered how much credit would be given for certain tasks accompanying a college course? Indeed, report cards themselves can be considered behaviorist in nature.

There is ongoing debate between those who believe humanism is the best approach to education and those who believe behaviorism is the best approach. Humanists subscribe to the idea that the most meaningful motivations are related to the internal satisfactions that come from doing well and that students learn to work for their own intrinsic feelings of accomplishment. For example, the inward uplifting feeling you get from presenting a well-prepared report is far more motivating and satisfying than receiving an external reward from the professor (although that is comforting as well). In the behaviorist classroom, students learn to work for rewards given by the teacher.

We take no sides on the humanism versus behaviorism issue. Both have strengths, and both have limitations. You will study these theories in detail in later courses, after which you can make up your own minds.

Information Processing

information processing theory A cognitive psychology that explains learning by manipulation of sensory register, short-term memory, and long-term memory.

cognitive psychology The psychological approach that explains behavior by examining mental processes.

Information processing theory focuses on how the brain processes information by attending to stimuli, receiving information, processing information, storing information in working (short-term) and long-term memory, and retrieving information. According to the information processing approach (often called cognitive psychology), people have the ability to manipulate information in thinking, problem solving, and other intellectual operations by using three basic mental processes: attending to sensory input in

A good example of the influence of behaviorism in the classroom is programmed instruction, a method of teaching attributed to B. F. Skinner because of his concern about the difficulty in providing suitable academic reinforcements to each student in a class. In programmed instruction, the unit or lesson is broken into a series of very small steps that are presented in sequence. Each step requires a response from the students. If a student is correct, the teacher provides some form of reinforcement, such as "Good for you!" "Yes!!!" "Great job!" and the like, and the student is permitted to move to the next step. If the student is incorrect, he is referred to material designed to teach the concept.

In the 1950s and 1960s, programmed instruction was presented in text form. When computers became available, the system was computerized. Typically, in these early forms of electronic programmed instruction, a piece of information was presented on the screen and the student was asked to enter a response to a question about the information. The computer gave feedback that the answer was a "Correct" or "Incorrect" response. If the response was correct, the computer provided positive reinforcement in the form of praise. If the response was incorrect, the computer referred the student to additional screens that reteach the information; after reviewing this additional material, the student tried a similar question.

Perhaps you recognize this type of format from video games. The elements of operant conditioning—reward and punishment—are used in a wide variety of educational games and simulations that are quite a bit more sophisticated than the initial programmed instruction applications available when personal computers first found their way into schools. Color and animation, nonlinear progression through the program, and access to customizable options make these educational games fun and engaging. They are extremely accessible for home use in gaming systems and online. Also, with the availability of personal technologies such as smartphones and tablets, these programs are now highly portable.

---

the sensory register, encoding the attended information in the working memory, and retrieving information from the long-term memory.

Information processing psychology was developed in the late 1950s, when computer technology was being developed. It was formed partly as a reaction to limitations seen in the behaviorist approach to education and partly to use the computer as a model for the way people think.

According to the information processing theory, people first take information into their brains by paying attention (attending) to stimuli coming their way. The information enters the cognitive processing system through the senses and is taken into the sensory register. If the individual does nothing with the information in the sensory register, it is lost. This occurs, for example, when the teacher is lecturing and the student is daydreaming; the teacher's words reach the student's ears and stimulate the hearing receptors, but nothing happens to them beyond the sensory register. On the other hand, if the person pays attention to the information, it is transferred to working (or short-term) memory where it can be processed and transferred to the long-term memory. Or, if nothing is done to process the information, it is soon lost. Once in long-term memory, the information is never lost (although it may be difficult to retrieve) (see Figure 2.4).

According to the information processing theory, processing begins in working memory, where new information and information retrieved from long-term memory interact with each other. The result is a change in memory. It is the teacher's responsibility to help students develop processes that support the

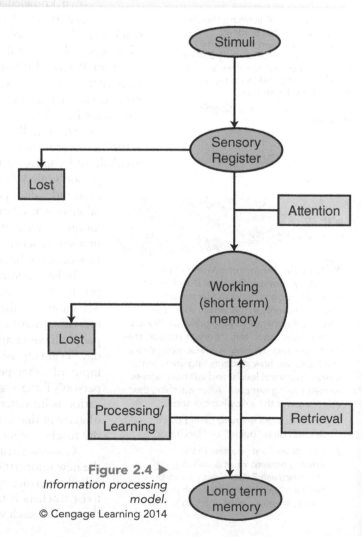

Figure 2.4 ▶
Information processing model.
© Cengage Learning 2014

View the TeachSource Video Case, "Using Information Processing Strategies: A Middle School Science Lesson." In this video, you'll see how middle school teacher E. J. Beucler translates theory into practice as he demonstrates to his students how to absorb information, process it, and apply it to a chemistry lesson. Also be sure to watch the bonus videos. After watching the videos, answer the following questions:

1. What strategies does Mr. Beucler use to help his students process (repeat, review, rehearse) the information?

2. Why is it necessary to provide opportunities for students to access the information in several different ways?

3. What are some examples of the different ways students may need to access information so that they successfully process it, moving it from working memory to long-term memory?

constructivism A learning theory that proposes that students construct their own knowledge by combining information they already have with new information, so that new knowledge takes on personal meaning to the student.

schemata (sg. *schema*) Cognitive structures.

View the TeachSource Video Case, "Vygotsky's Zone of Proximal Development: Increasing Cognition in an Elementary Literacy Lesson." In this video, you'll see how developmental psychologist, Dr. Francis Hurley, draws upon this theory to support students' abstract thinking in a lesson on poetry. You'll also see how students engage with the lesson on several levels, and will have access to their writing samples. After watching this video, answer the following questions:

1. How does the learning taking place depend on a "guide" or "facilitator"?

2. How does what you saw in the video represent what is called *social constructivism*? (Consider that to be "social," learning has to be shared with at least one other person.)

needed changes in memory. This is carried out by employing strategies such as the following:

- Organizing information carefully
- Linking new information to existing knowledge
- Recognizing the limits of attention
- Recognizing the limits of working (short-term) memory
- Providing encoding strategies to ensure that new information is meaningful

It is important to note that the terms *sensory register, working memory,* and *long-term memory* refer to processes rather than actual structures. Medical and psychological research currently is taking place to ascertain the actual physiological workings of the brain; some day we may have information processing models that show how the brain cells themselves work in attending, perceiving, storing, retrieving, and manipulating information.

Constructivism

Constructivism is an approach to teaching and learning that asserts that people actively construct their own understandings of information—that learners combine new information with existing information such that the new knowledge provides personal meaning. In the constructivist viewpoint, people build their own knowledge and their own representations of knowledge from their own experience. Learning does not occur by transmitting information from the teacher or the textbook to the student's brain; instead, each student constructs his or her own personal and valid understanding of this information.

Jean Piaget (1896–1980), a Swiss child psychologist, gave structure to the idea of constructivism. Piaget viewed the acquisition of knowledge as a continually developing process rather than as an end state. He viewed the mind as an aggregation of cognitive structures he called **schemata** (singular: **schema**). Again, it is important to note that the term *schema*, as well as other terms in Piaget's theories, refers to processes rather than actual structures. According to the constructivist view, schemata are opened, enlarged, divided, and connected to one another in response to the influx of information into a person's mind. Because no two people have had the same experiences, the schemata each individual possesses are unique to that individual and are linked to one another in ways that represent the unique experiences the individual has had and the unique connections the individual has made between and among those experiences. In a sense, schema theory is like a set of computer files; each computer user labels files in his or her own way and groups them in folders unique to that person.

Independently, in the 1920s and 1930s, Lev Vygotsky (1896–1934), a Russian psychologist, also developed basic constructs of constructivism, but his work was not known to the Western world until much later. Whereas Piaget focused on the individual nature of constructing knowledge, Vygotsky emphasized the role other people have in an individual's construction of knowledge. In our computer analogy, Vygotsky would say that a person set up files in a unique way but used the input of other people to get started, resulting in some similarities between this person's filing system and that of others. Among Vygotsky's contributions to education is his description of a "zone of proximal development," which is the region of activity that learners can navigate independently, but with some assistance from the teacher, other people, and other sources.

Constructivist teachers help students make sense by helping each student attach the new information to information he or she already possesses. This process is often called constructing information, hence the term *constructivism*. The role of constructivist teachers is to facilitate learning—to provide a variety of learning experiences that enable each student to learn in his or her own unique way and to construct the information such that it makes sense to that individual. Constructivist teachers ask students for their conclusions and their explanations rather than repetitions of what the teacher presented. To constructivist teachers, it is far more important to listen than to tell.

As you know, this entire text is constructivist in nature. We have described the ways it is designed to engage students at the beginning of Chapter 1, and you will revisit this concept periodically throughout the text.

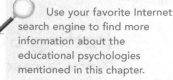 Use your favorite Internet search engine to find more information about the educational psychologies mentioned in this chapter.

Educational Psychologies in the Classroom

BUILDING BLOCK
2.10

Review your responses to the questions in Building Block 2.9. Do you still feel the same way? Are there any changes?

List two or three situations in which you believe your learning was facilitated using each of the following approaches to education:

- Humanism
- Behaviorism
- Information processing
- Constructivism

Your Philosophy of Education

You have examined several basic philosophies and psychologies of education and have looked at your own thoughts. Now, you are ready to develop your own tentative philosophy of education—one that is personal to you.

My Philosophy of Education

BUILDING BLOCK
2.11

Write a short preliminary philosophy of education. Consider these kinds of questions:

- What is the purpose of education? (What goals do you want your students to achieve?)
- What content should be taught? Why?
- How will you teach? Why?
- What are the teacher's roles and responsibilities?
- What are the students' roles and responsibilities?

Your philosophy should be a well-thought-out synthesis of your thinking about your own teaching, *not* merely a compilation of answers to these questions. The questions are offered only to stimulate your thinking.

Compare your philosophy of education with the primary philosophies and psychologies you explored in this chapter. With which one or ones does your philosophy most favorably compare? Briefly explain why.

This activity is deliberately given at the beginning of the course to give you a chance to reflect on your own thinking and to review your thoughts as you move along. As such, your statement will not be an all-inclusive opus, nor will it be definitively refined. Rather, it will be an expression of your ideas about the teaching/learning experience as you see it now. You will use this statement to guide you in your construction and reconstruction of your thinking about quality education as you progress through the course.

Save this philosophy statement; you will use it again later.

Putting Students to Work in the Classroom

Angela Teachey

Courtesy of Linda Winburn

When I began my teaching career in the mid-1990s, I taught mathematics the way I had been taught. My pedagogical choices were not really conscious decisions because I was never exposed to any other ways of teaching. Back then, I worked REALLY hard while teaching. I was in the front of the room with my trusty chalkboard and overhead projector, and I painstakingly developed every concept for my students and worked through seemingly thousands of examples in easy-to-follow steps. I thought I was doing a great job, but my students' achievement never seemed to meet my expectations.

For a long time, I blamed my students for their lackluster performance. I thought that they did not study enough and that they didn't do their homework. Sometimes, that may have been the case, but I eventually realized that there was more to the story. When I began graduate school, my experience as a teacher made me more thorough and reflective.

I realized that mathematics is learned by actually doing mathematics, not by watching others do it. When I discussed my thoughts with colleagues who teach in other disciplines, they said the same of their subject matter. In other words, learning is not a spectator sport. I began to formulate strategies for making my classroom a more active environment for my students.

Following are some suggestions from my own experience. First, it is very important to establish a classroom where active engagement is welcome and expected. At my school, our mathematics classrooms are arranged in pods of three or four desks, and we expect students to begin discussing homework problems in their pods immediately after arriving in class (whether or not the teacher has arrived). We establish this expectation in the early days of school, and we remain consistent throughout the year. Students are immediately engaged in content discussions. We often ask them to present their solutions to challenging homework problems; by explaining their thinking to others, students deepen their own understanding of concepts.

Equally as important is establishing an environment that honors and promotes student participation. At the beginning of the year, I ask my students to help create a list of classroom policies that require the respect for and participation of all students. I have found that students are much more likely to comply with policies that they have developed themselves than with policies that I impose on them.

In presenting material to students, I try to create structured investigative activities that allow them to explore the concepts for themselves. For example, I may ask students to use technology to look at a variety of graphs of functions, and I will provide some guiding questions that lead them to recognize the patterns I want them to detect. Toward the end of each investigation, we "debrief" by accumulating ideas on the board and by making as many relevant connections as we can. Students then work on additional practice for homework. I am by no means suggesting that it is possible to create investigative activities for every class period, and I understand that sometimes teachers have to move quickly through certain topics to meet curricular demands. In addition, creating effective and engaging investigations takes time and creativity. I suggest that teachers gradually create and incorporate them over a period of years.

Although my teaching style has numerous benefits, there are challenges of keeping students actively engaged in class. Teachers often discover that their students have not been required to work hard in their previous classroom experiences, and that they are resistant to change. Teachers who are committed to maintaining active learning in their classes have to be persistent in helping students to develop collaborative skills and encouraging them to exercise patience in figuring out challenging concepts on their own. Teachers have to remember that it is important for students to struggle with concepts, but they also have to be sensitive to times when students' struggles become overly frustrating. Often, a leading question or a little hint can point a group of students in the right direction without giving too much away.

To step away from the board and allow students to explore concepts on their own requires courage, confidence, and humility. Teachers have to be confident and brave enough to accept that class may not always proceed the way they planned it and to explore the various avenues that students' investigations may present. Sometimes, they have to admit that they may not know something if a student poses an interesting or difficult question that the teacher has never considered. Asking other students for input or assigning the investigation of the question as a research assignment are two strategies for dealing with this type of situation.

Managing student behavior can also be challenging in an active learning environment. Allowing student input in establishing class participation procedures is helpful, but it is also important for teachers to provide structure for activities and to make their expectations very clear. Be sure to hold groups accountable for their work by requiring them to present their findings to the class or by asking them to hand in work to be evaluated. Changing group assignments frequently (I do it after every test) keeps groups from becoming too social and from stagnating.

In my experience, the benefits of creating an active classroom far outweigh the challenges. Rarely do I hear a

(Continued)

student say, "I'm bored." Best of all, I love interacting with my students in the classroom. I can "eavesdrop" on their group discussions and gain insight into how they are thinking, and I often learn new ideas and perspectives from my students. I leave my classes excited, invigorated, and full of ideas for future activities. My students leave my class with greater confidence in their problem-solving skills and in their content knowledge.

Angela L. Teachey, PhD
North Carolina School of Science and Mathematics

Metaphors

One last comment dealing with your beliefs about education involves the use of **metaphors**. Researchers have looked at metaphors and teachers' latent beliefs about teaching as indicated by the metaphors they choose to characterize their role as a teacher (Mahlios, Massengill-Shaw, and Taylor, 2010; Taylor, 2010; Patchen and Crawford, 2011; Alger, 2009). For example, teachers characterizing themselves as "captains of their ships" may be very strong leaders, reluctant to transfer responsibility for learning to children.

metaphor A figure of speech in which two seemingly unlike objects or ideas are compared based on something they have in common.

Metaphors

BUILDING BLOCK
2.12

Take a minute or two and think about a metaphor you would use to characterize your role as a teacher. Do you consider yourself the captain of your ship? A bus driver? An explorer? A gardener?

Think about the metaphors that could be used to describe what a teacher does, and select one you believe most closely represents your current thinking about what a teacher's role is. Write it down and explain what it means.

Refer to the metaphor you choose frequently during this course; consider whether you want to change it. This may be one of the better indicators of how you are constructing the content of the course.

■ SUMMARY

- Philosophy is our way of knowing, and it encompasses metaphysics, epistemology, axiology, and logic.
- Educational philosophies and psychologies try to answer several basic questions: what should be taught, who should decide what should be taught, why should this material be taught, how should this material be taught, and what should the roles of the teacher and the student be?
- There are several basic schools of thought concerning education:
  - Perennialists believe schools should transmit the accumulated wisdom of past generations to today's students in a disciplined environment.
  - Essentialists believe students should learn basic material such as the "three Rs"; the teacher is the authority, and the students' job is to learn the material.

CHAPTER RESOURCES

○ Progressivists believe schools should develop thinking and problem-solving skills in students and should help students learn how to keep up with change; students and teachers are co-inquirers into areas of study that the school system and the teacher determine.

○ Existentialists believe schools should teach students to make responsible choices as free individuals and should encourage them to study what is of interest to them through individual discovery and inquiry; the teacher functions primarily as a facilitator.

○ Social reconstructionists believe it is the duty of schools to educate students to influence the reconstruction of society.

○ Education in the United States is driven by these Eurocentric philosophies. However, many students and teachers subscribe to non-Eurocentric perspectives, and their beliefs and expectations may differ from those governing mainstream education in the United States.

○ Most people are eclectic in their philosophical stances.

• There are several psychologies that describe beliefs about the way people learn. Humanists believe people are intrinsically capable and desirous of growing and learning. Behaviorists believe people's behavior is shaped by their environment and its extrinsic forces. Information processing theorists believe people learn through proper manipulation of the sensory register and short- and long-term memory functions. Constructivists believe people actively construct their own understandings by combining new information with prior experiences.

• In this chapter, you constructed your beginning philosophy of education, which will serve as a jumping-off point for your continued inquiries and constructions.

• Metaphors for teaching suggest the basic philosophies teachers possess.

■ Key Terms and Concepts

Axiology, 36
Behaviorism, 58
Classical conditioning, 58
Cognitive psychology, 58
Constructivism, 60
Cosmology, 36
Deductive reasoning, 38
Eclectic, 54

Epistemology, 36
Humanism, 57
Inductive reasoning, 38
Information processing
  theory, 58
Logic, 36
Metaphor, 63
Metaphysics, 36

Ontology, 36
Operant conditioning, 58
Programmed instruction, 59
Schemata (singular:
  schema), 60
Service learning, 51
Theology, 36

■ Construct and Apply

1. Suppose you are a sixth-grade teacher and you have to teach all the subjects. How would you set up your classroom if you were a
   a. Perennialist?
   b. Essentialist?
   c. Progressivist?

2. A high school English teacher has decided to teach a four-week unit on U.S. poetry.
   a. Describe how this teacher would teach this material if she subscribed to the essentialist philosophy of education.
   b. Describe how this teacher would teach this material if she subscribed to the progressivist philosophy of education.

3. Fill in the following columns with the major concepts pertaining to each educational philosophy discussed in this chapter. Then, fill in the last column to represent your own philosophical thoughts.

	Perennialism	Essentialism	Progressivism	Existentialism	Social Reconstructionism	Yours
What should be taught?						
Why should it be taught?						
How should it be taught?						
What should the teacher's role be?						
What should the student's role be?						

4. Suppose you were teaching a class of fourth graders. List several things you might do in your classroom that reflect each of the following approaches to teaching and learning:
   a. Humanism
   b. Behaviorism
   c. Information processing
   d. Constructivism

Deconstructing the Standards

1. Recall the InTASC standards associated with the objectives for this chapter:

   InTASC Standard #2: Learning Differences reads,

   "The teacher uses understanding of individual differences and diverse cultures and communities to ensure inclusive learning environments that enable each learner to meet high standards."

   InTASC Standard #9: Professional Learning and Ethical Practice reads,

   "The teacher engages in ongoing professional learning and uses evidence to continually evaluate his/her practice, particularly the effects of his/her choices and actions on others (learners, families, other professionals, and the community), and adapts practice to meet the needs of each learner."

   a. What part(s) of these standards does this chapter address?
   b. How will the concepts in this chapter help you apply these standards as a teacher?

2. Use your favorite search engine to find your state's standards for certification. When you find it, bookmark the site. You will refer to it often as you progress through this book.
   a. How are your conclusions about educational philosophy represented in your state certification standards?
   b. How do the InTASC Standards compare to your state's certification standards regarding educational philosophy?
   c. Do you believe the degree of representation concerning educational philosophy is adequate in your state certification standards? Why or why not?

▊ Your Portfolio

In this chapter, you have considered many factors dealing with several philosophies and psychologies of education. Select two or three pieces of evidence that show your mastery of this topic and put them in your portfolio. This evidence could include your educational philosophy statement, other work done in class, work done out of class, or field experiences where you have had the opportunity to demonstrate your philosophy by implementing some aspect of classroom activity based on your philosophy.

▣ Education CourseMate Resources

Check out this text's Education CourseMate website (at www.cengagebrain.com) for more information about philosophies and psychology of education, interactive study tools, and useful resources. You will find the TeachSource Videos, a guide for doing field experiences, glossary flash cards, activities, tutorial quizzes, direct links to all the websites mentioned in the chapter, and more.

PART II Student

IN PART I, you saw that many characteristics of effective teachers affect student achievement, and you saw that many different types of effective teaching are consistent with these characteristics. You saw yourself and your beliefs about effective teaching as primary influences on your understanding of the most effective ways of teaching. You added new experiences and understandings to your original beliefs and predispositions, building your preliminary philosophy of education.

In Part II, you will explore the most important element of education—the students.

We hear a lot about the many ways in which students are different. Phrases such as these permeate discussions about education:

- "*All* students must learn."
- "Individualize your instruction."
- "Teachers must meet the needs of *every* student."

Certainly students differ from one another in many ways. The concept of student uniqueness, however, has received so much emphasis that we tend to forget there are also ways in which students are alike.

It is important to understand differences among students so that you can tailor their education to meet their needs. It is equally important to understand commonalities among students, so that you can provide suitable motivation and learning experiences for all your students. The three chapters of Part II invite you to look at how students are alike, how they are different, and how you can accommodate *all* students in your classroom. In Chapter 3, you will investigate students' common needs and how these needs are related to motivation. In Chapter 4, you will investigate the unique perspectives students bring to school, and in Chapter 5, you will investigate students' unique abilities.

The Student: Common Needs

OTHER THAN YOURSELF, your experiences with school, and your beliefs about education, the most significant influence on your teaching is—and should be—your students. Students bring with them many different characteristics that affect their academic achievement. Yet they are alike in so many ways and have many common needs.

This chapter is devoted to the exploration of needs shared by all students. Among these are basic human needs, cognitive needs, and psychosocial needs. You will investigate each of these categories from the viewpoint of your own experiences and understandings and through the theories and conclusions of researchers. You will find ways these common needs can be satisfied for all students in your classroom.

Because motivation is a primary concern in teaching, and because motivation is closely linked to needs, you will investigate ideas about the relationships between needs and motivation. You will consolidate what you already know about students with the work of others to construct your own conceptualizations of students' common needs, how students are alike, and how they are motivated in school.

Students' Needs and Motivations

If you ask teachers, "What is the problem with our students today?" you are likely to hear answers such as "They're not responsible," "They're not disciplined," or "They're not motivated to learn." Often, teachers place the responsibility for student difficulties in the laps of their families or on their environments: "Her parents just don't care!" "He's from the bad part of town; what do you expect?" However, when students are in classrooms, it is up to the teacher to provide engaging instruction and motivate them to learn. But what affects student motivation to learn? To answer this question, let us investigate what motivation entails.

Your Motivation

What would it take to get you to put down this book, stand up, find a crowd of people, step out in front of them, and cluck like a chicken? Would $5 do it? How about $10? Maybe $50 or $100? What semi-outrageous act would you perform for $100? Why would you do it? What would *motivate* you to do such a thing?

BUILDING BLOCK

3.1

You might do this act for the money, assuming that the amount of money was enough to make the action worthwhile. Maybe you even said you *need* the money. You might even do it for free, just to make people laugh and get their attention. Whatever the reason, you would not perform this outrageous act unless you were *motivated* to do it.

The concept of motivation includes the perception of a *need* and an *action* taken to meet that need. If you perceived a need for extra money, that need would give you the drive to do whatever you had to do to get some money. Your behavior would be driven by your need, with the money acting as a motivational force. Similarly, the drive to meet a need motivates students to exhibit particular behaviors, including the behaviors associated with learning.

We want our students to be motivated to learn. But motivation can occur only after certain needs common to all students are addressed. These needs include basic human needs of survival and self-fulfillment,

What motivates student learning? For some students, awards encourage student learning and achievement.

cognitive needs, and psychosocial needs. Basic needs are those needs that people must have met to live satisfied and happy lives. Cognitive needs are those related to thinking and solving problems. Psychosocial needs are those associated with people getting along with themselves and with others. The nature of these needs changes with development, but these needs are essentially the same for all students at given developmental stages.

Basic Needs

All learners have the same basic needs, regardless of their differences in beliefs, interests, and goals. Whether and how these needs are met for any student affects that student's motivation to learn. Let us try to identify some of the common basic needs students bring to the classroom.

BUILDING BLOCK 3.2

Common Basic Needs

1. Imagine yourself as a three-year-old child. What are your needs? (Do not limit yourself to material things.)
2. Next imagine yourself as an early teenager. Do you still have the needs you identified as a three-year-old? Have any gone away? Are there any new needs?
3. Then think about yourself at your current age. How have your needs changed? Which, if any, have remained?
4. Finally, anticipate your needs as a senior citizen. Identify new needs and needs that will no longer exist.

Maslow's Hierarchy of Needs

In Chapter 2, you saw that people become actualized to accomplish higher learning only after they have fulfilled certain basic needs. What needs did you identify in Building Block 3.2? Which are associated with survival? Which are associated with protection? Which are associated with learning?

Psychologist Abraham Maslow (1968) identified seven categories of basic needs common to all people:

1. Physiological needs (needs for food, water, and shelter)
2. Needs relating to safety and security
3. Needs relating to love and belongingness
4. Needs relating to self-worth and self-esteem
5. The need to know and understand (cognitive needs)
6. Aesthetic needs (needs relating to creativity, beauty, or art)
7. Self-actualization needs (needs relating to the ability to fulfill one's potential)

Maslow represented these needs as a hierarchy in the shape of a pyramid (see Figure 3.1). A hierarchy is an arrangement that ranks people or concepts from lowest to highest. According to Maslow, individuals must meet the needs at the lower levels of the pyramid before they can successfully be motivated to tackle the next levels. The lowest four levels represent deficiency needs, and the upper three levels represent growth needs.

Physiological Needs

Notice that the physiological needs are the foundation of the pyramid. Why do you suppose these needs occupy this position?

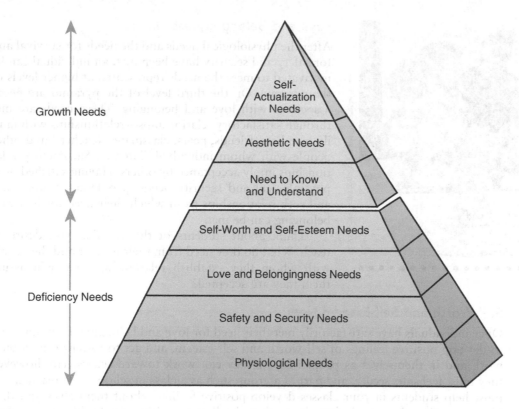

Growth Needs

Deficiency Needs

- Self-Actualization Needs
- Aesthetic Needs
- Need to Know and Understand
- Self-Worth and Self-Esteem Needs
- Love and Belongingness Needs
- Safety and Security Needs
- Physiological Needs

◀ **Figure 3.1**
Maslow's hierarchy of needs.
© Cengage Learning 2014

Maslow suggested that the first and most basic need people have is the need for survival: their physiological requirements for food, water, and shelter. People must have food to eat, water to drink, and a place to call home before they can think about anything else. If any of these physiological necessities is missing, people are motivated above all else to meet the missing need. Have you ever had a hard time paying attention to what the professor is saying when you are hungry? Some of your future students may not have had breakfast—or dinner the night before, and some may be homeless and may live in shelters or even cars. Free and reduced breakfast and lunch programs have been implemented in schools to help students meet their physiological need for food.

Safety and Security Needs

After their physiological needs have been satisfied, people can work to meet their needs for safety and security. (But the physiological needs must be met first.) Safety is the feeling people get when they know no harm will befall them, physically, mentally, intellectually, or emotionally; security is the feeling people get when their fears and anxieties are low. How does this relate to students in school? What threats to their physical, mental, intellectual, or emotional security might students perceive in school?

Have you seen metal detectors outside of schools? Police roaming the halls? These, of course, are deterrents to violence, thereby providing a degree of physical safety. Equally important is the assurance of intellectual safety. Intellectual safety is the feeling you get when you know that your responses and contributions in class will be received with intelligent respect. No one will pronounce your contributions wrong or dumb or use any other put-downs; in an intellectually safe classroom, all responses are equally valuable.

Emotional safety is similar to intellectual safety in that people feel they are accepted for who they are in the classroom, *no matter what*. Perhaps one of the most prevalent threats to the safety and security of your students is the incidence of bullying. Certainly, bullying has been at the forefront of concerns posed by media in recent years. As a teacher, it is your duty to address bullying not only in your classroom, but also throughout the school and its community. The topic of bullying is a powerful and emotion-packed one; you will explore this topic in detail in Chapter 8.

Students can meet each other's need for love and belonging by sharing and talking.

Love and Belongingness Needs

After the physiological needs and the needs for survival and for safety and security have been met, an individual can be motivated to meet the needs represented at higher levels of the pyramid. On the third level of the pyramid are needs associated with love and belonging. These needs are met through satisfactory relationships—relationships with family members, friends, peers, classmates, teachers, and other people with whom individuals interact. Satisfactory relationships imply acceptance by others. Having satisfied their physiological and security needs, people can venture out and seek relationships from which their need for love and belonging can be met.

Think about students of the age that you desire to teach. What do they need from their teacher and the people with whom they establish relationships that will assure them they are accepted?

Self-Worth and Self-Esteem Needs

Once individuals have satisfactorily met their need for love and belonging, they can begin to develop positive feelings of self-worth and self-esteem, and act to foster pride in their work and in themselves as people. Before they can work toward self-esteem, however, they must feel safe, secure, and part of a group such as a class in school. As a teacher, you must help students in your classes develop positive feelings about themselves and thus begin to satisfy their needs for self-worth and self-esteem. You can do this by attending to the environment that you create in your classroom. Students should be given opportunities to interact with one another, and they should feel that your classroom is a place where they will not be harassed, ridiculed, or humiliated by other students or by the teacher.

The Deficiency Needs

These first four levels of Maslow's hierarchy of needs are essential for a person's well-being and must be satisfied before the person can be motivated to seek experiences that pertain to the upper levels. If a student cannot meet one or more of these needs, that student is unlikely to be motivated to pursue any of the needs in the succeeding levels. Because of this, the first four levels of needs are called deficiency needs. Fortunately, many students come to school with the deficiency needs already met—at home; in peer groups; in church, scouting, athletic, or music groups; in other groups; or in some combination of these. However, some students who come to school do not have these needs met elsewhere and they look to the school for help in satisfying these needs. And *all* students must meet these deficiency needs in some way before they can successfully work at learning.[1]

The Need to Know and Understand

The fifth level of Maslow's pyramid represents an individual's need to know and understand. According to Maslow's hierarchy, motivation to know and understand cannot occur until the deficiency needs have been met to the individual's satisfaction. As you can imagine, the need to know and understand is a primary area of focus for education and is a topic on which we will concentrate. One of our primary jobs as educators is to motivate students so they will want to know and understand.

---

[1]While Madeline Cartwright was principal of a North Philadelphia elementary school, she took extraordinary steps to help children in her school meet their deficiency needs. Her account is chronicled in the book, *For the Children: Lessons from a Visionary Principal* (Cartwright and D'Orso, 1999).

Aesthetic Needs

Aesthetic refers to the quality of being creatively, beautifully, or artistically pleasing; aesthetic needs are the needs to express oneself in pleasing ways. Decorating your living room, wrapping birthday presents attractively, washing and waxing your car, and keeping up with the latest styles in clothing are all ways of expressing your aesthetic sense. People are motivated to meet this need only after the previous five needs have been met.

aesthetic Creatively, beautifully, or artistically pleasing.

The Need for Self-Actualization

At the top of the pyramid is the need for self-actualization, which is a person's desire to become everything he or she is capable of becoming—to realize and use his or her full potential, capacities, and talents. This need can be addressed only when the previous six have been satisfied. It is rarely met completely; Maslow (1968) estimated that less than one percent of adults achieve total self-actualization.

self-actualization The state of having become everything a person is capable of becoming, realizing one's full potential, capacities, and talents.

The Growth Needs

The upper three levels of the pyramid constitute a person's *growth needs*. Growth needs can never be satisfied completely. Contrary to the deficiency needs, for which motivation diminishes when a need is satisfied, as growth needs are met, people's motivation to meet them increases. The more these needs are satisfied, the more people want to pursue them. For example, the more one comes to understand a certain topic, the more one's motivation to learn more about that topic increases. Have you experienced this yourself? In what situation? We hope you are experiencing this increased motivation to learn in your introduction to education course.

Maslow's Hierarchy of Needs

BUILDING BLOCK
3.3

Look at the needs you identified at various ages in Building Block 3.2. For each need, identify one or more categories of needs from Maslow's hierarchy with which it can be associated:

- How does the pattern of needs change as age increases?
- What other patterns can you notice?
- For each of Maslow's needs, list some actions you could take to help you meet these needs yourself.

Other Basic Needs Theories

Maslow's hierarchy of needs is common to all people and is widely accepted as a model for understanding and explaining motivation. However, other researchers and theorists also have identified human needs common to all people.

© Bettmann/CORBIS

BIOGRAPHY

Abraham Maslow, psychologist (1908–1970), was one of the founders of the humanist psychology movement. He is most widely known for his view that people are motivated by successive hierarchical needs.

Born in Brooklyn, Maslow studied at the University of Wisconsin, where he received his B.A., M.A., and Ph.D. degrees in psychology. He taught psychology at the University of Wisconsin and later at Brooklyn College, where he came in contact with many European intellectuals such as Adler, Fromm, and other European psychologists. Maslow moved to Brandeis University in Waltham, Massachusetts, where he served as chair of the department of psychology until his retirement in 1969.

Noted psychologist William James (1892–1962), whose work Maslow studied, developed a theory that organizes basic human needs into three categories:

1. Material needs, including physiological and safety needs
2. Social needs, including the needs for belongingness and esteem
3. Spiritual needs

Mathes (1981) proposed three levels of motivational needs: physiological, belonging (including security and self-esteem), and self-actualization.

Alderfer (1972) developed a hierarchy based on Maslow's work, called the existence, relatedness, and growth (ERG) theory. In the ERG view, individuals must satisfy their requirements for existence (physiological and safety/security needs) and relatedness with other people (love/belonging and self-esteem needs) before they can grow in the areas of learning and self-accomplishment.

Alderfer correlated the needs in his hierarchy with actions typically required to meet these needs and ways people typically work to satisfy the needs. For example, to meet existence needs, Alderfer says individuals place a priority on acquiring material and psychological necessities, even if resources are limited. To meet relatedness needs, individuals participate in relationships with others in which they share ideas and feelings. For the growth needs, individuals act upon themselves or the environment to solve problems, leading to a creative product. These efforts engender a sense of accomplishment and contribution. Table 3.1 shows details of Alderfer's hierarchy of needs.

As noted in Chapter 1, Glasser (1993) identified five basic needs common to human beings:

1. Love (to care for and be cared for by others)
2. Power (to respect and be respected by others)
3. Freedom (to be allowed and encouraged to think for oneself)
4. Fun (to be able to laugh with others)
5. Survival (to make life secure)

In his choice theory, Glasser (1998) states that people are genetically predisposed to act to satisfy these five needs. In fact, Glasser argues that people choose how to behave partly as a result of this genetic influence.

Another group that has expanded on the basic needs that Maslow and others described is the Search Institute, a nonprofit organization that works to identify what every child needs for success. Through research conducted in the 1990s, the Institute has described sets of "developmental assets" of healthy and well-adjusted young people that represent the relationships, opportunities, and personal qualities that young people need

TABLE 3.1 Alderfer's Hierarchy of Needs (ERG Theory)

Need	Action Required	How Met
Existence	Acquire material and physiological necessities	Attain what is needed, which becomes a priority, even if resources are limited
Relatedness	Participate in relationships with others	Share ideas and feelings, give and receive respect, understand, accept, and validate acceptance by others
Growth	Act upon self or environment to make creative products	Solve problems, leading to a sense of accomplishment and contribution

© Cengage Learning 2014

to avoid risks and to thrive (Search Institute, n.d.). Forty separate developmental assets divided into *external assets* and *internal assets* have been described for several age and grade levels, including early childhood, middle childhood, and adolescence. Typical assets are family support, service, and concern for social justice. The Search Institute has determined that the more of these 40 assets individuals have, the more likely the individuals are to experience academic success and make positive life choices that will keep them from engaging in risky behaviors; that these assets are the building blocks of healthy development that assist young people in growing up to be healthy, caring, and responsible individuals. They have also found that, in the United States, regardless of region, most young people have less than 50 percent of the 40 identified assets (Search Institute, 2011).

Find the Search Institute on the Internet, and explore the 40 developmental assets identified by the Search Institute for the age student you wish to teach. Determine their impact on educational practice.

Basic Needs Revisited

BUILDING BLOCK
3.4

Look again at people's basic needs identified by Maslow, James, Mathes, Alderfer, and Glasser:

- What are the commonalities? Which needs (if any) are addressed by only one researcher?
- How do students meet these needs?
- How does the school help students meet these needs?
- How do teachers help students meet these needs in the classroom?

The Influence of Basic Needs on Academic Motivation

Recall your thoughts on how the satisfaction of physiological, safety, and social needs influences a student's motivation to study and learn. How do these needs affect your instructional decisions? Motivation is a requirement for effective learning, and the lack of fulfillment of basic growth needs hinders motivation. Teachers should provide an atmosphere to foster accomplishment of some of these needs such as the need for safety and security, the need for love and belongingness, and the need for self-worth. When teachers provide such an atmosphere, the motivation for learning is high. When teachers ignore the basic needs, the motivation for learning is low.

Cognitive Needs

Maslow's fifth level is the need to know and understand. As mentioned earlier, teachers focus primarily on this need; it is the one we are most prepared to help students meet. To do this, we must be aware that a student's potential for achievement is strongly influenced by the levels of cognitive development that all students go through, as well as socioeconomic status, English language proficiency, level of education achieved by parents, and other factors that also contribute to academic achievement (Christian, 2008). Motivation is promoted by giving students tasks that are within the learner's cognitive capabilities.

Cognitive Development

Cognitive development is the intellectual development of the mind. As people grow and mature, they progress through several increasingly sophisticated stages of cognitive

cognitive development The intellectual development of the mind.

development, representing increasingly complex abilities to think and process information. People progress through the stages in the same order, but individuals move through the stages at different rates. Thus, at certain ages, most students tend to be at certain cognitive stages, and they need to be taught with strategies that are appropriate for their cognitive level. Older students have more highly developed abilities to think and reason than young children do. For example, you would not try to teach algebra to first graders, and you probably would not require high school seniors to memorize nursery rhymes; these tasks normally are inappropriate for the cognitive levels of the students at those ages. Instead, you would teach algebra to older students and you would teach nursery rhymes to kindergartners to align the activities with the students' levels of cognitive development.

Let us consider the differences in people's cognitive capabilities as they grow and mature. To get an idea of cognitive growth, compare the reasoning ability of a three-year-old with your own reasoning as you think about the concepts presented in Building Block 3.5.

BUILDING BLOCK
3.5

Cognitive Readiness

Look at this magnificent second-grade riddle: Which weighs more, a pound of feathers or a pound of lead?

Did you catch yourself? You have a *pound* of each, of course! They weigh the same. The riddle is a trick question that might make a seven-year-old slip up because, based on experience, children of that age "know" that lead weighs more than feathers.

Let us try something else. Suppose you have two empty glass containers like those labeled *A* and *B* in the illustration. You also have a pitcher holding 500 milliliters of water. If you pour half of the water in container A and the other half in container B, which container has more water?

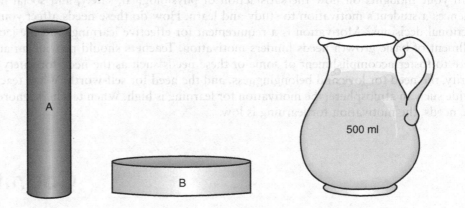

What was your answer? In fact, both containers hold the same amount of water: 250 milliliters. However, a three-year-old would have told you that container A holds more water. Why would the young child say that? Even if you measured the amount of water in front of the child and poured the same measured amount into each container, the child would say that container A holds more water and would give the same answer when the demonstration was performed again. Why? What is different about your cognitive abilities from those of a young child?

How would it affect the child emotionally if you, the teacher, kept performing this demonstration, asking the same question, and insisting that the volume of water in each container was the same? What *needs* does this child have with regard to instruction that is influenced by his or her stage of cognitive development?

The concepts demonstrated in Building Block 3.5 deal with conservation. Conservation is one of the defining characteristics of two of Piaget's cognitive stages; it is the ability to recognize that the amount of material does not change when its volume or shape changes. Young children are not able to reason that the different shapes of the containers make the volumes only appear to be different. There are many such examples of young children's reasoning abilities. Young children believe a nickel is worth more than a dime because the nickel is bigger. Young children believe there are more pennies in a row if there are spaces between the coins than if the pennies touch each other. Young children believe there is more clay in a cigar-shaped cylinder than there is in a ball from which the cylinder is made—even when they see the ball rolled out into the cylindrical shape.[2]

consevation With regard to cognitive development, the ability to recognize that the amount of material does not change when volume or shape changes.

Stages of Cognitive Development

According to Swiss biologist and psychologist Jean Piaget, all students progress through the same series of cognitive developmental stages as they get older. Piaget identified four stages, which progress from infancy through adulthood (Piaget, 1972). These stages, in the order in which students progress through them, are as follows:

1. Sensorimotor
2. Preoperational
3. Concrete operational
4. Formal operational

Table 3.2 shows the stages and the basic characteristics associated with each. Each stage represents more advanced capability (not accomplishment) for cognitive processing than the previous stages. Look at the characteristics associated with each level. How do your students' levels of cognitive development relate to their basic needs? How do the levels of your students' cognitive development affect your decisions about how to teach?

Sensorimotor Stage

The earliest stage, the sensorimotor stage, is characteristic of children in infancy. During this stage, children's thinking abilities consist largely of interacting with their

TABLE 3.2 Piaget's Stages of Cognitive Development

Stage	Approximate Age	Characteristics
Sensorimotor	Infancy	Information obtained through physical interaction with objects
Preoperational	Toddler and young child	Information obtained from increased use of symbolism and language Limited logic Egocentric perspective Difficulty in reversing and conserving
Concrete operational	Elementary and early adolescence	Information obtained from manipulation of concrete objects Logical and reversible thinking Concept of conservation develops
Formal operational	Adolescence and adulthood	Information obtained through manipulation of symbols generalized to abstract concepts

---

[2]Piaget developed several tasks to assess children's cognitive development. The tasks are given in Appendix A of Charlesworth and Lind (2010), *Math and Science for Young Children* (6th ed.), Belmont, CA: Wadsworth, Cengage Learning.

environment—what is around them. It is crucial to the intellectual development of children that they be given the opportunity to act on their environment in unrestricted (but safe) ways to start building the richest experiential bank they can. In later years, they will draw upon these experiences to make sense of what they are learning.

Preoperational Stage

The second stage is the preoperational stage, characteristic of toddlers and young children. During this stage, children begin to develop an understanding of symbols such as letters, words, numerals, pictographs, and the like. Perhaps the most significant area of development during this stage is the acquisition of language. Preoperational children are egocentric in perspective; their thought is based on what *they* see or experience, not on what someone else has done. They cannot put themselves in someone else's shoes and tell, for example, what Janie probably saw with the magnifying glass; they can only tell what *they* saw. They are not able to reverse operations easily. For instance, they can learn that 6 plus 2 equals 8, but they are not able to make the reverse operation spontaneously that 8 minus 2 equals 6. Preoperational children also lack the maturity of thought that allows for conservational thinking, as you saw in Building Block 3.5.

> We adults continue to be preoperational in our thought processes to a certain extent. How many people turn the map upside down when driving south? How many can follow directions to someone else's house but have difficulty finding their way back? And, to see how good you *really* are at conservation, go to an aquarium store and ask to see the various aquariums with, say, a ten-gallon capacity. It can be very difficult for us to believe that all the shapes hold the same amount of water.

Concrete Operational Stage

Piaget's third stage is the concrete operational stage, characteristic of elementary school and early adolescent children. During this stage, children must see, hear, feel, touch, smell, taste, or in some other way use their senses to *know*. "Seeing is believing" for concrete operational students. They must manipulate real objects such as globes, mathematics cubes, science apparatus, and the like to gain understandings of the principles involved. When thinking, they think in terms of real objects rather than abstractions without objects associated with them. For example, when concrete operational children think about proportions, they need to visualize goldfish in a goldfish bowl, or pizzas, or some other object; they have difficulty calculating proportions from mathematical abstractions. In their thinking, they must either actually see or manipulate objects or visualize manipulating them. Concrete operational children have difficulty thinking without this crutch. As they gain maturity, concrete operational people can reverse thinking, and they gain increased capabilities of conservation. Many adults remain at this stage, never fully developing their formal operational thinking powers. (Remember that a cognitive stage represents the *capability* of intellectual development. It does not represent the accomplishment of that level.)

Formal Operational Stage

The fourth and uppermost stage is the formal operational stage, characteristic of adolescents and adults. In this stage, people have the ability to think and reason abstractly without requiring concrete examples. For example, a person in the formal operational stage will be able to imagine what it would be like if there were no gravity. However, this stage is not limited to older people; many younger students in the concrete operational stage are capable of some formal operational thinking. In Piagetian theory, the ability to do formal operations is the ultimate achievement in human intellectual development.

Lawson (1978) identified five basic aspects of formal operational thought to help clarify what is meant by formal operations:

- *Proportional reasoning* (What are the proportions of boys and girls in your class?)
- *Isolation and control of variables* (If you are sick and take an aspirin, eat a bowl of chicken soup, and go to bed early, which made you feel better?)
- *Probabilistic reasoning* (What are the chances you will win the lottery?)
- *Correlational reasoning* (To what extent do people's heights correlate with the grades they earn in school?)
- *Combinatorial reasoning* (How many different words can you make from the letters in the word *mountains*?)

Notice that we illustrated the formal operations skills with concrete examples. What does that tell about our ability to think and reason in formal operations?

Students may arrive at each stage at different times and may take different amounts of time before they are ready to reason in the subsequent stage.

Use your favorite search engine to find out more about Piaget's stages of cognitive development. See if you can find more examples of different tasks that learners are able or not able to do in each stage. Have you noticed any of the children that you know exhibit abilities that represent cognitive development?

Cognitive Developmental Stages and Needs

BUILDING BLOCK 3.6

Go back to that three-year-old child and the water demonstration you thought about in Building Block 3.5. Using Piaget's stages of cognitive development, explain why the child would give the same incorrect answer again and again, even when you carefully explain that it is wrong. Recall the emotions you said the child would feel as you were attempting to explain this demonstration. How would the child's lack of understanding affect his or her motivation? As a teacher, what do you need to know about the cognitive development of the students in your class?

The Influence of Cognitive Needs on Academic Motivation

Recall your thoughts on how students' levels of cognitive development influence the kind of learning opportunities they need. How do these needs affect your instructional decisions? Motivation is a precursor to learning, and preparing activities and materials that are appropriate for the cognitive levels of development of your students is necessary for both motivation and learning. Asking students to work beyond their abilities will frustrate them. Asking them to work at levels below their abilities will bore them. Either of these emotions will crush any motivation students may have had.

BIOGRAPHY

© Farrell Grehan/CORBIS

Jean Piaget (1896–1980), a biologist and psychologist, was born in Neuchâtel, Switzerland, the son of a professor of medieval literature. At age 11, he wrote a short paper on an albino sparrow; that paper is considered the start of his brilliant scientific career. In high school, he narrowed his scientific interest to mollusks, and he maintained his interest in this area for the rest of his life. He received his doctorate in science in 1918, and worked in European psychology labs, where he questioned the "right-or-wrong" nature of intelligence tests and began to ask how children reason.

Piaget watched children at play, talked with them and recorded the conversations in detail, and conducted research with them to try to discover their reasoning processes and how their minds develop. His research focused on the child's concepts of space, time, number, causality, and perceptual and moral development. His work led to the now-famous four stages of intellectual development. Less known, but perhaps more important, are his theories of schema, equilibration, and personal constructivism developed from his exacting and thorough investigations.

Criticism of Piaget's Theory

Although widely recognized, Piaget's theory of cognitive development is not without its critics. Bohlin, Durwin, and Reese-Weber (2009) have compiled a list of the main criticisms and counterarguments, outlined as follows:

- Critics contend that Piaget underestimated the abilities of young children. In fact, children who are in the preoperational stage of development are able to perform concrete operational tasks if the instructions for the tasks are modified so that they can understand them. However, it is thought that these preoperational children are not able to perform the concrete tasks because they are thinking in concrete ways, but rather it is because they approach the task in preoperational ways. For example, suppose a preoperational child is presented with twenty poker chips, equally divided and arranged into two lines of ten. The top line of chips is spread out farther than the other. The preoperational child, not yet able to understand the concept of conservation, will report that the top line contains more chips. According to the critique, a preoperational child, given simplified instructions, will say that both rows have the same number of chips. However, it is thought that instead of using mathematical reasoning to understand number conservation as a concrete operational child would, a preoperational child simply counts the number of chips in both rows.

- When considering Piaget's stages of development, others have criticized the theory saying that the rate of progression through the stages cannot be accelerated. However, Piaget did not really focus on if or how these stages could be accelerated. He was more interested in what changes occurred in cognitive abilities as children develop. Piaget proposed that the rate at which children progress through the stages was dependent on previous experience.

- Piaget has been criticized for proposing "stages" of cognitive development when it has been observed that individuals do not acquire all the abilities of the next stage of cognitive development all at once, but rather might display only some of the abilities at first, acquiring others at a later time. In other words, children don't cross a line into the next stage of cognitive development all at once. It has been suggested that perhaps these stages are really "changes" that individuals go through as their cognitive abilities develop.

- Piaget has also been criticized for underestimating the impact of culture and prior schooling in his cognitive development theories.

- Finally, because of limitations in Piaget's research (such as the fact that he observed mainly his own children), critics have argued that his theory does not apply to other cultures. Counterarguments note that the developmental stages Piaget described have been exhibited by individuals all over the world, and that Piaget did acknowledge that culture and exposure to educational experiences affect the progression through the stages.

WHAT DO YOU THINK?

1. *How have you observed Piaget's different stages of cognitive development in individuals?*
2. *Do you remember experiencing them yourself? What do you remember?*
3. *What do you make of the criticisms and counterarguments regarding Piaget's theory?*

Psychosocial Needs

psychosocial development
Development of psychological and social factors within an individual.

A third way in which learners are alike is their progress through the stages of psychosocial development. Psychosocial development refers to the growth people experience in forming self-concepts, their ways of interacting with others, and their general attitudes toward the world. The development is both personal and social, and thus is termed *psychosocial*. Remember that a basic need of all people is to feel loved and to have a sense of belonging.

Schools and classrooms are social places. Individuals go through stages of psychosocial development, just as they go through stages of cognitive development. You have found that students' motivation and their potential for academic achievement are strongly influenced by both their basic needs and their level of cognitive development. The same is true of their level of psychosocial development.

Some Psychosocial Predicaments

Consider how you would respond in each of the following situations. Also consider how different responses might encourage or discourage future behavior in the student. Are these behaviors the kind you would want a learner in your classroom to exhibit?

Suppose a four-year-old reports that last year's teacher told her she must have grown a foot over the summer vacation. She then shows you a self-portrait with three feet, complete with shoes and socks on each. What will you say? What message will this send to the child? What behaviors will be encouraged and discouraged?

Suppose this same four-year-old child tells you her mother "goed to the store." What will you say? What message will this send to the child? What behaviors will be encouraged and discouraged?

Now imagine the child is in fourth grade and is hanging upside down on the playground's jungle gym. Alarmed, you yell at her, telling her to be careful and to hold on with her hands. What message will this send? What behaviors will be encouraged and discouraged?

Finally, imagine the child as a middle-school student asking a question such as, "Why is the sky blue?" Perhaps this question is a little off the topic being discussed, or perhaps the student has caught the teacher off guard. Suppose the teacher says, "Why don't you find the answer to that question for us and share it with the class tomorrow?" What message is the student receiving? Or suppose a student asks a question about something the class has already covered and is met with laughs and taunts from the other students. What message is this student receiving? What behaviors will be encouraged and discouraged?

Stages of Psychosocial Development

Erik Erikson (1968) believed that people develop psychologically throughout their lifetimes. This development depends on social interactions with their parents, siblings, peers, teachers, other adults, and other people who enter their life. His theory of development is called his **psychosocial theory** because development involves psychological development of the individual, which depends on the individual's social interactions. According to Erikson, individuals must address certain challenges or life crises at different periods of their lives, and other people play a large role in how individuals deal with these predicaments. Individuals are faced with specific tasks in each level of development that will enable them to resolve the predicament. Depending on how individuals are encouraged in their attempts to resolve a crisis, the individuals' needs for continued development are either met or not met, and motivation is correspondingly increased or decreased.

For example, the psychosocial development task prevalent in toddlers' lives is to develop a firm sense of autonomy—the certainty that they can control their environment. Toddlers want to try ideas for themselves (think of the so-called terrible twos) without always having to depend on others. It is essential that parents, teachers, and other adults permit toddlers to explore freely but safely and do things for themselves, while providing guidance and encouragement. Children who discover they *can* perform by themselves develop a sense of autonomy. Those who are discouraged, ignored, scolded, or punished develop a sense of shame for having demonstrated what they think is bad behavior, and they develop a feeling of doubt that they have the wherewithal to make things happen. For a child to progress in a healthy psychological and social manner to the next stage of life, this dilemma must be resolved such that the child develops at least some degree of autonomy. Thus, this stage is identified as the autonomy stage versus shame and doubt stage.

psychosocial theory Theory addressing the psychological and social aspects of identity development.

In Eriksonian psychology, each stage is represented by a continuum ranging from total positive resolution to total negative resolution. Of course, most people resolve their crises somewhere between the extremes, but the crises must be resolved in some manner before resolution of the successive stages can be achieved. This can either be positive or negative in nature. The manner in which the crises are resolved has a lasting effect on the individual's view of his world and of himself as a person, and affects the way the person resolves each of the subsequent stages. Table 3.3 shows Erikson's psychosocial stages in summary form.

TABLE 3.3 Erikson's Stages of Psychosocial Development

Stage	Age	Expected Resolution
Trust vs. mistrust	Infancy	Learns to trust that needs will be met by constants in the environment (parents, physical objects) or Will mistrust and will act to get needs met, even if the actions are inappropriate
Autonomy vs. shame and doubt	Toddler	Learns to control environment and self or Will experience shame and/or doubt regarding perceived inappropriate self-control
Initiative vs. guilt	Early childhood	Learns to explore and initiate activities and tasks or Will feel guilt regarding what they feel are inappropriate actions
Accomplishment/ industry vs. inferiority	Childhood	Learns to measure success by comparison to a standard or Will feel inferior when performance is below that standard
Identity vs. role confusion	Adolescence	Learns to identify a concept of self by associating with certain groups of people who have similar values or Will vacillate between several roles, never forming a definitive association or conviction
Intimacy vs. isolation	Young adult	Learns to commit to long-term relationships with others or Will retreat into isolation
Generativity vs. stagnation	Middle adulthood	Learns to contribute to or affect the environment or workplace so as to affect future generations; seeks satisfaction through productivity in career, family, and other interests or Will feel that work and efforts are leading to no significant contribution
Ego identity/ integrity vs. despair	Late adulthood	Looks back on life as well lived with little regret or Will feel life has been wasted

Erik Erikson (1902–1994) was born of Danish parents in Germany. In high school, he focused on becoming an artist; after graduating, he wandered around Europe visiting museums and sleeping under bridges, living a carefree and rebellious life. When he was 25, Erikson taught at an experimental school for American students, one of the early Montessori schools. While there, he developed his interests in psychology and sociology. In 1928, he began psychoanalytic training at the Vienna Psychoanalytic Institute, where Anna Freud was his analyst. Soon after graduating in 1933, Erikson left for the United States. He started a psychoanalytic practice in Boston, began research at Harvard, and later moved to the University of California at Berkeley.

At Berkeley, Erikson studied the Lakota and Yurok Indians, whose children and adolescents faced difficulties finding their place in the world because of conflicts between the very strong native traditions taught by their families and the instruction of the teachers in the American schools they attended. The children's white teachers found them difficult to work with, and their parents believed they had been corrupted by a foreign culture. Erikson's studies led him to analyze the conflicts people go through on their way to adulthood.

In 1960, Erikson took a position as a professor at Harvard, and he stayed there until his retirement in 1968. He is best known for his epigenetic principle, which says people develop through the unfolding of their personalities in eight stages, each of which involves certain developmental tasks that are psychosocial in nature.

Psychosocial Needs and Academic Motivation

In Eriksonian psychology, each stage must be resolved successfully in some manner before resolution of the successive stages can be achieved. Motivation depends largely on successful resolution of the predicament in each stage. Effective teachers work with their students to foster these resolutions. How do the ways in which students resolve their psychosocial needs influence their motivation to succeed in school? First, think about the questions presented in Building Block 3.8.

The Psychosocial-Sensitive Classroom

**BUILDING BLOCK
3.8**

In this activity, you will pay special attention to the psychosocial stages of initiative versus guilt, accomplishment/industry versus inferiority, and identity versus role confusion; these are the stages most children encounter while they attend school.

First, consider young children whose psychosocial struggles are with initiative versus guilt. How might you provide opportunity for your students to take initiative in your classroom without feeling guilty?

Next, consider elementary school children whose psychosocial struggles are with industry versus inferiority. How might you provide the opportunity for your students to be industrious in your classroom without suffering feelings of inferiority?

Finally, consider high school students whose psychosocial struggles are with identity versus role confusion. What kinds of classroom interactions could you provide to help students form their sense of identity? What effect would discouraging adolescents from social interaction have during this stage of development? What basic needs does forming a sense of identity through the establishment of relationships address?

The complete stages of Erikson's psychosocial theory are shown in Table 3.3. However, let us focus primarily on the stages teachers are most likely to encounter in their classes.

Initiative versus Guilt

Young children three to six years old are in the psychosocial stage of initiative versus guilt. As we have seen, children at this stage seek to improve their language skills and to explore their environments to learn what they can about what they live with every day. According to Erikson, those who are encouraged to explore and who succeed in their efforts develop positive feelings of initiative. Those who are discouraged, severely corrected, or punished for their explorations and language exploits develop negative feelings of guilt—guilt for having attempted something they believe they should not have tried. Success breeds motivation, and lack of success thwarts motivation.

Did you conclude that children in this stage of development need to be given multiple and varied opportunities to explore? These explorations can occur in the schoolyard, on field trips, at school assemblies, through play, in hundreds of interesting classroom activities, and at home.

Industry versus Inferiority

Children of elementary school age are in the psychosocial stage of accomplishment/industry versus inferiority. Their primary goal in life is to *do*—do anything. They want to learn all about everything, and they want to learn how to do everything, from swimming the breast stroke to playing chess to reciting the names of the constellations and identifying models of cars that go by. Successful accomplishment of these tasks fosters a desire to do even bigger and better things, resulting in feelings of accomplishment and industry and good feelings about themselves and their abilities. On the other hand, children who are discouraged from these extremely important developmental activities or who are criticized and scolded for doing them will develop feelings of inferiority—feelings they are not as good as others.

Did you conclude that elementary school children need to perform activities at which they can be successful? There are many different ways students can get involved, and there are many different activities students can use to learn basic concepts. These activities range from reading and writing to drawing, play acting, and even composing rap songs and producing mini operas. When a student's desire for industry is encouraged, that student will feel competent and capable, will be motivated to accomplish bigger and better feats, and will increase his or her expectation for success. However, if a student is made to feel inferior, he or she will experience a sense of failure and incompetence, leading to low motivation.

Identity versus Role Confusion

Adolescents have quite a different but equally difficult predicament in their lives: identity versus role confusion. Adolescents constantly ask the question, "Who am I?" Physical changes, coupled with cognitive changes and a growing sense of wondering about their identity, cause adolescents to turn away temporarily from their parents and to try out different roles among people of their own age to see what "fits." Concurrently (and often surreptitiously), adolescents look to parents and other adults, including teachers, for positive role models. At this age, students experiment with various educational, sexual, recreational, and occupational roles in their attempts to find and become themselves. Those who are successful in their search discover their personal identities; those who are not successful develop feelings of role confusion that must be addressed before they can progress through subsequent stages and live happy, successful, and contented lives.

Did you decide it is important to encourage multiple relationships in high school? These can be fostered through classroom-based interactions, group projects, participation in extracurricular activities, and a host of other means. When a student is helped to form a positive self-identity, that student develops the virtues of loyalty, commitment, self-reliance, and independence. But if they do not know which group to affiliate with or commit to, adolescents can find themselves spread so thin they become burdened with feelings of not belonging to *any* group. With which of Maslow's basic needs do you associate this level of psychosocial development? Is it a deficiency or growth need? What does that mean?

▶❚❚ TeachSource Video

View the TeachSource Video Case, "Social and Emotional Development: The Influence of Peer Groups." In this video, you'll observe how a drama teacher draws her students out on their experiences with peer pressure (such as feeling the need to identify with a particular social group) through open discussion. Then you'll see how students use drama to gain perspective on the real-life situations they encounter, the different choices they can make, and the potential consequences. Be sure to view the bonus videos as well. After watching the video clips, answer the following questions:

1. How could a teacher of basic subjects (mathematics, science, and the like) draw students out like the drama teacher did?

2. How much of her classroom time do you suppose the teacher devotes to these discussions of peer pressure?

3. What would she do if she had a prescribed curriculum she had to cover?

General Academic Needs

Let us put all of this together. You have made some important inferences about common needs of students. We hope you have found that all students have the same basic human needs and all students have needs that are affected by their levels of cognitive and psychosocial development. It is time to focus on how these needs are represented academically. We will start by imagining the first day of school or class. What needs must be met? What can the teacher do to alleviate concerns and ensure these needs are satisfied?

BUILDING BLOCK
3.9

The Scary First Day of School

Take a moment to remember the first day of school. It doesn't matter what grade level you focus on; it probably isn't too hard to recall the anxiety you may have felt. Make a list of the questions or concerns you had in your mind at that time.

Then think of the first day of the class in which you are using this textbook. What were you worried about? What did you need to know? Why did you need to know it? Did your teacher help you relax your anxieties? If so, how?

Now consider a student entering *your* classroom on the first day of school. What do you think that student needs? How do these needs affect the student's incentive to learn? How can you help meet those needs?

Other preservice teachers have reported that, on the first day of school, they were concerned about being in the right place, understanding what they were expected to do, and not being embarrassed. They wanted to be reassured that they were indeed in the right classroom with the right teacher, and they wanted to know how to behave in the classroom so that they fit in and didn't stand out from everybody else. Their teachers helped make them more comfortable by sharing their expectations, explaining classroom procedures, and establishing personal relationships with the students.

Even when you entered your college classroom, you may have had some of these same questions, concerns, and anxieties. These concerns are basically the same for students of all ages. In his seminal article, Brooks (1985) identified seven classroom questions that students need answered on the first day of school:

1. Am I in the right room?
2. Where am I supposed to sit?
3. What are the rules in this classroom?
4. What will I be doing this year?
5. How will I be graded?
6. Who is my teacher as a person?
7. Will the teacher treat me as a human being?

© Catherine Ledner/Getty Images

Peer relationships in middle and high school help students form positive self-identity, which encourages progress through the other stages of psychosocial development, according to Erikson.

How do the needs you listed in Building Block 3.9 compare to these questions? Were the seven needs met in the class you are now in? How about in other college classes? How will you respond to these concerns (most of which are never spoken aloud) with your future students?

Try to link these questions to the needs identified in Maslow's hierarchy. Many of them have to do with the needs for safety, love and belonging, and self-esteem.

From this exercise, you can tell that students share basic concerns when they begin a school year or a new class. These concerns stem from anxieties that their classroom needs might not be met—that the teacher might minimize or misinterpret students' basic human needs, cognitive needs, and psychosocial needs. Will the teacher make all students feel accepted and valued? Or is the teacher inclined to ridicule those who don't think as he or she does? Are the teacher's academic expectations appropriate for the students' age and experience levels? Or are those expectations too difficult or (equally disturbing) too easy? Will the teacher foster independence or require conformity to the rules?

Familiarity with these concerns helps us understand how we must structure our teaching and our interactions with students to satisfy their fundamental needs, thereby motivating students to maximum achievement. For, as you have seen, meaningful learning cannot take place unless the basic human needs, cognitive needs, and psychosocial needs of each student have been recognized and addressed.

The application of these fundamental needs in school settings can be combined into a few central principles of teaching. Jones and Jones (2013) listed academic needs that are basic to all students. Their list offers a good summary of where this chapter has been leading us. Students have the academic need to

- Understand and value learning goals.
- Understand the learning process.
- Be actively involved in the learning process and relate subject matter to their own lives.
- Take responsibility for their own learning by following their own interests and setting goals.
- Experience success.
- Receive appropriate rewards for performance gains.
- See learning modeled by adults as an exciting and rewarding activity.
- Experience a safe, well-organized learning environment.
- Have time to integrate learning.
- Have positive contact with peers.
- Receive instructions matched to their learning style.
- Be involved in self-evaluating their learning and effort.

How do these academic needs relate to the three categories of needs you have been investigating in this chapter? In Building Block 3.10, you will associate the academic needs listed by Jones and Jones with Maslow's needs hierarchy, Piaget's stages of cognitive development, and Erikson's psychosocial ladder.

BUILDING BLOCK 3.10

Academic Needs

The academic needs that Jones and Jones identified are shown in the left column of the following table. Read through the list and show how each might be related to Maslow's hierarchy of needs, Piaget's stages of cognitive development, and Erikson's psychosocial ladder by filling in the empty cells. Use the questions in the right column to guide your discussions; they are the kinds of questions competent teachers constantly ask themselves to be sure they are meeting their students' needs to maximize motivation and achievement.

Continued

What are the implications of this completed chart for you as a teacher?

According to Jones and Jones, students need to . . .	Maslow's Hierarchy of Needs	Piaget's Stages of Cognitive Development	Erikson's Psychosocial Ladder	Questions to Foster Discussion
Understand and value learning goals.				How could you help a student understand learning goals and attach value to them?
Understand the learning process.				What could you do to help students understand their learning?
Be actively involved in the learning process and relate subject matter to their own lives.				Why is being actively involved important? Why is it important for subject matter to be relevant?
Take responsibility for their own learning by following their own interests and setting goals.				How does giving students responsibility help meet some of their common needs?
Experience success.				How will the experience of success affect expectations?
Receive appropriate rewards for performance gains.				How will motivation be affected if a reward is meaningful to the student? What kinds of rewards are most meaningful?
See learning modeled by adults as an exciting and rewarding activity.				What common need does the reward of learning and understanding fulfill?
Experience a safe, well-organized learning environment.				How does a well-organized classroom lead to a feeling of security?
Have time to integrate learning.				What emotions can result from feeling rushed?
Have positive contact with peers.				How is peer contact important to psychosocial development?
Receive instructions matched to their learning style.				How does this relate to cognitive development?
Be involved in self-evaluating their learning and effort.				Why would having the opportunity to self-evaluate be motivating to a student?

Differentiating the Classroom

Brenda Zabel

Courtesy of Brenda Zabel

Effective teachers create opportunities for students to take control of their own learning. By designing lessons that allow students to explore a concept at a level and pace that is appropriate and that accommodates individual learning styles, teachers empower students to achieve in the classroom and beyond. Students who perceive they have choices in the classroom are much more motivated to become engaged and persevere in the face of challenge than are students who perceive their education as being force-fed as if from an already established, prescribed procedure.

When students are empowered to learn, rather than instructed to learn, they take ownership in the quantity and quality of the products they produce, whether those products be written documents, oral presentations, simulated models, or electronic multimedia performances. Students who feel they have some control over where, how, and how much they learn about a subject have a greater vested interest in the amount and quality of time and energy they are willing to devote to important curricular topics both inside and outside of the traditional classroom and the traditional school day. One of the most important things teachers do is provide opportunities for students to discover and communicate ways in which key instructional outcomes are relevant and applicable in the students' daily lives.

In the high school zoology and human physiology classes I teach, one nontraditional tool that I use to empower students is music. Music is a highly motivational medium for most teenagers. Early in the school year, my teaching colleagues and I provide a theme song to accompany each new learning unit. For example, prior to beginning a learning unit on reptiles, we might play Elton John's "Crocodile Rock" for all 300 of our students in a "concert hall" setting prior to a large-group class meeting. It usually doesn't take long for the students to begin suggesting their own theme songs for upcoming units. We honor these requests by playing the students' choices and reward their efforts to find real-world connections for the topics we deal with in class. The students take special pride in finding a song that is somehow connected to one of our more technical topics, such as roundworm parasites or the human respiratory system.

Another way in which I attempt to empower my students to learn is by providing them different options about how to demonstrate their understanding of an important learning objective. During a project that occurs in a unit on human histology, students first select a team of students with whom they want to work to research one specific type of human tissue selected by the team. The team members divide up the work of finding out what the characteristics of the tissue are, how the tissue functions when it is healthy, and how it functions when it is diseased, and they prepare a group presentation to share their information with other teams of students who did not research the same tissue. All through the project, the students have choices and control over their progress. The group presentation usually mirrors the individual and collective strengths of the members of each group. For example, a team of students with dramatic skills might choose to perform a short one-act play, while another team with more musicianship could compose and perform an original musical score. A team with an artistic flair might create an elaborate poster painting or three-dimensional model while a different team might choose to deliver their information as a television newscast. Regardless of the format of the final product, students appreciate and respond positively to being given the opportunity to show what they have learned in a variety of ways, determined by them, rather than in one standard pattern way determined by the teacher.

2005 Nebraska Teacher of the Year
Westside High School
Westside Community Schools
Omaha, Nebraska

Instruction that Addresses Student Needs

You have found that students are alike in many ways, possessing common basic, cognitive, and psychosocial needs. You have seen there are many successful approaches to teaching based on people's feelings, ideas, beliefs, and philosophical views. And you have identified characteristics of excellent teachers and effective teaching. Recognizing that numerous factors influence teaching and learning, you might ask, "How do we implement these factors in our classrooms?" To answer that question, let us correlate the characteristics of excellent teachers and effective teaching with the fundamental student needs discussed in this chapter.

Putting Together What You Know—Common Needs

Take a blank sheet of paper and turn it sideways (landscape orientation). Divide it into thirds horizontally by drawing two lines from top to bottom (see diagram). At the top of the first column, write *Students' Basic Human, Cognitive, and Psychosocial Needs*. List the basic needs you have found in this chapter to be common to all students.

Next, make a heading for the middle column of your paper: *Attributes of Effective Teachers and Excellent Teaching*. In this column, write the primary attributes you decided are characteristic of effective teachers and excellent teaching in Chapter 1. Finally, make a heading for the right column: *Students' General Academic Needs*. List the general academic needs you have found in this chapter to be common to all students. (See diagram.)

Students' Basic Human, Cognitive, and Psychosocial Needs	Attributes of Effective Teachers and Excellent Teaching	Students' General Academic Needs

Draw lines from each of the basic needs in the left column to one or more attributes of effective teachers and excellent teaching in the middle column that might help address that need. Similarly, draw lines from each of the academic needs in the right column to one or more attributes of effective teachers and excellent teaching in the middle column that might help address that need.

What does your paper look like? Are there many lines, all crisscrossing each other? Or are the connections few and far between? Can you modify or add to the list in the middle column to let you make more connections to the list in the left and right columns? If so, make those modifications or additions and connect them to the appropriate needs.

What teaching skills might accompany the connections?

In Building Block 3.11, you related basic student needs and basic academic needs to characteristics of effective teachers and excellent teaching. Now that you've done that, what do you believe are the most valuable attributes of good teachers? Which of these do you currently possess? Which do you believe you need to develop or refine?

As you continue your explorations in this course, keep in mind that students are alike in many ways, including their basic human needs, their cognitive characteristics, and their psychosocial development. Look for specific examples of ways in which students are alike, and look for how you can provide instruction and classroom environments that meet the needs common to all students.

Use your favorite search engine to find resources for teachers available on the Internet. You may have to get creative with your search terms, but you can find many materials that are already made or websites that let you create materials like handouts, calendars, rubrics, videos, and posters yourself.

In this chapter, you have identified needs that are common to *all* students. It is important for teachers to acknowledge these needs and meet them in their classroom environments and instruction. Teachers can use technology in addressing many of these needs.

Let us review Brooks's list of questions that students have on the first day of school:

_____ 1. Am I in the right room?

_____ 2. Where am I supposed to sit?

_____ 3. What are the rules in this classroom?

_____ 4. What will I be doing this year?

_____ 5. How will I be graded?

_____ 6. Who is my teacher as a person?

_____ 7. Will the teacher treat me as a human being?

Now, consider some of the technologies that were introduced in Technology and Education in Chapter 1:

A. Television programs and DVDs for students to view educational programs

B. YouTube for students to view clips of demonstrations, events, or educational programs

C. Online animations (such as those found in BrainPop) to present short content information cartoons and to assess student learning

D. Electronic slide shows with color, graphics, sound, video, and animation to present content

E. Content-area software on CD-ROMs for students to use independently or in groups

F. Content-related Internet sites projected for the class or viewed on individual computers

G. Teacher-made websites and blogs to post interesting content information, calendars, syllabi, and events

H. Word-processing and publishing programs to create neat and colorful handouts, signs, and bulletin boards

I. Assistive and adaptive technologies for students with special needs

J. Response system technology ("clickers") for on-the-fly assessments of student learning

K. Interactive whiteboard (such as Smart Boards) to present information for students

L. E-mail to communicate with parents and students

M. Electronic spreadsheets or databases to keep track of grades, attendance, and other data

N. Podcasts to provide additional content information for interested students

O. Applications that allow teachers to design and create online multimedia interactive posters

How do the technologies match up with the questions? How can these technologies help teachers answer these student questions effectively and efficiently? Write the letter of a technology in the blank by any of Brooks's questions that technology might help answer. You may have more than one letter per blank. You may have no letters in some blanks. You may be able to think of some technology that is not listed. By all means, write it in! There are myriad other technological applications we have not mentioned.

Most of the students' first-day-of-school questions have to do with a need to know. Teachers can use word-processing or publishing programs, PowerPoint, or other online resources and applications to create signs and posters informing students of the room number, the teacher's name, the subject(s) taught, and the bell schedule. Word-processing and publishing programs often contain templates for newsletters, which teachers can use to inform students and parents of classroom events and activities. Teachers can develop and maintain a class website, wiki, or blog with information, or the teacher can e-mail the information to students and their families. (Keep in mind, however, that not all of your students will have Internet access at home.) This initial communication with students and parents is invaluable in establishing an effective learning environment that will set the tone for the rest of the year.

What about the last question: "Will the teacher treat me as a human being?" The technologies teachers use to introduce themselves to a class can do the same for students. Students would welcome the opportunity to introduce themselves by writing a paragraph, sending an e-mail, creating a slide presentation or poster, or drawing an electronic picture using programs available on the Internet to give the teacher information about them beyond what is contained in student records.

How can technology help meet some of students' common needs? Using the technologies described earlier contributes to a safe and well-organized learning environment. Computer-assisted instruction allows students to be actively involved with their own instruction, often controlling the pace of their learning. Given guidelines and broad topics, students can search the Internet for information or use appropriate content-area software. This technology appeals to several learning styles, and can be visual, auditory, and tactile all at once. As teachers model the use of technology to find and present content information, students will feel comfortable and will be motivated to do the same.

Is technology absolutely necessary to meet needs you have learned about in this chapter? Of course not. But technology can help.

■ SUMMARY

In this chapter, you have investigated ways in which students are *alike*:

- All students have fundamental, common needs, and the fulfillment of these needs is prerequisite to successful motivation. Maslow developed a pyramidal hierarchy of seven basic needs common to everyone. According to Maslow, all people have these same basic needs, and people must fulfill these needs to some degree in order to exist as human beings. People must satisfy needs that are lower on the pyramid before they can be motivated to satisfy needs at higher levels. Other researchers' basic needs theories are similar to Maslow's hierarchy and to one another's.

- Piaget theorized that people pass through four increasingly sophisticated stages of cognitive development. Each stage represents higher levels of people's capacities to think, reason, and solve problems.

- Erikson theorized that people pass through several phases of psychosocial development. Each phase is characterized by a crisis that must be resolved; how a crisis is resolved may either foster or hinder a person's continued healthy development.

- All students have general academic needs that the teacher must meet to facilitate learning and maintain an effective learning environment.

- The theories of basic needs, cognitive needs, and psychosocial needs are all related to motivation.

Through your work in this chapter, you were able to relate common basic needs to common classroom and academic needs. Your final task was to recall characteristics of effective teachers and excellent teaching, and to correlate these characteristics with students' needs. Having completed this exercise, you can see why you must learn teaching skills and strategies that are effective for all students.

Although all students are alike in that they have similar needs, they are *un*like in that they bring unique perspectives and characteristics to these needs. These unique perspectives heavily influence how common academic needs are met. This is the subject of Chapter 4. Remember, however, that no matter how different those faces look and how unlike those abilities are, excellent teaching addresses the basic needs common to *all* students.

■ Key Terms and Concepts

Aesthetic, 73
Basic needs, 70
Cognitive development, 75
Cognitive needs, 70

Conservation, 77
Deficiency needs, 70
Growth needs, 70
Hierarchy, 70

Psychosocial development, 80
Psychosocial needs, 70
Psychosocial theory, 81
Self-actualization, 73

■ Construct and Apply

1. Think back to the teachers you identified as your favorite and your least favorite in Chapter 1. Identify several reasons why you chose these teachers. Which of these reasons relate directly to increasing or decreasing your motivation? What emotions did you experience in your interactions with these teachers in their classrooms? How were your needs met or not met in the classrooms of these teachers?

2. How do Glasser's five basic needs and Maslow's seven hierarchical needs relate to each other?

3. Suppose you have a student in your class whose parents have just divorced. What needs will this student most likely express in the classroom? What can you do in an academic situation that would help to meet these needs?

4. Consider your experience in higher education. How have your professors met or not met your academic needs? What suggestions do you have for them?

5. Because behavior is driven by needs, students may display unacceptable or inappropriate behavior if their needs are not being met. Describe the kind of behavior you might observe in

your classroom if the following needs were *not* being met. Then describe what the teacher might do to alleviate these concerns:

a. The student needs to know he is in the right place.

If he is unsure, he might _____.

The teacher can solve this anxiety by _____.

b. The student needs to know who you are and whether you're a nice teacher.

If she doesn't know, she might _____.

The teacher can solve this anxiety by _____.

c. The student needs to know what he is expected to do in this class.

If he doesn't know what the teacher's expectations are, he might _____.

The teacher can solve this anxiety by _____.

d. The student needs to know that she is not going to be embarrassed in this class.

If she is afraid she will be embarrassed, she might _____.

The teacher can solve this anxiety by _____.

e. The student needs to know how to act and behave in this class.

If he doesn't, he might _____.

The teacher can solve this anxiety by _____.

Deconstructing the Standards

1. Recall the InTASC Standards associated with the objectives for this chapter:

   InTASC Standard #1: Learner Development reads, "The teacher understands how learners grow and develop, recognizing that patterns of learning and development vary individually within and across the cognitive, linguistic, social, emotional, and physical areas, and designs and implements developmentally appropriate and challenging learning experiences."

   InTASC Standard #3: Learning Environment reads, "The teacher works with others to create environments that support individual and collaborative learning, and that encourage positive social interaction, active engagement in learning, and self-motivation."

   a. Which part(s) of these standards does this chapter address?

   b. How will the concepts in this chapter help you apply these standards as a teacher?

2. Use your favorite search engine to find your state's standards for certification. When you find it, bookmark the site. You will refer to it often as you progress through this book.

   a. How are your conclusions about students' common needs represented in your state certification standards?

   b. How do the InTASC Standards compare to your state's certification standards regarding meeting students' common needs?

   c. Do you believe the degree of representation concerning student needs is adequate in your state certification standards? Why or why not?

Your Portfolio

For your portfolio, include evidence that shows you understand the common needs of students. You may have been able to address specific students' common needs at some time. If so, add a narrative of what you did and why you did it. You may wish to use the material you prepared in Building Block 3.11.

What activities have you been involved in that help students experience a sense of love or belonging? In what ways have you helped students satisfy the need to know or understand? How have you helped a particular student see his or her own potential and talent? Do you have evidence of these interactions? Reflect on your experiences and use them as evidence in your portfolio.

Education CourseMate Resources

Check out this text's Education CourseMate website (at www.cengagebrain.com) for more information about common student needs, interactive study tools, and useful resources. You will find the TeachSource Videos, a guide for doing field experiences, glossary flashcards, activities, tutorial quizzes, direct links to all of websites mentioned in the chapter, and more.

CHAPTER

4

The Student and the Teacher: Acknowledging Unique Perspectives

FOR YOUR STUDENTS to learn, they must know that you care about them. In Chapter 3, you found that all students have certain common needs. Yet every student has a unique perspective and is different from every other student in many ways. How can you demonstrate to *all* your students that they are important and that you care about them?

Among students' common needs are the needs to feel a sense of belonging, acceptance, respect, and self-esteem, as well as the need to feel loved. Students need to know you hear them, see them, care about them, and recognize them as human beings.

For your students to know that you really care about them, you must recognize, acknowledge, and honor the unique characteristics and perspectives each individual brings to the classroom. These characteristics and perspectives influence how students learn and how their needs can be met.

Students come to our schools with tremendously diverse backgrounds, traditions, values, expectations, experiences, strengths, limitations, and preferences. They are different in countless ways, some of which are easier to identify than others. Many of these differences have been shown to influence academic achievement. In this chapter, you will investigate student diversity, including several unique perspectives that impact learning. And you will investigate how you can teach acknowledging these perspectives so that each student feels accepted, respected, and motivated to learn.

Diversity The condition of being different from one another.

Chapter Objectives

As a result of your explorations in this chapter, you will be able to:

1. Investigate the nature of diversity.
   InTASC Standard #1: Learner Development; Standard #2: Learning Differences

2. Describe the nature of cultural diversity, and suggest teaching techniques that acknowledge cultural diversity.
   InTASC Standard #1: Learner Development; Standard #2: Learning Differences

3. Describe the complexities associated with English language learners, and suggest teaching techniques that acknowledge English language learners.
   InTASC Standard #1: Learner Development; Standard #2: Learning Differences

4. Describe the variety of religions in the United States and the challenges this variety brings to schools, and list teaching techniques that acknowledge religion.
   InTASC Standard #1: Learner Development; Standard #2: Learning Differences

5. Describe the nature of socioeconomic status, and suggest teaching techniques that acknowledge socioeconomic status.
   InTASC Standard #1: Learner Development; Standard #2: Learning Differences

6. Describe gender equity, and list teaching techniques that acknowledge gender differences.
   InTASC Standard #1: Learner Development; Standard #2: Learning Differences

7. Describe the nature and types of sexual orientation, and suggest teaching strategies that acknowledge sexual orientation.
   InTASC Standard #1: Learner Development; Standard #2: Learning Differences

The Nature of Diversity

Let us begin by investigating what you already know. The following activities and simulations will help you reflect on your knowledge and beliefs about diversity and draw conclusions about the diversity represented in classrooms.

BUILDING BLOCK 4.1

Teachers and Students as . . . Shoes

Try exploring the diversity you find among the shoes in your closet.

Consider every pair of shoes you own. Go to your closet and have a look. Select one shoe from each pair you own and put the shoes you selected in a pile. Also, if you can, gather one of each pair of shoes belonging to everyone in your household; add these shoes to the pile.

Separate the shoes in your pile into two groups. What characteristics did you use to separate them?

Then separate the shoes in each of the two groups into two subgroups for a total of four piles. What characteristics did you use to separate them?

One more time: If you have enough shoes in the four piles, separate each into two piles or at least separate one of the piles into two. This should give you between five and eight piles of shoes. Name each group with a descriptive name such as *sports shoes, brown shoes, canvas shoes, high-heeled shoes, children's shoes,* and so on.

What if each shoe was a student? Each shoe-student would have the characteristics of the shoe, complete with the material it is made of, its color, its size, its purpose, and whether it is a right or a left shoe. Each shoe-student would be in a group with a label that describes the group's purpose or characteristics. None of these can be changed; they are who they are.

Look at the shoes you have on. Suppose the shoes you are wearing represent the teacher. This shoe-teacher has the purpose, the looks, and the characteristics of your shoes, and none of these things can be changed. You, the shoe-teacher, are who you are.

Now suppose you, the shoe-teacher, plan a unit for your students, the shoe-students. The lessons are to be active, requiring student participation. What activity are your shoes particularly well suited for? Suppose the first lesson includes this activity. As the shoe-teacher, you are able to conduct and participate in this activity fairly easily and successfully. Is the same true for your shoe-students? For example, suppose you have on hiking boots. Your first lesson might include a five-mile hike on rocky terrain. Which of your shoe-students can participate easily in this lesson? Which will give it a fairly good try? Are there shoe-students for whom you would need to make special accommodations? What would these accommodations be?

Suppose day two involves walking three miles. Which of your shoe-students can participate easily in this lesson? Which will give it a fairly good try? Are there some shoe-students for whom walking three miles would be too easy? What accommodations would you make for the students who might find this activity too hard or for whom this activity might not be challenging enough?

Suppose the final day of your unit has your shoe-students going on a job interview. Which of your shoe-students can participate easily in this lesson? Which will give it a fairly good try? Are there shoe-students for whom you would need to make special accommodations? What would these accommodations be?

Now, consider your own shoes. If you make the assumption that the shoe-students in your classroom have the same preferences you have and learn in the same way you do, you are ignoring the unique characteristics and perspectives of your shoe-students.

Is it fair or appropriate for teachers to make assignments based on their own learning or teaching preferences? What could you do as a teacher to accommodate all your shoe-students within a unit of study? Would it be possible to accommodate all the shoe-students within a single lesson?

From the activity in Building Block 4.1, you can infer that everyone in a classroom, including you, is unique and has a unique set of characteristics that affect how he or she approaches learning. Many of these characteristics cannot be changed and must be accommodated in the classroom. This applies to students in all classes (including the students in your introduction to education class). We hope that you also discovered that it is possible to make accommodations so *everyone* can participate in the lessons.

To effectively teach all children, teachers must recognize their own assumptions and beliefs about diversity.

Jim West/The Image Works

Building Block 4.1 used the analogy of comparing shoes to students to prompt you to draw conclusions based on appearances and characteristics. However, no matter how good an analogy is, at some point, it breaks down. Making assumptions and then decisions based on students' outward appearances can be very dangerous. Let's explore this further in the next Building Block.

BUILDING BLOCK 4.2

Classroom Diversity

Suppose you have been given your first teaching job and it is the first day of school. You have been assigned a class of 29 students.

You already have looked through student records to get some background information about your students, and you now spend some time watching your students and talking with them as they interact with you and with one another. You make the following observations:

- There are 15 boys and 14 girls in your class of 29 students.
- Of the boys, two seem indifferent to team sports.
- There is one girl who seems to be a bit of a bully or tomboy.
- Seven students are Hispanic.
- There are six African Americans.
- Four students are Vietnamese.
- Twelve students are white.
- One student wears a yarmulke (a skullcap worn by Jewish males).
- The special education coordinator has identified several students as having special needs: Four of your students have a learning disability and two students are gifted.
- One student has muscular dystrophy and is in a wheelchair.
- Your examination of the school records tells you that 14 of your students come from single-parent homes.
- One student comes from a home with single-sex parents.
- Ten students are considered "middle class," and 19 are identified as either "working class" or "poor."

Just as you separated your shoes, these students have been categorized and labeled for you based on their observed characteristics. Suppose you are a high school math teacher. For which of these students are you able to predict grades? Go down the list, bullet by bullet. How well would each of these students perform in your class? What if you are an elementary physical education teacher? A music teacher? Remedial reading? Advanced Placement physics? Go ahead and write down your initial assumptions about these students. It is important that you be honest and forthcoming doing this. You won't be asked to share your ideas. How might these assumptions affect the expectations you have for these students regarding their learning and performance in your classroom?

Keep in mind that your predictions were based on your assumptions, which were, in turn, based on your prior knowledge and experiences regarding students' unique characteristics.

Students' Unique Perspectives and Characteristics

As you have seen, students differ from one another in a great many ways. Some individual characteristics are readily apparent; others are more subtle. All these characteristics affect how students approach learning—and therefore how you should teach them.

The goal of education in the United States is that *all* children learn, regardless of their differences. A primary goal of your teacher preparation program is for you to become skilled in planning and implementing ways to accommodate these differences as you motivate students to learn in your classroom. To be able to teach in ways that acknowledge student diversity, you must first acknowledge your own experiences and beliefs that may have given rise to assumptions, expectations, stereotypes, and even prejudices. We will explore several unique perspectives and ways in which your experiences and beliefs influence student learning. Before we begin, we should note that many of the characteristics used to classify students into subgroups of unique perspectives are social constructs, not fixed attributes. Remember that in the previous chapter, we explored how students are mostly alike, possessing common needs. For the most part, you can be assured that all of the students you will teach in the future are of one species: human beings (although you may wonder about a few at times). But, identifying classifications of unique perspectives is helpful in identifying trends, preferences, and patterns that are influenced by the perspectives and that should impact instructional decisions and practices (Lee and Buxton, 2010).

In his blog, *Can a White Man Speak with Authority on Diversity?*, Visconti (2011) writes "[The] mindset for majority-**culture** people requires an epiphany or evolution in thinking that brings one to understand the extent of the discrimination around all of us that is perpetuated mostly by the majority culture. . . . In this country, the majority culture is defined as white, male, heterosexual, Christian, and not having an ADA[1]-defined disability." He writes that all of us, regardless of perceived differences, must come to the realization that "I am not different *from* you; I am different *like* you."

You can access the Diversity.com website through the direct link on the Education CourseMate website. This site has facts, figures, and discussions about many aspects of diversity.

> **stereotype** A standard image or idea that represents an uninformed opinion or biased attitude toward a group.

Cultural Diversity

When we consider cultural diversity, many of us think of race. But a person's culture includes much more than race. The dictionary defines *culture* as "the customary beliefs, social forms, and material traits of a racial, religious, or social group . . . the set of shared attitudes, values, goals, and practices" (Merriam-Webster, 2012). An individual's culture is composed of several attributes, including race, ethnicity, social aspects, and religion. Let us look at some aspects of the wide cultural diversity present in our world.

> **race** A group of people that possesses traits that are inherited and sufficient to characterize the group as a distinct human type.
>
> **culture** The customary beliefs, social forms, and material traits of a racial, religious, or social group.
>
> **ethnicity** Affiliation with a group that has general customs, language, and social views and based on common racial, national, tribal, religious, linguistic, or cultural origin or background.

Population Diversity

According to the Population Reference Bureau, in July 2010, the world's population reached almost 7 billion people, and it is expected to be between 9.15 and 9.51 billion by 2050 (Brenner et al., 2010). If we could take the data from the Population Reference Bureau and shrink it to just 100 people while maintaining the ratios, we would have the following information (The Miniature Earth Project, 2010):

- Sixty-one of the 100 are Asian.
- Thirteen are from Africa.
- Eight are North Americans.
- Five are from South America and the Caribbean.
- Twelve are from Europe.
- One is from Oceania.
- Fifty are men and fifty are women.
- Forty-seven live in urban areas.
- Twelve are disabled.

---

[1]Americans with Disabilities Act.

- Thirty-three are Christian (Catholic, Protestant, Orthodox, Anglican, and other Christian denominations).
- Twenty-one are Muslims.
- Thirteen are Hindus.
- Six are Buddhists.
- One is a Sikh.[2]
- One is a Jew.
- Eleven are nonreligious.
- Eleven practice other religions.
- Three are atheists.
- Forty-three live without basic sanitation.
- Eighteen live without an improved water source.
- Fourteen are hungry or malnourished.
- Twelve cannot read.
- Twelve have a computer.
- Eight have an Internet connection.
- One adult (15 to 49 years old) has HIV/AIDS.
- Twenty people hold 75 percent of the entire world's income.

Where do you fall in this representation of the world's population? How are the majority of global inhabitants like you? How are they different from you?

The population of the United States is growing rapidly and is becoming more and more diverse. Figure 4.1 shows forecast trends in the racial and ethnic makeup of the U.S. population from 2000 to 2050.

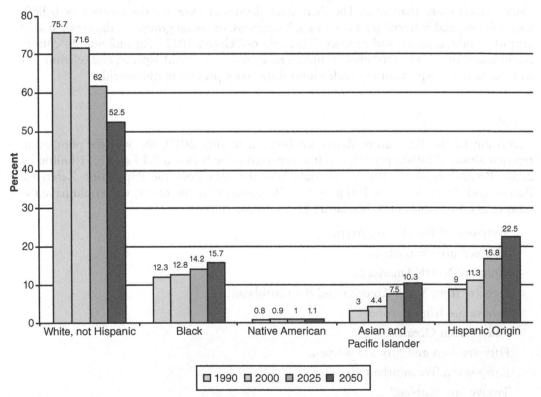

Figure 4.1 ▶
U.S. population trends by race and ethnicity, 2000–2050.
(From data in Day, 2001.)
© Cengage Learning 2014

---

[2]Sikhism is a 500-year-old religion with foundational beliefs in one god and in the equality of all human beings (Brar, 2003).

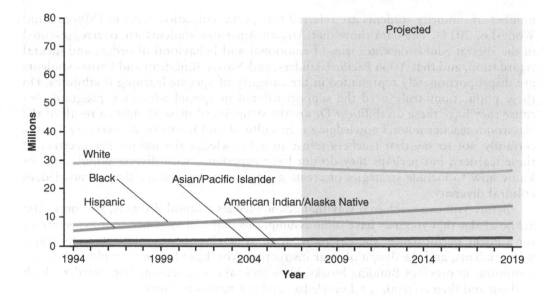

◄ **Figure 4.2**
Percentages of public school students by race, 1994–2019.
(From National Center for Education Statistics, 2010a.)
© Cengage Learning 2014

Similarly, the population of students in American schools is becoming increasingly multicultural. In 2008-2009, the enrollment in U.S. public schools was 54.9 percent white, 16.9 percent black, 21.5 percent Hispanic, and 7.7 percent other ethnicities (National Center for Education Statistics, 2009a). Figure 4.2 shows the trend in racial makeup of schools from 1994 to 2007 with known data, and then projected through 2019 (National Center for Education Statistics, 2010a). If this trend in the ethnic makeup of public school students were to come to fruition, when would the so-called minorities of today overtake the white students in school population?

Diversity and Educational Perspectives

Philosophies of education often are based on cultural heritage and vary greatly from one cultural group to another. Some believe that education is a joint endeavor among school, community, teacher, students, and family; others believe that education is the professional purview of teachers and that families need to stay out of the way of teachers. The educational philosophy of some African Americans emphasizes that students must learn to be responsible for themselves. Hispanic culture often holds the family as the most important cultural factor. Native American educational philosophies often embrace a holistic view of teaching and a profound respect for ancestors, elders, and nature; they do not necessarily like to be singled out for attention or praise but rather value sharing and cooperation over competition. Many Asian American families view teachers as authorities whose job is to ensure that students learn. The predominant educational philosophy of European Americans is that school is a joint venture between the parents and teachers.

What do these perspectives mean to the academic needs of these cultural groups? How might an African American parent who subscribes to the philosophy of self-responsibility perceive a highly structured, teacher-dependent classroom? Why might some teachers feel "abandoned" when seeking collaboration or input from Asian American parents who see teachers as authoritative? How might a Native American learner feel about a review game involving competition played in a class preparing for a test? These are broad, generalized questions, but it is important to realize that parents and students from different cultural groups may value different aspects of schooling, teaching, and learning.

Teaching That Acknowledges Cultural Diversity

How important is it that you, as a teacher, address the unique cultural perspectives of the learners in your classroom? Recent research has indicated that a disproportionate number of minority students are referred for special education services (Moreno and Wong-Lo, 2011). The data show that African American students are overrepresented in the special education categories of emotional and behavioral disorders and mental retardation, and that Asian Pacific Islanders, and Native American and Latino students are disproportionately represented in the category of specific learning disabilities. Do these populations truly need the support offered in special education programs because they have these disabilities? Or are the struggles of these students a result of the classroom teacher not acknowledging their cultural and linguistic differences? That is certainly not to say that teachers refuse to acknowledge the unique perspectives of these learners, but perhaps they do not have experience with diverse populations or know how to include strategies or create a classroom atmosphere that acknowledges cultural diversity.

Before you can teach in a way that acknowledges cultural diversity, you must first acknowledge that you may have some assumptions that will influence your expectations for student performance, the environment of your classroom, your communications with students, and the design of your instruction. You have begun to explore these assumptions in previous Building Blocks. Now let's take a closer—perhaps harder—look at them and then recognize, acknowledge, and put names to them.

BUILDING BLOCK 4.3

Identifying Assumptions and Expectations

Think about your favorite grocery store. What types of people frequent the store? Can you recall your last trip there and the kind of people you saw? Are they the types of people you would expect to find? How well do the people who go to your grocery store represent your community? How well do they represent the kind of person you are? Do you see children in the store? By looking around your grocery store, could you tell which of the children you see there are probably good students and which are probably troublemakers?

Think about a shopping mall you may patronize. What are your favorite stores? What kinds of people would you expect to see in those stores? How are they like you? How are they different from you? How are the people who patronize the higher-priced stores like you or different from you? What about the people in the lower-priced stores? Do you think they went to college? Why or why not?

Consider the discount department store most convenient to where you live. Have you noticed the type of people that frequent that store? How are they like you? How are they not like you? Have you made some assumptions about the people you may have seen shopping there based on what they look like? Possibly, assumptions were made about level of income, education, and intelligence. How would you expect these people to perform in your classroom if you were their teacher?

Are there some neighborhoods where you can only dream of living? What kinds of people live there? What do you suppose their children are like? What kinds of students would you expect these children to be? What do you think the children will do when they grow up?

Are there some "bad" neighborhoods where you can't imagine living? What are the people like who live there? What do you suppose their children are like? What kinds of students would you expect these children to be? What do you think these children will do when they grow up?

Diversity in the Community

Another way to explore more about the cultural diversity of your students is to get out and explore the community of the school. Perhaps the most effective way to discover your beliefs is to talk face-to-face with people who are different from you. Although such conversations may be uncomfortable at first, they can reveal both misunderstandings and congruence. Education professor Sonia Nieto says, "The unfortunate thing is when people walk on egg shells, afraid to talk about diversity . . . part of it is that they fear it will bring up conflicts. And perhaps it will, so all of us . . . need to be more tolerant, to learn to talk frankly with one another" (Kitagawa, 2000, p. 162).

It should be clear that culture and ethnicity of students and their families are expressed in the community in which the students live. Just as important as the personal characteristics that describe individual students is getting to know *where* students come from. Many teachers do not live in the same community as the school in which they teach. Yet, they expect to know their students well enough so as to be able to meet the needs of those students. Visiting the community or communities in which your students live can provide you with valuable insights into their backgrounds, experiences, values, and expectations. Indeed, community and family influence on learners is receiving increasing attention in education.

Dr. Xae Alicia Reyes, Associate Professor of Curriculum and Instruction in Puerto Rican and Latino Studies and Interim Director of the Puerto Rican and Latin American Cultural Center at the University of Connecticut at Storrs states, "As future teachers, you need to be committed to meeting the needs of all students; the process needs to begin with deeper knowledge about the communities in which your students live and socialize. . . . Recently, students' cultural backgrounds and prior experiences [have been] recognized as important factors when discussing pedagogy and curriculum design. What seems to be missing in this equation is a clear understanding that context—outside of the school—also matters as much if not more than all of these elements" (Kellough and Carjuzaa, 2009, p. 42).

Dr. Reyes suggests that, in an effort to become more involved in the school and students' community, teachers should attend events such as fairs, festivals, exhibits, and town meetings. In this way, teachers will be able to identify cultural, social, and political issues that affect the community, the school, families, and learners.

We teachers make plenty of assumptions and hold many expectations. Some of these assumptions and expectations may reflect prejudices and biases that we need to address. Do you *really* believe that everyone can learn? Or is the notion lurking somewhere that there will always be one or two students who, for whatever reason, simply will not succeed in school? You might, for example, believe that adolescent students who are unkempt and show signs of drug or gang activity will not be able to achieve because they have other activities on their minds. Or you might believe that young children who come from broken homes, who have a parent in prison, or whose parents seem disinterested in their education will have serious difficulties with academic achievement because the cards are stacked against them. Do you believe all ethnic groups and races are equally capable of learning? Or do you believe deep down inside there are some groups that just won't make it? Students of different cultural backgrounds have had different life experiences and thus bring different perceptions, understandings, and characteristics to the classroom. Although these perspectives are *different*, teachers should not view them as a hindrance to learning and academic achievement. To be sure, there is a well-documented achievement gap between minority and majority students in schools. But we can't assume that the reason for this discrepancy is due to limitations of the individual students because of their cultures. Yet, we may carry these assumptions into our classrooms so that they affect teaching.

Cultural Paradigms: Deprivation and Deficits

The assumptions we make that relate cultural diversity to teaching and learning may be categorized as "multicultural paradigms." According to Vang (2010), a multicultural paradigm is a model for explaining cultural diversity. James A. Banks, professor and director of the Center for Multicultural Education at the University of Washington at Seattle, is one of the most respected experts in his field. He proposed a model called the

cultural deprivation model A multicultural paradigm that assumes that nonmainstream students may fail to achieve because their culture deprives them of resources and experiences.

cultural deprivation model (Banks, 2008). In this model, it is assumed that students representing minority groups may fail to achieve academically due to being *deprived* of the language skills and experiences afforded to students representing the dominant culture. In this way, their culture doesn't give them the opportunity or exposure to experiences that would support their success on the same level as students representing the majority culture.

cultural deficit model A multicultural paradigm that assumes that nonmainstream students may fail to achieve due to deficits that are imposed on them by their culture.

This notion is somewhat consistent with the cultural deficit model that originated in the 1960s. This model implies that a student's culture imposes a deficit that must be overcome in the classroom. The differences in language, social skills, values, customs, and traditions create a hole from which minority students must struggle to climb out of to achieve (Manning and Baruth, 2009).

The implication of a cultural deprivation or deficit model is that there is a desired standard that culture prohibits some students from attaining. This standard is that of the white, middle- or upper-class citizen. Indeed, we usually refer to groups other than white, middle- or upper-class citizens as "minorities." The term *minority,* and its opposite, *majority,* usually references number. In society, however, minority status is determined not only by numbers, but rather primarily by perceived *power.* And power in society can be determined by socioeconomic status and level of education, which may be correlated to cultural diversity (Bohlin et al., 2008). For this reason, rather than use the terms *majority* and *minority,* it may be more useful and more accurate to use the terms *mainstream* and *nonmainstream,* where mainstream students are representative of the dominant culture. In school, the nonmainstream students may experience environments that are very different from their home environments in terms of language, thinking skills, social interactions, and expectations. The mainstream students have the advantage in that the culture of school is consistent with the culture of home (Lee and Buxton, 2010).

socioeconomic status A position influenced by a combination of social and economic factors including income, education, occupation, and place in the community.

white privilege The idea that the white race is afforded unearned advantages and positive treatment due to race.

Perhaps you have heard the term "white privilege." Vang (2010) says that in every nation in which multiple cultures and languages are represented, people of one race have more privileges than the others. Privilege is represented by unearned advantages and positive treatment. The privileged race has more social prestige and institutional privileges than other races (Lee and Buxton, 2010). In her classic article, "White Privilege: Unpacking the Invisible Knapsack" (1989), Peggy McIntosh, a feminist and antiracism activist, provides many examples of white privilege as she perceives it. A few examples include:

1. Being able to use cash, credit, or checks to make a purchase without the color of your skin working against the appearance of your financial responsibility
2. Facing a person of your own race when you ask to speak to the "person in charge"
3. Buying "flesh-colored" bandages and expecting them to match the color of your skin

Vang (2010) offers a couple of ways you might consider to see for yourself the existence of white privilege. First, think of any friends or acquaintances that you have who are Asian. What are their names? Often, students who are foreign adopt "Americanized" versions of their names or even American names. Instead of Shuin, a Chinese girl may choose to go by "Sharon." A boy from Pakistan named Syeedur may choose to go by "Lenny." Why would they do this? What are the perceived advantages? Even if you concede that the Americanized name might be easier for some to pronounce, why would this be important?

A second interesting occurrence that indicates the presence of white privilege exists in schools. Often, as a part of efforts in multicultural education, teachers invite students representing minority cultures to share their own customs, traditions, meals, and lifestyles. Yet, no one asks mainstream students to share their white culture with minority students. Why do you suppose this is? What are the implications?

Do you believe there is a culture of being white? Use your favorite search engine, and check out the website, Stuff White People Like. Also, search for websites similar to Stuff White People Like for other cultures. Is there one for a culture with which you identify? Do you find any of it familiar? Do you find any of it offensive?

Cultural Paradigms: Differences and Mismatches

When people subscribe to the paradigm that minority learners have a deficit to overcome, they imply that the fault lies within the learners. Of course, this is not true. What may be more applicable to education is the cultural difference model (Banks, 2008). This model attributes gaps in educational achievement between majority and minority groups to the differences between the culture of the minority learner and the culture in the school. Similar to this is the cultural mismatch model, which states that nonmainstream students may struggle to achieve in schools that are dominated by mainstream culture. The cultures of the students and the school do not match. Certainly, advantages rooted in white privilege are not attributable to any individual white learner. Rather, these paradigms leave room to acknowledge the strengths that different cultures bring to the classroom, and emphasize that these strengths should be acknowledged and brought into the classroom as a part of the environment, curriculum, and instruction. It is absolutely essential that teachers acquire cultural sensitivity. To do this, you must first examine your own culture and your own beliefs about other cultures, similar to what you did when you were identifying qualities of effective teaching and your philosophy of education in the first two chapters of this book. You can accomplish this self-examination in several ways. One way is to take a self-test dealing with your feelings about diversity. Several such tests can be found on the Internet.

cultural difference model A multicultural paradigm that assumes that nonmainstream students may fail to achieve due to differences between their culture and the culture of the classroom.

cultural mismatch model A multicultural paradigm that assumes that nonmainstream students may fail to achieve due to a mismatch between the students' culture and the culture of the classroom.

Use your favorite search engine to find self-awareness tests about biases available on the Internet.

Multicultural Education

In 1988, Banks proposed four approaches to multicultural education:

1. *The contributions approach.* Teachers using this approach include appropriate information about other cultures and representative individuals on holidays and other events. During black history month, for example, a teacher might create a special bulletin board featuring prominent African American inventors and their inventions. The teacher might read to the class about Mexican history on Cinco de Mayo and share traditional songs, food, and dances.

2. *The additive approach.* In this approach, teachers integrate relevant information from other cultures at appropriate places in the curriculum. For example, it might be part of the curriculum for students to learn about the events that led to the first Thanksgiving. Including a Native American perspective on Thanksgiving would be an additive approach to multicultural education. The curriculum itself is not modified; rather, it is supplemented with multicultural information. The dominant culture is still the focus of the learning.

3. *The transformation approach.* As its name implies, this approach transforms the curriculum. An investigation of multicultural perspectives is an objective of the study as students consider multiple points of view.

4. *The social action approach.* In this extension of the transformation approach, students not only explore topics but also participate in activities that intend social change as an outcome. Students might investigate a social issue such as poverty and then take action on the issue, such as writing letters to political figures or undertaking a charity drive (Banks, 1988).

As you consider these approaches to multicultural teaching, how does the philosophy of multicultural education move toward the social reconstructionist philosophy (see Chapter 2)? Which of these approaches is most consistent with viewing

You will see a wide range of cultures represented in your students.

cultural differences as strengths rather than from a cultural deficit model? Also, when reading about the additive approach, did it occur to you that when incorporating this approach, a teacher should acknowledge when Caucasian individuals made certain contributions? What does *not* doing so imply about the "dominant culture"?

Ladson-Billings (1994) first proposed the term culturally relevant pedagogy to describe teaching that bridges students' home life and school life, acknowledging their experiences and influences of community and culture in the design of lessons and activities. In her studies of effective teachers of African American students, she found that regardless of their students' race, these teachers worked on developing a community of learners that included the students and the teacher. They believed that their students could learn and succeed, and they did not use language that conveyed a belief that the students' culture was a hindrance to their ability to achieve. They worked to understand what a typical day was like for students in school, at home, and in the community, and they made an effort to understand the many facets of the students' cultures. She proposes four "pillars" for multicultural teaching (Ladson-Billings, 2009):

1. Teacher attitudes and expectations
2. Cultural communication in the classroom
3. Culturally diverse content in the curriculum
4. Culturally congruent instructional strategies

Lee (2012) suggests five things teachers can do to create an antiracist classroom—one in which expectations for all students are raised and in which differences are not simply tolerated but, rather, are valued:

1. Don't ignore race.
2. Seek out established community organizations.
3. Remember that communities of color are not monolithic.
4. Read!
5. Self-awareness is the key.

You may have noticed that the characteristics of teachers and approaches we have examined in this section are not recent. Indeed, this information has been "out there" for decades! So, you have read about it before or even experienced it as a student yourself, right? Probably not. Why do you suppose that is? Why is it that these approaches, strategies, and teacher qualities may not be more evident in all schools and classrooms? Why is it important that you, as a new teacher entering the profession in the near future, be very familiar and comfortable with the information in this section?

Something else you may have noticed is that the approaches for effective teaching and the characteristics of effective teachers of culturally diverse populations of students apply to *all* cultures of learners, including the perceived "mainstream" or "dominant" culture of being white. Keep in mind that what you have already learned about acknowledging the different cultures of students in your teaching is also applicable to the other unique perspectives that you will examine in the rest of this chapter.

culturally relevant pedagogy
Teaching that acknowledges students' culture in the design of lessons.

View the TeachSource Video Case, "Culturally Responsive Teaching: A Multicultural Lesson for Elementary Students." We live in a multicultural society. Yet, classroom discussion of diverse societies often get short shrift in this age of high-stakes testing because many teachers worry about squeezing as much curriculum as possible into a school day. In this video, you'll see how Developmental Psychologist Dr. Francis Hurley weaves a lesson on multiculturalism into a traditional lesson on the five-paragraph essay. After watching this video, answer the following questions:

1. How does Dr. Hurley bring multiculturalism into the lesson for her students?
2. How does Dr. Hurley think that thematic teaching lends itself to multicultural education?
3. Where do Dr. Hurley's methods fit into Banks's approaches to multicultural education?
4. What ideas do you have for themes that you might work into multicultural education in your future classroom?

English Language Learners

English language learner A person learning to speak English whose primary language is other than English.

With the increasingly multicultural complexion of America's population, it makes sense that the number of languages spoken in schools is also increasing. English language learners (ELLs) are students who are actively attempting to learn the English language with support from school programs (National Council of Teachers of English, 2008). It

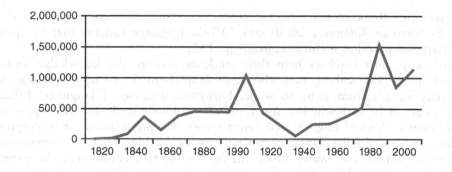

◀ **Figure 4.3**
Number of people obtaining legal permanent resident status in the United States, 1820–2010.
(From U.S. Department of Homeland Security, 2011.)
© Cengage Learning 2014

is estimated that in the United States, approximately 10.8 percent of students enrolled in grades K–12 in the 2008–2009 school year were English language learners. The five states with the highest percentages of ELLs were California, Texas, Florida, New York, and Illinois (National Clearinghouse for English Language Acquisition, 2011). And according to a report issued by the U.S. Census Bureau in 2009, one in every four children under the age of five in the United States is raised in a home where a language other than English is spoken (Lee, Lee, and Amaro-Jiménez, 2011). In the 2000–2001 academic year, more than 400 different languages were spoken by students; besides English, the most common was Spanish (Padolsky, 2002). This proliferation of languages, of course, is to be expected. Except for a decline in the early 20th century and another decline in the late 20th century, the number of people seeking legal permanent resident status in the United States has increased regularly (see Figure 4.3). Between January 2000 and March 2010, 13.1 million immigrants, both legal and illegal, came to the United States (Camarota, 2010).

Predominant languages vary greatly by region in the United States, but there may be many different languages spoken in any one school. For example, John C. Diehl Elementary School in Erie, Pennsylvania, serves a total of 450 students in kindergarten through eighth grade. In this relatively small population, students speak Bosnian, Vietnamese, Spanish, Arabic, Albanian, Russian, Ukrainian, Sudanese, Turkish, Somalian, Swahili, Romanian, and Maay-Maay (John C. Diehl Elementary School, 2012). So it is evident that there is great diversity in the native languages spoken by U.S. students.

Even the designations we use to label students who do not speak English as their native language are numerous and varied. The following list contains some common acronyms and terms that are used when referencing this population of learners (Beare, 2012):

- *English language learner (ELL)* is used to refer to students who are actively learning English with support from school programs.
- *English as a second language (ESL)* is a support program of instruction for ELLs.
- *Limited English proficiency (LEP)* is used to refer to individuals who lack the mastery of English to be successful in a mainstream classroom. This term is not a preferred term because it implies that these individuals are deficient. Instead, ELL is preferred because it acknowledges the individuals as learners.
- *English as a foreign language (EFL)* is used to refer to individuals who are learning English in a country where English is not the native language.
- *1.5 generation students* is used to refer to individuals who have graduated from a high school in the United States and who have entered higher education while still learning English.

Teaching ELL students presents unique challenges. It is important to realize that just because two different students may be classified as English language learners, they may not have the same needs in the classroom and therefore may not be served well by the

English as a second language (ESL) A support program of instruction for ELLs.

limited English proficiency (LEP) Refers to individuals who lack the mastery of English to be successful in a mainstream classroom. This term is not a preferred term because it implies that these individuals are deficient. Instead, *ELL* is preferred because it acknowledges the individual as a learner.

English as a foreign language (EFL) Individuals who are learning English in a country where English is not the native language.

1.5 generation students Refers to individuals who have graduated from a high school in the United States and who have entered higher education while still learning English.

same strategies. Remember that they each will bring their own unique perspectives with them. As Nieto (in Kitagawa, 2000) says, "All the language varieties that we speak are really part and parcel of multiculturalism" (p. 162).

Not only must teachers help their students acquire the knowledge and skills required in the curriculum, they also must help them do so in a language whose familiarity ranges from none to some. However, because of language difficulties, teachers cannot be sure whether any academic problems students have represent low achievement or limited English proficiency. Given this predicament, it is tempting for teachers to view English language learners as low achievers. It is correspondingly tempting for teachers to "water down" the curriculum to accommodate these students. This is "a simply indefensible solution" (Gersten et al., 1998, p. 70) because this practice denies English language learners "access to quality instruction and, ultimately, academic opportunity" (p. 70).

To help you imagine the challenges of learning in an English-speaking classroom if you do not speak English, do the activity in Building Block 4.4.

BUILDING BLOCK 4.4

A Second Language

Following are the instructions to play a simple game. A short quiz follows the instructions. Read the instructions, complete the game, and take the quiz.

Instruksjoner: Spillet er for 2 spillere: en som er X og en som er O. Objektet får 3 Xs eller 3 Os i et vertikalt, horisontal, eller diagonal ledning.

1. Tegn 2 vertikal parallell linjer.
2. Nå tegn 2 flere parallell linjer det krysset det for det første i den grad at de ligne denne: #.
3. Det for det første spilleren merkene en X inne ettall av boksene dannet av det linjer.
4. Så, sekundet spilleren merkene en O inne en annen bokse med.
5. Spillerne fortsette tar dreier til ettall spilleren har Xs eller Os inne en vertical, horisontal, eller diagonalt line.

Prøve:

1. Hvem vant spillet?
2. Kunn De leker dette spillet alene?
3. Hva er det største antallet Xs mulig om O drar først?
4. Hva er det største antallet Xs om X drar først?

Did you enjoy the game? How did you do on the quiz questions? Did you figure out what the game was? There are some familiar characters that may serve as clues if you read through the instructions carefully.

Translation (The language is Norwegian.):

Directions: This game is for 2 players: one is X and the other is O. The object is to get 3 Xs or 3 Os in a vertical, horizontal, or diagonal line.

1. Draw 2 vertical parallel lines.
2. Now draw 2 more parallel lines that cross the first so that they look like this: #.
3. The first player marks an X in one of the boxes formed by the lines.
4. Then, the second player marks an O in another box.
5. Players continue taking turns until one player has 3 Xs or 3 Os in a vertical, horizontal, or diagonal line.

Quiz:

1. Who won the game?
2. Could you play this game alone?
3. What is the greatest number of Xs possible if O goes first?
4. What is the greatest number of X if X goes first?

Teaching That Acknowledges English Language Learners

At this point, it is important to recall the information you investigated in the previous sections: The concepts of cultural diversity, your assumptions, the multicultural paradigms, white privilege, and mainstream versus nonmainstream students all apply here because the task of learning English as a new language often accompanies the characteristics of nonmainstream race and ethnicity.

In 1968, Congress passed the Bilingual Education Act, which created services for students with limited English-speaking ability. More recently, the No Child Left Behind (NCLB) Act has augmented the Bilingual Education Act to require states to include ELLs in assessments taken by all students and to administer English language proficiency tests. Provisions allow the state assessments to be given in a student's native language for the first three years after enrollment in a school in the United States, but the test must still be aligned with the state standards. Yet, students normally take five to seven years to acquire a language (Dickenson, 2012). The NCLB Act also provides funds for language instruction, called Title III funds.[3] In fact, Robinson (2010) has found that, on standardized tests of mathematics, providing ELL with students' tests translated into their primary language results in improvement of the test scores.

As we have indicated, ELL students are fully capable of achieving in the subject areas; their primary difficulty is with language. Consequently, it is necessary to employ teaching strategies that help ELL students compensate for their deficiency in English. If you are bilingual or have some familiarity with a foreign language, by all means, use it with your future students. However, a person does not need to speak other languages to be an excellent teacher. As is the case with culturally diverse students, attitude is the first and foremost consideration in providing effective education for students with emerging or limited proficiency in English. Teachers must develop the same positive attitude toward ELL students that they have for *all* students—the attitude that all students can learn and can achieve their high expectations.

Lee, Lee, and Amaro-Jiménez (2011) suggest the following strategies for teaching mathematics to young children who are English language learners; these strategies could just as well be applied to teaching any subject to ELLs at any grade level.

- Make use of children's own stories.
- Integrate conversational language and language that is familiar to students.
- Promote children's native language.
- Allow children to think aloud to promote their understandings.
- Integrate nonlinguistic materials to facilitate academic language.

Bilingual education is education that includes subject-matter instruction in both the student's native language and in English. Educators have approached bilingual education in four basic ways:

1. *Immersion.* ELL students are immersed in English-speaking classes where teachers attempt to use very basic language so students can learn the content and the language at the same time. Note that immersion does not really fit the definition of bilingual education because no instruction is offered in the student's native language.

2. *English as a second language (ESL).* ESL is similar to the immersion approach, except students may receive some instruction in their native language. ESL classes typically

---

[3]In *Lau v. Nichols* (1974), the U.S. Supreme Court unanimously decided that schools could *not* deny access to a meaningful curriculum to English language learners: "There is no equality of treatment merely by providing students with the same facilities, textbooks, teachers, and curriculum; for students who do not understand English are effectively foreclosed from any meaningful education." In other words, for ELL students, the *same* treatment does not constitute *equal* treatment; schools bear an obligation to address both the language and curricular needs of the students (Hakuta, 2011).

bilingual education Instruction provided in both a student's native language and in English.

View the TeachSource Video Case, "Bilingual Education: An Elementary Two-Way Immersion Program." Many students learn to become proficient in Spanish or English in school. What's especially interesting about this video is that you'll get to meet two teachers and their students who are involved in a two-way bilingual program: All students learn to read, write, and communicate in both English and Spanish in all subject areas.

After watching this video, answer the following questions:

1. What are your thoughts about the two-way immersion program?
2. What are the advantages?
3. What are the disadvantages?
4. Why would you choose to participate or not participate in a program such as this?
5. What would you have to do to prepare if your principal informed you that you would be co-teaching in a two-way immersion program beginning next fall?

In this New Mexico school, teachers instruct students in both English and a Native American language.

Bilingual Education

Bilingual education is not without controversy. Some people believe that non-English speakers in the United States should learn to speak English. They say that ELL students should be immersed in English-speaking classrooms and that no special and expensive bilingual education programs should be necessary. They maintain that the job of the school is not to promote the native language and culture of the student, but rather to help all students achieve academically through the development of English language skills (Callaghan, 2010). Proponents of bilingual education note that, in our increasingly global society, being bilingual would be an asset to nonnative English speakers. It would also benefit native English speakers to be bilingual (Olsen and Spiegel-Coleman, 2010). Others say that providing instruction in the native language means students may graduate without the necessary English skills (Fuller, 2010). Another concern is that teachers need to be qualified to teach ESL. In fact, it has been suggested that one reason English learners fall behind in academic achievement may be because they are not taught English effectively (Callaghan, 2010). Immigrants are divided on whether or not they believe their children should be taught in English immersion or in bilingual education programs. Sixty-three percent of those surveyed believed that all classes should be taught in English, whereas 32 percent believed that students should receive some instruction in their native languages (Public Agenda Online, 2003).

Bilingual education is such a controversial issue that some states have adopted legislation that virtually eliminated bilingual programs. California voters approved Proposition 227 in 1998, which resulted in English language learners being placed in immersion programs. Arizona passed a similar measure in 2000, as did Massachusetts in 2002. Colorado voters, however, did not approve similar propositions. At the national level, the Obama administration favors an approach that transitions learners from their native language to English as quickly as possible. Research has shown that this approach, called "transitional bilingual education," has been effective. Students in bilingual education programs demonstrate greater gains in achievement than those in English-immersion programs. But once again, this effectiveness is strongly dependent on the quality of the teacher (Fuller, 2008).

WHAT DO YOU THINK?

1. *Should ELL students be immersed in English-speaking classrooms to learn content? Why or why not?*
2. *Should ELL students be provided with English language instruction as part of their regular school day? Why or why not?*
3. *What would be the advantages and disadvantages of pulling ELL students out of the regular classroom and providing them with content instruction in their native language (not necessarily from a content-certified teacher)?*

▶️ **TeachSource** Video

View the TeachSource Video from the CBS/BBC Motion Gallery, "The Debate over Bilingual Education." Because Proposition 227 virtually outlawed bilingual education in California, many English language learners in the state are now being taught in English-only schools. However, some schools have worked to keep bilingual programs. After watching this video, answer the following question:

If you were to begin teaching in Oceanside, California, this fall, would you be among those who fight to maintain the bilingual programs that Proposition 227 outlawed? Why or why not?

consist of students with many different primary languages. Students may attend only one ESL class a day, which focuses on developing their English skills, or they may attend up to a full day of classes that work on both English and content.

3. *Transitional bilingual education.* Students receive some instruction in their native language and also instruction in how to speak English in concentrated classes. The intent is for students to become proficient enough in English so they can make the transition into English-speaking classes in a matter of a few years.

4. *Developmental bilingual education.* Students receive instruction in their own language as they learn English as a second language.

In some schools, students take certain subjects in English for half of the day and other subjects in their native language for the other half of the day. In a variation of this scheme, some schools switch language days each week.

The National Association for Bilingual Education (2009) reports that bilingual education programs that focus on developing students' skills in their native language lead to increased achievement in English. As with any educational program, however, bilingual education must be well designed and well implemented. Also, the effectiveness of such programs is better when the teacher uses the language in the context of learning (rather than just providing translations), and when the goal of the program is really to develop bilingual skills (rather than just to get the learner up to the mainstream standard). Adequate materials and resources are important, as is the support from administrators, school boards, parents, and the community.

Teaching All Learners
Bonnie Robb

Every year, there they are. Those eager first-grade faces. They are full of promise and ready for learning. Every year, I take a moment to stop and reflect on the joys, challenges, and possibilities waiting for me and my students over the next nine months. I've spent most of my career teaching high-poverty, high-ELL populations, and my students have both loved and have had high achievement in math. I have found there are a few important points to consider as teachers of these young mathematicians.

Don't let your past become their present! We all have stories about how we learned math that usually include a failure or disappointment. I have sat in many parent-teacher conferences and heard parents say, "I am so bad at math." I have heard classroom teachers say the same thing, in front of students! "Don't worry John," they say, "math was hard for me too." Teachers might think they are making the student feel better, but really, we are enabling him to fail. Young learners will rise to our expectations, but we need to "sell it"! Students are watching our attitudes and expressions—if we don't like something, they won't either. Don't deny a child a future in mathematics because math was hard for you as a student.

Keep your expectations high and your excuses low. Mathematics is one of the gateways to opportunities in life. Our children of poverty and color need more, not fewer, opportunities for their future. We need to provide them more math instruction, on par to the time we spend on literacy. New national standards in mathematics are more rigorous than ever. For young learners, we need to teach math every day, and expect them to achieve at a high level. Yet, we know some students struggle. In order to reach all students, I use several key strategies.

Put students "in the picture" of math. Many students from poverty have not seen mathematics in life. They do not play math games at home, use dice or cards, count everyday objects, help shop or cook. My job is to let them see themselves as mathematicians every day. If you cannot see yourself doing something, you will never achieve it! Much of my work in the classroom has been based around Viconic Language Strategies.™ From the first day of school, I draw pictures of the students in the classroom space doing what is expected of them. I draw them "thinking" about math, talking about math, using math tools. When I draw these stick cartoons, in real time,

I see my students' bodies becoming still, mouths closing, hands not touching. Once students understand how to look like a mathematician, then they can begin to *be* a mathematician.

Keep math relevant and in context. We all learn best when we can relate to what we are learning on a personal level. All learning begins with the preoperational: How do I relate to this? When people put themselves in the math picture, it becomes more relevant to them. Once we have put ourselves in the picture, we can see others in the picture and then can move to concrete representations.

We often skip the preoperational in math and move straight to the concrete. In the classroom, I often begin math with a story. For example, "Mathematicians, yesterday I went to the store to buy some bananas for my banana bread recipe. Have any of you gone to the store before? You have? Take your piece of paper and quickly draw a picture of a time you went to the store and what you needed to buy at the store. When you finish, find a partner and tell them about your picture. I am going to finish my story now. I knew I needed seven bananas for my recipe. When I saw bunches of bananas, I found one with five bananas. Mathematicians, I wonder, did I need more bananas, or less in order to have my seven bananas." This may seem lengthy, but it is so much more meaningful than a page of equations. Find a way to put a person into the math, and your students are much more likely to remember the math.

All students can achieve in math. When I was in college, there was no Internet and the best way to contact someone quickly was with a pager. When my parents were in college, they wrote papers on typewriters and used a nickel in a payphone. The world is changing so fast; by helping your students achieve in mathematics, you prepare them for the possibilities of a future we cannot begin to imagine. They deserve nothing less.

2008 Milken National Educator Award, Oregon
2011 Kappa Delta Pi Teacher of Honor K–5
Math Achievement Coordinator, Portland Public Schools
Portland, Oregon

Religion

Just as there are differences in ethnicity and native language, there are differences in religious beliefs among the students in our schools. Can you think of instances in which religion has affected education? Some examples include the legal issue barring prayer from schools and the controversy over studying the theories of evolution and creationism in science classes. But how would a student's individual religious beliefs affect his or her learning or perspective on an ordinary educational task? Why is it important to be aware of your students' religious beliefs?

There are some 10,000 distinct religions in the world, of which approximately 150 have a million or more followers. Within Christianity, there are more than 33,000 different denominations (Barrett et al., 2001). Major religions by percentage of members in the United States and in the world are shown graphically in Figure 4.4.

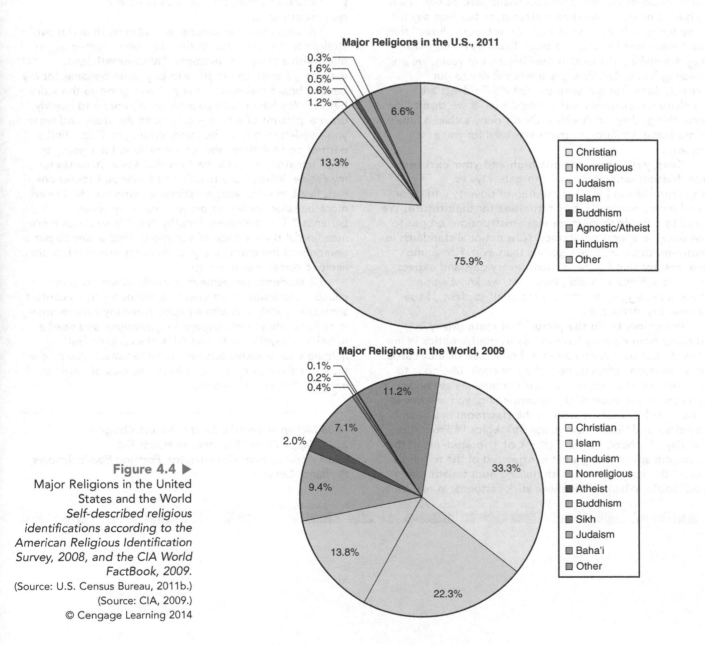

Major Religions in the U.S., 2011

0.3%
1.6%
0.5%
0.6%
1.2%
6.6%
13.3%
75.9%

- ☐ Christian
- ☐ Nonreligious
- ☐ Judaism
- ☐ Islam
- ☐ Buddhism
- ☐ Agnostic/Atheist
- ☐ Hinduism
- ☐ Other

Major Religions in the World, 2009

0.1%
0.2%
0.4%
11.2%
7.1%
2.0%
33.3%
9.4%
13.8%
22.3%

- ☐ Christian
- ☐ Islam
- ☐ Hinduism
- ☐ Nonreligious
- ☐ Atheist
- ☐ Buddhism
- ☐ Sikh
- ☐ Judaism
- ☐ Baha'i
- ☐ Other

Figure 4.4 ▶
Major Religions in the United States and the World
Self-described religious identifications according to the American Religious Identification Survey, 2008, and the CIA World FactBook, 2009.
(Source: U.S. Census Bureau, 2011b.)
(Source: CIA, 2009.)
© Cengage Learning 2014

© Michael Newman/PhotoEdit Inc.

Along with the diversity in your classroom comes a diversity of holidays your students do and don't celebrate.

With this great diversity of religions, coupled with students' great diversity of national origins and ethnic backgrounds, it should come as no surprise that many different religions are represented in our schools. How do religious beliefs influence students' attitudes and expectations?

Religions

BUILDING BLOCK
4.5

Talk to a person whose religion is different from the religion you know best to learn about their basic beliefs, rituals, and observations. Focus on the following questions:

- What are the religion's primary beliefs?
- Where and when does worship take place?
- What are the required rituals? What do they represent?
- What are the major feasts or celebrations? When do these occur? How do adherents observe them? What do they represent?
- What are the major fast days or periods? When do these occur? How do adherents observe them? What do they represent?

Now ask yourself these questions:

- What are your own beliefs? How do they compare with the beliefs of this person?
- Can you assume a position of neutrality with respect to religious beliefs?

Teaching That Acknowledges Religions

As you might imagine, religious convictions and observations strongly influence students' expectations and performance at school. During the course of a school year, events occur and topics are studied that may be inconsistent with the values of certain religions. The study of evolutionary theory is a major example. Some religious groups object strongly to this theory, saying that it directly contradicts the Bible's account of the creation of Earth and humanity. What does this mean to the science teacher planning a unit of study on evolution, as may be required in the state curriculum? What if your own religious beliefs put you at odds with teaching evolutionary theory? (You will investigate the controversy surrounding the teaching of evolution versus creationism in Chapter 11.) As another example, in the United States, it is common to celebrate holidays such as Valentine's Day, Halloween, Thanksgiving, and Christmas. However, not all students celebrate the same holidays, nor do they celebrate religious holidays at the same time. In fact, some students do not celebrate any holidays at all—not even birthdays. Individual schools and school districts establish policies concerning observance of religious holidays in school, and teachers are expected to adhere to these policies.

You must become sensitive to the fact that there will be several different religions represented in your classroom, and you must recognize and honor them all. Referring to the basic needs that Maslow outlined (see Chapter 3), you can see that doing so helps foster the positive feelings of safety and security, belongingness, and self-esteem that must be satisfied before students can focus on learning. Once again, go back and review the qualities and characteristics of effective teachers that help them create an environment of acceptance in their classrooms and design instruction that acknowledges unique perspectives. Those characteristics also apply (and are required) as you consider the values and experiences of students who are influenced by their religious beliefs.

It is neither desirable nor possible to advance the beliefs of the religions you will encounter in your classroom. Unless you will be teaching in a religious school, the most appropriate attitude to adopt concerning religion is one of neutrality.

Socioeconomic Status

We often consider that people who are financially very well off or who are financially struggling belong to their own cultures. As a society, we even use terms such as *upper class, middle class,* and *lower class* to denote financial categories of individuals and families. Break the word *socioeconomic* into its parts. What do you think the word means? What do you think the term *socioeconomic status* (SES) means? What characteristics or qualities make up a person's socioeconomic status?

The following demographic characteristics can be used as descriptors of socioeconomic status in the United States (Woolfolk, 2010):

- Household income
- Parents' occupation
- Parents' education
- Parents' attitude toward education
- Parents' aspirations for their children
- Intellectual activities of the family (including trips to educationally stimulating locations such as museums, zoos, historical sites, and so on)

It should be noted that financial status is only one of the determinants of socioeconomic status. Recall that you learned earlier that SES is an expression of perceived power. How do the demographic characteristics listed above contribute to the power of an individual, family, or group in society?

Socioeconomic Status and School

Suppose you were asked to describe the socioeconomic status of a family and its environment. Using the characteristics listed previously describe a high-SES family and a low-SES family. How would the environments you described for high- and low-SES families affect a child's educational "readiness" to enter school with a set of experiences that would form a foundation upon which to build? How would the environments you described affect a student's attitude toward learning and education?

Money is the characteristic most often used to describe socioeconomic status. Among the descriptors used is poverty level. Poverty level is defined in terms of annual income and ranged in 2011 from $10,890 for a single person living alone to $37,630 for a family of eight; these levels are slightly higher for the states of Alaska and Hawaii (Federal Register, 2011). In 2010, 15.1 percent of the U.S. population was living below the poverty level (U.S. Census Bureau, 2011c). This number is up from 12.5 percent in 2007, and from 11.3 percent in 2000. Whites made up 13.0 percent of those identified, 27.4 percent were black, 12.1 percent were Asian and Pacific Islander, and 26.6 percent were Hispanic. Twenty-two percent of children in the United States were living below the poverty level in 2010, up from 20.7 percent in 2009 (Walt, Proctor, and Smith, 2011). (See Figure 4.5.)

poverty level The minimum amount of income that is determined to be adequate.

As you saw in Chapter 3, all students have common human needs, and the most basic of these needs are the survival and safety needs represented in the foundational levels of Maslow's hierarchy. You also saw that these common needs must be met before students can turn their attention to learning and pursue self-actualization. For families identified as having a low socioeconomic status, priority often must go to fulfilling the deficiency needs of survival and safety.

Studies have indicated that there is a correlation between low socioeconomic status and low achievement. As with some of the populations with unique perspectives we have already examined in this chapter, a lack in language skills as compared to the mainstream population may play a part in low-SES students' struggles to succeed (Aikens and Barbarin, 2008). You don't have to be a person for whom English is a "foreign" language; many Americans have difficulty with English (as evidenced by the number of Americans who cannot read). Research has shown that

Active, stimulating learning experiences in preschool can promote future academic achievement for students.

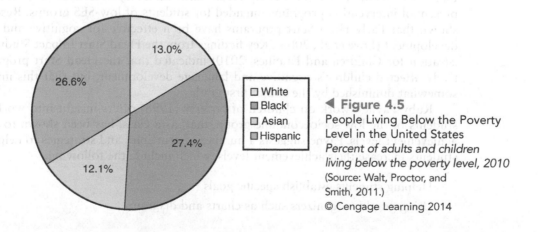

◀ **Figure 4.5**
People Living Below the Poverty Level in the United States
Percent of adults and children living below the poverty level, 2010
(Source: Walt, Proctor, and Smith, 2011.)
© Cengage Learning 2014

Legend: White, Black, Asian, Hispanic

Values shown: 13.0%, 26.6%, 27.4%, 12.1%

students who live in low-SES homes are slower to develop basic skills needed for academic success than those from higher-SES families (Morgan, Faras, Hillemeier, and Maczuga, 2009). The environment of a low-SES household is associated with low literacy levels and high stress levels, which can affect the development of academic skills before preschool (American Psychological Association, 2011). Children who come from lower-SES families have been found to have learning disabilities about twice as often as students from higher-SES households (Morgan et al., 2009). Although we have acknowledged that socioeconomic status is more complex than merely considering household income, financial concerns may contribute greatly to stress levels in a low-SES household. Finances may prohibit low-SES families from affording some of the resources such as computers, books, and the opportunity to participate in educational activities that contribute to the development of academic skills (Orr, 2003; Aikens and Barbarin, 2008). Whereas children from middle- and high-SES families might have education-related trips to places like museums and educational toys available to them, the parents of lower-SES families are forced to place precedence on housing, food, and other necessities. The result is that children from lower-SES households have less exposure to experiences that prepare them for the educational environment. Being "ready" for school contributes greatly to initial success. And, as you have observed, success is vital for motivating students to achieve. The high school dropout rate was 16.7 percent among low-SES students compared to 3.2 percent for high-income households in 2007 (National Center for Education Statistics, 2008a).

Teaching That Acknowledges Socioeconomic Status

Students of different economic and social backgrounds have different expectations and career goals, which are influenced by their parents and communities. You, the teacher, also may have different expectations of students, depending on your beliefs about the SES group they come from. Recall Building Block 4.3, where you thought about neighborhoods in which you dream of living and neighborhoods in which you cannot imagine living. Was there a difference in your expectations when you were thinking about the students who live in these neighborhoods?

Would you agree that there is a culture associated with socioeconomic status? If that is so, then you must realize that all of the information you have considered so far in this chapter with regard to culture—the multicultural paradigms (cultural deficit model, cultural mismatch model, and so on), the recommendations for acknowledging the unique perspectives of your students, and the importance of involving the community in education and yourself in the school's community—are applicable here as well.

You have seen that students' motivations often vary according to social classes, which affect achievement. You also have seen that the extent to which young children are prepared to enter school correlates with their achievement in school. Because of this, federal and state programs have been initiated to help prepare young children to enter school. Examples include Head Start, Early Head Start, the Perry Preschool project, and other preschool intervention programs intended for students of low-SES groups. Research has shown that Early Head Start programs have been effective for cognitive and language development (Love et al., 2005). Key findings from the Head Start Impact Study (Administration for Children and Families, 2010) indicated that the Head Start program positively affected children's cognitive and language development, but that this impact was somewhat diminished by the end of first grade.

Ruby Payne's work on children of poverty (1998) offers insight into working with students of the low socioeconomic group, that, as a class, has been shown to have low achievement levels. Payne suggests a number of principles and strategies to help low-SES students increase their achievement levels, which include the following:

- Helping students establish specific goals
- Using graphic organizers such as charts and diagrams

- Helping students associate content with their personal experiences
- Helping students utilize what they already know in the learning process
- Using "hands-on" approaches
- Helping students evaluate their own performance
- Teaching students how to ask questions dealing with the content
- Helping students sort relevant information from irrelevant information

How do these strategies help students fulfill their common and academic needs? Remember, students of poverty are likely to need reinforcement in the most basic needs such as physiological needs, safety, security, love, and belonging.

Payne's work has made major contributions to the understanding of economic classes and students from poverty. Swan (2004) found that the use of Payne's instructional framework in a widely diverse school district was associated with an increase in student achievement. However, many in the field of multicultural education believe her work actually contributes to classism in schools instead of promoting class equity because of her emphasis on the difference between the lower and upper classes (Gorski, 2005). Kunjufu (2006), an African American educator, has written an entire book disputing many of Payne's hypotheses when it comes to African American children. And Bomer, Dworin, May, and Semingson et al. (2008) write that Payne's work may be contributing to lower expectations of poor students, resulting in poor students being more likely to be placed in lower ability groups where their education is likely to be dominated by memorization exercises.

Additional studies have found that traditional, teacher-centered approaches seem to be less effective with students from lower incomes. Approaches that work include making the students responsible for their learning, setting clear and reasonable goals, using student-centered strategies such as cooperative learning and hands-on activities, giving students autonomy, and assessing learning regularly (Patrnogich-Arieli, 2009).

Teaching Students of Poverty

BUILDING BLOCK 4.7

Review the strategies Payne suggested for teaching students of poverty. Go back and review ideas you had and information you considered for effective teaching in previous sections of this chapter and in Chapter 3. How are these strategies consistent among all populations of students? How do these strategies foster heightened relationships between students and teachers? How do they help students meet their common and academic needs?

Gender

It has been said that males and females speak different languages. Maybe you have felt this way when trying to communicate with someone of the opposite sex. Because the behavioral differences between genders seem so pronounced, you might even consider them to be separate cultures. Of course, genders are not separate cultures, but there certainly are generalizations associated with being male or female. What are some of these generalizations? To what extent do you fit them? Are there any general impressions about your gender that do not apply to you? What impact, if any, do you think gender has on learning? Do you think boys are better than girls at some subjects? Do you think girls are better than boys at some subjects?

BUILDING BLOCK 4.8 — Activities for Boys and Girls

The following activities are listed on various websites constructed by troops of the Girl Scouts of America and the Boy Scouts of America. Can you guess which activities came from which sites? Mark the activities you think came from the Girl Scout sites with a *G* and those that you think came from the Boy Scout sites with a *B*. Be sure to record your immediate, initial response. (This activity can also be found on the CourseMate website so you can print it out or record your responses electronically.)

_____ Archery
_____ Axe throwing
_____ Tie-dying
_____ New ways to wear a bandana
_____ Woodcraft
_____ Bedding materials
_____ Bicycle maintenance
_____ Birdhouses
_____ Oil changing
_____ Homemade compasses
_____ Cooking contests
_____ Deduction in tracking
_____ Fire building
_____ Hiking
_____ Insect collecting

_____ Knot tying
_____ Loom and grass mats
_____ Acting
_____ Surfing
_____ Sailing
_____ Rock climbing
_____ Photography
_____ Map and compasses
_____ Measurement and estimation
_____ Night tracking
_____ Rope making
_____ Sign language
_____ Animals
_____ Creative composing
_____ Food fun

_____ Safety
_____ Sounds of music
_____ Space exploration
_____ Sports and games
_____ Science wonders
_____ Snakes
_____ Stalking and observation
_____ Storytelling
_____ Teepee building
_____ Tomahawk throwing
_____ Weather wisdom
_____ Art to wear
_____ Math fun
_____ Puppets, dolls, and plays

G: Tie-dying, New ways to wear a bandana, Oil changing, Acting, Surfing, Sailing, Rock climbing, Photography, Animals, Creative composing, Food fun, Safety, Sounds of music, Space exploration, Sports and games, Science wonders, Art to wear, Math fun, Puppets, dolls, and plays

B: Archery, Axe throwing, Woodcraft, Bedding materials, Bicycle maintenance, Birdhouses, Homemade compasses, Cooking contests, Deduction in tracking, Fire building, Hiking, Insect collecting, Knot tying, Loom and grass mats, Map and compasses, Measurement and estimation, Night tracking, Rope making, Sign language, Snakes, Stalking and observation, Storytelling, Teepee building, Tomahawk throwing, Weather wisdom

Look again at the activities. Which did you associate with girls? Which did you associate with boys? Based on these associations, which gender do you suppose would be better at math? At language? Science? Social sciences?

Many of the activities in Building Block 4.8 can be easily assigned to one gender or the other based on our stereotypical notions of traditional gender roles. However, it might surprise you to learn that some of the activities we traditionally associate with boys, such as computers, tying knots, and archery, can be found on Girl Scout websites. Making an upside-down cake in a can and participating in a songfest were activities suggested on Boy Scout websites.

Why is it that we so readily associate certain activities and subjects with gender? Are there really gender-specific differences in academic aptitudes? Are girls really better readers and writers? Are boys really better at math?

Research shows that girls tend to be better in language skills—spelling, verbal skills, reading, and writing, although these differences decrease as students progress in school. Boys tend to be better in math and spatial skills such as mental rotation (being able to think of how an object would look from different angles), although girls tend to narrow the math gap in middle school (Robinson and Lubienski, 2010).

It is interesting to note that the differences between genders in cognitive and social skills have actually decreased in the past couple of decades. This seems to indicate that socialization and experiences affect gender development (Cook and Cook, 2009).

The gender roles of boys and girls begin to be differentiated very early in life. Boys and girls learn at an early age what their gender roles are, and they learn that the genders are treated differently. Teacher and parent behaviors may influence performance by boys and girls on various tasks (Bohlin, Durwin, and Reese-Weber, 2009). For example, gender stereotyping by parents and teachers may discourage girls from pursuing activities, areas of study, or even careers that are generally thought of as masculine, such as participating in certain sports, studying the pure sciences or mathematics, or pursuing a career as an engineer or astrophysicist.

Children often exhibit stereotypical, gender-specific roles very early in their development.

Within their families, boys and girls receive different treatment, and their parents communicate different expectations for them, both verbally and nonverbally. Male children are handled and played with more roughly than girls, even as infants, and this differential treatment continues as children get older. Boys are given different toys to play with than girls are and they are dressed differently to play with these toys (Parke and Gauvain, 2008). Think about the toy section of a familiar department store. Can you see that there is an aisle for boys' toys and an aisle for girls' toys? Perhaps you can make this distinction based on such subtleties as the predominant color of the toys displayed in the aisle. Chances are you can apply this same method for identifying the section for boys' clothes and girls' clothes in the same store. And which clothing would you say encourages children to go outside and get dirty versus stay inside and keep clean (Huffman, 2011)? This differential treatment may help to foster some personality traits that are stereotypical in boys and girls. Traits that are thought of as masculine include being active, competitive, dominant, independent, and aggressive. Feminine stereotypical traits include being considerate, selfless, emotional, passive, and nurturing (Berk, 2000).

However, research suggests that genetic factors may predispose males to act in masculine ways and females to act in feminine ways (Blum, 1999; Kreeger, 2002). It appears masculine and feminine behaviors result from a combination of genetic inheritance and socialization.

So, strong social influences may contribute to gender bias in the classroom. These influences seem to encourage girls toward "softer" subjects, such as reading and social studies, and boys toward mathematics and science. In classrooms and in society, girls are discouraged in both subtle and overt ways from participating in activities and studies traditionally associated with being male, and boys are discouraged from activities traditionally associated with being female.

Let us look at some representative data. The Program for International Student Assessment (PISA) is a system of international assessments that measures capabilities of 15-year-olds from 65 countries in reading, science, and mathematics every three years. The result of the 2009 mathematics test showed that U.S. boys scored slightly higher than U.S. girls in mathematics literacy. In reading literacy, U.S. girls scored slightly higher than U.S. boys. And in science, U.S. boys outscored U.S. girls by only a slight margin (Fleischman, Hopstock, Pelczar, and Shelley, 2010). The National Assessment of Education Progress (NAEP), also known as *The Nation's Report Card,* administers subject-matter assessments annually to randomly selected schools in the United States. The most recent results available show that boys outscored girls in mathematics in both fourth grade and eighth grade (National Center for Education Statistics, 2009a), and that girls outscored boys in reading in both fourth grade and eighth grade (National Center for Education Statistics, 2009b). In science, boys outperformed girls overall in fourth grade and in eighth grade (National Center for Education Statistics, 2009b).

Teaching That Acknowledges Gender

Now that you have seen that gender influences the way students learn, it is clear that teaching strategies must acknowledge gender differences. Boys' early orientation toward exploration gives them experience interacting with concepts associated with science and mathematics. In science and mathematics classes, therefore, many boys approach the content with more experience and confidence than some girls. Similarly, girls' early orientation toward caring and kindliness gives them experience and confidence in the "softer" behaviors many girls bring into their school years.

One of the challenges teachers face is to foster the achievement of both boys and girls in *all* areas. In the classroom, research shows that boys receive more active instruction than girls, and that names, experiences, and examples using males outnumber those using females in curricular materials in all subject areas (Zittleman and Sadker, 2009). Teachers call on girls less, and when they do, the questions girls are asked tend to require a lower level of knowledge to answer. When girls do answer, the feedback they receive from the teacher is less constructive than feedback given to boys (Sadker, 2002).

Research has shown that when preschool teachers used gendered language in the classroom, the children tended to express gender stereotypes and to choose children of their own gender to play with. In other words, if the teacher made statements such as, "Girls play with dolls and boys play with trucks," the children tended to express the same stereotypical beliefs and behaviors (Moskowitz, 2010). And, in elementary school, if a female teacher is anxious about math, it is thought that she can actually transfer this anxiety to her female students who then don't perform as well (Beilock, Gunderson, Ramirez, and Levine, 2010), although these findings have been disputed (Plante, Protzko, and Aronson, 2010).

Teachers can use a number of strategies to ensure that both boys and girls have the same opportunity to learn, whether the material is traditionally more associated with girls (such as the language arts) or boys (such as science and mathematics). Teaching for gender equity is not about making either sex superior to the other; it is about removing gender restrictions from both boys and girls so that *both* genders can move forward (Zittleman and Sadker, 2009; King, Gurian, and Stevens, 2010). Following are some of these strategies:

- Involve girls and boys equally as classroom assistants and helpers.
- Recognize the academic achievements of girls and boys equally.
- Recognize the extracurricular achievements of girls and boys equally.
- Talk equally about prominent women and men.
- Call on girls and boys with equal frequency.
- Include both girls and boys in cooperative learning groups.

► II TeachSource Video

View the TeachSource Video Case, "Gender Equity in the Classroom: Girls and Science." In this video segment, you'll see how Robert Cho, a middle school teacher, promotes science learning for all his students: boys and girls. Rob describes how he keeps the girls in his classroom interested in science. He also reflects on the importance of a role model or mentor. After watching this video, answer the following questions:

1. How effective were Mr. Cho's strategies?

2. How could you model the intent of Mr. Cho's methods in your content area?

Gender Equity: Single-Sex Classrooms and Schools

One approach to offering both boys and girls equal opportunity to succeed in schools may be to separate them by sex. For example, girls and boys would take math in separate classrooms and with separate teachers in an effort to reduce some of the social pressures that both sexes might feel with regard to expectations based on gender. Same-sex schools—mostly private schools—have been around for years. But in public schools, girls are separated from boys primarily for physical education and health/sex education classes. Using federal Title IX funds made available in 2006, many schools have implemented the use of single-sex instruction to take advantage of the opportunities these funds may offer. Among these opportunities are:

- Using teaching strategies that have been shown to be particularly effective for either males or females and using resources with gender-specific examples.

- Eliminating distractions like flirting and gender-based competition that may be present in co-ed classrooms.

- Removing the fear of being ridiculed by the opposite sex for comments or incorrect answers so that learners can concentrate on performance rather than what others' think.

- Creating a classroom environment in which males and females concentrate on learning rather than on how they look or performing to get the attention of others.

- Having a safe atmosphere for boys to tackle new problems so that they don't have to worry about looking like failures or appearing too feminine in front of girls.

- Giving girls the chance to explore interests in "traditionally male" subjects such as math, science, and technology. (Gurian, Stevens, and Daniels, 2009)

Offering single-sex science and math courses may serve girls, especially, in encouraging not only their participation in studying the discipline, but also in pursuing careers in science, math, technology, and engineering. Many schools have taken advantage of federal funding, and for the 2010–2011 school year, at least 506 public schools had single-sex courses (National Association for Single Sex Public Education, 2011).

You can access the website of the National Association for Single Sex Public Education through the direct link on the Education CourseMate website. There you will be able to access the research, nature of single-sex schools, and many other facets of single-sex education programs.

WHAT DO YOU THINK?

1. *Would you like to learn in a single-sex classroom or school? (Perhaps you have had this experience.) Why?*
2. *Would you like to teach in a single-sex classroom or school? Why?*
3. *What advantages would there be for you as a teacher? For the students in your class? What challenges would there be?*

Understanding the nature and development of gender-based stereotypical roles and the value placed by students and adults on these roles is a good first step toward reducing gender-based expectations in school.

Before you start drawing conclusions about methods that make content accessible to both genders, it might be useful to explore your own assumptions and expectations regarding gender.

Your Gender Biases

BUILDING BLOCK

4.9

Take the test for gender bias at the Implicit Association Test on the Internet. Use the direct link to this battery of tests on this textbook's Education CourseMate website. Select the Gender-Science IAT.

Reflect on your results. What do the results tell you about stereotypical gender biases you may have?

From Building Block 4.9, can you tell what you *really* believe about gender roles? Do you really believe that males make better scientists than females? Do you really believe that females make better writers? What would *you* do to ensure that gender inequalities do not exist in your classroom?

Sexual Orientation

As you survey your classroom, many of the student perspectives and characteristics we have discussed so far may be apparent, but you may not be able to discern a student's sexual orientation. Indeed, some students go to great lengths to hide this attribute. Nonetheless, a student's sexual orientation can have a profound impact on his or her motivation to participate in your classroom.

There are several sexual orientations, including heterosexual, homosexual (gay and lesbian), bisexual (sexual orientation toward both sexes), and transgender (having the characteristics of the opposite sex), and questioning (for those not ready to identify a sexual orientation). Although most people are heterosexual, many, including students in our schools, identify with alternative orientations. Of these, homosexuality predominates. Homosexual people have been called the "invisible minority." Not only is their orientation not readily discernible, but they are also unlikely to disclose it, largely out of fear of others' reactions.

Recall the basic needs of all students: love, security, belonging, and self-esteem. What unique issues do gay students bring to getting these needs met by teachers and other students?

Some individuals are less accepting of the homosexual orientation than others, so students with nontraditional sexual orientations may have good reason to keep their orientation secret. The 2009 National School Climate Survey (Kosciw, Greytak, Diaz, and Bartkiewicz, 2010) reports the following about lesbian, gay, bisexual, transgendered, and questioning (LGBTQ) students:

LGBTQ Lesbian, gay, bisexual, transgendered, and questioning.

- Almost nine out of ten LGBTQ students were harassed at school because of their sexual orientation. Eighty-five percent reported this as verbal harassment and 40 percent as physical harassment. Almost 64 percent of LGBTQ students were verbally harassed and 27 percent were physically harassed because of their gender expression.

- Nearly 20 percent of LGBTQ students reported being physically assaulted because of their sexual orientation and 12.5 percent because of their gender expression.

- Seventy-two percent of LGBTQ students frequently hear derogatory comments toward homosexuality in the halls and classrooms.

- Sixty-one percent reported feeling unsafe due to their sexuality, and 40 percent felt unsafe due to their gender expression.

- One out of three LGBTQ students skipped a class at least one time, and 30 percent skipped school during the month preceding the survey out of fear. (For comparison, a national sample of high school students showed that 8 percent skipped a class and 6.7 percent skipped a day of school.)

- Grade point averages of students who were harassed due to sexual orientation were almost a half grade lower than those who reported they weren't harassed as frequently.

These statistics describe a situation in schools that is unacceptable. No student should feel unsafe in school. Some students have gone to extreme measures to escape the harassment they have experienced due to their real or perceived sexual orientation. In 2009, two 11-year-old boys hanged themselves within two weeks of each other—one in Georgia and one in Massachusetts—as a result of experiencing gay bullying (Simon, 2009 and GLSEN, 2009). There were five teen suicides across the country in a period of three weeks in 2010, as a result of pressures related to their real or perceived sexual orientation (Hubbard, 2010). In fact, suicide among sexual minority youth is a major social issue (Robinson and Espelage, 2011). What you must realize, as a future teacher, is exactly what we have been saying throughout this entire chapter: You have an obligation to *all* students to do what you can in your classroom to help them feel loved, accepted, and respected so that they can move on to the business of learning.

Direct links to the Parents, Families, and Friends of Lesbians and Gays (PFLAG) association website and the Gay, Lesbian, and Straight Education Network (GLSEN) are available on the Education CourseMate website.

Teaching That Acknowledges Sexual Orientation

As with religion, people's beliefs about sexual orientation are strongly influenced by the environment in which they were raised. As with gender, society has exerted strong influence on perceptions of alternative sexual orientations. And, as with culture, language, religion, SES, and other individual differences, teachers have an obligation to students with different sexual orientations to demonstrate positive regard in meeting their needs as students and as human beings. Robinson and Espelage (2011) report that LGBTQ students who experienced teasing, but who perceive school as being a positive force in their lives, had lower depression, suicide, and alcohol and drug use rates than those who are bullied and perceived their school climate to be negative. The teacher can make a difference. Shah (2012a) reports that fewer than half of the 1,100 elementary teachers surveyed said they would feel comfortable responding to their students' questions about sexual orientation. Recall the characteristics of effective teachers you identified in Chapter 1. Chances are that you agreed with the researchers and others that tolerance for *all* people is a desirable characteristic—one that is normally found in effective teachers. Does your tolerance extend to people with alternative sexual orientations? The way you teach people with alternative sexual orientations should not differ from the way you teach the other students in your class. Review the strategies you have identified that contribute to the creation of an effective learning environment for *all* students. How do these strategies serve to meet the needs of LGBTQ students or those students who are questioning their sexuality? Of course, there is no specific list of strategies to teach gay students. The strategies you have already identified help meet the needs of each and every student in your classroom.

And, above all, you should *not* participate in intimidating or harassing students, however subtly, whose alternative sexual orientation you know.

Your Sexual Orientation Biases

BUILDING BLOCK 4.10

Take the Sexuality Implicit Association Test (IAT) available on the Internet. The Sexuality IAT assesses for sexual orientation bias. Access the test through the direct link available on the Education CourseMate website for this textbook.

Reflect on what your results tell you. What do you think contributed to the beliefs you hold that contributed to your score? If you have discovered that you hold certain biases toward people with alternative lifestyles, what can you do to neutralize those biases and be an effective teacher?

Putting It All Together

You have examined many aspects of diversity, including culture, language, religion, socioeconomic status, gender, and sexual orientation. You have investigated each of these issues and you have attempted to identify your own personal beliefs, predispositions, biases, and prejudices. You must realize as well that some students will bring

I n this chapter, you have found that, although students have common needs, each student brings a different perspective to the classroom. It might seem daunting to acknowledge all the different perspectives in any one classroom, but technology can assist teachers in meeting this challenge effectively.

Using instructional technology can help teachers understand and acknowledge different cultures, religions, and languages. Teachers can use the Internet to research the cultures and religions represented in their classrooms to gain a better understanding of students' perspectives. Imagine the validation a student might feel knowing that the teacher cared enough to learn about his or her culture or religion! When a teacher does this, what common needs is the teacher helping to meet? Which of Brooks's questions does the teacher's action help to answer (Chapter 3)? Keep in mind that other students could also access the same information to learn more about their classmates and themselves. Take the time to educate yourself about other unique perspectives you have learned about in this chapter, taking advantage of the Internet's vast resources.

Technology affords teachers many resources to help teach English language learners (ELLs). We all know that a picture is worth a thousand words. Technology provides teachers with access to countless images, diagrams, and videos that can be projected or printed when giving instructions or illustrating an idea. And what you cannot find,

you can draw. Don't worry if you are not an artist. Software is available to help you draw anything from a straight line to a complex diagram.

Software for language learning is also available. ELL students can use such packages to help them learn English, and English-speaking students can use them to learn other languages. Online language courses exist, some of which are free. Translation software and websites let teachers translate work they produce for students, as well as letters to and from parents. Again, some online translation sites are free; others charge a fee. What kind of online language courses or translations sites can you find?

Content-area software frequently offers different language options. DVDs and CD-ROMs, for example, may have Spanish language tracks. Many websites are also available in two or more languages. If English-speaking students find content-area websites in a language other than English, an ELL student who speaks that language can translate the site and share it with other students, thereby learning and practicing both language and technology skills.

Teachers can use technology as a valuable tool to acknowledge the unique perspectives students bring to the classroom. Tools and software are available to aid in communication, understanding, and learning.

new perspectives to your classroom that we haven't addressed in this chapter. As a teacher in today's pluralistic society, it is essential that you maintain a diverse perspective in your classroom. This may mean thinking differently about what is acceptable and what is not acceptable on the part of students and teacher alike and what cultural and diversity characteristics are promoted in the classroom.

As a teacher, you have a responsibility to be sure you are *not* contributing to racism, classism, sexism, homophobia, and other elements of diversity that may create a hierarchy and define a norm. Rather, you must see that all your interactions with students foster personal and educational equity.

**BUILDING BLOCK
4.11**

Metaphors Revisited

Refer to the metaphor you selected to describe yourself as a teacher in Chapter 2. In light of the investigations you have made in this chapter, ask yourself this question: "Does my metaphor imply unconditional equity?"

■ SUMMARY

In this chapter, you investigated several differences that affect the ways students learn and, ultimately, their achievement:

- *Diversity* includes numerous ways in which people are different from one another. Some of these ways are visible and immediately recognizable. Others are less visible but just as important.

- The student population of schools in the United States is becoming increasingly diversified relative to both race and ethnicity. This diversity requires teachers to be sensitive to culture-based differences in approaches to learning.

- Multicultural paradigms are models that explain cultural diversity. The cultural deprivation paradigm says that nonmainstream students fail to achieve academically because they have been deprived of knowledge and experiences they need to succeed. The cultural deficit model proposes that nonmainstream students are actually at a deficit due to their cultural identification. Other paradigms include the cultural difference and cultural mismatch models, which hold that nonmainstream students struggle because the culture of the classroom is different or is a mismatch from the minority culture of the learner.

- The primary difficulty of English language learners is their lack of fluency with the English language; however, teachers can assist ELL students with a few appropriate instructional adjustments.

- Many religious beliefs are represented in our schools, and teachers must recognize this fact and assume an attitude of neutrality when it comes to religion.

- Students' socioeconomic backgrounds have a tremendous influence on the students' preparedness for school, their attitudes toward school, and their achievement; and different socioeconomic backgrounds present unique instructional challenges.

- Gender roles tend to be perceived stereotypically in schools; skillful teachers teach for gender equity.

- Teachers must show tolerance and respect for students who identify with alternative sexual orientations.

- Biases and prejudices often exist toward people with perspectives perceived as "different." Teachers must identify their own viewpoints and work toward acceptance of *all* students, regardless of their unique characteristics and perspectives, to provide a safe, respectful, and equitable classroom environment that allows students to focus on learning.

- The learning strategies identified are useful in meeting the needs of *all* students, not only the needs of single groups.

It is not necessary to provide separate lists of specific ways of teaching to acknowledge the unique learning needs presented by each different perspective or characteristic. Although certain strategies can be identified for managing certain perspectives, all students have similar needs. Teachers must show students that the material being taught connects to their individual lives. This connection arises largely from the teaching and learning relationships developed in the classroom.

Many factors bear on students' ability to learn, and the factors discussed in this chapter represent selected examples. By now you can see that no two people are the same and no two people learn in precisely the same way. You will continue this exploration into the next chapter, where you will consider cognitive differences.

Key Terms and Concepts

1.5 Generation
  Students, 105
Bilingual education, 107
Culture, 97
Cultural deficit model, 102
Cultural deprivation
  model, 102
Cultural difference
  model, 103
Cultural mismatch
  model, 103

Culturally relevant
  pedagogy, 104
Diversity, 94
English as a foreign language
  (EFL), 105
English as a second language
  (ESL), 105
English language learner
  (ELL), 104
Ethnicity, 97

LGBTQ (lesbian, gay,
  bisexual, transgender, and
  questioning), 120
Limited English proficiency
  (LEP), 105
Poverty level, 113
Race, 97
Socioeconomic status
  (SES), 102
Stereotype, 97
White privilege, 102

Construct and Apply

1. List five factors you consider to be "identifiers" about yourself. These can be physical characteristics, information about your history or background, or a role you occupy as a citizen or family member. Which factors indicate a difference between you and most other people?

2. Why do you suppose traditionally minority populations cite their minority characteristic as defining?

3. For each unique student characteristic and perspective you investigated in this chapter, describe how these students can be expected to provide for their basic need of love and belonging and how you would expect them to motivate *themselves* to learn. Are your expectations reasonable for the age you wish to teach?

4. What are your thoughts regarding the cultural paradigms presented in this chapter? How do you feel about the presence of white privilege?

5. Make a list of teaching strategies effective for teaching *everyone* in all groups discussed in this chapter.

Deconstructing the Standards

1. Recall the InTASC Standards associated with the objectives for this chapter:

   InTASC Standard #1: Learner Development reads, "The teacher understands how learners grow and develop, recognizing that patterns of learning and development vary individually within and across the cognitive, linguistic, social, emotional, and physical areas, and designs and implements developmentally appropriate and challenging learning experiences."

   InTASC Standard #2: Learner Differences reads, "The teacher works with others to create environments that support individual and collaborative learning, and that encourage positive social interaction, active engagement in learning, and self-motivation."

   a. Which part(s) of these standards does this chapter address?

   b. How will the concepts in this chapter help you apply these standards as a teacher?

2. Use your favorite search engine to find your state's standards for certification. When you find it, bookmark the site. You will refer to it often as you progress through this course.

   a. How are your conclusions about students' unique perspectives represented in the state standards?

   b. How do the InTASC Standards compare to your state's certification standards regarding students' unique perspectives?

   c. Do you believe the degree of representation concerning students' unique perspectives is adequate in your state certification standards? Why or why not?

Your Portfolio

Use your work in the activities suggested in this chapter to show your developing awareness of the differences among students in our schools.

Reexamine the philosophy of education you wrote in Chapter 2. Make any revisions or additions that seem appropriate as a result of your work in this chapter, highlight these changes, and replace your former philosophy with your new one in your portfolio.

To enhance your increasing awareness of diversity, try a few enrichment activities. Here are some suggestions:

- Some colleges offer language courses specifically designed for teachers. Check one out.

- Immerse yourself in a cultural experience. Attend services at a synagogue or church. Volunteer to tutor underprivileged kids.

- If there is an International House on your campus, visit it and pick up some literature to include in your portfolio.

- Refer to a newspaper or the Internet to examine the population demographics of the school systems in your area. Include the material you find in your portfolio.

- Find a student on campus or at your field placement school who identifies with a culture different from yours. Talk with the student about his or her educational experience. Write a brief reflection to include in your portfolio.

- Find out if the software in your campus or in your field placement school (or both) is available in languages other than English.

- Attend an event—fair, festival, or farmers market—in the community in which a school that you would like to teach at is located. Observe the activities, materials, and people at the event. How do they translate into the school environment? Write up your observations and reflections and include them in your portfolio.

Education CourseMate Resources

Check out this text's Education CourseMate website (at www.cengagebrain.com) for more information about working with the diverse populations of our schools, as well as interactive study tools and useful resources. You will find the TeachSource Videos, a guide for doing Field Experiences, glossary flash cards, activities, tutorial quizzes, direct links to all the websites mentioned in the chapter, and more.

©Ellen B. Senisi/The Image Works

CHAPTER 5

The Student and the Teacher: Acknowledging Unique Abilities

WE ALL KNOW every student has unique abilities. Some of these abilities are expressed artistically; others may be expressed intellectually. Like the unique perspectives students bring to class that are influenced by culture, race, ethnicity, language, religion, socioeconomic status, and sexual orientation, these abilities also contribute to diversity in the classroom. Step into any classroom and you will encounter a broad spectrum of physical, sensory, cognitive, and behavioral differences. As a teacher, you always strive to create a learning environment that will allow *all* students to use their unique abilities to succeed.

This chapter asks you to familiarize yourself with some unique abilities and learning styles and investigate the nature of these abilities. You will consider ways of teaching to foster maximum achievement for students with diverse abilities. You will explore some of the ways in which learning abilities can be classified, beginning with the categories of exceptionality covered by the Individuals with Disability Education Act. You will examine how students with unique abilities are served by special education, with a special focus on students with learning disabilities, attention deficit/hyperactivity disorder, and autism. Although teachers and schools frequently emphasize traditional measures of intellectual ability such as IQ, you will investigate some alternative (but influential) views of intelligence. You will also explore learning styles and other individual differences among learners that have been shown to have pronounced influences on student achievement.

Chapter Objectives

As a result of your explorations in this chapter, you will be able to:

1. Investigate ways in which variations in ability are classified according to the Individuals with Disabilities Act.
   InTASC Standard #2: Learning Differences

2. Identify characteristics of learning disabilities and other disorders that may affect learning, and describe some teaching strategies that are effective for these disabilities and disorders.
   InTASC Standard #2: Learning Differences

3. Identify characteristics of cognitive abilities, learning preferences, and learning styles, and describe some teaching strategies that are effective for these abilities and preferences.
   InTASC Standard #2: Learning Differences

4. Describe the theory of multiple intelligences and show how this theory can be used to help *all* students learn.
   InTASC Standard #2: Learning Differences; Standard #8: Instructional Strategies

5. Identify the three primary learning modalities and explain how teachers can use each in the classroom.
   InTASC Standard #2: Learning Differences; Standard #8: Instructional Strategies

6. Investigate best teaching practices to help all students learn by acknowledging their unique abilities and using co-teaching and differentiation strategies.
   InTASC Standard #8: Instructional Strategies

7. Identify relationships between constructivist teaching and learning and acknowledging students' unique abilities.
   InTASC Standard #2: Learning Differences

Exceptional Children and the Individuals with Disabilities Education Act

No two children are identical, but exceptional students are those who differ from societal norms to the extent that they require some form of modification to a standard educational program. These differences can vary from physical impairments to emotional and behavior disorders to intellectual giftedness. Special education refers to instruction specially designed to meet the unique needs of students who are recognized as exceptional (Gargiulo, 2011).

Students with exceptionalities have not always been well served by our nation's public schools. Before the mid-20th century, it was common practice to bar children with disabilities from attending school. However, the rise of the civil rights movement in the United States marked a turning point for securing the rights of citizens with disabilities. In the past 50 years, the federal government, in a series of landmark pieces of legislation, has helped to define the current special education policies and practices of our schools.

exceptional students Students who require some form of modification to the standard educational program.

special education Instruction that is specifically designed to meet the unique needs of students who are recognized as exceptional.

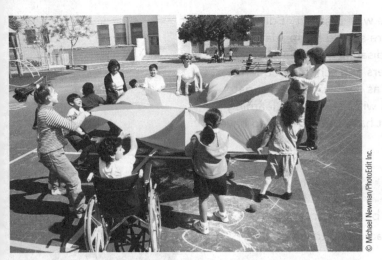

According to federal law, children with special needs must receive full and appropriate education and be educated with their typical peers in the least restrictive environment possible.

In 1975, Congress passed Public Law 94-142, the Education of All Handicapped Children Act, which required each state to develop and implement policies that assure a free and appropriate education for all students with disabilities. In 1986, Congress passed amendments to include children attending preschool. In 1990, the Individuals with Disabilities Education Act (IDEA) was passed into law to amend the 1975 law; this act was amended in 1997 and was reauthorized in 2004.

The IDEA requires states to provide services for all children with disabilities so these children can receive a "full and appropriate education." The law extends to many different types of disabilities, including cognitive disabilities and physical disabilities. Among the categories covered under the IDEA are the following:

- Learning disability
- Mental retardation
- Emotional disturbance
- Autism
- Speech or language impairment
- Visual impairment
- Hearing impairment
- Physical impairments, including orthopedic impairments, multiple disabilities, and traumatic brain injury

IDEA Disability Categories

Nearly 6.5 million students aged 3 through 21 received services for various disabilities in the 2008–2009 school year. The following list shows these disabilities and the percentage of students receiving services for each (National Center for Education Statistics, 2011a):

• Specific learning disabilities	38.2%
• Speech or language impairments	22%
• Intellectual disability	7%
• Emotional disturbance	6.5%
• Hearing impairments	1%
• Visual impairments	less than 1%
• Orthopedic impairments	1%
• Other health impairments	10%
• Autism	5%
• Traumatic brain injury	less than 1%
• Multiple disabilities	2%
• Deaf–blindness	less than 1%
• Developmental delay	5.5%

The law requires that schools provide all students with disabilities with at least the following:

- A full and appropriate education
- Education in the least restrictive environment
- An individualized education program (IEP)
- Due process
- Nondiscriminatory assessment
- Parental participation

individualized education program A plan for meeting the educational needs of an individual student who may have disabilities.

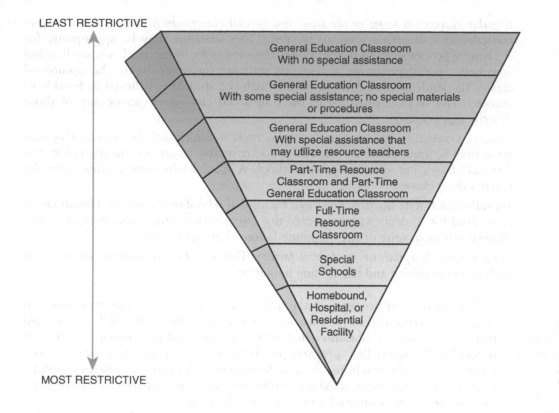

LEAST RESTRICTIVE

General Education Classroom
With no special assistance

General Education Classroom
With some special assistance; no special materials
or procedures

General Education Classroom
With special assistance that
may utilize resource teachers

Part-Time Resource
Classroom and Part-Time
General Education Classroom

Full-Time
Resource
Classroom

Special
Schools

Homebound,
Hospital, or
Residential
Facility

MOST RESTRICTIVE

◀ **Figure 5.1**
Cascade system of special education services. (Adapted from Gargiulo, 2006.)
© Cengage Learning 2014

The least restrictive environment provision means that students with disabilities must be educated to the greatest extent possible in general education classrooms. We can think of the least restrictive environment concept as an inverted tree that depicts a cascade of special education services, as shown in Figure 5.1.

As you can tell from the diagram, the degree of services provided for students with disabilities varies from inclusion in traditional classroom programs with no special assistance, to homebound with no school attendance at all. At some point in your own educational experience, you may have heard the terms mainstreaming or inclusion. *Mainstreaming* is a now-outdated term that was used to describe the integration of children with disabilities into general education classrooms. The word *inclusion*, a more current term, has replaced *mainstreaming*, and suggests that schools are getting closer to total integration of children with disabilities. In practice, inclusion may occur in varying degrees:

- *Regular classroom with no special assistance.* This situation may be most appropriate for students with very mild disabilities that do not prevent them from pursuing challenging work, although advocates of full inclusion believe that all children with disabilities should be served in general education classrooms.

- *Regular classroom with some special teaching assistance but no special materials or procedures.* This situation may be appropriate for students with mild disabilities who require some special treatment, either in the form of accommodation of physical handicaps (vision-impaired, hearing-impaired, and so on) or special teaching techniques. Teachers of these students expand their repertoire of teaching techniques to include all students in their classes.

- *Regular classroom with assistance from special education teachers or other specialized teachers.* This situation may be appropriate for students who can attend traditional classes but who need special planning and special instruction to accommodate their disabilities. The classroom teacher may rely on resource teachers to deliver special instruction on the topics being studied. Special materials often are provided.

mainstreaming Placing a disabled student in regular school classes.

inclusion The practice of assigning students with below-normal or above-normal IQs or disabling conditions to the same classrooms they would attend if they were not disabled.

full inclusion The strategy of including students who may have exceptionalities in with the population of all students in all classes and activities.

- *Regular classroom some of the time and special classroom (usually taught by special education teachers) some of the time.* This situation may be appropriate for students who can succeed in traditional classrooms for some academic studies, but who need special programs and special teaching for other areas. The traditional classes the students attend are those in which the student is believed to be able to succeed. The services provided in the traditional classroom can be any of those described previously.

- *Resource classroom full time, with no time spent in traditional classrooms.* This situation may be appropriate for students who are unable to attend and succeed in traditional classes but who can attend school. A special education teacher normally teaches these classes.

- *Special schools with no attendance in a traditional school or classroom.* This situation is reserved for students with handicaps that prevent them from functioning in a traditional school in spite of any accommodations that can be made.

- *Homebound, hospital, or residential facility.* This situation is reserved for students with severe cognitive and functioning limitations.

A second major provision of the IDEA is the requirement of an individualized education program (IEP) for each student with disabilities. The IEP is a detailed plan for a student's education that will meet the student's unique educational needs. The IEP normally is prepared jointly by the special education teacher, classroom teachers who will be involved in the student's education, the student's parents or guardians, and someone who can interpret the results of the assessment tests, such as the guidance counselor or school psychologist.

A third major provision of the IDEA is the assurance of due process. This means parents or guardians:

1. Have the right to examine all of their child's school records;
2. Must be given notice before any change in placement or classification is made; and
3. Must give their consent before their child is evaluated or placed.

The fourth major provision of the IDEA is the "nondiscriminatory assessment provision." This means that students must be evaluated using several types of assessments that have been shown to be free of bias.

The fifth major provision, called the "parental participation provision," requires that parents or guardians participate fully in the decision-making process.

Adapting instruction for students with learning disabilities includes clearly specifying learning objectives, presenting lessons in a step-by-step format, and providing frequent assessments of student learning.

Courtesy of Bill Lisenby

CONTROVERSIES in Education

Special Issues in Special Education

There is a great deal of controversy over the concept of inclusion in education. Some believe that inclusion helps to minimize perceived differences between students who have disabilities and those who do not. Others believe that inclusion can result in an inferior education for students with disabilities because they are required to keep up with the rest of the class. There is also disagreement about how much time special education students should spend in a general education classroom, and there is a question of how effective inclusive classrooms actually are for students with disabilities (McCleskey and Waldron, 2011).

Controversy also surrounds the labeling of students. Some people believe that labeling helps educators prepare the most appropriate educational programs. Others believe that labels can be stigmatizing or even penalizing and misrepresent the true nature of individuals. In Chapter 4, you saw that unique perspectives tend to be identified with labels. In this chapter, you will find that students with different kinds of disabilities and abilities as well are labeled.

The use of "person-first" language is stressed in education. "Person-first" language means that you first reference the learner, then whatever label is attributed to the learner. For example, instead of saying that you have three gifted students in your classroom and two learning-disabled students, you would say that you have three students who are gifted and two students who are learning disabled in your classroom. Do you see the difference?

WHAT DO YOU THINK?

1. *What do you think are the benefits of inclusion for students with special needs?*
2. *What are the benefits of inclusion classrooms for "regular" students?*
3. *What drawbacks exist for both groups of students?*
4. *What are the challenges for the classroom teacher?*
5. *Why is having to pay close attention to the way you refer to your students important?*
6. *How are referring to the person first and the exceptionality (or culture or other label) second consistent with meeting the common human needs of all learners? What do you think about labeling in general? Remember that the goal of education is to provide the best possible learning opportunities for all students to maximize their achievement.*

Learning Disabilities

Learning disabilities are the most commonly occurring handicapping condition. The term learning disability (LD) refers to a disorder that can cause a person to have difficulty learning and using the skills of language (reading, writing, listening, and speaking), reasoning, and mathematics (MedicineNet.com, 2012). Students with learning disabilities are included among those who qualify for special education services. As of 2009, almost 2.1 million school-age children attending public schools in the United States were classified as having a learning disability (National Center for Learning Disabilities, 2011).

learning disability (LD) A disorder that interferes with the learning process.

Learning disabilities are hard to diagnose but are usually suspected when there is a gap between a student's ability and his or her performance. Some signs that a student may have a learning disability include coordination problems, difficulty with concentration, and consistent problems with handwriting, remembering newly learned information, staying organized, or speaking so that he or she is understood. It is important to note that most students with learning disabilities are of average or above-average intelligence (National Center for Learning Disabilities, 2011); in fact, some are considered gifted and talented.

Response to Intervention

School personnel often use a method called "Response to Intervention" (RTI) to help diagnose a learning disability. If they suspect that a student's lack of achievement in the classroom may be the result of a learning disability, teachers, parents, and administrators design an individual and increasingly concentrated intervention that involves supporting

response to intervention (RTI) A method used for the early identification of students who may have special needs that employs deliberate strategies to impact learning. If the student does not respond to the intervention, it may be determined that the student has a learning disability.

the student in various ways, including instructional methods. The intervention is implemented early in the student's academic career, and frequent measurements of progress are made. After a predetermined amount of time, if the student does not respond to the intervention, the conclusion may be drawn that a learning disability may be involved and the student may be referred for special education services (Cortiella, 2011).

Dyslexia

dyslexia A learning disability in which an individual has difficulty with reading comprehension and writing.

Learning disabilities are as individual as the students who have them. Dyslexia is one example of a learning disability with which you may be familiar. Students with dyslexia have severe difficulties with reading comprehension, failing to understand the relationship between sounds and letters. They often sequence letters incorrectly in words while they are reading or writing, and they interchange words and numerals. To begin to understand what a person with dyslexia sees while reading, try to read the passages in Figure 5.2.

Figure 5.2 ▶
*What a dyslexic student might see.
(Adapted from kidshealth.org.)*
© Cengage Learning 2014

Thew ord sare n otsp aced cor rect ly.

We spell wrds xatle az tha snd to us.

Sometimesallthelettersarepushedtogether

The translation of above passage is:

3. Sometimes all the letters are pushed together.

2. We spell words exactly as they sound to us.

1. The words are not spaced correctly.

Attention Deficit/Hyperactivity Disorder (ADHD)

attention deficit/hyperactivity disorder (ADHD) A disorder characterized by not being able to maintain attention or to control impulses. Often includes incidence of increased distraction and energy resulting in not being able to stay still.

Although attention deficit/hyperactivity disorder (ADHD) is not formally a learning disability, this disorder can affect academic performance and should be acknowledged in the classroom. Students with ADHD have an inability to maintain attention, to plan ahead, or to ignore impulses and distractions and stay still. As of 2007, 9.5 percent of children between the ages of 4 and 17 were diagnosed with ADHD (Pastor and Reuben, 2008). The rate of diagnosis of ADHD has increased an average of 3 percent every year between 1997 and 2006, and 5.5 percent between 2003 and 2007 (Centers for Disease Control, 2010). According to the American Academy of Child and Adolescent Psychiatry, just about every teacher has at least one student with ADHD in class. In fact, teachers may be the first ones to suspect that a child who is struggling may have ADHD. The behaviors that may cause a teacher to wonder if a student should be evaluated for ADHD include distractibility, inability to focus, disorganization, forgetfulness, procrastination, incomplete assignments, and frequent daydreaming. Most students demonstrate only the attention deficit component of the disorder (termed attention deficit disorder, or ADD), although some show the hyperactivity component in the form of fidgeting and an inability to sit still through a structured lesson, and blurting out answers. The most severe cases involve students showing both the attention deficit and hyperactivity components (Dunne, 2005).

attention deficit disorder (ADD) A disorder characterized by not being able to maintain attention or control impulses. Usually not accompanied by the hyperactivity component of ADHD.

With the significant increase in the rate of diagnosis of ADHD, teachers must be aware of some of the myths associated with the disorder. The following lists some common myths about ADHD as well as some suggestions for teaching techniques.

Myths about ADHD

- **ADHD is only a childhood disorder.** In fact, children who have been diagnosed with ADHD often carry the disorder into adolescence and adulthood. Also, adults may be diagnosed with ADHD.
- **ADHD is overdiagnosed.** Advocates note that an increase in general awareness of the disorder and changes in special education legislation may have led to the misconception that ADHD is overdiagnosed.
- **Children with ADHD are overmedicated.** There has been an increase in the rate of prescription of the leading drug for ADHD, Ritalin, consistent with the increase in rate of diagnosis. And most children with ADHD are not medicated.
- **ADHD can be caused by poor parenting.** Although poor parenting techniques can cause ADHD symptoms to be aggravated, other factors have been found to be more influential in causing ADHD. Studies have shown that genetics play a contributory role in ADHD.
- **Minority children are overdiagnosed with ADHD and are overmedicated.** Research has shown African American students appear to be underserved in diagnosis and treatment of ADHD.
- **Boys have higher rates of ADHD than girls, and ADHD in boys is more severe.** It is thought that girls may be diagnosed less frequently with ADHD than boys because ADHD in boys may manifest itself in behaviors that result in conduct referrals. However, several studies comparing girls and boys with ADHD have indicated that girls suffer more severe internalized disorders involving mood, anxiety, distress, and depression, which affect them socially and academically.

Source: Adapted from Adesman and Ellison, 2007.

Suggested techniques to help you teach students with ADHD follow.

Techniques for Teaching Students with ADHD

- Incorporate advance organizers that review previous lessons.
- Provide clear and simple instructions that include expectations for learning and behavior as well as time management.
- State what materials will be needed for participation.
- Use technology to provide audiovisual information.
- Use prompts and cues to signal appropriate participation.
- Monitor students throughout the lesson in an attempt to prevent or quickly address circumstances that have the potential to cause frustration or distractions.
- Provide additional directions individually.
- Address information in smaller chunks and highlight the key points.
- Provide additional time allowed to take tests.
- Encourage participation in cooperative learning activities.
- Provide warnings that the time to conclude the lesson is approaching.
- Check student work for completion and accuracy.
- Provide a preview for the upcoming lesson.

Source: Adapted from U.S. Department of Education, 2004b.

A PBS website called Misunderstood Minds offers a simulation of what it might be like to have your attention constantly thrown off track while trying to learn. Go to the site, click on the section for ATTENTION, and choose to try the visual activity, the auditory activity, and the attention video.

Autism

Autism is a developmental disorder that affects how people communicate with others, how they relate to others, and how they perceive the world around them. Autism is characterized by abnormal social interaction and communication, by moderate to severe behavior problems such as irritability and aggressiveness, and by restricted and repetitive

autism A spectrum of disorders in which communication, social interactions, and the ability to participate in relationships is impaired.

behavior. These characteristics are seen in early childhood. The incidence of autism is rising, and teachers are increasingly likely to have one or more children with autism in their classroom. As a matter of fact, in early 2012, the highest rate of autism in the U.S. ever was reported. One in eighty-eight children were reported to have autism or a related disorder (Begley, 2012). Suggested techniques for teaching children with autism follow.

Techniques for Teaching Children with Autism

1. Use visuals and reminders liberally for instruction.
2. Use hands-on activities in class instead of "lecturing."
3. Use body language as opposed to verbal instructions.
4. Provide flexibility in assignments.
5. Structure lessons clearly.
6. Use concept maps and other visual cognitive strategies.
7. Announce impending transitions clearly.
8. Link material to the students' interests.
9. Provide opportunities for the students with autism to memorize facts.
10. Use computers as much as possible.
11. Allow breaks.
12. Offer rewards as appropriate.
13. Model social skills.
14. Be aware of distracting background noise and clutter.
15. Make expectations and consequences clear.
16. Ignore the small stuff that can't be changed, and focus on teaching and learning.

Source: From Jay and Jay, 2008.

Teaching That Acknowledges Disabilities

From your investigations into ways to accommodate students with other unique characteristics and perspectives in the classroom, you can probably think of some effective strategies to accommodate students with disabilities.

BUILDING BLOCK
5.1

Teaching Students with Disabilities

Select a specific student disability, such as hearing impairment, learning disability, ADHD, orthopedic impairment, or other disability you might encounter among the students in a class you would teach:

- What teaching strategies would foster these students' motivation to learn?
- How are the strategies similar to those you have suggested for students with other unique characteristics and perspectives?
- How do they foster heightened relationships between the students and the teacher?
- How do they help students meet their basic and academic needs?

assistive technology Technology that individuals with disabilities may use to perform tasks that would otherwise be difficult or impossible.

People with disabilities have special learning requirements that teachers must provide. Understanding the unique characteristics and perspectives of students with disabilities helps teachers tailor their classrooms to meet the needs of these students, as well as all the

The Technology-Related Assistance for Individuals with Disabilities Act of 1988 offered the first legal definition of assistive technology (AT). Although the Assistive Technology Act of 1998 replaced this act, the definition for AT remained the same: technology that individuals with disabilities may use to perform tasks that would otherwise be difficult or impossible (National Center on Accessible Information Technology in Education, 2011). Certainly we are familiar with assistive technologies that help students perform daily living activities such as wheelchairs, hearing aids, and motorized lifts on school buses. What classroom and learning tasks might be difficult for students with disabilities? Think about learners with vision impairments. How about orthopedic impairments? How about learning disabilities involving higher-order thinking skills, reading comprehension, and writing skills? What technology can you think of that might assist these learners?

Examples of assistive technologies that you may see in the classroom include voice recognition software, specially adapted keyboards and input devices, built-in magnifiers, audiobooks, modeling software, simulations, and virtual environments. A student's IEP may identify assistive

Students with physical disabilities and other special needs can use technology to facilitate classroom learning. A specially adapted keyboard is an example of assistive technology.

technologies as part of the support needed to perform tasks in school (Family Center on Technology and Disability, 2010). Portable technologies such as PDAs, MP3 players, cell phones, and tablets can also assist students with disabilities. (Keep in mind that these technologies assist all learners by making information and data accessible.)

others. Here are some specific instructional strategies teachers use to adapt instruction for students with special needs:

1. Identify the specific competencies students are to achieve.
2. Ensure that students have previously achieved the skills and understandings they need for success in the lesson.
3. Modify reading levels to meet students' capabilities.
4. Prepare explicit and specific introductory and summary activities.
5. Deliver introductory and summary activities in small pieces.
6. Provide the information of the lesson in small pieces.
7. Identify and define any new vocabulary words that may come up.
8. Assess student achievement frequently and be aware of students' progress and understanding.
9. Develop alternative forms of assessment.
10. Provide an assortment of methods students can use to demonstrate their understanding.
11. Adapt physical facilities (furniture, storage areas, and other facilities) for use by all students.
12. Ensure that everyone works on the lesson's activities.
13. Modify equipment and materials as needed so all students can use them.
14. Enlarge aisles and areas of movement to accommodate all students.
15. Provide assistive and adaptive forms of technology resources.

▶Ⅱ TeachSource Video

View the video TeachSource Video Case, "Assistive Technology in the Inclusive Classroom: Best Practices." In this video, you'll meet five-year-old Jamie, a kindergartener with cerebral palsy who uses assistive technologies to help her learn the same curriculum content as the other students in her class. You'll also hear her teacher and the inclusion facilitator share their insights about how best to teach Jamie and how assistive technologies can enhance her learning. Be sure to view the three bonus videos. After watching these videos, answer the following questions:

1. What assistive technologies have you seen in schools?
2. What kinds of assistive technologies are free or inexpensive? What would they be used for?
3. How can assistive technologies enhance learning?

Inclusive environments encourage interaction between students with special needs and their peers. Full and appropriate educational opportunities for students with disabilities might not be possible if not for legislation like the IDEA.

Compare these strategies with those you listed in Building Block 5.1. Are there similarities? Which of the strategies for students with ADHD would be beneficial for students with other learning disabilities? Which of all the strategies in this section would be good for *all* students in your classroom?

Cognitive Abilities

You have investigated learning disabilities. These disabilities affect how students learn, but they are not necessarily indicative of intelligence, which is what we mean by cognitive ability. Indeed, some learners who have been diagnosed with a learning disability are also academically gifted. Let's explore cognitive abilities further.

You have seen that characteristics such as race, ethnicity, language, gender, socioeconomic status, and sexual orientation can affect how—or even whether—a learner approaches a learning task. Certainly these differences affect classroom climate and the way we teach. However, if we were to ask, "What single student characteristic most accounts for differences in student achievement?" your first inclination might be to reply "intelligence." Intelligence is "the ability to learn or understand or to deal with new or trying situations" (Merriam-Webster, 2012). When teachers say "intelligence," they normally are referring to a student's cognitive (or intellectual) ability. What exactly is intelligence, and how is it measured?

cognitive ability The ability to learn, know, and understand.

Aptitude tests such as the Otis–Lennon School Ability Test (OLSAT), the Cognitive Abilities Test (CogAT), and intelligence quotient (IQ) tests like the Stanford–Binet and Weschler IQ tests, are used to measure cognitive ability, aptitude, and potential for success of students in school. These tests gauge linguistic, mathematical, and spatial abilities by posing questions that require linguistic, mathematical, and spatial thinking, together with memory skills. Educational decisions are made partly on the basis of student IQ as measured by the tests. How valid are these tests?

Intelligence Tests

Use your favorite search engine to find "free IQ Tests." Select one and take it. After you are done, analyze your score and answer the following questions:

- Look at the questions. What background knowledge do they presuppose you have? Are there any ambiguous questions (questions that can have more than one meaning)?
- How did you score? Do you believe that this score accurately reflects your intellectual ability? Why or why not?
- How valid do you believe the IQ score is? Why do you think so?

Measuring Cognitive Ability

There are concerns about IQ tests and, therefore, about decisions made on the basis of IQ scores. Primary among these concerns is the cultural bias that seems to be embedded in many IQ tests, and which may result in inaccurate scores for individuals whose experiential and cultural backgrounds differ from those that govern the tests' development. For example, a test question might ask when people are most likely to go swimming. Students whose experiences with swimming primarily deal with the school swim team might answer *winter* rather than the "correct" response of *summer*. Or what about a question that asks what materials—wood, metal, grass, or stone—would be good to build a house out of? Depending on your previous experiences and familiarity with houses, which may be dependent on your culture, there could be several correct answers. Did you find questions with experiential or cultural bias in the sample tests you took in Building Block 5.2?

Some IQ tests do not allow for creative thinking and therefore may not represent the full extent of a student's ability to solve problems. In fact, some of the greatest thinkers of our time, such as Thomas Edison and Albert Einstein, did not perform well on traditional measures of intelligence.

Nevertheless, educational decisions continue to be made using IQ scores. Among those decisions is the categorization of students into intellectual ability groups. IQ scores between 70 and 130 represent normal intelligence. You can expect most of the students in your classroom to fall in this range. IQ scores below 70 indicate mental retardation, and IQ scores above 130 represent exceptional intelligence.

Naturally, the further away from the normal range an IQ score is, the fewer people have that IQ. The complete distribution of IQ scores can be represented by a graph in the shape of a bell, called the bell-shaped curve or the normal curve. On the normal curve, IQ is represented on the horizontal axis, and the percentage of people is represented on the vertical axis. The normal curve for IQ is shown in Figure 5.3. Study this graph and familiarize yourself with the distribution of IQs.

bell-shaped curve The bell shaped graph of a distribution that may and may not be symmetrical.

normal curve The symmetrical, bell-shaped curve of a normal distribution.

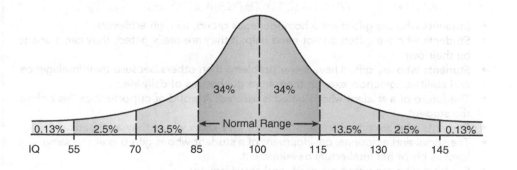

◀ **Figure 5.3**
Normal curve showing relative percentages of the general population in each major cognitive ability group.
© Cengage Learning 2014

People Who Are Gifted and Talented

Students who are gifted and talented have potentially outstanding abilities that allow them to excel in one or more areas. As of 2006, 6.7 percent of students in public elementary and secondary schools were categorized as gifted or talented (U.S. Department of Education, Office of Civil Rights, 2008). The National Association for Gifted Children (2008) defines gifted individuals as "those who demonstrate outstanding levels of aptitude or competence in one or more domains." A "domain" is "any structured area of activity with its own symbol system (e.g., mathematics, music, language) and/or set of sensorimotor skills (e.g., painting, dance, and sports)."

Consistent with this are the abilities included in the definition of giftedness provided in the Jacob K. Javits Gifted and Talented Students Education Program. These abilities are seen in students who demonstrate outstanding competency in activities that are intellectual, artistic, creative, or academic in nature. The Javits Act also acknowledges giftedness in leadership abilities and notes that the students who demonstrate these capabilities may not be fully served in a general education classroom. The Javits Act provides federal funding for programs designed specifically for gifted and talented individuals, especially for students who are economically disadvantaged, have limited English proficiency, or are disabled.

The most common method of identifying students who are classified as gifted is the use of tests. Because giftedness frequently is dependent on high intelligence, schools often use IQ scores to label the intellectual ability of gifted and talented students. The ranges are as follows:

130 to 144	Gifted
145 to 159	Highly gifted
160 and above	Profoundly gifted

Note that the IQ score for students who are gifted and talented starts with 130, which is the beginning of the upper 2.63 percent of the population (see Figure 5.3).

Although tests of intellectual ability are often used to identify intellectual giftedness, general intellectual ability is just one dimension of giftedness and talent. As you have seen, giftedness also manifests itself in other ways and thus depends on other factors. Consequently, a greater variety of assessment tools is used to identify students who are gifted and talented in one or more areas, thereby reducing the likelihood that minority students who are gifted and talented are overlooked (as may be the case when identification depends largely on traditional intelligence tests).

Often, students who are gifted stand out from other students as being really smart, maybe even being labeled as "nerds." Students and teachers alike may make certain assumptions about students who are gifted based on their exceptional intellect, talent, or both. The following shows some myths and truths about students who are gifted.

Common Myths about Students Who Are Gifted

- Students who are gifted are a homogeneous group, all high achievers.
- Students who are gifted do not need help. If they are really gifted, they can manage on their own.
- Students who are gifted have fewer problems than others because their intelligence and abilities somehow exempt them from the hassles of daily life.
- The future of a student who is gifted is assured: A world of opportunities lies before the student.
- Students who are gifted are self-directed; they know where they are heading.
- The social and emotional development of a student who is gifted is at the same level as his or her intellectual development.
- Students who are gifted are nerds and social isolates.

- The primary value of a student who is gifted lies in his or her brainpower.
- The family of a student who is gifted always prizes his or her abilities.
- Students who are gifted need to serve as an example to others, and they should always assume extra responsibility.
- Students who are gifted can accomplish anything they put their minds to. All they have to do is apply themselves.
- Students who are gifted are naturally creative and do not need encouragement.
- Children who are gifted are easy to raise and are a welcome addition to any classroom.

Truths about Students Who Are Gifted

- Students who are gifted are often perfectionist and idealistic. They may equate achievement and grades with self-esteem and self-worth, which sometimes leads to fear of failure and interferes with achievement.
- Students who are gifted may experience heightened sensitivity to their own expectations and those of others, resulting in guilt over achievements or grades they perceive to be low.
- The chronological age and social, physical, emotional, and intellectual development of a student who is gifted may be at different levels. For example, a five-year-old may be able to read and comprehend a third-grade book but may not be able to write legibly.
- Students who are gifted may be so far ahead of their chronological age mates that they know more than half the curriculum before the school year begins. Their boredom can result in low achievement and grades.
- People who are gifted make up as much as 20 percent of the prison population.
- Students who are gifted are at high risk for dropping out of school; 20 percent of high school dropouts have tested in the gifted range.
- Children who are gifted are problem solvers. They benefit from working on open-ended, interdisciplinary problems, such as how to solve a shortage of community resources. Students who are gifted often refuse to work for grades alone.
- Students who are gifted often think abstractly and with such complexity that they may need help with concrete study and test-taking skills. They may not be able to select one answer in a multiple-choice question because they see how all the answers might be correct.
- Students who are gifted and who do well in school may define success as getting an A and failure as getting any grade less than an A. By early adolescence, these students may be unwilling to try anything if they are not certain of guaranteed success.

Source: From Berger, 2006.

How do you suppose teachers could work to meet the basic needs of love and belonging, respect, and self-esteem of gifted and talented students? How might giftedness influence students' desire to learn? How might the label *gifted* affect the social aspects of school for gifted students?

Teaching Students Who Are Gifted and Talented

BUILDING BLOCK
5.3

Review the myths and truths about students who are gifted and talented. What teaching strategies would provide motivation for these students to learn? How could teachers foster student perception that the material being studied is meaningful and relevant? How could they foster heightened relationships between student and teacher? How could they help students meet their basic and academic needs?

Why do you suppose people who are gifted are overrepresented in the high school dropout and prison populations?

Although detailed federal mandates exist to provide services for students with disabilities, the federal legislation specific to students who are gifted and talented consists primarily of grants and rules governing the distribution of this grant money. Each state adopts its own definitions, laws, and policies concerning the nature and services provided for students who are gifted and talented. At the federal level, the Jacob K. Javits Gifted and Talented Students Education program awards grants to help students who are gifted develop their abilities and reach high levels of achievement.

Depending on state and local policies, special programs may be offered to students identified as gifted or talented. These programs may take the form of special learning environments and experiences offered at special times on certain days, often in special classrooms. Or they may take the form of the inclusion model in traditional, general education classrooms, similar to the inclusion model used for integrating students with exceptional needs.

 You can access the U.S. Department of Education Jacob K. Javits program site through a direct link on the Education CourseMate website. This site has full details of the Javits program.

> ## State Legislation for the Education of Students Who Are Gifted and Talented
>
> All 50 states have rules, regulations, policies, and /or legislation that address the education of gifted learners (Passow and Rudniski, n.d.). Additionally, most states offer special endorsements for gifted and talented teaching specialists who provide special programs for qualifying students. However, traditional classroom teachers can expect to have students who are gifted and talented in their classrooms for much of the school day. Teaching students who are gifted and talented requires presenting them with challenging work, building on their interests, allowing large blocks of time for them to pursue their projects, and encouraging continued work in out-of-school arenas.

Multiple Intelligences

When you have an important test coming up, how do you choose to study? Does the room have to be quiet and free from distractions? Do you find that you learn the information best if you recopy your notes or if you try to explain it to someone else? Have you ever thought that you could have done better on an oral exam over the information rather than the paper-and-pencil test your teacher just gave you? In the classroom, is there a particular way that the instructor provides information that seems to help you understand and remember it? Maybe you do best with pictures or charts. Do you consider yourself to be a "math person"? All of these are examples of multiple intelligence preference.

Perhaps you have heard the assertion that instead of asking, "How smart are you?" we should ask, "How are you smart?" Howard Gardner has argued that humans have at least eight distinct intelligences, not only the two or three measured in traditional IQ tests. The eight intelligences are spatial, bodily–kinesthetic, musical, linguistic, logical–mathematical, interpersonal, intrapersonal, and naturalistic. Gardner also is investigating other possible areas of intelligence—existential, spiritual, and moral. So far, only existential intelligence has been fairly well supported, though Gardner is hesitant to include it with the others because it meets some but not all of his criteria for an intelligence (Smith, 2008).

Spatial intelligence involves our ability to perceive accurately what we see, to interpret this in our own mind, and to represent what we experience in visual formats. We use *bodily–kinesthetic intelligence* when we perform physical actions. *Musical intelligence* involves hearing music almost continuously and representing our thoughts in musical terms. *Linguistic intelligence* has to do with the use of language. *Logical–mathematical intelligence* involves working with numbers and solving problems logically and scientifically. We use *interpersonal intelligence* when we interact with other people, understanding and responding to them accurately and appropriately. *Intrapersonal intelligence* involves knowing ourselves, knowing who we are, being comfortable in our own skins, and acting on our knowledge of ourselves. *Naturalistic intelligence* is used by people who exhibit true and internalized appreciation of and sensitivity to the natural world. Finally, *existential intelligence*, not yet formally included as one of the intelligences in multiple intelligence theory, is demonstrated by the ability to look at the "big picture," seeing connections between details and components across ideas or topics.

How do the inferences you made in Building Block 5.4 compare with these descriptions?

Figure 5.4 shows the theory of multiple intelligences in diagrammatic form.

Figure 5.4 ▶
The basic intelligences identified by Howard Gardner.
© Cengage Learning 2014

J. Gardner, copyright 2003

Howard Gardner's Biography in His Own Words

I was born in Scranton, Pennsylvania, in 1943, the son of refugees from Nazi Germany. I was a studious child who gained much pleasure from playing the piano; music has remained very important throughout my life. All of my post-secondary education has been at Harvard University. I was trained as a developmental psychologist and later as a neuropsychologist. For many years, I conducted two streams of research on cognitive and symbol-using capacities—one with normal and gifted children, the second with adults who suffered from brain damage. My effort to synthesize these two lines of work led me to develop and introduce the theory of multiple intelligences in my 1983 book *Frames of Mind*. Since the middle 1980s, I have been heavily involved in school reform efforts in the United States. In 1986, I began to teach at the Harvard Graduate School of Education while continuing my long-term involvement with Project Zero, a research group in human cognition that maintains a special focus on the arts. With colleagues, I have begun a study of the nature of interdisciplinary work as it is carried out in precollegiate and collegiate settings, and in research institutions, and a study of the role of trust and trustees in contemporary American society.

Source: Courtesy Project Zero, Harvard University.

Note that the existential intelligence is included—in anticipation of a conclusive resolution by Gardner.

Gardner defines intelligence as "the capacity to solve problems or to fashion products that are valued in one or more cultural setting" (Gardner and Hatch, 1989, p. 5). His identification of different intelligences has brought about the theory of multiple intelligences (MI). This theory suggests that all people have all intelligences; the strength of each intelligence varies from person to person. For example, one person may be an absolute whiz at mathematics (strong logical–mathematical intelligence) but unable to "carry a tune in a bucket" (weak musical intelligence). Another individual may be terrific at understanding other people (strong interpersonal intelligence), understands herself and who she is (strong intrapersonal intelligence), and inquires logically into scientific problems (strong logical–mathematical intelligence), but has difficulty in writing reports and compositions (weak linguistic intelligence).

Although you might have one predominant intelligence, you probably use all of the intelligences at one time or another to learn. You can strengthen any of the intelligences by using it more and more. Furthermore, your predominant intelligence can change over time.

theory of multiple intelligences (MI) A proposition by Howard Gardner asserting that traditional measures of intelligence are limited and that individuals possess different types of intelligences. These intelligences include spatial, bodily–kinesthetic, musical, linguistic, logical–mathematical, interpersonal, intrapersonal, and naturalistic intelligences.

Teaching That Encompasses Multiple Intelligences

Teachers should become sensitive to the idea that students can learn through different intelligences and use this sensitivity in their interactions with students. MI theory asks teachers to recognize the several intelligences students have and to develop a repertoire of instructional approaches that capitalize on each. According to MI theory, students do not learn just through the written word and mathematics. Learning can occur through any of the other intelligences as well, and teachers must teach to their students' strongest intelligences.

The primary idea behind the theory of multiple intelligences is to respond to the needs of every student by making alternative learning strategies available based on the different intelligences. The goal is *not* to teach each concept using each of the intelligences or to ensure every student develops every intelligence.

Table 5.1 summarizes characteristics, examples, and ways to acknowledge each of the intelligences in education settings.

TABLE 5.1 Characteristics, Examples, and Teaching Strategies to Accommodate Multiple Intelligences (Adapted from Martin, 2012.)

Intelligence	Characteristics	Frequently Found in . . .	Teaching and Learning Strategies
Spatial	Ability to perceive the visual–spatial world accurately and represent this in one's own mind	Architects Artists Sculptors Cartographers Anatomists Boy Scouts and Girl Scouts Examples: Michelangelo Frank Lloyd Wright Salvador Dali Georgia O'Keefe	Draw maps Study maps Make models Draw pictures Solve mazes Do activities in graphics arts
Bodily–kinesthetic	Ability to use one's body or body parts, such as hands and fingers, to solve problems and express ideas	Athletes Dancers Actors Mimes Examples: Tom Hanks Meryl Streep Magic Johnson Michael Jordan Mia Hamm	Dance Pantomime Play act Play with blocks Work with construction materials Play sports
Musical	Ability to think in music, hear music almost continuously, and recognize musical patterns, remember them, and transform them	Musical performers People who love to play musical instruments People who love to sing People who enjoy listening to music Examples: Ludwig van Beethoven Michael Jackson Elton John	Sing songs Learn tunes Write tunes Write rap songs Engage in rhythmic games and activities Dance Play musical instruments Create rhymes Play classical music in the background (the so-called Mozart effect)
Linguistic	Ability to use language effectively, either in oral or written form, to express ideas to others	Writers Poets Storytellers Lawyers Editors Journalists Examples: Ernest Hemingway Maya Angelou	Read Write Send e-mail Play board or card games Listen to recordings Participate in discussions and conversations Use computers Search the Internet Write poetry, news reports, fiction

(Continued)

TABLE 5.1 (*Continued*)

Intelligence	Characteristics	Frequently Found in . . .	Teaching and Learning Strategies
Logical–mathematical	Ability to use numbers and operations mathematically and to reason logically	Mathematicians Accountants Statisticians Scientists Computer programmers Examples: John Forbes Nash, Jr. John Glenn Marie Curie Steve Wozniak Sally Ride	Argue points successfully Classify and sequence Play number and logic games Solve puzzles Draw and interpret cognitive maps Draw graphs Interpret graphs Express conclusions in mathematical formats Search the Internet
Interpersonal	Ability to understand other people, to interpret their verbal and nonverbal behavior correctly, and to exhibit sensitivity to their moods and feelings	Teachers Clergy Salespeople Politicians Examples: Ronald Regan Bishop Desmond Tutu Mother Teresa Mahatma Gandhi Eleanor Roosevelt	Lead discussions Participate in discussions Participate in cooperative games Participate in group projects and discussions Participate in dramatic activities Role-play Ask clarifying questions Study with a partner
Intrapersonal	Ability to understand oneself, know who one is, know one's own strengths and limitations, and act in accordance with this self-knowledge	People who exhibit self-discipline People who exhibit personal authenticity Examples: Dalai Lama Martin Luther King, Jr. Deepak Chopra Karen Horney	Participate in independent projects Read books Write in journals Lead discussions Be a friend Help resolve quarrels Organize games Direct play activities Work in cooperative groups Find quiet places for reflection
Naturalistic	Ability to discriminate among living things and exhibit sensitivity to one's natural surroundings	Botanists Zoologists Ecologists Explorers Farmers Hunters Examples: Charles Darwin Jack Hanna Dian Fossey	Explore nature Group according to natural surroundings or environment Find origins Study objects found in nature Collect objects from nature Mount and label specimens from nature
Existential	Ability to see the big picture and make connections among ideas	Politicians Philosophers Examples: Confucius Albert Einstein Jesus Christ Nelson Mandela	Draw interdisciplinary connections Take content into the community

Multiple Intelligences

Select an area of content you plan to teach, and describe an activity pertaining to that lesson you might develop specifically for each intelligence.

How would designing classroom activities and lessons in a way that gives students opportunities to use their primary intelligences help to motivate them by meeting their needs?

Learning Styles

As you might suspect from your explorations of multiple intelligence theory, people learn more and retain it longer when the material they are learning is taught in a manner that is comfortable to them. To demonstrate this to yourself, do the activity in Building Block 5.6.

Your Comfort Zones

Sit with your body relaxed and your hands folded in your lap or on your desk. Then, unfold your hands and refold them the other way—so the other thumb is on top.

Which way was more comfortable?

Do the same thing with crossing your legs and folding your arms. Is one way more comfortable to you than the other?

You can do the same for choosing which ear you bring the telephone to, which shoe you put on first, and other habitual actions.

In Building Block 5.6, you demonstrated to yourself you have strong personal preferences for a number of things you do. These preferences often are so strong (such as folding your arms one way) that it is difficult—perhaps nearly impossible—to do these simple tasks differently from the way you are used to doing them.

The same principle is true of learning: Learners have distinct preferences for the ways they learn most comfortably.

It has been shown that people take in information in several fundamental ways to process it. These ways are called learning styles or learning modalities, and generally one modality is stronger than the others (Dunn, 1988). There are three main learning modalities: visual, auditory, and tactile–kinesthetic. People for whom the visual learning modality is strong are termed *visual learners*; people for whom the auditory learning modality is strong are termed *auditory learners*; and people for whom the tactile–kinesthetic learning modality is strong are termed *tactile learners* (referring to touch) or *kinesthetic learners* (referring to movement, although the term *kinesthetic learners* often is used to include both the kinesthetic and tactile modalities).

Visual learners learn best by seeing—pictures, diagrams, graphs, charts, films, and the like. Auditory learners learn best by hearing—the voice of the teacher or colleagues, the oral discussion led by the teacher, the responses of other students, and the like. Tactile–kinesthetic learners learn best by feeling things—touching, manipulating items, and the like.

To understand how people use learning modalities, let us explore them in action in Building Block 5.7.

learning style An individual's preference about how information is presented and taken in. Learning styles include visual, auditory, and tactile.

learning modality See **learning style**.

Exploring Learning Modalities

The following activity will help you discover what it is like to have each of the three primary learning modalities.

Find a friend, classmate, or family member. Looking into the eyes of your partner, record the direction your partner's eyes move—up, straight ahead, side, down and left, or down and right—as you ask him or her the reflective questions that follow:

1. What is your favorite television program?
2. What is your favorite movie from the past year?
3. Who is your favorite relative?
4. What is your favorite song or piece of music?
5. What is your favorite sport to watch?
6. Who is your favorite actor?
7. Who is your favorite actress?

If your partner's eyes moved upward or were focused straight ahead as he or she reflected on the answers, the individual probably is a predominantly visual learner. If your partner's eyes moved to either side or down to his or her left, the individual probably is a predominantly auditory learner. If your partner's eyes moved down toward his or her right, the individual probably is a predominantly tactile–kinesthetic learner (Laborde, 1984; Bandler and Grinder, 1979). See Figure 5.5. Ask your partner to describe what he or she thought of when deciding on the response to each question. What memories were recalled? Because the way people recall information is congruent with the way they perceive and process information (the way they learn), these descriptions reveal the ways in which visual, auditory, and tactile–kinesthetic individuals learn.

How would you describe a visual learner? An auditory learner? A kinesthetic learner?

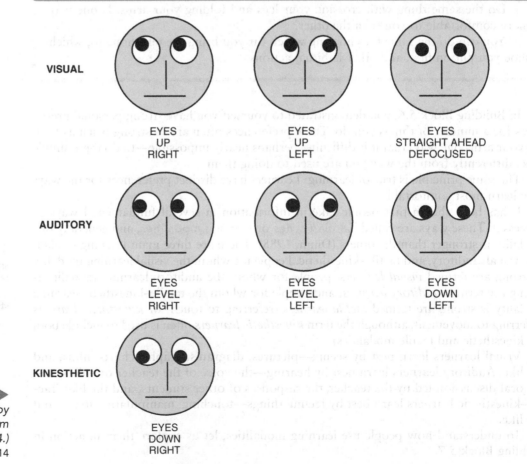

Figure 5.5 ▶
Learning modality revealed by eye movement. (Adapted from Laborde, 1984.)
© Cengage Learning 2014

People often process information in two or even all three modalities at the same time. However, one of the three tends to be stronger—in many cases, much stronger than the others. For example, a student may be listening intently to someone describe how the Grand Canyon was formed (auditory learning) but also is reinforcing that information by looking at the pictures and video clips of the Grand Canyon the teacher is providing (visual learning). The teacher may also pass around samples of different rocks that came from the Grand Canyon for people to feel (tactile learning) and look at (visual learning). However, this student is getting most of the information through the spoken descriptions. Others may rely mostly on pictures and video clips for their information and will daydream during verbal presentations.

Teaching That Includes the Primary Learning Styles

Achievement is fostered when teachers use strategies compatible with students' primary learning modalities (Felder, 2010). As you have seen, students learn and process information in different modalities. However, because it is not always possible to tell which modality is the strongest for each student in a given situation, teachers must teach in a manner that accommodates all the modalities. Effective teachers combine all three modalities in their lessons to the extent possible by ensuring that appropriate stimuli are present.

But how are multiple intelligences different from learning styles or modalities? You might think of it this way: Learning modalities are ways that students prefer to take in and process information. Multiple intelligences may be thought of as ways students are skilled at expressing their understanding. So, as a student, you may prefer to learn information by listening (as an auditory learner), and then express your understanding in a spatial representation such as a poster or collage.

Learning Styles in the Classroom

BUILDING BLOCK
5.8

Review the visual, auditory, and tactile–kinesthetic learning styles you investigated. Select an area of content you plan to teach, and describe an activity you might develop specifically for each modality.

How do these strategies foster heightened relationships between the student and the teacher? How do they help students understand that the material being studied is meaningful and relevant? How do they help students meet their basic and academic needs?

Just as each student has his or her own unique style of learning, teachers also have their personal learning styles, and they tend to incorporate these comfort zones into their teaching. Ebeling (2000) writes, "Our own learning style often becomes our most comfortable teaching style" (p. 247). The implication is that teachers tend to want to teach using their own dominant learning style, thus requiring the students to adopt the teacher's learning style in their class. It may be a bit uncomfortable for you to design a lesson that incorporates learning styles that may not be your predominant style, but as one who aspires to be an effective teacher, it is your job to consider and acknowledge the unique abilities of all the students who will learn in your classroom. And, with practice and experience, it will soon become second nature to incorporate methods that appeal to and facilitate the learning of all of the students in your class.

Teaching That Acknowledges Unique Abilities

You have considered strategies that will promote engagement and achievement of learners with disabilities, ADHD, special talents, and particular preferences for learning and demonstrating their knowledge of information. Have you considered that it is most likely that all of the students you have read about in this chapter will be in your classroom at the same time? It is also likely that you will not be the only teacher in your classroom if you have students with special needs included in your classroom. Together, you and another teacher will plan and implement lessons to support all of the learners in your classroom. You must therefore be familiar with the concepts of co-teaching and differentiated instruction.

Co-Teaching

co-teaching Two or more certified teachers (such as a general education teacher and a special education teacher) teaching a class together.

As learners with special needs are increasingly included into the general education classroom, more and different kinds of support is required to meet those needs. In co-teaching (also known as collaborative teaching, cooperative teaching, or team teaching), a general education classroom teacher and another certified teacher work together to plan, implement, and evaluate lessons that acknowledge the unique abilities and perspectives of the student population. You should review the information in Table 5.2 to gain an understanding of what co-teaching in an inclusion classroom involves.

TABLE 5.2 What Co-Teaching Is and Is Not

Co-Teaching is . . .	Co-Teaching is not . . .
Two or more coequal (preferably credentialed) faculty working together.	A teacher and an assistant, teacher's aide, or paraprofessional.
Conducted in the same classroom at the same time.	When a few students are pulled out of the classroom on a regular basis to work with the special educator. It is also not job sharing, where teachers teach different days.
Conducted with heterogeneous groups.	Pulling a group of students with disabilities to the back of the general education class.
When both teachers plan for instruction together. The general education teacher (GET) is the content specialist while the special education teacher (SET) is the expert on individualizing and delivering to various learning modalities.	When the general education teacher (GET) plans all lessons and the special education teacher (SET) walks in to the room and says, "What are we doing today and what would you like me to do?"
When both teachers provide substantive instruction together; having planned together, the SET can grade homework, teach content, facilitate activities, and so on.	When the special education teacher walks around the room all period as the general education teaches the content. Also, not when the SET sits in the class and takes notes.
When both teachers assess and evaluate student progress. IEP goals are kept in mind, as are the curricular goals and standards for that grade level.	When the GET grades "his" kids and the SET grades "her" kids, or when the GET grades all students and the SET surreptitiously changes the grades and calls it "modifying after the fact."
When teachers maximize the benefits of having two teachers in the room by having both teachers actively engage with students. Examples of different co-teaching models include team teaching, station teaching, parallel teaching, alternative teaching, and "one teach, one support."	When teachers take turns being "in charge" of the class so that the other teacher can get caught up in grading, photocopying, making phone calls, creating IEPs, and so on, or when students remain in the large group setting in lecture format as teachers rotate who "talks at them."
When teachers reflect on the progress and process, offering one another feedback on teaching styles, content, activities, and other items pertinent to improving the teaching situation.	When teachers get frustrated with one another and tell the rest of the faculty in the teachers' lounge or when one teacher simply tells the other teacher what to do and how to do it.

Source: From *The High School Journal*, vol. 86, April/May Issue. Copyright © 2003 by the University of North Carolina Press. Used by permission of the publisher. www.uncpress.unc.edu.

Teaching *All* Students through Leadership

Eloise Stewart

Teaching is a profession that reinvents itself when we get a new class each fall, change grades, or develop a new curriculum. We model all day long how to teach, but perhaps the most important thing we can model is how to learn. I view a teacher leader as a listener, a model, a facilitator of processes, and a builder of relationships and mutual respect with her students. Creating a positive classroom culture is the key to success.

Teachers are the ones who touch students and interact with them. They have complete power over the process that takes place in the classroom. I teach study skills to students with special needs at Randolph High School, and also job training skills to students with special needs enrolled in the transitional program. When students first enter my classroom, I believe it is important for them to understand that they are special and important. Asking questions and getting to know their likes, dislikes, and learning styles help me make a personal connection with them. By creating an environment of trust within the classroom, I am able to greatly affect student learning.

I provide leadership to my students by creating lessons that incorporate concepts such as respect, tolerance, courage, trust, diversity, and responsibility. Designing lessons that help students make connections to their daily lives can also help students make decisions that reflect their personal values. Often, the students I work with in study skills and the transitional program come to school with various degrees of background knowledge. My responsibility is to provide multiple learning opportunities that are geared toward their learning styles. All students can learn, and certain teacher behaviors motivate students' thinking. These behaviors are often found in the questioning technique used to gather information. I structure questions to promote student thinking. For example, "What do you think causes ...?" "Based on what you know, what can you predict about ...?" These types of questions allow students to understand the material after they had an opportunity to talk about it. As a teacher, I began accepting solutions to problems as plausible, understanding that students take risks in providing answers. I found that the level of anxiety and competition between the students declined. There were no right or wrong answers. Students soon realized that, in Dr. Stewart's class, it was alright to think through a process. Sometimes more than one answer can solve a problem.

I believe that the way I structure my classroom has direct bearing on student behavior, learning, and most importantly, motivation. Students should be active learners and encouraged to use higher-level thinking skills. Lessons should foster creativity and discovery learning, and should foster good problem-solving skills. I like creating situations in the class where students have the opportunity to work in group situations. By giving students a clear objective and a clear set of directions, students are able to engage in meaningful learning. One person may be artistic, another may be an excellent communicator, and another may be able to put pen to paper effectively. Creating multiple assessment models can also be a motivator to students. Not all students are great test takers. Some may require an oral test versus a written test, whereas others may need to demonstrate their understanding of a concept through optional means of assessment. Students are motivated to do well when they truly believe that their teacher understands their learning style and is willing to go that extra distance to help them excel in their academics.

It is important to provide leadership and motivation to students. I believe motivation leads to greater achievement. My goal as an educator is to not only be a leader and motivator for my students, but also to leave a lasting impression of a love for learning on each and every student who enters my classroom.

Eloise Stewart, Ed.D.
Kappa Delta Pi Teacher of Honor
Randolph High School
Randolph, New Jersey

Chances are you will have the opportunity to be a part of a co-teaching team. The most important goal of effective co-teaching is to keep the needs of the students the priority. Cooperation, collaboration, and professionalism are keys to success for a co-teaching team.

Differentiated Instruction

differentiated instruction Instruction that is tailored to the different needs of individual students.

As you know, students in a classroom have many differences. We could say that students are differentiated based on their unique perspectives and their unique abilities. It follows that the instruction teachers provide should be differentiated as well. Under the leadership of Carol Ann Tomlinson, the concept of differentiated instruction is becoming well known. Differentiated instruction is an instructional strategy based on the teacher's awareness of the needs of individual students. It calls for teachers to have "clear learning goals that are rooted in content standards but crafted to ensure student engagement and understanding" (Tomlinson, 2008, p. 26).

How can you differentiate instruction? Perhaps multiple intelligences and learning styles came to mind. That's good! Including different learning styles and multiple intelligences in a lesson is one good way to differentiate the instruction. For each characteristic, we have suggested teaching strategies that acknowledge that characteristic. You saw that there are some common denominators that span all or most of the characteristics. In differentiated instruction, teachers plan and teach lessons that incorporate as many of the strategies as possible to acknowledge the different characteristic of the students in their class. Differentiated instruction includes tailoring content to meet the capabilities, experiences, and interests of the students. Differentiated instruction makes available alternative routes to achieving lesson objectives. Differentiated instruction provides meaningful ways for students to demonstrate their understandings. Differentiated instruction includes variations in the learning environment based on the needs of individual students. Differentiated instruction does not call for teachers to create separate lesson plans for each student. Rather, it asks teachers to look for patterns of need and then group students with similar needs or interests so the teacher can work with these individual groups.

Table 5.3 shows elements of differentiated instruction and their implications.

TABLE 5.3 Critical Elements in a Differentiated Classroom and Their Implications

Goal or Element	Implications for Teachers	Implications for Students
Students need to . . .	*The teacher . . .*	*Students . . .*
Work in small groups with classmates.	• Will ensure that all groups have assignments that work for the group so all students can learn what they need to learn. • Will ensure that each group has clear directions. • Will ensure that students know how to work together effectively. • Will provide directions for moving furniture to allow for a variety of groupings.	• Will focus on what their group should do rather than pay attention to what others are doing. • Will ensure that they understand and follow the directions given to their group. • Will contribute to the effectiveness of their group and ask for help when there is a problem the group cannot solve. • Will monitor their conversations so noise doesn't detract from learning. • Will move furniture smoothly so groups have appropriate spaces to work.
Work with the teacher individually or in small groups.	• Will know what each student requires to learn at a given time so the groups support learning.	• Will be able to start and stop individual and small group work efficiently to meet with the teacher when necessary.

TABLE 5.3 (*Continued*)

Goal or Element	Implications for Teachers	Implications for Students
Students need to . . .	*The teacher . . .*	*Students . . .*
	• Will ensure that student directions are clear and that students have ways to get help when he or she is busy with a small group or individual. • Will keep track of student needs, work, and growth and help students do the same for themselves.	• Will not interrupt the teacher when he or she is working with individuals or groups. • Will know how to get help when the teacher is busy with groups or individuals. • Will keep track of their own learning goals and work.
Spend different amounts of time on a task in order to learn well.	• Will provide a place for students to turn in completed work and get it checked if necessary. • Will provide options for important student work when a task is finished.	• Will follow directions about turning in work or getting it checked when it's finished. • Will work with anchor activities smoothly and effectively when an assignment is completed.
Work with different materials in order to learn well.	• Will provide a variety of materials that work for students' different entry points, including reading needs, interests, and formats. • Will help develop a way to make sure students know which materials to use at a particular time and where materials will be stored.	• Will help make sure materials are cared for and returned to the place they belong after an activity is completed. • Will help the teacher know which materials (or kinds of materials) work best for them as individuals.

Source: From *Leading and Managing A Differentiated Classroom* (p. 59), by Carol Ann Tomlinson & Marica B. Imbeau, Alexandria, VA: ASDC. © 2010 by ASCD. Reprinted with permission. Learn more about ASCD at www.ascd.org.

A Final Word about Unique Perspectives and Abilities

In Chapter 4 and in this chapter, you investigated ways of teaching students with unique perspectives and abilities. In the teaching strategies you considered throughout these chapters, you sought to accomplish several objectives:

- Motivate students.
- Enable students to develop a relationship with the teacher, thereby fostering their relationship with the academic material.
- Enable students to reinforce and satisfy their basic and academic needs.
- Foster learning and achievement.

You have investigated how the teaching strategies suggested for one group of students are similar to those suggested for other groups. Now it is time to put this all together.

Teaching All Students in the Classroom

BUILDING BLOCK
5.9

Prepare a grid. Across the top, list the characteristics of students you investigated in Chapter 4 and in this chapter. Down the left side, list various teaching strategies you suggested. A few examples of teaching strategies are provided to help you get started. The grid will look something like the example that follows.

Teaching Strategy	Cultural Diversity	ADHD	Autism	English Language Learners	Religion	Socioeconomic Status	Gender	Sexual Orientation	Students with Disabilities	Gifted and Talented Students	Multiple Intelligences	Learning Styles
Ensure topics relate to students' lives												
Slow down the pace of the class												
Provide hands-on activities												
Use the Internet												
Prepare charts and diagrams												

- Use check marks to show the characteristic or characteristics for which each strategy is appropriate.
- What teaching strategies seem to be appropriate for *all* students? Identify one or two teaching principles you believe to be most appropriate for teaching all students.

Constructivism and Teaching Students with Unique Abilities

You have investigated many characteristics and perspectives that students bring to the classroom. You have wrestled with ways of teaching to accommodate each of these exceptionalities. You have seen that numerous strategies apply to all students, regardless of exceptionality, and that certain strategies seem appropriate for certain situations. With so many differences in students and so many different ways to teach them, it may seem that the teacher has an impossible and complex job.

In your investigations, you have sought ways to meet students' basic needs and academic needs and ways to help students relate content and material to their own lives, thus making the material meaningful to them and increasing their chances of learning.

This brings us to what we believe is the bottom line in teaching.

David Ausubel wrote, "The single most important factor influencing learning is what the learner already knows" (Ausubel, Novak, and Hanesian, 1978, p. iv). In other words, effective teachers do in their classes exactly what you have been doing in this course: help students relate new material to what they already know.

As we indicated in Chapter 2, Piaget, Dewey, Vygotsky, and numerous others have concluded that knowledge cannot be transmitted from one person to another; people must construct their own understandings and their own knowledge. Learners construct this knowledge as they wrestle with new information and integrate it into their existing knowledge framework. When students are encouraged to relate new information to what they already know, the self is recognized, relevance is established, and learning occurs. This is constructivism. You may recall from your inquiries in Chapter 1 that each activity suggested in this textbook, and indeed this textbook itself, is constructivist in orientation.

©Elizabeth Crews/The Image Works

In a constructivist classroom, all students are actively engaged in learning.

constructivism A learning theory that proposes that students construct their own knowledge by combining information they already have with new information, so that new knowledge takes on personal meaning to the student.

To see firsthand what constructivist teaching and learning are all about, look at how you have been approaching this course. In all instances, you have brought your own knowledge, thoughts, and prior information to the surface before you looked at what others have said. You then combined your existing understanding with new information to form refined, revised, and sometimes new conceptualizations.

Constructing Information

Review the work you have done so far in this course. In what ways were you asked to bring your existing knowledge, ideas, and understanding to the surface of your mind? In what ways was new information provided? In what ways were you asked to combine the new information with information you already had to form new and refined conceptualizations?

How is the work you have done so far constructivist in nature?

BUILDING BLOCK

5.10

Constructivist educators, including the authors of this textbook, believe that all learners must construct meaning for themselves—that learning can take place only when it is connected to each individual's already existing knowledge, experience, or conceptualizations. What students learn in school is not a copy of what they observe and hear in class; it is the result of their own thinking and processing.

In an address to the Holmes Group in 1987, Judith Lanier, then dean of the College of Education at Michigan State University and president of the Holmes Group, made these remarks:

> Competent teachers jump into the heads of their students to see how they are constructing information. ... Competent teachers combine content knowledge with a flexible and creative mind, constructing and reconstructing subject matter in multiple ways as they teach the children. They get inside the children's heads. They listen to them. They remain alert to students' interpretations and the ways they are making sense. (Lanier, 1987)

This is the essence of constructivism. Teachers who want to ensure learning teach in this way.

BUILDING BLOCK
5.11

My Philosophy of Education Revisited

Part I of this textbook dealt with yourself as a future teacher. Part II has dealt with students.

Revisit the philosophy of education you prepared at the end of Chapter 2. Do you still have the same beliefs? Would you like to make some changes?

Rewrite your philosophy to reflect your thinking at this point in your investigation of American education.

■ SUMMARY

- The Individuals with Disabilities Education Act (IDEA) outlines requirements that must be met to provide a "full and appropriate education" for students with disabilities.

- Attention deficit/hyperactivity disorder (ADHD) is a serious disorder that affects many students. Teaching accommodations include strategies for gaining and maintaining students' attention.

- The incidence of autism is increasing and teachers need to know how to teach students with autism. Techniques include being very detailed, focusing on the students' areas of interest, and providing appropriate avenues for their cognitive excursions.

- Human intelligence ranges from low to high, and most students can be taught in the regular classroom regardless of their basic intelligence, although a few adjustments in teaching strategies may be appropriate.

- According to Howard Gardner, people have several different kinds of intelligences, the relative strengths of which strongly influence how they learn and demonstrate their achievement.

- People have different learning styles; they are visual, auditory, and tactile–kinesthetic. These learning styles correspond to the ways students find are most comfortable in approaching learning tasks. Basic needs and fundamental academic needs are the same for everyone, regardless of any differences students may exhibit. Although a few specific teaching techniques apply to specific student needs, the techniques of teaching are essentially the same for everyone if teachers seek to foster relevance.

- Constructivist teaching acknowledges individual abilities in that learning experiences are tailored to meet the needs of each individual student.

We trust you will always bear in mind that the best teachers are those who can tailor the instruction to meet the needs of *all* their students—no matter who those students are.

■ Key Terms and Concepts

Assistive technology, 135
Attention deficit disorder (ADD), 132
Attention deficit/hyperactivity disorder (ADHD), 132
Autism, 133
Bell-shaped curve, 137
Cognitive ability, 136
Constructivism, 153
Co-teaching, 148

Differentiated instruction, 150
Dyslexia, 132
Exceptional students, 127
Full inclusion, 129
Gifted and talented student, 138
Inclusion, 129
Individualized education program (IEP), 128
Learning disability, 131
Learning modality, 145

Learning style, 145
Mainstreaming, 129
Normal curve, 137
Resource classroom, 130
Response to intervention (RTI), 131
Special education, 127
Theory of multiple intelligences, 142

Construct and Apply

1. Referring to your investigations of humanism in Chapter 2 and Chapter 3, would Rogers and Maslow approve of the strategies you suggested in Building Block 5.9 for meeting the needs of students with unique perspectives and abilities? Why or why not?
2. How might your own learning preferences affect your teaching style?
3. What common teaching strategies have you identified that would help *all* students achieve in your classroom?
4. Consider this scene: A student in a traditional classroom approaches his teacher. He says, "The gifted students are going on a field trip to the zoo. The special education kids are having a party where they get to dress up like jungle animals. I get to come in here and take notes." What is the implication? To what degree are the methods used for gifted and special education students appropriate in the traditional classroom?

Deconstructing the Standards

1. Recall the InTASC Standards associated with the objectives for this chapter:

   InTASC Standard #2: Learning Differences reads, "The teacher uses understanding of individual differences and diverse cultures and communities to ensure inclusive learning environments that enable each learner to meet high standards."

   InTASC Standard #8: Instructional Strategies reads, "The teacher understands and uses a variety of instructional strategies to encourage learners to develop deep understanding of content areas and their connections, and to build skills to apply knowledge in meaningful ways."

   a. What part(s) of these standards does this chapter address?

   b. How will the concepts in this chapter help you apply these standards as a teacher?

2. Use your favorite search engine to find your state's standards for certification. When you find it, bookmark the site; you will refer to it often during this course.

   a. How do your conclusions about teaching learners with different abilities compare to the state standards?

   b. How do the InTASC Standards compare to your state's certification standards?

   c. Do you believe the degree of representation concerning educational philosophy is adequate in your state certification standards? Why or why not?

Your Portfolio

Use your work in the activities suggested in this chapter to show your developing awareness of best practices in teaching.

Summarize one or more instances from your field experience where you or your cooperating teacher used certain teaching techniques to accommodate the needs of students with unique abilities.

Volunteer to tutor a student with special needs and reflect on your experiences.

Education CourseMate Resources

Check out this text's Education CourseMate website (at www.cengagebrain.com) for more information about working with students with diverse abilities, interactive study tools, and useful resources. You will find the TeachSource Videos, a guide for doing field experiences, glossary flash cards, activities, tutorial quizzes, direct links to all of the websites mentioned in the chapter, and more, including material about locus of control and field dependence/field independence, both which are additional student differences.

PART III School

IN PART I, you investigated your *self*, your experiences with teaching and learning, and your thoughts about excellence in teaching and learning. Your ideas and beliefs informed your initial philosophy of education. You saw that there are several different ways of looking at education, depending on the expected outcomes. Part II helped you see that all students have common personal, cognitive, and social needs, and that teachers must consider the unique characteristics, perspectives, and abilities each student brings to the classroom to identify effective teaching strategies that facilitate equality and achievement.

In Part III, you will broaden your sphere of inquiry to include the schools themselves. You will investigate the purposes of schools, how schools are structured to fulfill their purposes, how students work within these structures to fulfill their needs, and how teachers work within these structures to meet the needs of the students they serve.

CHAPTER 6

Purposes of Schools

CHAPTER 6 INVITES you to explore different kinds of schools and their purposes. Schools can have many different purposes, depending on several factors. You will identify some of the factors that influence schools' purposes, and you will examine how these factors exert their influence on the purpose of the place we call "school."

Schools' purposes range from developing students so they will fit in with existing society to providing students with the skills needed to change society, from mastering basic skills and concepts to keeping up with the times, from preparing students to enter the work force to preparing them to affect culture and society. Some purposes seem to be common to all schools, even though individual schools may go about accomplishing these goals in different ways.

On the surface, it might seem that schools all have the same underlying purposes—that they all have the same basic goals. But do they? Just as students have common academic needs, schools have common purposes. However, as each student brings unique characteristics and perspectives to the classroom, each school also has unique characteristics and perspectives. In this chapter, you will explore these factors and the ways in which they determine the basic purposes of schools.

Common Purposes of Schools

To start off, look at your thoughts about the purposes of schools.

Questions about the Purposes of Schools

BUILDING BLOCK 6.1

Consider the age group of students you wish to teach.

- What are the primary purposes of sending these children to school? Bear in mind that there are many ways to think about this issue. Try not to rely too heavily on personal experiences and thoughts because there are many kinds of schools that exist in addition to the kinds you attended, and there are many personal experiences in addition to the ones you have had.

- From your list of primary purposes, write a statement of what you believe are the major purposes of schools.

- Compare your responses with those of other students in your class. What are the commonalities? What are the differences?

Schools serve communities, and the purpose of a school reflects the community it serves. Most communities are made of businesses, industries, services, government, residents, families, and friends, in addition to the faculty, administration, and students in the schools. In deciding on the purpose of its schools, a group comprising representatives from all parts of the community, including educators, debate several important questions, ultimately resolving these issues into a singularity of purpose. The result is a statement of the purpose of the school, which is similar to statements developed by parallel groups across the country but that differs in the way the purpose reflects the individual community. Many government agencies, blue-ribbon panels, and educators have described what they believe are the fundamental purposes of schools.

Purposes of Schools as Seen by Government Agencies

The federal government has officially been in the education business since 1953, when President Dwight D. Eisenhower established the Department of Health, Education, and Welfare and named Oveta Culp Hobby its first secretary. In 1979, President Jimmy Carter formed the first cabinet-level Department of Education and appointed Shirley Mount Hufstedler as its secretary.

A Nation At Risk

One of the first attempts of the federal government to identify the purposes of schools came in the form of a report titled *A Nation At Risk,* published in 1983. This paper was the result of two years of work by the National Commission on Excellence in Education created by the secretary of education in the Ronald Reagan administration. The report started with one short sentence, "Our nation is at risk," meaning that the United States was at risk for losing its place as the world's leader in educational attainments. (This report is discussed in more detail in Chapter 10.)

Goals 2000

In 1989, following the publication of *A Nation At Risk,* President George H. W. Bush and the nation's governors met, for the first time in the history of the United States, to discuss national educational policy. Their discussion was summarized in the now-famous Goals 2000, which comprised six national goals for public education. Two additional goals—one dealing with teacher education and professional development and the other with parental participation—were added to the original six goals, resulting in an expanded Goals 2000: Educate America Act that was passed into law in 1994 under the Clinton administration.

As listed in the act, the goals are as follows:

1. *School readiness.* By the year 2000, all children in America will start school ready to learn.
2. *School completion.* By the year 2000, the high school graduation rate will increase to at least 90 percent.
3. *Student achievement and citizenship.* By the year 2000, all students will leave grades 4, 8, and 12 having demonstrated competency over challenging subject matter, including English, mathematics, science, foreign languages, civics and government, economics, arts, history, and geography, and every school in the United States will ensure that all students learn to use their minds well, so they may be prepared for responsible citizenship, further learning, and productive employment in our nation's modern economy.
4. *Teacher education and professional development.* By the year 2000, the nation's teaching force will have access to programs for the continued improvement of their professional skills and the opportunity to acquire the knowledge and skills needed to instruct and prepare all U.S. students for the next century.
5. *Mathematics and science.* By the year 2000, U.S. students will be first in the world in mathematics and science achievement.
6. *Adult literacy and lifelong learning.* By the year 2000, every adult American will be literate and will possess the knowledge and skills necessary to compete in a global economy and exercise the rights and responsibilities of citizenship.
7. *Safe, disciplined, and alcohol- and drug-free schools.* By the year 2000, every school in the United States will be free of drugs, violence, and the unauthorized presence of firearms and alcohol and will offer a disciplined environment conducive to learning.
8. *Parental participation.* By the year 2000, every school will promote partnerships that will increase parental involvement and participation in promoting social, emotional, and academic growth of children.

 You can access the full text of *A Nation At Risk* and Goals 2000, progress reports, and supplemental material through direct links on the Education CourseMate website.

Goals 2000 provided purpose and direction for U.S. education. Although we have passed the year 2000, Goals 2000 continues to be influential.

From these statements, what do you suppose were the federal government's ideas about the purposes of school? Which of the school purposes outlined in Goals 2000 are the same as the school purposes you identified in Building Block 6.1?

No Child Left Behind

The No Child Left Behind Act of 2001 (NCLB) was passed into law in 2001, under the George W. Bush administration. This act constituted the reauthorization of the Elementary and Secondary Education Act (ESEA) originally signed into law during the Lyndon Johnson administration in 1965. (You were introduced to this law in Chapter 1.) Although NCLB is due to be replaced, its provisions remain in force and its effects on education continue to be strong.

One principle of NCLB is increased accountability for states, school districts, and schools for students' achievement. This provision calls for challenging state standards and annual testing in reading and mathematics for all students in grades 3 through 8 (U.S. Department of Education, 2002a), and testing all students in science at least once in the elementary grades, middle grades, and high school grades. The pressure for students to perform well on these standardized achievement tests (that have been implemented in response to the accountability provision of NCLB) is tremendous. Indeed, the consequences of children's failure to perform on these tests are so serious that many teachers and schools do not want to stray too far from emphasizing the basic skills the tests assess. As a result, most elementary schools have the common goal of emphasizing the so-called three Rs: reading, writing, and arithmetic.

Concerns exist about this emphasis:

1. Other subjects, such as science, social studies, art, music, and physical education, take a secondary position or are left out completely because of the time devoted to the three Rs.

2. There is little consideration for adapting teaching to individual needs; the pressure for success on standardized achievement tests appears greater than the need to accommodate children's individual needs.

3. There is little consideration for the development of social skills.

Many people see the No Child Left Behind Act as challenging schools' independence, stifling teachers' creativity and teaching abilities, and placing tremendous pressure on schools and teachers to demonstrate increasing standardized achievement test scores. Thus, the term *high-stakes testing* has risen to prominence in educational discussions.

The purpose of schools, according to the federal government, includes teaching students the three Rs—reading, writing, and arithmetic, as demonstrated in legislation like the No Child Left Behind Act and Goals 2000.

Blueprint for Reform and NCLB Waivers

NCLB was scheduled for reauthorization by Congress in 2007, but as of this writing, it has not occurred. However, President Barack Obama and Secretary of Education Arne Duncan have new and different ideas about the way the federal government should support education.

These new and different ideas began with Race to the Top, funded by the American Recovery and Reinvestment Act of 2009, and awarded to states on a competitive basis.

This program emphasizes four areas:

■ Decisions about teaching children based on data
■ Talent(s)
■ Turning around chronically low-performing schools
■ Tailoring the teaching to the needs of the community

The plan for the actual reauthorization of ESEA is embodied in *The Blueprint for Reform* (U.S. Department of Education, 2010a), presented by President Obama in

March 2010. The *Blueprint* "builds on significant reforms already made in response to the American Recovery and Reinvestment Act of 2009 [Race to the Top]," (ibid. p. 3) and introduces major changes "with the goal of becoming the most educated country in the world" (Richardson, 2009, p. 24).

The *Blueprint for Reform* emphasizes four areas:

1. Improving teacher and principal effectiveness to ensure that every person has a great teacher and every school has a great leader
2. Providing information to families to help them evaluate and improve their schools, and to educators to help them improve their students' learning
3. Implementing college- and career-ready standards and developing assessments aligned with those standards
4. Improving student learning and achievement in the lowest-performing U.S. schools by providing intensive support and effective interventions

Of particular note is the desire of the administration to shift the focus of the standardized tests to measuring the growth of each student, regardless of the performance at which he starts.

There are concerns with this new proposal. The National Education Association (NEA) and the American Federation of Teachers feel that the *Blueprint* signals an increase in federal control and that, although it provides teachers with more responsibility, it provides no additional authority. In addition, the professional organizations see a continued reliance on standardized tests that, as we have seen, are intrinsically unreliable measures of achievement.

Because the No Child Left Behind Act has not yet been reauthorized, and because schools need to know what the "rules" are for the current school year, the secretary of education has established a policy of granting waivers for certain provisions of NCLB. To be granted a waiver for exemption from NCLB, states must make a formal application that is reviewed by a committee of peers; Secretary Duncan makes the final decision.

The topic of federal influence on education is hotly debated, and, to the extent possible, you should keep yourself apprised of happenings with respect to the federal laws.

 You can access the No Child Left Behind Act home page and a website that has the full text of the act, progress reports, and supplemental material through direct links on the Education CourseMate website.

Purposes of Schools as Seen in Mission Statements

mission statement A written public statement crafted by the stakeholders in an organization (such as a school) that identifies the organization's perceived purpose.

One place to get a glimpse into the purpose of schools is in their mission statements. It makes sense that the teachers, administrators, parents, officials, and the interested public might be involved in writing such statements. And, it is interesting to note how the statements differ from school to school, indicating variations in purpose.

BUILDING BLOCK
6.2

School Mission Statements

Find the mission statements of two or three public and private elementary, middle, or secondary schools in your area. Use the Internet to search for the school's name, and then look for its mission statement. Sometimes this document is called a *mission* or a *mission statement*; sometimes it is called a statement of *vision*, a *philosophy*, *values,* or a similar term. You may wish to examine the mission statement of a school you attended so you can compare that mission statement with your actual experiences at that school. (Of course, the time difference may be a factor if the mission statement was written since you attended the school—but the school's essential mission probably has not changed significantly.)

In the mission statement, look for these factors:

1. The school's predominant educational philosophy or approach
2. What the school expects of its students as a result of attendance
3. How the school provides for students' basic, academic, and developmental needs
4. Any special population mentioned
5. Any particular curriculum mentioned
6. Any particular instructional methods mentioned
7. Attention given to the needs of the community the school serves

From your investigations, determine the school's primary purpose. How does the mission statement of a school you attended compare with your experience at that school?

Mission statements can inform us about the purposes that individual schools see for themselves. A school's mission statement is a short document that describes the school's purpose, focusing on what the school wants to be, what it wants to do, and what its values and principles are. It reflects the shared vision and values of the learning community, including the faculty and administration. It becomes the criterion by which everything that happens in the school is measured. A mission statement is a living document that the learning community continually reviews, refines, and keeps up to date to reflect current thinking about the school. (Recall that, in Chapter 2, you read the mission statements of several schools to infer the philosophies that guided those schools' operations.)

Anyone reading a school's mission statement can learn the school's primary goals, how these goals are implemented, and what the school expects its students and graduates to know and be able to do. Although there may be some discrepancy between a school's mission statement and its actual practice, the mission statement specifies why the school exists and establishes the scope of its activities (Dottin, 2001). It provides a description of the present and a direction for the future.

Your explorations thus far have enabled you to identify some common goals or purposes of schools and schooling. Did you find that some of your ideas were different from those of your classmates and those cited in the preceding literature and quotations? What influences your ideas? How strongly do your personal experiences and philosophy of education influence your ideas about the purposes of school? You bring your own unique perspectives to your ideas.

The Purposes of Schools

BUILDING BLOCK 6.3

You have seen many different thoughts about the purposes of schools from several different points of view. Look at the purposes you identified in Building Block 6.1 and make any changes you think are appropriate. Write a revised school purpose statement.

Developing a Mission
Bev Abrams

Courtesy of Bev Abrams

I was the sixth person hired to teach a class of first through third graders in a brand new, open structured, constructivist public school, the Santa Barbara Charter School. Teachers left as quickly as they were hired, and over 50 percent of the original families had abandoned the school. All had invested tremendous energy into opening the doors for the start of school, but there was no coherent educational vision or definition of staff and parent roles.

Within days of my hire, the small staff sat down to draw up a document that defined the role of teachers in our school; within months, we also wrote a mission statement. The school community readily adopted both statements because all parties were having trouble living in the programmatic vacuum that existed. The school's founding teacher provided our initial inspiration with her passion for teaching academics through the arts. The other teachers lent a deep commitment to progressive education and a love of wordsmithing to the process. Once we articulated the school's mission, conflict dissipated. By the third year, families were choosing our school with some understanding of what we offered. We found it easier to focus our limited resources on the things that mattered.

The mission statement revealed the school's core values. The school was begun as a parent cooperative, hence the statement that the school would build the interests and skills of both students and their families. As progressive educators, we believed that good education is an ongoing process, rather than a moment in time during which students demonstrate their mastery of a collection of facts, so we stated that we would "nurture lifelong learners." Finally, we consciously chose to list "arts, academics, and relationships" in that order because we wanted "arts" and "relationships" to stand out. In light of the standardization of education in the United States, our articulated commitment to arts, academics, and relationships has kept us from being swept along with the radical narrowing of public school curriculum.

Our mission statement provides coherence, both in individual classrooms and to the school as a whole. Decision making about the use of classroom time, hiring of specialists, and purchase of supplies often refers to our mission. Though some arts opportunities vary from year to year, all elementary students participate in a fiber arts program and all students are part of an annual class play. Visual arts and music are part of the weekly curriculum, and dance and recorder are taught in some grades. Arts are taught both for their own sake and to develop other academic understandings. At times, an entire class does an art activity; at other times, just a few students are engaged. Teachers, students, and parents initiate art experiences in the classroom.

Time is devoted to cultivating relationships and building community. Communication and conflict resolution skills are facilitated based on schoolwide policy and curriculum. Class meetings are held in the lower school program, and students meet in councils in the middle school program. The first thing that visitors notice about our school is that "both children and adults are very kind." Many families have found that family dynamics shift as they use the communication strategies that children and parents learn at Santa Barbara Charter School. The school recently received a grant based on the work that we do in this area.

We have had several opportunities to revisit our mission. The first time was when we planned our expansion to middle school. All of the stakeholders were involved, and a committee member who was a professional writer drafted the final statement. Unfortunately, this statement faded into oblivion because it was too long to remember or use when making daily decisions or promoting the school. Additionally, we found that having a separate mission statement distracted from creating a cohesive kindergarten through eighth-grade program. A few years later, we looked at the match between the mission and implementation during our authentic assessment process. At that time, we examined each area of the mission and evaluated how well the school was implementing its mission based on a parent survey, observation by an outside evaluator, teachers' plan books, and student feedback. Happily, we found that there was a high degree of consistency between the mission and the education our students were receiving. Most recently, a financial crisis forced us to look again at our program, in light of both finances and our mission during a process of long-term strategic planning (LTSP). Ultimately, the recommendations of the LTSP committee reflected a commitment to the values stated in the mission, and these were considered when planning the budget.

Our mission statement has served as the organizing principle at Santa Barbara Charter School. Other documents, such as our education plan, further articulate our vision. Although our mission doesn't really convey the intensity with which we work to keep children at the center of all decisions, it does help us plan the program and provision the school to best meet students' needs and enrich their lives.

Santa Barbara Charter School Mission Statement:

Santa Barbara Charter School nurtures lifelong learners by cultivating the interest and building the skills of both students and their families in the arts, academics, and relationships.

Bev Abrams
Santa Barbara Charter School
Santa Barbara, California

© Cengage Learning 2014

Factors Influencing the Purposes of Schools

Let us now explore the effects specific influences and unique perspectives have on schools' purposes.

Unique Perspectives and Purposes of Schools

BUILDING BLOCK 6.4

What influences the purposes of schools? Take a moment to brainstorm, listing as many factors as you can think of that might influence a school's stated purpose. Write these down to compare to those considered in this chapter.

Influence of Grade Level on School Purpose

One factor that influences the purposes a school sees for itself is its span of grade levels. When we think of grade levels, we often think in terms of elementary, middle, junior high, and secondary schools. Elementary schools normally encompass the lower grades, typically preschool through fifth or sixth grade. Junior high schools usually include grades six (if not included in elementary school), seven, and eight. Middle schools normally include grades 6, 7, and 8. And finally, secondary schools ordinarily include grades 9 through 12. Figure 6.1 depicts the general structure of education in the United States.

How do the purposes of schools reflect the grade levels they include?

Elementary Schools

Purposes and Goals of Elementary Schools

BUILDING BLOCK 6.5

Recall some of the activities in which you participated while in elementary school. What were the purposes of these activities? (You may wish to refer to Building Block 6.1.)

- What do you think was the basic purpose of your elementary school?
- What do you think are the basic purposes of a typical elementary school?
- How does the elementary school meet the needs of the students who attend it?
- What does the typical elementary school expect of its students as a result of attending school?

Historically, elementary schools were established to teach children the three Rs: reading, writing, and arithmetic. Children needed to know how to read so that they could read the Bible. They needed to be able to write and do basic mathematics so that they could carry out their future livelihoods of farming or managing a small business.

As the American colonies expanded, towns, cities, businesses, and transportation all grew. The need for educated citizens also grew, and the country needed more and better educated individuals to promote social progress. Therefore, secondary schools and colleges were established to provide education at higher levels. Accordingly, it became the primary purpose of most elementary schools to prepare children for success in these higher grades, teaching them how to think and readying them for a useful and productive life of citizenship in the society in which they would live. (See Chapter 10.)

These purposes of typical elementary schools seem to be the same today: namely, to prepare children for success in higher grades, teach them how to think, and equip them for a useful and productive life of citizenship in the society in which they will live. Among the skills children master in the elementary school are reading, writing, and mathematics. These skills are considered paramount today, and children's success in these areas has become the number-one priority in elementary schools. As you have seen, the No Child

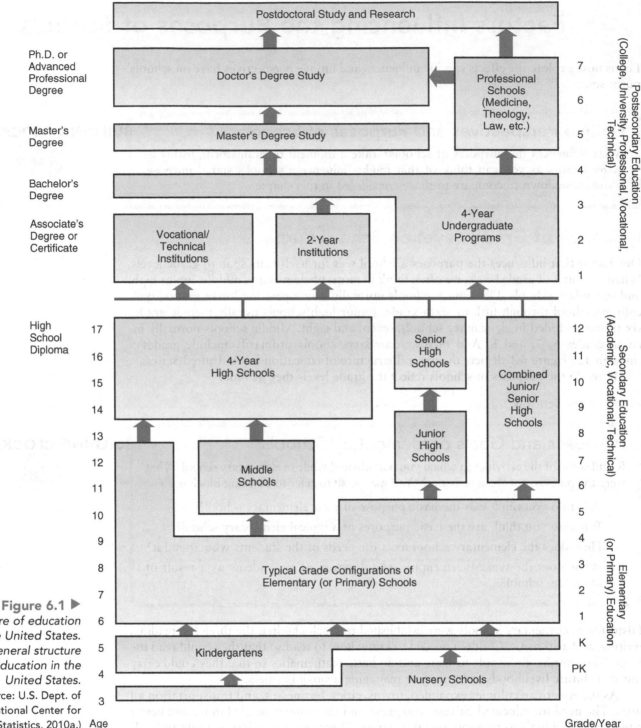

Figure 6.1 ▶
The structure of education in the United States. General structure of education in the United States. (Source: U.S. Dept. of Education, National Center for Education Statistics, 2010a.)

Left Behind legislation of 2001 requires that all public school students achieve grade-appropriate proficiency in reading and mathematics.

Middle Schools

Did you go to a junior high school or a middle school? Think about the name of each: *junior high* school and *middle* school. If you know what a high school is like, what do suppose a *junior* high school is like? And, if students go to a *middle* school after they go to elementary school and before they go to high school, what do you suppose a middle school is like?

Adolescent Needs and the Purposes and Goals of Middle Schools

Think about students in grades 6, 7, and 8:

- What are their ages?
- Name some characteristics that you associate with these young adolescents.
- What activities—desirable and undesirable—interest young adolescents?
- How do you think these characteristics and interests could affect academic needs?
- Recall Piaget's cognitive and Erikson's psychosocial developmental stages. What are some unique characteristics and needs of adolescents?
- What implications do these adolescent developmental stages have for teaching and learning?
- What do you suppose would be the primary purpose of a school designed with young adolescents in mind?

Many people do not differentiate between middle schools and junior high schools. However, the two are fundamentally different and have fundamentally different purposes. Junior high schools first appeared in the early 1900s, in response to overcrowding in high schools. At that time, elementary schools consisted of grades 1 through 6, and secondary schools consisted of grades 7 through 12. The first junior high schools took over grades 7 and 8 and functioned essentially as high schools did, but with a younger population of students. The main purpose of junior high school was to bridge the gap between elementary school and high school.

The middle school, on the other hand, recognizes that early adolescent learners have unique needs unlike those found in either elementary school or high school. The middle school was developed to align the educational environment with these unique needs.

The 1989 Carnegie report, *Turning Points: Preparing American Youth for the 21st Century* (Carnegie Council on Adolescent Development, 1989), identified the unique characteristics of young adolescents and described this population as one struggling with tremendous opportunities for social, intellectual, and psychological development, and also with vulnerability and uncertainty. The report concluded that existing junior high schools did not meet the needs of young adolescents and that radical reform was needed, suggesting a purpose and direction for this reform:

Effective middle schools provide adolescent students with rich learning environments customized according to students' unique physical, emotional, social, and cognitive needs.

> The middle grade school proposed here is profoundly different from many schools today. It focuses squarely on the characteristics and needs of young adolescents. It creates a community of adults and young people embedded in networks of support and responsibility that enhance the commitment of students of learning. (Carnegie Council on Adolescent Development, 1989, p. 36)

The middle school became the preferred school concept for the education of young adolescents, almost completely replacing the junior high school. The Association for Middle Level Education (AMLE, formerly called the National Middle School Association; 2010) expanded the original concept of focusing on student needs by suggesting a set of specific educational objectives to guide the development of middle schools' purposes and missions. AMLE recommends that the middle school provide learning experiences for adolescents that achieve the following goals:

- Address adolescents' varied intellectual, physical, social, emotional, and moral development
- Help them make sense of themselves and the world around them
- Be highly integrated and connected to life
- Include adolescents' questions, needs, developmental issues, and ideas
- Involve them in rich and significant knowledge about the world
- Open doors to new ideas that evoke curiosity, the desire to explore, and at times, awe and wonder
- Challenge students and encourage them to take maximum advantage of educational opportunities
- Develop caring, responsible, and ethical citizens who practice democratic principles

 You can access the home page of the Association for Middle Level Education through a direct link on the Education CourseMate website.

As you can see, much of what is advocated as the purpose of the middle school recognizes the unique needs and characteristics that accompany being an adolescent.

Secondary Schools

You may have wonderful memories of high school, but then again, maybe not. Certainly, high school offered a variety of experiences for everyone who attended. But what do you suppose is the purpose of high school?

BUILDING BLOCK 6.7

Purposes and Goals of Secondary Schools

Recall some of the activities in which you participated while in high school:

- What were the purposes of those activities?
- How were these activities different from those in junior high school or middle school?
- What do you think are the basic purposes of a typical secondary school?
- How does the secondary school meet the needs of the students who attend it?
- What does the typical secondary school expect of its students as a result of having attended school?

High schools as we know them—free, public, and open to all—have been around since the 1800s. Recall what you know about American society at that time. What happened to industry and the economy in the 19th century? What would people need to know and do to live and thrive during that time? How might this affect the purpose of education beyond elementary school?

After the Civil War, a demand arose for workers who possessed the knowledge and skills needed to work in a society marked by industrial growth. There was also an influx of immigrants who needed education in the ideals of the United States, their new country, in addition to the knowledge and skills needed for the marketplace. High schools responded to these needs with practical curricula whose purpose was to educate the masses (Webb, Metha, and Jordan, 2000).

Today's high schools serve a more comprehensive purpose, addressing a variety of educational goals and representing all aspects of society. As a nation, we regularly examine the purpose of our secondary schools and often engage in debates about whether these schools should prepare students for college or careers. The secondary school is the last level of schooling for students who do not continue to college or who do not complete some other postsecondary education, such as a trade school. As such, most secondary schools have two purposes: one for students who will go to college, and one for those who will not go to college. Most high schools have curricula that include a college preparatory program, a basic education program for those choosing not to continue their education past high school, a vocational or industrial education program, and programs that prepare support personnel for business (Webb Metha, and Jordan, 2000).

However, in the past few years, there has been an emerging consensus that all students should graduate from high school and then go on to some sort of higher education—college or university, community college, two-year college, trade school, and the like (Balfanz, 2009). It is probable that we will see changes in stated purposes of high schools as this consensus builds. For example, New York State is reforming its high school graduation requirements based on a revised high school general purpose of "college and career readiness" (George, 2011, p. 1).

Influence of School Location on Its Purpose

Another factor that influences a school's purposes is school location. The location of a school has a great influence on its purpose, as envisioned by its community, faculty, and administration. For example, consider the school system in Oak Ridge, Tennessee. Oak Ridge is the home of the Oak Ridge National Laboratories, established in 1943 as a site of the Manhattan Project and charged with producing the fuel for the first atomic bomb. As you might imagine, many of the students in the local schools have at least one parent with an advanced degree in science. How do you think this context affects the purposes the Oak Ridge schools see for themselves?

The National Center for Education Statistics (2011a, p. B-3) has identified 12 general locations of public schools:

- *City, large:* A territory inside an urbanized area with a population of 250,000 or more
- *City, midsize:* A territory inside an urbanized area with a population of less than 250,000
- *City, small:* A territory inside an urbanized area with a population of less than 100,000
- *Suburb, large:* A territory outside a principal city and inside an urbanized area with a population of 250,000 or more
- *Suburb, midsize:* A territory outside a principal city and inside an urbanized area with population between 100,000 and 250,000
- *Suburb, small:* A territory outside a principal city and inside an urbanized area with a population less than 100,000
- *Town, fringe:* A territory inside an urban cluster[1] that is less than 10 miles from an urbanized area
- *Town, distant:* A territory inside an urban cluster that is 10 to 35 miles from an urbanized area
- *Town, remote:* A territory inside an urban cluster that is more than 35 miles from an urbanized area

---

[1]An urban cluster is a geographic area consisting of a central core and adjacent to densely settled territories with a combined population of between 2,500 and 49,999 people and a population density of at least 1,000 people per square mile (U.S. Department of Transportation, 2003).

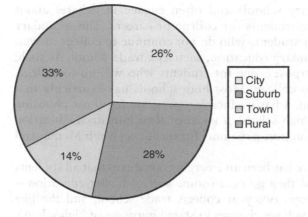

Figure 6.2 ▶
Percent of U.S. Schools by
General Locale, 2009–2010
(Source: National Center for
Education Statistics, 2011a).
© Cengage Learning 2014

26%

33%

14%

28%

☐ City
▨ Suburb
☐ Town
▨ Rural

■ *Rural, fringe:* An area designated as "rural" by the U.S. Bureau of the Census that is less than 5 miles from an urban cluster

■ *Rural, distant:* An area designated as "rural" by the U.S. Bureau of the Census that is 5 to 25 miles from an urban cluster

■ *Rural, remote:* An area designated as "rural" by the U.S. Bureau of the Census that is more than 25 miles from an urban cluster

Statistics are aggregated into the four main categories of city, suburb, town, and rural. In the 2009–2010 school year, there were 88,214 public schools in the United States (Chen, 2011). The schools were distributed by location as follows:

■ City: 26 percent

■ Suburb: 28 percent

■ Town: 14 percent

■ Rural: 33 percent

School location can influence the school's purpose. In small rural areas, the schools often serve fewer students. What might be the purpose of this rural school? In larger urban area schools, more students are served and the community may dictate the purpose. Would this urban school provide more academic opportunities than its rural counterpart? Why?

This distribution is shown in graphic form in Figure 6.2.

As you have seen, a school's mission or purpose reflects the desires and needs of the community it serves. Consider a school in a small city or a large suburb. What population would this school serve? What needs would the population have? Urban schools tend to have larger enrollments and a higher concentration of students from low-income families than rural schools. Many of these students have difficulty speaking English and are thought to have less supportive home environments and less positive school experiences than students from other schools. However, urban schools' larger enrollments and greater

student diversity enable these schools to offer a wide variety of programs and specialties, helping to offset student disadvantages. What do you suppose are the primary purposes of schools in urban communities?

Enrollments are smaller in rural schools than in urban schools. Many rural areas are experiencing population loss, and schools in such areas find it difficult to provide students with the opportunities for higher-education preparation that are available in urban schools. What value do you think rural schools place on preparation for higher education? DeYoung (1995) notes that although statistics may portray rural areas as disadvantaged, rural populations tend to place a higher value on keeping family members nearby than on them leaving the area for high-paying jobs or careers. Indeed, Seal and Harmon (1995) noted that in rural areas, the school may become a focal point for the town, suggesting that the community may value extracurricular activities more than academic achievement. From this, what can we conclude about the comparisons of basic purposes of urban and rural schools?

Nontraditional Schools

A third factor that influences a school's purposes lies in the school's basic function. In addition to the traditional elementary, middle, and secondary school configurations, many specialized schools have become prominent. These specialized schools are particularly attractive to people who have specific goals or needs. Examples include the following:

- Charter schools
- Magnet schools
- For-profit schools
- Home schools
- Alternative schools
- Vocational schools
- Private schools
- Online and virtual schools

Charter Schools

Charter schools are public schools that operate with freedom from one or more of the regulations that apply to traditional public schools. Charter schools enjoy a degree of autonomy not available to other schools; in return, they are accountable for producing positive academic results. Charters, granted by state educational agencies, typically last for three to five years and are renewable. The primary goals of charter schools are as follows:

- To realize a specific educational vision, such as focusing on a particular subject or focusing on interdisciplinary curricula without regard to subject-matter boundaries
- To gain autonomy so faculty and administrators can provide educational services they believe best serve the needs of their school's specific population
- To serve a special population in curriculum, methodological approaches, or both

In the 2009–2010 academic year, there were 4,952 charter schools in the United States, equivalent to 5 percent of the total number of public schools (National Center for Education Statistics, 2011a). A hybrid model that combines the face-to-face instruction of charter schools with online instruction is gaining momentum and will likely replace the total brick-and-mortar charter schools of today (Quillen, 2012). States with provisions for charter schools are shown in Figure 6.3.

charter school A school that has been granted permission by state educational agencies to operate with freedom from one or more of the regulations that apply to traditional public schools.

▶❚ TeachSource Video

View the TeachSource ABC News Video, "Rethinking How Kids Learn: KIPP (Knowledge is Power Program) Schools Use Effective Schools Correlates." KIPP schools are teaching students in ways that guarantee success. This small network of charter schools is sending students to college at an outstanding rate. After watching the video, answer the following questions:

1. What is the KIPP school's policy about homework?
2. What characteristics are needed for successful teachers in KIPP schools?
3. What do the KIPP schools believe is the chief motivator of their students?

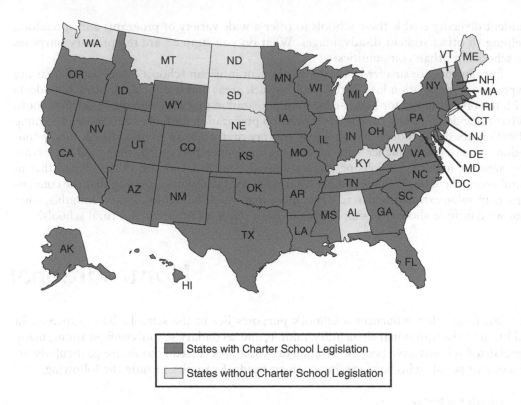

Figure 6.3 ▶
States with charter school legislation.
(From National Charter School Directory from the Center for Education Reform, 2009)
© Cengage Learning 2014

☐ States with Charter School Legislation

☐ States without Charter School Legislation

BUILDING BLOCK
6.8

Charter Schools in Your State

What are the provisions for charter schools in your state? (Go to the website of your state Department of Education or your local school system.)

What are the laws, rules, and regulations governing charter schools in your state?

If your state does not yet recognize the charter school concept, what steps, if any, are being taken in this direction?

Magnet Schools

magnet school A school that focuses on specific curricular areas—such as the arts, math, or science—to attract students with special aptitudes and interests in those areas.

Magnet schools focus on specific curricular areas to attract students with special aptitudes and interests that the school can foster (hence the term *magnet* school). Magnet schools are school choice options that provide the parents or the students themselves the opportunity to choose the programs best suited to their interests and abilities.). Because magnet school programs reside in specific schools (and not every school) in a district, they normally accept students from outside their traditional school boundaries; school transportation sometimes is provided and sometimes is the responsibility of the parents. Further, most magnet schools require applications for admission. The primary purpose of magnet schools is to provide students with the opportunity to acquire the knowledge and skills that will enable them to realize their full potential. In magnet schools, students explore their special talents and interests while concentrating on strong academics. In the 2009–2010 school year, there were 2,213 magnet schools in the United States, equivalent to 2.2 percent of the total number of public schools, serving 3 percent of the total public school population (National Center for Education Statistics, 2011).

Magnet schools exist at elementary, intermediate, and secondary levels. Although they offer a complete curriculum, each magnet school has a particular theme, focus, or emphasis that is integrated throughout the curriculum. Themes may include science, mathematics, technology, music, visual arts, performing arts, computers, or any of a number of other areas of concentration. For example, in 2011, the magnet school system in the state of Minnesota offered the following magnet programs in elementary schools, middle schools, and high schools:

- Environmental studies
- Science, technology, engineering, and mathematics (STEM)
- Career and technical education
- Fine arts
- World cultures
- Montessori
- International baccalaureate[2]
- Language immersion

You can access the International Baccalaureate Organization website through the direct link on the Education CourseMate website.

▶II TeachSource Video

View the TeachSource ABC News Video, "A Positive School Climate Reduces the Achievement Gap." A Boston magnet school provides a positive school climate for 220 minority and low-income students. After watching the video, answer the following questions:

1. How do people know that the approach used in the Match School works?

2. What has the Match School done to meet students' basic needs?

Education Management Organizations

Education management organizations (EMOs) are corporations that assume responsibility for some or all facets of school management, including curriculum, instruction, building maintenance and operation, administration, and other aspects of running schools. EMOs can be either for-profit or nonprofit corporations.

As their name suggests, for-profit EMOs operate schools to make a profit; indeed, some have publically traded stock. The primary goals of for-profit EMOs are to raise student achievement and to make money. They operate on the principle of free enterprise that emphasizes competition as a way of improving performance, and they accept the challenge to improve student achievement performance. A school run by a for-profit EMO can be thought of as a business where students and parents are the customers. Their operating model is that of big business, and, accordingly, planning focuses on optimizing profits as a result of student success in school.

In the 2009–2010 school year, 98 for-profit EMOs (up from 51 in 2004) were operating 728 public schools (up from 534 in 2004), serving over 363,000 students (up from 242,400 in 2004) (Molnar, Miron, and Urschel, 2010). Among the leaders is EdisonLearning, Inc., a for-profit EMO that has been in business since 1992. This corporation has achieved a degree of success in turning the Philadelphia school system around and in offering online virtual high schools (EdisonLearning, 2011a).

Imagine Schools, founded in 2004, is the largest for-profit EMO in terms of the number of schools it manages—75 different schools in 12 states and the District of Columbia during the 2009–2010 school year. The mission statement of Imagine Schools is as follows:

As a national family of public charter school campuses, Imagine Schools partners with parents and guardians in the education of their children by providing high-quality schools that prepare students for lives of leadership, accomplishment, and exemplary character.

Based on that statement, how would you describe the predominant philosophy of the Imagine Schools?

Nonprofit EMOs operate like their for-profit counterparts except that their fee schedule does not contain a profit element. Another difference is that nonprofit EMOs focus

education management organization A corporation that assumes responsibility for some or all facets of school management, including curriculum, instruction, building maintenance and operation, and administration.

---

[2]The International Baccalaureate Diploma is a program headquartered in Geneva, Switzerland. It assists schools worldwide in developing and implementing challenging international education curricula to facilitate their graduates' admission to colleges and universities. Students who complete this program are awarded the International Baccalaureate diploma. Many of the courses carry college credit.

CONTROVERSIES in Education

Education Management Organizations

As you have seen, the number of schools operated by education management organizations (EMOs) is increasing steadily. Combining the for-profit and the non-profit EMOs, we find that in the 2009–2010 school year, 235 separate EMOs were operating in 1,541 schools in the United States, serving 600,000 students in grades K–12.

EMOs contract with public school districts to use tax money and, in the case of for-profit EMOs, venture capital funds as well, to operate schools. Most are charter schools that operate with a degree of autonomy, but some for-profit EMOs contract with school districts to operate all the schools in that district, bringing rigor, new curriculum and instruction ideas, and technology to increase the achievement of the students.

Contracting with EMOs generally is more costly than the ordinary school budget. The question is: Are EMOs worth the money? Those who support the idea of EMOs argue that, with their higher fees, the EMOs can engage in research and development activities to form better and more effective education systems. Supporters also note that because EMOs are in competition with each other, each one tries to create an emphasis that enables it to stand apart from the others, including such areas as innovative curriculum and instructional practices, emphasis on diversity, and the like. And because EMOs are actual businesses, they have intrinsic business-related incentives to ensure that student achievement increases.

Those who are skeptical about using school district funds for EMOs cite the lack of long-term systematic studies, and note that the studies that have been done show mixed results relative to student achievement. Fleischman and Heppen (2009) concur that there is a lack of definitive evidence about the effectiveness of EMOs. In fact, Shah (2011) writes that a new national study on the effectiveness of EMOs found that achievement of EMO-operated schools is not significantly better than achievement in regular public schools. However, Garcia, Barber, and Molnar (2009) found that student achievement in reading vocabulary was slightly greater in EMO-operated charter schools, but that achievement in reading comprehension was lower. Opponents also say that the EMOs have it backward: that the goal of education is to educate, whereas the goal of EMOs is to make money (and be profitable in the case of for-profit EMOs). Opponents also point out that the "extras" such as extracurricular clubs, band and chorus, sports teams, and the like often are eliminated to keep costs down.

Educators and the public have been debating the EMO issue for years.

WHAT DO YOU THINK?

1. *What do you think are some advantages of EMOs?*
2. *What do you think are some disadvantages of EMOs?*
3. *Suppose you were the superintendent of schools in a district that had just received approval to implement several charter schools that are based on the principles of magnet schools. Would you consider contracting the management of these schools to an educational management organization? Why or why not?*

Use the Internet to find information about a school operated by an EMO—one in your area, if possible. (Go to your state Department of Education website.) See if you can answer the following questions to gain a good understanding of what EMOs do:

- What is the school's curriculum?
- How much does it cost to attend?
- How is it funded?
- What is the length of the school day? What is the school calendar?
- Are there admissions criteria? What are they? What does the application process require?

almost entirely on management of charter schools whereas for-profit EMOs also include district schools and entire school districts among their clientele. A third difference is that whereas the number of for-profit EMOs has leveled off in the past few years, the number of schools operated by nonprofit EMOs has increased markedly. In the 2009–2010 school year, 137 nonprofit EMOs were operating 813 public schools with over 237,000 students in America's schools (Miron and Urschel, 2011).

EMO-operated schools tend to have longer school days and school years; they also tend to be high-tech. For example, in schools operated by EdisonLearning, all students are provided access to computers, and all students within a given Edison school are connected to one another using the Edison Intranet so they can correspond with one another on academic matters (EdisonLearning, 2011b). However, because the bottom line of these schools is profit, they may find it necessary to reduce the number of teachers and support personnel to minimize costs.

Home Schools

Home schooling is an educational alternative in which children learn under the general supervision of their parents at home rather than attend a conventional school. As of 2007, approximately 1.5 million (or 2.4 percent) of America's children were being home-schooled in grades K–12 (National Center for Education Statistics, 2011a). Home schooling is legal

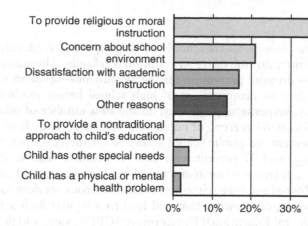

To provide religious or moral instruction

Concern about school environment

Dissatisfaction with academic instruction

Other reasons

To provide a nontraditional approach to child's education

Child has other special needs

Child has a physical or mental health problem

0% 10% 20% 30% 40%

◀ **Figure 6.4**
Top reasons for homeschooling.
(Source: National Center for Education Statistics, 2011a)
© Cengage Learning 2014

home schooling An educational alternative in which children learn under the supervision of their parents at home rather than at a conventional school.

in all states, and most states require regular reports of curriculum taught, days attended, evaluations, standardized test results, and other data required from schools.

People choose to home-school their children for many different reasons. Among these reasons are religious beliefs, lack of safety in regular schools, a poor fit between regular schools and their children, desire for increased family time, desire to supervise the content of their children's education, desire to provide education more suitable for their children's special needs or learning styles, and many others. Figure 6.4 shows the top reasons why people elect to home-school their children.

Although students who attend school at home study a rigorous curriculum, there are concerns about home schooling, including limited access to equipment and materials, the teaching parents' lack of required professional education background, limited access to extracurricular activities, and questionable development of healthy social skills. To address these concerns, home-schooling parents often work with other parents in large, well-formed groups to provide their children with maximum advantages. In addition, numerous publications, curriculum programs, and instructional ideas and aids are available in print and on the Internet to help parents provide the best possible education for their children. Regarding extracurricular activities, many states have equal-access laws that permit children who are home-schooled to participate in the public schools' interscholastic and extracurricular activities, including sports teams, music and drama programs, and social and academic clubs. Each state may have different requirements for eligibility to participate, such as dual or part-time enrollment in the school, permission of the local school district, or approval of the home-school program (Home School Legal Defense Association, 2011).

You can access the American Homeschool Association website through the direct link on the Education CourseMate website. This association maintains a great deal of information about home schooling.

Home Schooling

BUILDING BLOCK
6.9

Use the Internet to find information about home schooling in your state. (Go to your state Department of Education website.)

- What are the requirements for parents who wish to home school their children?
- What reports does your state require?
- How can students who have been home-schooled through high school satisfy your college's or university's admission requirements?
- What are the advantages of home schooling? What are its disadvantages?
- Would you consider home-schooling your child?
- Would you send your child to a neighbor or friend to participate in home schooling? What factors would influence your decision?

Alternative Schools

alternative school A school with the primary purpose of educating students who, for various reasons, do not thrive in traditional schools.

Alternative schools are schools whose purpose is to educate students who, for one reason or another, do not thrive in traditional schools. Alternative schools often see their missions as dropout prevention for at-risk students—students who are considered at high risk for failing or dropping out of high school before graduation because of poor grades, truancy, suspension, pregnancy, or any of a number of other reasons. In the 2007–2008 school year, 64 percent of public school districts had alternative schools, serving 645,500 (1.3 percent) of public school students. Of these, 63 percent were housed in a separate building, and 37 percent were housed within a regular school. Seventeen percent used distance learning as an instructional mode (Carver and Lewis, 2010).

Most alternative schools provide numerous services to students, including academic counseling; coursework that will lead to a regular high school diploma; preparation for the General Educational Development (GED) exam, a high school equivalency exam; and vocational skills.

The following are some major benefits of alternative schools:

■ More responsive and flexible environment
■ More curricular options
■ Smaller class sizes
■ More informal teacher–student relationships
■ High standards for attendance, behavior, and performance
■ Flexible scheduling

Alternative schools operate within the school district of the students they serve and are financed by the district like the other schools under district control (Carver and Lewis, 2010).

Vocational Schools

vocational school A public high school that provides various types of vocational education programs in addition to an academic curriculum; also called career and technical schools.

Vocational schools (also referred to as *career and technical schools*) are public high schools that provide various types of vocational education programs in addition to an academic curriculum. In the 2008–2009 school year, 5 percent of public schools were vocational schools (National Center for Education Statistics, 2011a).

private school A school that restricts its population of students to those who meet certain criteria established by the school.

The number of students in vocational education programs is declining, partly because the U.S. government is urging every student to complete high school and get technical or vocational training in postsecondary institutions, and because of the increased cost of vocational education programs, declining public perception that vocational education is desirable, and fewer rural schools offering vocational programs.

Private Schools

Private schools restrict their population of students to those who meet certain, specific criteria established by the school. These schools must meet the demands of two masters:

1. The government, with its emphasis on testing, the three Rs, and student achievement
2. The school foundations that give the schools their reasons for existence and the finances they need

© Craig Witkowski/Getty Images/Photolibrary

Educating students according to a religious philosophy, according to gender, or according to a college preparatory curriculum are the purposes of some private schools.

Numerous kinds of private schools exist; each has its own specific purposes, goals, and objectives.

Types of Private Schools

Take a moment to list as many types of private schools you can think of. Perhaps you or someone you know attended a private school. What are some possible reasons for attending a private school?

- What is the primary purpose for each school you listed?
- What purposes are common to all the private schools?
- How do these common purposes compare with the common purposes of schools you listed earlier in this chapter?
- What purposes are unique to specific kinds of private schools?

Students in classes like yours listed the following types of private schools:

- Boarding schools
- All-male schools
- All-female schools
- College preparatory schools
- Schools with religious affiliations
- Montessori schools
- Military schools

In the 2009–2010 school year, over 4.7 million students (10 percent of all U.S. students) attended private schools in the United States. Of these, over 1.7 million (36 percent) attended Catholic schools (National Center for Education Statistics, 2012).

Advantages of private schools include the following:

- Fostering academic excellence and high achievement
- Educating the whole child within a values-based setting
- Providing a safe and secure environment (Council for American Private Education, n.d.)

Online Learning and Virtual Schools

A virtual school is a school that teaches its curriculum mostly or entirely online using the Internet. Online learning is classroom learning that takes place over the Internet instead of in a classroom. Virtual schools are staffed by specially trained teachers, and can involve 100 percent of the teaching done online or can be a hybrid where some of the teaching is done online and the rest is done face-to-face in a "brick-and-mortar" classroom setting. Depending on the hardware people have, the teaching may be offered through webcams or through the written word on dedicated websites and/or bulletin boards. Online learning is offered in colleges (you may have taken one or more courses online—maybe even this one). More surprising is that online learning and virtual schools encompass all school grades, from kindergarten through high school.

Virtual school experiences are very appropriate for students who are homeschooled; who attend low-performing schools; who attend rural, inner city, alternative schools, or other schools that may have limited course offerings; who want to earn their high school diploma earlier than usual; and who are homebound because of illness or

virtual school A school that offers most or all of its curriculum online using the Internet.

online learning Learning that takes place online using the Internet.

other factors. The virtual school is particularly useful for students in rural areas where online classes help fill in the gaps in courses offered in the upper grades and help provide sound education for elementary grade children who may not be able to make it to school regularly, and for students who live in remote areas where school is not available (such as Kodiak Island in Alaska where seven of the school district's 14 schools are accessible only by air or boat [Gordon, 2011]). Most virtual schools are fully accredited by the same organization that accredits brick-and-mortar schools, and most virtual high schools offer high school diplomas.

Online learning is growing rapidly. The number of K–12 students using online education was more than two million during the 2008–2009 academic year, and is expected to grow to 10.5 million students by 2014 (Nagel, 2009). In 2009, 5 percent of high school graduates had taken courses for credit online (Buckley, 2011). Online learning has received positive endorsements from the research. For example, the U.S. Department of Education conducted a meta-analysis of research studies that investigated online learning between 1996 and 2008, and found that, on average, students in online learning conditions performed better than those receiving face-to-face instruction (U.S. Department of Education, 2010b).

Many states have one or more centralized virtual schools that are available without cost to any student enrolled in the state's system. And these schools are fully accredited. For example, Florida has a virtual school that offers over 90 online courses to students in grades 6 through 12; these courses are taught by over 1,100 specially certified virtual school teachers who also hold Florida teaching certificates in the subject(s) they teach (Florida Department of Education, n.d.). Minnesota operates a Virtual Academy, also known as K¹², that offers online programs for students from kindergarten through the senior year of high school. In fact, 46 of the 50 states plus Washington, DC, have state virtual schools or other online initiatives including individual virtual schools, or both. States are beginning to require online learning experiences of their students. As of this writing, Michigan, Alabama, and Florida require a virtual learning credit for high school graduation (Devaney, 2011), and Idaho has made it a requirement for high school students to complete at least two one-semester online courses as a condition for graduation (Cavanagh, 2011b).

The use of the Internet for online learning and virtual schools is a rapidly growing trend and you should make it a point to keep up with it.

WebQuest A learning activity in which some or all of the information with which students interact comes from the Internet, similar to a scavenger hunt.

wiki A collaborative website on which content can be edited by anyone who has access to it.

Your Hypothetical School

Now it is time to pull together the ideas you have thought about in this chapter. What do you consider to be the most important purposes of schools?

BUILDING BLOCK 6.11 — Mission of a Hypothetical School

Suppose you had to write a hypothetical mission statement for a school of your choosing. Consider your current thinking about yourself as the teacher, the students with their common and diverse needs, and the purposes of schools.

Write an abbreviated mission statement for the school you conceive. Be sure to include references to the school's primary goals, how you envision the implementation of these goals, and what you expect for the students and graduates of your school (that is, what you expect them to be able to do while they are students in your school and after they leave it). Keep this statement for use in later chapters.

Retrieve the philosophy statement you wrote in Chapter 2 and updated in Chapter 5. Compare this philosophy statement with your mission statement. In what ways are the two statements alike? How are they different? If you wish, update your philosophy statement again to show the progression of your thinking so far.

blog A blend of the terms *Web* and *log*. Individuals can develop blogs online that contain text, audio, photo, and video postings on a particular subject.

podcast (pod = play on demand) An audio broadcast over the Internet that may be recorded for later access.

vodcast (vod = video on demand) A video broadcast over the Internet that may be recorded for later access.

Technology offers students (and teachers) many opportunities to learn and build knowledge. Certain factors—such as distance, location, and financing—might prevent a school from providing its students with specific learning experiences, but technology can help fill the gap. Consider a school that does not have a teacher certified to teach chemistry, or a group of students interested in advanced placement (AP) courses who attends a school at which AP courses are not offered, or a remote area in which many students live too far away from the school to attend. Virtual field trips, distance education, and virtual schools are three ways technology might help students in these situations (see the previous section titled "Online Learning and Virtual Schools").

Virtual field trips are structured online experiences that help students increase their knowledge of a subject or concept. A teacher who is teaching a lesson on the Grand Canyon, for example, might assign a virtual field trip. To deter students from searching aimlessly for websites about the Grand Canyon, the teacher structures this part of the lesson by providing students with an explanation of the task (or "trip"); a list of websites or places to visit; an "itinerary"; things each student must do at the virtual destination; and list of artifacts or "souvenirs" for each student to collect at each website. Students on virtual field trips freely explore to enhance their learning, and they do so without regard for distance or expense.

Distance learning may involve transfer audio over phone lines and live or recorded video via cable TV. More commonly, however, the Internet is used for distance learning: webcams, e-mail, websites, school-based chat rooms, and video and audio streaming all facilitate e-learning. Distance education can take many forms. A group of students might meet regularly at a remote location while a teacher in a distant classroom explains a topic. In this case, the distance learning is *synchronous*, meaning that the students are "tuned in" at the same time the instruction is taking place. In another form of distance learning, students might use individual workstations (or a home computer) to access the teacher's discussion and accompanying information at their leisure. This is an example of *asynchronous* distance learning. Of course, many online courses are a mixture of both synchronous and asynchronous instruction. For example, students might access information the teacher has posted on the Internet and then be required to log in to a school-based chat room on a certain date and time. Academic chat rooms provide real-time interaction among students and between students and the teacher. Schools that are completely online are called *virtual schools* and have course offerings for all grade levels. Often, home-schooled children attend virtual schools. And online coursework is being offered during summers to help students make up missed work and to extend learning for advanced students (Rapp, 2011).

To use distance education effectively, teachers must be able to organize information and design instruction to make it suitable for transmission and for student-centered learning. Teachers must also be familiar with the technology, not only to create the courses but also to troubleshoot and solve problems. Students must also contribute to their learning and the learning environment. Some of the current technologies that foster online learning include the following:

- *WebQuest.* A WebQuest is an activity designed by teachers in which some or all of the information with which students interact comes from the Internet. It is a semidirected outline of activities that students use in independent investigations. The format of a WebQuest is as follows (Dodge, 1995):

  1. An introduction that sets the stage for the inquiry

  2. A basic task

  3. A set of information sources including links to Internet sites, e-mail conferencing, searchable databases, computer programs, books, magazines, and other available resources

  4. A description of the process the students should go through in accomplishing the task, broken into steps

  5. Guidance on ways to organize the material

  6. Conclusion that also includes ideas for further study

  7. Evaluation through a rubric that is part of the WebQuest

- *Websites.* Both teachers and students can develop private websites that contain information pertinent to the specific class being taught such as student enrollment, homework, helps, notices of class activities, results of investigations, and the like.

- *Wikis.* A wiki is a collaborative website on which content can be edited by anyone who has access to it. A familiar example is *Wikipedia*. Wikis are very useful because teachers and students alike can write their observations or thoughts on the wiki, ask for responses and critiques from others, respond to the entries of other people, and edit what anyone (including themselves) has written. A wiki is sort of like an open online chalkboard where all people can write their own thoughts.

- *Blogs.* The word blog is a blend of the terms *Web* and *log*. It is a website that contains text, audio, photo, and video postings on a particular subject. Both students and teachers can develop their own blogs to share with one another and/or other members of an online class. A blog most often is used to express opinions, thoughts, and reflections. Students in virtual schools can use blogs to demonstrate their understanding of a concept and/or to ask questions and seek clarification.

- *Podcasts and vodcasts.* A podcast (pod = "play on demand") is an auditory broadcast over the Internet. It is one-way only, and the listener cannot communicate with the broadcaster. Many podcasts are recorded for later access. They are primarily used to explain or describe some concept or point, and often are found on blogs. A vodcast (vod = "video on demand") is a video broadcast over the Internet. As with podcasts, vodcasts are one-way only, and many vodcasts are recorded for later access. They are primarily used to describe or explain some concept or point and are often found on blogs. Both teachers and students can create podcasts and vodcasts for the benefit of the classes.

- *Internet telephone and video calling software* (such as Skype), often available at no cost, enables anyone in the world to make free video and voice calls to anyone else in the world who has installed the same software. This type of software may be used for video conferencing and for virtual face-to-face discussions between the online teacher and one or more students.

These technologies are increasing at an extremely rapid pace. By the time this book is published, several new applications will have been developed. This is a field you must be sure to keep up with.

■ SUMMARY

- Schools have different purposes, some of which are common to all schools.
- The federal government has passed and implemented laws and has funded programs to foster its beliefs about the purposes of schools.
- A school's purpose is seen in its mission statement, which reflects the school's basic philosophy.
- Factors influencing the purpose of a school, and therefore its operation, include grade levels it serves, its location, its special interests, the special expertise it offers, and numerous other factors.
- Nontraditional schools fill special needs and interests of a community, and include charter schools, magnet schools, schools operated by commercial education management organizations, home schools, alternative schools, vocational schools, private schools, and the rapidly increasing virtual schools.

In this chapter, you have investigated the nature of elementary, middle, and high schools. You have looked at several kinds of nontraditional schools, and you have explored their advantages and disadvantages. In doing so, you have come to your own informed conclusions, and you have applied the acid test: *Would you want to teach at this school?*

Although a school must have a stated mission as a foundation on which to build, it must also have the resources, facilities, personnel, and organization to carry out that mission. In Chapter 7, you will identify what schools and teachers need to carry out their mission effectively. You will examine various school structures, and resources from personnel to materials and equipment to schedules, and you will draw conclusions about how a school's organization relates to its effectiveness.

■ Key Terms and Concepts

Alternative school, 176
Blog, 179
Charter school, 171
Education management
    organization, 173
Home schooling, 174

Magnet school, 172
Mission statement, 162
Online learning, 177
Podcast, 180
Private school, 176
Virtual school, 177

Vocational school, 176
Vodcast, 180
WebQuest, 179
Wiki, 179

■ Construct and Apply

1. The primary purpose of any school is to provide its students with the opportunity to learn. What other factors might influence a particular school's stated purpose?
2. Consider where you currently live. What do you suppose are the purposes of your neighborhood schools? What influences these purposes? How do you suppose the purposes of your neighborhood schools have changed in the past 50 years? What may have caused these changes?
3. Some students in small, rural towns may aspire to careers they believe are beyond what the local school is able to prepare them for (for example, robotics, computer programming, and sonogram and CAT scan technician training). What responsibility does the school have to these students? How can the school serve them? How could you, as a teacher, assist them?
4. Prepare a chart, listing the types of schools you have investigated across the top. Below each type of school, list the primary purpose(s) of that kind of school. Look at your chart to find purposes that are common to all schools.
5. What factors might influence you to choose a nontraditional school for your child? What advantages might a nontraditional school have over a traditional one?

■ Deconstructing the Standards

1. Recall the InTASC Standard associated with the objectives for this chapter.

   InTASC Standard #3 reads. "The teacher works with others to create environments that support individual and collaborative learning, and that encourage positive social interaction, active engagement in learning, and self-motivation."

   a. Which part(s) of this standard does this chapter address?

   b. How will the concepts in this chapter help you apply this standard as a teacher?

2. Use your favorite search engine to find your state's standards for certification. When you find it, bookmark the site; you will refer to it often during this course.

   a. How are your conclusions about the purposes of school represented in your state standards?

   b. How do the InTASC Standards compare to your state's certification standards?

■ Your Portfolio

Add a copy of your field experience school's mission statement to your portfolio. Compare the school's mission statement with your own philosophy statement. Describe how, if you were a teacher at that school, you could contribute to the fulfillment of the mission.

■ Education CourseMate Resources

Check out this text's Education CourseMate website (at www.cengagebrain.com) for more information about school purposes, nontraditional schools, virtual schools and distance learning, and interactive study tools and useful resources. You will find the TeachSource Videos, a guide for doing field experiences, glossary flash cards, activities, tutorial quizzes, direct links to the websites mentioned in the chapter, and more.

7

Structure of Schools

IN CHAPTER 6, you investigated the purposes of schools. As you recall, the purpose of a school represents its fundamental reason for existence. You saw that many factors influence a school's purposes, such as the grade levels and community being served, location, population, specialties offered, and the like. You also saw that a few purposes seem to be common to all schools, such as helping students learn to read and write, develop language literacy, develop mathematical skills, prepare to live in today's (and tomorrow's) society, develop technological skills, prepare for work, and prepare for college.

To accomplish their purposes, schools require certain facilities, materials, equipment, and personnel. For example, a magnet school focusing on science needs laboratory space and equipment. Schools also need to develop routines and schedules that will meet the needs of their students and the community they serve. In this chapter, you will examine factors that contribute to the inner workings of a school. These factors include facilities (materials, equipment, technology resources, other resources), personnel, and scheduling. You will examine these inner workings from the point of view of what a school needs to fulfill its purpose.

Chapter Objectives

As a result of your explorations in this chapter, you will be able to:

1. Identify the necessities all schools must have to fulfill their purposes.
   InTASC Standard #3: Learning Environments

2. Describe the various physical facilities needed by specific types of schools and explain why these facilities are necessary for the school to carry out its mission.
   InTASC Standard #3: Learning Environments

3. Discuss the roles and responsibilities of professional and nonprofessional personnel in schools and describe how these people help the school carry out its mission.
   InTASC Standard #3: Learning Environments

4. Describe the various kinds of scheduling of the school year and the school day and show how scheduling helps a school carry out its primary purpose.
   InTASC Standard #3: Learning Environments

Needs of Schools

As you have found, many different types of schools exist; these schools serve many different groups of people and have many different purposes. Schools have very complex inner workings, involving both physical facilities and people. As a student who has experienced and is currently experiencing "school," you might take these intricate workings for granted, never thinking to ask how it all works.

Do you think about the parts of your car and how they all work together before you get in, start it up, and drive off? Probably not. You just want it to start and take you where you need to go. But if you stop and think about it (even with limited knowledge of car engines), an automobile is a pretty amazing machine. Let us consider schools in the same way.

We have already established that the purposes of schools are as different as the populations they serve. A school's structure and organization must be arranged so the school can achieve its purpose. If different schools have different purposes, the structure and organization of those schools must also differ. For example, schools designed to serve very young children are not the same as schools designed for high school students, and rural schools differ from urban schools.

Let us think about a school's overall structure. What parts are needed to make it work? If you were asked, you could probably name a few parts of a car engine. But if you thought about it a little more, you might be able to get more detailed about the parts that you name, citing some smaller, less visible, but nevertheless important parts that are vital to an engine's function. Building Block 7.1 asks you to think about a typical school in the same way.

Parts of a School

**BUILDING BLOCK
7.1**

Think of a particular kind of school:

1. Brainstorm and list some of the necessities the school requires to fulfill its purposes. List both large and small items—everything you can think of.
2. Compare your list with your classmates' lists:
   a. How do they compare?
   b. What made them different?
3. To what extent did your list depend on the type of school you were thinking of?

Your list probably included such categories as the building, classrooms, materials and equipment, teachers, administrators, paraprofessionals, specialists, and the like. You also may have referred to technology requirements in view of its increasingly important role in education. Let us consider three basic aspects of school structure: physical facilities, human resources, and scheduling.

Physical Facilities

Physical facilities refer to the school building itself. Did your list from Building Block 7.1 contain classrooms? "Of course!" you say. But this question may not be as silly as it appears. In the 1960s, some schools were built without classroom partitions to accommodate a need for flexibility in forming adjustable groups of students (Anderson, 1966). These *open classroom* schools were popular for a while, but are no longer being built.

The great architect Louis Sullivan wrote, "Form should follow function" (in Boudreaux, 1993, p. 1). In other words, a structure's purpose should determine its design. This principle is as appropriate for designing a school as it is for designing any other architectural structure. As you investigate the elements of school structure (buildings, materials and equipment, personnel, and scheduling), keep this dictum in mind: The purpose and goals of a school determine its design.

Let us investigate this principle relative to the schools whose purposes you examined in Chapter 6.

BUILDING BLOCK 7.2

Identifying a School's Structure from Its Purpose

In Chapter 6, you investigated the purposes of several different kinds of schools, including traditional schools (such as elementary schools, middle schools, junior high schools, and high schools) and nontraditional schools (such as charter, magnet, schools operated by education management organizations, home schools, alternative schools, vocational schools, private schools, and virtual schools).

Select one kind of school:

- What two or three characteristics distinguish this school from other kinds of schools?
- How might you design the building so the school could achieve its purposes?

The purpose of the school should determine its design. Based on the design, what kind of school could this be?

© Michael Newman/PhotoEdit, Inc.

The Middle School as an Example

A good example of applying the "form follows function" principle can be seen in the middle school. As you recall, the purpose of the middle school is to align the educational environment with the unique needs of early adolescent learners. In elementary school, students spend most of each day with the same teacher and the same peers. Each grade-level classroom is usually on the same hall with others of the same grade. In high school, teachers and students change with each class, and classrooms are grouped by subject. How might a school organization "in the middle" of these two look?

When the middle school concept was developed, many junior high schools were converted to middle schools. Converting a junior high school required not only a change in curriculum and philosophy, but also a change in physical structure. As new school buildings were built, designers paid attention to developing the structure and organization that would best facilitate the middle school's purpose. The result was

TECHNOLOGY & EDUCATION
Use of Technology in Schools

The federal government has worked to support the implementation of educational technologies in our schools. A major area of support has been the development of educational technology plans for the nation. The first National Educational Technology Plan was released in 1996, and was followed by two updates that reflected the tremendous rate of growth in technology and the change in thinking about educational technology from an expensive fad with questionable results to an essential element of instruction. The fourth National Educational Technology Plan, released in 2010, is titled *Transforming American Education: Learning Powered by Technology*. This plan urges schools to use technology to (1) promote increased student learning; (2) assess student achievement; (3) improve teaching; (4) make knowledge available to everyone; and (5) improve efficiency in the use of resources (Office of Educational Technology, 2010). The following shows the basic principles of this plan:

A Model of Learning Powered by Technology

Basic Principles of the National Education Technology Plan of 2010

1. **Learning: Engage and Empower** All learners will have engaging and empowering learning experiences both in and out of school that prepare them to be active, creative, knowledgeable, and ethical participants in our globally networked society.

2. **Assessment: Measure What Matters** Our education system at all levels will leverage the power of technology to measure what matters and use assessment data for continuous improvement.

3. **Teaching: Prepare and Connect** Professional educators will be supported individually and in teams by technology that connects them to data, content, resources, expertise, and learning experiences that enable and inspire more effective teaching for all learners.

4. **Infrastructure: Access and Enable** All students and educators will have access to a comprehensive infrastructure for learning when and where they need it.

5. **Productivity: Redesign and Transform** Our education system at all levels will redesign processes and structures to take advantage of the power of technology to improve learning outcomes while making more efficient use of time, money, and staff.

Not everyone believes that technology can be used to help educate our children. Oppenheimer (2003), an award-winning journalist and outspoken critic of educational technology, shows many examples in which technology either has failed to improve student learning or has failed to work. Consequently, he suggests that education would be better served by increasing attention to the real-life experiences of the students rather than virtual experiences. However, Burns (2005/2006) urges that before we dismiss computers as an expensive fad, educators should ensure they are using computers to their maximum instructional potential in fostering student learning. And Friedman (2005) takes the position that the most important force of change in the late 20th and early 21st centuries has been the explosion of technology. More recently, a report on the use of technology in schools (International Center for Education Statistics, 2010) showed that, of the 97 percent of U.S. teachers who had computers in their classrooms, 69 percent said they use computers in their instruction, and, of those who attended professional development programs, 88 percent said that the use of technology supported the goals and standards of their state, district, and school.

You can access the National Clearinghouse for Educational Facilities through the direct link on the Education CourseMate website. This site has many references dealing with technology in U.S. schools.

---

the now-familiar middle school building in which the rooms are arranged in "pod" form, with classrooms for each of the main subjects taught in a particular grade clustered in the same general area.

Middle school teachers work in interdisciplinary teams of four or five. A team normally comprises a social studies teacher, a mathematics teacher, a language arts teacher, a science teacher, and sometimes a reading teacher. Ideally, these teachers work in adjacent classrooms, and the team's students move from one class to the next in the same general area. Thus all students on a team have the same teachers.

Perhaps you are familiar with junior high schools rather than middle schools. The structure of a middle school is more like an elementary school than a high school, whereas junior high schools have a structure more similar to high schools. How do you suppose the structure of a junior high school differs from the middle school about which you have just read?

Physical Requirements of Schools

Schools have major physical necessities. They require an extensive array of classrooms: teaching space for special subjects; room for after-school programs; playgrounds and/or athletic fields; technology equipment and materials; materials, equipment, and supplies to support teaching and learning; and space for administration, teachers of special subjects, and support personnel.

Did your list of requirements from Building Block 7.1 include trailers or portable classroom space? Or did you assume that school buildings are large enough to accommodate students? No matter how forward-thinking school-facility designers try to be, the population often grows faster than anticipated, causing overcrowded conditions. One solution to this problem has been to use portable classrooms. More than a third of U.S. schools use portable classrooms (U.S. Environmental Protection Agency, 2009). The Modular Building Institute estimated that public school systems used over 300,000 portable classrooms in 2006 (National Clearinghouse for Educational Facilities, 2011). The primary reasons for using this temporary instructional space are overcrowding caused by a large influx of people, and school districts attempting to comply with state laws limiting class size.

Did your brainstorming list include rooms or areas for special offerings such as art, band, orchestra, chorus, physical education, vocational education, technology education, theater, and other specialized subjects? Did your list contain facilities for after-school programs (ASPs), extracurricular activities, and community programs? For many years, offering after-school and weekend programs and extracurricular activities—to students, families, and the community at large—has been a priority of educators and the federal government. Such activities are designed to help students, their families, and members of the community learn new skills and discover and develop new abilities. Services offered typically include tutorial services, academic enrichment activities, youth development activities, counseling and character education, and adult programs.

The federal government offers support in the form of grants; the 21st Century Community Learning Centers program is one example. This program supports the development of community learning centers that provide opportunities for academic enrichment during nonschool hours; it focuses especially on centers designed to attract students who attend high-poverty and/or low-performing schools. Grant awards range from a few million dollars to tens of millions of dollars (U.S. Department of Education, 2011b).

Federal legislation requires all school buildings be accessible to students with disabilities. Accessibility ramps, elevators, and other building modifications are examples.

Did your list for Building Block 7.1 have provisions for technology? From your experience as a student, you are probably aware that most schools have a variety of technologies available for students and teachers. There are computer labs and/or laptop carts that usually contain a class set of computers (one per student in a class). Teachers can reserve the labs or carts for use with their classes. Also, the teacher usually has a desktop computer that is connected to a projector and/or an interactive whiteboard, and classrooms may contain at least one or several computers for student use. Of course, the school usually has wireless Internet access.

Did you include adaptive and assistive technology devices in your plan? (You investigated this technology in Chapter 5.) You also saw in Chapter 5 that the Individuals with Disabilities Education Act (IDEA) requires that all children be educated in the least restrictive environment, regardless of special need. This act extends to technology, and schools must provide students with access to technology such that *all* students can use it.

Did your list contain facilities for students with special needs? What kinds of disabilities did you consider? What provisions for these disabilities did you list? Such provisions can range from wheelchair ramps, to space and equipment accommodations in regular classrooms, to special rooms with special facilities for students with severe handicaps.

Perhaps you took the time to consider those smaller—though no less important—requirements of a school, such as supplies for teachers, students, administrators, and custodial staff. Did you remember that all the people in a school typically eat lunch there each day? What resources are required for the formidable task of feeding everyone associated with a school? (Chapter 12 provides specific material about school lunches.) And did you remember that most schools need gymnasiums and auditoriums?

Personnel

Next, let us consider human resources.

Recall our analogy of the car engine. What happens if one of the parts does not work quite right? Perhaps it does not fit well, or is the wrong size or shape, or is old and worn. What does this mean for the engine? Perhaps the part works well enough that the engine starts but runs jaggedly or unevenly. Eventually the engine could stall, refuse to restart, and bring everything to a complete halt.

For your car to run smoothly, the parts must be in good shape and must all work together in a well-oiled machine. What is necessary for a school to run smoothly? Sure, there are glitches in any school year and even in every school day. But for the most part, schools succeed extremely well in carrying out their functions and achieving their purposes. To do so requires that all parts of the school you have considered—those that make up the structure and resources of the school, including personnel—be organized effectively.

Review the list you made in Building Block 7.1. What human resources did you see as necessary for the school to fulfill its purpose?

Schools require many different kinds of personnel. Of course, different kinds of schools and schools with different purposes require different kinds of personnel. Regardless of a school's nature and purpose, however, all schools require people with certain qualifications.

Teachers

Probably the predominant person you listed as necessary to a school was teacher. How many teachers should a school have? During your own experience of school, perhaps you have been in some very small classes, and perhaps you have attended very large classes, such as the lecture courses often found in colleges and universities. An important consideration in the organization of a school is the student–teacher ratio, the number of students assigned to one teacher in a class, on average. For example, a student–teacher ratio of 21:1 means that, on average, there are 21 students in each class assigned to a teacher.

student–teacher ratio The average number of students assigned to one teacher.

Optimal Class Size

Based on your experience, what do you think is the optimal student–teacher ratio for each of the following classes? Why?

- Preschool class
- High school trigonometry class
- Chorus
- Middle-grades physical education class
- Third grade
- High school study hall

BUILDING BLOCK
7.3

- High school science laboratory
- Special education class for students with moderate disabilities
- College-level introductory literature class

What do you think is the optimal class size in general? What factors are important to consider when making decisions about student–teacher ratio?

What is the maximum class size for your school system or state? (Check your state's Department of Education website.)

Do local school systems provide information about the general student–teacher ratios in their schools? What is the range of these ratios? Would knowing this ratio be important to you in deciding whether to accept a teaching position? Why?

Student enrollment in public schools increased steadily in the 20th century, except for a slight decline during the 1970s and 1980s. The number of teachers also has increased steadily. However, the increase in teachers has occurred faster than the increase in student population. This has resulted in a steadily decreasing nationwide average student–teacher ratio from 32:1 in 1920 to 15.2:1 from 2008 and 2009 (World Almanac Books, 2011). Note that all instructional staff are included in this ratio, even those who have few students because of their specialties. The individual state ratios vary from a high of 22.9:1 in Utah to a low of 10.6:1 in Vermont (National Center for Education Statistics, 2011h). The U. S. Department of Education estimates that the average class size in the 2008–2009 school year was close to 25 students (Sparks, 2010). However, these figures include special education and other specialized teachers who normally have much smaller classes than regular classroom teachers. Figure 7.1 shows the national average of student–teacher ratios since 1955.

The student–teacher ratio in private schools tends to be smaller than the national averages. For example, the student–teacher ratio for private schools in the 2008–2009 school year was 13.1:1, compared with the national average for public schools of 15.9:1 (National Center for Education Statistics, 2010a).

How do the national averages of student–teacher ratios compare with the classes you attended in elementary school, middle school, and high school? What might account for any discrepancies?

Many studies have shown that reducing class size improves student achievement. Smaller class sizes enable teachers to spend the time and energy needed to help each child

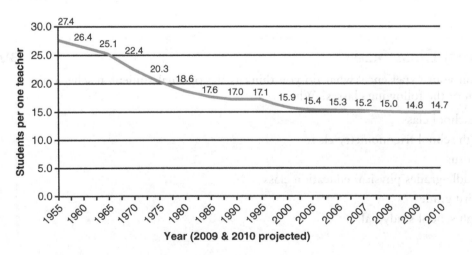

Figure 7.1 ▶
Student–teacher ratios: National averages from 1955 to 2010.
(Source: National Center for Education Statistics, 2010a.)
© Cengage Learning 2014

CONTROVERSIES in Education

Does Class Size Matter?

You have been investigating the inner workings of a school, including class size. To parents and the general public, class size seems to be the "litmus test" of the quality of a school. Schools with small class sizes are perceived as being better than schools with large class sizes. Randi Weingarten, president of the American Federation of Teachers, said surveys show that parents care more about class size than anything else except school safety (Dillon, 2011a). After all, if a teacher has only 15 or so students in a class, it is far more possible for that teacher to provide individual attention to each student. None will be left behind, and none will have to fare forth on their own. On the other hand, teachers of class sizes of 30 or so students simply cannot teach to each individual student. These teachers have huge numbers of papers to grade, grades to calculate, makeup work for students who are absent, parents to contact, and e-mails to answer. Furthermore, discipline is much more difficult: For example, students may be able to doze in class without the teacher knowing it, and surely the teacher cannot correct every student who shows evidence of daydreaming.

Yet, according to the experts, of the factors that make a school a good one, class size is a distant fourth after solid teacher training, a clear and well-sequenced curriculum, and a staff that is well supported and regularly evaluated (Tyre, 2011).

Is it true that smaller classes are better? Let us look at some evidence. You have already seen some of the figures, and you have looked at Project STAR, considered the "gold standard" of class size research. Smaller class sizes enable teachers to spend the time and energy needed to help each child succeed, and enhance safety and discipline in the classroom. This project and many other research projects tell us that smaller classes are better, but only if the teacher is very good (Rotherham, 2011). *Education Week* (2012) says the research in general tells us that smaller classes are better, but primarily when (1) students attend smaller classes for three or more consecutive years; (2) students are living in poverty; (3) students are minority students; and (4) class size is cut down to 16 or so students.

Additionally, it appears that very large class size reductions (on the order of 7 to 10 fewer students per class) are needed for long-term effects on achievement, and that this effect is greatest when the smaller classes are introduced in the early grades and for students from less-advantaged families.

Many states have legislated class size limits in the belief that smaller classes foster greater student achievement. For example, Texas established a student–teacher ratio of 22:1 (Marchiechay, 2010), and Florida amended its state constitution to limit class size to 18 for kindergarten through third grade, 22 for fourth grade through eighth grade, and 25 in high school classes (Albright, 2005). However, in times of economic stress, lawmakers have to consider budgetary constraints, and smaller classes mean more teachers. Consequently, the student–teacher ratio is beginning to increase in 2011.

So, the question becomes: "Are the gains from reducing class size worth the extra expense?" To give you an idea of the extra expense involved, the Brookings Institute has estimated that decreasing the student–teacher ratio in the United States by one student would cost at least $12 billion in teacher salaries alone (Whitehurst & Chingos, 2012). Many states have loosened legal restrictions on class size. For example, *The New York Times* reports that, in the 9th grade in Los Angeles schools, the average size of English and math classes has increased from 20 to 34 students, and 11th- and 12th-grade English and math classes now have an average of 43 students in each (Dillon, 2011b).

Consequently, the bottom line of the debate about class size and student–teacher ratio is an issue of mixed research results versus expense. Class size does seem to matter, but teacher effectiveness matters more.

WHAT DO YOU THINK?

1. *What qualities of an excellent teacher are most important when dealing with large classes?*
2. *If class sizes change from large to small, what changes in school facilities need to be considered?*

succeed, and enhance safety and discipline in the classroom. Much of the research about how class size affects achievement comes from Project STAR (Student–Teacher Achievement Ratio), an experiment that took place in Tennessee in the late 1970s (The CSU Institute for Education Reform, 1996). In this project, kindergarten students were randomly assigned either to small classes of 13 to 17 students or to large classes of 22 to 26 students; students stayed in these classes for 4 years through the third grade. A follow-up study of several thousand students found that those in the small classes made better academic gains, especially in reading, were more likely to graduate from high school, and were more likely to attend college than those who had been in the large classes. However, the effect was seen only in students who had attended the small classes for all 4 years; 1 or 2 years were not enough to make a difference. The researchers attributed the higher

Courtesy of David Ottenstein Photography

More individual attention for students, more classroom space, and increased student achievement are benefits of smaller class sizes. In which of these classrooms would you prefer to teach?

success rate of students in the small classes to increased individual attention and the inability to avoid teacher attention (Sparks, 2005).

How do the optimal student–teacher ratios you established in Building Block 7.3 compare with the optimal class sizes just discussed?

We all have had experience with "regular" or "general" classroom teachers, but you probably also identified other types of professional personnel who are present in schools in Building Block 7.1. Some may be specialized teachers, some may have responsibilities that extend throughout the school rather than in a particular classroom, and some may have administrative responsibilities. In addition, you may have identified some nonprofessional personnel.

Teachers with Specialties

There are many different teaching specialties. The higher a school's grade levels, the more specialized the teachers are relative to subject matter. Teachers in elementary schools generally are prepared to teach all subjects, whereas middle school and high school teachers specialize in one or two subjects. However, special teachers are found in most schools. Elementary schools generally have art, music, and physical education specialists. These teachers are responsible for teaching their subjects to large numbers of students in a school—often all the students. Middle schools and high schools employ specialty teachers to implement specialty programs, such as band, chorus, orchestra, art, computers, business, agriculture, culinary arts, and others. In the upper levels, the presence of specialty teachers directly reflects the school's purpose and mission statement.

One example of teachers with specialties is the special education teacher. Special education teachers are found in most schools: elementary, middle, and high schools. Some teach students in their own self-contained classrooms; others work in conjunction with regular classroom teachers in inclusion classrooms to accommodate the needs of learners with exceptionalities who can be included in regular classrooms (see Chapter 5). The United States is currently experiencing a critical need for special education teachers due to increased enrollment of special education students, teacher retirement, and legislation that broadens the scope of special education and extends it to very young children. Also, as more students with special needs are included in regular classrooms, schools need more special education teachers to work with these students. Teachers who specialize in special education typically complete a focused program in which they learn to facilitate the teaching and learning of students with special needs.

A Special Education Teacher

Katherine Spung

When pursuing my bachelor's degree in elementary education, I had the option to add a minor in special education. The rumor among preservice teachers was that this endorsement would help ensure a job offer, but once placed in a special education position, teachers could not get out. Good special education teachers are in big demand, and the burnout rate is high. I had worked with students with significant learning disabilities and I greatly enjoyed it, yet I intentionally did not complete the last nine hours I needed to complete this additional certification. A year later, I was offered a position in a small rural elementary school for a start-up self-contained special education classroom. I accepted and was hired on a waiver and condition that I would complete the hours needed to be certified that year.

Several years later, I have absolutely no regrets. Although I have faced tremendous challenges, I know that I have greatly improved the lives of my students. Despite the fact that this was a start-up program, no budget for supplies had been considered. I started with nothing and spent several hundred dollars of my first-year salary on supplies. I faced resistance from some coworkers regarding whether a program for my students should exist. The most important thing I learned that year was that I was the voice and advocate for my students and I was obligated to fight for their needs. The next year I made sure I had a sufficient budget and voiced my students' rights for an equal education to those who spoke out against them.

I also learned that using traditional textbooks and teacher-centered instruction was not what my students needed. Hands-on experiential learning resulted in greater understanding time after time. This also meant that I needed to develop a curriculum for my students that would generate knowledge. Frequently, I teach students for consecutive years, sometimes for most if not all of their years in my building, so the curriculum must change from year to year. The curriculum had to be fun, engaging, individualized, meet state standards, and guide students to construct meaning. This was a tall order. I knew that I needed to learn more in order to serve my students' needs, and I have been enrolled in graduate classes almost every semester since.

Each of my students is a unique learner with unique needs and backgrounds. I believe this is true in every classroom. My students may have a disability label but the label is only words. Two students with the same diagnosed disability are not the same and are different learners. I have very high expectations for my students, yet they have continued to surprise me. My first year teaching in my current position, I was told that one of my students "would never read." I was disgusted at this teacher's statement. Of course she could read. She was missing some foundational skills on which to build upon, but by the end of the year, she was proudly reading "easy readers" to the principal.

I was asked once how I continue to come up with ways to guide my students with learning. I learn from other teachers; I read continually; I borrow someone's idea and tweak it to meet the needs of my students; and most importantly, I never give up. I help learners construct meaning with every chance I get. While reading a book aloud to the class about the Statue of Liberty in a unit I developed on national symbols, one of the students asked why they chose to paint the statue that color. That statement led to a science experiment with pennies, salt, water, vinegar, and air. Students recorded their own observations and concluded why the statue is the color it is. Students in my classroom partner to collaborate on assignments and we play games to help the learning process. I developed separate centers for each continent that contain books, maps, coins, stamps, and flags. Students work in small groups to discover knowledge and respond about what they learned. This is just a short list of what my classroom looks like. Teachable moments are everywhere. The trick is to find those moments, let students come up with ideas for learning, let them inspire you, keep expectations high, and never give up on their ability to show you how much they know.

Katherine Spung
Kappa Delta Pi Teacher of Honor, 2011
Special education teacher/learning behavior specialist
Chrisman Elementary School
Chrisman, Illinois

Courtesy of Katherine Spung

Another example of teachers with specialties is the bilingual educator. Bilingual educators not only work with students to help them learn English, but they also assist students with the translation of books and other materials and with understanding information presented by regular teachers, and they help teachers design instruction to make information more accessible to all students. Bilingual education programs are known by several names, including TESL (teaching English as a second language), TEFL (teaching

Use the Internet to find which endorsement programs in education your state recognizes. Which do your college or university offer? What are the requirements for these endorsements? What endorsement programs do neighboring institutions offer?

English as a foreign language), TESOL (teaching English to speakers of other languages), ESL (English as a second language), EFL (English as a foreign language), and ESOL (English for speakers of other languages). To earn the bilingual education specialty, teachers study specialized programs.

Many classroom teachers develop interests in other areas and can earn specialized endorsements or add-ons to their teaching certificates. Examples include early childhood special education specialists, technology specialists, reading specialists, mathematics specialists, science specialists, and gifted education specialists. Most recently, states are beginning to offer endorsements in online teaching (Quillen, 2012a). Others specialties are available; these vary from state to state.

Administrators

Did your list include school administrators? When you think of the school principal, what comes to mind? Many people think of discipline, because when we went to the principal's office, it usually meant we were in trouble.

Depending on its size, a school may have a principal and one or more assistant principals, each of whom has a specific role and set of responsibilities. The principal is the administrative head of the school—the person to whom teachers and other school personnel report and who is ultimately responsible for the operation of the school. Indeed, the principal and the administrative staff have many responsibilities that help maintain the school's function and achieve its stated purpose. What do you think a principal's responsibilities are?

BUILDING BLOCK 7.4

The Principal's Jobs

Imagine it is early on a Monday morning and you are the school principal just arriving at work. List the items you need to do for the day. Be sure to include time for scheduled meetings or appointments. Suppose you find you have an hour of uncommitted time in your day. What would you do with it?

Next, list items you have to do for the week.

Look at your lists and generate some categories for a principal's responsibilities.

Many sources list school principals' roles and responsibilities. The U.S. Department of Labor uses the term "educational administrator" to describe someone who provides instructional leadership and manages the day-to-day activities in schools. The department lists the following duties and responsibilities for educational administrators:

- Sets educational standards and goals
- Establishes policies and procedures to achieve the standards and goals
- Supervises personnel
- Develops academic programs
- Monitors students' educational progress
- Trains and motivates teachers and other staff
- Manages career counseling and other student services
- Administers record keeping
- Prepares budgets
- Handles relations with parents and the community (U.S. Department of Labor, 2011)

How does the list of principal's duties you made in Building Block 7.4 compare with this list of responsibilities?

School principals are responsible for supporting student learning and providing leadership to teachers and other school personnel. As a new teacher or student teacher, the principal together with an experienced teacher can provide you with career guidance and advice based on their extensive experience as educators.

The principal traditionally has been seen as the school's leader, the person who supervises faculty and staff, interacts with students, makes discipline decisions, and oversees everything from student achievement, faculty performance, and staff development to building maintenance and the purchase of materials and supplies.

However, the principal's role is changing. Whereas principals formerly were considered school managers, they are now being asked to function as educational leaders, as you can tell from the job description.

Regardless of how you currently view the school principal's role, as a teacher you will want to avail yourself of your principal's expertise. After all, he or she has been in education for a long time and has solved many problems. Principals want to help; they especially want to help new teachers. The principal evaluates your performance, but it is also the principal who provides much-needed assistance and advice.

Teachers versus Administrators

BUILDING BLOCK

7.5

What is the difference between a teacher and an administrator? What do you feel the difference *should* be between a teacher and an administrator?

Often the principal is considered the "boss" in the school. In your view, is this a valid characterization? To what extent should the principal exercise his or her authority? To what extent should teachers and administrators work collaboratively? Do some situations require the principal to make independent decisions? What are they?

Professional Support Personnel

Schools employ many people besides teachers and administrators. These individuals possess experience and special degrees or endorsements that allow them to fulfill their roles within the school building. The library media specialist (LMS), for example, knows about library science and various media, including computer technologies. In the Information Age, the job of library media specialist has changed significantly from that of librarian. The lead teacher and the learning support specialist (LSS) provide curricular and instructional help to teachers and special instruction to groups of students selected on the basis of some common need. Technology specialists provide much-needed support in maintaining technological equipment and instructing teachers and students in the use of technologies. Curriculum specialists help interpret the system-mandated curriculum in terms of its most appropriate application for the students in individual schools.

Guidance counselors and school psychologists have various duties, which depend on the needs of the school and its students. They are found in all levels of schools, from elementary

library media specialist (LMS) Professional educator whose specialty includes library science and multimedia management.

lead teacher A teacher whose responsibilities include assisting teachers in developing and implementing strategies to reach all types of learners and whose focus is on aiding teachers.

learning support specialist (LSS) A teacher whose responsibilities include assisting teachers in developing and implementing strategies to reach all types of learners and whose focus is on aiding individual students.

school through high school. As their titles imply, they are available to counsel students and advise them on issues such as personal and academic problems and postsecondary or vocational plans. These professionals also administer and interpret tests to help identify students with special needs and assist in developing individualized education programs.

You can probably think of other professional support personnel whose areas of expertise meet the needs of some special students. These personnel might include speech therapists, nurses, social workers, truant officers, and police officers. As you know, it is the school's responsibility to meet the needs of *all* students. Sometimes, meeting those needs requires the collaboration of a staff with qualifications as varied as the students they serve.

Nonprofessional Personnel

paraprofessional A trained teacher's aide.

Teacher's aides (teacher assistants), also known as paraprofessionals, often provide assistance in the classroom. Paraprofessionals typically assist the classroom teacher with a variety of instructional and noninstructional tasks. Under the teacher's guidance, paraprofessionals may provide large-group, small-group, or individual instruction, including assisting students with special needs or English language learners. They may supervise laboratory activities, computer lessons, and other activities, including lunch and recess. In addition, a paraprofessional might assist in record keeping. Based on what you have already observed in your field experience, you can probably see just how valuable a paraprofessional might be in the busy life of a classroom teacher.

© Michael Newman/PhotoEdit, Inc.

Parent and community volunteers provide teachers with instructional support, and provide students adult supervision in class. What is this volunteer doing to help in the classroom?

Parents or other community members sometimes volunteer to work in the schools. Classroom volunteers provide another set of hands, ears, and eyes that can help teachers give more students individual attention. With another adult in the room, teachers can incorporate activities that require close adult supervision, such as dissections, outdoor lessons, or activities that require the use of many different materials.

Other support personnel include the front office staff, the custodial staff, and cafeteria workers. You may also find volunteers in the front office answering phones and monitoring the comings and goings of students. Some teachers will argue that the school's staff is what keeps the place up and running.

As you have observed, a school contains many different adults with many different responsibilities. It may be surprising to learn just how many people can be at work in a school. Remember that people like those described here contributed to your own schooling experience. And soon you will be one of those people, working in a collaborative and cooperative environment to help your students and your school achieve.

Scheduling

Have you ever heard anyone say that a car engine's timing is off? In an automobile, "bad timing" might mean that the car stalls at a stop sign or races when it idles. Sometimes, a car with bad timing lurches or lags. A car engine's timing must be adjusted for the car to run smoothly. Can you apply this analogy to organizing the schedule that governs the students, personnel, and resources in a school? When people talk about school scheduling, they may be referring to the times school is in session during the year or to the time periods of the school day.

Annual Schedule

Let us first consider ways of scheduling the school year. Schools typically operate on a schedule that requires students to be in school for 180 days during the fall, winter, and spring, but not during the summer. This scheme was developed in the 19th century so that school-aged children could be at home and help on the farms during the busiest time of the year.

For students, the primary advantages of a nine-month school year include summers off for rest and regrouping, the ability to attend summer camps, and the possibility of gaining significant workplace experience. Primary advantages for teachers include summers off for rest and regrouping and the ability to take summer courses for professional development, certification renewal, or the pursuit of an advanced degree. Primary disadvantages include discontinuity of education because of the long summer vacation (students have three months to forget what they learned during the preceding year) and the need of some teachers to find summer work.

Many states and school districts are moving toward new and creative scheduling plans that include year-round education. There are many ways to implement year-round education. One example is the trimester system, in which students go to school for three months, have one month off, and repeat this cycle three times a year. Another method involves devising several tracks in which sequencings of school time and vacation time differ for different students and teachers, all within the same school. Primary advantages of year-round systems include increased school capacity, relief from overcrowding, an enhanced instructional pace, and flexible vacation options. Primary disadvantages include increased need for faculty, staff, materials, and storage facilities; more "start-ups" and "endings" to the academic year; and a nontraditional calendar.

Among those who oppose year-round school are the owners of resorts and summer vacation attractions. These people fear that year-round school could cause them to lose business and revenue. These business owners point out that they also pay taxes to support education.

There are many variations on the annual schedule. Some school districts start the school year in late July or early August and end it in May, with several breaks scattered throughout the year. Some start in early August and end in late May, with several one-week breaks scattered throughout the year. And the Park City, Utah, high school offers a flexible schedule centered around the winter sports seasons so students can hone their skills and enter competitions.

Yearly School Schedule

BUILDING BLOCK

7.6

What annual school schedule do you think is best? Take the position of a teacher and describe the kind of annual school schedule you feel would be best for a teacher and tell why.

Do the same from the viewpoints of a parent, an elementary school student, and a high school student.

Daily Schedule

Next, let us look at ways of scheduling during the day. Your outlook on this topic will depend on the level of school at which you are planning to teach. Each level has its own unique situation and its own unique ways of solving scheduling problems.

Schools typically meet five days a week, with the same classes meeting on the same schedule every day for an academic year. In high school, a typical student attends seven different classes in discrete periods of 50 to 55 minutes, attending these same classes every day for a full academic year, although some courses meet for only one semester, and half-day release time may be provided for certain work and apprenticeship programs. High school teachers typically teach five classes and deal with 125 or more students each day.

In an effort to provide more flexibility in using the time students are in school, many high schools have implemented innovations such as block scheduling. There are numerous variations to the concept of block scheduling. In one of the more common models, a school's daily schedule is organized into large blocks of time—so that students schedule four 90-minute classes a day for the first semester in the school year and four 90-minute classes a day during the second semester. This allows students to take eight classes a year instead of the traditional seven, and gives teachers the flexibility to pursue topics in greater depth than is possible in the shorter class period. And there is the perennial concern that students might be more alert in class if school were to start later. Kirby, Maggi, and D'Anguilli (2011) have shown that there is a lack of synchronicity between school start times and the circadian rhythm of adolescents—enough so that later start times can be justified and implemented with minimal difficulty.

Middle schools are also moving to block scheduling, citing the same reasons for doing so as high schools.

Elementary schools typically have all-day scheduling in which students stay in their assigned classrooms for a full day all year long, except for those times when they go to other rooms for music, art, physical education, and other special subjects. The day's scheduling within a particular classroom may be determined by the teacher. Some flexibility is available to elementary school teachers in the form of cooperative teaching, looping, and multiage education. Cooperative teaching allows individual teachers to teach subjects that they prefer and in which they have expertise, while other teachers take responsibility for subjects in their areas of expertise. This arrangement maximizes teachers' strengths and provides flexibility in forming groups. Several cooperative teaching models exist. In one, teachers of a particular grade or cluster of grades form teams; different teachers in the teams teach those subjects in which they have particular interest or expertise. In another model, subject matter specialists are responsible for teaching their subject to all children in a grade level or group of grades; this model is close to the subject specialists' model used in the middle schools and high schools. In a third model, teachers plan together in an interdisciplinary and cooperative manner, and each assumes the responsibility for a portion of the unit being taught (see also Chapter 5).

In looping, the same teacher is assigned to the same group of students for two or three years. Looping has been used with increasing frequency in elementary schools and in some middle schools. This practice has the advantage that teachers get to know their students deeply. It allows teachers to challenge the students in ways a teacher less familiar with students' capabilities may not, and it enables teachers to provide remedial work for those who need it without having to wait for assessment results.

In multiage education, students of several ages are clustered together in one class. Groups are formed on the basis of ability and professed interest, helping teachers provide appropriate classes because all students have approximately the same ability.

block scheduling A scheduling system in which a school's daily schedule is organized into large blocks of time.

cooperative teaching A method of distributing teaching responsibilities in elementary schools such that teachers assume responsibility for their areas of expertise.

looping A system of assigning students in elementary schools to the same teacher for two or more consecutive years.

multiage education A system of clustering students of different ages in elementary schools in the same class.

BUILDING BLOCK 7.7

School Schedules

If you were in charge, would you make changes to school scheduling? What would these changes be? Why would you make them?

Which type of daily school schedule do you believe is best for elementary schools? Which type do you believe is best for high schools? Describe the schedule and tell why you believe it is the best schedule.

Putting It All Together

In this chapter, you have been investigating some of the complex factors that enable schools to achieve their purposes (the topic of the previous chapter). Now it is time to put these elements together.

Structure of Your Hypothetical School

BUILDING BLOCK
7.8

In Building Block 6.11, you developed a hypothetical mission statement for a hypothetical school. What would your hypothetical school need to function?
Answer the following questions:

1. What kind of school (urban or rural; elementary, middle, or high school) is your hypothetical school?
2. What are its basic purposes?
3. What physical facilities will this school require? Think of materials and equipment and the physical structure your school will need.
4. How will your school building be laid out?
5. What personnel will your school require? What are their duties? How many of each type of professional and nonprofessional worker will your school need?
6. What requirements are specific to this school? How do they help the school fulfill its basic purpose? How do the requirements for this school differ from the requirements for other schools?

■ SUMMARY

- A school's needs are based in large measure on its educational goals. School is a very complex entity that requires both physical facilities and specialized personnel.

- The physical facilities of a school include the building itself, classroom space, space for special subjects, materials and equipment needed for teaching, and equipment for technology.

- Several types of personnel are needed in a school. The number of teachers depends on the course offerings and the student–teacher class size ratio. Many teachers have earned specialty endorsements. Administrators are viewed as the school's educational leaders. Support personnel such as library media specialists, counselors, and lead teachers support the educational programs of the school, as do nonprofessional personnel such as paraprofessionals and lunchroom people. Secretaries and the custodial staff are essential to make the school "go."

- Annual scheduling is steeped in the farming tradition where students go to school during the fall, winter, and spring, and have summers free. Schools are moving to variations in the annual schedule to save money and make more efficient use of the time available. Many variables influence daily scheduling. In the elementary grades, most schools have full-time self-contained classrooms for each grade, although there is some flexibility within a group of grades. Middle-grades schedules tend to have students moving from room to room for their classes. High schools may have period-based or block scheduling.

This chapter asked you to think about the place called *school*. In previous chapters, you have thought about teachers, teaching, and students. In the next chapters, you will look at the relationships among all three elements: teachers, students, and the school. You will examine how the school serves the common and unique needs of its students, learn what the school expects from its teachers, and discover what you can expect from the school where you decide to teach.

◼ Key Terms and Concepts

Block scheduling, 196
Cooperative teaching, 196
Lead teacher, 193

Learning support specialist
(LSS), 193
Library media specialist
(LMS), 193

Looping, 196
Multiage education, 196
Paraprofessional, 194
Student–teacher ratio, 187

◼ Construct and Apply

1. How would you feel if your classroom were in a trailer? What are some of the advantages and disadvantages of teaching in a trailer? Do you believe having a class in a trailer can affect learning? How? Why?
2. Many people with many different kinds of responsibilities interact in a school, and the number of people in a given role varies with the type of school. How many people in each role would you expect to see in different schools?
   a. Look at the following chart of schools and personnel. Indicate on the chart the extent to which the various personnel would be present in a school. Use a double check mark (✓✓) if many are present, a check mark (✓) if some are present, and a dash (—) if none are present.
   b. Look at each column. What accounts for the different numbers of personnel in different types of schools?

	Elementary School	Middle School	High School	Private School	Alternative School	Vocational School	Virtual School
Teacher							
Principal							
Assistant principal							
Lead teacher							
Learning support specialist							
Library media specialist							
Counselor							
Paraprofessional							
Special education teacher							
Technology specialist							
Volunteer							
Nurse							
Custodial staff							
Cafeteria staff							
Other (write in)							

3. Do you believe planners should continue to try to reduce the current teacher–student ratio? Why? What do you believe is the optimal student–teacher ratio?

Deconstructing the Standards

1. **InTASC** Standard #3 reads, "The teacher works with others to create environments that support individual and collaborative learning, and that encourage positive social interaction, active engagement in learning, and self-motivation."
   a. How does this chapter address this standard?
   b. How will the concepts in this chapter help you apply this standard as a teacher?

2. Use your favorite search engine to find your state's standards for certification. When you find it, bookmark the site; you will refer to it often during this course.
   a. How do your conclusions about the structure of schools compare to the state standards?
   b. How do the InTASC Standards compare to your state's certification standards?

Your Portfolio

1. Add a copy of the floor plan of the school where you are doing your field experience to your portfolio. Provide a reflection of how the school's physical structure enables it to carry out its function.
2. What technology does your field experience school have available for students and teachers? How does the school make this technology accessible for the users? Reflect on the availability and accessibility of instructional technology, and comment on how you might manage the use of the available technology with students.

Education CourseMate Resources

Check out this text's Education CourseMate website (at www.cengagebrain.com) for more information about the structure of schools, roles and responsibilities of personnel, interactive study tools, and useful resources. You will also find the TeachSource videos, a guide for field experiences, glossary flash cards, additional activities, tutorial quizzes, direct links to all of the websites mentioned in this chapter, and more.

The School and the Student: Expectations and Responsibilities

SO FAR, you have considered yourself, the student, and the purposes and structures of schools. It is in this place we call *school* that the relationship between you (the teacher) and your students must be established and nurtured. In this environment, all the participants in the educational experience have certain expectations of one another. As a student, you have expectations of your teacher and your school. As a teacher, you have expectations of your students and the school in which you will work. Let us take the opportunity to explore these expectations and how schools meet them.

Students spend about a third of their day in school. In fact, "aside from their sleeping hours, most children spend more time in the presence of their teachers than they spend in the presence of their parents" (Eisner, 2002, p. 648). Students bring more than their bodies to school; they also bring their individual thoughts, feelings, experiences, backgrounds, and beliefs.

You have investigated how students' unique perspectives and abilities affect their performance in the classroom. Consider as well that students must function effectively and congenially in the school atmosphere. Recall Maslow's hierarchy of needs: There are many challenges to students' feelings of safety, love and belonging, and self-esteem, both inside and outside the classroom and the school. And recall Erikson's psychosocial developmental stages: Students may experience issues with trust, autonomy, and initiative as they attempt to interact within the culture of the schools.

Students can hardly be expected to devote their attention to schoolwork if these needs and issues have not been satisfied and resolved.

In this chapter, you will explore the responsibilities and relationships that exist between the school and the students. You will investigate how students, teachers, and others in the school work together to create an environment that is inviting, safe, and maximally conducive to student learning. As in previous chapters, you will integrate your personal experiences with the theories and thoughts of others to enable you to draw some important conclusions and construct your understandings of how the school helps students learn.

Chapter Objectives

As a result of your work in this chapter, you will:

1. Describe life in school as the student experiences it in terms of physical, intellectual, and emotional safety, and describe possible threats to student safety.
   InTASC Standard #3: Learning Environments

2. Provide examples of school responses to ensure the physical, intellectual, and emotional safety of each student.
   InTASC Standard #3: Learning Environments

3. Describe the teacher's role in meeting students' needs through effective classroom management.
   InTASC Standard #3: Learning Environments

Student Safety in the School

What is life in school like for students? We all have definite ideas about this question based on our own experiences. How can we make students feel comfortable and safe in school? What can we do so they will be able to focus their energies on learning?

We have said the primary purpose of schools is to help students learn. Before students can be motivated to learn, their needs must be met. One of these needs is the need for safety and security. This need includes not only physical safety but intellectual safety and emotional safety as well. Schools are responsible for *all* aspects of safety and security for their students.[1]

Physical Safety

It is obvious that students should be assured of their physical safety at school. Building codes, inspections, and many other measures ensure that schools are safe. Fire, tornado, and earthquake drills become part of students' lives so they can react in an orderly way if there is a threat of disaster or danger. Additional threats come from individuals who, for whatever reason, wreak havoc in schools by theft, violence, terrorist acts, assault, or other criminal actions.

---

[1]The entire September 2011 issue of *Educational Leadership* (Volume 69, Number 1) is devoted to safety in schools.

School staff as well as city and state personnel can help ensure student safety on school premises. Did the schools you attended take extra precautions to ensure your safety?

Sadly, shooting tragedies have occurred all across the country. You may recall incidents at Columbine High School in Littleton, Colorado (1999); Red Lake High School in Red Lake, Minnesota (2005); and West Nickel Mines Amish School in Nickel Mines, Pennsylvania (2006). Shooters in these schools caused multiple homicides and extensive injuries to both students and teachers. In the case of Columbine and Red Lake High Schools, the shooters were students enrolled at the schools. The shooter at the Amish school in Pennsylvania was an outsider. The National School Safety Center's Report on School Associated Violent Deaths (2010) indicates that between the 1992–93 and 2009–10 school years, 348 students and teachers were killed in school shootings.

Criminal acts can seem commonplace in our schools. Most are nonfatal. Although there has been a decrease in the number of nonfatal crimes committed at school during the past decade, in 2008, more than 1.2 million nonfatal crimes, including rapes, sexual assaults, robberies, aggravated assaults, simple assaults, and thefts, were committed against students ages 12 to 18, and these crimes were committed while the victims were in school (Robers, Zhang, and Truman, 2010; see Figure 8.1). Additional threats and potential threats to the physical safety of students were noted in a report from the U.S. Department of Education and the U.S. Department of Justice. In 2009, for students in grades 9 through 12:

- Eight percent reported that they were threatened or injured with a weapon (knife, gun, or club).
- Eight percent of males and 3 percent of females reported carrying a gun on school grounds.
- Twenty-three percent reported that drugs had been made available.
- Four percent reported drinking alcohol and 5 percent reported using marijuana.
- Thirty-one percent reported that they had been in a physical fight (Robers, Zhang, and Truman, 2010).

Nonetheless, the reality is that "America's public schools are *very safe*, even those in high crime neighborhoods" (Fowler, 2011, p. 16). Still, any act of violence in a school is a cause for concern. How can schools work to be safer places?

BUILDING BLOCK 8.1   Safe Schools

None of us is a stranger to media reports of school violence. Perhaps you have thought about possible threats to your personal safety as you consider a career in teaching. School officials are responsible for assuring the physical safety of their students and personnel. This responsibility, of course, includes taking measures not only to thwart heinous attacks such as those we hear about in the news, but also to protect against natural hazards such as fire and severe weather, provide for the security of students' and staff's personal belongings, and ensure safety in the school buses that transport students to and from school.

- What are some of the ways school officials work to ensure the physical safety of students and personnel?
- How are these efforts different from those taken by your school when you were a student?

Hold on to your ideas; you will examine how schools work to ensure student physical safety later in this chapter.

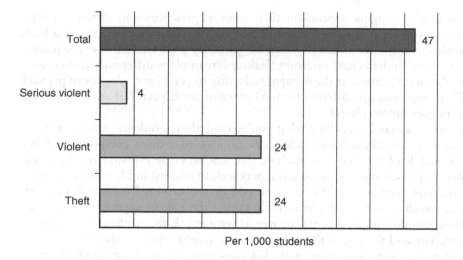

◀ **Figure 8.1**
Student-Reported Nonfatal Crimes against Students occurring at school (age 12-18), per 1000 Students: 2008.
Note: "Violent crimes" include simple assaults, whereas "serious violent crimes" include rape, sexual assault, robbery, and aggravated assault. Serious violent crimes are included in violent crimes.
Source: Robers, Zhang, and Truman, 2010
© Cengage Learning 2014

The National School Safety Center is an excellent source of additional material on school safety. You can access their website through the direct link on the Education CourseMate website.

Intellectual Safety

A second type of safety that schools must provide is intellectual safety. Have you ever spoken up in class with what you thought was a good answer, only to have it dismissed as wrong? Although your answer made perfect sense to you, it was devalued because it was not the response the teacher sought. After several such incidents, you are likely to start believing that your thinking is not good. You find you must respond in a way that pleases the teacher, rather than expressing your own thoughts. Your intellectual safety has been compromised. You no longer feel safe to express your thoughts. Recalling Erikson's stages of psychosocial development, how likely are you to take the *initiative* in classroom discussions or activities?

As teachers, we must preserve not only the physical safety of our students, but also their intellectual safety. This means we must seek, respect, and value our students' thinking as much as our own. How do we do this?

Intellectual Safety

BUILDING BLOCK 8.2

1. Look at Figure 8.2 and describe what you see.
2. Select one of the following words, and note the *first* concept that comes to mind when you see it.

   FAN   FLAG   PLANT

3. What are two of your favorite TV shows?

Compare your answers with others in your class. Are there differences? Why?

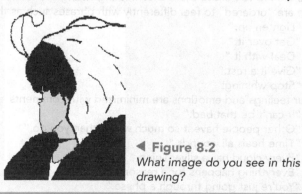

◀ **Figure 8.2**
What image do you see in this drawing?

Because people's thoughts depend on their prior experiences and different people have different experiences, it is highly likely that students will interpret the same academic situation in different ways. A student may solve a geometry problem in a way the teacher did not expect. Some students may interpret Shakespearean plays differently from others. Some small children may cringe at the thought of having to pet a furry classroom pet such as a gerbil. Their responses are different from what we might expect. But are they wrong? Or are the responses simply *theirs*?

At this point, you may be recalling what you've read about students' unique perspectives. What did you learn about how teachers can acknowledge those perspectives? It is a fundamental principle of excellence in teaching that teachers *listen* to students. By listening to students' responses and discussions, teachers seek to understand how their students are learning and how they are constructing their conceptualizations. Teachers must create a classroom in which students feel comfortable taking the risk of saying what they are thinking. Before you dismiss a student's answer as wrong, ask the student to explain his or her thinking. You and the rest of the class may gain insight into that student's perspective and you may even learn something new! Teachers who do this ensure students' intellectual safety.

Emotional Safety

A third type of safety is emotional safety. Emotional safety is what we feel when we know that others understand and accept our emotions. When others, such as students, teachers, or parents, fail to validate a student's emotions, the student learns to distrust his or her own feelings. Teasing, ignoring, judging, or diminishing another's feelings may cause this invalidation. The ensuing distrust may lead to anxiety, depression, and the repression of individuality, confidence, and creativity.

Emotions are personal. When someone's feelings are validated and understood by other people, that person feels emotionally safe. As a result, he or she feels safe telling others about feelings of enthusiasm, excitement, fear, elation, worry, anger, devastation, or shame. But when a person fears criticism or ridicule of his or her feelings, that person feels emotionally unsafe. He or she still has feelings but hides them. It is important that people's feelings be validated and that they not be criticized, corrected, or condemned by others for their emotions. Note that we are not saying that teachers must agree with the emotions students express, but rather just understand and accept them. For example, you don't have to swoon over the current teen idols that the students in your classroom are crazy about, but you can certainly understand the fun they are having. There is no need to tell them they are just being silly.

Ways in Which Emotions Can Be Invalidated

The following list shows different situations in which emotional safety is at risk (Hein, 2003):

- We are told we shouldn't feel the way we feel.
- We are told we are too sensitive, too "dramatic."
- We are led to believe there is something wrong with us for feeling how we feel.
- We are "ordered" to feel differently with phrases such as these:
  - "Lighten up."
  - "Get over it."
  - "Deal with it."
  - "Give it a rest."
  - "Stop whining!"
- Our feelings and emotions are minimized with comments such as the following:
  - "It can't be that bad."
  - "Other people have it so much worse than you do."
  - "Time heals all wounds."
  - "Every cloud has a silver lining."
  - "Everything happens for a reason."
  - "You're just going through a phase."

- Our feelings are judged by comments such as the following:
  - "You're a crybaby."
  - "You're too sensitive or thin-skinned."
  - "You're overreacting."
  - "You always make a big deal about little things."

Researchers have found a close correlation between harbored negative feelings and violent acts at school. For example, a study jointly conducted by the National Threat Assessment Center (a division of the U.S. Secret Service) and the U.S. Department of Education reported that in many of the incidents of school shootings investigated between 1974 and 2000, the attackers felt "persecuted, bullied, threatened, attacked, or injured" (Vossekuil et al., 2002, p. 20). When students develop negative feelings and negative emotions and cannot express these feelings or obtain validation of them from peers and adults, they may be inclined to express their feelings in inappropriate and sometimes dangerous ways.

Bullying

There are many threats to emotional safety, but among the more powerful and far-reaching are bullying and harassment.

Bullies and Bullying

BUILDING BLOCK
8.3

Do you remember any bullies at your school? Maybe you were picked on at one time or another, or perhaps you witnessed some students ganging up on another student. Maybe you were the bully . . .

- How would you recognize bullying if you saw it in the hallway or on the playground of a school in which you were teaching?
- What makes a person a bully? What characteristics does a bully have?
- What are some different types of bullying? When does teasing become bullying? Can spreading rumors be bullying?

Dan Olweus (2011), an authority on bullying and the developer of the Olweus Bullying Prevention Program, notes that bullying occurs when a person is exposed repeatedly to negative actions on the part of one or more other people, and has difficulty defending himself or herself.

    The power that bullies use to intimidate others can come from social and/or financial status, age, or physical strength. Some individuals get the power to be bullies by association—just from hanging out with people who have one or more of these powers (Quiroz, Arnette, and Stephens, 2006). The federal government recognizes four categories of bullying; any single act of bullying may fit into more than one category. They are:

1. Verbal—teasing, name-calling
2. Social—social exclusion or isolation, spreading rumors
3. Physical—hitting, pushing
4. Cyber—using technologies such as the Internet and mobile devices to cause harm to others (StopBullying.gov)

Boys tend to participate in direct physical bullying. Girls tend to use verbal and social tactics such as exclusion, name-calling, and gossip (Quiroz, Arnette, and Stephens, 2006). Both boys and girls engage in cyberbullying. Did your responses in Building Block 8.3 include these factors?

bullying One or more people repeatedly exposing another person to negative actions against which the person has difficulty defending himself or herself.

A Safe Learning Environment

Linda L. Eisinger

Courtesy of Linda Eisinger

Students have the ability to reach their full potential in a safe and structured classroom environment. It is important that families and communities expect and demand a safe classroom and safe school.

Most people equate a safe school and a safe classroom with physical safety. Although I agree this is very important, when I say *safe school* and *safe classroom*, I am thinking of an environment where children know they can take academic risks and they will not be embarrassed by peers or an insensitive teacher. Teachers must provide this safe learning environment, where students are prepared and can take risks that let them demonstrate their skills and knowledge successfully.

I began my career as a special education teacher in a middle school. Students would have to leave their classrooms for math remediation. I can still see them coming to my room very upset and with tears in their eyes because their teachers had embarrassed them in front of their classmates by telling them they were not smart. I immediately made up my mind that each and every child placed in my classroom would always have a successful experience.

Charlie came into my life on Valentine's Day. His mother dropped him off at school with nothing. We were having Valentine parties that day and he came with no valentines to share. I hurriedly scrambled and got some construction paper and we cut and pasted valentines throughout the day, with some student helpers helping him finish.

After seeing how Charlie handled that day, I had a special place for him in my heart. I knew he had been disappointed many times in his young life and he really didn't expect anything. How sad it must be to be eight years old and not let yourself get excited about things because you know they will never come true.

I was having difficulty getting Charlie to take risks in his learning. He seldom volunteered an answer, and if he did he would always preface it with the comment, "I know this is wrong. . . ." One day I was teaching a science lesson and was preparing to show a video when the remote control wouldn't work. I started to do something else when Charlie spoke up and told me he could fix it. He fiddled with it a minute, and it was working! The class started to clap and cheer and Charlie just beamed. I knew I could use this experience to help with his self-esteem.

The next day before science, I stood up in front of the class and asked the children if they remembered how Charlie had fixed the remote. They cheered again. I told them I had discovered that Charlie had turned the remote into a magical one. I had Charlie's attention! I then made the statement, "A habitat is the environment . . ." and I pointed the remote at the students and said, "Rewind and replay." The class immediately caught on and repeated the statement. Charlie loved it, and we often used "Charlie's Magic Remote" to review for tests and lessons.

Charlie stayed with me for the rest of the year. He came to summer school that year, and I would often see him helping the slower children, repeating words or phrases I had used with him.

Charlie moved on after summer school and I truly missed him the following year. He had felt so comfortable in our school and I imagine he had to start all over again at a new school until he felt secure and safe with his learning. I wish the best for him and hope to see him again.

Teachers must do all they can to make each child's year in their rooms a safe and successful one. All students come that first day of school wanting to learn. I have never seen a year start without that energy and potential. Ineffective and insensitive teachers must be weeded out and removed. They cannot be allowed to affect students adversely.

When a teacher creates that safe learning environment, the rewards for the students and the teacher are immeasurable. In the classroom, I have been thrilled to observe a student reading an entire sentence without one mistake for the first time. The joy expressed on this student's face was indescribable. On one occasion, a student who had been struggling for weeks with multiplication finally looked up from his paper and said, "I get it!" The entire class broke into spontaneous applause. These are exciting moments in my profession, and I have contributed to them by creating that learning environment where students feel comfortable about taking academic risks. I cannot envision a more important task than for a teacher to create an emotionally and intellectually safe classroom.

Linda L. Eisinger
Missouri Teacher of the Year, 2004–2005
West Elementary School
Jefferson City, Missouri

According to the report, *Indicators of School Crime and Safety: 2010* (Robers, Zhang, and Truman, 2010), students aged 12 to 18 reported the following for the 2007–2008 school year:

- Ten percent reported hearing hate-related words directed at them.

- Thirty-five percent reported seeing hate-related graffiti.

- Thirty-two percent reported being bullied while at school. The types of bullying included:
  - Verbal bullying—21 percent
  - Being the subject of rumors—18 percent
  - Physical bullying—11 percent
  - Threats of physical harm—6 percent
  - Being socially excluded/isolated—5 percent
  - Being forced to do things they didn't want to or having their property purposely destroyed—4 percent

- Five percent reported being afraid of attack or harm.

- Three percent reported avoiding an activity, and six percent reported avoiding a particular place in school out of fear of attack or harm.

Bullying and harassment can detrimentally affect the victim's social and emotional well-being. What might a teacher do to deter bullying like this against other students?

A recent study found that sexual minority students—those who identified as gay, lesbian, or bisexual—were bullied two to three times more often than heterosexual students but were less likely to do any bullying themselves (Nationwide Children's Hospital, 2010). In fact, sexual minority students are 1.7 times more likely than their peers to report being threatened, injured, or assaulted, and almost three times as likely to miss school due to fear (Friedman et al., 2011).

Brewster and Railsback (2001) reported that teachers seem to be mostly unaware of the prevalence of bullying or, if they were aware, they took no serious action to stop it. Bullying has led victims to depression, anxiety, delinquency, vandalism, fighting, truancy, and even suicide. In an effort to help inform federal practice, raise awareness, and suggest bullying prevention strategies, the federal government has begun holding a series of annual Bullying Prevention Summits (U.S. Department of Education, 2011c).

Cyberbullying

Did you think of cyberbullying? Cyberbullying is defined as the act of bullying through email, text and picture messages, websites, posts on social networking sites and chat rooms, and cell phones. The same negative action, repetition over time, and power imbalance that is present with person-to-person bullying is present with cyberbullying (Kowalski et al., 2008). The Internet has become a setting for this practice, also called virtual bullying. Students have created websites devoted to humiliating classmates and have used instant messaging and chat rooms to harass individuals. These activities may be unmonitored by adults and represent a serious concern for school officials and parents.

Studies have found that, in 2010, about 20 percent of students aged 11 to 18 years had been victims of cyberbullying; about the same percentage admitted to being cyberbullies themselves; and 10 percent said they were both victims and perpetrators (Lenhart et al., 2011; Hinduja & Patchin, 2010a). Victims of cyberbullying are less willing to go to school, start getting poor grades, and suffer from lower self-esteem and health issues as a result of bullying. The very public and tragic suicides of three teens, Megan Meier in October 2006, Phoebe Prince in January 2010, and Jamey Rodemeyer, who was gay, in September 2011, were all linked to cyberbullying. In fact, one research study involving 2,000 randomly

cyberbullying Bullying that takes place using electronic technology such as cell phones and computers.

selected middle-grades students found that 20 percent of those who reported being victims of cyberbullying seriously considered suicide. An additional, even more frightening statistic is that 19 percent of those participating in the study reported *attempting* suicide (Hinduja & Patchin, 2010b). In 2010, the National Education Association warned teachers that cyberbullying would be one of the top challenges that teachers will face (Flannery, 2010).

Harassment

Harassment means "to annoy persistently" (Merriam-Webster, 2012). Harassment can take many forms, but sexual harassment may be the most disquieting. Other forms of harassment usually are treated as aspects of bullying.

Sexual harassment is illegal, whether it is student-to-student or adult-to-student, and whether it involves members of opposite sexes or members of the same sex. The U.S. Department of Education, Office for Civil Rights (2008) defines sexual harassment as behavior that is sexual, unwelcome, and that affects a student's participation in or benefit from the educational opportunities a school offers. Examples include propositioning or pressuring students for sexual favors, inappropriate touching of students, touching oneself or making crude gestures or noises in front of others, telling dirty jokes, showing writings, pictures, drawings, printed materials, or graffiti that is sexual in nature, spreading rumors about students regarding sexual activity and/or performance, and distributing or showing emails or websites that are sexual in nature.

Research has found that over a third of middle and high school students surveyed reported being sexually harassed. Boys were harassed as frequently as girls, but sexual minorities (gays, lesbians, bisexuals, and transgendered students) experienced harassment more frequently (Gruber & Fineran, 2008). This same research has shown that even though bullying is more prevalent, sexual harassment has more detrimental effects on students' emotional and physical health than does bullying. And again, sexual minority students are harassed more frequently than their heterosexual peers.

Sexual harassment is always wrong, and students should be encouraged to tell an adult if they are victims. Adults and other school officials can take the necessary actions to stop such harassment. School districts are required to have clear policies and procedures that address the sexual harassment of both students and employees, whether students or employees commit the harassment (Walsh, 1999). Schools activate these procedures as needed.

What do you suppose these girls are giggling about?

School Responses to Safety Issues

In your experience, how have schools responded to safety issues? You may have gone to a school that took precautions to prevent the threats to safety that you have read about, and you may have seen or read in the news about some policies or actions schools have taken. Let's examine several ways schools try to meet the expectations that students have to be kept safe.

Increased Security and Prevention

One way that schools have responded to threats to safety is to intensify security measures using such procedures as the following:

- Surveillance cameras and video cameras
- Door and key controls

- Locked doors
- Metal detectors
- On-campus police officers
- ID cards
- Communications devices
- Warning codes
- Duress alarms
- Video cameras on school buses
- Profiling and identifying students who may have a higher-than-normal risk of committing violent acts and keeping track of their activities
- Inspecting book bags or banning book bags altogether
- School uniforms or strict dress codes
- Drug and weapons sweeps by police and canines
- Visitor check-in/check-out with IDs

Did the list you compiled in Building Block 8.3 contain these measures? Should it? Many of these procedures are put in place to apprehend students who may bring weapons or other contraband to school.

Figure 8.3 shows the increase in severity measures between 2000 and 2008.

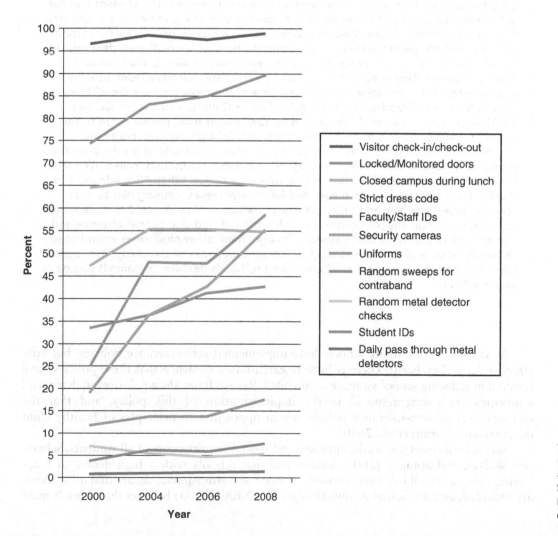

◀ **Figure 8.3**
Percent of schools using various security measures, 2000–2008.
Source: Adapted from U.S. Census Bureau, 2011b
© Cengage Learning 2014

Zero-Tolerance Policies

zero-tolerance policies Policies that entail a strict and swift disciplinary response to students or school personnel who engage in violent activities, who bring to or use weapons in school, or who bring or use controlled substances.

Numerous schools have zero-tolerance policies in place that entail a strict and swift disciplinary response to students or school personnel who engage in violent activities such as fighting, who bring or use weapons such as firearms and other dangerous objects to school, or who bring or use controlled substances such as alcohol, tobacco, or other drugs. It is estimated that almost 75 percent of schools have adopted zero-tolerance policies (Borum et al., 2010). These policies apply not only to students, but also to teachers and other adults. For students, consequences of zero tolerance vary with the offense but usually entail some degree of suspension from school, expulsion, or the involvement of law enforcement agencies.

Should Tolerance Be "All or None"?

Zero-tolerance policies are not without their critics. Although it is hard to imagine a legitimate reason for a student or adult to bring a firearm or a controlled substance such as alcohol to school, some criticize the policy's strict interpretation. For example, in 2010, a North Carolina high school senior who excelled in academics and playing soccer was suspended from school for having a knife in her lunchbox (FoxNews, 2010). The paring knife was found during a search conducted by officials who were going through students' belongings looking for drugs. The student did not realize that the knife was in her lunchbox; in fact, the lunchbox didn't even belong to the student. It was her father's lunchbox and it contained not only the knife but also a whole apple for which the knife was intended. The student and her father had identical lunchboxes and the student mistakenly grabbed the wrong one. Regardless, school officials cited their zero-tolerance policy for weapons on school grounds, and the paring knife was considered to be a weapon. The student missed the remaining portion of her senior year and was charged with a misdemeanor. There are several similar cases from around the country that have resulted since the implementation of zero-tolerance policies. One of the most tragic is the 2011 case of Nick Stuban of Woodson High School in Fairfax County, Virginia (St. George, 2011). Nick was a 15-year-old dedicated football player who, perhaps due to the stress of dealing with his mother's advancing Lou Gehrig's disease, made the mistake of purchasing from another student at school a capsule of a substance that produces a marijuana-like effect. Though the synthetic compound, called JWH-018, is not illegal, it violated the school's zero-tolerance policy. When Nick admitted to making the purchase, he was suspended for several weeks, causing him to miss school-related activities and other activities in which he was involved that were held on school grounds. His relationships with friends suffered due to that absence and due to rumors that were being spread. Though many other challenges contributed to the situation and to Nick's struggles, the consequences of the disciplinary action taken by the school system have been linked to Nick's decision to commit suicide in January 2011.

Use your favorite search engine to find whether your local school system has implemented a zero-tolerance policy. Go to your state's department of education website to learn whether your state has statewide zero-tolerance laws. What are the policies and laws? What are the consequences of violating them?

As you have seen, many schools have implemented zero-tolerance policies; but how effective have they been? There is little research-based evidence that these policies have resulted in reducing school violence as intended. Research has shown, however, that racial minorities are overrepresented in the implementation of this policy, and that the consequences of zero-tolerance policies are in opposition to principles of healthy child development (Borum et al., 2010).

Safe schools meet the needs, interests, and special requirements of all students. Schneider, Walker, and Sprague (2000) have found that schools with a high degree of long-lasting safety are well led, have a positive climate and atmosphere, ensure that *all* students are included, and are academically effective. The NEA (2003a) believes that schools must address the root causes of violence among students through developing and implementing strategies to achieve the following goals:

- Reduce and eliminate bullying and harassment
- Expand access to counseling, anger management, and peer mediation
- Provide ways for students to communicate with adults about rumors and threats
- Develop instruction that teaches such values as respect and responsibility

Anti-Bullying Programs

Recalling the statistics you have read about bullying and cyberbullying, it is probably not surprising to know that 47 states now have laws against bullying (Bully Police USA, 2011). Many schools have adopted anti-bullying policies, and some have implemented anti-bullying programs. For the most part, the policies define bullying to include the concepts of cyberbullying and harassment, and identify the responsibilities of those involved in the policy such as students, teachers, administrators, counselors, parents, and other stakeholders. They also outline the consequences and describe the procedures for reporting acts of bullying.

Some systems have purchased programs developed by specialists to implement in their schools. These programs stress the importance of teaching students not only what bullying is, how to prevent it, and how to respond to it, but also the importance of involving the whole school and community (Quiroz, 2006). The Olweus Bullying Prevention Program claims to be the "World's Foremost Prevention Program." It is research-based and authored by Dr. Dan Olweus (whom you saw above is a leading authority on bullying). The program consists of a collection of materials for students, teachers, administrators, and other stakeholders to help them prevent and address bullying by teaching strategies to victims and witnesses. In the biggest study of its kind (involving 56,137 students and more than 2,400 teachers from 107 schools over a two-year period), researchers evaluated the effectiveness of the Olweus Program and noted a reduction in reports of bullying and more positive attitudes of students regarding bullying (Schroeder et al., 2011).

You can probably imagine that cyberbullying is more difficult to address. Parents may not have the technology "know-how" to understand how their children use their computers and other technologies to harass and bully others. Also, cyberbullying is most often done in private and anonymously, preventing any witnesses to the event. Again, addressing this particular type of bullying requires the concerted effort of several people: adults, other students, the community, and in this instance, social media companies (Hinduja & Patchin, 2010a).

Chances are that you will do a field experience, student teach, and/or work in a school with an anti-bullying policy or program. It will be your responsibility to not only be familiar with the policy or program, but also to enforce and employ it.

AP Images/Dan Loh/Pool

Are popular methods of reducing school violence, like school police and metal detectors, enough to prevent school violence against students, teachers, and school staff?

▶❚❚ **TeachSource** Video

View the TeachSource Video, "Cyberbullying." Cyberbullying is a growing problem in schools as traditional bullying has migrated onto computers. Some social networking sites have set up safeguards to prevent cyberbullying, and there are services that can allow parents to monitor their children's use of social networking sites. After you view the video, answer the following questions:

1. Should schools have a say when bullying happens beyond the school ground?
2. In what ways can schools and teachers help to prevent cyberbullying?
3. How might restricting access to computers or certain Internet sites in an effort to prevent cyberbullying also affect instruction?
4. Would the restrictions' effect on instruction be worth preventing potential episodes of cyberbullying?

GSA or No GSA

To provide a safe space for those who, according to research, experience harassment and bullying most often, some schools have included Gay-Straight Alliances (GSAs) among their organized extracurricular clubs. These organizations typically meet after school, on school grounds, and are meant to bring together gay, lesbian, transgendered, questioning, and straight students in an atmosphere of support. As of 2008, over 4,000 GSAs were registered with the Gay, Lesbian, and Straight Education Network (GLSEN, 2011). Not surprisingly, such clubs are often associated with controversy. In some instances, students want to start GSAs, but the school won't approve the organization. Such was the case in Flour Bluff, Texas, in 2011. According to a local news station (Curtis, 2011), a student and an adult advocate proposed forming a GSA on the campus of the high school. The school district decided to suspend all extracurricular clubs until they could be reviewed for approval. Although it seems that this decision was in response to the proposal for a GSA, the school district issued a press release stating that the legal review of all clubs was part of their regular policy and practice. The school board's action drew counter responses from students and parents who support the GSA as well as the other extracurricular organizations, and the director of the Texas Civil Rights Project threatened legal action.

On March 2, 2011, the American Civil Liberties Union sent a letter to the school board demanding that they allow the proposed GSA to form and to hold meetings (ACLU, 2011a). A free website devoted to starting, joining, and supporting social change in which anyone can initiate a petition about any subject and viewers can "sign" with those they agree, hosted an online petition that garnered over 57,000 signatures to support the recognition of the Flour Bluff High School GSA. On March 9, the ACLU reported that the school district had voted to approve the GSA late the night before (ACLU, 2011b).

In other instances, the schools approve the GSA, but the community protests. A group of students petitioned to form a GSA in a high school in North Carolina for the 2005–2006 school year. Over 700 community members, parents, and students gathered to protest. As a result, the school board adopted a policy to ban any school clubs based on "sexuality" (Evans, 2006). GLSEN responded to this, saying

© Custom Life Science Images/Alamy

that calling a GSA a "sexuality-based club" was a gross mischaracterization (GLSEN, 2006). Supporters threatened to sue the board on the basis of the federal Equal Access Act, which states that curriculum- and noncurriculum-based clubs must have equal access to school facilities. The North Carolina Family Policy Council, an organization that "defends traditional family values" and provides information on public policy affecting families, noted that "Gay-Straight Alliance clubs have been a key weapon in the arsenal of the homosexual movement for spreading its message to youth" (Evans, 2006, p. 1). The Council contends that GSAs' message is that "it's okay to be gay," and that this message is in contrast to the moral and religious teachings of parents and church.

WHAT DO YOU THINK?

You might have difficulty asking yourself whether you would be active in or even support a GSA at a high school or school district you might work in one day. Remember that your first consideration should always be your students' well-being, including physical and emotional safety. Does the inclusion of GSAs in schools help serve this purpose?

You can access the website where you can enter or join a petition of just about any topic through a direct link on the Education CourseMate website.

The Teacher's Role

The efforts discussed so far to ensure student safety in schools have primarily been school-level policies and procedures. As a teacher, you also have a big part to play in addition to teaching and assessing. It has been said that the teacher is the most important person in responding to bullying in the classroom (Quiroz, 2006). Certainly, teachers must implement and enforce anti-bullying policies and programs, as mentioned previously. But the way teachers manage the classroom and implement instruction can go a long way to preventing bullying, which in turn can prevent its escalation into further violence and tragedy.

Of course, your responsibility as a teacher extends beyond addressing student safety. You are also responsible for your students' learning! Let us take a look at what students can expect from teachers.

Helping Students Feel Safe

BUILDING BLOCK 8.4

Think of the following needs for students at the age level you plan to teach:

- Safety and security needs
- Love and belonging needs
- Cognitive needs
- Psychosocial needs

For each, list two or three *specific* actions you could take with regard to instruction and classroom climate that would strengthen your relationship with students and help them to meet these needs. (Compare these actions with the qualities of good teachers you identified in Chapter 1, and the instructional strategies you suggested in Chapters 3 and 4.)

- Reduce your list to the four or five most important actions teachers can take to build positive and supportive relationships with students.
- How might these actions help ensure the safety of students?

From Building Block 8.4, you can see that teachers can do a lot to help their students meet their needs and feel safe and comfortable in school.

Classroom Management and Discipline

As a teacher candidate, one of your biggest concerns is probably how to manage your students' behavior. Implementing a fair and firm classroom management plan is among a teacher's most important activities. The first step in designing a classroom management plan is to create a caring classroom environment. And the first step in creating this environment is getting to know your students. You read about this early in this chapter. The good news is that knowing your students and letting them know that you care about them and their learning will go far in preventing a lot of misbehavior. However, students often act out because they feel a lack of security that comes from not knowing what is expected of them or where the boundaries are. As a teacher, you can help students by providing structure and routine.

You will need to develop structures, procedures, and routines as a part of your classroom management plan. These are meant to help the classroom run as a cooperative, collaborative learning community and prevent the misbehavior that might result when students feel unsure of what is expected of them. Well-defined classroom procedures and routines help satisfy students' need for safety, security, and belonging. For most students, the procedures and routines are enough to meet these needs; they know what to expect and what is expected of them.

Other students, however, might have greater needs. Some may feel they need an extraordinary amount of attention, either from peers or from the teacher. They might go to extraordinary—and disruptive—lengths to get this attention. Some, reacting to feeling controlled, might act out against these authority figures in an attempt to gain power. The behavior that results from attempts to satisfy such needs may be disruptive and unacceptable in the classroom environment. For this reason, teachers must also develop consequences as well as rules as part of their classroom management plans.

Students sometimes refer to life in school as "prison-like." Why do you think they feel this way? Might it be because, as in a prison, they feel their behavior is being controlled? Surely rules and regulations are necessary at school. We have them in our general society, and we need them at school. This is partly because of legal considerations (see Chapter 13), and it is partly because schools must keep order. Structure is necessary in the school environment to enable the classes to run smoothly. Having rules, policies, and procedures is part of life in school and helps students know what is expected of them and where the boundaries are.

The teacher's method of maintaining order in the classroom is known as *behavior management*. Behavior management has two fundamental goals:

1. To permit the teacher to teach
2. To provide each student with the maximum opportunity to learn

Unfortunately, there is no magical plan that will ensure golden behavior from all of your students all of the time. However, you can examine some strategies and methods and observe the behavior management system used in your field experience classroom to gain insights on how to manage behavior effectively.

BUILDING BLOCK 8.5

Discipline in the Classroom

Have you ever been in a class in which there seemed to be no discipline?

- What was it like?
- How did it make you feel as a student about the classroom environment?
- What did you think about the teacher?
- How did this lack of discipline affect your attitude toward the content you were supposed to be learning?

Have you ever been in a class in which the discipline was so strict that nobody dared to do anything the teacher might not like?

- What was it like?
- How did it make you feel as a student about the classroom environment?
- What did you think about the teacher?
- How did such strict discipline affect your attitude toward the content you were supposed to be learning?

There are many ways to manage behavior in the classroom, and these depend on the classroom climate the individual teacher wants to maintain. To gain an idea of the kind of behavior you expect in the classroom, do the activity in Building Block 8.6.

BUILDING BLOCK 8.6

Classroom Behavior Expectations

Different teachers have different ideas and expectations about order in the classroom. To learn your own basic conception, take the inventory that follows. Mark each statement in accordance with the following scale:

4 = True all or almost all the time.
3 = True much of the time.
2 = True less than half the time.
1 = Never or almost never true.

1. _____ Students should be assigned seats in the classroom—often in alphabetical order.
2. _____ Seating assignments in the classroom should be negotiated between students and the teacher.
3. _____ Students should be given opportunities to make choices.
4. _____ Students must follow teacher directions, whether they like it or not.
5. _____ Students should remain quiet in the classroom except when the teacher calls on them to respond to a question.
6. _____ Students should be allowed to talk to one another, providing their discussions deal with the topic under study.
7. _____ "Controlled chaos" is okay in the classroom.
8. _____ The best way to get an unruly class to quiet down is to yell at them.
9. _____ The teacher makes the classroom rules, and students should follow them.
10. _____ If a student falls asleep in class, the teacher could bang a book on the desk to wake up that student.
11. _____ Teachers must not show any weaknesses lest their behavior management systems collapse.
12. _____ During the first week or two of class, teachers should work at negotiating rapport and mutual respect with the students.
13. _____ Teachers should nurture students' own creativity and self-expression as much as possible.
14. _____ It is okay for a teacher to laugh at himself or herself in front of the class.
15. _____ When a student violates rules, the teacher should punish that student appropriately and immediately.
16. _____ When a student violates rules, the teacher should threaten the student with punishment.
17. _____ When a student violates rules, the teacher should ignore this behavior because there really isn't anything the teacher can do about it anyhow.
18. _____ If a student doesn't turn in homework on time, the teacher should record a zero.
19. _____ The teacher should keep the invitation open for students to submit homework, even if it is late.
20. _____ The goal of effective discipline is obedience.
21. _____ The goal of effective discipline is for students to be responsible.
22. _____ Really bad students need to be put in their place.
23. _____ The teacher should ignore the really bad behavior of students, as not much can be done about it anyway.
24. _____ Students need to have the freedom to let off steam and express themselves.
25. _____ Teachers must always treat students with dignity, regardless of students' behavior.
26. _____ Students can usually be expected to ignore class rules.
27. _____ Students don't have a right to get angry in school.
28. _____ There are always a few students whose behavior the teacher cannot control.
29. _____ The teacher should post crystal-clear limits and behavior expectations on the classroom wall and enforce them.
30. _____ Teachers can expect that students will behave in class; after all, students have been brought up to respect authority, respect peers, and behave properly.
31. _____ Teachers need to keep a tight rein on the students in their classes; bending the rules only encourages further infractions.
32. _____ When a whole class decides to be unruly, there is nothing the teacher can do about the situation.
33. _____ It is okay for students to interrupt the teacher and one another if they have legitimate comments.

34. _____ The teacher is always right.
35. _____ It is good to let students win arguments when they have valid points.
36. _____ Students should never argue with the teacher.
37. _____ The teacher should reprimand students for huffing and puffing, rolling their eyes, and similarly disagreeable behaviors.
38. _____ It is fine to enforce classroom rules some days and ignore them on other days; after all, teachers are human, too.
39. _____ Students should develop the class rules by themselves; after all, it is *their* class.

Scoring: Put the number you placed by each question in the following corresponding blank, and find the total for each group. The results will show you what your current thinking is about behavior management in schools.

Group I	Group II	Group III
1. _____	2. _____	8. _____
4. _____	3. _____	10. _____
5. _____	6. _____	13. _____
9. _____	7. _____	16. _____
11. _____	12. _____	17. _____
18. _____	14. _____	23. _____
20. _____	15. _____	26. _____
22. _____	19. _____	28. _____
27. _____	21. _____	30. _____
31. _____	24. _____	32. _____
34. _____	25. _____	33. _____
36. _____	29. _____	38. _____
37. _____	35. _____	39. _____

Totals: _____

Chart the totals on a bar graph using a template such as the one that follows:

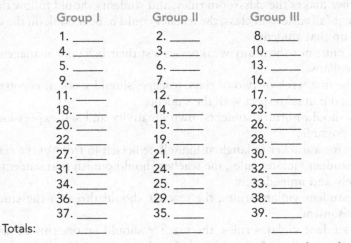

	Group I	Group 2	Group 3
55			
50			
45			
40			
35			
30			
25			
20			
15			
10			
5			
0			

autocratic teacher A teacher who controls every part of the classroom and student behavior, demonstrating no flexibility or receptiveness to student input.

collaborative teacher A teacher who solicits and uses student input in the creation of classroom rules and procedures, demonstrating respect for all.

permissive teacher A teacher who lets students get away with anything in the way of classroom behaviors, causing a stressful and chaotic classroom environment.

Group I consists of statements that represent the autocratic teacher. How would you describe an autocratic teacher's management style?

Group II consists of statements that represent the collaborative teacher. How would you describe a collaborative teacher's management style?

Group III consists of statements that represent the permissive teacher. How would you describe a permissive teacher's management style?

A teacher's expectations about classroom behavior management can be placed on a continuum that ranges from autocratic on the left to permissive on the right (see Figure 8.4). The center of the continuum represents a collaboration between student and teacher. Based on the inventory you took in Building Block 8.6, where do you put yourself on the continuum?

◄ **Figure 8.4**
Continuum of classroom behavior management styles.
© Cengage Learning 2014

The far left represents the classroom of an autocratic teacher. The teacher sets rules and expects students to obey them. No debate, bending, or negotiation is allowed. Students are expected to be quiet except when responding to teacher questions. Nobody moves around unless the teacher grants permission. Students must be in their assigned seats on time and must stay there until the teacher dismisses them.

The far right represents a teacher who is so permissive that students can do anything they want. Students talk when the teacher is trying to teach, disturb other students, move about the room at will, do things totally unrelated to the instruction. The teacher tries tactics such as:

■ Discipline-related questions that have no answers, such as "Why are you touching her?," "How many times do I have to tell you . . . ?," or "What am I going to *do* with you?"

■ Yelling: "Stop that right now!"

■ Cajoling: "Oh, c'mon—I know you can be better than this."

■ Begging: "Puhleeze, won't you try to be a little quieter when I'm talking?"

■ Bargaining: "If you do your work, you can have a half hour to do whatever you want."

■ Making threats that cannot be carried out: "Do that one more time and you'll stay after school every day for a year!"

None of the teacher's actions produces any positive results. The students are running the class.

Somewhere in the middle is the teacher who relies on teacher–student collaboration to develop and maintain good order and discipline in the classroom. These teachers respect their students—even the worst students—and treat them with respect (not permissiveness). These teachers have a few rules of classroom behavior designed to enable the teacher to teach and the students to learn. Often, these teachers solicit student input for the design of classroom procedures, rules, and consequences. They enforce the rules fairly and consistently; when a student violates a rule, the teacher makes the appropriate correction right away. These teachers are never sarcastic, never make idle threats, and do not cut students down. They are honest and authentic.

FROM THE FIELD

Becoming a Classroom Manager
Christie Daniels

Courtesy of Christie Daniels

From the first day that I stepped into a public school classroom, the concept of classroom management has been drilled into my head as the single most important factor in determining a teacher's success in the classroom. After nine years of teaching the most challenging students available, I have learned that classroom management is not about discipline. It's not about organization. It isn't a methodology. Effective classroom management is, purely and simply, the process of creating an environment in which students want to learn. A teacher's classroom management skills are directly proportional to the extent to which they are willing to go to great lengths to capture and maintain their students' attention.

While serving as a mentor to a first-year teacher, I was asked the question, "Dr. Daniels, do you ever wonder if you are *really* making a difference with these kids?" I laughed as I remembered the many times that I drove home thinking and asking out loud, "Why did I even get out of bed today?" I no longer ask that question. When those nagging doubts arise, I simply close my eyes for a moment and think about Michael. Michael is a former student who helped me realize that I had finally become an effective classroom manager.

I will always remember the date—Friday, October 17, 2003. I was a behavior modification teacher at the Picayune, Mississippi Center for Alternative Education. My students had all been referred to my class as a result of having exhibited severe behavior problems in their regular classrooms. Many of my students had experienced very little, if any, success at their "home" schools.

On this particular day, Michael, one of my fifth-grade students, did not show up for school at the expected time. This was unusual because he was the only student in my class who had not missed a single day of school. I walked into the principal's office and asked whether his mom had called to let us know he was going to be absent. My principal told me that there had been an accident. I immediately panicked, but she assured me that Michael was unharmed. She explained that Michael's bus had had a minor accident on the way to pick him up, and that by the time the bus reached his stop, he was not there. We both assumed that his mother had probably gone to work and that he had, most likely, simply decided to stay at home for the day.

At about 9:45 a.m., as my students were getting ready to take a class picture, Michael walked in soaking wet and out of breath. I looked at him incredulously and asked him if it was raining outside. He looked at me and said, "No, I walked." Michael had walked approximately six miles from his home to our school. I asked him "Why?" and he smiled and said, "I just couldn't miss one single day of your class." My principal and I cried together that day, our hearts swelled with pride for the progress Michael had made and by his newfound commitment to learning. Yes, October 17, 2003, was an important day for me. It began a new era for me—one in which I no longer question my commitment to teaching.

Christina Ross Daniels
2005 Mississippi Teacher of the Year
Picayune Center for Alternative Education
Picayune, Mississippi

© Cengage Learning 2014

They know what they want, expect it, and get it. These teachers are collaborative teachers.

Canter (1985) uses the term *assertive* to describe the teachers who are most successful in managing classroom behavior. He says that assertive teachers take this stand about classroom management:

1. I will not tolerate behavior problems in my class. There is *no* excuse good enough for you to stop me from teaching. I will not tolerate you stopping me from teaching for any reason. You *can* behave and you *will* behave in my classroom.

2. I will not tolerate you stopping someone else from learning. Every student in my class has the opportunity to learn—free from disruptions.

3. No student will engage in behavior that is not for the good of themselves and one another. You will not threaten, bully, or attack other students.

You must set your own discipline program to suit yourself and the students in your class. However, your discipline plan must be congruent with the school's discipline code. Any discipline plan you set must include the overarching school-wide rules. For example, suppose you don't care whether students chew gum in class, but the school says that students are not allowed to chew gum in school. Your personal plan must include a "no gum chewing" clause.

No single classroom management formula works for everyone. However, the most successful teachers are those who are collaborative, assertive, respectful, and consistent, and who have high expectations for student achievement.

As you prepare to enter the classroom, be sure to study Canter's propositions and internalize their full implications. Work to eliminate any worries you might have that children will not behave in your class. If you have any lurking reservations, work at getting rid of them now.

You probably found from the inventory in Building Block 8.6 that your classroom management beliefs reflect each of the positions on the continuum. However, you probably also found that your beliefs cluster around one of these positions. We do not like to assert that only one approach to behavior management is right and the others are wrong. There are times when you will want to invoke systems other than your preferred system. For example, you might prefer to be collaborative in your overall approach, but sometimes you will have to be autocratic and at other times you will want to be more permissive. Use the classroom management system that works best for you. The only criteria are that you can teach and your students can learn—free of disruptions.

Finally, let us mention the practice of sending misbehaving students to the principal. As you know, one of the school administration's duties is to deal with students who exhibit unacceptable behavior. But the teacher can and should handle the vast majority of discipline problems in the classroom. Reserve requesting the principal's intervention for only the most serious cases—cases that are potentially harmful to the student, to other students, or to you. You want to become known in your school as a teacher who can handle his or her own discipline. Then, if you send a student to the office, the principal will know that the student presents a serious problem.

Involving the principal in discipline problems should be reserved for serious behavioral issues, like those in which the teacher or other students are in danger.

A s the saying goes, "If you can't beat them, join them." Today's students at virtually all grade levels have electronic gadgets of every description, and many students bring them to school, much to the consternation of their teachers who view these gadgets as distractions from the serious work at hand. According to *The Washington Times*, the use of cell phone technology used to access the Internet has jumped to 46 percent of African Americans and 51 percent of Hispanics as compared with 30 percent of whites (Washington, 2011). Even though many families do not have high-speed computers with Internet access at home, almost all of their children have smartphones that can be used to access the Internet.

We mentioned earlier that one of the challenges in education is to effectively use the technology to which students have become accustomed. This use not only provides comfort to the students because they are learning with something that is already familiar to them, but it also expands the repertoire of teaching resources available to teachers. However, as you can guess, the use of technology in schools isn't restricted to teaching and learning. You have already read about cyberbullying. How does having technology available in schools and classrooms affect the incidence of cyberbullying? And what about the newest gadgets—smartphones, tablets, media players such as the iPod, e-readers, laptops, and other similar portable electronic devices that students bring to school? It's easy to see how these devices can be used for less than honorable intentions. How can they can be used to expand the repertoire available to teachers?

Because students tend to bring their smartphones and, to a lesser extent, their tablets, e-readers, notebooks, and laptops to school, let us concentrate on educational uses of these devices. At this writing, over 200,000 apps are available for the Apple iPad, and over a half million apps are available for iPhones. Let's look at just a few types of apps, together with ways they can enhance the repertoire of teachers:

- *Note-taking apps* enable students to create and edit text notes. Students can use this app to take initial class notes and edit them later.
- *Calculator apps* range from simple to very sophisticated, and students can use these to ensure mathematical accuracy and to solve difficult problems.
- *Voice-to-text apps* verbally enable students to dictate information that will be displayed as text.
- *Text-to-voice apps* read written text aloud, which provides teachers an option to help poor readers and assist learners with visual impairments.
- *To-do lists* help students get their tasks in order, and the app reminds them what has to be done and when.

- *Content-oriented apps* can act as resources and references. For example, there are astronomy applications that help students to learn the night sky while observing actual and virtual scenes of the night sky at various times of the year. Other content-oriented apps are available to help students do things like learn Spanish, practice algebra, view world maps, review vocabulary, and much more.
- *News apps* are available from virtually every newspaper, as well as TV and radio stations. Yes, they have sports and recipe sections, but they also have news of the day and commentaries from experts.
- *Reference apps* provide a quick and easy way for students to access resources like dictionaries, encyclopedias, world and U.S. population statistics, maps, quotes, sign language, and much more.

These are just a few of the types of apps available for help in academic settings. You may notice that we haven't listed music, movie, TV show, or gaming apps; these are primarily meant for entertainment and not academic inquiry. If your students need an app they can't find on the Internet, why not challenge them to write one themselves? They can use free software from the Internet.

In addition to apps, more and more books, newspapers, and magazines are accessible through smartphones, tablets, and e-readers. In fact, publishers are working to create electronic versions of classroom texts so students can access the material on tablets or e-readers (see Brezicki, 2010/2011) without having to carry the books themselves. And the federal government has unveiled a plan to get schools to switch from print to digital textbooks by 2017 (Tomassini, 2012).

And don't forget the social networking sites. Perhaps, the first thought that comes to your mind might be that students may use these sites to bully and harass other students. But can they be used to help teachers? Ways in which experienced teachers have used social media in their classes include course assignments and other curriculum matters, end-of-unit reviews prior to unit-end tests, integrating real-work applications into teaching, collaborative learning, distance learning, cross-cultural communication, language learning, professional development, networking with colleagues anywhere in the world, parent communication, and community outreach (Stansbury, 2011).

The field of technological applications available to students is getting larger by the day. As a person interested in becoming a teacher, you should keep up with these advances so you will be on par with your students when you enter the classroom and so that you *and they* can be aware of how to use them for learning, not ill will.

■ SUMMARY

- A school is a complex system designed to foster maximum student learning. To learn, students must become an integral part of that system. They must have their basic needs met by the school and have the freedom to express their individuality within conventional boundaries; at the same time, students must conform to safety and behavior standards set by the school and its teachers.

- Safety considerations include physical safety, intellectual safety, and emotional safety.

- The school, with the help of its students and outside agencies, can provide reasonable assurance of students' physical safety. Schools often increase security measures in an effort to prevent threats to physical safety. Some of these measures include installing security cameras and metal detectors, requiring students, personnel, and visitors to carry visible identification, and random searches for contraband. Several schools have also adopted zero-tolerance policies, but it is unclear whether these policies are effective. Indeed, they are controversial due to their sometimes strict interpretations that do not leave room for extenuating circumstances.

- Intellectual and emotional safety arise from positive interpersonal interactions between students and teachers. Emotional safety is fostered through positive teacher–student interactions and through the reduction or elimination of bullying and harassment.

- Bullying, including cyberbullying and harassment, has been linked to incidents of school violence, including school shootings and student suicides. Most states have anti-bullying laws, and schools have adopted anti-bullying programs and policies. If these policies and programs are to be effective, they must involve not only the students, teachers, and administrators, but also all school personnel, parents, and the community. Some large-scale anti-bullying programs are available for purchase by schools and school systems and have been shown to be effective.

- Teachers have the responsibility to contribute to school safety and can do so by implementing effective classroom management plans. The first step in creating an effective classroom management plan is to establish a safe and caring classroom environment where the teacher and students treat one another with dignity and respect. The second step in creating a classroom management plan is to design a discipline plan to help manage student behavior.

When the school personnel–student system provides for students' safety and security, cognitive, and psychosocial needs; insists on behavior that allows the teacher to teach and students to learn; and undertakes academic challenges that engage all students, then students can aspire to their highest levels of achievement.

■ Key Terms and Concepts

Autocratic teacher, 216	Collaborative teacher, 216	Permissive teacher, 216
Bullying, 205	Cyberbullying, 207	Zero-tolerance policies, 210

■ Construct and Apply

1. Address Erikson's stages of psychosocial development as they relate to students' needs for individuality and acceptance. How can the school not only accept but also protect students' expressions of individuality? How can you, as the teacher, foster this healthy development?

2. Imagine you are assigned to a debate team focused on one of the issues discussed in this chapter. Choose a pro or con position and write a paragraph supporting your choice. Suggestions include the following:

   a. Metal detectors, searches, campus police, and so on.

   b. Zero-tolerance policies.

   c. Having a Gay-Straight Alliance (GSA) at the school.

3. Explain how too much discipline in the classroom can be as ineffective as too little in creating an environment conducive to learning.
4. A common adage given to new teachers regarding classroom behavior management is, "Don't smile before Christmas!" Is this good advice? Why or why not?
5. You are currently a student in college. What is your favorite way to be taught? Think carefully. Is the method you cited your favorite because you learn the material best that way? Or is it because it helps you perform well on traditional tests? Or is it both? Explain.
6. What expectations and responsibilities does the school have to the student? What expectations and responsibilities does the student have to the school?

■ Deconstructing the Standards

1. Recall the InTASC Standard associated with the objectives for this chapter:

   InTASC Standard #3 reads: "The teacher works with others to create environments that support individual and collaborative learning, and that encourage positive social interaction, active engagement in learning, and self-motivation."
   a. What part(s) of this standard does this chapter address?
   b. How will the concepts in this chapter help you apply this standard as a teacher?

2. Use your favorite search engine to find your state's standards for certification. When you find it, bookmark the site. You will refer to it often during this course.
   a. How are your conclusions about the expectations and responsibilities of schools and students represented in your state standards?
   b. How do the InTASC Standards compare to your state's certification standards?
   c. Do you believe the degree of representation concerning expectations and responsibilities of schools and students is adequate in your state certification standards? Why or why not?

■ Your Portfolio

1. Include a copy of the information students and parents are given regarding school policies and rules, and a copy of the classroom rules where you are doing your field experience. Write your reflections on the necessity of these rules for the safety of the students and school personnel. Relate your reflection to meeting students' needs for safety and belonging.
2. Include resources from your community that help students build character, such as Boys Clubs, Girls Clubs, YMCA or YWCA, Boy Scouts, Girl Scouts, volunteer programs, and the like. Include a list of these resources in your portfolio.
3. Begin to design your own classroom management plan, including room arrangement, routines and procedures, and classroom rules. Include your plan in your portfolio to show that you are aware of what an effectively managed learning environment might be.

🖥 Education CourseMate Resources

Check out this text's Education CourseMate website (at www.cengagebrain.com) for more information about student safety and the school's responsibilities. You will find the TeachSource Videos, a guide for doing field experiences, glossary flash cards, activities, tutorial quizzes, direct links to the websites mentioned in the chapter, and more.

CHAPTER 9

The School and the Teacher: Expectations and Responsibilities

IN CHAPTER 8, you investigated the role of the student in the complex relationship between school, teacher, and student. You saw that students can expect to receive much from the school, including fulfillment of basic needs and the opportunity to learn. You also saw that students are expected to give to the school in such areas as helping to ensure safety, adhering to school rules and regulations, and respecting the classroom management systems of individual teachers. The school has responsibilities to the students, and the students have responsibilities to the school.

Similarly, the school has expectations of and responsibilities to the teacher, and the teacher has expectations of and responsibilities to the school.

In this chapter, you will investigate the relationship between the school and the teacher. You will find that the teacher's primary responsibilities are instructional. You have already investigated the teacher's instructional responsibilities in this textbook, but teachers also have other responsibilities, some of which you have previously identified. You will focus on two basic questions:

1. What does the school expect of the teacher?
2. What does the teacher expect of the school?

Chapter Objectives

As a result of your explorations in this chapter, you will be able to:

1. Describe the school's expectations of the teacher, including instructional and noninstructional duties, certification, and professional development.
   InTASC Standard #7: Planning for Instruction; Standard #9: Professional Learning and Ethical Practice

2. Describe the teacher's expectations of the school, including salary administration, job security, working conditions, materials and resources available, and support.
   InTASC Standard #7 Planning for Instruction; Standard #9: Professional Learning and Ethical Practice

The School's Expectations of the Teacher

Let us first look at the professional life of a teacher. What tasks are teachers expected to do? Certainly, they teach their classes. But what else do they do?

BUILDING BLOCK 9.1

A Teacher's Life in School

Think back to your earliest years in school—as far back as preschool or nursery school if possible. What do you remember your teacher doing? Think of what a teacher does during the school day and throughout the school year. Which of these activities were routine? Which occurred periodically or only from time to time? Which occurred only once or twice? Similarly, recall what your teachers did in the lower elementary grades, upper elementary grades, middle school or junior high school, and high school. Use the table that follows to list some activities.

	Nursery School or Preschool	Lower Elementary	Upper Elementary	Junior High or Middle School	High School
Routine activities					
Periodic activities					
Rare activities					

What trends did you notice in the general thrust of teachers' activities as you progressed through the grades? Does it seem that teachers of young children spend a lot of time dealing with children's personal needs, whereas teachers of older students focus more on the subject matter?

Teachers' Tasks

You have tried to recall the activities of the teachers you had in school, and you have been observing the activities of your cooperating teacher in your field experience. Now, try to get more specific about what is expected of teachers from day to day.

Make a list of the tasks and activities that a teacher in the grade level that you are interested in teaching might do during a typical 24-hour day. Categorize each task as either instructional or noninstructional in nature.

Then, estimate the approximate percentage of a teacher's time in school that is spent on instructional duties and the approximate percentage spent on noninstructional duties. Does the amount of time teachers spend on noninstructional tasks seem reasonable?

instructional duties Teacher duties directly associated with planning, instruction, and evaluation.

noninstructional duties Teacher duties not directly associated with instruction of students.

In Building Block 9.2, you may have encountered some difficulties in separating instructional from noninstructional activities, because many of these activities are interdependent. For example, parent conferencing, often considered a noninstructional task, and assessing student work, an instructional task, support each other. Being the advisor or coach of a club, team, or some other extracurricular activity is a noninstructional task when compared to the daily teaching load, but it can be an instructional task when considered as a part of overall student learning.

The specific duties of teachers are established by states, school districts, and schools. Use your favorite search engine to find the duties of teachers in your location. You may have to look for a statewide teacher assessment instrument and infer the duties from rubrics used to assess teacher performance.

Does your finding accurately reflect what, in your experience, teachers do?

Instructional Duties

First and foremost, schools expect teachers to teach. Elsewhere in this textbook, you have investigated some of the features of teaching—planning, preparing interesting lessons that meet the needs of *all* students, implementing the teaching in ways that involve students meaningfully, assessing student progress as you go along, and the like.

Depending on the grade level, teachers can be responsible for teaching all the academic subjects, or just one or two. They can teach an average of up to 30 or more students in the public elementary schools, or they can teach an average of up to 130 or more students a day in public secondary schools (National Center for Education Statistics, 2010a).

The actual act of teaching takes up most of a teacher's day. But many tasks lead up to and follow teaching. Perhaps you thought of some of these tasks in the Building Blocks you completed earlier. Teachers must organize and sequence objectives and lessons for the day, the week, the grading period, and the school year. They must design assessments appropriate for the instruction. Few nonteachers realize the time that goes into planning and evaluating.

Did your list of teacher instructional duties include work done at home? Teachers do a great deal of the planning, preparation, and evaluation work needed for successful teaching during evenings, weekends, and holidays. They take work home because the school day is so filled with tasks related to students that there is not enough time to finish planning and grading as well. Elementary school teachers are particularly challenged because they normally do not have built-in planning time—they have the occasional period of free time when their students go to art, music, physical education, and other special classes, but even then they

Teaching not only involves instruction time, but also time spent planning instruction and evaluating student learning. These co-teachers are planning instruction for their elementary class.

Courtesy of Bill Lisenby

This teacher sponsors the chess club at his school. What other options exist for teachers to participate in extracurricular activities?

are responsible for walking their students to the special classroom. Teachers in middle school and high school typically have one or two class periods built into their schedules for use in planning, grading, and report writing. But, due to meetings, parent conferences, paperwork, and other tasks that require their attention, they are often not able to use their planning time for its intended purpose: planning and grading.

The need to take work home is especially acute for new teachers while they are developing and refining efficient routines. As you gain experience, you will find efficient ways to accomplish the teacher tasks so you can provide rewarding educational experiences for your students while preserving your personal time. But you will probably never be able to do everything during school hours. There will always be work to do when students are not around, and this will have to be done after school or at home.

Noninstructional Duties

Besides teaching, schools expect teachers to perform noninstructional duties. Noninstructional duties are those duties not directly associated with the instruction and supervision of students. You listed several examples previously. Noninstructional responsibilities assigned to teachers differ markedly between states in which teacher unions are strong and states with little or no union influence. Teacher unions work to keep teachers' noninstructional supervisory duties to a minimum. Union states insist that teacher contracts define precisely which duties are assigned to teachers and require school districts to provide extra pay for duties not stipulated in the general contracts.

In some schools, the less desirable noninstructional duties may fall to new teachers. In some jurisdictions, however, school boards, unions, and teacher associations have written policies stipulating that the majority of these duties should *not* be assigned to new teachers because these teachers need all the time they can get for planning, discussions with experienced teachers, and professional development. Often, unions and teachers associations influence district school boards to develop policies dealing with noninstructional duties. For example, the New Hanover County, North Carolina, Board of Education policy states in part:

> Principals shall minimize the assignment of noninstructional duties for all teachers to those duties essential to the operation of a safe and orderly school. Special consideration, by limiting such assignment, shall be given to beginning teachers and teachers with at least 27 years of experience. A compelling need exists to provide beginning teachers with as much time as possible to develop their instructional skills and to interact with experienced teachers for the purpose of professional growth. (New Hanover County, North Carolina Board of Education, 2011)

Some noninstructional duties typically assigned to teachers in the elementary and secondary schools are shown in Table 9.1. What other noninstructional duties have you seen teachers perform that you can add to this list?

Many people believe that noninstructional supervisory duties, although necessary to ensure safety and order, could be performed by lower-paid, nonteaching personnel. Some

TABLE 9.1 Some Noninstructional Duties Typically Assigned to Teachers

	Elementary Schools	Middle Schools	Secondary Schools
Outside of the classroom	• Monitoring car riders during morning drop-off and afternoon pick-up • Bus duty • Lunchroom duty • Club sponsor • Science fair judge • In-school suspension duty • Chaperone at school functions • Volunteer at school fairs, concession booths, etc. • Serving on committees	• Monitoring car riders during morning drop-off and afternoon pick-up • Bus duty • Lunchroom duty • Club sponsor • Yearbook, school newspaper sponsor • Science fair judge • In-school suspension duty • Chaperone at school functions • Volunteer at school fairs, concession booths, etc. • Serving on committees • Emergency coverage for another teacher during planning periods • Detention duty	• Monitoring car riders during morning drop-off and afternoon pick-up • Monitoring student parking lot • Bus duty • Lunchroom duty • Club sponsor • Yearbook, school newspaper sponsor • Science fair judge • In-school suspension duty • Chaperone at school functions • Volunteer at school fairs, concession booths, etc. • Serving on committees • Emergency class coverage for another teacher during planning periods • Freshman, sophomore, junior, or senior class sponsor • Detention duty
In the classroom	• Taking attendance • Managing paperwork, such as permission slips, student records, etc. • Accompanying students as they move from class to gym, other classes, special classes, lunch, etc. • Parent conferences	• Taking attendance • Managing paperwork, such as permission slips, student records, etc. • Accompanying students as they move from class to gym, other classes, special classes and lunch, etc. • Parent conferences • Advising	• Taking attendance • Managing paperwork, such as permission slips, student records, etc. • Parent conferences • Advising

© Cengage Learning 2014

schools are moving in this direction by requiring paraprofessionals to take on many of these tasks; using other nonprofessional personnel, such as bus drivers, in monitoring capacities; and hiring personnel specifically for these tasks.

In addition to noninstructional supervisory duties, teachers normally are asked to perform many other noninstructional functions. Parent conferences are among these duties. How did you classify parent conferences—as an instructional or a noninstructional activity? There are good reasons for either classification. Parent and family conferences are common in elementary school and middle school and occur frequently in high school. They are an occasion for the exchange of information between family and teacher about the student. The parent conference is viewed as a necessary supplement to the report card. Preparing for and holding conferences with all the parents of students in a class takes a great deal of time. But the value of these conferences is so high that teachers willingly allow for the time and effort needed to prepare and conduct them. Strictly speaking, of course, the parent conference is a noninstructional duty. But the courts have consistently held that parent conferences are part of normal school operations and it is reasonable to expect teachers to hold them (*Fox v. Board of Education*, 1977).

If you plan to teach in a middle school or a high school, you can almost count on being given detention duty. School administrators normally assign detention to students as a punishment for some rule infraction. In some schools, detention is an

Courtesy of Bill Lisenby

Bus duty is a noninstructional teacher responsibility. Why is it important to have teachers and other personnel present when buses arrive and depart?

after-school affair of silence; in others, the time is used to help students with their homework and to provide extra tutoring assistance. In-school suspension is a form of detention that occurs in a designated room during school hours. Students assigned to in-school suspension are removed from their regular classes as a punishment, but they receive assistance as required to complete their assigned work during the time they are on in-school suspension.[1] Some schools assign full-time teaching professionals to this duty; others require that teachers give up some of their planning time to staff the designated room.

Participating in professional development or continuing education, being a reflective practitioner, and implementing the rules, policies, and regulations of the school system and state department of education may also be considered part of a teacher's noninstructional duties.

Reconsider the list of activities you generated in Building Block 9.2. Would you recategorize any of the activities as instructional (associated with planning, instruction, and evaluation) or noninstructional (not directly associated with instruction of students)?

BUILDING BLOCK 9.3

Extracurricular Activities

Think back to your days as a student—in elementary school, middle or junior high school, or high school. What extracurricular activities were available to you? Which were available during school hours? Which were limited to after-school hours? In which extracurricular activities did you participate?

Now consider how teachers might get involved in these extracurricular activities. Do you think teachers should be required to participate in these activities? Should they volunteer for such duties? Should they be paid for extracurricular duties?

What opportunities for involvement in extracurricular activities did you suggest? Teachers may coach sports teams or collect tickets at games, concerts, or plays. They may sponsor clubs or chaperone field trips or school dances. Most extracurricular activities occur before or after regular school hours and outside the regular instruction of students, but some may occur during the school day. Teachers normally are paid a stipend for sponsoring certain extracurricular activities such as team sport coaching. For other types of activities, however, teachers may be expected to volunteer. As we have said, most school district policies limit the number of extracurricular activities in which new teachers can participate; however, in cases of compelling need such as lack of adequate personnel to

---

[1]For example, administrators at Rockville High School in Vernon, Connecticut, a school with a mixed population base, have shown that in-school suspensions (ISS) are more likely to be honored by students than out-of-school suspensions (OSS), and that ISS helps students increase their educational time because students are serving the suspension in the school building instead of out of school. The program is staffed by a full-time facilitator and a part-time paraprofessional who coach the students on their class work and their standards of behavior (Damon, 2011). The Baltimore City Schools showed that the graduation rate of African American boys increased from less than 50 percent to over 67 percent in the six years of ISS implementation (Sundius & Dove, 2011).

carry out the school's commitments, the administration may require teachers, including new teachers, to take on extracurricular responsibilities.

Which extracurricular activities would you like to be involved in at your future school? To make a positive impression during an interview, let the principal or personnel director know that you are willing to work with students and support them outside of the classroom. In hiring, school administrators look for qualified people who can not only teach well, but who also can bring other activities to the students.

Schools expect teachers to teach and to be accountable for their students' learning. They also expect teachers to carry out noninstructional duties and participate in extracurricular activities. Teachers must be well-educated, highly qualified individuals to live up to these expectations.

Certification

Schools expect their teachers to be certified. Students in our schools deserve to have competent teachers as much as they deserve competent doctors and dentists. Teacher certification is a state's official recognition that a person has met the requirements to be a professional teacher in that state. Each state sets its own requirements for teacher certification, and these vary significantly from state to state. However, most states have the following minimum requirements:

- At least a bachelor's degree; some states require a master's degree
- Completion of an approved and accredited teacher preparation program
- A major or minor in education for elementary education majors
- A major in the subject area or areas in which the teacher plans to teach for middle or high school teachers
- Passing scores on state licensure examinations

teacher certification A state's official recognition that a person has met the requirements to be a professional teacher in that state.

The Education CourseMate website has a direct link to an interactive website you can use to find the specific certification requirements and methods of acquiring certification for each state. The site is maintained by the University of Southern California.

Several routes to teacher certification exist, depending on your state's regulations. Many people choose the university preparation route; some universities offer their programs entirely or partially online. However, there are other routes to certification: the postbaccalaureate route, the master's degree route, and several different alternative routes that are especially appealing to individuals seeking to change careers. The key is that, whatever the route, candidates must ultimately be endorsed by the teacher certification arm of the state's education department in order for them to be eligible for state teacher certification.

Regardless of your route to certification, you must build solid constructions and understanding of the teaching profession. The material in this textbook and the constructions you make while investigating this material are vital for every preservice teacher.

Exactostock/SuperStock

The university certification route includes professional education courses prescribed by the college, department, or school that offers the education major.

University Certification Route

The university route to teacher certification typically entails a four-year program of study leading to a bachelor's degree (see Chapter 1). The program includes core courses required by the college or university and content and professional education courses prescribed by the college, school, or department that offers your major. Although these programs traditionally have been offered on college and university campuses, some institutions of higher education are offering them online.[2]

BUILDING BLOCK
9.4

My Teacher Preparation Program

If you have not yet done so, be sure to contact your advisor or the advisement center at your college or department of education, and obtain an advisement sheet for your major. What content (math, science, language arts, social studies) and professional courses (teacher education) are required? What field experiences are required? How much time do they take? When do they occur in your program?

You can use this sheet as the basis for outlining your complete course of study.

Postbaccalaureate Certification Route

The postbaccalaureate route to teacher certification is designed to enable students who already have a bachelor's degree to earn teacher certification at the undergraduate level. If you hold a bachelor's degree in a specific content area such as mathematics, a science (biology, chemistry, physics), English, or history, it is often only a matter of taking professional education courses and participating in field experiences to receive certification at the secondary level. More coursework may be required to obtain certification at the elementary or middle grades level, and even more may be required if your bachelor's degree is in an unrelated content field such as accounting, nursing, communications, psychology, or economics. Some postbaccalaureate programs lead to a second bachelor's degree in addition to qualification for state certification. Some lead only to state certification.

Master's Degree Certification Route

Some states and institutions have developed graduate-level programs that lead to initial certification at the master's degree level. In these programs, an individual with a bachelor's degree who does not have teacher certification can earn it together with a master's degree. Students who pursue this path find they must spend a great deal of time in field experiences during their programs, and may not be able to have an outside job (except in cases where the field work can be combined with on-the-job experience). For this reason, the professional education coursework and the field experience work may be compressed into two semesters, sometimes with summer sessions added, resulting in relatively rushed class work and intense field work when compared to the university route or the postbaccalaureate route. Because of this compression, students may not have sufficient time to construct their own conceptualizations.

Alternative Certification Route

In response to teacher shortages, numerous alternative teacher preparation programs have sprung up in the last decade or so. Although the postbaccalaureate and master's degree routes technically are forms of alternative teacher preparation, the term *alternative certification* more commonly refers to highly compressed teacher certification programs in which students undergo brief, intensive teacher training, and then complete a supervised teaching internship, often during their first year of professional teaching.

Such alternative routes provide opportunities for people from various educational backgrounds and walks of life to become teachers, usually specializing in the subject or

---

[2]When checking online teacher preparation programs, be sure they are fully accredited by a national accrediting agency as described in Chapter 1, and that the program leads to clear and renewable certification in the state where you want to teach.

area of their prior education and experience. As of 2010, all states except Alaska, Oregon, and the District of Columbia had alternate routes to teacher certification in place (National Center for Alternative Certification, 2010). Each state has its own version of these programs. Critics of alternative certification programs argue that teachers who complete these programs may lack adequate pedagogical skills; supporters point to the superior subject matter knowledge and experience these teachers can bring to the classroom (Otuya, 1992). In a recent national study of alternative teacher preparation programs, Humphrey and Wechsler (2005) found that, to prepare teachers fully, alternative programs need to focus on strengthening the mentoring component, establishing systems to help struggling participants, and linking coursework to the on-the-job training participants receive. There is little actual research on the success of students taught by teachers who took alternative routes to certification because these routes are extremely varied. But a study completed in 2005 by the American Educational Research Association showed that there is little difference between alternatively and traditionally prepared teachers (Feistritzer and Haar, 2008.).

Troops to Teachers

Troops to Teachers is a federal government initiative that helps eligible military people become certified teachers. The program's primary focus is to recruit teachers for schools that serve low-income families, especially in high-need areas such as science, mathematics, and special education. Troops to Teachers is not a teacher preparation program; rather, it provides participants with financial assistance, logistical assistance, counseling, and job placement services. Participants earn their teacher certification through one of the established teacher preparation programs in their state.

You can access the Troops to Teachers website through a direct link available on the Education CourseMate website.

Teach For America

Teach For America is a nonprofit, private organization that recruits recent college graduates to teach for two years in urban and rural schools in the United States. New corps members (as they are called) attend a rigorous pre-teaching training institute, receive ongoing coaching and professional development throughout their two-year commitment, and have access to online resources to help them become effective classroom teachers. Corps members can earn certification in the state where they teach, and the training program is considered to be an alternative path to certification. Because of the compression of the pedagogical studies and preservice experiences, there is a high rate of turnover in the Teach For America corps, with many corps members leaving the field within the first three years (Hopkins, 2008). However, a study by Donaldson and Johnson (2011) showed that a substantial number of corps members remain in the teaching profession, and many remain in their low-income placement schools beyond their two-year commitment.

You can access the home page of Teach for America through a direct link available on the Education CourseMate website.

Temporary, Provisional, and Emergency Certification

Some states offer temporary, provisional, or emergency teaching certification that authorizes people to hold professional teaching positions provided they pursue regular certification through an accredited teacher preparation program. These certificates normally are granted for teaching high-need subject areas such as mathematics, science, or special education, and for teaching in high-need geographic areas such as urban schools, schools that serve children of poverty, and remote rural schools. The regulations governing temporary and emergency certificates vary from state to state and the certificates are limited in the length of time for which they are valid. Depending on the region, it can be difficult to complete an accredited teacher education program while you are teaching full-time. If you are considering a provisional certificate, you should ensure that there are reasonable options and opportunities for completing permanent certification requirements.

Teacher Certification Examinations

In addition to completing an approved teacher preparation program, candidates for teaching credentials must pass the teacher certification examinations prescribed by the state in which they are seeking certification. Many states require the appropriate Praxis exams, although increasing numbers of states are developing their own exams. Exams include a basic skills test of some sort depending on the area of certification sought, and one or more subject-area competence tests. The Praxis tests are developed and assessed by Educational Testing Service (ETS). ETS offers the Praxis I test, a preprofessional basic skills test, and many subject-area tests. The ETS website publishes state requirements and *Test at a Glance* publications that give the objectives and topics covered in the tests.

 You can access the Educational Testing Service website through a direct link on the Education CourseMate website. The ETS site describes ETS teacher certification exams required by your state.

Reciprocity

Most states have reciprocal teacher certification agreements with other states. In these reciprocity arrangements, a person who has earned a teaching certificate in one state can qualify for a similar certificate in another state, providing he or she meets certain additional requirements. These requirements normally include passing the new state's teacher certification test and taking special courses. To find the reciprocity agreements and requirements for each state, talk with the teacher certification officer at your institution or access the National Association of State Directors of Teacher Education and Certification website.

You can access the National Association of State Directors of Teacher Education and Certification reciprocity website through a direct link available on the Education CourseMate website.

Professional Development

Teachers are expected to keep up with the latest developments in education, just as physicians must keep up with the latest developments in medicine. You would not want a doctor to treat you based on the medical practices of the 1970s, and you would not want your child to be taught using curriculum, methodologies, and assessment strategies of the 1970s.

Today's schools differ from earlier schools in many respects. Curriculum has been updated to reflect new knowledge. Methodology has been updated to foster student construction and ownership of knowledge rather than memorization of information presented by the teacher. Contemporary education places greater emphasis on students' development of thinking and problem-solving skills. Assessment includes student-constructed responses and evaluation of student-focused activities, especially applied *during* the instruction to see how the students are doing, rather than solely fact-based, objective tests given at the end of a unit. Technology is used to assist in instruction and to help teachers in their administrative tasks.

Because of frequent and rapid changes in education, states require a certain amount of formal professional development work to maintain teaching certification. This work can involve taking college courses, taking in-service programs offered by your school district, or completing other programs approved by the state. Some of these programs can lead to certification add-ons, and some can lead to advanced degrees. But all help you to keep up with the latest developments in education.

Besides formal work, a teacher has numerous informal options for keeping up-to-date. Schools, school districts, colleges, universities, private and governmental agencies,

certification add-ons Additional areas of certification typically added onto an existing certification area by an individual completing the certification requirements for the area.

The First Practicum

Steven Webb

I can still hear his voice: "Be you, be creative, learn [about] your students, and they will come to learn the standards." The next day was to be the start of my first experience as a practicum student teacher. I was nervous, as any young man or woman would be, on the verge of being placed in a position in which I would be responsible for the academic well-being of a classroom full of delicate young minds for the first time. I was confident in my abilities due to the wonderful training and guidance I had received from the majority of my professors in preparing me for the task at hand. And that word of advice from one of those positive professors was a summation of the type of guidance I had received which provided me with such confidence. These simple words would indeed prove priceless in less than 24 hours from that moment and in the weeks and months to come.

I had expected that the first few days of my first practicum experience would consist of observation and note taking of the performance of my mentoring teacher. My expectations could not have been more misconceived. I indeed sat and observed and took notes for the entirety of one class period, at the conclusion of which my mentoring teacher turned to me and said I was welcome to teach the second class the lesson she had just concluded with the first class. Ten minutes later, I experienced a rush of adrenaline I had never before felt as I stood in front of a class of 20 students who did not know me from Adam. I froze for a brief second as I searched for my opening statement. A boy in the front row raised his hand and posed the question, "Do you like pie?" I was speechless; then I smiled. I answered with a simple, "Sure," and quickly began to improvise and link the student's question about pie to the lesson objective of the day, which dealt with using pie charts to show probabilities. I was off and running. This was certainly not the way I had envisioned the start of my first class, but the student had broken the ice and I had in turn made my first connection with and step toward learning how to reach my students through their thoughts. As I progressed through my practicum, I came to lean on this first experience as guidance whenever I questioned my next move. During this field experience, my mentoring teacher missed many classes due to a family issue, and I was depended upon to teach the class without her full-time guidance and tutoring. This perceived inconvenience came to be a blessing to me as I had the full responsibility of the class thrust upon me and it became a matter of sink or swim.

I swam, and the experience I gained is and always will be another priceless anecdote from my education training program. It is this type of positive learning experience that strengthens my belief that the true mark of any education program is the effectiveness by which it places its students in effective, real-world field settings. Any future educator's mastery of classroom leadership and teaching effectiveness can only increase with increased exposure to on-the-job training in such settings. They are the lifeblood of successful programs.

I call myself one of the lucky ones when speaking of my experiences in my education program. By that, I mean that I consider myself blessed to have completed my education in a program whose focus is not to pump out robots trained to simply teach the standards and material a specific way without flexibility or creativeness. My program and professors have instilled in my classmates and me the fine art of using our creativity and personalities in such a way as to teach each student the standards and content in a way that reaches each student on a humanistic level and on a personable basis.

So my education program has been flawless? No! Far from it. There was the professor who insisted on delivering humdrum lectures day in and day out with not the slightest call to creativity or offering up a single word of inspiration. Then there was the highly unorganized, perfectionistic practicum advisor. I can still feel the fury that raged inside me as she walked away following her first observation of one of my lessons. I knew from that moment by her snide comments that neither I nor any other practicum student of hers would ever live up to her expectations. I decided I would not even try—I would rather strive to be effective than to achieve her perfection. Unfortunately, in many education programs today, there are times when the words *illegitimi non carborundum* come to mind and education majors must focus on the good of the program to avoid being pulled down by those who are unwilling to embrace a pedagogy that works.

I call myself one of the lucky ones also because I have been fortunate to let the negatives of my school's education program roll off my back and allow the positives to shine through. Each time I step into a classroom, I use these positives and the type of instruction I have gained from them to connect with my students so that they form a sense of responsibility to themselves to learn the material at hand—all by simply being me, being creative, and learning my students, and they do in turn succeed in learning the standards, the material, and then some.

Steven Webb
*Senior at Tennessee Tech University, Cookeville, Tennessee
Majoring in education with a concentration in middle school grades 4 through 8*

▶⏸ TeachSource Video

View the TeachSource Video Case, "Mentoring First-Year Teachers: Keys to Professional Success." In this video, you will see new teacher, Dania Diaz, working with her mentor teacher, Abdi Ali. Throughout, Abdi observes Dania as she interacts with her students and colleagues, and then reflects on her teaching practice. Be sure to watch the two bonus videos for more detail.

After you view the videos, answer the following questions:

1. What does a mentor teacher do?
2. Why is mentoring important for the new teacher?
3. What is a reflective journal and what is its value to the new teacher?

mentor A trusted and experienced guide in the profession.

and professional organizations offer workshops that can last from an hour or two to a week or two. But, professional development does not have to involve workshops, institutes, and other similar programs. Nieto (2009) suggests that teachers establish partnerships with other teachers and groups that have similar interests so people can learn from one another. There are several vehicles for doing this, including social media, personal websites, and blogs and wikis.

Schools receive professional journals that are available for teachers. There are professional societies for all areas of education, and they publish their own professional journals and magazines. Teachers can keep up with the latest developments and best practices in any field of education through perusing these journals.

The literature shows that, by far, the most meaningful professional development for a new teacher is having a *mentor*. Mentors show the new teacher the ropes, help with lesson preparation, help find materials, share successes, offer critiques, provide suggestions and hints for behavior and time management, and do all sorts of things the new teacher needs help in doing. Mentoring is *critical*. In their study of factors that influence teachers' thoughts about their own professional growth, Gabriel, Day, and Arlington (2011) found that three main factors lead to teachers feeling supported, trusted, and valued as professionals:

1. Participation in professional development programs—courses, workshops, seminars, and the like
2. Mentor or collaborative peer support where teachers can share ideas and reflect out loud
3. "Engaged autonomy" where administrators allow teachers freedom but don't leave them completely on their own

Keeping up with your profession is essential. You are making a good start in this course, and you need to keep the momentum going throughout your teaching career. As a school superintendent once said, "There are two kinds of teachers who have been in the business for 20 years: Those with 20 years of experience, and those with one year of experience 20 times." Which do you want to be?

Examples of professional development include attending school-sponsored workshops and discussion groups and earning college credit toward an advanced degree.

© Spencer Grant/Photo Edit, Inc.

Professionalism

What kinds of professional behaviors are expected of teachers? Choose the best available answer to each of the following questions. (More than one answer may be "correct.") We will start with a few items about expectations for professional behavior in your field experience.

1. As long as I am only observing in my field placement classroom, I may
   a. Dress as I would if I were going to one of my college classes.
   b. Quietly study for a test.
   c. Sit quietly and unobtrusively in the back of the room.
   d. Eat a snack quietly if it is my normal lunchtime.

2. During my field experience, it would be appropriate for me to
   a. Initiate involvement by asking my cooperating teacher how I can help.
   b. Request the opportunity to teach a class by myself.
   c. Correct my cooperating teacher in front of the students if I know he or she has given them misinformation.
   d. Correct my cooperating teacher in private if I know he or she has given students misinformation.

3. If my cooperating teacher has a computer in the classroom, I may
   a. Search the Internet for information relevant to the current lesson.
   b. Enter grades for the students.
   c. Check my cooperating teacher's e-mail account to rid it of spam.
   d. Not use it unless given permission by the cooperating teacher.

4. If I am dissatisfied with my field experience situation, the best option for me is to
   a. Go to the school principal.
   b. Discuss my placement with others in my college class.
   c. Talk with the instructor of my college class.
   d. Move to another teacher in the school who has a better classroom.

5. If I suspect a student in my field placement classroom is being abused, the best option for me is to
   a. Report my suspicions to the school counselor.
   b. Report my suspicions to the instructor of my college class.
   c. Report my suspicions to my cooperating teacher.
   d. Do nothing because I have no authority in the matter.

6. If I see my cooperating teacher behaving inappropriately toward a student, I should
   a. Report the incident to the principal.
   b. Report the incident to the instructor of my college class.
   c. Ask other students in my class what they would do.
   d. Do nothing because I have no authority in the matter.

7. When arriving at my field placement school, I should park my car
   a. In a spot reserved for the teaching staff.
   b. In a spot reserved for visitors.
   c. In any available spot.
   d. In an open spot not likely to be used by others who come to the school.

8. If my cooperating teacher is not providing me with the opportunities I believe I need to get the most out of my field experience, I should
   a. Show a copy of my field experience evaluation form or the course syllabus to my cooperating teacher and ask for advice as to how I can demonstrate my achievements.
   b. Discuss the matter with the instructor of my college class.
   c. Ask for a new placement.
   d. Find out what other students in my class would do in my situation.

9. Professional school dress for women includes
    a. Shorts and a halter top.
    b. A skirt and a long-sleeved blouse.
    c. A skirt and a tight-fitting sweater.
    d. Jeans and a T-shirt.
10. Professional school dress for men includes
    a. A shirt, tie, and jacket.
    b. Shorts and a T-shirt.
    c. Jeans and a T-shirt.
    d. Sports running wear.
11. When a student disagrees with me, I should
    a. Tell him, "Shut up!"
    b. Threaten him.
    c. Ask him to elaborate.
    d. Ignore him.
12. When a student is disruptive, I should
    a. Talk with the student.
    b. Report her to the principal.
    c. Tell other teachers in the teachers' lounge.
    d. Tell my next-door neighbor.
13. When a student does something really funny but inappropriate in my class, I should
    a. Keep quiet about it.
    b. Relate the incident to my friend in the grocery checkout line.
    c. Laugh about it in the teachers' lounge.
    d. Share it with other students.
14. If I decide to go to a nightclub with my friends for an evening, I should choose one that is
    a. Close to school.
    b. Close to home.
    c. In town.
    d. In a different school district.
15. If I decide to have a drink at a restaurant and the parents of one of my students stops by to say "Hello," I should
    a. Push the drink away.
    b. Hide the drink.
    c. Act normally.
    d. Say the waitress must have brought the wrong order.
16. If school starts at 8:05 A.M., I should be there at
    a. 8:05 A.M.
    b. 7:30 A.M.
    c. 8:30 A.M., providing I call in late.
    d. 6:00 A.M.
17. If I go to a late party Sunday evening and feel under the weather Monday morning, I should
    a. Go to school anyway.
    b. Call in sick.
    c. Show up late.
    d. None of the above; I shouldn't go to late-night parties on school evenings.
18. When I am exasperated with a student, I should
    a. Complain about this student in the teachers' lounge.
    b. Complain to my best friend.
    c. Ask another teacher confidentially for advice.
    d. Keep quiet about the situation.

19. When a mother asks me in the grocery store how her child is doing in my class, I should
    a. Tell her.
    b. Suggest she arrange for a parent conference.
    c. Refer her to the principal.
    d. Say, "I have no idea!"
20. When I disagree with a school policy, I should
    a. Discuss my concern with the principal.
    b. Complain about the policy in the teachers' lounge.
    c. Bring up my concern at a PTA meeting.
    d. Bring up my concern at a school board meeting.
21. When a kindergartener comes up to a male teacher and gives him a big hug around his knees, the teacher should
    a. Return the hug.
    b. Gently disengage from the hug.
    c. Tell the child *never* to touch an adult!
    d. Nothing—he should shake the child's hand *before* the child has the chance to hug him.
22. When a student in my first-grade class shows affection to me in a public place, I should
    a. Return the affection to the child.
    b. Recognize the child in a businesslike manner.
    c. Turn away.
    d. Pretend I don't know the child.
23. When I am responsible for collecting lunch money and I decide to go to the rest room while my class is at art, what should I do with the money?
    a. Put it in my pocket and carry it with me.
    b. Put it in my purse and leave it in my room while I am gone.
    c. Hide it in my desk drawer.
    d. Deposit it in the office on my way to the rest room.
24. When a high school teacher is asked to tutor one of her students in the same subject she teaches, she should charge
    a. Nothing.
    b. The going rate for tutoring.
    c. Half the going rate for tutoring.
    d. None of the above—she should *not* tutor one of her own students on a private basis.
25. When a high school teacher is asked to tutor one of his students in a subject that is different from the subject he teaches, he should charge
    a. Nothing.
    b. The going rate for tutoring.
    c. Half the going rate for tutoring.
    d. None of the above—he should *not* tutor one of his own students on a private basis.
26. My email address is usexythang@internet.net. When I begin my field experiences, I should
    a. Keep that address for correspondence with my cooperating teacher because I've had it for years.
    b. Use my official student email, even if I don't check it too often.
    c. Use my official student email, check it often, and keep the old email address for my crazy friends to use.
    d. Use my official student email, check it often, and get rid of, or change the old email address.

27. When one of my students says something really clever, I should
    a. Respond appropriately in the classroom, but protect his privacy outside of the classroom by not sharing the remark.
    b. Be sure that I post it on social networking site with a picture of the student, giving him credit for the remark.
    c. Post the remark on a social networking site, but say only that "one of my students" said it.
    d. Post it on a social networking site, but be sure not to be "friends" on the site with that student.
28. It's OK for me to post pictures from my wild birthday party on a social networking site because
    a. I'm over 21 and I can do what I want to.
    b. None of the pictures actually show ME doing anything questionable.
    c. I am not friends on the site with any of my students or their parents, so there is no way they would see the pictures.
    d. Maybe it's not a good idea for me to post pictures from my wild birthday party on a social networking site.
29. If I receive a text message while I am observing in a teacher's classroom, I should
    a. Disregard it, not even taking my phone out to observe who it is from, until I am out of the classroom and away from students.
    b. Quickly check it to ascertain whether I should step out of the room to read and answer it.
    c. Inform the teacher ahead of time that I will silence my phone but that I will most likely get a message that I will step out to check.
    d. Go ahead and step out of the room to check out the message.
30. Which of the following could be classified as Internet plagiarism?
    a. Using the Internet to get ideas about planning a lesson
    b. Making a copy of an article found on the Internet and including it as your own work in a paper you are writing
    c. Copying a test from the Internet-based site of a textbook you are using
    d. Copying a blog entry found on the Internet and attaching it to a report you have to write.

Discuss these situations and your responses with others in your class. Suggested "best" answers follow.

There may be disagreement among students regarding answers. Use these disagreements as opportunities for discussion.

This activity can also be found on the Education CourseMate website so you can print it out or answer the questions electronically.

1. c; 2. a & b; 3. d; 4. c; 5. c; 6. b; 7. d; 8. a & b; 9. b; 10. a; 11. c; 12. a; 13. a; 14. d; 15. c; 16. b; 17. d; 18. c; 19. b; 20. a; 21. b; 22. b; 23. d; 24. d; 25. d; 26. b; 27. a; 28. d; 29. a; 30. b.

© Cengage Learning 2014

professionalism The ethical behavior exhibited by teachers.

As you saw in Building Block 9.5, professionalism has many faces. As a professional, you are expected to model good behavior to your students and exhibit highly professional behavior at all times. In Chapter 13, you will find that the U.S. Supreme Court and lower courts have consistently held that, because of their influence on young people, teachers can and should be held to higher standards of behavior than other adults.

You can start exhibiting high standards of professional behavior in your current field experience. If you have any questions or uncertainties about professionalism in the field, you should discuss these with your professor or university supervisor. Normally, it is *not* appropriate to discuss issues of professionalism with your cooperating teacher, and it is *never* appropriate to discuss them with other teachers in the building. The following list contains professional behaviors you need to be especially concerned with in your field experience, taken from instruments used to evaluate preservice and in-service teachers.

To demonstrate professional behavior, you should:

- Demonstrate leadership and initiative.
- Demonstrate flexibility.
- Participate in positive interpersonal relationships with students, peers, parents, and administrators.
- Dress appropriately.
- Follow school rules, procedures, ethical and legal regulations.
- Respect the confidentiality of conversations and records concerning students, teachers, parents, and administrators.
- Communicate effectively.
- Cooperate and collaborate with others willingly.
- Accept and respond positively to constructive criticism.
- Accept responsibility for action and inaction.
- Be punctual and regular in attendance.
- Meet deadlines.
- Demonstrate willingness to become a lifelong learner.
- Demonstrate respect for family, community, and cultural values.

As a teacher, you can establish and maintain a valuable relationship with your students without crossing the line of professionalism.

Most professions have a code of ethics to guide professional behavior, and education is no exception. The National Education Association (NEA) has issued a *Code of Ethics of the Education Profession* that governs the ethics of teachers throughout the nation (National Education Association, 1975). The code is divided into two parts:

1. Ethics involving the teacher's commitment to the student
2. Ethics involving the teacher's commitment to the profession

Each state also has a code of ethics for teachers. You should become familiar with both the NEA code and your state's code of ethics. The complete NEA *Code of Ethics* is reproduced in Figure 9.1. It has not been revised since it was originally ratified in 1975.

Legal Requirements

Teachers are subject to certain legal requirements, with which you *must* become familiar. You will investigate these in Chapter 13, but two of them are so important they are included here:

Suspected child abuse. You *must* report to school authorities any instance of suspected child abuse. The suspicion can come from a student telling you about abuse, from noticeable but unexplained bruises, from other students telling you, and the like. This is not to say that you should look for evidence of child abuse in every student you see. But if you have reason to suspect that a student has been the victim of child abuse, you must report your suspicion. In most states, failure to do so is a

Figure 9.1 ▶
NEA Code of Ethics
Source: Courtesy National Education
Association (2012).

PREAMBLE

The National Education Association believes that the education profession consists of one education workforce serving the needs of all students and that the term *educator* includes education support professionals.

The educator, believing in the worth and dignity of each human being, recognizes the supreme importance of the pursuit of truth, devotion to excellence, and the nurture of the democratic principles. Essential to these goals is the protection of freedom to learn and to teach and the guarantee of equal educational opportunity for all. The educator accepts the responsibility to adhere to the highest ethical standards.

The educator recognizes the magnitude of the responsibility inherent in the teaching process. The desire for the respect and confidence of one's colleagues, of students, of parents, and of the members of the community provides the incentive to attain and maintain the highest possible degree of ethical conduct. The Code of Ethics of the Education Profession indicates the aspiration of all educators and provides standards by which to judge conduct.

The remedies specified by the NEA and/or its affiliates for the violation of any provision of this Code shall be exclusive and no such provision shall be enforceable in any form other than the one specifically designated by the NEA or its affiliates.

PRINCIPLE I

Commitment to the Student

The educator strives to help each student realize his or her potential as a worthy and effective member of society. The educator therefore works to stimulate the spirit of inquiry, the acquisition of knowledge and understanding, and the thoughtful formulation of worthy goals.

In fulfillment of the obligation to the student, the educator—

1. Shall not unreasonably restrain the student from independent action in the pursuit of learning.
2. Shall not unreasonably deny the student's access to varying points of view.
3. Shall not deliberately suppress or distort subject matter relevant to the student's progress.
4. Shall make reasonable effort to protect the student from conditions harmful to learning or to health and safety.
5. Shall not intentionally expose the student to embarrassment or disparagement.
6. Shall not on the basis of race, color, creed, sex, national origin, marital status, political or religious beliefs, family, social or cultural background, or sexual orientation, unfairly—
   a. Exclude any student from participation in any program.
   b. Deny benefits to any student.
   c. Grant any advantage to any student.
7. Shall not use professional relationships with students for private advantage.
8. Shall not disclose information about students obtained in the course of professional service unless disclosure serves a compelling professional purpose or is required by law.

PRINCIPLE II

Commitment to the Profession

The education profession is vested by the public with a trust and responsibility requiring the highest ideals of professional service.

In the belief that the quality of the services of the education profession directly influences the nation and its citizens, the educator shall exert every effort to raise professional standards, to promote a climate that encourages the exercise of professional judgment, to achieve conditions that attract persons worthy of the trust to careers in education, and to assist in preventing the practice of the profession by unqualified persons.

(Continued)

In fulfillment of the obligation to the profession, the educator—

1. Shall not in an application for a professional position deliberately make a false statement or fail to disclose a material fact related to competency and qualifications.
2. Shall not misrepresent his/her professional qualifications.
3. Shall not assist any entry into the profession of a person known to be unqualified in respect to character, education, or other relevant attribute.
4. Shall not knowingly make a false statement concerning the qualifications of a candidate for a professional position.
5. Shall not assist a noneducator in the unauthorized practice of teaching.
6. Shall not disclose information about colleagues obtained in the course of professional service unless disclosure serves a compelling professional purpose or is required by law.
7. Shall not knowingly make false or malicious statements about a colleague.
8. Shall not accept any gratuity, gift, or favor that might impair or appear to influence professional decisions or action.

Adopted by the NEA 1975 Representative Assembly.

criminal offense punishable according to the appropriate state statutes, and teachers can and have been prosecuted for trying to protect students and respect their confidences. You don't have to look very hard to find examples of this.

Drugs, alcohol, and firearms. You must report to school authorities any student who brings drugs, alcohol, or firearms to school. Teachers are required to report students who bring these items to school, and you must uphold the law regardless of your personal feelings.

Schools have procedures for reporting these and other infractions and require that you submit these reports in writing. Be sure to keep a copy of any written form or correspondence so you can demonstrate that you have acted in accordance with school policy and the law, should the need arise.

The Teacher's Expectations of the School

You have been investigating what schools expect of teachers. Now let us examine what teachers expect of schools.

The Teacher's Expectations

Why are you thinking about becoming a teacher? We suspect it is not for the money, although educators can earn reasonable salaries, especially as they gain experience. There are other advantages to being a teacher, and it is reasonable to expect that the school in which you work will provide these.

What do you expect of the school? Brainstorm your responses to this question and share them with others in your class.

BUILDING BLOCK
9.6

Teacher Salaries

It is said that teachers are underpaid and overworked. How true! Yet we *do* expect to be paid for our labors. How much can we expect to be paid? How does this compare with other professions? How are raises administered? As with certification and program requirements, teacher pay and its administration are state functions and vary greatly among states.

Normally, teachers are paid on the basis of degree held and prior experience. Each school district establishes an actual pay scale for that district; this pay scale is public and should be available either on the Internet or from the district central office. The pay scale is a table of actual salaries in steps for each year of service within columns showing level of preparation. Within a state, district salaries vary greatly. The state pays a certain base salary, and the district adds a supplement to that base. The amount of the supplement is determined independently by the district and is funded by local property taxes and, in some cases, sales taxes (see Chapter 11). Districts in less wealthy areas normally add lower supplements than wealthier districts. Why do you think that is?

<table>
<tr><td>BUILDING BLOCK
9.7</td><td>School Salary Scales</td></tr>
</table>

Select several school districts in which you might like to teach. Or, if you have no preference at present, select the school district in which you are doing your field experience. Obtain copies of the district's salary schedules from either the district offices or the Internet; teacher salary schedules are publically available information. Make it a habit to update this information annually.

- What is the salary for a beginning teacher with a bachelor's degree and no experience?
- What is the salary for a beginning teacher with a master's degree and no experience?
- What salary increase is awarded for each year of experience or service?
- Is there a top salary? What is it? What are the requirements to earn this salary?
- What salary do you think is reasonable for you to earn after you have gained some experience?
- How long would it take you to earn this salary in the school district you are investigating?

The traditional method of teacher salary administration in the United States is to use a salary scale such as the one you just investigated. A beginning teacher with no experience can expect to earn the salary associated with the degree he or she has at the salary scale step of zero years of experience. For each year of experience, the salary increases by a certain amount in a steplike fashion—usually the same dollar amount for each year. The entire salary scale may or may not increase to keep up with inflation and provide salary incentives. Often the pay increases teachers receive depend on the state's economy. Thus, although teachers can expect their salaries to increase to the next step in the salary scale each year, they do not always get cost of living or other general increases, unless the state or school board increases the scale.

An applicant's experience is discussed when a teacher is first employed by a school district; once agreed upon, this experience establishes the entry salary step. Thus, someone with a bachelor's degree who has taught successfully for three years at one school can expect a salary at the fourth step at the bachelor's degree level at a different school in the same district. However, school districts often factor in other experiences when deciding salary offers—such as military experience, classroom paraprofessional experience, experience in the business world, or other experience that would enhance that teacher's performance. In addition, signing bonuses may be offered to applicants for teaching in poor districts or low-performing schools and for teaching high-need subjects such as mathematics, science, and special education.

Teacher salaries are higher than they used to be. The average starting salary for newly graduated education majors in 2011 was $37,830, with a range from $31,495 to $42,980; this was an increase of 2.1 percent over the average starting teacher salary for 2010 (National Association of Colleges and Employers, 2012). The overall average teacher's salary in the United States for the 2009–2010 school year was $55,202, with a range from $38,837 to $71,633; this was an increase of 1.6 percent (National Education

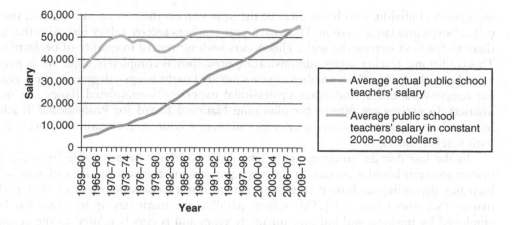

◀ Figure 9.2
Estimated average salary of teachers in public elementary and secondary schools, 1959–2010 in current dollars and 2008–2009 dollars.
Source: National Center for Education Statistics, 2010b.
© Cengage Learning 2014

Association, 2011). However, although salaries have increased, so has inflation. The graph in Figure 9.2 shows average teacher salaries between 1959–60 and 2009–10, and the same average teacher salaries in 2008–09 dollars with an adjustment for inflation. The line for current dollars shows the increase in the actual amount of money teachers were paid. You can see that this amount increases steadily. However, we have to factor in inflation, which means a dollar had less buying power in 2010 than it did in 1959. Taking inflation into consideration produces the line labeled "2008–09 dollars."

Just for fun, compare the salaries in Figure 9.2 with those offered by the District 1 Old Center School in Burlington, Vermont, in 1813. Teachers in this school were paid $6 to $9 a week, and in 1910, almost a century later, they were paid $11 to $15 a week (Miller, 1999). Compare these salaries also with the average monthly salaries of teachers in several states in 1847, as shown in Table 9.2.

As you have seen, considerable differences can exist between the state base rates and the district scales. As you look for your first teaching job, keep in mind that different districts offer different pay scales. Many sources compare teacher salaries among all states. To gain an idea of where your state stands in the nation, check one of the many surveys published on the Internet.

TABLE 9.2 Average Monthly Salaries (Including Board) of Teachers in 1847

State	Men	Women
Connecticut	$16.00	$6.50
Indiana	$12.00	$6.00
Massachusetts	$25.44	$11.38
Michigan	$12.71	$5.36
New Hampshire	$13.50	$5.65
New York	$14.96	$6.69
Ohio	$15.42	$8.73
Pennsylvania	$17.02	$10.09
Vermont	$12.00	$4.75

Source: Eakin, 2000.

Salary Increases

Salary scales are normally revised each year to reflect inflation and an increased base pay rate for teachers. Most school districts have followed a policy of awarding annual salary increases to individuals to bring them to the next step on the revised salary scale, the so-called "steps and lanes" system. Thus, each year, teachers receive salary increases that take them to the next step on the scale. This occurs without regard to quality of performance. This traditional teacher salary administration procedure is completely objective in nature, awarding salaries based on number of years having taught (steps), degrees earned, graduate coursework taken, and other professional experiences completed (lanes). In many districts, incentives are offered for obtaining National Board for Professional Teaching Standards certification, and many offer incentives to recruit and/or retain teachers in fields with teacher shortages.

In the last decade, however, many school districts have been moving from the step system to merit-based increases. In the merit pay system, teachers receive different salary increases depending on how the building administrators assess the merit of their performance. (See also Chapter 1.) This system parallels the merit pay system that has been employed by business and industry for many years and is closely related to the accountability provision of No Child Left Behind.

Although details of merit-based salary administration vary among school districts, the common aim is to encourage teachers to meet preestablished goals. For example, in the early 2000s, the Denver, Colorado, public school district piloted a salary system that rewarded teachers for producing student growth and provided bonuses to proven teachers who took on the toughest teaching assignments (Gratz, 2005). In this system, the teachers themselves established their own performance goals.

A great deal of controversy exists over merit pay systems for teachers. Those who favor such systems feel that outstanding teachers should be rewarded for their efforts, contributions, and successes. They feel that merit pay will increase teachers' effectiveness and eventually weed out those who are ineffective. Those opposed to merit-based pay systems cite favoritism, unrealistic and immeasurable goals, and potentially biased appraisals of teachers' performance. Opponents feel that all teachers do fundamentally the same job and should be paid on an objective, not a subjective, basis.

Tenure

Like other workers, teachers want job security. This security is provided through the vehicle of tenure. Tenure represents a teacher's status when that teacher is considered a permanent member of the faculty in a school district. Tenure is granted by state law, and the type and amount of protection vary from state to state. Tenure is awarded to individuals by the school board upon the individual's successful completion of a probationary (nontenured) period, normally two or three years. The primary purpose of tenure is to provide teachers with job protection by permitting them to request school board hearings if their administrators do not renew their contracts. Tenured teachers can be transferred within a school district; it is the district and not the individual school that awards tenure. If a teacher transfers to a different school district, he or she must earn tenure all over again, although it may take less time. Many people are under the impression that tenured teachers cannot be dismissed. This is incorrect. Districts that want to dismiss tenured teachers for incompetence can do so, but typically they must undertake a lengthy process of hearings and appeals, the results of which may be challenged in court. District personnel are reluctant to go through this potentially expensive and drawn-out procedure, and do so primarily when the evidence is clear and rapid decisions can be expected. Thus, it often is assumed that once a teacher has been awarded tenure, that teacher can keep his or her job in the school district for life, regardless of quality of performance.

As a matter of fact, it has been so difficult to discharge incompetent tenured teachers in New York City that special rooms dubbed "rubber rooms" have been set aside for these teachers to spend normal school hours doing nothing at all while drawing full salaries. They stay there while their case is being prepared or until they get tired of doing nothing and resign. As of summer 2010, about 700 teachers and administrators in New York City were assigned to these "reassignment centers," costing the city $30 million a

CONTROVERSIES in Education

Merit Pay

Education experts agree that one of the most important factors in the education of our nation's youth is the quality of the teacher, and many experts believe that the best way to attract and retain high-quality teachers is to pay them more. These concepts have led to proposals to reward good teachers and penalize bad ones. The proposals are termed merit pay (sometimes called pay for performance).

But there are difficulties with the merit pay system that have led to one of the most contentious controversies in the teaching profession.

First, let us look at some of the pros and cons of merit pay. Arguments in support of merit pay for teachers include the following:

- Americans reward hard work.
- With merit pay, teachers will work harder and get better results.
- Merit pay programs will help recruit the brightest minds into the teaching field and help retain them.
- Merit pay would inspire people to become teachers.
- Because education in the United States is in crisis, we should be trying anything new in the hope of making positive changes in education.

Arguments in opposition of merit pay for teachers include the following:

- It would be a bureaucratic nightmare to design and implement a merit pay system.
- The good will among teachers would be compromised.
- Success is difficult—maybe impossible—to define and measure.
- A better solution to the low pay of teachers is to pay all teachers more.
- A merit pay system would encourage dishonesty and corruption (from About.Com Elementary Education, 2012).

For many years, merit pay systems have been the staple of other professionals: factory workers, salespeople, lawyers, professional athletes, and the like. Why is this concept so contentious in the teaching profession? Let us consider some of the problems involved:

1. Teachers have no control over who is assigned to their classes. Everyone knows that teachers are better teachers when they have a "good" class than they are when they have a "challenging" class. So, it follows that teachers who have good classes will be perceived as more outstanding than teachers who have challenging classes.
2. Objectivity is necessary for a merit salary administration system to work. This means measuring the same things the same way for every teacher. But what should be measured? Most proposals for merit salary increase

systems hinge on students' standardized tests outcomes. But, as you know, there are a multitude of problems with standardized testing.

3. If teachers work for merit increases, they know they will be rewarded for high performance on the given criteria, and it is human nature to concentrate on the area(s) that count the most. This means that other tasks associated with excellence in teaching won't get done.
4. Testing is only one measure of teaching effectiveness; thus it is necessary to develop a measurement rubric that includes other factors as well. But, such a rubric will be extremely complicated as it tries to account for and give different weights to these many factors (Gonzalez, 2012).
5. Merit pay systems can be demoralizing and can foster an unhealthy sense of competition among faculty members, resulting in the erosion and ultimate destruction of the sense of school-wide community that is so important to quality.

You have seen that the Denver, Colorado school system implemented a pilot program of merit salary administration that was developed largely on the basis of input from the district's own teachers. The teachers were almost unanimously in favor of the system, and they worked hard to make it a success. But studies undertaken after the pilot was complete showed that strategies that work the best for measurement undercut good educational practice. So, although Denver's was a good pilot plan, the results showed that pay-for-performance based on test data doesn't work (Gratz, 2005). New York City implemented a pilot program in the mid-2000s, in which the city offered performance bonuses. But the program was discontinued after three years when it was shown that the performance bonuses had no effect on either test scores or student grades (Otterman, 2011).

These and many other programs have shown that merit pay salary administration systems do not work. Nonetheless, federal education policy fosters the pay-for-performance idea, and the Race to the Top and the NCLB waiver programs require states making proposals to link evaluation and pay of teachers to student performance.

What Can Be Done?

On behalf of the National Governors Association, Koebler (2012) says that, for merit systems to work, the following are necessary:

1. Create fair evaluation systems based on student assessments that measure growth in learning, and create data systems that are capable of linking student outcomes to individual teachers.

2. Do not rely solely on tests (that is not fair).

3. Form strong partnerships that include teachers in every step of the development and implementation process.

Milanowski (2012) writes there are three elements necessary in evaluation systems that are fair:

1. Formal teacher evaluation observations

2. Teacher work samples

3. Classroom walkthroughs

Critics of the currently used step system argue that the system is unfair because it can lead to mediocrity by rewarding outstanding and poor performance the same. However, advocates of the current system point out that a teacher's performance depends on many factors that cannot be isolated to determine who is truly outstanding and who is not.

Critics of the merit system fear that it is not possible to develop a truly objective evaluation system and that it will lead to favoritism. Advocates argue that merit pay encourages both outstanding and poorly performing teachers to become better, the result of which is that students benefit through increased learning.

Someday someone will come up with a merit-based salary system that is fair to *all* teachers and that truly discriminates the quality of teacher performances.

Most people agree that the current system, despite its many flaws, is about as objective as a salary administration system can possibly get. Yet, there is no distinction made between the outstanding teacher and the teacher who really ought to find a different profession.

WHAT DO YOU THINK?

1. *Based on what you have read and experienced, do you believe merit pay for teachers is a good idea or bad idea?*

2. *If a merit pay system were implemented at a school in which you were employed, what might you do in an effort to secure higher monetary rewards?*

3. *To what extent should student achievement scores be factored into merit pay? How would you figure merit pay for teachers of subjects such as music, art, and physical education that are not addressed by standardized testing?*

4. *On what factors do you think teacher pay should be based?*

merit pay A teacher's salary that is based on the quality of the teacher's performance; see also **pay for performance**.

pay for performance *See also* **merit pay**.

year. The centers were done away with effective fall 2010, and the incompetent teachers have been assigned to administrative work or other nonclassroom duties instead (Medina, 2010).

Tenured teachers have the advantage of full due process of law if their contracts are not recommended for renewal. This is not true for nontenured teachers. A school district may choose not to offer a nontenured teacher a contract for the following year, without citing any particular cause. Nontenured teachers do not have the right to school board hearings and appeals (although they always can pursue their grievances through legal channels).

As late as the mid-1990s, all states had some form of tenure in place. However, this teacher security mechanism is being eroded. Neither Nebraska nor South Dakota has tenure. Idaho eliminated tenure entirely in 2011, and 17 additional states changed their tenure laws to make tenure more difficult to acquire or to base tenure on performance (Cavanagh, 2011a).[3] Other states are considering eliminating or revising their tenure laws. The primary reason cited is to reduce the difficulties involved in terminating incompetent teachers. Because the statutes defining competence in teaching are vague, ambiguous, and subject to multiple interpretations, the elimination of the tenure protection makes it easier for school districts to dismiss incompetent teachers, and, thus, raise the quality of the teachers they provide for the education of the students in their district. Tenure is thoroughly explored from a legal standpoint in Chapter 13.

You can access a chart showing teacher tenure and/or continuing contract laws for each state through the direct link available on the Education CourseMate website.

---

[3]States that revised their tenure laws in 2011 are Alabama, Connecticut, Florida, Idaho, Illinois, Indiana, Maine, Michigan, Minnesota, Missouri, Nevada, New Hampshire, North Carolina, Ohio, Oklahoma, Tennessee, Wisconsin, and Wyoming.

Working Conditions

In Building Block 9.6, did you list factors that contribute to positive working conditions? How would you define positive working conditions? What working conditions do you feel your school should provide?

BUILDING BLOCK 9.8

Let's Get Specific: What Do You Need?

This textbook has focused a great deal of attention on how teachers and schools meet student needs. But, as a teacher, what do you need? If schools and society expect you to be accountable for your students' learning, what must you have to be able to meet that expectation? Consider such factors as class size, students, other teachers, support personnel, the administration, the building and physical plant, equipment, materials and supplies, and working hours.

- What items on your list are specific to grade level?
- What items are specific to content area?

Materials and Resources

You probably indicated that you would need a well-ventilated building with good-sized classrooms, navigable hallways, and adequate cafeterias, gymnasiums, art and music rooms, playgrounds, athletic fields, and other physical attributes. You probably also said you would need textbooks with teachers' editions; student workbooks; general classroom materials; computers and other technological materials and equipment; supplies such as paper, pencils, folders, markers, and other office supplies. You investigated some of these material needs in Chapter 7. You may have felt, however, that you need more materials than are ordinarily supplied. After all, although it is possible to be an effective teacher with a paucity of materials, it is far easier to teach if you have what you need. There is a lot of "stuff" associated with being a teacher. As a matter of fact, some people feel one of the advantages of being a teacher is that you get abundant "stuff" to work with—books, office supplies, posters, markers and pens, mathematics and science gadgets, maps, charts, and globes—the list goes on.

The school will meet most of your needs for paper, copies, and other office supplies. Often, however, teachers invest their own money in materials they feel they need for their students or for themselves that the school does not provide. They buy materials for seasonal activities, supplies for science and social studies activities, materials to use in making mathematics manipulatives, software for computer-based activities, and materials for many other activities. The National School Supply and Equipment Association reported that, in 2009–2010, teachers spent an average of $356 of their own money on school supplies and instructional materials (Nagel, 2010).

Teachers can minimize the amount of their own money they spend on materials for school. In the spring, schools normally ask teachers for a list of the equipment, materials, and supplies they will need for the following year, and they attempt to meet everyone's needs equitably and within budget. If there still is a need (and there probably will be, especially for unanticipated events), teachers can ask the PTA for donations, ask students' parents to donate materials (not money), create holiday "wish lists" to share with parents in a class newsletter, take advantage of free educational materials available to teachers, and write grant proposals. Many small grants are available for teachers to purchase equipment and materials for use in class projects. Some grants also pay for teachers to participate in professional development activities.

Suggestions for writing small winning grants for education are shown on the Education CourseMate website.

A s a teacher, we hope you have access to the good stuff—computers, interactive whiteboards, projectors, laptops, tablets, and other cutting-edge technology. You have repeatedly read in this textbook and elsewhere that the use of technology by the teacher should always serve to enhance instruction—never to replace it. Let us look at a few technological innovations that you can use to enhance your instruction. We will mention only a few to whet your appetite; you are sure to know of others—maybe you have even used some:

- **"Clickers"** (also known as **classroom response systems - CRS)** are the same as those gadgets you see on TV shows where the entire audience is asked to respond to a question. You can program the software so it flashes questions and multiple-choice answers on a screen. Students select what they think is the best answer, and the summary is projected onto the screen. This system has several purposes, including fairly instant feedback so teachers know right away what the students did and did not understand. You can even program the device so you will know who provided what response, enabling you to provide individual help. The clicker system may be used in both large and small classes.

- **Interactive whiteboards** are connected to a computer and have a touch-sensitive surface. Any image that is on the computer is projected onto the whiteboard for classroom viewing. Using a "pen" that comes with the board or even with a finger, you can write on the surface of the whiteboard with digital ink. This digital ink can even be erased with the accompanying eraser. Tapping the surface of the board is like clicking the computer's mouse. It is possible to click and drag objects with a finger, much like you would if you were using a mouse on a computer. Lesson plans that use an interactive whiteboard are available, as is software that allows teachers to create their own lessons. Teachers can also write notes on the interactive whiteboard and save a copy to the computer's hard drive or even print a copy.

- **Tablet computers** have numerous uses, especially via various apps (see Chapter 8). Tablets are becoming so popular that some schools issue them instead of paper and pencils for in-class activities and sometimes even in place of textbooks. Teachers in the elementary schools in a Connecticut school district use iPads to record observations of individual students as they move about the classroom. This provides immediate feedback and rich data that can be used to enhance individual instruction (Ash, 2012).

- Textbook publishers are producing digital versions of their textbooks. Students can use their tablets, computers, or smartphones to access the text and do the reading from an electronic version or online. An Indiana school district, having been unable to find textbooks that met all the needs of the district, turned to digital formats that incorporated a "Curriculum Loft" where teachers posted successful lesson plans and other materials to ensure the content is up-to-date. Students found their courses to be more relevant and 21st-century in nature (Nelson, Arthur, Jensen, and Van Horn, 2011). Using digitization of their education materials, publishers can update the content regularly, can prepare made-to-order materials, and can tie ancillaries to the basic materials.

- Science labs are becoming more digitized. Using simulations of experiments or dissections, students can execute investigations that would have been impossible a few years ago. They can manipulate variables and conduct multiple repetitions of experiments to see what happens without worrying about safety issues or running out of materials or resources.

These are but a few of the many new hardware and application technologies available for use in schools. In addition, there are innumerable sources to ensure you are correct and up-to-date with your information and to provide both interest and relevance to students:

- Videos and animations are available online, most often for free. Some sites that are specifically for teachers may include lesson plans, background information, suggestions for assessments, and other resources.

- Three-dimensional technology such as 3D video games, 3D representations of animals, and 3D nonverbal communications activities are being used to help autistic children learn to read and acquire communication and social ability skills (Alelo, 2012).

- Science fairs that used to be held in elementary school classrooms or high school gymnasiums are now being held online. Students anywhere in the world, ages 13 to 18, can participate in the annual Google worldwide science fair (National Science Teachers Association, 2012).

As you have seen, there is a lot of instructional technology out there. What is there is always changing and there is always more to come. You must become familiar with what is available, and, especially, how new technologies can help teachers enhance their instruction so *every* student learns. Keep a digital notebook in which you list what is available, where to find it, how it is used, and other details, and use this as a running list.

You can access sites referred to here through direct links on the Education CourseMate website.

Support

Did you include support in your list of needs? Many teachers will tell you that they will make do with the materials they have as long as they have cooperation, collaboration, and support from their colleagues and administration. Of course, some of this support provides supplies and needed resource personnel. However, teaching is a tough job and we also need other kinds of support.

Recall that as a teacher, you are responsible for ensuring your students' safety—physical, intellectual, and emotional. As a teacher, you also have the right to expect your physical, intellectual, and emotional safety to be ensured. Schools employ policies and strategies to address the physical safety of students; these policies apply to teachers, as well. What do you think intellectual and emotional safety for teachers entails?

Teaching is an intellectual activity. Teachers spend a great deal of time and intellectual energy developing lessons designed to involve and excite students. You have explored many teaching methods in previous chapters. Some of these methods stray from tradition and may earn the teacher who practices them some strange looks or critical comments from other teachers or parents. No teacher should feel pressured or threatened by the criticism of others, as long as he or she knows, and can show, that students are learning. Teaching is an intellectual process, and its product should be protected. Schools provide for the intellectual safety of their teachers through such vehicles as Teacher of the Year (TOTY), inviting teachers to share new and successful strategies at faculty meetings, and the like. In what other ways can a school provide for the intellectual safety of its teachers?

Not only is teaching an intellectual process; it is also emotional. Just as teachers expect their methodologies, curricular innovations, and assessment methods to be respected by others in the school, they have the right to expect they will be respected as professionals. Teachers expect and need support from colleagues who will respect the feelings they take into and out of the classroom. As with students, the emotional safety of teachers can be threatened when a teacher's feelings are invalidated. Schools provide for the emotional safety of their teachers through such vehicles as developing a school culture of honoring new and successful ideas, promoting classroom research, honoring confidences, and helping teachers to find ways of implementing their new ideas. In what other ways can schools provide for the emotional safety of their teachers?

Interactions with students can engender feelings of excitement, disappointment, hope, and anger. A teacher's biggest fear is that he or she will encounter an unmanageable class of students, the kind where students hurl insults and behave so badly the teacher is driven (sometimes literally) to tears. You can prevent this through effective classroom management techniques, such as those you explored in Chapter 8. The administration and other teachers will assist you. You expect this support from the school; it is necessary to ensure your emotional security. Remember, you are seeking respect from your students, not popularity. When this respect is earned, your emotional well-being relative to students is assured.

It is often necessary for teachers to share their feelings safely. Sometimes a teacher shares his or her emotions with the steering wheel on the drive home. Sometimes, a spouse or friend becomes a sounding board. Often, a teacher's best resource is another teacher—someone who really understands, or at least someone who has chocolate!

Perhaps the most important support a teacher can have within the school building comes from the administration. Teachers make hundreds of decisions every day. They need to know they have the trust and backing of the administration in these decisions, and they have the right to expect this backing.

Learning is a social activity and, therefore, so is teaching. Talk about teaching with others; share your excitement and setbacks; learn from your experiences and those of other professionals.

Courtesy of Bill Lisenby

Teachers are responsible for supporting and nurturing students in school. How can schools support and nurture teachers? How are teachers' emotional needs met in school?

Joys of Teaching

Among the advantages of being a teacher is the teacher's ability to fulfill the highest levels of personal development. Recall Maslow's hierarchy from Chapter 3. You surely have met your physiological needs when you go to work. Your safety and security needs, your love and belonging needs, and your esteem needs are met at school through your interactions with students and adults. You are satisfying your need to know and understand during your teacher preparation program, and you continue to meet this need through your implementation of best teaching practices in your school, continued professional development, and personal and collaborative reflections of your practice. You have the opportunity to satisfy your aesthetic needs in your own classroom, which you will decorate, arrange, and personalize. It is the self-actualization level in which teachers work. As you have found, the teacher's responsibility is to facilitate student learning. To do this successfully requires self-actualization. No one is going to teach for you. A day when you feel you have been in concert intellectually with your students is an extremely satisfying day, and it occurs because of you, the teacher, and your implementation of teaching practices that work.

The teacher is working toward resolution of Erickson's generativity versus stagnation stage of psychosocial development. If you stagnate, it is virtually impossible to be an effective teacher. Teaching is exciting, and it requires much originality, imagination, and creativity to succeed. Teachers, therefore, are in the ideal position to nurture their generativity aspects.

Schools provide for teachers' physical, intellectual, and emotional safety through procedures, respect, and support. In addition, schools are the ideal venue for teachers to work at the highest levels of personal development, thereby achieving the highest levels of personal satisfaction.

Ryan (1986) identifies four stages of teaching:

1. Fantasy: the stage when new teachers believe that all they need to do to be successful is relate and be a friend to their students
2. Survival: the stage when teachers do whatever is necessary to make it through the day
3. Mastery: the stage when teachers know how to achieve student success through employing effective practices
4. Impact: the stage when teachers know how to make an impact on their students through employing best practices (p. 5)

During your first year or two of teaching, you will develop a repertoire of management strategies, lessons, and instructional methods. As you gain experience and confidence, and if the school meets your expectations for support, you will reach the later stages that Ryan identifies; at the same time, you will meet the school's expectations of you.

■ SUMMARY

- Schools have expectations of teachers, and teachers have expectations of schools.
- Schools' expectations of teachers include instructional and noninstructional activities, certification, professional development, expertise in educational technology, and professional and ethical behavior.
- Noninstructional duties vary from school to school and state to state; some are compensated financially and some are not. In either case, noninstructional duties are part of teaching.
- Once a teacher is certified, he or she is expected to grow professionally through professional development activities. These activities are offered by many sources and are available to all teachers in nearby locations.
- Expectations teachers have for schools include reasonable salaries; job security; good working conditions; material support; and physical, intellectual, and emotional safety.

Teachers are busy, are held to high expectations, and are accountable for student learning. They are, themselves, lifelong learners. Effective teachers achieve these lofty goals, and you can, too. First, finish this book and the class in which you are using it. Then, complete your teacher education program. Your assignments and field experiences will help you gain knowledge and skills to bring to your classroom. Although teaching may be one of the few professions in which you are expected to have all the knowledge and skills on the first day, the more experience you acquire the more you can expect to benefit from the noble profession of teaching.

■ Key Terms and Concepts

Certification add-on, 232	Merit pay, 245	Professionalism, 238
Instructional duties, 225	Noninstructional duties, 225	Teacher certification, 229
Mentor, 234	Pay for performance, 245	Tenure, 244

■ Construct and Apply

1. Reflect on the "gray line" that exists between instructional and noninstructional duties. What tasks do teachers undertake that might be instructional but do not necessarily occur in the presence of students? Compare the teacher's instructional and noninstructional duties to the rehearsal and the opening night of a play.
2. Compare and contrast the different routes to teacher certification. What are the advantages and disadvantages of each?
3. Why is it important for teachers to stay current? Describe the classroom of a teacher who is "still in the dark ages."
4. Comment on teacher salaries. Consider that teachers are paid for 9 to 10 months of work. What would a monthly paycheck be before taxes? What would the monthly starting salary be for a teacher in your local school system if pay were distributed over 12 months? How does the teacher's annual salary compare to other professions?
5. What are advantages and disadvantages of tenure? Should tenure be retained in today's schools? Why or why not?
6. Recall the basic and academic needs of students that teachers and the school must meet. What are teachers' basic and academic needs? How does the school meet these needs?

■ Deconstructing the Standards

1. Recall the InTASC Standards associated with the objectives for this chapter: **InTASC** Standard #7 reads, "The teacher plans instruction that supports every student in meeting rigorous learning goals by drawing upon knowledge of content areas, curriculum, cross-disciplinary skills, and pedagogy, as well as knowledge of learners and the community context." **InTASC** Standard #9 reads, "The teacher engages in ongoing professional learning and uses

evidence to continually evaluate his/her practice, particularly the effects of his/her choices and actions on others (learners, families, other professionals, and the community), and adapts practice to meet the needs of each learner."

   a. How does this chapter address these standards?

   b. How will the concepts in this chapter help you apply these standards as a teacher?

2. Use your favorite search engine to find your state's standards for certification. When you find it, bookmark the site; you will refer to it often during this course.

   a. How are your conclusions about educational philosophy represented in your state certification standards?

   b. How do the InTASC Standards compare to your state's certification standards regarding educational philosophy?

   c. Do you believe the degree of representation concerning educational philosophy is adequate in your state certification standards? Why or why not?

Your Portfolio

1. Add copies of the NEA *Code of Ethics of the Education Profession* and your state's code of ethics for teachers to your portfolio for frequent reference.

2. Collect the information you have gathered throughout this chapter on professional development opportunities and teacher resources. Include them as appropriate in your portfolio.

3. Utilize technology whenever and wherever appropriate to complete assignments and activities and to make presentations to peers and professors. Include evidence of your technology-related knowledge and skills in your portfolio and reflect on how you will use these as a teacher to manage your work and instruct your students.

4. Make a special effort to collect evidence of your professional behavior as you progress through your program.

Education CourseMate Resources

Check out this text's Education CourseMate website (at www.cengagebrain.com) for more information about the teaching profession. You will find the TeachSource videos, a guide for doing field experiences, glossary flash cards, activities, tutorial quizzes, direct links to the websites mentioned in the chapter, and more.

PART

IV Society

IN PART I, you investigated your *self* and your ideas and beliefs about education. In Part II, you investigated students and their common and unique needs and talents. In Part III, you investigated the nature of schools and the complex relationships among the school, students, and teachers.

Part IV extends your investigations of education in the United States to the larger sphere of social influences. You will investigate the historical foundations of education in the United States, ways in which schools are managed and financed, some social issues that affect teaching and schools, legal issues that impact American education, and current reform activities relative to curriculum, assessment, and teaching.

CHAPTER
10 Historical Perspectives

SCHOOLS ARE SOCIAL INSTITUTIONS. They are profoundly affected by historical developments, governments, legislation, sources of finance, diverse goals set by diverse populations, religious beliefs, social mores, folkways, expectations, and much more.

In previous chapters, you investigated the complex school system. You saw that schools have definite and specific purposes and are structured to fulfill these purposes. Today's schools result from the continuous evolution of educational thought. U.S. schools began in colonial times, and today's schools resonate with the purposes, goals, structures, and teacher–student interactions as they have changed over time. These changes have been made in response to society's needs and the thinking of prominent educators.

The current concept of K–12 schools is one with which you are intimately familiar. You probably could trade tales out of school with friends, classmates, and new acquaintances, finding similarities in your stories and experiences. We all have our own definite ideas of what school is, and you have begun to articulate your beliefs about what schools should be. However, we cannot ignore what schools have been in the past. Studying the history of education and schools helps us to understand the past and offers insights into both the present and the future.

In this chapter, you will explore schools in various historical contexts to develop your understanding of how we got where we are and why schools are the way they are.

As a result of your explorations in this chapter, you will be able to:

1. Describe changes in school population, influences of society, changes in curriculum and instruction, and significant historical events that affected U.S. education in colonial times.
   InTASC Standard #9: Professional Learning and Ethical Practice

2. Describe changes in school population, influences of society, changes in curriculum and instruction, and significant historical events that affected U.S. education during the young nation period.
   InTASC Standard #9: Professional Learning and Ethical Practice

3. Describe changes in school population, influences of society, changes in curriculum and instruction, and significant historical events that affected U.S. education during the progressive nation period.
   InTASC Standard #9: Professional Learning and Ethical Practice

4. Describe changes in school population, influences of society, changes in curriculum and instruction, and significant historical events that affected U.S. education during the postwar period.
   InTASC Standard #9: Professional Learning and Ethical Practice

5. Describe changes in school population, influences of society, changes in curriculum and instruction, and significant historical events that affected U.S. education during the modern period.
   InTASC Standard #9: Professional Learning and Ethical Practice

6. Describe the trends and issues in the education of minorities in the United States.
   InTASC Standard #9: Professional Learning and Ethical Practice

Basic Educational History Considerations

There are many ways to divide the history of education into manageable pieces. In this chapter, we focus on the following time periods:

- Colonial period (1620–1750)
- Young nation period (1750–1900)
- Progressive nation period (1900–1950)
- Postwar period (1950–1980)
- Modern period (1980–present)

You will explore the history of U.S. education in the context of questions similar to those you considered in developing your philosophy of education in Chapter 2. For each time period, you will consider several questions:

- What was happening in the United States?
- Who went to school?
- What was taught?
- Who decided what should be taught?
- Why was this material taught?
- How were students taught?
- What were the schools like?
- Who were the influential educators and what were their contributions?

The answers to these questions have changed over time in response to the social needs of our nation as it developed into a world power. These needs have resulted in changes in legislation; changes in how schools are funded; changes in skills needed by graduates; changes in the expectations of local, regional, and national communities; changes in religious beliefs; and changes in the ways prominent educators and others view education, its curriculum, and its methodology.

To begin, read the account of the following educational dilemma.

Schooldays

A young boy goes off to school. He is called on for an oral recitation covering his written assignment. Later, the class breaks for lunch. In the afternoon, his class practices written exercises. At the close of the day, he returns home and is greeted by his father, who inquires how he did in school. The boy proudly recites what he has learned and shows off samples of his work. The father is pleased. Later that evening, the youth leaves a reminder that he be awakened early in the morning. He is anxious about getting to school on time.

The next day, so the account continues, the boy's mother hands him two rolls for his lunch and he hurries off to the schoolhouse. But, for reasons unexplained, he is delayed en route and arrives late for his first class. The attendance monitor is waiting at the door and orders the boy to report to the principal. Heart pounding in fear, the youth complies. As it turns out, besides being tardy, he failed to complete his homework. The irate principal administers a sound thrashing.

Thereafter, matters go from bad to worse. The rest of the day is given over mainly to beatings for still other infractions: for slovenly appearance in violation of the school's dress code, for speaking out of turn, for standing at ease and leaving his assigned seat without permission, for lapsing into the vernacular during a foreign language class, and finally, for loitering about on school grounds after hours.

The boy now dreads school and begins neglecting his lessons. His teacher, thoroughly disgusted, eventually abandons all pretense of trying to teach the youth anything, and threatens his dismissal. The boy's father is distraught; his son is on the verge of becoming a school dropout. In a last, desperate effort to settle matters, he hits upon the idea of inviting the principal home for a conference.

The schoolmaster is treated royally upon his arrival. He is led to the seat of honor and wined and dined. Gifts are pressed upon him. On cue, the lad begins to recount all he has learned in school. Then the father joins in, lavishing praise on the teacher for his unsparing efforts on the boy's behalf. This stratagem proves successful. By now greatly mollified and in a mellowed mood, the principal launches into a long, windy speech, thanking his host for his generosity and parental concern. In a paroxysm of enthusiasm, he winds up with words of praise for the young student's supposed academic accomplishments. Everyone is greatly relieved and a crisis is averted.

From Lucas, C. J. (1980). The more things change. *Phi Delta Kappan 61*(6), 414–16. Reprinted with permission.

When do you suppose this account was written? There are few clues in the text about its origin. Actually, this is a loose translation of the "Schooldays" composition restored from about 20 separate cuneiform tablets dating back some 4,300 years to the very dawn of civilization. Can you tell from this account what was taught in early Sumerian schools? What were the schools like?

Jumping ahead a couple of millennia, we find the writings of the ancient Greek philosophers. Socrates felt the primary purpose of schooling was for people to become moral beings (McCambridge, 1977). Plato and Aristotle believed the primary purpose of schooling lay in discovering what it means to be human, so that people could live a good life in accordance with their human nature.

Plato Wrote:

By education, then, I mean goodness in the form in which it is first acquired by a child. . . . But if you consider the one factor in it, the rightly disciplined state of pleasures and pains whereby a man, from his first beginnings on, will abhor what he should abhor and relish what he should relish—if you isolate this factor and call it education, you will be giving it its true name.

Aristotle Wrote:
Pleasure induces us to behave badly, and pain to shrink from fine actions. Hence the importance (as Plato says) of having been trained in some way from infancy to feel joy and grief at the right things: true education is precisely this.

But education was destined to change.

Education in the Colonial Period

TIMELINE 1620–1750 Colonial Period

1635	First Latin Grammar School
1636	Founding of Harvard College
1642	Massachusetts Act of 1642
1647	Old Deluder Satan Act
1689	Friends Public School, Philadelphia
1690	New England Primer
1692	Salem Witch Trials

© Cengage Learning 2014

Color Key:
- General Historic Topics
- Durational Topics
- Education Topics

Colonial Schools

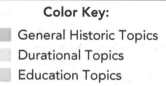

BUILDING BLOCK 10.1

Think about what U.S. schools must have been like in the colonial period (1620–1750).

- What was life like during colonial times? What did the colonists value?
- What was happening in the colonies during this time?
- What did people need to know and be able to do to function and thrive in their society?
- Did everyone need the same knowledge and skills?
- What do you think students were required to learn in school?
- How do you think students learned during this period?

You may recall from your studies of U.S. history that 17th-century colonies were settled in three different regions. The New England colonies included Massachusetts, Rhode Island, Connecticut, and New Hampshire. The Middle Atlantic colonies were centered in Pennsylvania and also included New York, New Jersey, and Delaware. The southern

Figure 10.1 ▶
The 13 original American colonies.
© Cengage Learning 2014

colonies included Maryland, Virginia, North Carolina, South Carolina, and Georgia (see Figure 10.1). Each region had its own unique characteristics, and schooling evolved differently in each.

Colonists settled in America for several reasons, among which religious freedom was of great importance. It is not surprising, then, to note that the primary purpose of education in the American colonies of the 1600s and early 1700s was to perpetuate religion. In the New England colonies, this meant maintaining Protestant religious beliefs; the Middle Atlantic colonies embraced several religious practices, although the people were basically all Protestants; and the prevailing religious practice in the southern colonies was patterned after the Anglican Church.

Because the colonies comprised three separate regions, each with its own unique thoughts about education, it is appropriate to look at each region separately.

New England Colonies

The overriding purpose of schooling in the colonial period was to ensure pupils' religious salvation. The very strict Calvinist Protestant ideas embraced by the New England Puritans viewed human nature as depraved. The Puritans believed that schools should instill religious conformity and religious values. To this end, students were required to learn to read and write English, Latin, and Greek so they could pursue theological studies. Of course, the colonies were still under British rule, and the educational institutions had been transplanted from class-conscious Europe and England. Consequently, there were two educational tracks, each represented in a different kind of school. One was the vernacular school for lower-class males that taught reading, writing, arithmetic, and religion; the other was the Latin grammar school for upper-class males. These two tracks were separate; students did not move from one to the other.

The religious purpose of education was made plain in two early laws. The Massachusetts Act of 1642 required that parents and masters see that their children know the principles of religion and the laws of the Commonwealth. The other law, the Massachusetts Act of 1647, was known as the Old Deluder Satan Act, and is reproduced here in its original language.

Old Deluder Satan Act

It being one chief project of that old deluder, Satan, to keep men from the knowledge of the Scriptures, as in former times by keeping them in an unknown tongue, so in these latter times by persuading from the use of tongues, that so that at least the true sense and meaning of the original might be clouded and corrupted with false glosses of saint-seeming deceivers; and to the end that learning may not be buried in the grave of our forefathers, in church and commonwealth, the Lord assisting our endeavors.

It is therefore ordered that every township in this jurisdiction, after the Lord hath increased them to fifty households shall forthwith appoint one within their town to teach all such children as shall resort to him to write and read, whose wages shall be paid either by the parents or masters of such children, or by the inhabitants in general, by way of supply, as the major part of those that order the prudentials of the town shall appoint; provided those that send their children be not oppressed by paying much more than they can have them taught for in other towns.

And it is further ordered, that when any town shall increase to the number of one hundred families or householders, they shall set up a grammar school, the master thereof being able to instruct youth so far as they may be fitted for the university, provided that if any town neglect the performance hereof above one year that every such town shall pay five pounds to the next school till they shall perform this order.

Source: From *Records of the Governor and Company of the Massachusetts Bay in New England* (1853), II: 203.

What Do You Think?

- What were the primary provisions of the Old Deluder Satan Act?
- What were the heads of families in towns of 50 or more families required to do for the education of their children?
- What were the heads of families in towns of 100 or more families required to do for the education of their children? How were these responsibilities accomplished?

To put the religious zeal of the New England colonists in perspective, one need only to look at the Salem, Massachusetts, witch trials of 1692 that resulted in convictions and executions of men and women for witchcraft. Consorting with the devil was considered a felonious crime in the 17th century. The punishment for the crime was hanging. Altogether, 19 men were hanged, seven people died in prison, and one man was pressed to death with rocks during torture (Salem Witch Museum, 2011).

Look also at the hornbook and the *New England Primer*, the primary reading books used in school. The hornbook was not a book but a small wooden paddle with a single sheet of paper glued to it, covered with a very thin, transparent layer of cow's horn for

vernacular schools Schools in the New England colonies for lower-class males that taught reading, writing, arithmetic, and religion.

Latin grammar schools Schools in the New England colonies for upper-class males that taught the subjects necessary for admission to college.

Massachusetts Act of 1647 The "Old Deluder Satan Act" that required towns with at least 50 households to hire a schoolmaster to teach children to read and write, and required towns of 100 households or more to have a school that would prepare children to attend Harvard College.

Old Deluder Satan Act Nickname for the Massachusetts Act of 1647

hornbook A single-faced wooden paddle used to teach reading in colonial times.

New England Primer A small book used to teach reading in the New England colonies.

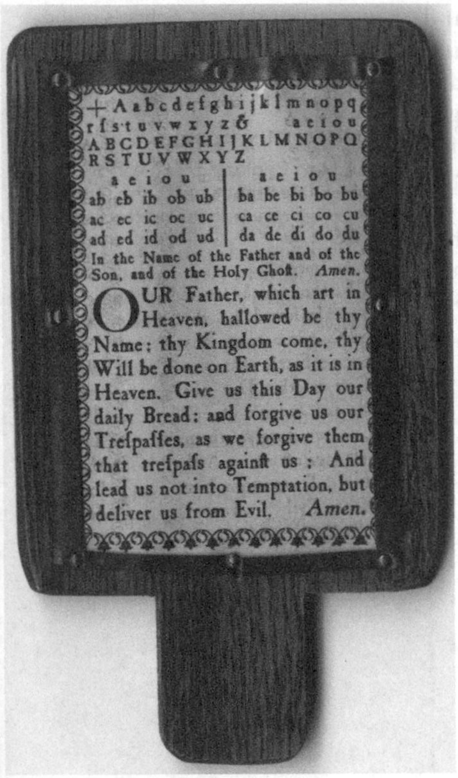

The hornbook text reads:

† A a b c d e f g h i j k l m n o p q
r s t u v w x y z &   a e i o u
A B C D E F G H I J K L M N O P Q
R S T U V W X Y Z

a e i o u | a e i o u
ab eb ib ob ub | ba be bi bo bu
ac ec ic oc uc | ca ce ci co cu
ad ed id od ud | da de di do du

In the Name of the Father and of the
Son, and of the Holy Ghost. *Amen.*

OUR Father, which art in
Heaven, hallowed be thy
Name; thy Kingdom come, thy
Will be done on Earth, as it is in
Heaven. Give us this Day our
daily Bread: and forgive us our
Trespasses, as we forgive them
that trespass against us : And
lead us not into Temptation, but
deliver us from Evil. *Amen.*

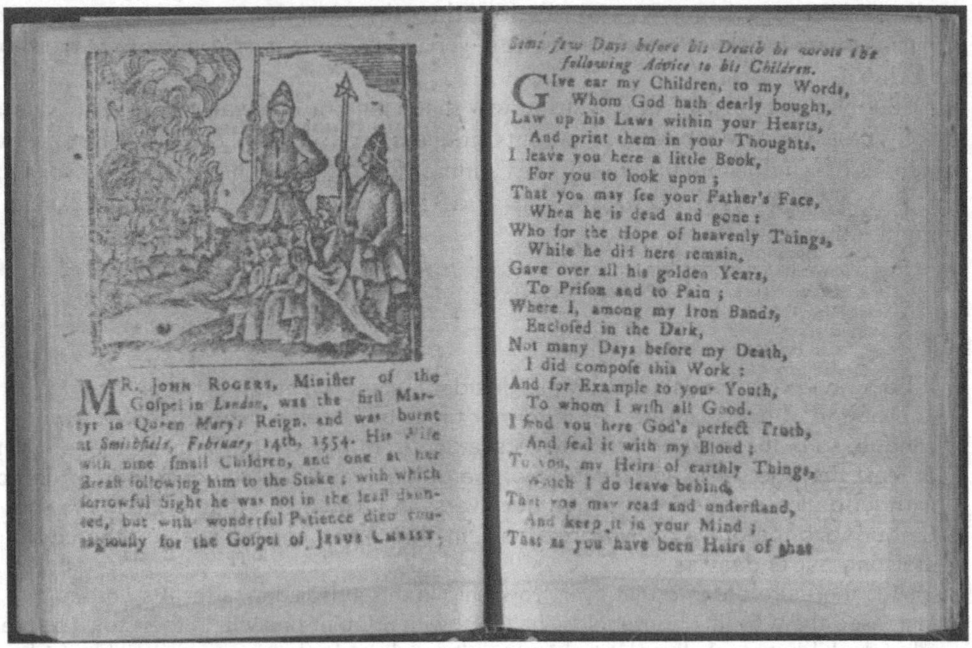

An early American hornbook, and pages from the New England Primer.

dame schools Colonial schools for girls.

protection. The paper had the ABCs, some pairs of letters, and a religious verse, often the Lord's Prayer, printed on it and was used to teach reading and writing. Hornbooks were used through the mid-1700s.

The *New England Primer* was first published in 1690, and combined the material of the hornbook with religious catechism, using words, couplets, and text to teach reading. It was shorter than 90 pages and approximately three by four inches in size (see photos). The *New England Primer* was used continuously through the early 1800s.

Formal schooling was reserved for boys of European descent in the northern colonies, although some girls attended the primary schools. The boys started school at age six or seven and went for three or four years. Most girls who attended school went to women's homes, where they learned housekeeping skills. These schools were called dame schools and served both day care and educational purposes.

After young boys had learned to read (by age nine or ten), there were essentially two paths available to them:

1. Attendance at a Latin grammar school to prepare them for college
2. Apprenticeship or training in the father's occupation at home

The first Latin grammar school was established in 1635, and its purpose was to prepare upper-class boys for the entrance test to Harvard College, where they would begin their theological studies. Founded in 1636, Harvard College was the only college available. The following shows admission requirements for Harvard College in 1642 and 1700:

Harvard College Admission Requirements in 1642
When any Schollar is able to Read Tully or such like classicall Latine Author
ex tempore, and make and speake true Latin in verse and prose suo (ut aiunt)

Marte, and decline perfectly the paradigmes of Nounes and verbes in the Greeke tongue, then may hee bee admitted into the College, nor shall any claime admission before such qualifications.

Harvard College Admission Requirements in 1700

Everyone competent to read Cicero or any other classic author of that kind extemporaneously, and also to speak and write Latin prose and verse with tolerable skill and without assistance, and of declining the Greek nouns and verbs, may expect to be admitted to the College: if deficient in any of these qualifications, he cannot under any circumstances be admitted.

Schools consisted of one room for 20 to 30 boys, where the primary motivators were praise and punishment. Teachers were required to have academic, religious, moral, and political qualifications; they were hired by boards of trustees from personal interviews and others' recommendations. Education was financed by royal donations, work and land rent, direct taxation, and some tuition.

The second path, primarily available to young boys of lower social or economic classes, was apprenticeship, which lasted approximately seven years. As an apprentice, the boy learned all the tasks of a trade from a master and often was required to make monthly payments to him. Because of the cost, the length of time required, and the inconvenience, most boys did not take this route. Instead, most lower-class boys trained at home in their fathers' occupations; such training was free, convenient, and productive.

Middle Atlantic Colonies

In the Middle Atlantic colonies, education took on a more practical nature than was prevalent in the north, subscribing to the principle that children should learn a useful trade in addition to reading, writing, arithmetic, and religion. Several different churches and denominations coexisted in the Middle Atlantic colonies. Consequently, instead of having a uniform system of education, as was prevalent in New England, the schools and the curriculum were established to meet local needs, including the needs of the churches, and thus were different from one area to another. Also, because of the growth of business, a middle class was emerging. The curriculum included both religious and practical subjects; various religious groups and the teacher jointly decided the actual program.

Although public schools in the Middle Atlantic colonies were meant primarily for boys, the education of girls was considered important. In fact, the Society of Friends (popularly known as the Quakers) accepted both boys and girls into their

© Bettmann/CORBIS

A colonial one-room schoolhouse. How does this sketch depict education in early America? Who is being educated, who is teaching, and what motivators for student learning are identifiable in this sketch?

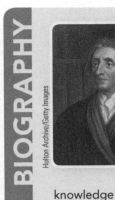

John Locke (1632–1704) was an English philosopher and doctor. His writings greatly influenced education during the 1600s and 1700s, and continue to occupy an important place in educational thought today. Unlike the early Greek philosophers, who felt people were born with all the knowledge they needed, Locke argued that knowledge is *not* innate; rather, knowledge is carried to people's minds through their sensory experiences. In his *Essay Concerning Human Understanding*, published in 1690, Locke wrote, "Let us suppose the mind to be . . . without any ideas; how comes it to be furnished? To this, I answer with one word: from EXPERIENCE" (in Kreis, 2000, p. 1). Influenced by Locke's writings, school programs began to move away from the God-centered curriculum to one with secular, humanistic, and practical approaches.

Not only was Locke influential in education; his writings on social order and government strongly influenced Thomas Jefferson and the framing of the Declaration of Independence and the U.S. Constitution.

private schools, having started the Friends Public School in Philadelphia in 1689, to educate all children until they could be apprenticed to learn a trade. The school offered many kinds of classes in keeping with people's needs. The school charged tuition to those who could pay; otherwise, school was free. Teachers were paid by the parents.

By the early 1700s, many private-venture schools had arisen, and many schools became ethnically and religiously segregated as a result of the national, cultural, religious, and racial influences.

Southern Colonies

The southern colonies treated education as a private matter, separate from the state, and offered education largely to wealthy children to prepare them for college. People in these colonies believed that the most important training children could receive was in the home; there, children could be inducted into the values of their society. The purpose of education was to create a college-educated elite. There was no middle class in the antebellum south—only plantation owners, poor whites, and slaves. Poor whites who worked on farms had no access to education, and slaves were prohibited from learning to read or write.

The first southern school was founded in Virginia in 1636. It was a private free school made possible by the estate of one Benjamin Symms, who left 200 acres plus eight cows to establish a free school. Other schools followed in 1655, 1667, 1675, and 1689; all were private and paid for by individuals' contributions. One reason for the slow growth in the number of schools was that the population was dispersed; often an area held too few children to justify a school. Teachers were tutors who traveled long distances between towns to teach at town schools. The growth of schools continued at this slow pace until the founding of the College of William and Mary, the nation's second oldest college, in Virginia in 1693.

BUILDING BLOCK
10.2

Your Thoughts about Colonial Education

■ How do the inferences you made about colonial education in Building Block 10.1 compare with the descriptions you investigated in this section?

■ How did colonial education mirror what was going on in the country at the time?

■ Which educational philosophy or philosophies prevailed during colonial times?

Education in the Young Nation Period

1750–1900 Young Nation Period

1749	The Academy
1750–1850	Industrial Revolution
1775–1783	Revolutionary War
1776	Declaration of Independence Adopted
1787	U.S. Constitution Adopted
1791	Bill of Rights Ratified
1810	Monitorial System of Teacher Preparation
1830	Common School
1839	Massachusetts State-Funded Teacher Preparation School
1852	Massachusetts Compulsory Attendance Law
1861–1865	Civil War
1862	First Morrill Act (Land Grant Colleges)
1890	Second Morrill Act

© Cengage Learning 2014

Color Key:
- General Historic Topics
- Durational Topics
- Education Topics

Let us next consider U.S. education from the end of the colonial period to the end of the 19th century.

Schools in the Young Nation Period

BUILDING BLOCK 10.3

Think about the time period from 1750 to 1900.

- What was happening in the United States during this time? List some major events.
- What knowledge and skills did individuals need to be able to respond to these events and to contribute to the society of a growing nation?
- Did everyone need the same knowledge and skills?
- How do you think schools and teaching changed from colonial times in response to societal changes?
- How do you think students learned during this period?

As you might expect, the American Revolution, the Declaration of Independence, the Constitution, and the Bill of Rights all had enormous influence on the purpose and nature of education during the late 1700s and early 1800s. The Civil War, immigration, reconstruction, and the Industrial Revolution had equally powerful influences on education during the late 1800s. During these times, U.S. education expanded to include a sense of nationalism as well as preparation for a trade, in addition to the traditional studies of reading, writing, arithmetic, and the Bible. This expansion included shifts in educational goals toward occupational proficiency and the ability to participate in a democratic society. The emphasis on religion declined, and the need for job-related training became increasingly important.

Changing Purpose of Education in the Young Nation Period

To foster occupational proficiency, science—a subject new to schools—began to emerge. In 1749, Benjamin Franklin founded The Academy in Philadelphia, which later became the University of Pennsylvania, where both the classical subjects and the subjects needed for occupations were taught. Franklin felt that neither religion nor tradition should determine the purpose and character of education. The Academy was intended to cultivate trades as well as "more useful culture of young minds" (Tyack, 1967, p. 73). Franklin's Academy instituted a double track in the same school: one for vocational preparation and one for preparation for college.

In the late 1700s, Thomas Jefferson believed that the country needed a supply of college-educated people who could take leadership roles and make good decisions for the country, especially in the territories created by western expansion. Education was beginning to reflect a sense of nationalism. Schooling began to stress the scientific and practical education emphasized by Franklin and the political and civic education emphasized by Jefferson.

BUILDING BLOCK 10.4

Educational Thought in the Middle Atlantic and Southern Colonies

Benjamin Franklin came from the Middle Atlantic colonies and Thomas Jefferson came from the South. How did the traditions established in each of those regions in the 1600s influence thinking about education in the next century?

Expansion

The United States saw many changes in the 19th century. The country was expanding westward. Industrialization brought such innovations as coal-gas lamps, electric lights, the phonograph, the steam engine, the transcontinental railroad, dynamite, the telegraph, the telephone, and the development of the Standard Oil Company. Increasing numbers of immigrants settled in America. All of this activity resulted in the expansion of the nation's schools to accommodate more students and to prepare these students for life in the growing industrialized nation. Consequently, all schoolchildren were taught basic knowledge, the virtues of patriotism and morality, and the skills they would need in life.

Because of growing immigration, schools began to emphasize civics, citizenship, history, geography, and moral development. Because of growing industrialization, subjects dealing with science, mathematics, thinking abilities, and vocational education appeared in the curriculum. Additionally, reading, writing, spelling, penmanship, arithmetic, and the classics continued to be prominent areas of study. In the larger towns, schools added algebra, American history, bookkeeping, geometry, and surveying to their programs; students took these courses in addition to Latin, Greek, general history, rhetoric, and logic.

McGuffey Readers Primary reading texts in the 19th century.

For many students in the mid-19th century, *McGuffey Readers* were the primary texts for reading instruction. Each book in the McGuffey series was graded according to reading level. Not only did each book in the series provide an eclectic mix of poetry and prose, but the books also stressed moral, ethical, and religious principles.

common school Elementary school in the 19th century that was free and public.

The common school was an elementary or primary school that came into existence in the period between 1830 and 1850, reflecting the common school movement that began in the early 19th century. This movement was based on the belief that free education would strengthen the nation and that all children had the right to a free, public education. The common school movement represented the beginning of compulsory education for everyone, although "everyone" was interpreted to mean primarily white boys, with a few girls and a few black children. Mary Lyon (1797–1849) worked hard to provide women with the same opportunities for education that were available to men, founding Mount Holyoke College, which became a model for women's colleges.

The first general law legislating the attendance of children at school was enacted in Massachusetts in 1852. This law required that children between the ages of 8 and 14 attend school for at least 3 months out of each year. Three weeks of this 3-month period had to be consecutive. Enforcement was loosely provided by individual cities. It took another 20 years to form enforcement procedures and hire truant officers to check absentees. By 1918, all states had passed compulsory attendance laws.

During the 1800s, public schools started to be funded through state and local taxes, making schools free to all students. School system superintendents were introduced to manage everything from curriculum and teaching methodology to hiring and firing personnel, maintaining the school buildings, and ensuring attendance.

The Loomis Chaffee School

An example of a 19th-century school that disregarded the restrictive educational traditions of the time is the Loomis Chaffee School. The Loomis Institute, as it was originally called, was chartered in 1874 by five Loomis siblings, who had lost all their children and were selflessly determined to found a school as a gift to the children of others.

The roots of the school go back to 1639, when the Loomis family (from which this textbook's coauthor Kim Loomis descended) settled in Windsor, Connecticut. The Loomis Institute was built on the original Loomis homestead. It offered both vocational and college preparatory courses, had no religious or political admission criteria, and admitted both boys and girls; each of these practices represented a major departure from tradition. In the early 20th century, the girls' division was named the Chaffee School. In 1970, the boys' and girls' divisions reunited and the school acquired its present name.

Courtesy of Kimberly Loomis

The original Loomis homestead on the campus of the Loomis Chaffee School.

Teacher Preparation in the Young Nation Period

Around 1810 to 1820, the monitorial system of providing training for teachers, which had been developed in England, was introduced in the United States. Monitors were older and better students, who were taught by experienced teachers and who instructed younger pupils. This system provided low-cost education, helped train children for future jobs, and provided hands-on experience for the monitors, many of whom went on to become teachers themselves.

The first state-funded teacher preparation school was established in Lexington, Massachusetts, in 1839. Before this time, teachers in the primary schools were selected largely on the basis of their knowledge of the subjects they were to teach and their demonstrated morality. Schools devoted to teacher preparation were known as normal schools. These schools focused on teaching methodologies, especially the humanistic and individualistic approaches developed by Johann Pestalozzi (discussed later in this section). These approaches represented a radical departure from the existing method of learning by rote

monitorial system Teacher preparation program wherein future teachers received training by older and better students in the schools they, themselves, attended.

normal schools Schools in the late 19th and early 20th century for the preparation of elementary school teachers.

memorization. Normal schools were based on a belief that teaching was a "science" that could be taught and could be learned, and they emphasized the psychology of child development.

The course of teacher preparation in normal schools lasted from a few months to two years but dealt only with teaching in the primary grades. Preparing teachers for the academically more rigorous secondary schools was left to liberal arts colleges.

During this time, teachers were expected to do literally everything connected with the school, and students were expected to be obedient. Rules for teachers and rules for students thought to have been in effect in 1872 are shown below.

1872 Rules for Teachers

1. Teachers will fill the lamps and clean the chimney every day.
2. Each teacher will bring a bucket of water and a scuttle of coal for the day's session.
3. Make your pens carefully. You may whittle nibs to the individual tastes of the pupils.
4. Men teachers may take one evening each week for courting purposes, or two evenings a week if they go to church regularly.
5. After ten hours in school, the teachers may spend the remaining time reading the Bible or other good books.
6. Women teachers who marry or engage in improper conduct will be dismissed.
7. Every teacher should lay aside from each day's pay a goodly sum of his earnings. He should use his savings during his retirement years so that he will not become a burden on society.
8. Any teacher who smokes, uses liquor in any form, visits pool halls or public halls, or gets shaved in a barber shop will give good reason for people to suspect his worth, intentions, and honesty.
9. The teacher who performs his labor faithfully and without fault for five years will be given an increase of 25 cents per week in his pay, providing the Board of Education approves.

Source: From Kalman, 1947, Early Schools. Crabtree., p. 42–43. (p. 260)

1872 Rules for Students

1. Respect your schoolmaster. Obey him and accept his punishments.
2. Do not call your classmates names or fight with them. Love and help each other.
3. Never make noises or disturb your neighbors as they work.
4. Be silent during classes. Do not talk unless it is absolutely necessary.
5. Do not leave your seat without permission.
6. No more than one student at a time may go to the washroom.
7. At the end of the class, wash your hands and face. Wash your feet if they are bare.
8. Bring firewood into the classroom for the stove whenever the teacher tells you to.
9. Go quietly in and out of the classroom.
10. If the master calls your name after class, straighten the benches and tables. Sweep the room, dust, and leave everything tidy.

Land Grant Colleges

Morrill Act of 1862 Land Grant College Act that gave land to states to develop colleges.

The Morrill Act of 1862, also known as the Land Grant College Act, gave every state a grant of 30,000 acres of public land, to be used for colleges, for every senator and every congressman in its congressional delegation. The states were to sell this land and use the proceeds to establish colleges in engineering, agriculture, and military service. This act resulted in the establishment of more than 70 colleges and universities. The second Morrill Act, signed into law in 1890, expanded the land grant system to southern states to include black institutions. Many liberal arts colleges and universities in the United States still stressed the classical Greek and Latin language and literature curriculum. But the Morrill acts made college education available to people in all social classes, improving the lives of millions of citizens. Although conceived as technical and agricultural schools, many of the original land grant institutions have grown into large public universities, sponsored by increasing state funds.

Influential Educators in the Young Nation

Let us look at some individuals who were particularly influential in education during the 18th century. Several, both in the United States and abroad, made highly significant contributions to educational thought and procedure.

BIOGRAPHY

Johann Pestalozzi During the 18th century, Johann Pestalozzi (1746–1827) first wrote about the importance of children learning through their senses and through concrete situations, stressing that schools should show love and acceptance of children. A Swiss educational reformer, Pestalozzi continued to influence schools well into the 19th century. He advocated sympathetic understanding of students, rather than harsh punishment. He stressed creating learning environments conducive to the maximum development of every child's natural talents, believing that students' natural intellectual powers develop from within. He reacted against the memorization/recitation method of teaching by grouping students into classes so that everyone in the group could receive the same instruction. In his view, the curriculum should include not only reading, writing, and arithmetic, but also music, geography, and nature study to help students develop their mental, moral, and physical talents. He considered preparation for life the primary purpose of education (Binder, 1974).

Pestalozzi emphasized the use of concrete objects, which were to be analyzed according to their form, number, and name. From their experiences with objects, students were led to drawing and tracing, and then to writing.

BIOGRAPHY

Horace Mann (1796–1859) has been called the father of American public education. He was appointed secretary of the nation's first state board of education, created by the Massachusetts legislature, and he toured the state to collect best practices and diffuse this information. Mann was a zealous advocate of free public education, nonsectarian education, teacher training schools, and the abolition of corporal punishment. He strongly supported the normal school for teacher preparation, and, with Henry Barnard, saw the development of many such schools throughout the country.

BIOGRAPHY

Johann Friedrich Herbart (1776–1841) was a German philosopher who advocated a well-organized curriculum and a five-step teaching method as follows:

1. Preparation for new lesson
2. Presentation of new lesson
3. Association of new material with ideas learned earlier
4. Use of examples
5. Assessment

Herbart's ideas came to the United States and were used in the normal schools. His five-step teaching method was a forerunner of today's lesson planning.

Your Thoughts about Education in the Young Nation Period

- How did the inferences you made about 19th-century U.S. education in Building Block 10.3 compare with the descriptions you investigated in this section?
- How did education mirror what was going on in the country?
- What do you think was the primary goal of education during this time?
- Which educational philosophy seemed to predominate?

Education in the Progressive Nation Period

TIMELINE **1900–1950 Progressive Nation Period**

1857	National Education Association (NEA) Founded
1873	First U.S. Kindergarten
1891	Committee of Ten
1893	Committee of Fifteen
1895	Committee on College Entrance Requirements
1900	College Board Formed
1901	Nobel Prizes Began
1903	Wright Brothers First Flight
1905	Einstein's Theory of Relativity
1913	Beginning of Progressive Movement
1914–1918	World War I
1915	Seven Cardinal Principles of Secondary Education
1916	American Federation of Teachers (AFT) Founded
1929	Start of Great Depression
1931	*Star Spangled Banner*
1937	Yellow School Bus
1938	First Child Labor Law
1939–1945	World War II

Color Key:
- General Historic Topics
- Durational Topics
- Education Topics

Schools in the Progressive Nation Period

Consider the events and issues associated with the progressive nation period (1900–1950).

- Think about developments in industry and technology that occurred as a result of war. What knowledge and skills do you think people needed to function and to contribute to society during this period?
- Who was expected to go to school to gain this knowledge and these skills?
- What do you think school was like?

A number of events affected U.S. education during the first half of the 20th century. World War I, the economic boom of the Roaring Twenties, the Great Depression, and World War II all influenced education. During this period, the Model T Ford replaced the horse and carriage. The yellow school bus appeared for the first time in 1937. This now-familiar mode of transportation helped to solve the problem of students who quit school rather than having to travel long distances, and they allowed school systems to consolidate widely scattered schoolhouses into central locations. The first Nobel Prizes were awarded in 1901. The Wright brothers made the first flight in 1903, the same year that baseball's first World Series was played. Einstein proposed his theory of relativity in 1905. The League of Nations was established in 1919, and was replaced by the United Nations in 1945. Babe Ruth hit 60 home runs in a single season in 1927, establishing a record that stood for 34 years. The nation adopted *The Star-Spangled Banner* as its national anthem in 1931. Throughout the period, the United States was establishing itself as an industrial nation, propelled by science and technology and operated by factories.

The increasing number of factories required an increasing amount of manpower to operate them. This need affected both school attendance and curriculum. Many children dropped out of school at an early age so that they could work and contribute to the family income. It has been estimated that, in 1900, at least 18 percent of U.S. children ages 10 to 15 were employed in industry; in the south, 25 percent of cotton-mill employees were below the age of 15, with half of these children below the age of 12 (Yellowitz, n.d.)—education was considered less important than money. Child labor organizations and individuals such as Mary Harris "Mother" Jones (1830–1930) fought for children's rights, saying that children must be freed from the workshops and sent to school. However, despite the fiery efforts of Mother Jones, child labor laws were slow to appear. The first federal law restricting child labor was passed in 1938, as part of the Fair Labor Standards Act, and was amended in 1949. Meanwhile, the Depression brought a tremendous decrease in available jobs, and children found themselves out of work. Consequently, they were put back in school, causing increased class sizes and severely strained facilities.

In the early 1900s, over half the school population was rural. Conditions in early rural schoolhouses were primitive. The typical schoolhouse may have been a log cabin, a wooden building, or a sod house with a crude and leaky door. Windows often were small slits without glass and, in the winter, covered with paper rubbed with lard to make it translucent.

© CORBIS

Children at work in a cotton mill circa 1900. Before child labor and compulsory education laws were established, children often worked instead of attending school.

The one-room schools typically housed 30 to 40 students of all ages and levels, taught by one teacher. As increasing numbers of children attended school, the one-room shacks could no longer handle the demand. This led to the construction of new buildings with numerous classrooms; some even had additional facilities such as lunchrooms and gymnasiums. School officials tried to determine the best way to group the children according to their ages, levels, and needs. The solution was to combine children of approximately the same age in one classroom, a system still in operation today.

Most teachers were women. In 1870, 65 percent of all classroom teachers were women. By 1900, the number of female teachers had grown to 75 percent, and the peak occurred in 1920, when 86 percent of all teachers were women.

Standardization of Education

By the end of the 19th century, schools throughout the United States had widely varying curricula, widely varying student populations, and widely varying community needs. Little consistency existed in the education of students across the country. Many students sought admission to universities, but admission officers had a very difficult time deciding who was eligible.

Two national movements emerged to address problems with education. One, the National Education Association (NEA), focused its attention on curriculum and other educational concerns. The other, the American Federation of Teachers (AFT), focused its attention on labor.

The NEA had been founded in 1857 in Philadelphia as a forum in which educational leaders would meet and discuss common concerns. By the early 20th century, the issues of a standardized school curriculum and college entrance requirements were at the forefront of the NEA's agenda. To address these issues, the NEA sponsored several major committees, described in the sections that follow.

Committee of Ten

In 1891, the Committee of Ten was formed to establish a standard high school curriculum. The committee was chaired by Charles Eliot, president of Harvard University, and included the U.S. commissioner of education, university administrators, and public school personnel. The committee determined that the purpose of high school was to prepare intellectually capable students (usually assumed to be white boys) for higher education. The committee recommended that education in the United States comprise eight years of elementary school and four years of secondary school. (Does this sound familiar?) It recommended that high schools offer both classical and contemporary programs. The classical track included Latin and Greek classical studies; the contemporary program included studies of modern languages and English, and was considered inferior to the college-preparatory track. The subjects of art, music, physical education, and vocational education were ignored. The committee decided that the goal of high school was to prepare all students, regardless of track, to do well in life, contributing to their own well-being and to society's good, and to prepare some students for college. The curriculum tracks established by the committee still exist in many of today's schools and are viewed the same way with regard to academic versus vocational programs.

Committee of Fifteen

The NEA's next task was to look at elementary education. In 1893, the organization convened the Committee of Fifteen, also chaired by Charles Eliot. The committee also proposed reducing elementary school from ten grades to eight, and recommended that the curriculum include grammar, literature, history, and geography, in addition to the "three Rs." The committee recommended that elementary schools teach hygiene, culture, vocal music, and drawing once a week for an hour, and that they teach manual training, sewing and cooking, algebra, and Latin in the seventh and eighth grades. The committee rejected the ideas of reformers who asserted that children's needs and interests should be considered when developing curriculum, and they rejected the idea of including kindergarten in elementary school.

Committee on College Entrance Requirements

The Committee on College Entrance Requirements, chaired by Chicago's superintendent of high schools, was formed in 1895 to standardize college entrance requirements. Prior to this time, the college president had interviewed college applicants to test the candidates' knowledge of classical languages, specific readings, and moral character. The basic high school course requirements the committee recommended consisted of a four-year course of 16 units. A unit was defined as a full year's work in a subject taught four or five periods a week. The Carnegie Foundation for the Advancement of Teaching accepted this same idea, giving rise to the term Carnegie unit. The committee recommended the following standard requirements for admission to college:

Carnegie unit Unit of credit awarded to students for the completion of a full year's work in a subject taught four or five times a week.

- Four units of a foreign language
- Four units of mathematics
- Two units of English
- One unit of history
- One unit of science
- Four units of electives

How do the college entrance requirements of 1895 compare with the college entrance requirements of today?

College Entrance Examinations

The College Entrance Examination Board, now known as the College Board, was formed in 1900, to foster uniformity in college preparation by administering examinations in which candidates could demonstrate their understanding of specific subjects. Thus, both the high school curriculum and the university entrance examinations became uniform across the country. The Scholastic Aptitude Test (SAT) was first administered in 1926 to test college applicants' ability to succeed in college. Based on the principles of Binet's IQ test, the SAT assessed aptitude, whereas earlier college entrance examinations had assessed subject-matter understanding.

Seven Cardinal Principles of Secondary Education

In 1915, the Commission on the Reorganization of Secondary Education issued the seven Cardinal Principles of Secondary Education to be used as the primary guide for education throughout the United States. The seven Cardinal Principles are as follows:

1. Health
2. Command of fundamental principles (reading, writing, and mathematics)
3. Worthy home membership
4. Vocation (knowing oneself to be able to choose from a variety of potential careers)
5. Civic education
6. Worthy use of leisure
7. Ethical character

How do the seven cardinal principles resonate in today's schools? How do they compare with today's goals of education?

Working Conditions of Teachers

Another major issue addressed in the early 20th century was the labor practices and working conditions of teachers, an issue on which the American Federation of Teachers (AFT) focused. Founded in 1916, the AFT sought to improve teaching conditions, increase wages, and provide benefits for teachers.

One of the founders of the AFT was John Dewey. Dewey, the philosopher and progressive educator, stressed that workers and employers should serve one another; he was

In the 1900s, future teachers studied education at institutions of higher education.

concerned that teachers were left out of the decision-making process. The AFT was formed, in part, to remedy that situation, and it continues to uphold the right of teachers to help form school policies.

Literacy

Of the men who were drafted into military service during World War I, some 25 percent were illiterate. Alarmed about the low literacy rate of the nation's young men, the NEA, in conjunction with the American Legion, decided to act to raise public awareness of the importance of education. One of their first actions was the declaration of American Education Week, first observed in 1921. This led to steps to improve how schools teach and handle the curriculum and, ultimately, to increased literacy. American Education Week is celebrated annually to this day during the first full week before Thanksgiving.

Teacher Preparation

In 1900, there were fewer than 50 normal schools in the United States. However, institutions of higher education, such as liberal arts colleges, teachers' colleges, state universities, and private universities, began to offer teacher preparation courses and programs. Teacher education went from being the subject of a single course to departments, schools, and entire colleges within universities. Teaching had arrived as a profession.

Progressivism

In the early 20th century, the United States saw a progressive movement in political and educational thought. During the presidency of Theodore Roosevelt (1901–1909), the nation was determined to industrialize and become a world economic leader. As a result of the emphasis on industrialization, factories throughout the country needed better-educated workers. This led to a restructuring of education.

The early 1900s were a time of reform, when efforts were made to control the corporate trusts and monopolies and to prevent corrupt politicians from running schools. Progressives, mainly from the middle class, were political, social, and educational reformers.

John Dewey was a key player in the progressive movement, especially in education. Considered the father of progressivism in education, Dewey subscribed to the following ideas:

- Education must foster the participation of all of society's members on equal terms and put students in a place of primary importance.
- The purpose of education is to prepare students to be lifelong learners in an ever-changing society.
- The emphasis of education is on the role of the child in a social setting.
- The teacher is the facilitator.
- The student's role is to learn and develop new understandings continually, through his or her own discoveries.
- Schools should encourage collaborative work and the use of new technologies.

Dewey thought that learning is a process that begins at birth, builds unconsciously, and comes from the demands of society (for example, the need to learn a new language). He said that education must begin with insights into the children's capacities, interests, and habits. He believed that students should be given opportunities to solve problems using a scientific method of complete thinking. According to Dewey, the school should be a form of community life and a representation of realistic life. (See Chapter 2 for details about progressive educational philosophy.) How has Dewey's progressivism movement influenced today's thinking about education?

Your Thoughts about Education in the Progressive Nation Period

BUILDING BLOCK
10.7

- How do the inferences you made about education in the progressive nation period in Building Block 10.6 compare with the descriptions you investigated in this section?
- How did education mirror what was going on in the country?
- What do you think was the primary goal of education during this time?
- Which educational philosophy seemed to predominate?

Education in the Postwar Period

TIMELINE 1950–1980 Postwar Period

1944	GI Bill
1945	End of World War II
1949	Beginning of Cold War
1950–1953	Korean War
1957	Sputnik
1958	NASA
1958	National Defense Education Act
1960	Zinjanthropus
1961	Supreme Court: Prayer in School Violates 1st Amendment
1965–1975	Vietnam War
1965	Elementary and Secondary Education Act
1969	Neil Armstrong on Moon
1972	Title IX

Color Key:
- General Historic Topics
- Durational Topics
- Education Topics

© Cengage Learning 2014

Schools in the Postwar Period

Think about U.S. society and schools during the postwar period (1950–1980).

- What was happening in the nation during this time?
- On what major concerns and goals was society focused?
- What knowledge and skills do you think students needed to learn in school to help address these concerns and meet these goals?
- Who was expected to go to school to gain this knowledge and these skills?
- What do you think school was like?

Many events during the postwar period shaped the nature of education in the United States. World War II ended in 1945. The Soviet Union's successful atomic test in 1949 ushered in the Cold War. The Korean War began in 1950, and lasted until 1953. The involvement of U.S. troops in the Vietnam War lasted from 1965 to 1975. In 1957, Russia successfully launched Sputnik, the first artificial satellite. NASA was founded in 1958. In 1962, John Glenn became the first American to orbit the earth, and in 1969, Neil Armstrong became the first man to set foot on the moon. In 1960, Louis Leakey found the skull of *Zinjanthropus* (called *Nutcracker Man* because of its giant molars), suggesting that human evolution began in Africa, not in Asia as previously thought.

The kinds of schools we attend, the curriculum we study while we are there, and the diversity of students' faces we see in the classroom all reflect this period's changes in social and cultural life, politics, law, and technology.

Federal Involvement in Education

The emergence of federal involvement in education may have been one of the most important post–World War II developments in U.S. education.

Servicemen's Readjustment Act

GI Bill A federal act that provides funds to returning war veterans to attend college.

The first major federal aid package for higher education was the Servicemen's Readjustment Act of 1944, better known as the GI Bill. This act provided funds for returning World War II veterans to attend college. The current version of the bill is called the Montgomery GI Bill and provides up to 36 months of education benefits for college, business, technical, correspondence, or vocational courses; apprenticeship or job training; or flight school. It provides assistance for members of all U.S. armed service personnel, including those on active duty and those in the selected reserve.

National Defense Education Act

National Defense Education Act (NDEA) Enacted in 1958, the NDEA provided federal aid for education in the United States at all levels, for public and private schools.

In 1958, President Dwight Eisenhower signed the National Defense Education Act (NDEA) to provide federal aid for education in the United States at all levels, public and private. The launching of Sputnik the year before pointed to urgent needs for advances in U.S. science and mathematics education. The bill was primarily intended to stimulate the advancement of education in science, mathematics, and modern foreign languages, and it specifically prohibited federal direction, supervision, or control over curricular matters, administration, or personnel. Furthermore, the United States was in a Cold War arms race that represented an atomic threat to the country. The education of the nation's youth supported by the NDEA was considered vital to the national security.

Elementary and Secondary Education Act

Elementary and Secondary Education Act (ESEA) Enacted in 1965, the ESEA provided federal guidance and funds to school districts with large numbers of disadvantaged students; reauthorized in 2001 as the No Child Left Behind Act.

In 1964, President Lyndon Johnson declared a nationwide war on poverty and the causes of poverty. In 1965, as part of this war on poverty, President Johnson signed into law the Elementary and Secondary Education Act (ESEA), which provided federal guidance and funds to school districts with large numbers of disadvantaged students. The ESEA helped to establish continuing expectations concerning the federal government's responsibility in supporting education. The act has been reauthorized every five to seven years; the latest reauthorization was passed by Congress in 2001, and is known as the No Child Left Behind Act of 2001. In 2011, frustrated with the inaction of Congress to reauthorize NCLB by the beginning of the school year, the Obama administration announced that states would have the opportunity to be relieved of some of the key provisions of the law. To get this relief, states must demonstrate their willingness to accept educational reform and apply formally for the "waivers." (See Chapter 6.)

ESEA was amended in 1968 with Title VII, the Bilingual Education Act, which provided federal aid to local school districts to help them address the needs of students with limited English ability, stressing language development for students in both English and their native languages. This has been replaced by the English Language Acquisition Act passed by Congress in 2002 under the umbrella of the No Child Left Behind Act of 2001, and stresses that schools should focus on English only (Crawford, 2002).

Higher Education Act

Recognizing the challenges that educationally and economically disadvantaged students face in pursuing higher educational goals, the Higher Education Act was enacted by Congress in 1965 to provide funds for loans, work study, and institutional aid in postsecondary institutions. Approximately 95 percent of the funds goes to student aid in the form of Pell grants for economically disadvantaged students. The act has undergone reauthorization approximately every five years, but Pell grant funding has not grown as rapidly as college costs, so the grants pay far less of today's college costs than originally intended (Baum, 2003).

You can access the federal government's Pell grant website through the direct link on the Education CourseMate website.

Title IX

Title IX of the Elementary and Secondary Education Act was signed into law by President Richard Nixon in 1972. It protected people from discrimination based on sex in education programs and activities that receive funding from federal sources (U.S. Department of Education, 2011e). "No person in the United States shall, on the basis of sex, be excluded from participation in, denied benefits of, or be subjected to discrimination under any education program or activity receiving Federal assistance" (U.S. Department of Labor, n.d.). Commonly thought of in terms of including girls in sports, the act actually applies to all federally funded education programs at all levels.

Curriculum

Education in the 1950s and 1960s was influenced by many theorists and psychologists, many of whom you have investigated elsewhere in this textbook. Education was especially affected by the emphasis on inquiry-oriented, problem-based curriculum and on the development of higher-order thinking skills. Lessons were designed to foster reconciliation of new material with students' prior knowledge; multiple textbooks were used instead of the traditional single textbook; and the use of multimedia became standard in classrooms. Television, which evolved into educational technology, made its way into the nation's classrooms; in the early 1960s, entire high schools would crowd into an auditorium with one small TV set on a stage to watch important world events unfold before them. Inquiry-based curriculum was emphasized through such innovative programs as SCIS (Science Curriculum Improvement Study),

Title VII A federal program that provides financial aid for the education of students with limited English ability (also known as the Bilingual Education Act).

Higher Education Act A federal program that provides grants and loans to students in college (often in the form of Pell grants).

Pell grants A federally sponsored grant system for post-secondary education.

Title IX A federal act providing for equal opportunities regardless of gender.

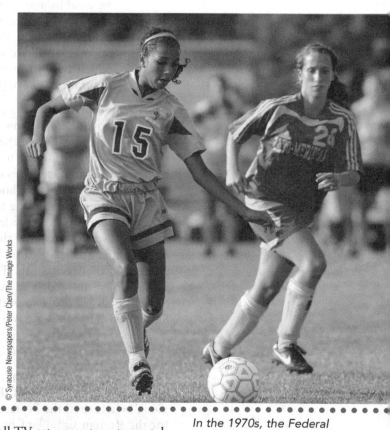

© Syracuse Newspapers/Peter Chen/The Image Works

In the 1970s, the Federal Education Act was amended to allow girls to compete in high school sports.

whole language writing, modern math, BSCS (Biological Science Curriculum Study), issue-centered social studies, and other hands-on, inquiry-based programs.

The *curriculum reform movement,* as it came to be known, gave students subject-matter choices, flexible scheduling, individualized instruction, and non-graded schools. However, college entrance test scores began to drop, school enrollments began to fall, and public confidence in teaching began eroding. By the 1970s, there was a general feeling that the education system had lost sight of its basic purpose. As a result, the nation's focus returned to the pursuit of traditional academic studies in the liberal arts, mathematics, and sciences.

Education and Religion

The question of the influence of religion in education has a long history. The First Amendment of the U.S. Constitution states that "Congress shall make no law respecting an establishment of religion, or prohibiting the free exercise thereof. . . ." This declaration was in response to the religious persecution Americans felt in England from the state-established church and says that the government will not proclaim a national religion. It ensures religious freedom, protecting the church from governmental influence.

"Separation of church and state" is a phrase originated by Thomas Jefferson in his "Wall of Separation" letter to the Danbury Baptist Association of Connecticut written January 1, 1802. Jefferson wrote:

> Believing with you that religion is a matter which lies solely between man and his God, that he owes account to none other for his faith or his worship, that the legitimate powers of government reach actions only and not opinions, I contemplate with sovereign reverence that act of the whole American people which declared that their legislature should make no law respecting an establishment of religion, or prohibiting the free exercise thereof, thus building a wall of separation between Church and State. Adhering to this expression of the supreme will of the nation in behalf of the rights of conscience, I shall see with sincere satisfaction the progress of those sentiments which tend to restore to man all his natural rights, convinced he has no natural right in opposition to his social duties. (From USConstitution.net.)

The interpretation of "separation of church and state" by the public and by the courts has had a major impact on schools. In 1961, the Supreme Court ruled that prayer in schools was a violation of the First Amendment. In a 1963 case, the Superior Court ruled that it is unconstitutional to read the Bible and recite the Lord's Prayer as part of the regular program of exercises in public schools. As a result, public schools discontinued the practice of classroom or school-wide prayer, and many replaced prayer with a moment of silence at some point during the day, during which students may pray silently if they wish. It may be hard to keep students from prayer, however. A popular bumper sticker reads, "As long as there are tests, there will be prayer in schools."

Another challenge came in 2002 when a California father, an atheist, filed a suit that contended that reciting the Pledge of Allegiance with its phrase "Under God" in school was unconstitutional. The case was dismissed on a technicality. The complex and emotionally charged problem of the relationship between religion and education in the United States is still debated today.

Education of Catholics

During the 19th-century industrialization boom, great numbers of people immigrated to the United States. Many of these immigrants were Catholic. Catholics had different religious beliefs than the Protestant majority, and many feared that their children's support for the Roman Catholic Church would diminish if the children attended public schools. This concern led to the establishment of Roman Catholic parochial schools. The Church tried to obtain government money to support its schools but was unsuccessful because such requests went against the principle of the separation of church and state.

There is much debate over the use of federal funds to support religious schools. Have you been in a situation touched by these debates? What are your thoughts about this topic? Why?

Your Thoughts about Education in the Postwar Period

- How do the inferences you made about postwar education in Building Block 10.8 compare with the descriptions you investigated in this section?
- How did education mirror what was going on in the country?
- What do you think was the primary goal of education during this time?
- What educational philosophy seemed to predominate?
- What factors during postwar times have influenced contemporary education? Which do you feel have had positive influences? Which do you feel have had negative influences?

Education in the Modern Period

TIMELINE   1980–2013 Modern Period

1975	Public Law 94–142
1983	*A Nation At Risk*
1986	*A Nation Prepared*
1988	Pan Am Lockerbie Explosion
1988	*A Nation Still At Risk*
1989	*GOALS 2000*
1990–1991	Persian Gulf War
1993	Siege of Waco
1995	Oklahoma City Bombing
1997	IDEA Reauthorization
2001–Present	Invasion of Afghanistan/War on Terror
2003–2010	Iraq War
2004	IDEA Reauthorization
2006	Saddam Hussein Executed
2008	Barack Obama Takes Office
2009	Stimulus Package Law
2011	Osama bin Laden Killed

Color Key:

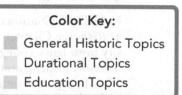
General Historic Topics
Durational Topics
Education Topics

Schools in the Modern Period

Consider the period from 1980 to modern times. Think about what has happened in our country since 1980.

- What were some significant events during this period?
- On what concerns and goals has society focused?
- What knowledge and skills were necessary for people to function, thrive, and contribute to society in the 1980s? The 1990s? Beyond 2000? Beyond 2010?
- To what extent do you think citizens of the United States believe that *everyone* should have this knowledge and these skills?

Let us reflect on some of the events that have occurred since 1980. To an extent, violence has characterized this period. In 1988, a Pan Am Boeing 747 passenger jet exploded from a terrorist bomb over Lockerbie, Scotland, killing all 259 people aboard. The Persian Gulf War began in 1990, and lasted 3½ months. The siege in Waco, Texas, ended in tragedy in 1993. The Oklahoma City bombing occurred in 1995, and the World Trade Center underground bombing occurred in 1993. On September 11, 2001, terrorist-flown planes crashed into the World Trade Center, the Pentagon, and a field in Pennsylvania, killing some 3,000 people, about 2,800 at the World Trade Center. Combat operations began in Afghanistan shortly thereafter to rout the seat of al Qaeda, the terrorist group responsible for the attacks of September 11. The United States invaded Iraq in 2003. Saddam Hussein, president of Iraq, was captured by U.S. forces in 2003 and was executed 2006. In 2011, the mastermind of the attacks on the World Trade Centers, Osama bin Laden, was killed in a raid by U.S. special forces. The first African American president of the United States, Barack Obama, was elected to office in 2008. World population reached seven billion in 2011.

How do you suppose these events have affected whom and what is taught in the nation's schools?

As you may have gathered, education in the United States has become increasingly available to all children. Remnants of midcentury segregation linger, but black activist and other groups are working to foster opportunities for African Americans that are equal to those of whites. However, there has been nationwide sentiment against allowing children of illegal aliens to attend our free public schools.

Elementary education has begun to include public preschools for children four years old or even younger. Middle schools are replacing junior high schools, and secondary schools are phasing out much of the former vocational track in favor of college-preparatory programs (see Chapter 7).

Public Law 94-142 was enacted in 1975, to assure that all handicapped children receive a free and appropriate public education in the least restrictive environment. This law was replaced in 1990 by the Individuals with Disabilities Education Act (IDEA), which was renewed in 1997 and in 2004. In 2006 and 2008, regulations in the part directed toward students age 3 to 21 were modified. The reauthorization of the IDEA has focused national attention and resources on ensuring that all children receive the best possible education. It is not unusual to see two teachers in one classroom, one working with children with special needs, to see a signer translating for a student with a hearing impairment, or to see portable voice recorders in use as students with vision impairments record lectures (see Chapter 5).

Educational Reform during the Modern Period

In 1983, the National Commission on Excellence in Education issued its report, *A Nation at Risk* (see Chapter 2). The commission was composed of 18 members, including university presidents, college professors, teachers, school board members, school administrators, business leaders, and even a Nobel Prize winner in chemistry.

The report essentially endorsed the traditional academic model of the college-preparatory high school, and made five recommendations for attaining excellence in education:

1. "Five new basics" should be added to the curriculum of secondary schools:

    Four years of English

    Three years of mathematics

    Three years of science

    Three years of social studies

    One-half year of computer science

2. More rigorous and measurable standards should be adopted.

3. The school year should be extended to make the time needed to learn the "new basics."

4. The teaching should be improved through enhanced preparation and professionalism.

5. Accountability should be added to education.

As a result of this report, many states strengthened their high school graduation requirements. Do the recommendations of *A Nation at Risk* sound familiar?

Despite intense nationwide reform efforts, another educational summit was held in Washington, D.C., in 1988, to discuss continued concerns over the state of education in the United States. Its findings were summarized in *A Nation Still at Risk: An Education Manifesto*. The summit was attended by William Bennett, then secretary of education; prominent educators from universities and public schools; and prominent business leaders. The manifesto asserted that, whereas our nation did not currently face imminent dangers of economic decline or technological inferiority, the state of our children's education still was far from where it should be.

President George H. W. Bush hosted a governors' summit in 1989; this summit launched a follow-up initiative to strengthen the curriculum of public school education and to increase the accountability of schools. The nation's governors identified six sweeping national goals in GOALS 2000 (see Chapter 6).

Because GOALS 2000 was a federal law, the federal government awarded grants to universities and professional organizations to develop standards in most curriculum areas and developed an Office of Assessment to measure progress toward meeting the goals. Thus, the development of national standards and educational accountability became a major undertaking in the 1990s. Each discipline convened task forces to develop standards. Results included national standards in all subject areas and grade levels. The standards were intended as guides and were intentionally written to provide the flexibility needed to accommodate the needs of individual students and the environments of individual communities (see Chapter 14). Nonetheless, there was concern that national standards could be perceived as a national curriculum, and that such a curriculum would work in opposition to programs designed to meet individual and local needs.

In November 2009, President Barack Obama introduced "Race to the Top" funds to support innovative programs and strategies in education that were designed to increase student achievement as well as school and school system productivity and effectiveness. States competed for a share of the $4.35 billion Race to the Top grants by proposing education reforms that would result in "making substantial gains in student achievement, closing achievement gaps, improving high school graduation rates, and ensuring student preparation for success in college and careers" (U.S. Department of Education, 2009b). Winners of the funds were announced in phases. Initial winners were Delaware, Tennessee, the District of Columbia, Florida, Georgia, Hawaii, Maryland, Massachusetts, New York, North Carolina, Ohio, and Rhode Island.

Improvement of Teaching

The improvement of teaching was another major educational focus of the late 1980s and 1990s. In 1986, the Carnegie Forum on Education and the Economy released the report *A Nation Prepared: Teachers for the Twenty-First Century*. The report called for stronger preparation of teachers in both subject matter and pedagogy and recommended the formation of the National Board for Professional Teaching Standards (NBPTS) and national board certification for exemplary teachers. The NBPTS was formed in 1987, with a primary goal of establishing standards for teaching and certifying exemplary teachers at the national level. NBPTS standards are listed in Chapter 1.

One of the major advances in education in the United States during the modern period is the use of instructional technology. Over the years, many new technologies have been developed and introduced to society. These technologies made their impact on society and, as a result, there were high hopes that they could also contribute to education in various ways.

Perhaps when you think of technology, you think of computers, smartphones, and other handy devices. Consider that at one point in time, silent films were brand new and exciting technology! You may not remember, but chances are you have relatives who remember when teachers loaded a 16-mm film cartridge on a projector to show a movie that elaborated on some concept. It was great because teachers then could add motion, pictures, and sound to their instruction. However, films were expensive, and showing them required the use of expensive, noisy, and undependable projectors. Furthermore, teachers didn't necessarily like darkening their classrooms for an extended period of time either!

The advent of television brought another new technology into consideration for education. Instructional television programming became popular, but teachers were restricted not only to being able to show a program when it was broadcast, but also to the small television screen that made showing it to the whole class difficult. Videocassette tapes enabled recordings of shows so that they could be shown at the teacher's discretion. However, although screens were getting bigger, they were still not large enough to accommodate average-sized classroom populations. Even as videocassette recordings were being shown in classrooms, the technologies of CD-ROMs and digital videodiscs (DVDs) were emerging.

In the 1980s, microcomputers were becoming more available to the general population, and they found their way into the classroom. When teachers use computers to help present information, it is called computer-enhanced instruction (CEI) or computer-assisted instruction (CAI). Students may participate in CEI or CAI without the teacher as well, or they may use computer-based instruction (CBI). There are also computer-based labs (CBLs) and computer-based tests (CBTs).

There were problems though: Software that was suited to teachers' needs was not readily available and was expensive. The machines themselves were expensive, which meant that teachers had to figure out how to manage instruction so that every student had a chance to use one. The computers quickly became outdated and replacements were expensive. And often, school personnel did not have the technological knowledge to solve the problems that always arose.

In the 1990s, the Internet gave teachers access to a multitude of resources for themselves and for their students. Computers became more powerful, portable, and affordable. Students of all ages now come to school with technology skills and access to computers, tablets, and a myriad of portable devices with access to the Internet. Today, school personnel often includes technology specialists, and teachers can be certified and earn degrees in instructional technology.

It won't surprise you to know that, initially, new technologies are met with a lot of "hype." New technologies typically go through a period of early adoption hype before the excitement wears off a bit. Revision and modification of technology have led to the release of a second generation of the technology, and as best practices and methodologies are developed, more and more individuals and institutions adopt the technology and begin to use it productively. Westera (2010) contends that the educational system tends to get in on the hype too late and gets out too early. By nature, the education system is conservative and is slow to accept new technology that does not fit into existing definitions and ideas of effective pedagogy. If the integration of technology doesn't produce positive effects on student achievement, a factor for which teachers are held directly accountable, teachers tend to step away from it.

The development of new technologies has increased at a rapid pace in the past three decades. Today's students have integrated technology into many aspects of their lives, and they expect educators to acknowledge this in their teaching and in their classrooms. The good news is that the Internet has opened up a vast array of resources including video, audio, images, real-time data, simulations, and many others. And the technologies that can access and use these resources are not only more readily available, but more and more people also possess the basic knowledge and skills to use them (and to problem-solve and fix them when things go wrong).

Your job as a teacher is to motivate your students so that they want to learn and stay engaged. Engaged students are less likely to think of ways that they can get into trouble by picking on other students. One way to engage students in your instruction is to use instructional technology effectively.

BUILDING BLOCK 10.11 — Your Thoughts about Education in the Modern Period

- How do the inferences you made about modern education in Building Block 10.10 compare with the descriptions you investigated in this section?
- How does education mirror what is going on in the country?
- What do you think is the primary goal of education during this time?
- Which educational philosophy seems to predominate?

TIMELINE 1740–2013 Education of Minorities

1743	School for Slaves in South Carolina
1794	African Free School in New York City
1824	Office of Indian Affairs
1829	First Antiliteracy Law (Georgia)
1857	Dred Scott Case
1861–1865	Civil War
1863	Emancipation Proclamation
1865	13th Amendment Abolishment of Slavery Ratified
1868	14th Amendment Citizenship to All Except Native Americans Ratified
1870	15th Amendment Elimination of Race for Suffrage
1879	Carlisle Indian Industrial School
1896	Plessy v. Ferguson
1917	Rosenwald Schools Started
1924	Citizenship for Native Americans
1954	Brown v. Board of Education
1965	Affirmative Action Law
1965	Native American Control of Their Schools
1973	Keyes v. Denver School District
1990	Initiative on Educational Excellence for Hispanics
2003	US Supreme Court Endorses Race as a Factor for College Admissions
2004	Minorities Comprise 42 Percent of PK–12 Enrollment
2010	Renewal of Initiative on Educational Excellence for Hispanics
2011	White House Initiative on American Indian and Alaska Native Education
2012	US Supreme Court Considers New Limits on Affirmative Action Programs

© Cengage Learning 2014

Color Key:
- General Historic Topics
- Durational Topics
- Education Topics

The education of minorities has been slow to arrive in the United States. African Americans, Native Americans, Alaska natives, Hispanic Americans, Chinese Americans, Japanese Americans, and other ethnic groups were not afforded educational opportunities equal to those of the white population until the mid-20th century, and some still do not have equal educational opportunities. Recall from Chapter 4 that the term *minority* is really no longer applicable to the populations that have traditionally been referred to as such. Nowadays, these populations no longer number in the "minority," and they may instead be referred to as "nonmainstream" populations. The groups you will read about in this chapter did represent minority populations in the historical context of education in the United States, however.

Education of African Americans

The road to the education of African Americans has been long, arduous, bumpy, and often violent.

From colonial times through the Civil War, African Americans were slaves, considered property, not people. Although there were slaves in the northern and central colonies as well as in the South, the view of African Americans as property was particularly strong in the South, where black people were forced to do work that supported various industries, especially cotton.

In general, slaves were not educated, largely out of fear that slaves who could read would demand freedom. In the mid-1700s, however, religious groups in Virginia, believing that literacy was a prerequisite for baptism, began to teach slaves to read. A school for slaves was opened in South Carolina in 1743, but the legislature, concerned with the consequences of literacy movements, enacted a law prohibiting any person from teaching slaves to read or write. In 1829, Georgia enacted a similar law, and this was followed rapidly by antiliteracy laws in Louisiana, North Carolina, Virginia, and Alabama. In 1834, South Carolina enacted a law prohibiting slaves from being taught to read or write, but Quakers (or the Society of Friends) of North Carolina urged that this law be repealed, saying that "religion should be taught to the colored population to lead to kindness of the masters and faithfulness of the slaves, promote the morality of the white population, and furnish slaves with light and hope" (Lewis, n.d., p. 386).

Financial support for the education of African Americans fluctuated. In 1794, New York City opened the first school in the nation for blacks, and it was free. Named the African Free School, it was supported by the Manumission Society, a philanthropic organization devoted to the abolition of slavery. By 1843, there were seven African Free Schools, and they were eventually incorporated into the public school system (African American Registry, n.d.). After the abolition of slavery in 1865, and as late as 1890, African Americans enjoyed relative equality in educational funding. For example, in Alabama, African American children constituted 44 percent of the school-aged population and received 44 percent of the state's appropriations for education (Anderson, 2003). Nearly equal benefits for black children and white children also occurred in North Carolina, Mississippi, and elsewhere in the south. By 1900, more than 50 percent of southern blacks were literate, compared with 10 percent literacy in 1800, just a century earlier. This rapid rise in literacy,

Prior to significant school desegregation, African American children in the South attended segregated schools, like these students attending Annie Davis School in Tuskegee, Alabama, circa 1902.

coupled with the fear that blacks might take jobs that whites felt belonged to them, precipitated the reversal of equality in the late 19th and early 20th centuries. The black-to-white ratio of per-pupil educational expenditures declined in every southern state between 1890 and 1910. During the first half of the 20th century, the dominant white South used state power to repress the development of black public education. In Alabama in 1930, African American children, who constituted 40 percent of the state's school-aged population, received only 11 percent of the school funds (Anderson, 2003), a major reversal from just 40 years earlier. One after another, southern states enacted legislation to pay teachers on the basis of the certification they held, enabling, for example, the state of Mississippi to pay $55 a month to white teachers but only $25 a month to African American teachers in the early 20th century, partly because black teachers taught only black students. In 1910, Mississippi budgeted only 20 percent of its annual school budget for African Americans, who constituted 60 percent of the school-aged population.

Discriminatory state budgets did not deter southern blacks from educating their children. In 1917, Julius Rosenwald, president of Sears, Roebuck, & Company and a friend of Booker T. Washington, initiated a school-building program to help solve the problem of educational opportunity for African American children. Over the next 15 years, Rosenwald contributed more than $4 million, and the black community raised a matching amount, to build more than 5,000 elementary schools, called *Rosenwald schools,* across the South. By the time the school-building program was discontinued in 1932, 90 percent of elementary school–aged black children attended school, compared with 91 percent of white children of the same age. This was an increase of 54 percent in a single generation— in 1900, only 36 percent of black children and 55 percent of white children attended school. However, unlike the schools for white children, which focused on academics, the Rosenwald schools focused on vocational education.

Southern blacks were largely excluded from secondary education. Between 1904 and 1916, the number of secondary schools in Georgia, for instance, increased from 4 to 122, but these were schools for whites. There were no four-year public secondary schools for blacks, even though African Americans constituted 46 percent of the state's secondary school–aged population. The same situation was true in the other southern states, and held true even at the beginning of World War II, when 77 percent of the high school–aged southern black population was not enrolled in high school.

The challenges of African American education were not limited to the South. Blacks were considered inferior to whites in the northern colonies, and this adversely affected African Americans' education.

The free and equal education of African Americans could not take place until the African American population was, itself, freed from past bondage. Key 19th-century decisions are shown in Table 10.1.

The *Brown v. Board of Education of Topeka* decision, which required desegregation of schools across the United States, was issued in 1954. In this decision, the Supreme Court ruled unanimously that separate schools for whites and blacks were inherently unequal and thus violated the 14th Amendment. In the Court's decision, Chief Justice Earl Warren wrote, "In the field of public education, the doctrine of 'separate but equal' has no place. Separate educational facilities are inherently unequal" (*Brown v. Board of Education,* 1954, p. 5).

Desegregation was difficult. In 1957, President Eisenhower sent the National Guard to Little Rock, Arkansas, to force desegregation of public schools by escorting nine African American children into a white high school. In 1961, President John F. Kennedy sent federal troops to enforce integration at the University of Mississippi after riots occurred. In 1965, affirmative action became law; in 1967, a federal court ordered that governors and state boards of education integrate all schools that year. In 1971, the Supreme Court upheld a measure to bus children to force integration in public schools.

Despite these constitutional advances, much opposition arose to awarding equal rights to African Americans. Notable among the dissenters was the Ku Klux Klan, which was first formed secretly in Tennessee in 1866 to terrorize blacks.

Among the many early civil rights leaders, two names stand out for their contributions to education: W. E. B. DuBois and Booker T. Washington. W. E. B. DuBois was the first African American to receive a Ph.D. from Harvard. Founder of the National Association for the Advancement of Colored People (NAACP), DuBois believed that African Americans needed intellectual training to prepare for leadership positions, and his many books written during the early 20th century helped make great strides in the African American community. Booker T. Washington, born a slave in Virginia in 1856, founded the Tuskegee Normal School for Colored Teachers, which later became the

TABLE 10.1 Key 19th-Century Decisions Affecting the Education of African Americans

Date	Decision
1857	In the *Dred Scott* decision, the U.S. Supreme Court ruled that a slave was *not* a citizen.
1863	President Abraham Lincoln issued the Emancipation Proclamation, freeing all slaves.
1865	The 13th Amendment, abolishing slavery, was ratified.
1868	The 14th Amendment, granting citizenship and civil rights to all persons born or naturalized in the United States, including blacks but *not* Native Americans, was ratified.
1870	The 15th Amendment, eliminating race as a bar to voting, was ratified.
1896	In *Plessy v. Ferguson*, the Supreme Court ruled that "separate but equal facilities" were constitutional under the 14th Amendment. This case dealt with Homer Plessy, who rode in a railroad car designated for whites, breaking Florida law. He was arrested and found guilty by Judge John Ferguson. Plessy argued that the separate car law violated his civil rights, but the Supreme Court upheld Judge Ferguson's decision. The concept of "separate but equal" was to remain the law of the land until 1954, when the Court reversed the decision.

© Cengage Learning 2014

Tuskegee Institute. Washington headed the Tuskegee Institute and taught the newly freed African Americans to be teachers, craftsmen, and businessmen, preparing African Americans for employment with practical skills. DuBois fostered solid academic preparation of African Americans, and Washington fostered their vocational education.

Education of Native Americans

Native Americans were used as slaves during the colonial period in the north. During the 19th century, Native Americans were taught farming, mechanical skills, and domestic chores, and they were taught religion to ensure their salvation and to "civilize" them. Native Americans were not granted citizenship until 1924, almost 60 years after all other residents (including African Americans, Hispanics, Asian Americans, and other immigrants) had been granted that privilege.

The education of Native Americans was controlled from Washington, D.C., by the Office of Indian Education, a branch of the Bureau of Indian Affairs organized in the late 1800s. It was established to "carry out the federal government's commitment to Indian tribes" (Office of Indian Education Programs, n.d.). Under the control of the Bureau of Indian Affairs, Native American children were placed in boarding schools taught by white teachers to acculturate Indian youth into "American" ways of thinking

W. E. B. DuBois

Booker T. Washington

Apache children on arrival at the Carlisle Indian School in Pennsylvania wearing traditional clothing (left), and Apache children at the Carlisle School four months later (right).

and living. For example, the Carlisle Indian Industrial School was opened in Pennsylvania in 1879 by Brigadier General Richard H. Pratt, who wanted to educate Native Americans rather than subjugate them. The school's most celebrated student was Jim Thorpe, an Olympic gold medalist. The school's goal was the assimilation of Native Americans into white culture; it taught the Native American students how to be American citizens and provided education in basic academic subjects and vocational training.

In 1965, Native Americans demanded control of the schools that taught their children, and they created tribal schools where Native American cultures were taught to preserve those cultures and their traditions. These schools were federally funded. Today, schools for Native Americans are locally controlled but are operated by the Office of Indian Education. Besides core subjects, the curriculum often includes instruction in native languages, English as a second language, and tribal history and culture.

In 2011, President Barak Obama created the White House Initiative on American Indian and Alaska Native Education. The purpose of the initiative is to improve educational outcomes for American Indian and Alaska Native students, including opportunities to learn their native languages, cultures, and histories (The White House, 2011).

Education of Hispanic Americans

From the mid-18th century to the early 20th century, Hispanic Americans were discriminated against, along with African Americans, Native Americans, and people from other ethnic groups. Hispanic students were taught religion, but neither the English language nor American or Hispanic cultures. Although they often had freer access to schooling than blacks or Native Americans, they were frequently segregated into the predominantly black urban schools. In 1973, the Supreme Court decided, in the case of *Keyes v. School District No. 1, Denver, Colorado* (Legal Information Institute, n.d.), that Hispanic students have a right to attend desegregated educational facilities and a right to bilingual education to help them become proficient in English.

In 2010, President Barack Obama signed an executive order to renew the Initiative on Educational Excellence for Hispanics, which was originally established in 1990 by President George H. W. Bush. The initiative was governed by a commission that focused on efforts to eliminate inequities and increase opportunities in education for Hispanic students. Over time, the initiative has focused on actively engaging Hispanic students and their families along with organizations and the community toward working on improving the educational experience for Hispanic learners.

Remembering Lawrence Cremin
Burt Saxon

Courtesy of Burt Saxon

Lawrence Cremin came along just when I needed him most—or perhaps I should say his ideas came along just when I needed them most.

The year was 1975, and I had just finished my fifth year of teaching at Lee High School, a desegregated school in New Haven, Connecticut. I was completely exhausted, and somewhat discouraged. Most of my Jewish students were generally doing great, but most of my African American students were not doing nearly as well. I had tried as hard as I could to help all my students acquire the academic skills they needed, but it seemed that most of my African American students lagged far behind.

I needed to regroup for a couple of years. I enrolled in a doctoral program at Teachers College of Columbia University and I took Lawrence Cremin's History of American Education course.

Lawrence Cremin is, without a doubt, one of the greatest historians of American education. He was not only one of the great professors at Teachers College, but he was also the president. He had taken the presidency only on the condition that he would be allowed to continue teaching his History of American Education course.

I was not sure how I would react to Professor Cremin's ideas. Somehow I believed he was a celebrationist, extolling the virtues of public education in America without seeing any flaws. But his lectures presented a different perspective. Cremin believed that, historically, over time, American public education had become more democratic, more tolerant, and more responsive to all minorities. He believed this was similar to the historical trend in America in general, but he also observed that public schools caused this trend as much as they reflected it. He certainly did not see the public schools as flawless, but he did see them as one of the key institutions in our democracy.

Once I asked him this question: "You once mentioned in passing that your own ancestors were poor eastern European Jewish peasants. Now you are president of Teachers College. Is it possible your own personal experiences have led you to overestimate the amount of social mobility in America directly due to public education?"

Professor Cremin said he had never thought about this issue. He noted that historians must be very aware of their own biases and that he would think seriously about this matter.

I needed to do some serious thinking about this matter myself. My own ancestors, like Professor Cremin's, were eastern European Jewish peasants. None of my four grandparents went past the sixth grade. Yet my father, born in America, became a lawyer, and his brother became a doctor. My mother's family was even more remarkable. My grandmother bore 17 children, nine of whom died before their fifth birthday. My mother was the second surviving child born in the United States. Like her sisters, she almost finished college. Her two brothers did finish college. One became an auditor, the other an engineer. The engineer became president of his company a year before he retired. My brother, a surgeon, called me one day to say that Uncle Bud's company was on the Fortune 500 list. We had always thought it was a mom-and-pop operation.

In other words, my own family history provided a stark refutation to the radical thesis that social mobility through education was very unlikely in this country. Larry Cremin's restrained analysis of American educational history started to make more sense to me intellectually.

Professor Cremin's ideas affected me on levels far more important than the intellectual. His ideas helped restore my faith in public education. Faith was what Larry Cremin was really about. For many Americans, faith in the opportunities offered by public education has become a secular religion. I am one of those Americans. I know the public schools in America are not perfect, but they provide more hope than the schools we find in most other parts of the world.

I returned to the New Haven schools in 1977, and I have taught there ever since. My students are now almost all African Americans. My hopes for them are still great, but I realize that it will take a long time to rectify all the unfairness with which their ancestors were treated. We still have more than just vestiges of institutional racism. Some of the historical results of racism are societal, others psychological. But Lawrence Cremin was right: The long-term trend in America is positive. There is still hope, even though it is easy to become discouraged if you choose to spend your life in the urban classroom. To young teachers I would say, "Always choose hope over despair." Hope is what keeps us teachers going every day.

Burt Saxon, Ed.D.
Connecticut Teacher of the Year, 2004–2005
James Hillhouse Hig-h School
New Haven, Connecticut

Despite the federal support, Hispanics have a higher dropout rate than blacks or whites and, of those dropouts, only one in ten goes on to earn a General Educational Development (GED) credential, with is the equivalent of a high school diploma. Two in ten blacks and three in ten whites who have dropped out of high school eventually earn a GED (Fry, 2010). It is interesting to note, though, that there has been a recent increase in the number of Hispanics enrolled in college. In 2010, there was a dramatic increase of 24 percent in Hispanic enrollment. This increase is thought to have been a result not only of the growth of the Hispanic population in the United States (making it the biggest non-mainstream group in the country) but also of their educational strides.

Education of Asian Pacific Americans

The Asian Pacific community is comprised of three general, broad, and distinctive ethnic groups: (1) Pacific Islanders (Hawaiians, Samoans, and Guamanians); (2) Southeast Asians (Vietnamese, Thais, Cambodians, Laotians, Burmese, and Filipinos); and (3) East Asians (Chinese, Japanese, and Koreans) (Huang, 1994). Each group is characterized by its own distinctive and decidedly different customs, philosophies, and cultural and religious backgrounds. The Asian American population makes up approximately 5.5 percent of the 2010 population of the United States (Pang, Han, and Pang, 2011).

In the early 20th century, Asian Pacific Americans suffered discrimination in the United States, both in society and in the schools. Great numbers of Chinese immigrated to the west coast of the United States in the last half of the 18th century to work in the new gold mines and on the transcontinental railroad. But, responding to prejudices and concerns that the Chinese were taking jobs from white Americans, Congress enacted a series of laws in 1882, and lasting until the mid-20th century, that prohibited further Chinese immigration (Tamura, 2003). Soon after, San Francisco built segregated "Oriental schools" that Chinese students were required to attend (Chan, 1991). In the early 20th century, Japanese and Koreans replaced the Chinese as having the greatest immigration to the West Coast. Their children were enrolled in regular schools, but were segregated from other students, often being required to attend all-Asian classes in separate areas of the school buildings. In 1906, the San Francisco school board required Japanese and Korean students to attend the segregated Chinese schools, an order that was rescinded two years later as a result of diplomatic efforts (Tamura, 2003).

Institutionalized discrimination against Asian Pacific Americans continued until the end of World War II, when the federal government granted naturalization rights to resident Asians and relaxed immigration restrictions.

Education is extremely important to Asian Pacific Americans, and parents go to great lengths to ensure that their children attend the best schools (Wang, 2005). And it seems that this minority group has been socioeconomically successful as a result. U.S. Census Bureau data indicate that Asian Americans attain more college degrees, have more advanced educational degrees (professional or Ph.D.), have a higher median family income, and work in more executive, professional, and upper management positions than other populations, including whites (U.S. Census Bureau, 2010a). This success is due in part to immigration policies that favor successful and well-educated Asians, who in turn motivate their children to pursue advanced education and high-status professions. Such statistics support the notion that Asian Americans are the "model minority," working and studying hard to attain the American dream of socioeconomic success. In fact, some believe that the overrepresentation of Asian Americans on the campuses of the elite colleges and universities in the nation make it difficult for students of other races to gain acceptance.

These statistics can be misleading as well. It is important to remember that the term *Asian American* is used to refer to a population that is actually made up of several distinct groups, as you saw earlier. In fact, although there is a group that received college degrees at a rate higher than the U.S. average, there are others categorized as Asian American who fall behind in academic achievement. For example, a significant number of Hmong and Pacific Islanders did not earn college or even high school diplomas. Many Asian Americans do not do well in the challenging programs at which they are stereotypically supposed to excel, and end up having to drop out (Holland, 2008). Thus, the stereotype is not applicable to all Asian Pacific American students, and affirmative action efforts are being undertaken, largely within the Asian Pacific American community, to provide the educational support needed by the lower-achieving groups and to debunk the notion that the Asian Pacific community is a "model minority."

■ SUMMARY

Today's schools are the result of the continuous progression of educational thought from earliest times.

- Schools in the United States began in colonial times with a primary purpose of teaching children religion and literacy. The independence and early development of the nation resulted in the expansion of education to include occupational proficiency and the ability to participate in a democratic society.

- After the Civil War, the subsequent period of reconstruction and industrialization, and World War I, education again shifted its emphasis to teach the skills and dispositions required for an increasingly industrialized country.

- The early twentieth century saw the rise of progressivism, increased numbers of children attending school because of the depression, and the beginnings of modern education facilities, curriculum, and instructional practices.

- World War II and the subsequent Cold War underscored the need for heightened scientific and technological education; in response, the United States developed supportive federally funded educational initiatives. After the launching of Sputnik, education focused on science, mathematics, and technology even more than before. Curriculum and instruction were constructed to make learning as meaningful as possible, but heated discussions continued about the direction education should take—issues that continue to be debated today.

- Over time, the federal government has enacted several pieces of legislature to ensure equal opportunities in education for all, to guide curriculum, and to promote achievement.

- The education of minorities in the United States has been slow moving and sometimes misguided. As populations of minorities have increased, so has the attention to the removal of barriers and the increase of opportunities to education.

■ Key Terms and Concepts

Carnegie unit, 271
Common school, 264
Dame schools, 260
Elementary and Secondary
 Education Act
 (ESEA), 274
GI Bill, 274
Higher Education Act, 275
Hornbook, 259

Latin grammar schools, 259
Massachusetts Act
 of 1647, 259
McGuffey Readers, 264
Monitorial system, 265
Morrill Act of 1862, 266
National Defense Education
 Act (NDEA), 274
New England Primer, 259

Normal schools, 265
Old Deluder Satan Act, 259
Pell grant, 275
Title VII, 275
Title IX, 275
Vernacular schools, 259

■ Construct and Apply

1. How was education in colonial times similar to education today?
2. How was education in the young nation period similar to education today?
3. How was education in the progressive nation period similar to education today?
4. How was education in the postwar period similar to education today?
5. Complete the following table:

	Colonial Period	Young Nation Period	Progressive Nation Period	Postwar Period	Modern Period
Major events					
Who went to school?					
Curriculum					
Reasons for this curriculum					
Methodology					
Purposes of schools					

6. For each period considered in this chapter, answer the following questions:
   a. What factors during that period have influenced contemporary education?
   b. Which do you feel have had positive influences? Why?
   c. Which do you feel have had negative influences? Why?

▇ Deconstructing the Standards

1. Recall the InTASC standard associated with the objectives for this chapter:

   InTASC Standard #9: Professional Learning and Ethical Practice reads,

   "The teacher engages in ongoing professional learning and uses evidence to continually evaluate his/her practice, particularly the effects of his/her choices and actions on others (learners, families, other professionals, and the community), and adapts practice to meet the needs of each learner."
   a. What part(s) of this standard does this chapter address?
   b. How will the concepts in this chapter help you apply this standard as a teacher?

2. Use your favorite search engine to find your state's standards for certification. When you find it, bookmark the site. You will refer to it often as you progress through this book.
   a. How are your conclusions about educational philosophy represented in your state certification standards?
   b. How do the InTASC standards compare to your state's certification standards regarding educational philosophy?
   c. Do you believe the degree of representation concerning educational philosophy is adequate in your state certification standards? Why or why not?

▇ Your Portfolio

1. For your portfolio, write a reflection about how your field experience school mirrors elements of the history of education.
2. If possible, interview someone who attended a school when it was very different from how school is now. Ask what it was like, how the teacher accommodated the different levels of the

students, what nonacademic duties students and the teacher had to perform, and the like. Write up the results of this interview to add to your portfolio.

Education CourseMate Resources

Check out this text's Education CourseMate website (at www.cengagebrain.com) for more information about the history of education in the United States. You will find the TeachSource Videos, a guide for doing field experiences, glossary flash cards, activities, tutorial quizzes, direct links to the websites mentioned in the chapter, and more.

CHAPTER 11

School Governance and Finance

IN CHAPTER 10, you examined some questions about American education, and you investigated how the answers to these questions changed through history. The questions were similar to those you considered when you were formulating your personal philosophy of education. Who should go to school? What should students learn in school? How should they be taught? You now know that the answers to these questions have changed with time.

Here are some more questions: At any point in time, *who* had the answers to the questions you have been investigating? *Who* had the power to determine the answers? *Who* made decisions about the curriculum? *Who* made instructional decisions? On what were these decisions based? And *who* paid for all this?

In this chapter, you will explore how schools are governed, controlled, and financed. How are these topics important to you as a teacher? Knowledge of governance and finance is essential for you to understand how schools work. With this understanding, you can become a participant in school affairs, rather than being someone who focuses exclusively on the classroom and students while others control what happens in the school. To get involved, you must know how the school conducts its business, how it is managed (governed), and how it is financed.

As a result of your explorations in this chapter, you will be able to:

1. Identify stakeholders in education and describe the influence of these stakeholders on the processes and policies of education.
   InTASC Standard #10: Leadership and Collaboration

2. Describe the structure of educational governance at the school, local, state, and federal levels.
   InTASC Standard #10: Leadership and Collaboration

3. Explain how U.S. public schools are financed.
   InTASC Standard #10: Leadership and Collaboration

4. Identify and discuss issues pertaining to the governance, control, and financing of education, including issues of equity instructional technology, and school choice and voucher systems.
   InTASC Standard #10: Leadership and Collaboration

The Stakeholders in U.S. Education

Let us start, as always, by exploring what you already know.

BUILDING BLOCK 11.1

Who Is in Control?

Think about a school you attended and answer these questions:

A. The Classroom
  - Who was in control of the instruction in the *classroom*?
  - To what extent did this person make decisions about what was taught (curriculum) in the classroom?
  - To what extent did this person make decisions about instructional methods in the classroom?
  - Were these decisions left to the sole discretion of the person you identified? If not, who else in the school had input into these decisions?

B. The School
  - Who was in control of the instruction in the *school*?
  - To what extent did this person make decisions about what was taught (curriculum) in the school?
  - To what extent did this person make decisions about instructional methods in the school?
  - Were these decisions left to the sole discretion of the person you identified? If not, who else had input into these decisions?

Maybe you have been in some classrooms where it seemed that the students were in control. In other classrooms, it may have seemed that the teacher had so much control that the students saw the teacher as the "warden." Still other classrooms may have seemed to promote a democratic learning community, with teachers and students both contributing to curricular and instructional decisions.

When the bell rings, the teacher starts the class and teaches. But to whom is the teacher accountable? Who else has an impact on what happens in the classroom? In Building Block 11.1, could you identify a single person in the *classroom* who makes curricular and instructional decisions? Could you identify a single person in the *school* who makes these kinds of decisions? Maybe you initially thought of the teacher as the classroom's decision maker and the principal as the school's decision maker. But, you know many individuals are involved in running a school and that these individuals function at different levels within the school. The principal might be the ultimate person in charge, but there are also assistant principals, lead teachers, and department chairs, all of whom have a stake in decisions that are made at the building (school) level.

You also may have identified outside influences as decision makers in a school. Certainly the standards and mandates of state agencies and organizations affect the curriculum and instruction in a school. Who else has a stake in the decisions that affect school operations? Ah! The students! But do the students really have an impact on decision making?

The people and institutions with an interest in education are called stakeholders. This word often refers to people or agencies outside the school with a particular interest in the school. However, no one can doubt that teachers and students have a real interest in the school. Consequently, *stakeholder* refers to interested parties both inside and outside of the school.

When considering the stakeholders in education, it might be useful to divide them into two groups based on the level at which each group functions:

- Those who are in control of school decisions
- Those who are not in control but who are affected by the decisions

Teachers, principals, and school support staff all strive to positively influence and impact education.

stakeholder A person or institution with an interest in education.

Control and the Stakeholders

BUILDING BLOCK

11.2

Which individuals or categories of individuals are interested in a single school? List as many as you can, and categorize your list under the headings of "*Individuals or Categories of Individuals in Control*" and "*Individuals or Categories of Individuals Who Are Affected.*" (You may want to use a table like the one shown here to help organize your thoughts.) Next, add to your list people or categories of people interested in the entire school system. Again, identify those in a position of control and those who are affected by decisions. Finally, do the same for people or categories of people interested in the statewide school system.

	Individuals or Categories of Individuals in Control	Individuals or Categories of Individuals Who Are Affected
Building Level		
System Level		
State Level		

Whom did you put in the table? Where did you list students, teachers, administrators, parents, workers, bosses, business owners, service providers, professionals, citizens, and politicians? How does the number of stakeholders who are affected by the schools compare with the number of people in control of the schools? From this exercise, you probably have no trouble concluding that we must be both careful and informed about the people to whom we give the power to govern our schools.

Governance

governance How an organization is controlled, including who has the authority to exercise this control.

The governance of an organization refers to how the organization is controlled and who has the authority to exercise this control.

Discussions regarding organizational structures and management usually begin at the top level and then move down. However, that system is opposite from the way this book is organized. As you recall, we started our exploration of the huge topic of U.S. education by thinking about *you* first. After all, who knows more about you than you? Since that first chapter, we have expanded our field of consideration to include the student, then the school, and now, society.

So, instead of taking a top-down approach to discuss organizational structures, we will begin with what you know best. It probably is a safe bet that most of your experience with the management of U.S. education has been in a classroom and in a school building. (Perhaps some of us have had more experience than others with school management and policy in that part of the school building known as the principal's office.)

Building-Level Governance

Recall your previous thoughts about who is in control in any particular school building. Who controls the school? Certainly the principal can be thought of as the school's manager. If you review the principal's job responsibilities in Chapter 7, it is clear that the principal's job involves making decisions about governing the school so that the environment facilitates teaching and learning. In most schools, the principal is the head of the school. He or she is charged with the management of the school affairs; is responsible for compliance with national, state, and local school board policies; is responsible for the budget; and is accountable for student achievement.

In some schools, the principal is seen as the "boss"—sometimes despotic, always reserving the final word. In others, the principal is a leader who asks teachers for input into many school decisions that affect teaching and learning. In either case, the principal is responsible to both the staff and the other stakeholders. And as you found earlier, there are many stakeholders outside the school itself.

Can the principal do this job alone? *Should* the principal do this job alone? Many members of the educational community within the school building can contribute to its governance. Principals may have one or more assistant administrators to help with building-level tasks. Teachers may serve in administrative roles as team leaders and department chairs.

Teachers and principals collaborate in numerous ways. Many schools employ a school-based management system called site-based management. As you saw in Chapter 7, the idea behind site-based management is that those who will be affected by a decision should be involved in making the decision. If teachers have input into the decisions that affect their environment and their teaching, they are more likely to support those decisions. Further, those closest to the students are most capable of making important decisions that will lead to change and improvement. Of course, to have input into decisions, teachers need to understand how schools are run. In almost every state, there are school districts that practice site-based management to some

site-based management A system of management in which plans and decisions involve all employees in a site.

Language arts	Assessment
Reading skills	Authentic assessment
Writing skills	Assessment procedures to accommodate individual student needs
Language mechanics	
Math concepts and skills	Parent/community involvement
Mathematical application and problem solving	Parent/student/staff communication
	Professional development
Science skills	Discipline
Social studies skills	Attendance
Creative problem solving	Graduation rate
Curriculum development	Character development, citizenship
Curriculum alignment with standards	School climate/safe learning environment
Instruction	Lifelong learning
Technology as a learning tool	Money issues
Remediation	

◀ **Figure 11.1**
Some school improvement focus areas.
© Cengage Learning 2014

degree, and in five states (Colorado, Florida, Kentucky, North Carolina, and Texas), site-based management is mandated for every school (Education Commission of the States, 2011).

Teachers and administrators also collaborate through jointly preparing and monitoring the school improvement plan. A school improvement plan is a document that identifies a school's priorities for the coming years, how these priorities will be implemented, and how the results will be assessed. It guides resource allocation, staff development, instructional content and practice, and student assessment. The school improvement plan has a great effect on the school's operation and the teachers' expectations; it requires the collaboration of the teaching staff in its development. School improvement plans are required by state and federal regulations for schools that fail to make adequate yearly progress according to the No Child Left Behind (NCLB) statutes, and are optional for schools that are not in that academic status. However, most, if not all, schools develop school improvement plans every year. Figure 11.1 shows a list of some common school improvement focus areas from which individual schools and school districts have chosen their school improvement priorities. Look this list over: Do any of these areas sound familiar to you?

As you have seen, parents and other members of the community are affected by what happens at a school. But how can they provide input into school decisions? What role do parents and other members of the community play in school governance? Of course, the parents or guardians of an individual student can influence some decisions made about that particular student's education at the school, but parents can have input into the bigger issues related to school governance by becoming involved in organizations such as the parent–teacher association (PTA) or the parent–teacher–student association (PTSA).

PTA and PTSA organizations meet regularly for updates on school activities and operations and discussions regarding governance and finance. During these discussions, parents provide school decision makers with valuable input and feedback. In addition, parents, teachers, students, staff, and administrators can serve on school-based committees that work on fund-raising, planning, budgeting, support for school athletics, curriculum, and community services.

Some schools have school advisory councils. As the name implies, these groups advise schools on issues such as school policy, school improvement, and budgets. An advisory

school improvement plan A plan that identifies a school's priorities for the coming years, methods to implement these priorities, and ways to assess the results.

Parent-Teacher Association (PTA) A local school-based organization comprised of parents, teachers, and other school personnel who work for the improvement of the school.

Parent-Teacher-Student Association (PTSA) A school-based organization comprised of parents, teachers, students, and other school personnel who work for the improvement of the school.

Parent–teacher associations support parent involvement in schools and encourage home–school collaboration. Are there other ways parents can become involved in and influence education in their community, states, and nation?

council typically includes parents, teachers, members of the community such as business and industry leaders, and students.

As you can see, many people participate in school governance at the building level, and there are many ways teachers can (and probably should) get involved. But the administrative head of an individual school has the ultimate decision-making authority in that school; this head is the principal.

System-Level and Local Governance

You have seen that a school's principal has the ultimate responsibility for everything that goes on in the school, ensuring implementation of the school district's policies and regulations. A school district normally includes several schools (see Chapter 6). Typically they have several elementary schools that feed into neighboring middle schools or junior high schools, which in turn feed into centrally located, larger high schools. School districts can be very large enterprises, employing thousands of professionals in many school buildings to educate hundreds of thousands of students. Or they can be small, with fewer than 1,000 students.

BUILDING BLOCK
11.3

Your School District

Using reports issued by your local school district found on the Internet, answer the following questions:

- How many elementary schools does the district have? How many students are enrolled in these elementary schools?
- How many middle schools or junior high schools are there? How many students are enrolled in them?
- How many high schools are there? How many students are enrolled?
- How many professionals are on the staff of this school district?
- How does the number of schools compare with the number of large businesses in the area?
- How would you characterize the governance needs for this school district?

Who has decision-making authority for a school district? Who has influence over these decisions? To whom are school principals accountable?

school board (Board of Education) The official policy-making authority for the school district.

Local school districts are governed by a school board (also known as the Board of Education) and a superintendent of schools. The school board is the official policy-making authority for the school district, with the legal authority to make decisions about the operations of schools within the district and the responsibility to ensure that the schools in the district comply with local, state, and national laws, policies, and regulations. School board members act as officers of the state. Most districts select their school board members in nonpartisan elections by popular vote; however, in some school districts, the mayor or another elected official appoints citizens to the school board. The board has collective authority, and no individual board member has the power to make or change educational policy. All school board meetings (except those dealing with confidential and personal matters such as grievances and terminations) are open to the public. In this way, the people represented by the board members know what is going on in their school district and have the opportunity to express their thoughts.

The **superintendent of schools** is the head of the school district. (In some very large school districts such as New York City and Washington, DC, the superintendent is known as *chancellor*.) The vast majority of superintendents are appointed by the district board of education; in a few cases, however, they are elected by the community. The superintendent's authority as head of the school district is delegated by the school board, and he or she remains accountable to the board. The superintendent is responsible for ensuring that board-approved policies and procedures are carried out in all schools in the district, and for the district's overall operational and financial management. The superintendent of schools is responsible for all aspects of the school district, including programs, buildings, finances, personnel, adherence to state and federal laws, and the like. The superintendent works collaboratively with the school board, school personnel, and the community. Superintendents of schools normally devote most of their time and effort to school management and community matters, leaving issues of curriculum, instruction, and assessment to subordinates. To this end, in larger school districts, superintendents of schools may be noneducators who come from the world of business, politics, law, or the military.

In large school districts, the central office may include one or more assistant superintendents responsible for various aspects of the school district, such as elementary schools, high schools, special programs, personnel, finance, and the like. There may also be curriculum coordinators responsible for the development and implementation of subject-area curriculum, and other professional personnel.

Superintendents of schools are considered the educational leaders of the school district. Many have worked successfully to turn around weak school systems. For example, Michelle Rhee, chancellor, Washington, DC, public school system from 2007 to 2010, accepted the challenge of seeing that low-income urban students catch up with students in the suburbs. During her fiery tenure of three years, student test scores rose, and decades of enrollment decline stopped as she closed ineffective schools and fired inefficient personnel.

Several federal secretaries of education were once superintendents of schools. Arne Duncan (2009–present) was CEO of the Chicago Public Schools, and Rod Paige (2001–2005) was superintendent of the Houston Independent School District.

Remember that we are working our way up from the building-level of our organizational structure. Figure 11.2 shows a visual representation of how this structure looks so far.

State-Level Governance

To whom are superintendents and local school boards accountable? Recall that members of the school board are agents of the state. The U.S. Constitution does not specifically

superintendent of schools The head of the school district.

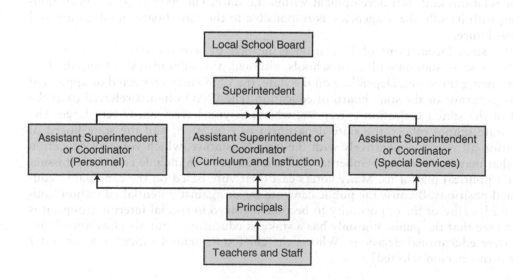

◀ **Figure 11.2**
Typical building- and local-level governance structure.
© Cengage Learning 2014

address education, but the Tenth Amendment gives the states any powers, including education, not constitutionally delegated to the United States:

> Amendment 10—The powers not delegated to the United States by the Constitution, nor prohibited by it to the States, are reserved to the States respectively, or to the people.

Thus, each state's constitution governs how education is to be implemented in that state. At the state level, several agencies and individuals have input regarding educational policy. The educational organizational structure varies from state to state, but we can identify some positions and responsibilities that are common to all states.

State Board of Education

Each state has a state board of education. State boards of education establish state school policies at all grade levels, from pre–K through postsecondary years. Members of state school boards can be appointed or elected; in most states, the members are appointed by the governor and confirmed by the state senate. The state board of education is responsible to the state legislature and the governor. The specific responsibilities of state school boards vary among states, but common functions include:

- Setting the standards for teacher certification.
- Setting the standards for accreditation of teacher preparation programs.
- Developing and establishing statewide curriculum and testing standards.
- Collecting, organizing, analyzing, and reporting school data.
- Making recommendations to the state legislature about the state's educational needs.
- Working with commissions appointed by the legislature on issues such as teacher education, financing, and redistricting.
- Formulating standards for school facilities.

State Department of Education

Department of Education (DOE) The state-level governing body for education policies developed by the state board of education including use of state and federal funds, teacher certification, curriculum, and testing.

Each state also has a Department of Education (DOE). Through the DOE, policies developed by the state board of education are put into practice. The DOE oversees all education in the state, distributes state funds appropriated for education, and monitors the use of federal education funds. The DOE also operationalizes and enforces the standards for teacher certification, teacher preparation program accreditation, and curriculum and testing developed by the state board of education. It is responsible for public relations and staff development within the state. The state Department of Education, with its subsidiary agencies, is responsible to the state board of education and the legislature.

chief state school officer (CSSO) The state superintendent of schools.

The state Department of Education is headed by a chief state school officer (CSSO) or state superintendent of schools, although this administrator's specific title varies among the states. Depending on the state, the CSSO may be elected or appointed by the governor or the state board of education. The CSSO often is referred to as the CEO of the state's education enterprise, which, as you have seen, is very large. The chief state school officer, the state department of education, and the state board of education all work cooperatively with the state legislature, which votes on education bills that may become laws. Gubernatorial candidates often include educational issues in their political platforms. Many voters cast their vote based on the candidates' educational positions. Because the public can vote for or against potential education leaders, and because of the opportunity to become involved in special interest groups, it is easy to see that the public not only has a stake in education—but also has some influence over educational decisions. Who is the chief state school officer in your state? How is this person selected?

CONTROVERSIES in Education

Textbooks and Evolution

In March 2002, hundreds of parents in Cobb County, Georgia, signed a petition protesting the contents of the school system's newly adopted science textbooks. They claimed that the books presented the scientific theory of evolution as fact and did not address other theories such as intelligent design. In response, the Cobb County school board approved a policy that required stickers to be placed on the covers of the textbooks stating, "This textbook contains material on evolution. Evolution is a theory, not a fact, regarding the origin of living things. This material should be approached with an open mind, studied carefully, and critically considered."

Three years later, a U.S. District Court judge heard a lawsuit filed by a group of six parents of students in the Cobb County school system. The suit claimed that the textbook stickers violated the establishment clause of the First Amendment, which states, "Congress shall make no law respecting an establishment of religion, or prohibiting the free exercise thereof." The judge ruled that the stickers violated the United States and Georgia constitutions, and that placing the stickers on the textbooks gave the impression that the Cobb County school board agreed "with the Christian fundamentalists" (Torres & Rankin, 2005). He ordered that the stickers be removed.

The lawsuit brought by the parents was originally filed in May 2002. From the time the suit was filed until the court's decision, several special interest groups spoke up in support of one side or the other. Among these were the National Academy of Sciences, which supported the removal of the stickers (MacDonald, 2002a), and a group of university professors, the Georgia Scientists for Academic Freedom, which encouraged critical examination of evolutionary theory (MacDonald, 2002b).

In a related issue, the Georgia state school superintendent came under fire for removing instances of the word *evolution* from the new state curriculum standards and replacing it with the term *biological changes over time*. The superintendent said that her intent was not to "appease Georgians who have religious conflicts with [the] scientific theory [of evolution]" but to avoid a controversial term (MacDonald, 2004a). The tactic seems to have backfired, however, as the superintendent drew criticism from science teachers, scientists, politicians, and the public in Georgia and many other states as the news story went national. The terms *evolution* and *big bang theory*, which had also been removed, were put back into the proposed state science standards, which were then approved by the state board of education (MacDonald, 2004b).

WHAT DO YOU THINK?

1. *Do you think evolution should be taught in high school?*
2. *Do you think intelligent design should be taught in high school?*
3. *Do you think school curriculum designers should accept at face value the majority opinion of the community members concerning controversial issues?*

Special Interest Groups

The public elects state legislators, but special interest groups lobby to influence the educational policies put forth in bills by the legislature each year. These special interest groups influence bills that cover such diverse topics as textbook adoption, curriculum, teacher tenure and salaries, and school calendars. Groups with a stake in decisions regarding these topics include teacher unions, religious and civil rights groups, parent groups, community groups, businesses, business associations, taxpayer associations, and colleges and universities. When these special interest groups bring pressure to lawmakers concerning their stands about particular topics, the special interest group is said to be lobbying. Lobbyists may or may not be paid for their work by the constituents they represent. Lobbying can represent large amounts of money; the costs involved in lobbying officials in the federal government reached a high of more than $103 million in 2008, but have declined since (Center for Responsive Politics, 2011).

One area greatly influenced by special interest groups is textbook selection. In several states, the state board of education is responsible for textbook adoption. This is a particularly contentious issue in California, Texas, and Florida, the three largest states in which textbook adoption occurs at the state level. Originally implemented so state funds could provide schools and students with free textbooks, the practice of state-level textbook adoption has attracted highly polarized special interest groups—and each one wants its own agenda incorporated into the adoption process. Among the more powerful of

lobbying The process of influencing local, state, or government policy.

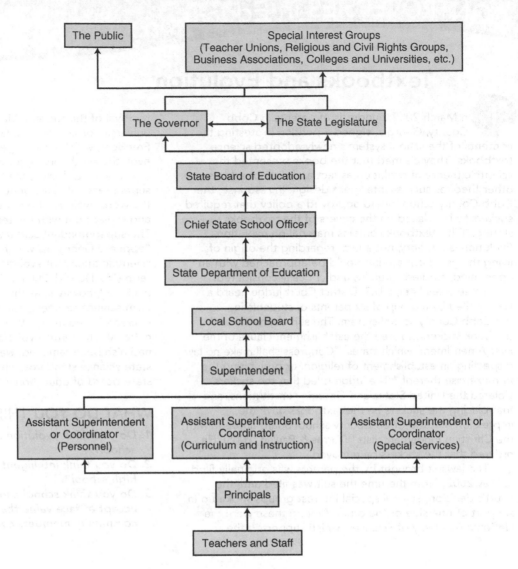

Figure 11.3 ▶
Building-, local-, and state-level governance structure.
© Cengage Learning 2014

these groups are the textbook publishers, who lobby textbook adoption committees in states with large student populations to try to convince them to adopt their textbooks; the publishers are even willing to censor and tailor their textbooks to meet the guidelines of these states to make the huge profits involved in textbook sales. Other special interest groups also can have a great influence on textbook adoption.

The issue of evolution in textbooks is very much alive. In 2011, the Texas Board of Education began hearings on whether alternatives to evolution should be included in the textbooks the state adopts, particularly electronic books (e-books) that would be used alongside the textbooks. But the board voted unanimously to adopt pro-evolution materials in e-books and to reject the inclusion of materials that call Darwin's theory of evolution into question (Clabough, 2011). Many other states continue to wrestle with this sticky issue in education.

Another example of the power of lobbying involves the coverage of plastic bags in high school chemistry textbooks in California. The revision of the textbooks includes a new section titled "The Advantages of Plastic Shopping Bags," to show a positive side of the plastic shopping bags that kill marine animals, leach toxic chemicals, and take an estimated 1,000 years to decompose in landfills (Rust, 2011).

What does our organizational structure look like now? We have extended our consideration from building- to local- to state-level governance (see Figure 11.3).

The Role of the Federal Government in Education

As mentioned earlier, the U.S. Constitution makes no direct provision for education; the Tenth Amendment delegates this responsibility to the states. However, there can be no doubt that the nation has a huge stake in education. Although states assume responsibility for education and local school districts operate the school systems, the federal government is involved in education through research, reports, recommendations, legislation, and, especially, funding. Many of these activities are carried out through the U.S. Department of Education and its subsidiary educational agencies.

The U.S. Department of Education became a cabinet-level federal agency in 1979, during the Carter administration. Previously, it had been called the U.S. Office of Education and was part of the Department of Health, Education, and Welfare. The first Department of Education was established in 1867 for the purpose of collecting information about best practices in teaching and schooling to help the states establish and govern their school systems. The Office of Education gave federal aid to the states for vocational education programs in the early and mid-1900s.

The mission of the U.S. Department of Education is to promote student achievement and preparation for global competition by fostering educational excellence and ensuring equal access. The department engages in four major types of activities:

1. Establishing policies related to federal education funding, administering distribution of funds, and monitoring their use.
2. Collecting data and overseeing research in U.S. schools.
3. Identifying major issues in education and focusing national attention on them.
4. Enforcing federal laws prohibiting discrimination in programs that receive federal funds. (U.S. Department of Education, 2009)

Although the U.S. Department of Education does not make education policy, it offers much assistance and some funding. The primary influence of the federal government in educational affairs comes in the form of conditions attached to funding. States and school districts must agree to federal conditions to qualify for federal funding. For example, to secure Title I federal funding, schools must demonstrate that they have a significant level of students of poverty. If a school chooses not to demonstrate this demographic, it will not receive Title I federal funding, regardless of the poverty level of the community it serves.

Some people believe that the Tenth Amendment should be followed to the letter. These individuals, including politicians and other influential people, believe that the U.S. Department of Education should be dissolved and that the states should have full control of education and the schools. Others maintain that education is so important to the nation that the federal government must be involved.

What do you think about this issue? Perhaps you are most familiar with the federal government's involvement in education through the No Child Left Behind Act. As you know, this legislation has had a huge effect on education in virtually every state. Yet, according to the U.S. Constitution, states are responsible for their own educational policies.

Much discussion and debate has centered on the No Child Left Behind legislation and, especially, the standardized testing program it requires. Many critics claim that the federal government offers insufficient funding to help states implement this federal law. But wait a minute—isn't it true that the federal government does not make educational policy? Yes, that is correct. But the federal government does provide a great deal of money to schools, districts, and states willing to abide by the federal statutes. If schools want to receive federal money, they must follow federal policies. Any state that refuses to abide by federal regulations loses the concomitant federal funding. It is possible for a state to decide that the funding is not worth compliance with the conditions imposed and choose to sacrifice federal funds in exchange for greater state control over education. That is exactly what the state of Utah did. In 2005, Utah's governor signed a measure defying the No Child Left Behind Act, saying it intruded on state education priorities; the bill empowered state education officials to ignore provisions of the federal law that conflict with the state's program. In doing so, the state faced the loss of $76 million in federal funding (*MSNBC News*, 2005). But, as you will see, federal funding accounts for about 9.5 percent of a typical school district's total educational costs Johnson, Zhou, & Nakamoto, 2011). And now, instead of having to defy the No Child Left Behind Act and run the risk of losing federal money, states can request waivers from certain constraining provisions. As of 2012, 19 states had been approved for NCLB waivers, and 36 more states plus the District of Columbia had formally submitted waiver requests (U.S. Department of Education, 2012a).

You have investigated school governance at the levels of the individual school, the school system, the state government, and the federal government. Now it is time to summarize your thoughts.

BUILDING BLOCK 11.4

Control and the Stakeholders . . . Again

Look back at Building Block 11.2. Use your new understandings to revise the chart you made, this time including the federal level. Use a table like the one shown here to help you organize your thoughts.

	Individuals or Categories of Individuals in Control	Individuals or Categories of Individuals Who Are Affected
Building Level		
System Level		
State Level		
Federal level		

- How does this table compare with the table you prepared in Building Block 11.2?
- How can you provide input for educational decisions at each of these levels?

Other Influences on Education and Schools

You have seen the influences stakeholders can exert on school policies and procedures. Let us consider two other factors that greatly affect schools: standardized test scores and teacher unions.

Standardized Tests

States use standardized tests to measure students' achievement to comply with the No Child Left Behind pillar of accountability (see Chapter 1), and standardized testing will continue under the waiver plan of the Obama administration. Student performance on standardized tests is of great concern not only to students and their parents, but also to states and the nation (see Controversy in Education, "Test Scores and Measures of Teacher Excellence," in Chapter 1). Standardized tests have long been part of the educational fabric as a way to measure student progress toward achieving state curriculum objectives. The No Child Left Behind legislation mandates the use of standardized tests to determine student achievement, teacher caliber, and school excellence.

If you can recall how many times you have seen references to No Child Left Behind in the news and have heard the term *accountability* referring to teachers and schools, you can get an idea of how strong the influence of standardized tests has been on education.

Furthermore, because student performance on those standardized tests is used to measure adequate yearly progress (AYP), and because schools and teachers are held accountable for student performance, you can understand the enormous influence that standardized tests have on teaching practices.

How do teachers respond to the pressures of accountability? Does the pressure for students to perform on the standardized tests affect what and how they teach? Certainly one skill teachers want their students to know is how to take a test. Some teachers prepare their students to take standardized tests by providing instruction on how to take tests. The testing atmosphere can be anxiety-ridden, and these anxieties can affect performance on the tests. By learning and applying test-taking strategies, students may feel less anxious and perform better. Teachers also may provide sample test questions for students to complete for practice. However, it is unclear whether preparation in test-taking strategies affects student performance. It is well documented that some teachers resort to cheating so their students will appear to have done well on the tests; perhaps the most widely publicized is the Atlanta, Georgia, Public School system where 178 teachers and principals in 44 schools tampered with the standardized test answer forms by erasing incorrect student answers and replacing them with correct answers (Severson, 2011).

There is much debate about standardized testing. Some people believe that the tests do not test what the curriculum teaches. They feel that, rather than testing the higher-order thinking skills emphasized in the curriculum, standardized tests require students to access memorized facts and concepts. As Kohn (2001) writes, "The intellectual life is being squeezed out of our schools as they are transformed into what are essentially giant test-prep centers" (p. 350). On the other hand, some people contend that standardized tests promote higher-order thinking skills in the context of the content being tested.

As you know, the Obama administration is granting waivers from the burdensome mandates of No Child Left Behind in lieu of the reauthorization of the Elementary and Secondary Education Act. Although standardized tests will still be required, they will not have the supreme power they have under NCLB.

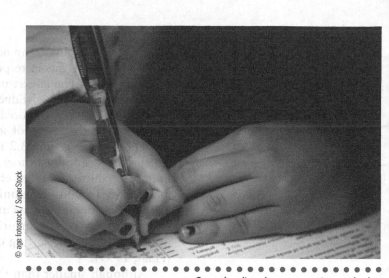

Standardized tests are intended to assess student knowledge acquired in the classroom. Student performance on various standardized tests influences school curriculum and federal school financing.

Use your favorite search engine to find which statewide tests your Department of Education requires and when students take them.

Standardized Testing

BUILDING BLOCK
11.5

What are your thoughts about the standardized testing programs in effect in your state?

- Can these standardized tests provide a valid measure of student achievement? If so, how?
- Can they provide a valid measure of a teacher's effectiveness? If so, how?
- Can they distinguish "good" schools from "poor" schools? If so, how?
- Can their scores enable the public to form valid opinions about the education their children are getting? If so, how?
- Can they accomplish the goal of accountability? If so, how?

From your inquiries, you can see that the people who work with and for schools have a tremendous interest in the *what, why,* and *how* of education. We have identified teachers, administrators, and other school personnel as stakeholders in education. It matters to them what is happening not only in their school buildings, but also in their school districts, their states, and the nation.

Teacher Unions

By definition, a union is "an organization of workers formed for the purpose of advancing its members' interests in respect to wages, benefits, and working conditions" (Merriam-Webster, 2012). The largest unions in the country for teachers and other education personnel are the National Education Association (NEA) and the American Federation of Teachers (AFT). You explored the backgrounds of these organizations in Chapter 10, and you have seen the results of some of their work throughout this textbook.

The NEA, boasting 3.2 million members, includes teachers from preschool to the college level, administrators, and other school personnel. It is the country's largest union for educators. It has chapters in every state and the District of Columbia, and in more than 14,000 communities across the nation (National Education Association, 2011a). National members are influential in federal politics, and state and local lobbyists have been very influential in shaping state and national education policies and practices and in supporting candidates for school board and state education positions (Haar, 1999).

Although smaller than the NEA, the AFT asserts similar positions on educational issues and also is influential in forming educational policy. The AFT has 1.5 million members in more than 3,000 local affiliates nationwide (American Federation of Teachers, n.d.). The AFT is affiliated with the American Federation of Labor–Congress of Industrial Organizations (AFL–CIO), a federation of 56 job-specific unions (AFL-CIO, n.d.).

The NEA is traditionally viewed as a professional organization that deals with general issues of educational policy and procedure, and the AFT is traditionally viewed as a labor union, but both are involved in collective bargaining activities as well as dealing with general education issues. The unions negotiate with school districts on behalf of teachers with respect to salaries, working conditions, transfers, staff development, and most other aspects of teacher benefits and working conditions. In many states, teachers are required to belong to a union; states in which union membership is required are often called "union states." In most union states, the unions can call for teacher strikes if they feel it is necessary to force the negotiation of teacher contract provisions, working conditions, and benefits.[1]

Individual states have their own state education associations; many of these are affiliated with national organizations and have student chapters in colleges and universities. You might have a student education association on your campus. Usually, the dues for joining a student chapter are minimal. There are certain benefits to student membership, such as liability insurance and free subscriptions to the association's educational journals. Not only will joining a student education organization provide you with access to important and current information and benefits, you will also have the opportunity to interact with other educators and individuals studying education.

In many union states, teachers are permitted to strike.

[1]Thirteen states permit teachers to strike: Alaska, California, Colorado, Hawaii, Illinois, Louisiana, Minnesota, Montana, Ohio, Oregon, Pennsylvania, Vermont, and Wisconsin (Alleghany Institute for Public Policy, 2011).

Teacher Unions

BUILDING BLOCK 11.6

This Building Block asks you to find information about teacher unions pertinent to your state:

- Is your state a union or a nonunion state for teachers?
- What is the general opinion regarding teacher unions in your state?
- What would be the advantages and disadvantages of living in a state where most teachers are members of a union?
- What would be the advantages and disadvantages of living in a state where teachers are not union members?
- Is there a student chapter of an NEA or AFT affiliate at your college or university?
- What is it called?
- What are its activities and goals?

Financing Education

You have identified a number of stakeholders in education and have examined how these stakeholders can influence the governance and control of education. You have an idea of the complexity and enormity of the governance of education in the United States. Can you imagine how much money is needed to operate just one school, let alone all the programs associated with it?

Adding It Up

BUILDING BLOCK 11.7

Make a list of everything you can think of in a school that requires money. Include personnel, facilities, equipment, material, and other costs associated with running a school. You might want to consider the school you used in Building Block 11.2, where you investigated who makes decisions.

Try to put a dollar figure on each person's salary and the costs of each support service item. Can you estimate a total annual cost for a school?

It is mind-boggling to try to think of everything that requires money in a single school. You probably identified teacher salaries as an expenditure. What about the cost of equipment, materials, and supplies? Electricity and water? Repairs? Landscaping? What about support personnel—administrators, nurses, cafeteria workers, custodians, bus drivers, and the like? And when you consider that in the 2009–2010 school year, the most recent year for which data is available, more than 49 million students attended almost 99,000 public schools (Chen, 2011), the numbers can be staggering.

The total expenditure for public school elementary and secondary education in the 2008–2009 academic year was $519 billion. Of this, 61.3 percent went to instruction (teacher salaries, textbooks, etc.), 34.6 percent went to support services (administration, media center, school maintenance, nurses, etc.), and 4.1 percent went to noninstructional expenses (food service, bookstores, etc.) (Johnson, Zhou, & Nakamoto, 2011). Figure 11.4 on the next page illustrates this breakdown.

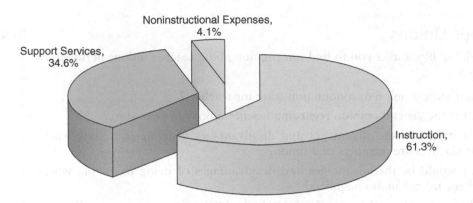

Figure 11.4 ▶
*Expenditures for public
elementary and secondary
schools by function, 2008–2009.*
© Cengage Learning 2014

Where does all this money come from? Revenues for public schools for the 2009–2010 fiscal year equaled $593 billion, with $453 billion coming from state and local governments, and $56.7 billion coming from the federal government. State sources accounted for 46.7 percent of this revenue, local sources accounted for 43.7 percent, and federal sources accounted for 9.6 percent (see Figure 11.5) (Johnson, Zhou, and Nakamoto, 2011).

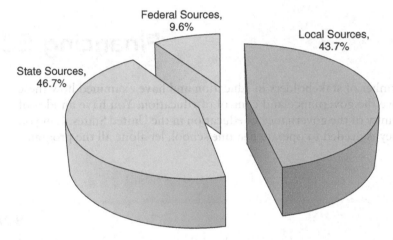

Figure 11.5 ▶
*Sources of revenue for public
elementary and secondary
schools, 2008–2009.*
© Cengage Learning 2014

Local Funding

More than 43 percent of school funding comes from local sources. But what are those local sources? Communities pay property taxes to support schools. In addition, in some areas, a portion of the sales taxes goes for school support.

Property taxes are taxes assessed on personal property, such as boats and cars, and real estate, such as homes, land, and commercial buildings. In any one community, therefore, the amount of money spent on schools depends on the value of the property in that community.

BUILDING BLOCK
11.8

Property Taxes and Equity

Think about the neighborhood where you live and its surrounding areas. Do some areas have huge, luxurious houses? Do other neighborhoods have less extravagant dwellings where middle-class people live? How about lower socioeconomic neighborhoods?

Now imagine that there is a school in the middle of each of those neighborhoods and suppose that the school is supported solely by a neighborhood property tax. What would the school in the luxurious neighborhood be like compared with the school in the lower socioeconomic neighborhood? What might you suggest to make the schools more equal? Would it be fair to tax the property owners in the less affluent neighborhood at a higher rate so its school could be better? Would it be fair to send some of the tax money from the luxurious neighborhood to the needy school?

Draw some inferences regarding the amount of support schools receive and the communities they are in. What are your conclusions regarding property values and school quality?

As you can tell, there can be huge discrepancies in school funding from region to region. Citizens can be taxed only so much. Schools are restricted in the education they can provide by the funds they have. Property taxes are assessed on property values; someone with more valuable property pays more than someone whose property is less valuable. On the other hand, everyone pays the same rate for sales taxes regardless of income, so those with lower incomes actually pay a higher percentage of their income in sales taxes than those with higher incomes. Can you explain why? Consequently, the amount of local funding available for schools is far greater in wealthy areas than it is in lower socioeconomic areas, and school districts vary tremendously in the quality of school buildings, amount of resources (including books), and level of teacher salaries, which include a supplement funded by local property and sales taxes in addition to the state-based salary (see Chapter 9). This disparity in funding is a very serious problem.[2]

State Funding

States provide about half of the funding for their schools. All states have sources of revenue used to finance education. In most states, this revenue comes from sales and income taxes, licensing fees, inheritance taxes, and other state sources. However, not all states have income taxes, and not all states have sales taxes.

BUILDING BLOCK

11.9

Sources of Revenue in Your State

- Does your state have an income tax?
- Does your state have a sales tax? If so, what is its percentage?
- What other sources of revenue does your state use to support schools?

States use several different methods to determine the educational financial aid each district receives. The most common method is based on a district's "average daily membership," which is based largely on attendance. In this system, the amount of financial aid a school district receives from the state depends on the number of students who are enrolled and actually attend school in the district. Thus, large school districts receive more state aid than small districts, but they also have more students to serve. Why do you suppose it is important for teachers to take attendance?

In the 2009–2010 academic year, states spent an average of $10,591 per student on education. Of this amount, an average of $6,436 (61.3 percent) went to instruction, $3,706 (34.6 percent) went to support, and $404 (4.1 percent) went to noninstructional expenditures (Johnson, Zhou, and Nakamoto, 2011). Table 11.1 shows a state-by-state listing of the average annual state-funded per-pupil expenditures for the 2008–2009 school year. As you can see, the per-pupil spending ranged from a low of $7,118 in Idaho to a high of $19,698 in the District of Columbia, a difference of $12,580. How does the average annual per-pupil expenditure for 2008–2009 in your state compare to other states and the national average?

---

[2]Jonathan Kozol's classic book, *Savage Inequalities* (1991), discusses the forces of equity and the extremes of wealth and poverty in the U.S. school system.

TABLE 11.1 State-by-State Full-Time Students and Per-Pupil Education Expenditures for 2009–2010.

State	Number of Full-Time Students	Total	Instruction	Support Services	Food Services	Enterprise Operations*
Total United States	49,003,001	$10,591	$6,456	$3,706	$404	$25
Alabama	739,198	$9,042	$5,273	$3,163	$607	0
Alaska	130,662	$15,353	$8,599	$6,277	$408	$69
Arizona	1,087,817	$7,929	$4,785	$2,738	$363	$43
Arkansas	478,965	$8,854	$5,140	$3,205	$500	$9
California	6,322,528	$9,503	$5,685	$3,441	$354	$23
Colorado	818,443	$8,872	$5,061	$3,375	$298	$48
Connecticut	567,198	$15,353	$9,594	$5,247	$379	$134
Delaware	125,430	$12,109	$7,378	$4,246	$484	0
District of Columbia	66,681	$19,698	$9,087	$9,985	$603	$24
Florida	2,631,020	$8,867	$5,361	$3,115	$391	0
Georgia	1,655,792	$9,649	$6,047	$3,093	$481	$28
Hawaii	179,478	$12,399	$7,714	$4,102	$584	0
Idaho	275,051	$7,118	$4,335	$2,429	$352	2
Illinois	2,026,925	$11,592	$6,815	$4,415	$361	0
Indiana	1,046,147	$9,254	$5,404	$3,460	$391	0
Iowa	470,537	$10,055	$6,159	$3,438	$449	$10
Kansas	471,060	$10,021	$6,162	$3,573	$465	0
Kentucky	651,370	$9,038	$5,353	$3,136	$528	$21
Louisiana	684,873	$10,625	$6,160	$3,891	$574	0
Maine	192,935	$12,183	$7,333	$4,415	$435	0
Maryland	843,861	$13,737	$8,470	$4,716	$361	$190
Massachusetts	958,910	$14,540	$9,461	$4,699	$380	0
Michigan	1,659,921	$10,373	$5,930	$4,103	$340	0
Minnesota	836,048	$11,088	$7,227	$3,387	$446	$28
Mississippi	491,962	$8,064	$4,731	$2,843	$489	$1
Missouri	892,436	$9,891	$5,943	$3,504	$443	0

Montana	140,936	$10,189	$6,122	$3,629	$420	$18
Nebraska	281,544	$10,846	$7,042	$3,066	$438	$300
Nevada	433,371	$8,321	$4,944	$3,105	$272	0
New Hampshire	197,934	$12,583	$8,084	$4,154	$345	0
New Jersey	1,381,420	$17,076	$10,084	$6,450	$380	$162
New Mexico	330,245	$9,648	$5,565	$3,680	$398	$5
New York	2,740,592	$17,746	$12,276	$5,097	$373	0
North Carolina	1,463,967	$8,518	$5,397	$2,660	$462	0
North Dakota	94,728	$9,802	$5,721	$3,260	$525	$296
Ohio	1,779,290	$10,902	$6,210	$4,328	$363	$1
Oklahoma	645,108	$7,878	$4,508	$2,835	$463	$72
Oregon	575,393	$9,611	$5,594	$3,684	$328	$4
Pennsylvania	1,775,029	$12,299	$7,437	$4,382	$427	$53
Rhode Island	145,342	$14,719	$8,812	$5,548	$358	$1
South Carolina	718,113	$9,928	$5,329	$3,400	$473	$26
South Dakota	126,429	$8,543	$4,958	$3,097	$449	$39
Tennessee	971,950	$7,992	$5,016	$2,580	$396	0
Texas	4,752,148	$8,562	$5,138	$2,979	$445	0
Utah	550,298	$6,612	$4,275	$1,959	$345	$33
Vermont	93,625	$15,096	$9,418	$5,258	$411	$8
Virginia	1,235,795	$10,928	$6,631	$3,895	$401	$1
Washington	1,026,023	$9,688	$5,830	$3,423	$316	$118
West Virginia	282,729	$10,821	$6,456	$3,769	$596	0
Wisconsin	867,035	$11,183	$6,846	$3,947	$390	0
Wyoming	86,709	$14,628	$8,602	$5,566	$452	$8

*Receipts from activities that are operated as a business such as school bookstores and certain after-school activities
Source: From the U.S. Department of Education, National Center for Education Statistics.

You can see there are large discrepancies among the amounts states spend on their students. What do you think causes these discrepancies? Remember that the primary sources of state funding for schools are sales taxes and income taxes. Therefore, the money that any particular state can allocate for education depends on the income of its residents and on the purchases made by residents, visitors, and tourists.

Some states supplement their educational funds with lotteries and other forms of gambling. Usually these revenues are intended to enhance specific educational programs, facilities, and operations. A typical example is the Florida lottery, which supports scholarships, school improvement programs, and new construction.

Federal Funding

The federal government contributes an average of 9.6 percent of school funding. There is great variance among the states, with the New England states receiving the lowest percentage and the southeastern states receiving the highest percentage (Owings & Kaplan, 2006). Funds are provided in three main ways: categorical grants, formula funding, and competitive grants. Federal funding is overseen by the U.S. Department of Education. Remember that the federal government cannot control the education programs or policies of states. But, it can (and does) develop needed programs that schools can implement if they choose. These programs are accompanied by funding. Only if the schools implement the federal programs will they receive the accompanying federal funding.

Categorical Grants

categorical grants Funding from the federal government to provide for elementary and secondary programs approved through federal legislation.

Categorical grants (sometimes called *block grants*) are provided by the federal government to help fund specific elementary and secondary programs approved through federal legislation. Programs provide financial aid for eligible schools for elementary, secondary, and college education; for the education of individuals with disabilities and those who are illiterate, disadvantaged, or gifted; and for the education of immigrants, American Indians, and people with limited English proficiency. Specific examples include the funding of arts education, bilingual education, Head Start programs, school breakfast and lunch programs, and the National Writing Project. Many of these programs have been discussed elsewhere in this textbook.

Formula Funding

formula funding Funding that is provided on the basis of the application of a formula that uses specific data to determine need.

Formula funding refers to grants the federal government provides to schools that show need; this need often is based on the number of free and reduced-price lunches they provide to their students. Examples include Title I funding, which is directed toward raising student achievement, Title II Part A funds that go toward improving teacher quality, and Title III funds that target language acquisition.

Competitive Grants

competitive grants grants awarded through a competitive process involving an evaluative review of proposals.

Competitive grants are provided by the federal government for specific projects and programs. States, school districts, and individual schools may submit proposals that compete with other proposals for funding for specific federal programs. The most prominent of these are the Race to the Top grants.

Another example of competitive grants, albeit less dramatic, is the National Science Foundation, which funds programs designed to improve student achievement in mathematics and science through innovative curriculum and teaching methodologies. Recipients must meet certain stipulations to receive some federal funds, and the funds are subject to restrictions.

Private Funding

Schools often obtain supplemental funds through fund-raising efforts, private grants, and commercial advertising. Fund-raising efforts raise money for specific needs, classes, or projects in individual schools. They may be sponsored by the PTA, school-based clubs, or students; examples include raising money for band uniforms, cheerleading camp, a new science center, an outdoor classroom, or any number of special projects a school could not otherwise afford. You have probably been involved in some school fund-raising efforts, on either the buying or the selling side. We have all had children (maybe even your own children) come to our doors selling magazine subscriptions, candy, or fruits to raise money for a school trip, new uniforms, or some other school project. School athletic clubs often solicit funds through booster clubs to help defray the expenses incurred by athletics programs.

Money from individual benefactors, private corporations, and foundations is available through the competitive grant application process. Grant awards range from small to very large. States, school districts, schools, and classroom teachers can apply for grants targeted toward specific programs. For example, grants from AOL/Time Warner fund programs that enhance teaching and learning with technology, and grants from the Intel Corporation fund programs that emphasize science, mathematics, and technology, especially those for women and the underserved populations. Toyota Tapestry grants are available for K–12 science teachers. Often, such grants are awarded preferentially to schools with populations that are underserved.

Many small and large grants are available from private foundations, commercial organizations, and educational organizations, such as the PTAs, PTSAs, colleges and universities, and professional associations. Teachers can (and should) apply for these grants to fund special projects in their classrooms. Large companies often provide support for education in other ways. For example, an office supply store may post a local school's supply list or a bookstore may stock books that are on the local school district's summer reading lists.

Some school systems have raised funds by allowing advertising on their property. You may have seen advertisements for local businesses on signs, scoreboards, and programs at athletic events. These ads can run from local business advertisements on school buses to ads that wrap around lockers and pyramid cards on lunch tables. For example:

- In Minnesota, wraparound ads on lockers earn $230,000 a year for each of the five schools in one district.

- In California, ads in the 15 high schools in one district are expected to bring in up to $1 million a year.

- In Colorado, ads on the sides of school buses in one district will generate $500,000 over four years. (Macedo, 2010)

Commercialism in the schools is a lucrative financial resource and allows schools to keep programs they would otherwise have to cut. But some find the practice problematic, believing that education should not be "tainted" with advertising. Critics claim

▶ ❚❚ TeachSource Video

View the TeachSource Video titled, "High Schools in Low-Income Communities Receive a Failing Grade" (Part 1). Nationwide, many schools are cutting educational funds. Schools face painful choices when their funding shrinks. They are increasing class sizes, reducing curricular offerings, and cutting teachers, all while under government pressure to increase students' performance. No Child Left Behind (NCLB) has been chronically short of the money it needs. Schools in Arlington, Massachusetts, had a $4 million budget cut and let go of 97 people including teachers, school counselors, and reading specialists. Private funding is being used to rescue local public schools. After watching the video, answer the following questions:

1. What will *not* be taught as a result of letting teachers go?

2. What will a reduced teaching force do for the education of our children?

Students and parents often initiate fund-raising efforts to supplement government funding for education. Why do schools need to pursue financing outside of municipal, state, and federal funds?

that children are being forced to view advertising in and around their schools without parental consent and are concerned that some advertisements may market unhealthy foods or use children as subjects of market research. Others believe that students are bombarded by commercialism anyway, so viewing advertising in school is not much different from the norm. Especially contentious is the cell phone industry that will pay schools handsomely for installing cell towers on school property. For example, in 2010, cell phone companies paid Hillsborough County, Florida Public Schools over $250,000 to lease school property for cell phone towers and antennas (Center for Safer Wireless, n.d.). However, parents are very concerned about the potential effect the electromagnetic radiation concentrated through the towers may have on the health of their children.

BUILDING BLOCK
11.11

Commercialism in the School

Look carefully at the school at which you are doing your field experience. Look at the hallways, the locker areas, the gymnasium, the lunchroom, the outdoor grounds, the buses, a few classrooms, and nonclassroom areas that are frequented by students.

What commercial advertising or suggestions do you find? Be specific as in the following chart:

Location	Type of Advertising or Suggestions	Product or Company Name	Product or Company Name	Product or Company Name
Hall _____				
Hall _____				
Locker area				
Gym				
Lunchroom				
Outdoors				
Buses				
Classroom _____				
Classroom _____				

Other				

- Is the advertising you found appropriate for the age of children who attend that school?
- Is the funding gained worth exposing the students to the advertising?
- Is school an inappropriate place for marketers to promote their products to students?
- How do you feel about commercialism in schools?

Some school systems have raised funds by allowing advertising on their property.

Issues in School Governance and Finance

As you have investigated school governance and finance, you have seen there are several issues about which educators and others involved in education have differing opinions. The degree to which the federal government should be involved in controlling and financing education, the degree to which state governments are involved, the activities of teacher unions, and the financing of education by private organizations are all controversial issues and frequent topics of debate. A few other issues warrant a closer examination.

Technology and the Digital Divide

You have seen the importance of technology in today's society and the importance of using technology in instruction. You have seen what the technology expectations are for teachers and students, and you have looked at the standards that detail these expectations (see Chapter 9).

Given the funding disparities among school systems, it should be no surprise that disparities exist with regard to instructional materials, including technology. The disparity in student access to technology, especially to computers and the Internet, is called the digital divide.

The most recent government study on computer and Internet use in the United States is tied to the 2000 census. The report, *A Nation Online: How Americans are Expanding Their Use of the Internet* (U.S. Department of Commerce, 2002), shows that the use of the Internet and other information technologies was growing rapidly across all geographic regions and all demographic groups. The implied message of this report is that the digital divide was no longer a major concern at that time (2002), and that would remain the case if the trends were to continue for the next ten years to 2012, when the next study was published.

Providing computers with Internet access in our public schools has progressed well. In the fall of 2008, 100 percent of public schools had instructional computers with Internet access (Gray & Lewis, 2009). This applies to all schools, regardless of size, location, socio-economic status, or percent of minority enrollment (National Center for Education Statistics, 2011a). The number of students per computer is a better indicator of how technology is being used in schools. In 1998, the overall ratio of students per instructional computer with Internet access was 12.1 students per computer; this decreased to an average of 6.6 students per computer in 2000 and 3.1 students per computer in 2008 (National Center for Education Statistics, 2011a). However, this ratio was higher in schools with the highest poverty concentrations than in schools with the lowest poverty concentrations; it was also higher in schools with the greatest minority enrollment than in schools with the lowest minority enrollment.

The fact that some students have access to modern technology while others do not is an equity issue. Many students do not have access at home to fast Internet technologies—or the Internet at all—and teachers must guard against assuming that all students can do technology-based projects easily. Knowing what you know about effective teaching, remember that the presence of technology alone does not ensure learning. Teachers must know how to integrate technology effectively into their instruction.

All students should have access to teachers who know how to use technology to teach effectively. This statement has direct implications for you as you progress through your teacher education program. It is not sufficient that you simply know how to turn on the computer, run some software, and surf the Internet. You must know how and when it is appropriate to utilize technology to enhance your instruction.

More and more students are using smartphones to access information on the Internet. Using a cellular phone to access the Internet is less expensive than having a computer with a modem. How does this factor affect the digital divide?

Today, there seems to be a new kind of digital divide—different from the one that defines *digital divide* in terms of access to and use of technologies. The digital divide today is really about digital literacy (Watkins, 2011). The digital divide today is generational, geographic, and ethnic in nature. For example:

- Blacks and Hispanics are using cellular phones to gain access to the Internet (in addition to many other uses), thereby cutting back on their Internet options (Washington, 2011). One reason may be that smartphones cost less than computers and Wi-Fi (James, 2011).

- Hispanics in California are on the downside of the digital divide—35 percent of adults do not use the Internet at all, and only 50 percent of those who do use the Internet have broadband access at home (James, 2011).

- Lower-income Americans and Americans in rural areas have slower Internet connections than people in more affluent communities. Slower connections make it difficult to download web pages, photos, and videos (Kang, 2011).

People on the downside of the divide may have the technology but do not know how to use it fluently. Current efforts are being directed toward helping people acquire digital literacy. For example, Minneapolis, Minnesota, has implemented a program called

Online Education for K–12 Teachers

Jacqueline Cahil

Online K–12 teaching is rapidly growing, because it offers students educational options that they could not otherwise attain due to (1) geographic location, (2) health issues, (3) courses not being offered at the brick-and-mortar school, (4) courses being full at the brick-and-mortar school, (5) scheduling conflicts, or (6) desire to attend a different school. Some students will be learning online for the first time, and others have been doing it for years: Teachers must have all of the information accessible for both types of learners. Effective online education requires savvy teachers. One pertinent online teaching strategy is implementing a student orientation that includes information on (1) how to be a successful learner, (2) discipline and motivation, (3) community building, (4) basic computer skills, (5) technology tools, (6) time management, (7) differences between online and brick-and-mortar courses, (8) expectations, (9) how to access technology assistance, (10) frequently asked questions, (11) skills and discipline readiness for online learning, and (12) lists of supplementary resources. Best practices include requiring an interactive student orientation and housing it as a resource for anyone to refer to throughout the year.

Time management lessons need to be taught, so students know how to (1) budget time, (2) set goals, (3) decipher priorities, (4) create weekly schedules, and (5) create daily schedules. An asynchronous interactive online tutorial that can be accessed and referred to throughout the school year is ideal. This way, the basic information is taught and students have templates to create and manage their information. Instructors can also access it to problem-solve time management issues.

A second important strategy is to have consistent expectations. Teachers can be expected to provide (1) a timeline for returning all forms of communication; (2) detailed, prompt, individualized feedback on written assignments; (3) a grading timeline; (4) assignments with clear instructions; (5) respect for diverse talents and ways of learning; (6) an effective syllabus; (7) teaching with active learning techniques; (8) proactiveness regarding behavior concerns, lack of participation, or grades; and (9) due dates with late penalties.

Students can be expected to follow (1) netiquette rules, (2) due dates with late penalties, (3) requirements for being online and checking communication tools, and (4) requirements for proactiveness regarding concerns. Clear and concise written expectations can prevent students and teachers from shutting down.

Teaching communication and collaboration while avoiding isolation are also important with online education. This can be accomplished by including (1) regular, interactive assignments; (2) a chatting area; (3) a question and answer section, and (4) community-building activities. Free online collaborative tools, such as applications within the suite of tools Google Apps for Education Edition, are options to utilize. A chatting area is where students can socialize with one another as they would in the hallway with a teacher standing nearby. The question and answer section is where anyone can post questions and answers; the teacher will need to oversee this section to make sure that all questions are answered correctly. Community-building activities need to occur frequently in the beginning of the school year and continue intermittently throughout, to create and maintain a warm and inviting community. It is also pertinent that instructors participate in the community-building activities, because this is one of the main ways students get to know and build a relationship with teachers. Crucial steps to effectively teaching an online course include implementing a comprehensive student orientation, providing interactive time management templates, establishing and following consistent instructor and student expectations, and creating a course that includes frequent communication and collaboration.

Jacqueline L. Cahill, PhD
Kappa Delta Pi Teacher of Honor Award 2010
Formerly K–12 Online Learning Specialist, Douglas County School District, Castle Rock, Colorado
Currently teaching online curriculum at Colorado State University Global Campus

"Digital Divide Initiative" (DDI) whose mission is to put computers with appropriate software in people's homes and to provide technological skills and knowledge to these people to help them succeed in an increasingly digitized world (Sherman, 2011).

Programs to help young people acquire digital literacy above what they can learn in school include after-school programs, summer camps, and summer workshops (Watkins, 2011). A major concern today is the number of people whose access to the Internet is slow—too slow to make good use of its capabilities. Consequently entire, the Obama administration has announced that federal funds will be used to connect the entire nation to the Internet (Kang, 2011).

School Choice and Voucher Systems

If some schools are getting more money than others, attracting the best teachers, and providing the best facilities and equipment, it would seem that a student from an underfunded, underachieving school would do well to transfer to the wealthier school. Of course, most students go to a school within their district. However, many parents choose to send their children to different schools for various reasons. This freedom to choose a school is called school choice.

School choice the freedom to choose which school children will attend.

According to Cookson (1994), there are six types of school choice:

1. *Intradistrict choice*: Parents choose to send their children to another school within their district.
2. *Interdistrict choice*: Parents choose to send their children to a school in another school district.
3. *Controlled choice*: Parents may choose another school, but their choice is restricted so as to maintain ethnic, gender, or socioeconomic status balance.
4. *Magnet schools*: Parents may choose to send their children to a magnet school to focus their studies. Recall from Chapter 6 that magnet schools focus on certain areas of the curriculum, such as mathematics, science, or the arts.
5. *Charter schools*: Although still responsible for documenting student achievement, charter schools are free to implement innovations with reduced government control. Recall from Chapter 6 that charter schools function more independently than other schools.
6. *Voucher plans*: Parents may choose to send their children to private schools (including those with religious affiliations) with funds for tuition made available by federal and state governments.

Of these six types, entire voucher plans have been the most controversial. Perhaps the biggest controversy surrounds the issue of the separation of church and state. Some contend that the federal government should not supply funds for students to attend private schools with religious affiliations. Thirty-seven states have constitutions that contain clauses or amendments that prohibit the government from providing aid to any organization with a religious affiliation. Nonetheless, many states have passed legislation to create or expand school voucher programs funded through voucher program tax credits and scholarships. As of the 2011–2012 school year, 18 states and the District of Columbia have approved school choice options, including the option of attending private schools funded by the state (Herbert, 2011). And a similar proposal is being put forward in Michigan (Cavanagh, 2011a).

Schools with more financial support may be able to provide better technology for their teachers and students. How might this affect school choice?

Some studies have shown that school choice results in increased academic achievement, higher graduation rates, greater parental satisfaction, and increased student safety (Burke & Sheffield, 2011). Proponents of school choice believe that the competition such choice creates among schools will force schools to become more effective. If schools want to keep their students, and therefore their federal funding, they must step up their efforts and improve their performance. Opponents say that the school choice program drains money from the public schools and has questionable results. They maintain that draining funds from schools manifests itself in failure, and that allowing any school to fail hurts the educational system as a whole. If a school loses students and money, it cannot be expected to improve.

What are your thoughts about the advantages and disadvantages of the school choice and school voucher programs?

■ SUMMARY

In this chapter, you have investigated systems of school governance and finance. As you have seen, governing and financing U.S. education are part of a very complex process.

- The stakeholders in a school are all the people with an interest in the school. In addition to the teachers and administrators, this includes parents, businesses, the community, and, yes, even the students. Stakeholders exert powerful influences over what goes on in a school.

- Governance in schools includes the local PTA and advisory boards, the school administration, the district superintendent and school board, the state chief education officer and the state board of education, and the federal Department of Education. According to the U.S. Constitution, education decisions are the purview of the states.

- School finance comes from states (46.7 percent), local sources (43.7 percent), and federal sources (9.6 percent). Additional funding is secured through grants, private funding, commercialism, and other means.

- The digital divide seems to be more a matter of technological literacy than equipment ownership.

- School choice is available to parents and often is funded by federal and state governments—even religion-based schools.

School governance and finance will always be an important and controversial issue in education. Remember that society is the ultimate stakeholder in education. Members of society fund education and elect those who hold power over education. Because of this, it is understandable that issues of current concern to society will make their way into schools, even though these issues might not relate directly to mathematics, science, the language arts, and social sciences. Because schools serve and are supported by society, however, they must respond.

■ Key Terms and Concepts

Categorical grants, 310
Chief state school officer (CSSO), 298
Competitive grants, 310
Department of Education (DOE), 298
Digital divide, 314
Formula funding, 310

Governance, 294
Lobbying, 299
Parent-Teacher Association (PTA), 295
Parent-Teacher-Student Association (PTSA), 295
School board (Board of Education), 296

School choice, 316
School improvement plan, 295
Site-based management, 294
Stakeholder, 293
Superintendent of schools, 297

■ Construct and Apply

1. Draw a table showing the governance structure in (a) a single school with which you are familiar, and (b) a school district with which you are familiar. For each entity, list the internal and external stakeholders who might influence decision making.
2. By law, standardized tests are here to stay. Do you believe standardized test scores can adequately assess the effectiveness of teachers for purposes of accountability? If not, what other information should be used? How should it be used?
3. Describe how education is funded by local, state, and federal funds.
4. Make a list of alternative sources of revenue for schools. Think outside the box and see how creative you can be.

■ Deconstructing the Standards

1. Recall the InTASC standard associated with the objectives for this chapter.
   InTASC Standard #10: Leadership and Collaboration reads, "The teacher seeks appropriate leadership roles and opportunities to take responsibility for student learning, to collaborate

with learners, families, colleagues, other school professionals, and community members to ensure learner growth, and to advance the profession."

  a. What part(s) of this standard does this chapter address?

  b. How will the concepts in this chapter help you apply this standard as a teacher?

2. Use your favorite search engine to find your state's standards for certification. When you find it, bookmark the site. You will refer to it often as you progress through this book.

  a. How are your conclusions about educational philosophy represented in your state certification standards?

  b. How do the InTASC standards compare to your state's certification standards regarding educational philosophy?

  c. Do you believe the degree of representation concerning educational philosophy is adequate in your state certification standards? Why or why not?

Your Portfolio

1. Prepare a diagram or flow chart showing the system of governance in your field experience school, district, and state. Include names for the positions you identify.

2. Obtain details, pictures, or other information about the unique ways your field experience school or classes in the school raise money; be sure to describe what the money will support.

3. Add a copy of your field experience school's school improvement plan to your portfolio.

Education CourseMate Resources

Check out this text's Education CourseMate website (at www.cengagebrain.com) for more information about the governing and financing of education in the United States. You will find the TeachSource Videos, a guide for doing field experiences, glossary flash cards, activities, tutorial quizzes, direct links to the websites mentioned in the chapter, and more.

CHAPTER 12

Social Issues and the School's Response

A PRIMARY PURPOSE of schools is to provide students with the knowledge and skills they need not only to function in the world, but also to become contributing members of society. In some cases, students may even be inspired to promote social change. In your investigations into the history of U.S. education, you explored what was happening in society during specific time periods. You extended the influences of these events to determine who went to school, what they learned, and how they were taught. As you have discovered, society has a strong and profound influence on schools and education. How can events happening outside the school building influence what goes on inside the school building? In this chapter, you will explore some significant current social issues and how the school responds to these issues. You will investigate the relationships among society, the school, and the community, and you will explore society's influence on you and your classroom.

As a result of your explorations in this chapter, you will be able to

1. Describe the nature of social issues.
   InTASC Standard #9: Professional Learning and Ethical Practices

2. Identify current social issues that may affect the emotional health of students and consider how schools may respond to these issues in an effort to prevent or address the consequences that the social issues may cause.
   InTASC Standard #1: Learner Development; Standard #2: Learning Differences; and Standard #9: Professional Learning and Ethical Practice

3. Identify current social issues that may affect the physical health of students and consider how schools may respond to these issues in an effort to prevent or address the consequences that the social issues may cause.
   InTASC Standard #1: Learner Development; Standard #2: Learning Differences; and Standard #9: Professional Learning and Ethical Practice

4. Identify current social issues that affect the communities that students live in and consider ways that schools may address these issues.
   InTASC Standard #2: Learning Differences; Standard #3: Learning Environments; and Standard #9: Professional Learning and Ethical Practice

Social Issues

You have heard the assertion that children are our future. As a society that recognizes this, we strive to nurture and protect our children. And, as a function of society, schools respond to issues that threaten students' well-being—emotional and physical—as well as to social issues that may affect the community in which the school is located.

BUILDING BLOCK 12.1

Social Issues

What is meant by a *social issue*? What social issues are we, as a society, concerned about right now? List them in order of their importance as you see it.

■ Which do you think schools ought to deal with?

■ Which do you think schools ought to leave alone?

As you were thinking about Building Block 12.1, you undoubtedly realized that issues change as society changes. Issues that were very important two or three decades ago have changed in importance or have been replaced by new issues. For example, technology has introduced some issues to society such as online identity theft and cyberbullying, neither of which existed even ten years ago. On the other hand, some issues seem to persist; for example, drug use by students was a concern in the 1960s and remains a concern today. Even so, when you begin teaching, you will encounter issues that do not exist today but that will affect your school and your students.

You have explored many social issues already in this textbook. For example, you investigated poverty in Chapter 4, and school violence, bullying, and sexual harassment in Chapter 8. Because we face numerous other social issues today, it is difficult to identify a few key issues on which to focus in this chapter. However, the chapter's purpose is for you to explore how social issues affect what goes on in schools.

Therefore, we will present some prevalent issues for you to grapple with. Your investigations into the relationships between these social issues and schools can equip you to apply your understandings to new or different social issues that may arise when you are in the classroom.

Look at the list of current social issues you generated in Building Block 12.1. Which of these have the potential to affect the emotional well-being of students? Which have the potential to affect their physical well-being? Which involve the entire community or segments of the community? To what extent is it the school's responsibility to address these issues?

Social Issues That Affect Emotional Health

Social Issues and Emotions

BUILDING BLOCK
12.2

Name as many social issues as you can that might be a threat to students' emotional health. (Emotional health involves feelings of security, safety, and the ability to cope with stress and difficult situations. Emotionally healthy individuals are able to use their abilities to help advance their lives and achieve their goals. Emotional health can be tied to self-esteem, self-efficacy, and optimism.) Recall your exploration of *the student* in Chapter 2 and consider what you learned about psychosocial development:

- How would struggling with issues that affect them emotionally affect a student's life in school? How might these effects be positive or negative, depending on the individual?
- What effect might emotional upset have on their relationships with other students and with teachers?
- How would it affect a student's motivation to learn?

Students struggle with a number of issues that can influence their emotional sense of well-being, thereby affecting both their performance in school and their motivation to go to school. Pressure from divorce and nontraditional family structures and feelings related to poverty, bullying, violence, child abuse, and other difficulties can cause some students to make a commitment to excel in school and others to drop out.

Changing Family Structure

Think of the people in your immediate family. Do you come from what mainstream culture considers a "nuclear" family—with both a mom and dad, and possibly other children? Perhaps your family also includes a pet or two? Certainly the notion of a traditional "family" is often represented as such. But it has to be acknowledged that family structures can change for a variety of reasons. Given that one of our basic common needs is to experience love and belonging, we must consider that changing family structure can ultimately impact a student's perspectives and motivation regarding learning. How many different *types* of families can you think of?

Divorce

According to data from the National Vital Statistics Reports (U.S. Center for National Health Statistics, 2010), the divorce rate in the United was 3.4 divorces per 1,000 people, down from 4.7 in 1990, and many of these divorces include children.

Students who come from divorced families tend to have trouble academically, socially, and emotionally. Specifically, one study found that children of divorce seem to fall behind in math skills and struggle with social skills such as making and maintaining friendships. They also battle feelings of anxiety, low self-esteem, and sadness (Kim, 2011). You can access a website that has suggestions for teachers supporting children from divorced families on the Education CourseMate website.

In the school environment, teachers can provide students from divorced homes with intellectual and emotional support, offering structure to help them address their scholastic concerns, encouragement in their social endeavors, and kindness and understanding regarding their emotions. They should be consistent in their expectations for participation as members of the classroom environment. They should provide structure for classroom routines and discipline to give students a feeling of security in knowing what is expected of them and what they can expect from the teacher, a feeling that they may not get from the adults at home. Teachers should also provide students from divorced families special opportunities to be successful in their academic work through focus on their competencies, thus helping with their self-esteem and feelings of inadequacy (New-2Teaching, 2011). To support students from divorced families, teachers should foster a partnership approach with the student and each member of his or her family, focusing on communication and mutual problem solving. To do this, teachers must work on their own attitude toward acceptance of all types of family structures and on becoming aware of the parents' attitudes toward the school environment.

Keep in mind that parents who have had positive school experiences will be more likely to become involved with the teacher and the school at the level needed to support the student through a difficult period of adjustment. With a partnership approach and an attitude of acceptance, teachers will find the door is open to create an atmosphere of support for students. Taking actions that include communicating with family members frequently in both formal and informal ways, sharing classroom activities and materials with parents, and encouraging all family members to participate in the student's educational experience will help children of divorce make the difficult transition into a new family structure while continuing to perform successfully at school (Leon and Spengler, 2005).

Of course, students from divorced families can and often should be referred to guidance counselors and school psychologists for help in resolving issues associated with the divorce. Together, the teachers and specialists can help these students come to grips with difficulties they may be experiencing.

Alternative Family Structures

Studies of the family and its impact on children are both broad and deep. And of course, a family whose structure has been determined by divorce is not the only type of family

The traditional family structure that once included a mother, father, and children has given way to primary caregivers who can be grandparents, extended family members, single parents, foster parents, and adoptive parents.

© LWA-Sharie Kennedy/CORBIS

structure in our society. There are many different family structures, and each functions differently in different cultures, different ethnic groups, and with different ages of children.

According to data from the U.S. Census Bureau, (2011a), in 2010, 69.4 percent of children under the age of 18 lived with both parents. Nearly one-quarter of the children (22.4 percent) lived with only their mother, 3.4 percent lived with only their father, and 4.1 percent lived with neither parent. The report classifies family structure into three categories—living with two parents, living with a single parent, and living with neither parent. These three categories are further subdivided, illustrating the varieties of family structures from which your students may come. The subcategories listed in the report are as follows:

- Living with two parents
  - Married parents
  - Unmarried parents
  - Biological mother and father
  - One biological parent and one adoptive parent (mother and father)
  - One biological parent and one stepparent (mother and father)
  - Two adoptive parents (mother and father)
- Living with one parent
  - Mother only (biological or adoptive)
  - Father only (biological or adoptive)
- Living with no parent
  - Grandparents only
  - Other relatives only
  - Nonrelatives only
  - Other

There are other family structures in addition to those listed here, such as those with same-sex parent families. In 2010, there were almost 650,000 same-sex households in the United States (U.S. Census, 2010b), with 17 percent of these households raising children (Gates and Cooke, 2011). However, research shows that the gay or lesbian family structure is least likely to be recognized as a family by preservice teachers, probably

© Fancy/Alamy

Other family structures in addition to the "nuclear" family include those with same-sex parents.

because of existing biases (Larrabee and Kim, 2010). Can you identify additional nontraditional family structures?

Studies have investigated effects of various family structures on student achievement in school and on student behavior, but these studies show that family structure varies so much that little direct correlation between types of family structures and student outcomes can be inferred. For example, Dunifon and Kowaleski-Jones (2002) found that single parenthood was associated with reduced mathematics scores and with juvenile delinquency, but only for white and nonminority children. These researchers did not find negative effects of single parenthood on African American children. DeLaire and Kalil (2001) found that teenagers living with unmarried adults were less likely to graduate from high school or attend college, but cautioned that not all such families are alike; teenagers living with a single mother or at least one grandparent have outcomes that are often better than those of teenagers living in traditional married families.

Concerns regarding children raised by same-sex parents include those relative to ability to form social relationships and difficulties in gender identity and personal development. In 2004, after reviewing relevant research, the American Psychological Association officially adopted a policy that states, "there is no scientific evidence that parenting effectiveness is related to parental sexual orientation: lesbian and gay parents are as likely as heterosexual parents to provide supportive and healthy environments for their children" (American Psychological Association, 2004).

Working Parents and "Latchkey Kids"

You are probably aware that some children, although they live with one or both parents, may have to spend a significant portion of their time at home alone. The U.S. Bureau of Labor Statistics reports that, in 2010, both parents worked in 58.1 percent of married couples with children. For single-parent families with children, 67 percent of mothers were employed and 75.8 percent of fathers were employed (U.S. Bureau of Labor Statistics, 2011a). Reviewing these statistics, it is clear that the children in these families probably spend some of their time at home, self-supervised depending on their ages, or under the supervision of a babysitter or teachers at an after-school program or day care center. Sometimes, unsupervised or self-supervised children in these situations are called "latchkey kids." They are called this because they must carry a key to their homes to let themselves in, as no one else will be there after school. It is estimated that, in 2005, almost 40 million children aged 5 to 14 years spent some portion of their week in "self-care" situations (Laughlin, 2010). One study found that students aged 11 to 14 years who had been left in self-care situations for more than three hours after school had a lower sense of well-being than children who weren't left home alone as long. The study reported that such feelings could eventually lead these children to choose to participate in high-risk behaviors (Mertens, Flowers, and Mulhall, 2003).

latchkey kid A child who spends unsupervised or self-supervised time after school.

From your examination so far, you may have discerned that family background has a significant impact on students' attitudes toward and achievement in school. Thus it is important that schools and teachers extend their attitude of acceptance to family structure.

The Struggling Economy and Unemployment

Certainly the struggling economy and the resultant effects on the housing market and unemployment have factored into placing some students and their families into emotional distress. The U.S. Bureau of Labor Statistics (2011b) reported that 14 million people were unemployed in September 2011. Figure 12.1 shows the distribution of those unemployed. Those who were unemployed for the long term (27 weeks or more) made up 44.6 percent of the unemployed population.

Many families have lost their homes and/or have had to declare bankruptcy due to unemployment. At the end of 2010, 4.6 percent of mortgage loans were in the foreclosure process (Mortgage Bankers Association of America, 2011). Over 1.25 million petitions for

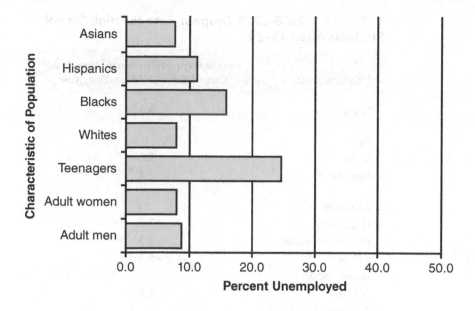

◀ **Figure 12.1**
Percent unemployment by characteristic of the unemployed, September 2011.
Source: Data from the U.S. Bureau of Labor Statistics, 2011b.

bankruptcy were filed in 2009 (Administrative Office of the U.S. Courts, 2011). Considering the stress that such actions cause a family, how do you think the social issues caused by the economy affect students in schools? You can probably imagine that many students who are of legal age—usually 16 years old—choose to or may even have to seek employment to help their families financially. Over 4 percent of the civilian labor force was made up of 16- to 19-year-olds in 2010 (U.S. Bureau of Labor Statistics, 2011c). How do you think leaving high school at the end of the day and then heading to a job and/or holding down a job on weekends might affect teenage students and their learning?

Consequences of Emotional Health Issues and the School's Response

Changes in family structure, the struggling economy, and other social issues put a lot of stress on families and children. The American Psychological Association reports that 32 percent of U.S. parents say that they experience extreme stress levels and that the majority of parents believe that the level of stress that they handle is unhealthy. Meanwhile, the children of these stressed parents reported that they too feel stress and reported feelings of being sad, worried, and frustrated (American Psychological Association, 2010). What consequences do you suppose these feelings have on life in school?

School Dropouts

Life's pressures, such as those from divorce, nontraditional family structures and having to work to help support the family can lead some students to choose to drop out of school. These students who might drop out of school when they can are termed at-risk students.

Most people would agree that education is key to survival in today's technological society. Adults must be literate, know how to use mathematics in everyday situations, and be well versed in technological skills to succeed. In many businesses, the minimum requirement for employment is a high school diploma.

High school dropouts are more likely to be unemployed and are more likely to be incarcerated than high school graduates. And, if they are employed, high school dropouts earn about $10,000 less annually than employees with a high school diploma (Whittaker, 2010).

Over 7,000 students drop out of high school every day. These students are primarily in big, urban school districts and are members of nonmainstream populations. Only 56 percent of Hispanic Americans finish high school and just 54 percent of African Americans and 51 percent of Native Americans earn their high school diploma. More females graduate than males; fewer than 50 percent of nonmainstream males graduate

at-risk student A student considered at high risk for failing to complete high school.

TABLE 12.1 2008–2009 Dropout Rate for High School Students Aged 15–24

Characteristic	Percentage of Students Who Drop Out of School When They Can
Total	8.1
Sex	
Male	3.6
Female	2.7
Ethnicity	
Hispanic	17.6
African American	9.3
White	5.2
Asian/Pacific Islander	3.4
American Indian/Alaska Native	13.2
Family Income	
Low income	8.7
Middle income	3.0
High income	2.0
Age	
16	2.2
17	5.0
18	7.8
19	9.9
20–24	9.5

Source: From the U.S. Department of Education, National Center for Education Statistics.

from high school (Swanson, 2010). Although the graduation rates have improved some over the past ten years or so, still far too many students drop out, constituting a dropout crisis (*Phi Delta Kappan*, 2011). See Table 12.1 for the percentage of high school students who dropped out of school before graduation during the 2008–2009 school year for each of several demographic characteristics (Swanson, 2010).

In their daily interactions with students, teachers can help those students who are thinking about dropping out of school choose to finish high school. Strategies they can employ include helping students see positive academic results, helping them overcome academic hurdles, and providing warmth, support, and encouragement.

BUILDING BLOCK 12.3

Reducing the School Dropout Rate

Consider what you have learned about stressors to students' emotional health and how the programs you have just read about address the needs that students may have due to this stress:

- What warning signs might elementary and middle school teachers see that suggest a student may be a likely candidate to drop out of high school?

- What actions can elementary and middle school teachers take to lessen the likelihood that at-risk students will drop out of school?

- Consider what you learned about students' common needs and unique perspectives. What specific actions might you take as a teacher to encourage a student at risk of dropping out to complete high school?

You have already identified that having an open mind and attitude of acceptance will convey an atmosphere of safety and security and love and belonging, to meet students' common needs. You also know that effective instruction and classroom management will help provide students with opportunities for success and structure. Along with programs such as the after-school program and mentoring at the school level, some schools have implemented programs to encourage at-risk students to stay in school and to help students who have dropped out get back into school.

More than 50 percent of students in schools in Los Angeles drop out. But one private school has implemented a tough curriculum that focuses on building study and writing skills needed for success in college, beginning in the sixth grade. The class sizes are smaller than they are in the public schools, and teachers are available for tutoring after school. In Philadelphia, schools focus on identifying warning signs in younger students to prevent dropouts, and provide transitional programs for students who have dropped out, but want to re-enter school. Philadelphia recently improved its graduation rate by 23 percent, more than any other city (Whittaker, 2010).

The Obama administration recognized the dropout rate in the nation and announced several significant federal funds in 2010 to prevent and address the problem. He acknowledged that students often choose to drop out of school because they find school irrelevant and not engaging. President Obama committed $3.5 billion to fund changes in persistently low-performing schools, $900 million to support School Turnaround Grants, and $100 million in a College Pathways program to promote college readiness in high schools, allowing students to earn a high school diploma and college credit at the same time (Office of the Press Secretary, 2010).

Students who feel emotional stress and who feel that they are not safe, supported, or successful in school or maybe even at home, may turn away from school-based opportunities and engage in activities that threaten their physical well-being. These activities are social issues in that they impact society either directly or indirectly, which means that we feel their impact in the school and the curriculum.

After-School Programs

As you have seen, due to changing family structure and/or the need for all adults in a family to work to provide financial stability, students may be subject to having to spend some time alone. The age of the student must be considered when examining the effects of this time alone. As you can imagine, younger learners may experience stress and worry if left to self-care whereas adolescents may find ways to occupy this time that are not necessarily beneficial to themselves or the community.

Many schools provide after-school programs (ASPs) as a response to the issue of students having to spend time without parental supervision. When you think of ASPs, you may get images of small children in nursery schools, but ASPs are available for all ages of students and provide all kinds of support—academic, recreational, and extracurricular activities such as sports and the arts. As many as 10 million children in the United States take advantage of after-school programs (Yohalem, Pittman, and Edwards, 2010). There are several documented benefits for students participating in after-school programs. Among them are improved academic performance (Naftzger et al., 2007), increased participation in healthy activities (Mahoney, Lord, and Carryl, 2005), decreases in classroom misbehavior (Huang, Leon, La Torre, and Mostafavi, 2008), and a decrease in drug use (Cunha and Heckman, 2006).

Having the option of participating in ASPs addresses several of the consequences of the social issues you have examined so far in this chapter. The safety, security, structure, supervision, and guidance these programs provide reduce the emotional stress that students may experience as a result of changing family structures or having to spend time alone.

Social Issues That Affect Physical Health

You have already explored ways that social issues can affect emotional health and well-being of students. Now let's examine how social issues can affect physical health. Good health is essential to successful living. Today's society tends to believe that teaching the fundamental principles of good health enables students to lead successful, productive adult lives, and that (with a few exceptions) the schools should undertake this education. Schools have taught such topics as exercise, nutrition, sleeping habits, and cardiovascular health to encourage healthy living for many years.

BUILDING BLOCK 12.4

Health Concerns

What are some current health issues? Jot a few down.

- Which of these issues have implications for students?
- What role should the school play in teaching these health issues?
- Do you think that schools should address some health issues and parents should address others?
- If you think that schools should teach some issues and parents should teach others, which issues belong in the schools and which belong at home? How did you make this determination?

The list you made in Building Block 12.4 is probably one that you could duplicate by reading newspaper headlines or watching television news: childhood obesity, drugs, sex, violence, and so on. Certainly, schools can address students' need to become educated about health issues. Let us take a look at some of these issues and how schools may respond.

Nutrition and Childhood Obesity

childhood obesity A condition of children being overweight.

One health issue that affects schools is childhood obesity. Statistics show that childhood obesity is on the rise in the United States. Several factors contribute to childhood obesity, such as eating junk food and getting limited exercise. People are calling for action to reduce childhood obesity, and schools are responding to that call.

Generally, childhood overweight and obesity are measured using body mass index (BMI). BMI is the relationship between height and weight, accounting for the age and sex of a child, and acknowledging the differences in body composition due to these variables. The Centers for Disease Control (CDC) defines an overweight child as one with a BMI at or above the 85th percentile but lower than the 95th percentile for children of the same age and sex. An obese child is one with a BMI at or above the 95th percentile for children the same age and sex (Barlow et al, 2007).

The latest statistics from the National Center for Health Statistics, a division of the CDC, indicate that an estimated 17 percent of children and adolescents aged 2 to 19 years are obese and that the number of overweight and obese children and adolescents is increasing. The data also indicate differences in rates of obesity between children from mainstream and nonmainstream cultures. Hispanic boys had greater rates of obesity than non-Hispanic white boys, and non-Hispanic black girls had greater rates of obesity than non-Hispanic white girls. In addition, children from low-income families have higher rates of obesity due to not having access to healthier food choices (Ogden and Carroll, 2010). Table 12.2 shows the percentage of overweight children and adolescents for selected years from 1963 to 2008. You can access a direct link to the CDC's *School Health Index for Physical Activity and Healthy Eating* through the Education CourseMate website.

TABLE 12.2 Prevalence of Overweight Children and Adolescents for Selected Years, 1963–2008

Age	1963–1970	1971–1974	1976–1980	1988–1994	2001–2002	2003–2004	2005–2006	2007–2008
6–11	4.2%	4.0%	6.5%	11.3%	16.3%	18.8%	15.1%	19.6%
12–19	4.6%	6.1%	5.0%	10.5%	16.7%	17.4%	17.8%	18.1%

Source: From the U.S. Department of Education, National Center for Education Statistics.

Recall that a significant percentage of today's families have reported being under extreme stress. It turns out that those families under great stress find that they have neither the time nor the willpower to manage stress by making healthy choices with regard to nutrition and exercise. In fact, children who are overweight and obese reported that they worry a lot and that their appearance is often the focus of this worry. These same children reported that their parents were under a great deal of stress "always" or "often" (American Psychological Association, 2010). Obese children tend to have high blood pressure and high cholesterol as well as type 2 diabetes. In addition, research has shown that being obese as a child has a significant impact on that child's health as an adult; among other issues, obese children tend to become obese adults and tend to have heart problems (Polhamus et al., 2011).

Organizations such as the CDC are recommending that schools and society focus on educating students about nutrition, encouraging youth to make good choices about eating, and getting everyone to watch TV less and to move more! Schools are reexamining their lunch and breakfast programs and their physical education programs. Several organizations have compiled resources and developed curricular materials and programs to help schools. For example, the CDC's Division of Adolescent and School Health has published the *School Health Index for Physical Activity and Healthy Eating: A Self-Assessment and Planning Guide*. This online resource allows schools to compare their own nutrition programs with other exemplary programs. Recognizing that children from low-income families may not get adequate nutrition, the National School Lunch Program provides low-cost or free nutritional lunches and a snack for after-school programs to students who qualify for this federally funded assistance. In 2010, 31 million students through the age of 18 benefitted from this program (Food and Nutrition Service, 2011).

First Lady Michelle Obama launched the "Let's Move" campaign in 2008, with the goal of raising a healthier generation of kids. Mrs. Obama's campaign seeks to empower families, provide healthy food choices in schools, provide access to healthy affordable foods for all families, and encourage families, schools, and communities to get physically active. As part of the focus on healthy eating, the federal government has updated the nutrition standards for school lunch and breakfast programs. The updated standards call for increased availability of fruits, vegetables, whole grains, low-fat and fat-free milk, and decreased levels of sodium and saturated and trans fats in school meals (Federal Register, 2012).

You have seen that after-school programs provide students with many opportunities to develop knowledge and skills in a variety of areas. ASPs are in a unique position to address nutrition and physical activity. Keep in mind that the students who take advantage of ASPs are oftentimes underprivileged and part of a population that we have already established as having a higher rate of obesity. The National School Lunch Program can provide funds for healthy snacks to offer students in ASPs. ASPs can also include physical activities for students during a time of day when they are often sedentary, and can encourage continuity between the nutritional and activity goals established at school and at home (Afterschool Investments Project, 2006).

Baerbel Schmidt/Getty Images/Stone

According to the Centers for Disease Control, more than 15 percent of children between the ages of 6 and 19 are obese. Healthier school lunch options and school-based nutrition programs can address this issue, but what can individual teachers do to further manage childhood obesity?

▶❚❚ **TeachSource** Video

View the TeachSource video, "Childhood Obesity and School Nutrition." The number of overweight children in the United States is on the rise. For three years, a Massachusetts school district has been eliminating junk food and providing healthier foods to students in alignment with national nutrition guidelines. After watching this video, answer the following questions:

• What are some of the advantages of providing healthier food options for students while they are at school? What might be some disadvantages?

• To what degree is it the school's responsibility to monitor student nutrition?

• What might be the implications for food choices available during school events other than mealtimes, such as items available for sale at concessional stands at extracurricular sporting events, and in vending machines?

Childhood and Adolescent Obesity

- Do you believe that childhood and adolescent obesity is a problem in today's society? To what extent?

- Is there something specific schools should do about childhood and adolescent obesity? If so, describe what you think might be a solution.

- Nutritious food choices help students to maintain a healthy weight, and exercise also plays a role. However, due to economic struggles, some schools are cutting back their physical education programs. Why do you suppose they are doing so? How can this be reconciled with the increasing rate of childhood and adolescent obesity?

Drugs and Alcohol

Drug and alcohol use by students has been a concern of parents, teachers, and society for many years. The percentage of illicit drug use, including alcohol, for students aged 12 to 17 increased to 10 percent in between 2008 and 2009, after having declined for the previous six years. Whites had the highest percentage of underage alcohol use (30.4 percent), and Asians had the lowest rate (16.1 percent) (Substance Abuse and Mental Health Services Administration, 2011).

Figure 12.2 presents figures about drug use by U.S. students between 2000 and 2011. The data represent illicit drug use (including alcohol) by grade level for eighth-, tenth-, and twelfth-graders at any time during their lives.

Other interesting information includes the following statistics concerning cigarettes and alcohol:

- Forty percent of students have tried cigarettes by the time they are in the twelfth grade. Eighteen percent (nearly one in five) have tried cigarettes by eighth grade. However, these are the lowest percents since the Institute for Social Research started the keeping data in 1975.

- Alcohol is the most prevalent of the illicit drug use, and 70 percent of students have consumed significant amounts of alcohol (more than a few sips) by twelfth grade. Thirty-three percent have consumed similar amounts of alcohol by eighth grade. In addition, half of twelfth-graders and 15 percent of eighth-graders have been drunk at least once. Nonetheless, these figures are the lowest since record keeping started in 1975 (Johnston et al., 2012).

We can probably all agree that *any* illicit teen drug use is contrary to the growth that will enable students to lead successful, productive lives. Schools can play a major role in educating youth about drug abuse. Have you seen evidence of this social issue in the schools?

In what class do students learn about drugs and their harmful effects? At which grade level? Do you believe schools should be involved in drug and alcohol abuse prevention programs? How are they involved now? What else, if anything, should they do?

Figure 12.2 ▶

Illicit drug use by 8th-, 10th-, and 12th-graders, 2000–2011.

Source: From Johnston, L. D., O'Malley, P. M., Bachman, J. G., & Schulenberg, J. E. (2012). *Monitoring the Future national results on adolescent drug use: Overview of key findings, 2011.* Ann Arbor: Institute for Social Research, The University of Michigan.

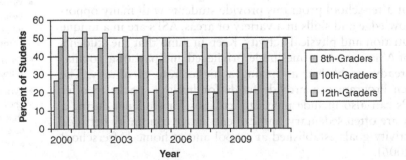

The Office of Safe and Drug-Free Schools, a division of the U.S. Department of Education, oversees federal funds for drug prevention programs. Drug-Violence Prevention grants are awarded to schools and other organizations to develop drug prevention activities for students. Several national organizations provide information and curricular materials about drug and alcohol abuse. For example, the National Institute on Drug Abuse (NIDA), the National Institutes of Health, and the U.S. Department of Health and Human Services offer free, science-based materials for teens, teachers, and parents. These materials help students understand the scientific basis for the harmful effects of drug abuse. NIDA hosts NIDA for Teens, which provides facts, real stories, and answers to frequently asked questions about drugs. Available for teachers are several curricular materials, including posters, DVDs, online modules of activities, and magazines for grades K–12. Parents can access information and activities to do at home. You can access the NIDA website titled "NIDA for Teens" through the direct link on the Education CourseMate website.

You probably have seen Just Say No posters in the halls of your field experience school, you may have observed National Red Ribbon Week, and you may have seen program materials from D.A.R.E. Former First Lady Nancy Reagan mounted the Just Say No campaign in the early 1980s to help raise awareness about the harmful effects of drug use and abuse. National Red Ribbon Week is held during the last week in October and is commemorated by individuals wearing or displaying red ribbons to signify their commitment to leading drug-free lives. The U.S. Drug Enforcement Agency sponsors National Red Ribbon Week, and the National Family Partnership coordinates activities. The National Red Ribbon Week campaign is the oldest and largest drug-prevention campaign in the country.

D.A.R.E. (Drug Abuse Resistance Education) is a drug abuse program designed to equip students in elementary, middle, and high schools with knowledge about drug abuse and its consequences, and skills for resisting peer pressure to experiment with drugs, alcohol, and tobacco. The program is taught in regular classrooms by uniformed police officers who create a positive atmosphere for interaction between students and the police officer. The D.A.R.E. program is used in 75 percent of the nation's school systems and in 43 countries (D.A.R.E., 2012).

BUILDING BLOCK 12.6

Drugs and Alcohol

You have noted that the overall use of drugs and alcohol by school-aged students seems to be decreasing.

- Do you believe that schools should be involved in drug and alcohol abuse prevention programs? Why or why not?
- How are schools involved in drug and alcohol abuse prevention efforts now?
- Is there something specific schools should do about the issue of drug and alcohol use and abuse by students? If so, describe what you think they might do.

Sex-Related Issues

The education of school-aged children in matters of sex and sexuality is a huge social issue, one that schools can help address. However, unlike schools' responses to childhood obesity and the use of drugs and alcohol, their responses to sexual issues are fraught with controversy.

What are society's concerns about sex? People are troubled by the potential for teens to become pregnant or to become infected with a sexually transmitted disease (STD). Some people also believe that premarital sex is morally wrong.

Teenage Pregnancy

The Centers for Disease Control has surveyed youth in ninth through twelfth grade every two years since 1990, as part of the Youth Risk Behavior Surveillance System (YRBSS). The survey's purpose is to assess the prevalence of risky behaviors by young people in several categories, including sexual behavior. According to the 2009 survey, the percentage of U.S. high school students engaging in risky sexual behaviors had not changed significantly since 2001

sexually transmitted disease A disease transmitted largely through sexual behavior.

risky behavior Behavior that may result in adverse consequences.

A s noted earlier, many school-aged children have smartphones that they carry with them at all times—including to school. Smartphones can be used for a multitude of applications, including a host of apps, voice messaging, texting, taking videos and photos, sending and receiving e-mails, and, yes, even making phone calls. Many school activities can be carried out using the smartphones. Teachers, of course, have to be careful to be sure the students are doing schoolwork on their equipment and not using their phones for something else.

One of the activities teenagers have used their smartphones for has been to engage in an activity called "sexting." Sexting consists of sending or receiving sexually explicit pictures or videos through the smartphone. This activity has parents, other adults, and law enforcement personnel concerned. The fear is that sexting will heighten sexual feelings and thoughts, and this will lead to undesirable or risky sexual behavior. But the research shows that only about one teen in 100 (one percent) has personally engaged in sexting, and that the practice is not as common as parents and educators might fear. Only 10 percent of the children who took sexually explicit pictures of themselves sent them to someone else, and only 3 percent of those who received such images forwarded them to another (eSchool News, 2011b).

Nevertheless, schools have written more stringent rules about cell phone use, and teachers are encouraged to provide information about the dangers of sexting, including legal ramifications and the permanent digital record it creates.

(Centers for Disease Control, 2010). In fact, the latest statistics on teen birth rates show that, for all races and ethnicities, teen birth rates decreased by about 37 percent between 1991 and 2009. Nonetheless, when compared with other industrialized countries, the United States has the highest rate of teen pregnancy (National Campaign to Prevent Teen Pregnancy, 2012).

What does a teenage girl do when she finds out she is pregnant? What does she do *after* she gives birth? Sometimes she continues regular school attendance until the baby is born; sometimes her options are limited to attending an alternative school or even dropping out of school altogether. A fact sheet provided by the National Campaign to Prevent Teen and Unplanned Pregnancy (2010) provides the following information:

- Parenthood is the leading cause of dropping out for teenage girls.
- Only 1.5 percent of women who were teenage mothers have college degrees by the time they are 30.
- The children of teen parents do poorly in school and are 50 percent more likely to fail and repeat a grade.

Schools around the country have responded to the social issue of teen pregnancy by hosting prevention and early intervention programs. There are many curriculum-based programs available that can be integrated into the school day or implemented as after school programs. Generally, these programs focus on helping teens understand that delaying sexual activity, *not* having sex, and/or using contraception consistently and carefully are ways to prevent teen and unplanned pregnancies. Many of these programs are tailored to specific populations based on ethnicity and socioeconomic status. It should be noted as well that some programs focus exclusively on females, some on males, and some on both (Suellentrop, 2011).

The National Campaign to Prevent Teen and Unplanned Pregnancy has noted that, contrary to what you might believe about peer pressure, students believe that guidance counselors and teachers are the *second* most reliable source of information about sex and sexuality—second only to their parents and families (National Campaign to Prevent Teen and Unplanned Pregnancy, 2004a). Teens say their parents influence their decisions about sex more than their peers (37 percent versus 33 percent, respectively). However, parents tend to believe that their teens' friends have the greater influence (47 percent versus 28 percent, respectively) (National Center to Prevent Teen and Unplanned Pregnancy, 2004c). Thus, it would seem that parents might safely take an increased role in the sex education of their children.

Do you believe that teenage pregnancy is a problem schools should address? What stance should the schools take on this issue? What, if anything, do you think schools should do about this problem?

Teen Pregnancy

One extremely controversial action taken by some schools in an effort to reduce teenage pregnancies, AIDS, and other sexually transmitted diseases (STDs) is the distribution of condoms in schools. The thinking behind this tactic is that having condoms available to students who decide to engage in sexual behaviors after having been educated about sex, pregnancy, and STDs will encourage them to make safe choices. On the other hand, opponents of this practice insist that students may feel free to engage in sexual behaviors simply because they can get condoms easily. However, in 2005, the American Academy of Pediatrics reaffirmed a policy statement regarding condom use by adolescents in which they noted that research has not shown that increased sexual activity results from condom availability (American Academy of Pediatrics, 2005).

Most experts feel that comprehensive sex education and AIDS-prevention programs should be continued in schools; these programs include content information and education about such factors as the perception of peer norms, teen beliefs and personal values about sex and condom contraception, and the ability to say "No" to having sex. *Education Week* reports that national standards about sex education were released in early 2012; they follow a format similar to that followed in the new common core

state standards. The standards suggest topics to be discussed for each grade level, kindergarten through grade 12. They were developed by a consortium of health education organizations (Shah, 2012a).

However, many schools are shifting away from comprehensive sex education and HIV-prevention programs because of the increased federal funding for abstinence-only programs (AIDS Alert, 2005).

WHAT DO YOU THINK?

1. *What do you think? Should schools provide contraceptives to students?*
2. *If schools were to provide contraceptives to students, at what grade level should it begin?*
3. *Do you believe that schools should teach sex education? Or should it be left up to parents? The church? Other community organizations?*
4. *At what grade level should students take sex education classes if they are offered in school?*

You can access the new National Sexuality Education Standards: Core Content and Skills (K–12) through a direct link on the Education CourseMate website.

Sex Education

You have investigated school-based sex education programs. Should the schools do more? Providing sex education courses in school is very controversial, mostly because of differing social mores and religious beliefs. Many parents want their children to have sex education in school, but it seems that everyone has his or her own idea of just what a sex education class should entail. Sometimes parental permission is required (even for learning facts about AIDS in science classes), but not all parents give their consent.

BUILDING BLOCK
12.7

- Do you believe schools should be involved in sex education programs? If so, on what topics should the programs focus?
- How are schools involved in sex education now?
- Is there something specific schools should do about sex-based issues? If so, describe what you think they should do.

Social Issues That Affect the Community

How do the consequences of the social issues you have investigated have the potential to extend into the community? Hundreds of social issues affect local communities, such as crime, gangs, illiteracy, vandalism, and you can probably think of many more. These issues can be the results of or compounded by students who are experiencing emotional distress and/or who are participating in the behaviors risky to their physical well-being, such as those you have examined. Certainly, there is an economic burden posed by health care for overweight

Figure 12.3 ▶

Law enforcement reports of gang activity, 2009.

Source: From data in Egley, Jr., Arlen, and Howell, James C. (2011). *Highlights of the 2009 national youth gang survey.* U.S. Department of Justice, Office of Justice Programs, Office of Juvenile Justice and Delinquency Prevention.

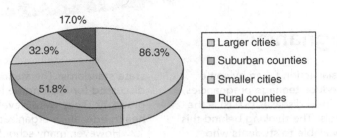

17.0%
32.9%
86.3%
51.8%

☐ Larger cities
☐ Suburban counties
☐ Smaller cities
■ Rural counties

and obese children, unplanned and unwanted teen pregnancies and births, and those who drop out of school and are unemployed. To help meet the need for safety and belonging, and searching for routes to drug and alcohol use, some juveniles might turn to gangs.

Gang Activity

It has been found that juveniles who join gangs may do so because they are experiencing problems and/or feel vulnerable in school, have experienced multiple transitions in caregivers, seek respect or money, feel unsafe in their community, or already know someone in a gang and are already engaging in unsafe behaviors (Howell, 2010). According to the Office of Juvenile Justice and Delinquency Prevention (Egley, Jr. and Howell, 2011), in 2009, there were 28,100 gangs and 731,000 gang members nationwide. Ninety-six percent of gang-related homicides occurred in large cities or suburbs (see Figure 12.3).

Who are the students who join gangs? Research has shown that these students are likely to have poor grades, are punished more frequently than others, and feel disconnected and uninvolved in school academics and activities. The schools these students attend typically are poorly performing schools that report greater levels of school violence and student and teacher victimization (Howell, 2010).

Gangs are posing an increasing threat to communities. In its 2011 National Gang Threat Assessment, the National Gang Intelligence Center reported that gang membership is greatest in the West and Great Lakes regions but that it has increased at the greatest rate in the Northeast and Southeast. The greatest level of gang-related violence occurs in major cities and suburbs, and is often associated with drug use and drug trafficking. Note that, in many communities, there has been an increase in of ethnic-based gangs (Eurasian, African, Caribbean, and Asian), and that the latest advances in technology have actually facilitated and assisted gang communication, coordination, and activity (National Gang Intelligence Center, 2011).

How can communities and schools address and prevent gang formation and membership? The Office of Juvenile Justice and Delinquency Programs (OJJDP) provides the following recommendations in its *Juvenile Justice* bulletin:

- Address risk factors for joining a gang.
- Strengthen families.
- Reduce conflicts that youth may experience and provide them with strategies that promote conflict resolution.
- Improve supervision of youth after school and at the community level by increasing the presence of adults and by providing recreation centers.
- Provide management training for teachers, resource officers, and parents that address management of disruptive and delinquent students.
- Review and soften school "zero-tolerance" policies to reduce the number of suspensions and expulsions.
- Punish delinquent gang behaviors, not gang apparel, signs, and symbols.
- Provide support for students who are struggling in school.
- Provide gang awareness training for school personnel, parents, and students. (Howell, 2010)

Service Learning

You have seen that sometimes juveniles choose to join a gang because they feel no connection with their school or community, and they believe that the school and the community do not care about them. Service learning activities are one way that the connection between student, school, and community may be established and strengthened through positive actions that benefit all involved.

Service learning engages students in meaningful service to their community through the integration of community issues with the school's curriculum. Service learning projects involve collaboration among teachers, students, and the community to identify, study, and propose solutions to community problems, often implementing the solutions and evaluating their results. The problems consist of social concerns that may affect small or large segments of the community.

The goals of service learning projects encompass improving academic performance that includes higher-order thinking; building social skills; providing character education; strengthening the connection between students, schools, and community; and promoting civic engagement. Service learning projects may include a variety of activities in the community and collaboration with community organizations, and may involve various numbers of participants from the school and the community. The following are examples of service learning projects that students of all ages have participated in (National Service Learning Clearinghouse, 2011):

Students who join gangs are those who are likely to have poor grades, who are punished more frequently, and who feel disconnected from school activities. How can you, as a teacher, help prevent students who are at risk?

- Elementary school students in a small town in Tennessee worked with community representatives to identify and publicize places of interest in their community in an effort to increase tourism in light of the struggling economy.

- Students in Boise, Idaho, worked with senior citizens to develop a historical representation of their community from with they created and sold note cards. Proceeds from the sales of the note cards went to an organization that helps seniors and disabled people in the community with the costs of pet adoption and veterinary care for their pets.

- In New York City, students learned about the energy-related advantages of using compact fluorescent light bulbs and then went out into their communities to educate and encourage community members to make the change from incandescent bulbs.

- In Fairbanks, Alaska, students worked with the Tribal Council and Elders of the Athabascan people to understand the historical and current importance of the area's watershed.

School-based service learning projects can encourage prevention of social issues like vandalism, pollution, arson, and crime. These students are involved in a service learning project that seeks to reduce vandalism in their community. How might a teacher integrate this service learning project into the curriculum?

FROM THE FIELD

Service Learning
Deb Perryman

If we were to research the mission statements of schools across the nation, we would find some mention of "creating citizens." But when do our schools actually provide students with the opportunity to act as citizens? The No Child Left Behind legislation calls for students to meet or exceed state standards—a worthy goal, as citizens must be educated and motivated to participate in today's society. Why not use the time we have in schools to actually show our young people how learning will apply to their lives? Why not allow our students to solve community problems and act as citizens? I have found a teaching strategy that allows me to fold learning standards into community action. This strategy is called *service learning*. To me, service learning is the ultimate teaching tool in the constructivist's toolbox. Service learning allows students to explore issues, formulate possible solutions, and implement and then evaluate those solutions. In the service learning model, the project students undertake is the shared responsibility of both the teacher and the student.

In service learning, students explore one or more aspects of a community issue. The teacher works to tie the exploration into a project that addresses the curriculum. For example, picking up litter near a creek on a monthly basis can be related to the Clean Water Act and therefore fits the environmental curriculum. The students are exploring a community issue (litter and its effect on creeks) while meeting state learning standards. My goal is for the students to find the source of that litter and outline a permanent solution to the litter problem. As their facilitator, I encourage them to implement their solutions and evaluate the outcomes.

Service learning is *not* community service. Although community service projects are wonderful and do provide positive student outcomes, they are not tied directly to curriculum. Take, as an example, one of America's most popular community service projects: the canned food drive.

Please tell me how placing collection boxes in a central location helps students meet learning standards. Think for a moment how this community service project can be transformed into a service learning project. First, have you ever looked at what is collected? Are the items collected really needed in food banks? Why not have the students work with the food bank and research the items most needed? Students can create graphics clearly depicting their research, and develop and implement a public outreach campaign to help the community better understand the issue of hunger. The bottom line of service learning is that it is cross-curricular and makes a great impact on our youth.

Planning a service learning project is as easy as planning a party. You have to think about who, what, where, when, and how. Whom do you want to be involved? What issue do you want your students to work on? Where and when will this project fit into your lesson plans? Where and when will it fit into the community? How will this fit into your curriculum, and how will the project be evaluated?

Please remember two additional tidbits: First, involve students at every stage of the project, including planning and evaluation. Second, make sure that the students are talking about a legitimate community need. Projects that are token projects are doomed to fail. Kids know when you are faking, so don't! As you might imagine, the first project is the most difficult. Once you get through one, I dare you to *not* find additional projects.

Deb Perryman
Illinois Teacher of the Year, 2004–2005
Elgin High School
Elgin, Illinois

■ Academically challenged third- and fourth-grade students in Fayetteville, West Virginia, spent part of their summer helping their park system continue its beautification projects. They cleaned up trash, weeded, painted, created rock gardens, and replaced light bulbs for the annual Christmas display.

Other projects, such as Habitat for Humanity and Trick or Treat for UNICEF are nationally and even internationally implemented. All of these projects promote civic engagement among students.

During the 2007–2008 school year, approximately 4.2 million students, including those with disabilities, participated in service learning activities (Spring, Grimm, and Dietz, 2009). Research has shown that the benefits to students include the following:

- Improved character and responsible behaviors
- Improved academic performance
- Increased feeling of connectedness to the community and school
- Better social and emotional skills
- Increased civic engagement (National Clearinghouse on Service Learning, 2011)

From this brief excursion into some of the many social issues that affect people today, you have seen that many such issues affect the children who attend our schools. Of course, there is no way that this textbook can identify and address every social issue that may impact life for teachers and students. As a teacher, however, it is your responsibility to be aware of the issues that your students may bring into the classroom. You can access websites dealing with these issues through the direct links available on the Education CourseMate website. The following briefly cites three situations that you will probably encounter among the children in your classroom:

1. *Immigration.* In the United States in 2004, there were some 1.7 million undocumented migrants under the age of 18, most of who attended public schools (Passel, 2005). Six states have passed harsh immigration control laws that will require undocumented immigrants to leave (Immigration Policy Center, 2012).

2. *Father's incarceration.* In midyear 2007, 1,599,200 school children had a father in prison. These children do not perform well in school, exhibit multiple behavior problems, are more likely to drop out of school, have a higher risk of suicide and substance abuse, display aggression, depression, loneliness, and disobedience, and are more likely to become incarcerated themselves (Collins, n.d.).

3. *Homelessness.* The federal government's definition of homelessness is used by all schools and includes "children and youth who lack a fixed, regular, and adequate nighttime residence" (National Association for the Education of Homeless Children and Youth, n.d.). Homelessness includes students living in shelters, transitional housing, cars, campgrounds, motels, and sharing the housing of others temporarily. Over 950,000 homeless students were enrolled in public schools during the 2008–2009 school year, a 20 percent increase from the previous year, and a 41 percent increase from the year before that. As you can imagine, homeless children face tremendous barriers to their education, even though school is a place where they can feel safe and welcome. Fewer than 25 percent of homeless children in the United States graduate from high school (Murphy and Tobin, 2011).

Recall that all students have common needs. It should be clear as you made your inquiries in this chapter that the issues you have explored both affect and threaten ways in which these needs are met. Remember that you as a teacher are in a uniquely powerful position to help students address these needs.

Society and the Schools

BUILDING BLOCK
12.8

In Building Blocks 12.1, 12.2, and 12.4, you listed some social issues that exist in today's society.

- Which of the issues on your list have prompted action by schools?
- Which issues have not prompted action by schools? Why do you suppose this is? Which of these issues do you believe schools should do something about? What should they do?
- Which issues have prompted controversy about school action? What kinds of controversy? Is there a commonality among the controversies?

■ SUMMARY

- Social issues such as changing and alternative family structures and the struggling economy and its impact on employment can affect the emotional health of students.

- Some students may spend time alone, self-supervised due to parents having to work.

- Stress on students and their families can sometimes lead students to decide to drop out of school so that they can get a job and contribute to the family's finances or simply because they don't see the purpose or relevance of education.

- To address the issues of self-supervision and dropouts, schools have implemented after-school programs, mentoring programs, and programs to identify and prevent at-risk students from dropping out. Some schools have developed programs to help students who have dropped out to reenter schools.

- Stresses on emotional health can translate into threats to physical health and well-being. There continue to be concerns in society with childhood obesity and unsafe behaviors that include risky sexual behavior and drug use.

- Schools have responded to these risky behaviors by implementing programs to guide nutrition and physical activity. To varying degrees, schools have also provided sex education to their students, with some schools taking the even more controversial step of providing condoms to students.

- The risky behaviors that students engage in carry out into the community, sometimes even to the extent of gang-related activities. Statistics regarding gang membership and violence are frightening.

- Schools can address gang activity in a variety of ways that involve prevention, intervention, and suppression.

- To help students form a meaningful connection not only with their school but also with their communities, teachers can employ various service learning activities that engage students' thinking, social, and emotional skills, and collaboration with members of the community, in order to identify and meet community goals.

■ Key Terms and Concepts

At-risk student, 325
Childhood obesity, 328
Latchkey kid, 324

Risky behavior, 331
Sexually transmitted disease
(STD), 331

■ Construct and Apply

1. How do issues such as divorce, family structure, and other issues that affect a student's emotional health influence that student's work in school?
2. Suppose you are the principal of an elementary school and you decide that health should be emphasized in all grades, but you can include only a single topic from these issues: childhood obesity, drug and alcohol abuse, and sex education. Which topic would you choose? Why? What would the topic be if your school were a middle school? A high school? Why?
3. If schools are to play a role in teaching students about sex, safety, and health issues, to what extent should teachers be held accountable for their own behavior in these areas?
4. To what extent is gang activity a concern in your community and/or in the community of your field placement? Does your school have any policies or rules regarding gang colors, symbols, or signs? Why do you think one of the recommendations for preventing gang activity is to punish the delinquent behavior rather than the display of gang colors, symbols, or signs? Do you agree with this proposition? Why or why not?
5. What are some ideas for service learning in which you might involve your future students? How would these activities benefit the students? The school? The community?

◼ Deconstructing the Standards

1. Recall the InTASC standards associated with the objectives for this chapter:

   InTASC Standard #1: Learner Development reads, "The teacher understands how learners grow and develop, recognizing that patterns of learning and development vary individually within and across the cognitive, linguistic, social, emotional, and physical areas, and designs and implements developmentally appropriate and challenging learning experiences."

   InTASC Standard #2: Learning Differences reads, "The teacher uses understanding of individual differences and diverse cultures and communities to ensure inclusive learning environments that enable each learner to meet high standards."

   InTASC Standard #3: Learning Environments reads, "The teacher works with others to create environments that support individual and collaborative learning, and that encourage positive social interaction, active engagement in learning, and self motivation."

   InTASC Standard #9: Professional Learning and Ethical Practice reads, "The teacher engages in ongoing professional learning and uses evidence to continually evaluate his/her practice, particularly the effects of his/her choices and actions on others (learners, families, other professionals, and the community), and adapts practice to meet the needs of each learner."

   a. What part(s) of these standards does this chapter address?

   b. How will the concepts in this chapter help you apply these standards as a teacher?

2. Use your favorite search engine to find your state's standards for certification. When you find it, bookmark the site; you will refer to it often during this course.

   a. How are your conclusions about how schools should respond to social issues represented in your state certification standards?

   b. How do the InTASC standards compare to your state's certification standards regarding the schools' response to social issues?

   c. Do you believe the degree of representation concerning social issues in schools is adequate in your state certification standards? Why or why not?

◼ Your Portfolio

1. Pay attention to the social issues and the school's response in your community. How do the schools in the area where you wish to be employed respond to these issues? Read the newspaper daily and become educated about the factors and people involved. Summarize the facts you find and write a reflection to include in your portfolio.

2. Review the philosophy of education statement you wrote in Chapter 2. Based on your examination of the effect of social issues on schools and the influence you may have as a teacher, consider revising this statement.

◼ Education CourseMate Resources

Check out this text's Education CourseMate website (at www.cengagebrain.com) for more information about social issues and how schools respond to them. You will find the TeachSource Videos, a guide for doing field experiences, glossary flash cards, activities, tutorial quizzes, direct links to the websites mentioned in the chapter, and more.

Teachers, Students, and the Law[1]

IN THIS TEXTBOOK, you have looked at a number of laws that affect teachers, students, and schools. Think back to previous chapters. Do you remember the requirements for the lengths of a school year and a school day? Do you recall the requirements of the Individuals with Disabilities Education Act (IDEA)?

You probably have heard about recent school legal issues from the media. If you have children or siblings currently in school, you have probably become familiar with still other legal issues, and you no doubt can recall legal issues from your own time in school. Think about the issues about which you have read or seen reports recently. What do you think is the purpose of each such law? What is its impact on schools?

Schools in the United States operate within a framework of laws and regulations that seek to ensure that all children within society can obtain an education that prepares them for a successful adult life. At the same time, schools operate in a litigious society, and lawsuits are common, involving all aspects of education. The decisions made in lawsuits and other court decisions help shape the educational environment and specify the exact meaning of laws.

---

[1]Dr. Linda Webb was primary author of this chapter in the first edition.

As a result of your explorations in this chapter, you will be able to:

1. Identify the system of laws governing education in the United States.
   InTASC Standard #9: Professional Learning and Ethical Practice

2. Explain teachers' legal rights and responsibilities.
   InTASC Standard #9: Professional Learning and Ethical Practice

3. Explain students' legal rights and responsibilities.
   InTASC Standard #9: Professional Learning and Ethical Practice

Sources of Laws and Regulations Impacting Schools

Let us start by exploring some of the laws that affect students, teachers, and schools. Think again about the laws and regulations you have encountered in this course. Think also about the laws and regulations you remember from your days in schools or that you know about from siblings, children, or the media. What are some of the laws affecting schools?

It's the Law!

BUILDING BLOCK 13.1

Take a few minutes to jot down some laws that affect schools. How do these laws affect teachers, students, or both? Make a chart with three columns:

- The law
- Its impact: How does the law affect the operation of a school?
- The consequences of violating it: What happens if someone breaks the law?

You may wish to use a table such as the one shown here to help you organize your thinking; we give an example to help you get started.

Law	Impact on School	Consequences of Violation
Teachers should not use illegal substances while at school.	A teacher under the influence would not be able to fulfill duties, responsibilities, and obligations associated with the job.	The teacher's employment could be terminated if this behavior continues.

> Compare your responses with those of others. Did you think of different laws? Did you think of the same laws but cite different impacts on teachers or students? Did you think of different consequences for the same laws? Keep your lists; you will refer to them throughout this chapter.

If you were to group the laws you cited in Building Block 13.1 into categories, you would find that the laws fall into several categories, such as the rights and responsibilities of teachers, rights and responsibilities of students, child abuse and neglect, and the rights of students with special needs. What categories would organize your list?

You probably generated a lengthy list of laws governing school life. Let us examine whether all the items you listed are laws. Some of them might be regulations. Others might be court decisions.

Laws and regulations come from federal, state, and local sources, and from the courts that, through numerous cases, have interpreted the laws. Let us see how this works. Some laws are based on the federal or a state constitution and are known as constitutional laws. Some are passed by the legislature at the federal or state level and are known as statutes. Some result from decisions made by the courts and are known as case law. Rules enacted by school boards and other state agencies to ensure compliance with the laws are called regulations.

constitutional law A law based on the U.S. Constitution or a state constitution.

statute A law passed by the federal, state, or local legislature.

case law A law that is the result of decisions made by the courts.

regulation A rule that is enacted by a state or local agency to ensure compliance with the law.

Federal Sources of Laws and Regulations

The U.S. Constitution is the supreme law of the land. The Constitution gives Congress the power to provide for the general welfare in the United States. Although the word *education* is not found in the Constitution, Congress has used the "general welfare" rationale to enact legislation providing for research and support of educational programs, providing financial assistance for education programs such as the Individuals with Disabilities Education Act (IDEA), and mandating safety regulations such as the Asbestos School Hazard Detection and Control Act of 1980. Think about the laws you listed in Building Block 13.1. Many of them probably concern federally controlled rights, such as employment discrimination and teacher rights. Federal legislation is a basis for many aspects of school life.

Most federal laws that directly affect education policies offer federal funds to the states but with conditions attached: If a school district wants the money that comes with a federal program, it has to implement that program according to federal regulations. For example, Title I funds must be distributed according to a formula whereby the school district gives the most money to the schools with the greatest need based on the size of the free and reduced lunch population. If the district gives more Title I money to a school with less need, all Title I money is withheld from the entire district. A state or a school that accepts federal money is bound by the conditions attached to those funds.

Title I funds Federal funds distributed to school districts to be distributed to schools with the greatest need, determined by free and reduced lunch program participation.

State Sources of Laws and Regulations

In the United States, public schools are a function of state government. The state's right to determine laws, rules, and regulations for public schools within its boundaries is derived from the Tenth Amendment to the U.S. Constitution which, as you have seen, states, "The powers not delegated to the United States by the Constitution, nor prohibited by it to the states, are reserved to the states respectively, or to the people." Because the U.S. Constitution does not specifically list education as a federal function and does not prohibit the states from regulating education, educational control is reserved for the states.

Each state enacts its own laws and regulations to establish the way education functions within its boundaries.

All state constitutions specifically address public schools and provide for a uniform, efficient system of public education. Unlike the federal government, the states have the power to make laws governing education to supplement their constitutional provisions; these laws are called statutes. For example, all 50 states have statutes requiring students within specified age ranges to attend school.

From these laws come regulations that ensure implementation of the laws. Regulations differ from laws in that they are not enacted by legislatures and are not part of a state's legal code. But regulations often carry the force of law. You are probably familiar with regulations in your state regarding certification and curriculum. Regulations governing facilities are less well known. For example, did you know that many state boards of education in the southern United States have mandated that all schools be air-conditioned?

Local Sources of Laws and Regulations

Although U.S. schools are controlled by the states, local boards of education administer the state laws, rules, and regulations. These boards often add their own local regulations, such as deciding that all teachers must attend specific staff-development activities. Local boards also formulate regulations covering such issues as the district student discipline policy, teacher attendance policy, and school year calendar.

Each state has layers of rules and regulations. But state law takes precedence. Figure 13.1 shows the layers of school control within the state.

The Courts

You have seen that there are two sources of law governing schools: state laws and federal laws. These laws are debated and passed by representative legislatures and do not rely on precedents. Remember the law enacted by some southern states that all school buildings must be air-conditioned? This law did not rely on any previous law or precedent. There were no previous examples to be considered.

A third type of law is case law. Case law results when judges rule on a legal dispute. IDEA, for example, has been the basis of numerous lawsuits wherein parents felt their children were not receiving the education to which they were entitled by law. When judges ruled on issues regarding IDEA, schools were required to provide specific services and act in specific ways. Thus, the determination of a court case had the impact of law. Courts tend to use previous case law to guide them in their decisions. Case law establishes precedents that guide arguments regardless of when or where the previous decision was handed down. Case law comes from state courts, federal courts, and the U.S. Supreme Court. In the latter half of the 20th century, there was an ever-increasing volume of lawsuits, and the resulting court decisions have affected virtually every aspect of school life.

Since the landmark *Brown v. Board of Education of Topeka* desegregation decision in 1954, the courts have assumed a significant role in education. Although court

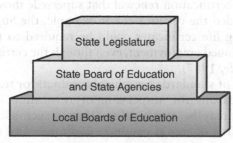

◀ **Figure 13.1**
Levels of school control in states.
© Cengage Learning 2014

decisions had affected schools before *Brown,* the latter half of the 20th century saw an unprecedented volume of lawsuits and resulting court opinions, affecting virtually every aspect of school life. As the impact of federal education legislation is felt across the nation, courts are certain to become involved in the areas of accountability, school choice, and local control. Court decisions on these issues will affect the daily life of all within schools.

Teachers and the Law

Teachers are affected by state and federal laws, the U.S. Constitution, state constitutions, and agreements negotiated between schools and teacher unions. Court rulings that interpret the laws have brought changes in what is required of teachers and have redefined teacher rights. Laws and their interpretations will affect almost every aspect of your professional life, starting before you are employed and continuing throughout your career.

Refer to the list of laws you developed in Building Block 13.1. Look specifically at the laws about teachers. Do you see categories? For example, do some of the laws you listed deal with employment? Do some deal with teacher rights? Teacher responsibilities?

Teacher Certification

Every state has laws and regulations that detail requirements for the certification and employment of teachers. Certification is the basic requirement for teacher employment and is based on professional preparation and other requirements determined by the state. The requirements for teacher certification have been tested in the courts and have consistently been allowed to stand. Consider some examples from the past: In *United States v. South Carolina* (1977), the court upheld the use of the National Teacher Examinations, even though the test had been shown to disproportionately disqualify minority applicants. In *Keyishian v. Board of Regents* (1967), the court ruled that teachers may be required to sign an oath pledging support for the federal and state constitutions and promising to faithfully perform their duties. In *Bay v. State Board of Education* (n.d.), the court ruled that finding a burglary conviction in an applicant's past was sufficient reason for the state to refuse a teaching certificate. Generally speaking, courts will not intervene in certification requirements unless a person's rights have been violated.

As you saw in Chapter 9, teaching certificates are issued for specific time periods to teach specific subjects and ages. Although the certification satisfies state requirements, local school districts may require additional training. To maintain a teaching certificate, a teacher must meet the state's requirements and, normally, acquire additional refresher education. Failure to meet continuing education requirements results in ineligibility for certificate renewal, which, in turn, can result in loss of employment. It's important to note that states may impose new conditions for certification renewal that supersede those that were in effect when the teacher was awarded the certificate. For example, the Supreme Court of Texas ruled that teachers holding life certificates could be required to pass a teacher examination as a condition of continued employment, even though the certificates were "permanent" (*State v. Project Principle,* 1987).

code of ethics A guide to acceptable professional behavior.

Every state has a code of ethics (a list of standards for ethical conduct) for teachers (see Chapter 9) and a description of reasons for suspension or revocation of the teaching certificate. A teaching certificate may be revoked for offenses such as *moral turpitude* (the blatant violation of standards of moral conduct), *unfitness,* and *felony criminal convictions.*

Revocation of Teaching Certificates

Several interesting legal cases illustrate reasons why teaching certificates can be revoked:

- A music teacher had her state certification revoked after she was convicted of stealing $3,000 from the booster club. It was also discovered that she intended to use the booster club's credit card on a cruise she was planning to take (Gibson, 2011).

- A 59-year-old Michigan teacher lost his state certification and was also convicted for exposing himself to a 12-year-old male student who was doing yard work for him (Carter, 2010).

- A music teacher in New York State lost his teaching license after he was charged with endangering the welfare of a child by engaging in inappropriate sexual conduct while in the presence of a student (Public Employment Law Press, 2010).

What basic cause of certificate revocation (moral turpitude, unfitness, or felony criminal conviction) underlies each of the preceding decisions?

Employment

Teachers are hired by the local board of education of that district, and not the individual school. The board hires and the board fires. Teachers work for the board. The board sets the employment requirements for teachers within the school district. The authority for employment and termination of teachers is exclusively vested in the local school board and cannot be delegated to any other body or official. For the most part, contracts of employment are offered only after the board has voted to employ the applicant.

However, state laws govern teacher contracts. Most teacher contracts contain salary and employment date information, stating only that the applicant is to be employed by that district for a specific number of days (usually 180 to 185) at a specific salary. Grade, specific school, and subject to be taught are not included, because the contract is a legal document for employment in the school district and not at a specific school within that district. When might a teacher want to break a contract? You can think of many reasons, such as being dissatisfied with your school placement, or wishing you were closer to home, or wanting to move to another state with your spouse. Or, you may suddenly realize you don't want to go into teaching after all, and you want out. A teacher may legally and ethically break a contract only by following approved procedures for contract release. In most states, this involves sending a written request for release. The local board then acts on the request. Failure to obtain proper release from a contract may result in monetary damages awarded to the school district (for the cost of locating and employing a replacement), loss of teaching certificate, and loss of employability in other school districts. In most states, teacher applications ask whether the applicant has also signed a current contract with another district. If so, the district to which she is applying will not consider the applicant for employment. If the applicant answers "no" but has in fact signed another contract, the applicant may be terminated by the district where she has the contract, and may even be prosecuted for lying on the new application.

After a teacher is employed by a school district, that teacher can legally be assigned to any school in the district, and the principal can legally assign the teacher to any grade level in the school, as long as the assignment is within the teacher's area or areas of certification. But, teachers normally interview with the principal of the school in the district that wants to consider the applicant for a position in that school, and, if hired,

contract An agreement with specific terms between two or more people or entities in which there is a promise to do something in return for a valuable benefit.

will in all probability be assigned to the school where the applicant was interviewed. Teachers sometimes want to specify the school, grade, and/or subject they will teach, especially after they have taken a year or two off. Schools often can accommodate individual requests, but not always.

Contracting for a Job

Teacher shortages in some areas have made it possible for qualified teachers to shop around for positions best suited to them. Consider the following scenario:

Mrs. Wilson, a mathematics teacher, has signed a contract to teach in the Lincoln County School District. Her husband has been reassigned to a job site 30 miles from their current residence, and they have decided to relocate to the new area, which is served by the Washington County School District. Not only is Washington County advertising for qualified mathematics teachers, but this district is also paying $2,500 more per year than Lincoln County for someone with Mrs. Wilson's level of experience. Washington County also offers a one-time signing bonus of $2,500 for science, mathematics, and special education teachers.

■ What are Mrs. Wilson's legal options?

■ What is her most ethical course of action?

Teachers may be transferred to different schools, but only when the decision is based on objective, *nondiscriminatory reasoning*, such as moving an English teacher from a school with a dwindling student population to one whose student population is growing. It would be illegal for a teacher to be transferred to another school just because he or she disagreed with and openly criticized school policies, but still obeyed them. This example above would constitute a transfer based on *discriminatory reasoning*, which was invalidated by the courts in the past (*Adcock v. Board of Education of San Diego Unified School District,* 1973). If a teacher did not obey the school policies that he or she was openly critical of, that may be a case of insubordination, which is covered later in this chapter.

Teachers may be legally required to undertake certain noninstructional duties, such as supervising the lunchroom.

Noninstructional Duties

Instructional duties include the act of teaching and those actions connected to teaching, such as lesson planning. You investigated teachers' instructional and noninstructional duties in Chapter 9. You saw that the courts tend to hold that noninstructional duties, such as lunch and bus duty, are part of normal school operations and that teachers must undertake such duties because those duties constitute a significant part of the school program. However, a court ruled long ago that teachers cannot be required to undertake duties that are not related either to their work or to school to keep their jobs. In its rulings on implied obligations of teachers, a New York court stated that any teacher may be required to supervise study hall and conduct conferences; English teachers may be assigned to direct school plays, physical education teachers to coach intramural and interschool athletic teams, and band directors to accompany bands on trips. A mathematics teacher, on the other hand, cannot be required to coach an athletic team, and no teacher may be required to perform services such as traffic duty, school bus driving, or janitorial services (*Parrish v. Moss,* 1951).

What Are My Assignment Options?

A principal has assigned a social studies teacher to coach the academic bowl team. The team meets twice weekly after school for two hours. Last year, the team won the state bowl and was invited to compete in the national bowl, but the national competition is held in another state. The social studies teacher declined the assignment on the grounds that child care issues prevented her from getting home late or traveling out of state.

- What are the teacher's legal options?
- What are the principal's legal options?

Tenure

Tenure is a state provision that grants teachers the right to continued, permanent employment status. Many but not all states award tenure to teachers. Teachers receive the right to tenure by state law, and tenure is awarded by local boards of education after two to five years of satisfactory teaching within a school district. Only those employed in regular, full-time teaching positions can receive tenure. Most commonly, tenure is awarded upon the successful completion of three years of teaching and the offer and acceptance of a fourth-year contract within the district. This system has been upheld by the courts. , Tenure has two primary advantages:

- The teacher has a reasonable assurance of continued employment.
- The teacher cannot be dismissed without cause, advance notice, and legal hearings.

However, many states are making it harder for teachers to get tenure and some states are doing away with tenure all together. The reason for this is that teachers are increasingly being held accountable for their performance, especially in response to the Obama administration's Race to the Top grants. As you can imagine, the teacher unions have responded very negatively to states' actions regarding tenure (Associated Press, 2012).

Dismissal

Before achieving tenure, teachers may be dismissed without cause at the end of a teaching year. *Without cause* means a teacher does not have to be given a reason for the decision not to reemploy him or her. Additionally, a nontenured teacher who is dismissed does not have the right to due process. The employment of nontenured teachers can be terminated simply through nonrenewal. Nontenured teachers have a one-year contract with a beginning date and an ending date, and the school system has no obligation to reemploy the teachers at the end of the contract term. The school system's only obligation is to provide teachers with a notice of intention not to reemploy by a specified date, which is mid-April in most states.

Teachers who have been awarded tenure cannot be dismissed without due process. Due process refers to a person's right to be adequately notified of charges or proceedings involving him or her and the opportunity to be heard at these proceedings. Due process includes the following:

due process A person's legal right to be adequately notified of charges or proceedings involving him or her and to be given the opportunity to be heard.

1. Notice of charges or reasons for dismissal
2. Prior notice of a hearing
3. The right to legal counsel
4. A hearing before an impartial party
5. The right to compel supportive witnesses to attend

6. The right to confront and cross-examine opposing witnesses, and to view evidence prior to the hearing

7. The right to testify in one's own behalf

8. The right to have a transcript of proceedings to use on appeal

Once a teacher has earned tenure, the school board is required to show good cause for dismissal and must provide the teacher with all the rights and procedures of due process. Boards cannot dismiss tenured teachers without just cause. The four most common reasons for dismissing a tenured teacher are incompetence, insubordination, immorality, and criminal activity.

Other actions are not so clear-cut and can be argued to have no effect on the teaching and learning process. When courts examine appeals by teachers who have been dismissed for cause, they generally examine whether the offense resulting in dismissal negatively affected the teacher's performance.

You may recall that tenure has been eliminated in some states and that other states are considering its elimination. In states that have abolished tenure, teachers gain due process rights after a certain number of years of employment. In states with strong teacher unions, a specific dismissal process is usually part of the union agreement.

Let us examine some of the most common reasons for teacher dismissal.

Incompetence

Have you ever had a teacher you considered to be incompetent? What did that teacher do (or not do) that showed incompetence?

BUILDING BLOCK 13.5

Is This Incompetence?

Mr. McDougal has been teaching mathematics at Broadview Middle School for ten years and was voted Teacher of the Year three years ago. During the seven months of the current academic year, Mr. McDougal has been habitually tardy and has submitted incomplete lesson plans. Numerous parent complaints suggest that his lessons are disorganized and that students have difficulties as a result. Observations of his teaching confirm this.

- Based on this scenario, do you believe Mr. McDougal is exhibiting incompetence? What is your reason?
- What are Mr. McDougal's legal options?
- What are the principal's legal options?

Incompetence has been broadly interpreted by the courts. It can include lack of subject-matter knowledge, inability to maintain discipline, the use of unreasonable discipline, unprofessional conduct, and willful neglect of duty. It can include attitudinal deficiencies; failure to get along with colleagues, parents, and administrators; neglect of duty; and even showing too many videos. Here are three situations that resulted in dismissals that were upheld by the courts:

- A teacher administered excessive punishment on three occasions (*Kinsella v. Board of Education,* 1978).
- A teacher had problems communicating material effectively to her students (*Johnson v. Francis Howell R-3 Board of Education,* 1994).
- A teacher had a messy classroom and produced unplanned lessons that were poorly communicated to students (*Blunt v. Marion County School Board,* 1975).

In each of these instances, the teacher was observed, evaluated, and offered opportunities to improve prior to his or her dismissal.

Most states have a clearly defined process to observe and evaluate teachers and then to provide tenured teachers with ample opportunity for remediation in the areas in which they have exhibited incompetence before they can be dismissed. The Obama administration's Race to the Top initiative has focused attention on teachers being "highly qualified" and competent. Teachers are increasingly being held accountable for their effective (or ineffective) classroom strategies. For example, in Washington State, 165 teachers were dismissed in 2010 for poor performance. This rate of dismal was the highest in the nation and was expected to be even more widespread in the state in 2011 (Dillon, 2011b).

Although dismissal for incompetence usually happens only after numerous instances of unsuccessful remediation efforts, teachers can be dismissed as the result of one action showing incompetence if that action is extremely serious. Such was the case of the teacher who wrote the word *stupid* across the forehead of one of his math students (DeVine, 2012).

Teaching performance is observed and evaluated by administrators. Teachers who demonstrate incompetence are often given opportunities for remediation and to correct their teaching practices.

Insubordination

Insubordination is defined by *Black's Law Dictionary* as "an act of disobedience to proper authority" (Garner, 2009). As with incompetence, dismissal for insubordination most often occurs after a series of actions. However, a single, sufficiently serious incident may be good cause. Here are instances of dismissal for insubordination that the courts upheld. Do you know of other examples?

insubordination an act of disobedience to proper authority (Garner, 2009).

- A teacher was fired for insubordination when he refused to offer an explanation for not allowing an injured student to go to the school clinic. He had the student wait in the hallway while other students in his class completed a quiz. A school staff member found the student and got help for her (Geary, 2010).

- A high school physics teacher was fired for insubordination when he refused to alter the failing grade he had given to a student who was sleeping in his class. After receiving the directions for the assignment, instead of beginning work, the student put his head down on his desk and went to sleep. When he turned the assignment in the next day, it was worthy of a good grade, but the teacher cut the grade in half due to the student's behavior in class the previous day. When the student and his parents complained, the school administration asked the physics teacher to reconsider and raise the grade. But the teacher refused, resulting in the charge of insubordination (Levs, 2005).

- A teacher in a religious school had taken an extended leave of absence for medical reasons, but was ready to return to her job. However, during her absence, the school had hired another teacher to fill her position. The teacher threatened to sue the school to get her job back but was subsequently fired for insubordination because the school officials said that her behavior during this dispute was disruptive and inconsistent with their belief that such matters should be handled by the church rather than in the court system. Because the teacher had received tenure after having taught there for three years, she couldn't be fired without cause. This case went to the U.S. Supreme Court, which ruled that religious organizations can hire and fire whomever they chose for criteria that they define (Graham, 2012).

As you can tell from the preceding cases, courts have looked at willfulness as the determinant of insubordination. Additionally, the courts look to see whether harm resulted, whether the punishment is appropriate to the insubordinate act, and whether the rule or order broken was reasonable and within the authority of the person making it.

Immorality

Historically, teachers have been viewed as being an example to their students. The rules of conduct and codes of ethics governing teachers are written guides to acceptable behavior, keeping teachers' exemplary role in mind. Courts have typically held the behavior of teachers to a higher standard than other people because of their interaction with impressionable children and youth. One court decision confirming the exemplary role of teachers says, "We note that statutes from colonial days forward recognize the unique position of teachers as examples to our youth . . ." (*Kilpatrick v. Wright*, 1977).

Changing lifestyles and disagreements about what constitutes moral behavior make it difficult to define proper teacher behavior. Generally, any act or behavior that substantially interferes with students' learning and impairs the teacher's fitness to teach serves as a basis for charges of immorality. Here are examples of court cases dealing with immorality:

- A teacher was dismissed on charges of immoral conduct when it was discovered that he had placed an ad soliciting sex on the Internet, complete with inappropriate pictures of himself (*San Diego Unified School District v. Commission on Professional Competence*, 2011).

- Charges of immorality were filed against a teacher after she admitted having sexual relations with another school official on school grounds (Cloonan, 2011).

- Two Catholic schools in Ohio fired an unmarried teacher when she became pregnant by artificial insemination. The teacher served as a technology coordinator for both schools. Although the reasons initially cited for the termination were that the teacher was single and pregnant, the schools became aware that firing the teacher for these reasons might violate state and federal laws, so officials cited the fact that artificial insemination was in conflict with the religious beliefs the schools (Perry, 2011).

Teacher immorality can be exhibited in unprofessional conduct, criminal activity, and certain types of sexual activities. Let us look at these three situations.

BUILDING BLOCK 13.6

Is This Immorality?

A tenured teacher tampered with the test results of the students in her class to raise the scores so they exceeded state goals. When this was discovered, she was dismissed (*Hanes v. Board of Education of City of Bridgeport*, 2001).

- On what grounds was she fired?
- What are this teacher's legal options?
- What are the principal's legal options?

Unprofessional Conduct

Unprofessional conduct is normally considered a breach of morality. Examples of unprofessional conduct include suggesting answers to standardized test questions, plagiarism, swearing at students in class, dressing inappropriately, and writing inappropriate e-mail. For example, the court upheld dismissal for immorality of a teacher who, after having been denied permission to attend a conference, did so anyway, and claimed upon her return that she had been absent due to illness (*Bethel Park School District v. Drall*, 1982).

Criminal Activity

felony A serious crime, usually involving violence, that is punishable by imprisonment.

misdemeanor A less serious crime than a felony, punishable by a fine and a possible jail term.

The courts view commission of a felony (a serious crime such as armed robbery or possession of drugs for resale) or even an arrest and being charged with a felony or a misdemeanor (a lesser crime such as public intoxication or shoplifting) as just cause for dismissal on grounds of immorality. Teacher dismissal cases can be based on charges of criminal activity and even circumstances in which the teacher is not formally charged; a school district does not have to wait for a conviction to initiate proceedings. For example, the court upheld a dismissal based on allegations that a teacher stole a teapot used as a prop in a school play, took 20 dollars from a basketball game's receipts, and stole a set of the school's books (Kimble v. Wroth County R-III Board of Education, 1984).

Sexual Activity

Although court decisions have been inconsistent, there has been a trend toward providing teachers more freedom in their private lives than has been the case historically. Community mores regarding morality vary, however; for example, activities that are acceptable in a metropolitan area may be viewed as immoral in a smaller, more rural area. Immorality decisions from the courts rely on individual case circumstances.

When examining reasons for dismissal involving sexual activity not related to students, courts try to determine whether the behavior has impaired the teacher's fitness to teach and whether the action was public or private. For example, the court ruled in favor of a teacher who had been dismissed for allowing male nonrelatives to stay overnight in her apartment (*Sullivan v. Meade Independent School Dist. No. 101*, 1976). A different ruling was handed down when a teacher's lifetime certificate was revoked after a plea bargain led to her conviction on charges of "outraging public decency" (committing an act so bad that the public's sense of decency is outraged); an undercover police officer had arrested the teacher at a private nightclub after watching her commit three separate sexual acts, a violation of the state's penal code. The court ruled that her behavior "certainly reflected a total lack of concern for privacy, decorum, or preservation of her dignity and reputation" (*Pettit v. State Board of Education*, 1973).

Decisions regarding dismissal for homosexual activity have increasingly centered on whether the acts in question were public or private. As gay rights have become more recognized, court rulings over teacher dismissal cases based on homosexual behavior have become less restrictive. The courts have ruled that homosexual people "are entitled to at least the same protection as any other identifiable group which is subject to disparate treatment by the state" (*Glover v. Williamsburg Local School District Board of Education*, 1998).

Sexual Activity Involving Students

The courts have been consistent in insisting that teachers be above reproach in their dealings with students. Not only do the courts generally uphold dismissals for sexual activities involving students, they also uphold publication of the dismissals and place no time constraints on when the impropriety occurred. The following rulings against teachers dismissed for sexual misconduct involving students illustrate the courts' strong position in this area:

- A female gym teacher in Ohio was convicted of having sex with at least five male students, some of them football players. Her plea of insanity did not hold up in court, and she was sentenced to four years in prison (*USA Today*, 2011).

- In 1998, a female elementary school teacher was convicted and sentenced to seven years in prison for the rape of one of her male students, with whom she began a relationship when he was in the sixth grade. Her initial sentence was suspended and she was placed on probation. She violated the probation, however, when she had contact with the student, and she went to jail to serve out her sentence. The teacher gave birth to the student's child while in prison for violation of the probation. She and her former student later married and had two children. She became a grandmother when her son from a previous marriage became a father. Her son is only one year younger than her husband, her former student (Jabali-Nash, 2011).

- In February 2012, a 61-year-old Los Angeles County elementary school teacher pled "not guilty" to charges that he took around 600 photographs of 23 young students in poses involving sexual situations and bondage (Duke, 2012).

- A male teacher at a Seventh-Day Adventist school in California was arrested and accused of the sexual molestation of a 15-year-old female student in June 2011. The teacher allegedly picked the student up at her house and then drove her to a nearby parking lot where the violations took place (Todorov, 2011).

You have seen that many actions fall under the category of *immorality* and that the major tests are whether the act will compromise the teacher's ability to complete his or her duties in an exemplary fashion and whether the act occurred privately or publically. Let us look at one more case.

BUILDING BLOCK
13.7

Is This Another Case of Immorality?

Mrs. Jackson, the cheerleader advisor, and Mr. Hughes, the football coach, were spotted one Saturday morning coming out of a motel room together in a town 35 miles from where they teach. The principal, who saw them on his way to visit a relative, confronted them. They admitted they had been having an affair for several months. The principal asked the board to dismiss Mrs. Jackson and Mr. Hughes, and to request revocation of their teaching certificates.

- On what basis do you believe the principal is seeking the teachers' dismissals? Why do you think so?
- Do you think a court would uphold the dismissal? Why or why not?
- Should the state revoke their teaching certificates? Why or why not?

Teacher Rights

We have been discussing reasons for the dismissal of teachers, especially tenured teachers. You need to know these factors so you won't fall unknowingly into a trap that might jeopardize your career. However, there is good news as well: Teachers have rights. Teachers enjoy the same constitutional rights that are afforded all citizens, such as the basic rights guaranteeing freedom of speech, freedom of the press, freedom to assemble, and due process. Teachers who have felt that their constitutional rights were violated can and have sued their board of education. Resulting court decisions have established a substantial body of common law, clarifying teachers' rights and responsibilities. You can access the National School Boards Association website, a great source of school law, through the direct link on the Education CourseMate website. Let us look at some of these rights in more detail.

common law Case law or precedent developed through decisions of courts.

Freedom of Speech and Expression

The First Amendment to the U.S. Constitution provides that the exercise of free speech cannot be restrained. The seminal case establishing teacher rights to freedom of expression involved a teacher's dismissal for having written a letter to a newspaper criticizing school officials' fund-raising practices. In this case, the Supreme Court ruled that, even though the letter contained inaccuracies, there was no evidence that the teacher inserted these inaccuracies knowingly or recklessly, so he could not be dismissed for exercising his right to speak on important public issues (*Pickering v. Board of Education,* 1968). Speech that is not protected and that can legally result in dismissal includes racial slurs made about or to students, vulgar remarks made to a school principal, and abusive language that consistently denounces school officials to teachers and other school employees.

freedom of expression The liberty to speak and otherwise express oneself and one's opinions, guaranteed by the First Amendment to the U.S. Constitution.

Freedom of Religion

BUILDING BLOCK
13.8

Celebrating the Teacher's Religion

Each day, Elaine wears a necklace with a cross on it. Her principal has asked her to stop wearing the cross to school. She has refused, saying that she has a right to wear the cross that her late father gave her.

- Do you think Elaine has a legal right to wear the cross?
- What legal arguments could she use?
- What are the principal's options?

Freedom of religion is a First Amendment right and includes all aspects of religious observance and practice. The Civil Rights Act of 1964 requires employers to make reasonable accommodations for an employee's religious practices and observances. For example, teachers must be allowed to use personal leave for religious purposes, such as observing a religious holiday. After teachers have used all available personal leave (normally two to three days a year), they must also be allowed to take additional days without pay for religious observances. However, the religious observance must be part of the teacher's religion, and the teacher may not claim simply any day as his or her Sabbath.

The issue of religious dress has attracted a great deal of litigation in recent decades. Decisions have varied in the different courts, but in the past there was a trend toward prohibiting teachers from wearing religious attire in the classroom. For example, the court ruled against a Sikh who sought to have her teaching certificate reinstated. It was revoked after she continually wore white clothes and a white turban to teach her sixth- and eighth-grade classes (*Cooper v. Eugene School District No. 41*, 1987). Another court ruled against a Muslim woman who sought to dress in traditional attire that covered her entire body except for her hands and face (*United States v. Board of Education for the School District of Philadelphia*, 1990). However, in 2010, legislation was passed in Oregon that repealed a 1923 law that prohibited teachers from wearing religious garb in the public schools (*Democrat Herald*, 2010). And the Pennsylvania legislature began action in 2011 to repeal a similar 1895 law that prohibited teachers from wearing any kind of religious insignia on jewelry or clothing (Andren, 2011).

Another aspect of religious freedom deals with participation in activities. For example, teachers may refuse to participate in the Pledge of Allegiance, even when reciting the pledge is a routine part of the school day, but they may not refuse to comply with curriculum requirements on the basis that such requirements violate personal religious beliefs. Teachers cannot use the classroom to disseminate their religious beliefs.

The courts have been careful to protect teachers' religious rights. At the same time, they have recognized a compelling state interest in educating children in an atmosphere that does not promote religion. The limitation of teacher religious freedom was clearly stated in *Palmer,* in which the justices wrote that education ". . . cannot be left to individual teachers to teach the way they please" and that teachers have ". . . no constitutional right to require others to submit to their views and to forego a portion of their education they would otherwise be entitled to enjoy" (*Palmer v. Board of Education of the City of Chicago*, 1980).

Right to Privacy

As you saw earlier, the courts have upheld the idea that teachers are exemplars. At the same time, however, teachers enjoy the right to privacy in their personal lives. Yet those rights end when a teacher's behavior adversely affects the teaching and learning process. If a teacher's private acts do not negatively affect his teaching, courts have ruled that they are not subject to employer scrutiny (*Erb v. Iowa State Board of Public Instruction*, 1974). When the courts view issues of teacher privacy, they seek to determine whether the conduct directly impairs the teacher's performance in the school and whether the conduct is the subject of such notoriety that it significantly limits the teacher's ability to meet his or her responsibilities.

A modern concern involving the right to privacy is e-mail. Nearly all teachers have e-mail available at their school. E-mail facilitates communication with parents and with others in the school system. Although many school systems do not prohibit teachers from using school e-mail for private communication, teachers should be aware that a school e-mail account is *not* private. Indeed, most school systems monitor e-mail, and inappropriate communication by teachers may result in disciplinary action.

Search and Seizure

The Fourth Amendment to the U.S. Constitution guarantees freedom from unreasonable search and seizure. As drug use has become more common in our society, some teachers have been faced with random testing for drugs and alcohol. Such tests are a form of

freedom of religion The right to choose a religion (or no religion) without interference by the government, guaranteed by the First Amendment to the U.S. Constitution.

search and seizure Examination of a person's premises by law enforcement officers looking for evidence of the commission of a crime, and taking articles of evidence (seizure and removal).

plagiarism Representing the writings, literary concepts (a plot, characters, words), or other original work of another as one's own product.

copyright The exclusive right of the author or creator of a literary or artistic property (such as a book, movie, or musical composition) to print, copy, sell, license, distribute, transform to another medium, translate, record, perform, or otherwise use (or not use) their work, and to give it to another by will.

Fair use provision of the copyright act The use of copyrighted materials determined to be fair and not an infringement of the copyright act based on four factors: (1) whether the use is commercial in nature or for nonprofit educational purposes; (2) the nature of the copyrighted work; (3) the portion used in relation to the copyrighted work as a whole; and (4) the effect of the use on the potential market value of the copyrighted work.

As a student, you know it is illegal to plagiarize others' work. Plagiarism involves taking the ideas of others and representing them as your own, without giving the proper credit. You have probably written a few papers in which you had to compile resources, synthesize ideas, and cite references. Giving authors credit for their ideas and writing is expected; not to do so is plagiarism. Schools have policies that contain stiff consequences for students caught plagiarizing.

Plagiarism used to consist of copying directly from books, encyclopedias, and other people's work, but now it includes copying directly from the Internet. Not only does the Internet contain a wealth of material, but many websites, called *essay mills* (or *paper mills*), offer essays, research papers, and the like for purchase. These essays have been previously written and are alleged to have received good grades. Some essay mills are careful to say that the materials they provide are for research only, but that does not mean that students will use the materials in this way.

According to research conducted by the Center for Academic Integrity between 2006 and 2010, 40 percent of students surveyed admitted to plagiarizing at least a couple of sentences for their assignments (Gabriel, 2010). However, 77 percent of the students surveyed did not think that plagiarism from Internet sources was a serious concern. *USA Today* (Terbush, 2012) reports that in a survey of 43,000 high school students conducted in 2011, more than half of the students admitted to cheating on a test during the preceding year, one-third admitted to cheating more than twice, and 33 percent admitted to using the Internet for plagiarizing assignments.

Instructors can use online services to help them find instances of plagiarism. These services compare student work with millions of the most frequently cited resources and can search the Internet rapidly for additional sources. The results of the comparison indicate the likelihood of plagiarism.

A great deal of material on the Internet is protected by copyright. Copyright means that the originator of the material—words, pictures, music, and so on—maintains the right to decide who can copy and distribute the material. Not only does using copyrighted material without proper attribution constitute plagiarism, it is also a copyright violation. A lot of Internet material is available to teachers without copyright protection; indeed, many copyright holders specifically waive protection to make their material freely available to teachers. But teachers must be careful about using Internet materials. Can you tell why?

Students and teachers alike must comply with the Fair Use Provision of the Copyright Act of the United States. According to the provision, copyrighted material used for "purposes of criticism, comment, news reporting, teaching (including multiple copies for classroom use), scholarship, or research is not an infringement of copyright" (U.S.

Copyright Office, 2009), but all other uses violate copyright laws. If you are not sure whether you are using copyrighted material fairly, the Fair Use Provision of the Copyright Act advises you to consider the following:

- The purpose and character of the use, including whether such use is of a commercial nature or is for nonprofit educational purposes
- The nature of the copyrighted work
- The amount and substantiality of the portion used in relation to the copyrighted work as a whole
- The effect of the use upon the potential market for or value of the copyrighted work

When in doubt, always provide a citation and obtain permission. Penalties for copyright infractions can be up to $150,000, even if you did not know you were violating the copyright.

Cheating in general is also on the rise. In a survey of 40,000 high school students conducted by the Josephson Institute of Ethics (2011), 59 percent admitted to cheating on an exam at some point during the preceding year and 34 percent cheated more than twice. And according to a 2011 *ABC Nightline* piece, nearly 70 percent of college students have admitted to cheating (ABC Nightline, 2010). This increase in cheating has been aided by the ever-growing capabilities of the Internet, especially custom paper writing. All you have to do is fill out an Internet form telling the company exactly what you want written and when, and they will write the paper for you. Oh, and you need money—lots of money. These papers cost between $14.00 and $60.00 per page (250 words) depending on the level of sophistication and urgency. Because they are custom-written, it is more difficult for a professor to detect the cheating, but it is not impossible. No matter what directions you provide, the writing style will not be your own.

Besides, remember that teachers are held to higher standards because of their influence on children. Do you think custom-written papers represent high standards?

Here is a paragraph taken from the *Chronicle of Higher Education*, written by one of the ghostwriters who writes papers for pay:

I, who have no name, no opinions, and no style, have written so many papers at this point, including legal briefs, military-strategy assessments, poems, lab reports, and, yes, even papers on academic integrity, that it's hard to determine which course of study is most infested with cheating. But, I'd say education is the worst. I've written papers for students in elementary-education programs, special-education majors, and ESL-training courses. I've written lesson plans for aspiring high school teachers, and I've synthesized reports from notes that customers have taken during classroom observations. I've written essays for those studying to become school administrators, and I've completed theses for those on course to become principals. In the enormous conspiracy that is student cheating, the frontline intelligence community is infiltrated by double agents. (Future Educators of America, I know who you are.)

Remember that teachers are held to the highest standards. As you adhere to these high standards, be sure to require the same of your students. Be sure your students understand what plagiarism is and that information on the Internet is intellectual property belonging to other people. Students should also know that you are familiar with essay mill websites, plagiarism detection sites, ghostwriting sites, and other methods of cheating.

search and have been called suspicionless because there was no reason to suspect the affected teachers were guilty of drug use. To a certain extent, random drug testing of teachers is legal. The reasoning behind decisions that allow random drug tests was expressed by Sixth Circuit Court of Appeals: " . . . the suspicionless testing regime is justified by the unique role they play in the lives of school children and *in loco parentis* [meaning in the place of a parent] role imposed upon them" (*Knox County Education Association v. Knox County Board of Education,* 1998). The courts also have ruled that school systems may use drug-detecting dogs and that a teacher's refusal to take a drug test after suspicion has been established by a dog sniffing a teacher's car is a legal cause for termination (*Hearn v. Board of Education,* 1999).

in loco parentis "In place of parents."

Legal Liability

In today's litigious society, teachers live with the constant concern that they may be sued and held liable for substantial damages. In legal terms, teachers are liable for tortuous acts. Simply put, a tort is a wrongful act, other than a breach of contract, for which relief may be obtained in the form of damages. Torts include a variety of actionable or civil wrongs committed by one person against another, and can be committed either by overt actions or by failure to act. Thus a tort can be intentional or the result of negligence. When a tort action occurs, one person (the plaintiff) brings a suit against another (the defendant) to obtain damages. The plaintiff usually requests damages in the form of money.

The most common intentional tort is assault and battery. Assault is a threat to use force, which causes fear. Battery takes place when physical contact occurs. Assault and battery lawsuits against teachers are most common in states that still allow corporal punishment; such cases generally result from a teacher's use of excessive punishment. Numerous court cases involving teachers who used excessive punishment have resulted in substantial awards to plaintiffs, but a decline in such cases has accompanied the decline in the use of corporal punishment. Whether or not a state allows corporal punishment, teachers should use force *only* to defend themselves from physical harm, and then only to the degree necessary. Other intentional torts include such acts as libel, slander, defamation, false arrest, malicious prosecution, and invasion of privacy.

By far the most common tort actions against teachers are for negligence. Within the negligence category, most actions stem from inadequate supervision. Lawsuits commonly maintain that harm occurred to students because a teacher failed to give adequate supervision. In many instances, such lawsuits are based on the idea that an accident would not have happened if the teacher had practiced proper supervision. Teachers have been found liable for student injury based on inadequate supervision in a wide variety of cases.

Negligence is not always cut and dried. Definite elements and conditions determine whether a teacher is negligent. Generally, the teacher must exercise a standard of care that a "reasonable and prudent" person would exercise under similar circumstances. In all circumstances, the teacher is responsible. Students must be supervised at all times, including during the school day while they are outside the classroom, before school, and after school while they are on school property.

Examples where the courts found negligence include the following cases:

■ A lawsuit was filed against a gym teacher who supervised an activity in which a student broke several vertebrae in her back. Earlier that day, another student was injured

liable (legal liability) A legal responsibility, duty, or obligation; the state of one who is legally bound to do something that may be enforced by legal action.

tort A wrongful act, other than a breach of contract, for which relief may be obtained in the form of damages.

plaintiff The person, people, or entity who files the lawsuit.

defendant The person, people, or entity against whom a lawsuit is filed.

during the same activity, which the same gym teacher was supervising. A witness said the gym teacher did nothing to modify the activity after the first injury occurred (O'Brien, 2011).

- In Chicago, a mother filed suit against the public school system as well as the teacher who left her seventh-grade students alone in the classroom for an extended period of time. While unattended, a fight broke out in which the mother's son was pushed forcibly to the ground, resulting in a broken femur. The mother contends that the teacher was negligent and disregarded student safety when she left the students alone for so long (Donovan, 2010).

- The parents of an eighth-grader at a Christian school sued the school and the teacher who admitted that he told their son in front of the rest of the class that he would become a "bigger and fatter moron" than he already was. According to the parents, their son went on a diet that caused him to lose 15 pounds in one month and that compromised his health. They claimed that the boy also suffered emotional effects due to being humiliated (Anasari, 2010).

Although there are defenses against liability lawsuits and the defendant can sometimes negotiate a reduction in the degree of negligence, you should be aware that, as a teacher, you may be subject to lawsuits and held liable for large amounts of money. If you should be found liable, the award to the plaintiff could take all your assets. Even if you should be found not liable, the cost of legal representation is substantial, often running into tens of thousands of dollars. Professional teacher organizations and teacher unions provide legal representation and liability insurance as membership benefits. The cost of membership is a small price to pay compared to the cost of defending against a tort suit.

Students and the Law

Thus far, you have been investigating school law as it applies to teachers. But the law applies to students as well as teachers, and much of the law is intended to protect students. U.S. public schools operate under the concept of *in loco parentis* ("in the place of a parent"); teachers and school officials exercise responsibility for the students under their supervision. Furthermore, throughout much of U.S. history, schools publicized rules and disciplined students with the view that education was a privilege and students' rights could be routinely restricted. However, in 1969 the U.S. Supreme Court held, in the landmark *Tinker* case, that students do not shed their rights at the schoolhouse door (*Tinker v. Des Moines Independent Community School District*, 1969). The *Tinker* case made clear that educators must respect students' rights and can restrict those rights only if there are legitimate reasons.

Due Process

As citizens, students are entitled to substantive and procedural due process rights. Over the past five decades, thousands of court cases have dealt with issues of due process. The basic due process requirements for dealing with students have been derived from decisions of the U.S. Supreme Court. In particular, two cases laid the groundwork for students' due process safeguards. The *Gault* case overturned the six-year reform school sentence of a juvenile convicted of making obscene telephone calls (*In re Gault*, 1967) because the student had not been given due process rights. The court noted that no appeal had been provided, no written charges had been presented, and protection against self-incrimination had been denied. This view of students' due process rights was strengthened a few years later when a court considered the case of a student suspended for ten days after a disturbance in the school cafeteria. In that case, the court ruled that the right to attend school is a legitimate right and a suspended student, even when the suspension was ten days or less, must be given notice of charges, an explanation of the evidence, and a hearing providing an opportunity to tell his or her side of the story (*Goss v. Lopez*, 1975). The court outlined informal procedures for cases of short suspensions but noted that expulsions or suspensions of more than ten days could require the formal due process procedure.

It might seem that the legal requirements make it impossible for teachers to exercise discipline. However, most school systems today provide students and parents with written discipline policies; such policies usually include an outline of student rights and a list of infractions and their consequences. By disseminating a sound discipline policy, schools protect themselves and ensure student rights.

Pregnancy and Marriage

In Chapter 12, you saw that pregnant students may have limited opportunities to attend school or continue their education. However, the courts have unanimously ruled to invalidate school rules that prohibit married or pregnant students from attending school or that cause them to be treated differently from other students.

Following are general guidelines for educators concerning pregnant or married students and students with children:

1. The courts have invalidated rules prohibiting married or pregnant students from attending school.

2. Married or pregnant students have the same rights as other students.

3. Only when compelling evidence of disruption, interference with school activities, or negative influence on other students is present can the school restrict married or pregnant students' attendance or participation in activities.

4. Only the student's physician can determine when the student should withdraw from and return to school.

5. Homebound instruction must be offered to students who withdraw from school because of pregnancy.

Freedom of Speech and Expression

BUILDING BLOCK

13.9

Is This Libel?

In early 2002, the Olympic Torch Relay passed down the street in Juneau, Alaska, on which the high school was located. The principal had permitted the students and staff to observe the relay from both sides of the street; teachers had responsibility for student supervision during this school-sanctioned "outing." As the torchbearers passed in front of the school, a group of students unfurled a large banner that said "BONG HITS 4 JESUS." The principal immediately directed the students to take down the banner, but the student who brought it to school refused to do so. The principal confiscated the banner and suspended the student for ten days.

The student appealed his suspension to the district administration, but it was upheld. He then filed suit, claiming that the principal and the Board of Education had violated his First Amendment rights. The Ninth Circuit Court agreed, and the case went to the Supreme Court.

What ruling do you think the Supreme Court handed down?

The U. S. Supreme Court reversed the decision of the Ninth Circuit Court, saying that the First Amendment does not require schools to tolerate student expression that contributes to [the dangers of illegal drug use] at school events (*Morse v. Frederick*, 2007).

As you have seen, the First Amendment provides for freedom of speech. But constitutional rights do not mean that students can behave in any manner they choose. The school's compelling interest is to maintain a proper atmosphere for learning. Thus, students can be prohibited from expressing themselves in ways that disrupt or harm the learning atmosphere. At the same time, a student may not be deprived of speech and expression that is not disruptive or harmful.

Tinker, cited earlier in this chapter, made clear that students have the right to express themselves, but that this expression must be done in an orderly way. However, court rulings that were handed down years ago established that students who cause a disturbance with their words or actions on the part of supporting a cause could be suspended by the school (*Blackwell v. Issaquena Bd of Educ* 1966; *Bethel School Dist No. 403 v. Fraser*, 1986). The courts held that schools may legitimately establish standards of civil and mature conduct, and a school that tolerated "lewd, indecent, and offensive" speech would find it difficult to convey those standards. Likewise, schools may prohibit students' use of fighting words and threats that have a direct tendency to cause acts of violence, such as hurling racial epithets. Student newspapers, plays, and literature fall within the realm of free expression. At the same time, schools do have some control. The key to determining the legality of prohibiting a particular expression can be found in the *Tinker* ruling: "To justify a prohibition of a particular expression of opinion, school officials must be able to show that their action was caused by something more than a mere desire to avoid the discomfort and unpleasantness that always accompany an unpopular viewpoint. There must be facts that might reasonably lead school authorities to forecast substantial disruption of or material interference with school activities" (*Tinker v. Des Moines Independent Community School Dist* 1969).

The following guidelines are useful in determining whether students' right to free speech and expression apply:

■ When deciding to prohibit expression or punish expression, determine whether there is evidence of significant disruption or potential disruption, indecent speech, or disregard for authority. When punishment is involved, provide due process.

■ Materials may be banned if they are vulgar, mock others' race, origin, sex, or religion, or if they are counter to the mission of the school.

■ The time and place of distribution of all materials may be regulated.

■ Legally defensible guidelines should be formulated regarding a school newspaper.

■ Determine whether a newspaper is to be an open forum or a curriculum-based publication. Students have greater freedom of expression in an open forum.

■ Develop a specific procedure whereby newspaper submissions must be reviewed before publication. Provide an appeals process.

Dress and Appearance

Dress is generally viewed as a form of self-expression. As such, it is a First Amendment right, and schools must show a compelling reason such as health and safety issues why restrictions on dress are necessary. The courts generally strike down vague or arbitrary dress codes. The courts uphold dress codes that aim to protect safety or prevent disruption or distraction that interferes with learning.

Schools may regulate dress and appearance where health and safety issues are concerned. For example, schools may prohibit long hair and jewelry and mandate safety glasses in shop classes or laboratories. Schools may also ban clothing, jewelry, or hairstyles that indicate gang affiliation. Immodest or suggestive clothing may be banned, as may T-shirts containing sexually vulgar messages. Some public schools have instituted the requirement that students wear uniforms. Generally, the argument for uniforms centers on educational and disciplinary issues. The constitutionality of uniforms was upheld in a case in which the court wrote that a uniform policy is constitutional if it furthers an important government interest, if it is not intended to suppress student expression, and if it is no more restrictive than is necessary to facilitate the school's educational interest (*Canady v. Bossier Parish School Board*, 2002).

Students in public schools may be required to wear uniforms provided there are compelling reasons. What reasons might be considered compelling?

However, the Supreme Court concluded that random searches of people and belongings by school officials are unconstitutional and violate the students' Fourth Amendment rights because random searches invade their expectations of privacy (*Doe v. Little Rock School District*, 2004).

Numerous court cases have also dealt with male hair and beards, but no conclusions can be drawn; courts have both upheld and ruled against school regulations based on a variety of arguments from both plaintiffs and defendants.

Search and Seizure

The Fourth Amendment to the U.S. Constitution prohibits unreasonable searches and seizures. Although students enjoy rights under that amendment, school officials are less limited than police in search and seizure practices. School officials need neither a warrant nor probable cause to initiate a search. *Reasonable suspicion* is a valid reason for school officials to initiate a search.

As the need to eliminate weapons, drugs, and other banned items has intensified and methods of detection have become more varied, issues of search and seizure in the schools have become more complicated. The Supreme Court established a standard of reasonableness for searches in schools in a 1985 case in which a teacher caught two students smoking in the bathroom. She took both to the principal's office. One admitted smoking, and the other denied she had smoked. The principal sought evidence by examining the second student's purse, finding marijuana and evidence of drug dealing. The student's parents sued, contending that the search was illegal because the principal did not have a search warrant (*New Jersey v. T.L.O.*, 1985). This court case is important because it concluded that reasonableness of search has two elements:

- Whether circumstances justified the action at its inception
- Whether the scope of the search was reasonable in relation to the situation

A search can be justified if a school employee has reasonable grounds to believe that the search will provide evidence that a student has violated the law or school rules. The scope of the search should be reasonable in terms of the situation and the age and gender of the students. School officials may search students' purses, book bags, lockers, packages, and automobiles parked on school property if there is reasonable cause to believe that evidence of some violation may be found.

Students themselves may be searched, although there is a higher standard for reasonable suspicion as the search process becomes more invasive. Courts have occasionally upheld strip searches of students. Personal searches and, especially, strip searches should be undertaken only when there is urgency based on a reasonable suspicion that the student possesses a dangerous object or substance. In 2009, the Supreme Court found that a strip search of a 13-year-old girl suspected of bringing prescription-strength ibuprofen to school violated the child's rights (*Safford Unified School District v. April Redding*; reported by Liptak, in the *New York Times*, 2009).

A modern kind of search is drug testing. The courts upheld the right of one school to require urinalysis drug testing for athletes (*Veronia School District 47J v. Action*, 1995), and of another school to require the drug testing of all students who participate in any extracurricular activity (*Board of Education v. Earls*, 2002). However, the Supreme Court has said that random searches of people and belongings by school officials are unconstitutional and violate the students' Fourth Amendment rights because random searches invade their expectations of privacy (*Doe v. Little Rock School District*, 2004).

The courts have disagreed on the use of canines in searches. The issue focuses on whether specially trained dogs can establish reasonable suspicion for a search. Broadly speaking, courts have upheld the use of canines to establish a basis for a search when there was a reasonable belief that some illegal substance or object was present. They have similarly upheld the use of dogs to sniff lockers routinely when parents had been advised of the probability of routine locker searches. The courts have even upheld the use of dogs to sniff students when a reasonable belief existed that a particular student had drugs. The courts have not upheld mass searches by canines or searches for which there was no reasonable basis.

The following guidelines are useful for educators:

■ All searches must be based on a reasonable suspicion that a student has violated the law or school policy. A student who looks guilty is not sufficient reason for a search.

■ Schools may undertake routine searches of lockers and desks, especially when parents have been notified that this is normal procedure.

■ The more invasive the search, the closer it comes to a need for probable cause.

■ Personal searches should be done in private and only by school officials of the same gender as the student being searched. If clothing is removed, the student should remove it and should be provided with alternative garments while clothing is searched. If you are searching only pockets, have the student turn his or her pockets inside out.

Privacy of Records

Family Educational Rights and Privacy Act of 1974 (FERPA) Guarantees parents and students confidentiality and fundamental fairness concerning the maintenance and use of student records.

The Family Educational Rights and Privacy Act of 1974 (FERPA) applies to all schools receiving federal money. Commonly referred to as the Buckley Amendment, this act guarantees parents and students confidentiality and fundamental fairness concerning the maintenance and use of student records. It prohibits the release of information about students under 18 years of age without parental consent. At the same time, it provides certain rights to parents and guardians of minor children.

With regard to school records, parents or guardians may legally:

■ inspect their child's school records.

■ challenge accuracy of information.

■ have corrections made.

■ request a hearing to contest information they perceive as inaccurate.

■ place a statement of disagreement in student records.

■ determine what confidential information is released and to whom.

■ receive prior notice of records subpoenaed by the courts.

- file a complaint with the U.S. Department of Education concerning alleged violations.
- seek relief in civil court.

Students 18 years of age or older control their own records.

FERPA applies only to identifying information about individuals. It does not apply to test data, special population data, or other general data gathered by schools. The key to the legal release of data is whether individual students can be identified. Individual students have a right to privacy.

Records of individual students can be released to the following in addition to parents and guardians:

- Other school officials or teachers in the system who have a legitimate interest
- Authorized representatives of government, including state education department personnel
- State and local officials collecting information required by state statutes
- Accrediting organizations

Students' right to privacy of records means that teachers must exercise care in revealing information. Teachers should discuss individual student grades, discipline issues, and other matters only with those who have a legitimate reason to know. Schools should have a clear procedure for releasing information, including the requirement for a written request for release of information and specific procedures ensuring timely compliance with parent requests. Schools and teachers should not post grades in any way that makes it possible to identify individuals.

Corporal Punishment

As of 2008, 30 states have banned corporal punishment (infoplease.com, 2007). Many individual school districts in other states have banned corporal punishment. Figure 13.2

corporal punishment The infliction of physical pain on someone as punishment for committing an offense.

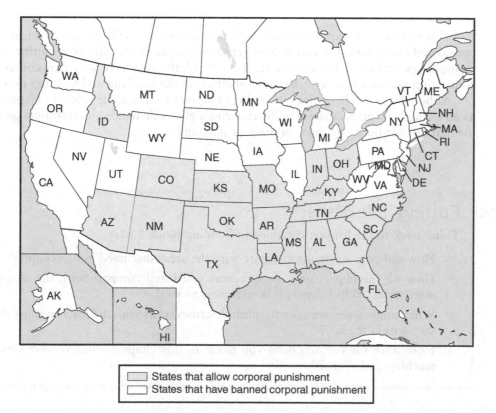

States that allow corporal punishment
States that have banned corporal punishment

◀ **Figure 13.2**
Status of state laws regarding corporal punishment as of 2008
Source: Infoplease.com, 2007
© Cengage Learning 2014

shows the current status of state laws and regulations regarding corporal punishment. Although the Supreme Court ruled a long time ago that corporal punishment of students is not constitutionally prohibited (*Ingraham v. Wright*, 1977), the trend in recent years has been to ban corporal punishment.

Where corporal punishment is not banned, school officials must be certain that due process is followed, that the punishment is not of excessive force, and that it is administered only by authorized individuals (usually the principal or other administrator). Most school boards require that a second adult be present as a witness during the administration of corporal punishment.

It is interesting to note that the United States and Australia are the only industrialized countries that still permit corporal punishment in schools. One hundred and sixteen countries, ranging from Afghanistan to Yemen and Zambia, prohibit corporal punishment in their schools, and 31 countries prohibit corporal punishment in the home (Center for Effective Discipline, 2010; Cleaver, 2011).

**BUILDING BLOCK
13.10**

What Are the Students' Rights?

The new principal at Mountain View High School has banned clothing with any kind of emblem or writing, including designer labels and corporate symbols. Parents have protested bitterly, and students have threatened a walkout.

- What are the students' legal rights?
- What are the principal's legal rights and obligations?
- Should the rule be reversed? On what basis?
- If the principal did not reverse the rule, do you think a court would uphold it? Why or why not?

Throughout your exploration of teachers and the law, you have seen that teachers are considered exemplars. The courts have repeatedly cited the legality of requiring teachers to model exemplary behaviors for students. Similarly, you have seen that courts seek a connection between teacher behavior and effect on the teaching and learning process.

Although the teacher enjoys the rights of a private citizen, the teacher's responsibility as an exemplar who is effective in the classroom places demands and restraints on behavior that are not borne by those in other professions.

**BUILDING BLOCK
13.11**

Putting it Together

Think back to the list you compiled in Building Block 13.1:

- How did your examples compare with the areas discussed in this chapter?
- How do the impact and consequences you listed compare with the chapter's discussions? Which legal areas were new to you?
- What single word would you think describes what you, the teacher, must do to stay within the law?
- How have the constructions you made in this chapter affected your view of teaching and schools?

■ SUMMARY

Laws and regulations that are relevant to education include those that affect the governing of schools, and the rights and responsibilities of teachers, other school personnel, and students.

- There are three basic types of laws in the United States: constitutional law based on the federal or state constitutions, statutes passed by legislatures, and case law resulting from decisions made by the courts. Rules and regulations promote adherence to the laws.

- Teachers need to know basic laws pertaining to schools so they can follow them. The laws teachers are primarily concerned with relative to themselves deal with certification, employment, tenure, and dismissal. Teachers have the same rights as any other citizen. But the exercise of these rights is tempered so as not to interfere with the education of children.

- Students are protected by laws such as due process, educational rights for mothers and pregnant women, freedom of speech and expression, and privacy of records. Laws pertaining to dress and appearance, search and seizure, and the use of corporal punishment are enforced to minimize disruptions in the teaching/learning process.

■ Key Terms and Concepts

Case law, 342
Code of ethics, 344
Common law, 352
Constitutional law, 342
Contract, 345
Copyright, 354
Corporal punishment, 361
Defendant, 355
Due process, 347

Fair Use Provision of the Copyright Act, 354
Family Educational Rights and Privacy Act of 1974 (FERPA), 360
Felony, 350
Freedom of expression, 352
Freedom of religion, 353
In loco parentis, 355
Insubordination, 349

Liable, 355
Misdemeanor, 350
Plagiarism, 354
Plaintiff, 355
Regulation, 342
Search and seizure, 353
Statute, 342
Title I, 342
Tort, 355

■ Construct and Apply

1. In view of everything you have explored in this chapter, who do you believe really controls schools in the United States? Do parents, through their elected board of education, determine what is taught and how? Does the local board of education? Does the state board of education? The state legislature? The federal government? What influence does the court system have on local schools? Think about the schools in your neighborhood and try to decide who determines what is taught and how. What examples can you think of to support your point?

2. From your inquiries in this chapter, it should be clear that teachers cannot be too circumspect in their behavior where students are concerned. The newspapers have provided ample coverage of situations in which teachers were accused of improper behavior with students. When a teacher was found to be innocent, what had been a front-page story became a fifth- or eighth-page paragraph. What basic principles or rules will you observe to ensure that you will not be accused of improper behavior with students?

3. Based on your explorations in this chapter, do you believe you will have to make any concessions to teach? Even if you don't perceive that you will have to make concessions, how will the role of teacher affect you in terms of such things as attire, personal lifestyle, and so on? What specific things can you think of that you will do to ensure that you serve as an exemplar?

■ Deconstructing the Standards

1. Recall the InTASC Standard associated with the objectives for this chapter.

   InTASC Standard #9 reads, "The teacher engages in ongoing professional learning and uses evidence to continually evaluate his/her practice, particularly the effects of his/her choices and actions on others (learners, families, other professionals, and the community), and adapts practice to meet the needs of each learner."

   a. Which part(s) of this standard does this chapter address?

   b. How will the concepts in this chapter help you apply this standard as a teacher?

2. Use your favorite search engine to find your state's standards for certification. When you find it, bookmark the site; you will refer to it often during this course.

   a. How are your conclusions about legal and ethical issues represented in your state certification standards?

   b. How do the InTASC standards compare to your state's certification standards regarding legal and ethical issues?

   c. Do you believe the degree of representation concerning legal and ethical issues is adequate in your state certification standards? Why or why not?

■ Your Portfolio

Develop a *personal* code of ethics to guide your behavior as a teacher. Include this in your portfolio.

■ Education CourseMate Resources

Check out this text's Education CourseMate website (at www.cengagebrain.com) for more information about the governing and financing of education in the United States. You will find the Teach-Source Videos, a guide for doing field experiences, glossary flash cards, activities, tutorial quizzes, direct links to the websites mentioned in the chapter, and more.

Note on Reading Legal Citations

This chapter cites many legal cases. A legal citation follows a standard format that lets you find cases, statutes, regulations, and law review articles. We cite two parts of each case in this chapter: the name of the case and the year in which the case was decided. In the case name, the plaintiff's name (name of the person bringing the case to course) appears first, and the defendant's name (the person or entity defending the plaintiff's charges) appears last. The year is the year in which the case was decided.

14 Education Reform: Standards and Accountability

IN THIS TEXT, you have investigated many topics related to education, schools, and teaching. You began each inquiry with an exploration of your thoughts, feelings, and what you already knew about the topic. After some further investigation, you formulated your ideas about the best way to handle that topic today.

In Part I, you identified characteristics of outstanding teachers and investigated the meanings and implications of major educational philosophies. In Part II, you listed teaching characteristics that support students' needs and teaching strategies that seem appropriate for students with a variety of perspectives and abilities.

In Part III, you wrote a hypothetical mission statement that described your hypothetical school. You explored the best ways to achieve successful and meaningful student–school interactions and you investigated the responsibilities teachers and schools have to one another.

In Part IV, you saw the impact of curricular and educational practices from a historical perspective and thought about the best ways to run a school. You also looked at the influence of society, social problems, and the law on school policies, procedures, and teaching.

In all these inquiries, you investigated the way things were, the way things are, and the way you believe things ought to be.

Changing education to make schooling what it ought to be is known as **education reform**. Education reform involves changing and refining the education system to meet the needs of the students and the society to which they belong. You are a member of society. What do you think is wrong with education today? What do you think should be changed? How do your views compare with those of others in society? These questions represent the topic of this chapter. You will investigate the general topic of education reform, the views of society as a whole, and areas in which steps are being taken to align education with current needs and views.

Chapter Objectives

As a result of your explorations in this chapter, you will be able to:

1. Describe the nature of education reform.
   InTASC Standard #9: Professional Learning and Ethical Practice

2. Summarize standards and curriculum reform movements in the core content areas of social studies, science, mathematics, and language arts, and apply conclusions to other areas such as foreign language, art, music, and physical education.
   InTASC Standard #4: Content Knowledge

3. Consider the implications of curriculum and standard reform on instruction and assessment.
   InTASC Standards #5: Application of Content; and #6: Assessment

4. Identify reform directions in teacher education.
   InTASC Standard #9: Professional Learning and Ethical Practice

What Is Education Reform?

You already have investigated numerous topics in this textbook that deal with education reform. To get an idea of what is involved in reform, look at Building Block 14.1.

BUILDING BLOCK 14.1

Education Reform Topics

Think about some of the investigations you have made and the conclusions you have reached using this textbook. Look at the following questions in light of what you have investigated so far:

- What curriculum do students study today that is appropriate and necessary for success in today's society?

- What instructional activities do teachers use to help students learn the content and skills they will need as outlined in the curriculum?

- What assessment opportunities do teachers provide that enable students to demonstrate this knowledge and these skills?

- To what degree should teachers be accountable for their students' classroom achievement and performance on assessments?

- What teacher induction elements prepare teachers to enter the workforce and provide their students with the most effective opportunities?

education reform Changing and refining the education system to meet the needs of the students and the society to which they belong.

In Building Block 14.1, you previewed the main topics of education reform. In its broadest sense, education reform consists of examining all aspects of education—curriculum, instruction, and assessment; teacher preparation; school buildings; scheduling the school day and year; and methods of governance and finance—and modifying all these to keep up with changing times. For some people, however, change is frightening, and they tend to want to hold onto their old ideas. Their schooling worked fine for them, so why should today's students need something different? Besides, educational change often reflects a change in educational goals and philosophies, and as you saw earlier, people tend to hold firmly to their philosophies and goals for schools.

Courtesy of Bill Lisenby

People have been talking about education reform since the first American schools opened. Recall from Chapter 10 that Benjamin Franklin's Academy added vocational education to classical and religious studies because of the growing needs of the country. Later, additional subjects were made available to reflect changing national priorities. In the late 19th and early 20th centuries, the National Education Association sponsored several committees to standardize the curriculum. Those committees made several decisions that still guide education today, such as:

Education reforms, including curriculum, instruction, and assessment innovation aim to improve all aspects of teaching to best promote student learning. How did education reform measures affect your education?

- High school graduation requirements
- Elementary education curriculum
- The Carnegie unit of credit
- Daily and yearly schedules of K–12 schools
- The separation of schools into elementary, junior high, and secondary schools

In the past 30 or so years, attention to education has intensified. In 1983, *A Nation at Risk* pointed to a decline in U.S. education excellence (see Chapters 2 and 10). Test scores were falling, and colleges and employers complained that high school graduates were inadequate in reading, writing, and calculating (see Chapter 2). The GOALS 2000 conference of 1989 and the resulting federal legislation passed in 1994 addressed these concerns by enumerating goals that all U.S. schools should strive to meet (see Chapters 6 and 10).

There are so many items on the school reform agenda that it is difficult to categorize them. However, in this chapter, we will look at the basic areas you saw in Building Block 14.1:

- Curriculum and instruction
- Assessment
- Teacher accountability
- Teacher preparation

Examination of these areas should provide a good overview of current reform efforts.

Curriculum and Instruction Reform

In school, students expect to obtain knowledge and skills that are meaningful and interesting. What they learn should help them achieve and succeed—not only as they progress in their education, but also in their chosen career and in life. They expect to be taught in ways that are effective and engaging so that they may achieve learning objectives. And they expect to be given the opportunity to demonstrate their learning in authentic ways.

The curriculum is the material taught in a school. Often it consists of a prescribed set of courses, with a scope and sequence for each. The scope of a course is the breadth and depth of the concepts covered, and the sequence is the order in which these concepts are introduced. The curriculum is usually prescribed by the state; individual school districts and schools normally interpret state-prescribed curricula.

BUILDING BLOCK 14.2

Meaningful Curriculum

John Dewey said, "Since there is no single set of abilities running throughout human nature, there is no single curriculum which all should undergo. Rather, the schools should teach everything that anyone is interested in learning."

- What does Dewey's statement imply about deciding what students should learn?
- How do you think curricular decisions are made?
- What do you remember learning in school? At the time, were you interested in learning these concepts and skills, as Dewey proposes?

You probably felt that some of the curriculum of the schools you attended was interesting, meaningful, and relevant, but some seemed meaningless, irrelevant to your life, and maybe even boring. It might have seemed that schools do not even care whether the curriculum suits their students. But this is not true. After all, a school establishes goals, purposes, and a mission to ensure it provides its students with the best possible education within its set of educational beliefs.

A great deal of work and input goes into developing curriculum. However, is the curriculum sufficiently flexible to respond to the needs of individual students? As you have seen, each student has a unique set of experiences and needs. The best teachers are those who meet students' needs by engaging them in meaningful and stimulating studies.

This means that you have to focus on instructional ways to make the prescribed curriculum interesting, meaningful, and relevant. Is this possible? Is it possible even to teach a topic described by the curriculum that students may not like in a way that makes it interesting and excites students about studying it?

BUILDING BLOCK 14.3

Hands-On Teaching

A middle-grades science teacher taught a lesson on weathering and erosion. The objective was for students to discover the effect of rainwater and rivers on mountains. She divided the class into groups of four or five students, gave each group a set of materials, and asked them to build a mountain in the plastic bin she provided using sand, sticks to represent trees, and pebbles to represent rocks. Using small sprinkling cans with holes of various sizes, the students poured water on the sand mountain to see what would happen. They did this activity several times, using a different approach each time. She then asked students for their observations and conclusions.

- What was the teacher's role in this lesson?
- What was the students' role?
- How was this lesson made interesting to the students? Meaningful? Relevant?
- What about this lesson engaged the students?

The activity you envisioned in Building Block 14.3 can be called a *hands-on* activity. The teacher selected the topic to be studied and encouraged students to branch out on their own to explore the topic in ways that were meaningful and relevant to them. Depending on students' age and degree of independence, they may receive different levels of guidance and support from the teacher. For example, students who can be thought of as independent learners (and who are in a well-managed classroom) may receive directions on how to set up the equipment and be told only to explore and observe. Other students who need more support may receive step-by-step instructions, with the teacher pausing and asking questions at appropriate times. The point is that the teacher considers students' individual needs and designs instruction to meet those needs. Instruction that is tailored to the different needs of individual students is often called differentiated instruction, a type of instruction you investigated earlier in this textbook. Lessons such as this are not only "hands-on," but are also "minds-on." This is one of the keystones of education reform—to have students inquire and think for themselves—a far cry from the memorization systems of generations past.

We have asked countless college students in teacher preparation programs which lessons in their precollege school years were the most memorable. And we always hear the same answer: The lessons students remember are those in which they *did* something. They dissected a frog, wrote a song, acted in a play, went on a field trip, collected leaves, looked at the stars through a telescope, painted a mural, made a video, built a website, and so on. Student involvement is key to long-lasting memories. It is difficult to separate curriculum (what is taught) from instruction (how it is taught). In earlier chapters, you investigated both curriculum and teaching methodology. This section combines these areas so you can investigate the current thinking about both. As you will see, curriculum and instruction are intertwined: We focus on the four major subjects of social studies, science, mathematics, and language arts, although standards have also been developed for all the other subjects (such as foreign language, art, music, physical education, and computer technology). Use the thinking you develop in this section to examine the other subject areas.

A major curriculum reform movement involves standards. In response to the concerns cited in *A Nation at Risk* and GOALS 2000, the federal government helped finance the development of nationwide standards for each subject taught in school. The standards are subject-specific and detail what students should know and be able to do as a result of studying that subject. Standards also suggest the most effective methods of teaching students to achieve those ends. They are guides to curriculum and instruction, and they present concepts and skills against which to measure achievement.

Individual states use these standards to develop their own statewide curriculum, which then becomes the official curriculum of the state. To provide consistency, standardized tests, based on the standards, assess student achievement in each state. The results of these tests provide data for judgments about achievement and program effectiveness. This thrust in education reform has become known as the standards movement.

standards movement An educational reform movement in which exemplary performances in specific areas of education are identified, especially in curriculum, instruction, and teacher preparation.

Common Core State Standards

In early 2009, the National Governors Association (comprised of the governors of each state) and the Council of Chief State School Officers (comprised of the state superintendents of education of each state) formed committees to work on standards in grades K–12 for English language arts; mathematics; and literacy in history, social studies, science, and technical subjects. The goal was to write a set of standards that each state would embrace. There were two different types of committees: a working group that developed the standards and their rationales, and a feedback group that solicited feedback from teachers and other educators and revised the standards based on this feedback. Committee members came from all areas of education: educational consultants, researchers, testing services, program developers, university faculty, and more. Public school teachers were heavily involved in the feedback phase.

View the TeachSource video, "Common Core Standards: A New Lesson Plan for America." A new approach would put kindergarten through twelfth-graders on the same track in math and reading across the country. National standards would increase consistency and accountability, and textbooks and testing would be more standardized.

After you view the video, answer the following questions:

1. What are some advantages of the Common Core State Standards?

2. What is the difference between the goals of the Common Core State Standards as presented by the National Governors Association and the goals of these standards as told in the video?

3. Do you agree with the "Nation's Lesson Plan" as described in the video? Why or why not?

Common Core State Standards The standards are designed to be robust and relevant to the real world, reflecting knowledge and skills that our young people need for success in college and careers" (Common Core State Standards Initiative, 2010).

After development, feedback, and revision, the final product—called the Common Core State Standards—was released in June 2010.

The Common Core State Standards intend to:

Provide a consistent, clear understanding of what students are expected to learn, so teachers and parents know what they need to do to help them. The standards are designed to be robust and relevant to the real world, reflecting knowledge and skills that our young people need for success in college and careers. With American students fully prepared for the future, our communities will be best positioned to compete successfully in the global economy. (Common Core State Standards Initiative, 2011)

The intent is for states to adopt the standards and merge them with state standards to produce a set of standards that are relevant to each state and that also includes a core of standards of excellence that are uniform for all states throughout the country. As of 2012, 45 states and the District of Columbia adopted these standards as the core of their curriculum (not surprising because the governors and state superintendents of education themselves oversaw their development and showed their commitment to them). States that have not yet adopted the common core standards as of this writing are Alaska, Minnesota (which adopted the English language arts standards only), Nebraska, Texas, and Virginia (see Figure 14.1).

The standards are based on research and evidence and reflect the high quality of education that young people in the United States need to compete in today's global economy. The standards address the question of what it will take for every U.S. child to be successful, and the standards answer that fewer, clearer, and higher standards will help us get there. In a sense, the Common Core State Standards represent the most recent effort in the current standards-based education movement, an effort that attempts to provide standards that are applicable to all states.

You have doubtless recognized that this chapter focuses on three sets of standards. Let us clarify. There is only one set of standards that direct the education in any given state,

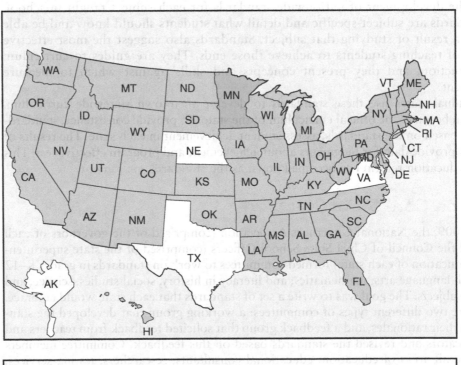

Figure 14.1 ▶
Common Core State Standards adopted by state.
Source: From Association for Supervision and Curriculum Development, http://www.ascd.org/common-core/common-core-standards.aspx.

☐ Have adopted the Common Core State Standards
☐ Adopted only the Common Core State Standards for English language arts

CONTROVERSIES in Education

The Common Core State Standards

There is some concern that the Common Core State Standards may come to be perceived as a "national curriculum," and that a national curriculum could work in opposition to individualized programs designed to meet the needs of students, their schools, and their communities. Many people believe that students throughout the nation should study the same curriculum so that everyone has a common knowledge base and parents can relocate to another state or school district without their children having to adapt to a new curriculum. However, many others believe that, to be meaningful, the curriculum must be tailored to reflect individual, school, and community needs and characteristics. For instance, the curriculum in Scranton, Pennsylvania, would differ from the curriculum in Santa Fe, New Mexico, because the students in each of these two communities have different needs and interests. (Recall your exploration of how the location of a school influences its curriculum in Chapter 6.)

Currently, every state has its own set of academic standards; this means that students in each state potentially are taught different concepts at different levels. However, proponents of common standards observe that *all* students must be prepared to compete not only with people from other countries around the world, but also with peers in other states. The Common Core State Standards will help prepare students with the knowledge and skills they need to succeed in such competition. Accordingly, the Common Core State Standards do *not* represent a national curriculum, but rather a uniform foundation on which the individual curricula of each state can be built.

Proponents say that the standards can foster competence and also provide the basis for measuring it; standards can facilitate learning and show students that their teachers believe they can meet expectations.

There are concerns with a common core curriculum:

- The assessment of the achievement of standards is often reduced to objective measures on tests such as multiple-choice questions.

- Standards can be applied in ways that shut down rather than foster learning, where the goal is to master the standard instead of broadening one's learning to the greatest possible extent.

- Standards may foster teachers' expectations to align their teaching with the standards rather than practice what fosters the greatest learning for each individual student (Rose, 2009/2010).

- Some people suggest that standards are more applicable to some students than to others.

Additionally, there is increasing concern that the standards will not have any significant effect on student achievement (Tienken, 2011a). Adoption of the standards and merging them with state standards will represent a great deal of change and will require a great deal of work (Porter, McMaken, Hwang, and Yang, 2011). But as Rose (2009/2010) says, "When standards are employed fairly, they can facilitate learning and show students that their teachers believe they can meet academic expectations" (p. 26).

WHAT DO YOU THINK?

1. *What are some of the primary advantages of having a common core of standards?*
2. *What are some of the primary disadvantages of having a common core of standards?*
3. *What is the difference between the goal of the common core standards as presented by the National Governors Association and the goal of these standards as told in the video?*
4. *Do you agree with the "Nation's Lesson Plan" as described in the video? Why or why not?*

You can access the Common Core State Standards so you can read them or download them through a direct link on the Education CourseMate website.

---

and that is the set of standards developed by the state for pupils going to school in that state. The Common Core State Standards provide guidance relative to topics to be covered and methods of instruction. When states adopt a common core curriculum, they are essentially agreeing to include these standards as the "backbone" of their state curriculum; such action makes it possible for all pupils in the United States to study essentially the same basic concepts in English language arts, mathematics, and literacy in history, social studies, science, and technology. The subject-specific standards also provide guidance to states as they develop their curriculum, but this guidance comes from experts in the subject-matter field. Once again, the state's curriculum is the one that is used to teach in that state.

Social Studies Curriculum

Social studies, which was introduced into U.S. schools to promote citizenship and civic competence, traditionally has focused on history, civics, geography, and economics.

Learning Social Studies

Think back to the social studies courses you have taken:

- List some of the topics you studied.
- What topics do you wish you had learned more about?
- Did you learn skills associated with social studies?
- What teaching methods helped you learn these social studies topics (and skills)?
- What method(s) of teaching social studies do you think was not helpful?
- Was your knowledge of these topics (and skills) useful to you later in life? Why or why not?
- Do you believe that the same topics (and skills) should be taught to students in today's social studies classrooms? Why or why not?

Chances are that you recall having had to learn names, dates, places, events, and other facts related to history, cultures, governments, civics, economics, geography, and social issues. Your study of these topics may have seemed isolated from other subjects and from your life, although topics taught in elementary school were probably less isolated from your life than those required in middle school and high school.

The aim of contemporary social studies education is "the promotion of civic competence—the knowledge, intellectual processes, and democratic dispositions required of students to be active and engaged participants in public life" (National Council for the Social Studies, n.d., p. 1). The discipline of social studies is viewed as more than a collection of facts to memorize. Today's social studies curriculum fosters understanding of how events came about and how people relate to one another, encouraging students to develop respect for different viewpoints and cultural beliefs. Today's social studies curriculum encompasses many disciplines and seeks reasons and connections rather than names, dates, and places.

In 2010, the National Council for the Social Studies (NCSS) released updated standards for social studies education in grades kindergarten through high school. The standards are not envisioned as a national curriculum, but rather as the core of state-developed curriculum where the content comes from the state requirements and the focus comes from the national social studies standards. The updated NCSS standards focus on the same ten integrated themes as the 1994 version of the standards but provide in-depth suggestions on the purpose of each, questions for exploration, what the students need to know and understand, what the student will be capable of doing, and how the students can demonstrate their understanding. The themes (called strands) are:

Teachers often post standards in their classrooms so that students know the objectives they are expected to achieve.

1. Culture
2. Time, continuity, and change
3. People, places, and environments
4. Individual development and identity
5. Individuals, groups, and institutions
6. Power, authority, and governance
7. Production, distribution, and consumption
8. Science, technology, and society
9. Global connections
10. Civic ideas and practices

The updated standards continue to urge teachers to employ teaching and learning strategies that require students to become active participants in the learning process, such as acquiring information and manipulating data; developing and presenting policies, debates, and stories; constructing new knowledge; and participating in groups. In Chapter 10, we have tried to present the history of education in a way similar to that suggested by the NCSS, complete with original writings for your interpretation. You can access the National Council of the Social Studies website through the direct link on the Education CourseMate website.

The National Council for the Social Studies outlined its vision for social studies teaching and learning in an influential position statement (NCSS, 2008) that says students must be able to use their prior knowledge and apply new learning as they think critically and solve problems creatively. To this end, social studies teaching and learning must be meaningful, integrated, value-based, challenging, and active. How is the teaching and learning different from memorizing names of important people and dates of important events?

There are concerns with the current social studies curriculum guidelines. The focus of the current curriculum is on solving problems rather than memorizing facts. How, critics wonder, will students learn factual information that everyone ought to know if they are not required to memorize these facts? In one study, the American Council of Trustees and Alumni surveyed seniors at top U.S. colleges and universities, as identified by the *U.S. New and World Reports* annual ranking of colleges, to assess the seniors' knowledge of high school–level U.S. history. The survey found the following:

- Only half of the students surveyed could identify George Washington as a U.S. general at the Battle of Yorktown.

- Only 42 percent could identify George Washington as "First in war, first in peace, first in the hearts of his countrymen."

- Less than one-quarter correctly identified James Madison as the "father of the Constitution."

- Only 28 percent could identify the phrase "Government of the people, by the people, for the people" as a line from the Gettysburg Address.

- Less than two-thirds could identify the U.S. Constitution as establishing the division of power in U.S. government.

- Little more than half (52 percent) knew that George Washington's farewell address warned against permanent alliances with foreign governments.

However, 99 percent of these students could identify Beavis and Butt-Head, and 98 percent were familiar with rap singer Snoop Dogg (Neal, Martin, and Moses, 2000, p. 2). You can access the American Council of Trustees and Alumni history survey report through the direct link available on this textbook's Education CourseMate website. The actual test referenced is shown at the end of the report, and correct responses and the percentage of students who chose each response are given.

The most contemporary assessment of students' knowledge of the social studies is the National Assessment of Educational Progress (NAEP), often referred to as the Nation's Report Card. Under the auspices of the federal Department of Education, students in grades 4, 8, and 12 are tested every four years on U.S. history and geography. The most recent test was given in 2010 to 7,000 fourth graders, 11,700 eighth graders, and 12,400 twelfth-graders nationwide. Twenty percent of fourth-graders, 17 percent of eighth-graders, and 12 percent of high school seniors demonstrated proficiency on the U.S. history test (National Center for Education Statistics, 2011a). On the geography test, 21 percent of fourth-graders, 27 percent of eighth-graders, and 20 percent of high school seniors demonstrated proficiency (National Center for Education Statistics, 2011b). Of particular interest was that only 2 percent of high school seniors correctly answered a question about *Brown v. Board of Education* (Dillon, 2011c).

Another concern about the contemporary social studies curriculum relates to textbooks. As you saw in Chapter 11, textbook publishers comply with the rules laid down by state boards of education and large school districts. Critics argue that social studies textbooks may leave out important information (such as omitting certain primitive aspects of Meso-American societies), distort historical data (such as portraying the controversial activities of the Chinese communist party and its leader, Mao Zedong, as a liberation movement), or interpret events in only one way, thereby denying students the opportunity to understand situations from multiple points of view (such as presenting only one perspective on Islam) (Thomas B. Fordham Institute, 2004). It is the responsibility of individual school districts to grapple with these contentious issues.

BUILDING BLOCK 14.5

Modern Social Studies Curriculum

Talk to an older (at least 10 years older) relative or friend about what he or she remembers about taking social studies in school:

- What courses did they take? How did they use technology, if at all? What strategies did the teacher use?
- Compare their answers with your own experience. What is different and what is the same? Is there anything that might be related to the standards reform you just read about?
- What else has recently impacted K–12 social studies education?

Students at San Lorenzo Middle School reenact the Civil War Battle of Bull Run. How does this learning activity reflect the standards of the National Council for the Social Studies?

Courtesy San Lorenzo Middle School

Science Curriculum

Science was introduced into U.S. schools as "natural history," whose purpose was to instill in students an appreciation for and an understanding of the natural world.

BUILDING BLOCK 14.6

Learning Science

Think back to the science courses you have taken:

- List some of the topics you studied.
- What topics do you wish you had learned more about?
- Did you learn skills associated with science?
- What teaching methods helped you learn these science topics (and skills)?
- What method(s) of teaching science do you think was not helpful?
- Was your knowledge of these topics (and skills) useful to you later in life? Why or why not?
- Do you believe that the same topics (and skills) should be taught to students in today's science classrooms? Why or why not?

After the launch of Sputnik, the appropriateness of the science curriculum began to be questioned. As you saw in Chapter 2, the scientific community urged that students should learn science in the same way scientists do science. This meant that science programs should focus on inquiry, exploration, problem solving, and higher-order thinking skills, rather than the memorization of facts.

In 1990, the American Association for the Advancement of Science responded to continuing concerns about the state of science education in the United States with Project 2061, named for the year when Halley's Comet will make its next pass near the earth. One product of Project 2061 was the publication of *Science for All Americans* (Rutherford and Ahlgren, 1990), which makes the following suggestions for teachers:

■ Treat science topics using an interdisciplinary approach.

■ Focus on systems and interrelationships among the disciplines, rather than isolated facts and concepts.

■ Proceed from the concrete to the abstract.

■ Start lessons with questions rather than answers.

■ Help students access information they have previously acquired.

■ Engage students in collecting evidence and answering questions.

The National Science Education Standards were published in 1996. These standards describe what students should know, understand, and be able to do as a result of their learning experiences in science. The standards call for inquiry-based science education programs, in which teachers facilitate learning rather than impart information, use multiple and authentic methods of assessment, provide learning environments conducive to inquiry learning, maintain high standards of intellectual rigor, and actively participate in the development and planning of their science programs.

The National Science Education Standards (NSES) outline eight categories of content for grades K to 4, 5 to 8, and 9 to 12 (National Research Council, 1996) as follows:

1. Unifying concepts and processes in science
2. Science as inquiry
3. Physical science
4. Life science
5. Earth and space science
6. Science and technology
7. Science in personal and social perspectives
8. History nature of science

These standards, together with Project 2061, were the driving force behind science education, yet we must recognize that a lot has changed since the NSES were developed. (Pluto is no longer a planet, cell phones and their relative technologies were not prevalent in 1996, and the field of biotechnology was nearly nonexistent.) The NSES were updated to focus on fewer content ideas and greater depth to provide students with the strong education needed to compete in college, the workplace, and the global economy (Achieve, Inc., 2012). The resulting Next Generation Science Standards (NGSS), as they are called, are meant for grades K–12, and are focused on both science content and processes. The states took a collaborative role in the development of the NGSS, basing them on the *Framework for K-12 Science Education*, which the National Research Council developed in 2011. This council is made up of scientists, science education researchers, cognitive scientists, and standards and policy experts, and the *Framework* identifies the science that all K–12 students should know. The revised standards were available at the end of 2012. You can access the National Science Education Standards and the Next Generation Science Standards through direct links available on the Education CourseMate website.

How well do current science education programs work? Remember GOALS 2000? Goal 5 states that, by the year 2000, U.S. students will be first in the world in math and science achievement. Standardized tests of mathematics and science achievement, named

Elementary students tend a class garden as part of their science curriculum. This activity promotes inquiry learning instead of rote memorization of facts.

Courtesy of Becky Stovall

the Third International Mathematics and Science Study (TIMSS), have been administered to students in grades 4, 8, and 12 in many countries since the mid-1990s. The test has been administered four times: in 1995, 1999, 2003, and 2007; a fifth administration was scheduled for 2011, but results were not available when this book was written.

Results of the science sections of the tests show that U.S. students in fourth grade consistently perform near the top, eighth-grade students consistently perform near the middle, and high school seniors perform near the bottom of international results. Some people have pointed out that interpreting these tests can present problems, citing the difficulties inherent in interpreting standardized tests for a worldwide population. Nonetheless, according to these results, the United States has fallen short of its goal that U.S. students be first in the world in math and science achievement. Table 14.1 shows the number of countries scoring above, near, and below the United States in both mathematics and science on the three international TIMSS tests.

TABLE 14.1 Number of countries scoring above, at, and below the United States on the TIMSS tests of science.

	Year (Number of Countries)	Number of Countries with Science Scores Significantly Higher than the United States	Number of Countries with Science Scores Not Significantly Different from the United States	Number of Countries with Science Scores Significantly Lower than the United States
Fourth-Grade Science	1995 (26 countries)	1	6	19
	1999 (not tested)			
	2003 (25 countries)	3	6	16
	2007 (36 countries)	4	7	25
Eighth-Grade Science	1995 (41 countries)	9	17	15
	1999 (38 countries)	14	6	18
	2003 (45 countries)	7	6	32
	2007 (48 countries)	9	4	35
High School Seniors: General Science	1995 (21 countries)	11	8	2
High School Advanced Mathematics and Science Students Taking Physics	1995 (16 countries)	14	2	0

Note: The term *significance* refers to statistical significance—the likelihood that the scores are true representations of students' knowledge and understandings.
Source: From the U.S. Department of Education, National Center for Education Statistics.

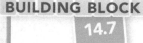

Modern Science Curriculum

Talk to an older (at least 10 years older) relative or friend about what he or she remembers about taking science in school:

- What courses did they take? How did they use technology, if at all? What strategies did the teacher use?

- Compare their answers with your own experience. What is different and what is the same? Is there anything that might be related to the standards reform you just read about?

- What else has recently impacted K–12 science education?

Mathematics Curriculum

As you recall from Chapter 10, mathematics (in the form of arithmetic) has been part of the curriculum of U.S. schools since colonial times. The goal of arithmetic was for students to be able to perform basic computations, a skill they needed to succeed.

Learning Mathematics

Think back to the mathematics courses you have taken:

- List some of the topics you studied.

- What topics do you wish you had learned more about?

- Did you learn skills associated with mathematics?

- What teaching methods helped you learn these math topics (and skills)?

- What method(s) of teaching mathematics do you think was not helpful?

- Was your knowledge of these topics (and skills) useful to you later in life? Why or why not?

- Do you believe that the same topics (and skills) should be taught to students in today's math classrooms? Why or why not?

Mathematics has always been considered one of the so-called "three Rs". People need quantitative skills to function as consumers, citizens, and employees in many professions. At the practical level, these skills allow us to balance a checkbook, estimate the cost of groceries, prepare a family budget, choose insurance, and the like. Similarly, people need to know how to use data and reason quantitatively to analyze problem situations, such as calculating the cost of gas for a trip, finding the amount of carpeting needed for a house, or doubling or halving a recipe. The extension of basic mathematical knowledge to rational numbers (fractions, decimals, and percentages) is also part of our daily life: think of baseball statistics, the lottery, election results, and public opinion polls.

The traditional method of mathematics instruction involved memorizing math facts using flash cards; drilling on computations by working countless pages of sums, differences, products, and quotients; going to the chalkboard to work out the answer to a problem; memorizing rules and procedures (for example, "When dividing fractions, invert the second fraction and multiply"); and working two-column proofs. Mathematics was taught in a very traditional way from the 1600s to the mid-20th century, when Sputnik spurred the call for drastic steps to improve both mathematics education and science education. As a result, the American Mathematical Society set up the School Mathematics Study Groups (SMSG), which was the most influential group in the development of the New Math

New Math A mathematics program in which students were taught the theoretical basis of mathematics through the use of actual mathematical language and notations.

curriculum. For much of the 1960s, this mathematics curriculum was used in classrooms at all levels. One impact of New Math was inclusion of calculus in high school. Common criticisms included that teachers weren't given professional development in teaching this new curriculum and that it included an overemphasis on formal mathematical language and algebraic notations before students were ready for this level of abstraction.

In keeping with the standards movement of the 1980s and 1990s, K–12 mathematics standards were developed. The National Council of Teachers of Mathematics (NCTM) led the standards movement with the publication of mathematics standards called *Curriculum and Evaluation Standards for School Mathematics* (National Council for Teachers of Mathematics, 1989). The most recent version is *Principles and Standards for School Mathematics* (NCTM, 2000), which describes "a future in which all students have access to rigorous, high-quality mathematics instruction" (NCTM, 2000). The ten standards include five content standards and five process standards. The content standards are

1. Number and operations
2. Algebra
3. Geometry
4. Measurement
5. Data analysis and probability

The five process standards are:

1. Problem solving
2. Reasoning and proof
3. Communication
4. Connections
5. Representation

You can access the National Council of Teachers of Mathematics math standards through a direct link on the Education CourseMate website.

This mathematics curriculum is interdisciplinary and seeks to help students understand how mathematics can help to explain scientific, social, and other natural phenomena. Contrary to the rejection of physical objects that characterized earlier math courses, today's mathematics urges the use of manipulatives so students can construct their own personal understandings. Examples of such manipulatives include geoboards, pattern blocks, counting blocks, and tangrams for lower grades, and relation shape forms, relational geometrical solids, Pythagorean theory manipulatives, and angle blocks for upper grades.

Of course, the most recent reform in mathematics standards is represented in the Common Core State Standards curriculum that you read about earlier. Is your state one that has adopted this new math curriculum? Find out and be sure to become familiar with your state's math standards.

BUILDING BLOCK

14.9

Modern Mathematics Curriculum

Talk to an older (at least 10 years older) relative or friend about what he or she remembers about taking mathematics in school:

- What courses did they take? How did they use technology, if at all? What strategies did the teacher use?
- Compare their answers with your own experience. What is different and what is the same? Is there anything that might be related to the standards reform you just read about?
- What else has recently impacted K–12 mathematics education?

Teaching the Standards
Billie Travis

In education, they say just stick around and you will see lots of changes—and everything will keep coming back around again and again. The biggest change for math occurred when NCTM adopted new standards in the early 1990s. This change was well received by many educators, and the standards and accompanying assessment tools have been widely accepted.

I teach middle school math. Math is a subject that lends itself to real-life application. It is easy to teach middle school students new math concepts by relating the new concept to their world. For example, one of my favorite units to teach is on using percentages. What better way to show students how to use percents than to have them practice using percents? I bring in menus, and we order our meal and add the tax and gratuity. This is such a simple idea but a great way for students to see the real application. They want to do more because they can see the application. When students want to do more, it is because they are excited or empowered by what they are learning. I encourage them to think of more ways to use the math they have just learned. Other examples of activities I use include sports, games, and shopping. Students can relate to all

these activities, and they can use the concepts and skills immediately outside the classroom. The students love it because they know why they are learning that particular concept or skill.

Then the ultimate happens: Students feel empowered because they know why. When the math standards and curriculum were aligned in the early 1990s, the math teacher's job was made easier. We know what to teach according the NCTM standards, so we have aligned our state and district curricula with the national standards and teach our concepts accordingly. That was the goal of NCTM. I do believe that these standards are powerful. And I enjoy teaching math because I can relate math to the students' worlds. Their worlds are then validated.

Billie Travis
2005 Kentucky Teacher of the Year
Georgetown Middle School
Georgetown, Kentucky

© Cengage Learning 2014

How do our students fare in mathematics when compared with students in other countries? (Remember that GOALS 2000 calls for U.S. students to be the best in the world in both science and mathematics.) As you can tell from Table 14.2, fourth graders performed near the middle in mathematics, and eighth graders also performed near the middle (although there was substantial improvement in the 2003 and 2007 tests). Clearly, the United States has a way to go to be first in the world in mathematics achievement.

TABLE 14.2 Number of countries scoring above, at, and below the United States on the TIMSS tests of mathematics.

	Year (Number of Countries)	Number of Countries with Mathematics Scores Significantly Higher than the United States	Number of Countries with Mathematics Scores Not Significantly Different from the United States	Number of Countries with Mathematics Scores Significantly Lower than the United states
Fourth-Grade Mathematics	1995 (16 countries)	4	6	16
	1999 (not tested)			
	2003 (25 countries)	11	1 (USA)	13
	2007 (36 countries)	8	5	23
Eighth-Grade Mathematics	1995 (20 countries)	2	5	13
	1999 (37 countries)	13	7	17
	2003 (35 countries)	9	11	25
	2007 (48 countries)	5	6	37

Note: The term *significance* refers to statistical significance—the likelihood that the scores are true representations of students' knowledge and understandings.
Source: Data from Office of Educational Research and Improvement, 1999 and 2001, and Gonzales et al., 2004 and 2008.

English Language Arts Curriculum

The language arts consist of the commonly used forms of communication, including reading, writing, listening, and speaking. Traditionally, language arts instruction in the early grades (pre-K, kindergarten, and early elementary grades) has focused on teaching children how to read, write, and convey meaning. In the later elementary grades, middle school, and high school, the focus was on developing meaningful and accurate communication, writing to learn, and reading to learn.

BUILDING BLOCK 14.10

Learning English Language Arts

Think back to the English language arts courses you have taken:

- List some of the topics you studied.
- What topics do you wish you had learned more about?
- Did you learn skills associated with English language arts?
- What teaching methods helped you learn these English language arts topics (and skills)?
- What method(s) of teaching English language arts do you think were not helpful?
- Was your knowledge of these topics (and skills) useful to you later in life? Why or why not?
- Do you believe that the same topics (and skills) should be taught to students in today's English language arts classrooms? Why or why not?

---

phonics A method for teaching reading and spelling that is based on interpreting the sounds of the letters.

whole language A constructivist approach to teaching reading and writing in which students learn from firsthand experiences.

Reading and writing are indispensable skills. As long as schools have existed, students have been taught to read and write. In the early 1800s, students were taught using the phonics method, by which they learned the sounds of letters and letter groups. In the mid-1800s, this system was replaced with a methodology in which students memorized entire words. When basal readers such as the McGuffey Readers and the Dick and Jane series were introduced, students learned to read using sight cards, ditto sheets, and workbooks keyed to the stories in the reader. The 1980s brought the introduction of whole language, a constructivist approach to teach reading and writing in which students learned by interpreting text and by freely expressing their ideas in writing, as in journals. Students read a wide variety of culturally diverse literature and acquired vocabulary through reading rather than memorizing weekly lists of vocabulary words. They read often, they read independently, they read aloud, and they read in groups. These literacy skills were integrated with the other content areas, and teaching skills that were not connected to meaning development (such as grammar and spelling) in isolation were de-emphasized.

The whole-language approach was very popular and used materials relevant to students, who were given choices about what to read and what to write about. Teachers used interdisciplinary thematic units to aid in teaching reading and writing meaningfully; the unit's topic served as the subject. By 1990, however, leaders of business and industry questioned students' reading and writing skills, complaining that they had to teach new hires how to read and write effectively. The public became upset that students did not master reading and writing skills in the earliest stages of learning, and was concerned about the decline of test scores on reading comprehension.

In 1996, the International Reading Association and the National Council of Teachers of English published Standards for the English Language Arts. The purpose of these standards is to "provide guidance in ensuring that all students are proficient language users so they may succeed in school, participate in society, find rewarding work, appreciate and contribute to our culture, and pursue their own goals and interests throughout their lives"

Courtesy of Becky Stovall

Effective reading and literacy instruction involves a balance of phonics and whole-language approaches. Were you taught to read and write using phonics, whole language, or a combination of both?

(International Reading Association, 1996, p. 1). The reading and language arts standards include the following 12 interrelated content areas shown in abbreviated form:

1. Students read a wide variety of print and nonprint texts.
2. Students read a wide range of literature.
3. Students apply a wide range of strategies to comprehend, interpret, and appreciate texts.
4. Students adjust their use of spoken, written, and visual language to communicate effectively.
5. Students employ a wide range of strategies in writing.
6. Students apply knowledge of language structure, language configurations, media techniques, figurative language, and genre to create, critique, and discuss print and nonprint texts.
7. Students conduct research and communicate their discoveries effectively.
8. Students use a variety of technological and information resources to gather and synthesize information and to create and communicate knowledge.
9. Students develop an understanding of and respect for diversity in language.
10. Students whose first language is not English use their first language to develop competency in English and develop understanding of content.
11. Students participate in a variety of literacy communities.
12. Students use spoken, written, and visual language to accomplish their own purposes.

Of course, the most recent reform in English language arts curriculum is the development of the Common Core State Standards. Not only do these standards address English language arts, but they also include expectations for literacy in the content areas. In the middle and high school grades, these standards emphasize learning to read in the content areas and making reading and writing connections, to produce meaning. For example, current thinking in literacy proposes that a science teacher's job involves more than just providing the content-area reading assignment for the students to complete, assuming that the student will "get it" just because the student knows how to read it. Rather, reading science content and making meaning from what is read requires certain strategies that the science teacher must know how to help the student acquire. To be able to construct meaning from content-area information that is read requires the use of higher-order thinking skills. The same is true for reading and literacy in all the content areas. You can access the English language arts standards through the direct link available on the Education CourseMate website.

TeachSource Video

View the TeachSource video, "School Reform: One High School Literacy Initiative." In response to an extremely high failing rate on the English and math sections of the Massachusetts high school exit exam, teachers at Brockton High School were called upon to engineer a back-to-basics curriculum they call the literacy initiative. Reading, speaking, reasoning, and writing were integrated throughout the curriculum. The failure rates in both English and math dropped significantly. The approach is now being studied by Harvard University and supported by the teachers union.

After you view the video, answer the following questions:

1. What did Brockton High School do in developing their literacy reform program?
2. What was a major aspect of their literacy reform movement?

TABLE 14.3 Number of countries scoring above, at, and below the United States on the PIRLS tests of reading literacy for fourth-grade students.

	Year (Number of Countries)	Number of Countries with Reading Literacy Scores Significantly Higher than the United States	Number of Countries with Reading Literacy Scores Not Significantly Different from the United States	Number of Countries with Reading Literacy Scores Significantly Lower than the United states
Fourth-Grade Reading Literacy	2001 (35 countries)	3	9	23
	2006 (45 countries)	10	13	22

Note: The term *significance* refers to statistical significance—the likelihood that the scores are true representations of students' knowledge and understandings.
Source: From the U.S. Department of Education, National Center for Education Statistics 2004, 2007

As with science and mathematics, international assessments have been conducted in reading. The Progress in International Reading Literacy Study (PIRLS) was first conducted in 2001, and was repeated in 2006. These tests assess reading literacy of fourth graders in many countries, using both multiple-choice and written response formats. In the 2001 administration, U.S. fourth graders performed close to the top, with children from only three countries (England, Bulgaria, and Sweden) recording higher performances (Ogle et al., 2003). In the 2006 test, U.S. fourth graders performed at about the middle, with ten countries recording higher performances (Baer et al., 2007). See Table 14.3.

BUILDING BLOCK 14.11

Modern Language Arts Curriculum

Talk to an older (at least 10 years older) relative or friend about what he or she remembers about taking English language arts in school:

- What courses did they take? How did they use technology, if at all? What strategies did the teacher use?
- Compare their answers with your own experience. What is different and what is the same? Is there anything that might be related to the standards reform you just read about?
- What else has recently impacted K–12 English language arts education?

The Impact of Reform on Instruction and Assessment

It should come as no surprise that if *what* students are to learn (curriculum) changes, then *how* they should learn it would also be affected (instruction). The methods by which students should demonstrate their learning (assessment) also will be impacted.

Instruction

One aspect about the reform efforts regarding standards that you may have noticed is that they emphasize problem-solving, decision-making, and higher-order thinking skills. Traditional teaching methods of direct instruction, such as lecture and note taking and then completing worksheets, or reading out of the chapter and defining bold print terms and answering questions at the end of the chapter, simply do not allow teachers to teach and learners to learn how to *think*.

Think about what you have learned about constructivism and constructivist-based teaching. In a constructivist-oriented lesson, students actively work to discover concepts. They observe, infer, hypothesize, and conclude—all elements of problem solving and decision making. In the end, they learn the content, and it belongs to *them* because they have worked to discover it. And, in the process of learning the content, they have also learned and practice the higher-order thinking skills associated with the standards.

What Would You Do with Curriculum?

BUILDING BLOCK
14.12

Brooks and Brooks (1999) offer 12 characteristics of constructivist teaching. Some deal with curriculum, some deal with instruction, and some deal with assessment. They are listed in abbreviated form in the following chart.

Give an example of how each characteristic can be applied in each of the major subject areas. You may wish to use a chart similar to the one shown here.

Characteristic of Constructivist Teaching	How It Is Applied in Social Studies	How It Is Applied in Science	How It Is Applied in Mathematics	How It Is Applied in Language Arts
1. Encourage and accept student autonomy and initiative.				
2. Use raw data and primary sources, along with manipulative, interactive, and physical material.				
3. Use cognitive terminology such as *classify, analyze, predict,* and *create.*				
4. Allow student responses to drive lessons, shift instructional strategy, and alter content.				
5. Inquire about students' understandings of concepts.				
6. Encourage students to engage in dialogue, both with the teacher and with one another.				
7. Encourage student inquiry.				
8. Seek elaboration of students' initial responses.				

Characteristic of Constructivist Teaching	How It Is Applied in Social Studies	How It Is Applied in Science	How It Is Applied in Mathematics	How It Is Applied in Language Arts
9. Engage students in experiences that might contradict their initial hypotheses, and then encourage discussion.				
10. Allow wait time after posing questions.				
11. Provide time for students to construct relationships and create metaphors.				
12. Nurture students' natural curiosity.				

Differentiated Instruction

We in the United States believe that everyone deserves an education. The current standards in all of the subject areas emphasize higher-order thinking skills as well as content. And effective teaching of these standards means that active, student-centered activities must be employed in the classroom. But as you recall from your inquiries about unique perspectives and abilities, teachers cannot teach all students the same way. A major thrust of current education reform is an emphasis on differentiation of instruction. You investigated differentiated instruction in detail in Chapter 5. As you will recall, differentiated instruction is an instructional strategy based on the teacher's awareness of the needs of individual students. It calls for teachers to have "clear learning goals that are rooted in content standards but crafted to ensure student engagement and understanding" (Tomlinson, 2008, p. 26). Lesson plans that include differentiated instruction are adapted to the readiness, interest, and strongest mode of learning for each individual student. Differentiated instruction is guided by five basic principles:

1. It is respectful of each student.
2. The material students are asked to learn is rooted in the critical ideas of a topic.
3. Teachers use flexible grouping.
4. Teachers use ongoing assessment to inform their instruction.
5. The learning environment supports students in taking the risk of learning. (Sousa and Tomlinson, 2011)

Differentiated instruction is an extremely important concept in current education reform. It would be worth your while to review what you have already learned about it and to pay close attention to what you learn in your future courses in teacher education. It is definitely a term you will hear again, and planning for differentiated instruction will be a skill that you will be expected to possess as a new teacher.

▶❚❚ **TeachSource** Video

View the TeachSource video, "Reading in the Content Areas: An Interdisciplinary Unit on the 1920s." How can teaching an interdisciplinary unit enrich students' understanding of both literature and history? In this video, you'll see how high school teachers join forces to create a unit focused on the Roaring 20s. Be sure to view the four bonus videos for more detail.

After you view the videos, answer the following questions:

1. How does the study of *The Great Gatsby* in the history class help students in their study of literature?

2. How does the study of *The Great Gatsby* in history class help students understand history?

3. What qualifications do teachers need to have to teach two subjects at the same time?

An Odyssey into 21st-Century Learning

Courtesy of Rayna Freedman

Being known as the teacher who takes risks, breaks out of the box, or does not fit the mold is something I pride myself on. So in 2003, when I approached my administration with our music teacher and art teacher, they were not surprised to hear what we wanted to do. Collaborating with two colleagues who had the same vision as I ended up in the creation of a most worthwhile project, and we began an odyssey into 21st-century learning.

The seed was planted when I read Chris Van Allsburg's *The Stranger*. The fantastical story leaves the reader wondering, "Who is the stranger"? Using context clues, students form their own opinions. They are exposed to the tale numerous times. They draw an illustration representing who they think the stranger could be. If they think he is autumn, you might see a picture of a leaf or shades of orange. If students envision the stranger as Jack Frost, they might draw the farmhouse window etched in frost or a snowman. Using their illustration as a guide, students write a free-verse poem, telling who they think the stranger is and why. They begin by writing a story, and through a writer's workshop in poetry, they are left with a free flow of words that share their experience of who the stranger is. Students create a slide show, initially created in a storyboard template, which they share with a larger audience. The first slide is a title card. Students are given the challenge to come up with a clever title. The next card is their hand-drawn illustration. The third card is an interpretation of the illustration drawn on the computer. The final card includes a background with a text box containing the free-verse poem.

Students are simultaneously meeting with the music teacher, working in small collaborative learning groups. Each group is assigned a scene and spends some time determining the mood of their scene. Their job is to create a soundtrack using instruments, voices, or other creative methods to portray the mood. Each group also chooses students to read their scene out loud. While one scene is being presented, the rest of the class is learning how to act out the scene using dramatic movements.

We then combine the slideshows, musical soundtrack, and dramatic piece into an hour-long presentation that includes a video that shows the audience the entire process from start to finish. As a group, students share their dramatic version of the story along with its musical soundtrack. Then they individually share their slideshows and read their poems. This leaves the audience hooked on the story and amazed at the work that went into this majestic project, which was completed along with all other curriculum expectations for the year.

This project can be done with any fiction or nonfiction book that inspires students to think. It also reaches more state standards than any individual unit we teach. You could do a slideshow on an event in the American Revolution, design a soundtrack for your event, and write a poem about it. A student could create a similar presentation on the lifecycle of the frog. Later, we attempted *Two Bad Ants*, also by Van Allsburg. Students were asked to take on the point of view of an ant, writing a story as if they were ants lost in our classroom. Imagine that a fan becomes a wind tunnel or the pencil sharpener becomes a fun house. With this project we also weaved in science by studying insects as well as math. Students designed sets for their play and had to make things to scale.

It is now eight years since our first project, and every year former students return to see what project we are doing. I am reminded that they took this odyssey with me and carry it with them in all they do. It inspired them to imagine, collaborate, think critically, problem-solve creatively, learn, grow, perform, and dream big. They saw their teachers face roadblocks along the way and hurdle over them or around them in order to see them succeed. By weaving together various disciplines, students began their own odyssey into 21st-century learning. I am proud to have paved that road for them.

Rayna Freedman
Jordan/Jackson Elementary
Mansfield, Massachusetts
Chamber of Commerce Teacher of the Year, 2011
Kappa Delta Pi Teacher of Honor, 2010

© Cengage Learning 2014

Keep this in mind: So far, you have investigated current reform trends in curriculum and instruction in the four disciplines of social studies, science, mathematics, and the English language arts. Visit the websites for the professional organizations associated with foreign language education, art education, music education, and physical education (PE) to learn about current standards in these areas and how they might integrate with the core content areas.

Interdisciplinary Instruction

The prevailing approach to curriculum at all levels involves the separation of the subject-area disciplines into discrete subjects, each with its own time slot, its own textbook, and its own program of study. However, what we now know is that showing students how subjects are integrated can appeal to their prior knowledge and interests. You will recall that one of the objectives in modern curriculum development is subject integration. An example of integrating content is the use of graphs (a mathematics topic) to interpret experimental data obtained in a science experiment. Another example is writing a story about a person living on the moon, combining science and language arts. The more subjects that are drawn into the study of a topic, the more sophisticated the approach becomes and the more interrelated the disciplines become. Johnson (2011) says that science is the application of math, and urges teachers to integrate science and mathematics to foster relevance, meaning, and usefulness. After all, scientific data cannot be analyzed without the use of math. You saw other examples of curriculum integration in the section on service learning in Chapter 12 and in the material on social reconstructionism in Chapter 2.

Assessment Reform

You have explored the concept of assessment in several parts of this textbook, and you have seen that the purpose of assessment is to obtain information about student achievement. Through assessment, students demonstrate their understanding. There are many ways to assess, and education reform efforts seek to strengthen assessment so it measures what students actually know and can do.

BUILDING BLOCK 14.13

Assessing Your Achievement

What kinds of assessments do you remember having had as a student? Write them down.

- Did these assessments give you the opportunity to show all that you knew about the topics?
- Considering current curriculum reform and emphases (content *and* skills), do you think the way that you were tested would allow students in today's classrooms to demonstrate the knowledge and skills in the standards?
- What do you believe teachers should do to find out what a student really knows and is able to do?

The primary goals of assessment in education are (1) to obtain and interpret information about what students know and can do, and (2) to use this information to guide instructional and educational decisions. Traditionally, the primary assessment method found in classrooms is the paper-and-pencil test, in which students select among multiple-choice or "true or false" test items, fill in blanks, or write an essay on a given topic. With the possible exception of open-ended essays, this form of assessment requires students to select which of several possible answers is the correct one. Multiple-choice assessments measure a student's ability to select a response; they do not necessarily show what the student knows and can do. In a multiple-choice test, students cannot generate their own responses and do not have the opportunity to explain their reasons for choosing a response. Would this type of assessment be the best way for students to demonstrate some of the knowledge and *skills* that are specified in the content-area standards you have considered?

Authentic Assessment

Learning theory holds that different people construct their understanding of material in different ways. Assessing student performance on tasks relevant to real-world activities is called authentic assessment. The subject-area national standards encourage the use of authentic assessment methods. These authentic assessments methods include portfolios, journals, interviews, observations, performance assessment, and human judgment. Further, teachers often weave assessment directly into the instruction with projects and presentations, instead of testing only with end-of-unit tests, midterms, and finals given after the instruction.

Portfolios are folders of evidence of students' accomplishments. You may be keeping a portfolio in this course to show evidence of your achievement of the basic course goals established by your professor or institution. Journals are records of a variety of information, such as reflections, descriptions of projects and laboratory inquiries, questions, answers, reports, stories, drawings, charts, tables, and many other things. Journals often are used in conjunction with other assessment methods to show what students have learned. When conducting interviews, teachers ask questions during a lesson to check for student understanding and to uncover alternative ways of thinking. Based on student responses to the questions, teachers can affirm student understanding or take appropriate steps to help students clarify their thinking.

Performance assessments are based on students' ability to demonstrate a skill such as playing a piece of music, labeling the parts of an actual dissected frog, doing a basic routine on uneven parallel bars, or writing a persuasive essay. Assessments based on human judgment might include having a classroom debate or having students critique a procedure or a campaign strategy. Notice that these authentic assessments include opportunities for students to demonstrate those higher-order thinking skills that content-area standards call for.

Many schools have replaced traditional methods of assessment with authentic assessment, because authentic assessment provides the information they really want—what students know and what they can do.

authentic assessment Education tasks that resemble the real-world applications of the skills and knowledge being assessed.

portfolio An authentic assessment method consisting of a container or folio of evidence that shows a student's progress toward achieving the knowledge and skills of a subject.

journal Students' writings, including what they did, what they learned, and their reflections, often used as an element of authentic assessment.

interview An assessment method that consists of a structured or open conversation between student and teacher in which the teacher asks questions relating to the objectives of a lesson.

performance assessment An assessment that requires the learner to actually demonstrate—or perform—the skill.

Summative and Formative Assessment

A major trend in assessment is the movement toward formative assessment. Typically, assessment occurs at the end of a unit of instruction. (Keep in mind that in this instance, a "unit of instruction" can mean a lesson, chapter, or sequence of related chapters.) Assessment at the end of a unit is called summative assessment, and it measures student achievement after the unit is complete—*after* the instruction and student inquiries have taken place. Its purpose is to determine if the required learning has been retained. What do teachers do if the assessment shows that the learning either did not occur or was not retained?

Formative assessment, on the other hand, is assessment that occurs *during* the course of the unit or lesson. Its purpose is to help both the teacher and students evaluate student achievement while they are still studying the unit so corrections can be made while there is still time. Formative assessment tells how the students are constructing (forming) their conceptualizations; summative assessment tests a summarization of the learning. Formative assessment gives us tools we can use to guide the design and implementation of our learning activities. Methods include observation, formal and informal interviews, asking questions, using "clicker" technology, and many other ways. Many experts say that formative assessment is the only way teachers can really know what the students are learning and how they are thinking. Current reforms in assessment focus on formative assessment.

formative assessment An assessment that is implemented during the course of instruction so that teachers and students may be informed of the students' progress in achieving objectives.

summative assessment An assessment that is implemented at the end of an instructional unit to measure student achievement of objectives.

One way teachers can assess student achievement authentically is to record observations.

Robert Stake (in Dirksen, 2011) said it best: "When the cook tastes the soup, that's formative. When the guests taste the soup, that's summative" (p. 26).

BUILDING BLOCK 14.14

Using Assessment Data

Use your current understandings of authentic assessment and standardized testing and experiences you may have had with these forms of assessment to answer the following questions:

- What kinds of authentic assessments have you experienced?
- How are authentic assessments different from pencil-and-paper tests?
- How are authentic assessments different from standardized tests?
- How could standardized tests be made to be authentic?
- How can educators use data from both authentic assessment and standardized tests to inform educational decisions?

Teacher Education Reform

Teacher preparation is a major element of education reform. Of course, reforms in curriculum, instruction, and assessment impact the way that future teachers are prepared to enter the profession. Much of what you investigated about teacher preparation and certification in Chapter 9 represents the current state of reform efforts. The No Child Left Behind legislation requires schools to place a highly qualified teacher in every classroom. The Ready to Teach Act of 2003 provides federal funding to improve teacher preparation so this goal can be accomplished (Boehner, 2003).

Teacher education reform efforts target five basic areas:

- Subject-matter knowledge
- Pedagogical knowledge and skills
- Methods of teacher preparation
- Incentives and accountability
- Teacher induction

Subject-Matter Knowledge

Educators agree that subject-matter knowledge is critical to effective teaching. When you investigated your teacher preparation program in Chapter 9, you probably found an emphasis on subject matter, regardless of the program you plan to pursue. In fact, some states are eliminating the undergraduate degree in education as a teacher certification requirement; instead, they require that future teachers major in a content area and some require an undergraduate degree in subject matter and a master's degree in education. However, most educators believe that the subject-matter understanding needed by teachers is different from the understanding needed by traditional majors; teachers need to know their subject in ways that make it teachable to others. Thus, teachers need to know and understand the pedagogy associated with teaching the content areas.

Pedagogical Knowledge and Skills

Pedagogical knowledge and skills comprise the "how to teach" component of teacher education. You probably know someone who is a whiz in his or her subject area but cannot teach it. There is controversy over the relative importance of subject-matter and pedagogical expertise to teaching effectiveness. The dominant view is that teachers need rigorous training in educational theory and pedagogical skills. For example, Wenglinsky (2000) found a high correlation between the performance of eighth-grade students in science and mathematics and teachers who emphasized hands-on learning, higher-order thinking skills, and individualized instruction in their teaching. He concludes, "what really matters [in teaching quality] is not where teachers come from but what they do in the classroom" (p. 32). He reported that strong subject-matter knowledge is particularly essential for science and mathematics teachers in high schools and middle schools in addition to pedagogical skills. The opposing view holds that teachers need only minimal exposure to education theory and pedagogy and that teachers best acquire their skills through on-the-job experience. (This is the view championed by the Thomas B. Fordham Foundation.)

Darling-Hammond (2000) reviewed research and evidence to ascertain relationships between teacher qualifications and student achievement. She found that teachers' subject-matter knowledge is critical, but that its relationship to student performance varies depending on grade level (the lower the level the greater the concentration on pedagogy that is needed) and level of student sophistication. She also found that, regardless of grade level or subject taught, student achievement relates strongly to teachers having full certification and a major in their field. Darling-Hammond concluded that preparing future teachers how to teach specific subjects has the greatest impact of all on student achievement.

pedagogical knowledge and skills The knowledge and skills of how to teach content information to learners.

Methods of Teacher Preparation

As you found in Chapter 1, teacher education programs must be accredited. This means that external reviewing agencies assess programs for compliance with the reviewing agency's standards. The two primary national teacher accreditation agencies are the National Council for Accreditation of Teacher Education (NCATE) and the Teacher Education Accreditation Council (TEAC). Both accredit teacher preparation programs on the basis of standards developed by the agency, subject matter and other education specialty organizations, and teacher preparation faculty; the standards are grounded in the education reform movements dealing with curriculum, instruction, assessment, and teacher preparation. For accreditation, teacher preparation programs must demonstrate that preservice teachers (teacher education students) are proficient in subject-matter knowledge, applying learning theories and teaching skills to planning and instruction, that impacts the achievement of *all* learners, and demonstrating professional dispositions. The emphasis in teacher education reform is on producing highly qualified teachers who are able to impact student learning. The thrust behind this emphasis is the current movement in education reform to hold teachers *accountable* for their students' performance.

Whereas national accreditation organizations evaluate the effectiveness of teacher preparation programs according to national standards, individual states are responsible for ensuring that the programs comply with state standards and requirements; this responsibility normally belongs to the state department of education.

Incentives and Accountability

Incentives tend to foster a desire to do things differently, and accountability measures the extent to which goals are met. The No Child Left Behind Act of 2001 turned the focus of education on accountability: Schools and teachers are held accountable for the performance of their students largely as measured by standardized tests.

Teacher Accountability

According to No Child Left Behind, teachers should be "highly qualified." It is left up to the states to figure out how they would define "highly qualified" and how they would measure teacher effectiveness for accountability. As a result, there are as many different systems to determine teacher accountability as there are states (Stecher, Vernez, and Steinberg, 2010).

There is little dispute that teachers should be held accountable for student achievement. Conflicts regarding reform movements in teacher accountability are primarily centered on *how* accountability is measured. To many, the way to judge a teacher's performance is by linking it directly to students' scores on achievement tests. But, from your investigations so far, you know that standardized test scores are unreliable for a variety of reasons.

So, how do we measure teacher accountability? Obviously, the assessment used must relate to the teacher's performance in the classroom.

In Chapter 9, you investigated teacher evaluation. And, as you know, different states have different methods of assessing teacher performance. One method that is drawing a lot of attention and controversy is called value-added analysis. It is a complicated statistical method that uses standardized test scores and other data. In the end, it can provide an indication of how well an individual student performed from year to year and from teacher to teacher. The idea is that if a teacher's students perform well according to a variety of indicators, that teacher must be effective. In 2010, the *Los Angeles Times* did a value-added analysis of student test scores of some 6,000 teachers in local elementary schools and published its findings (*Los Angeles Times*, 2010). The statistics indicated that there was a great deal of variance in student performance from year to year and from teacher to teacher. Students showed significant gains with certain teachers, and with other teachers, students did not perform as well. But, there are extraneous variables and anomalies that impact value-added analysis, and the statistical methods are complex. For these reasons, some believe that value-added analysis should not be the only evidence on which teacher effectiveness is judged. Rather, it is thought that value-added data might contribute to teacher evaluations as a percentage of the outcome along with evidence generated by other sources, such as observations by administrators and peers' documentation produced by the teacher.

> **value-added analysis** A statistical method that uses standardized test scores and other data to inform the evaluation of teacher performance.

Teacher Induction

Teacher induction involves support, guidance, and orientation programs for beginning teachers. Of these, personal guidance (called *mentoring*) provided by experienced teachers for the new teachers is by far the most important. New teachers are especially vulnerable to the seemingly indecipherable complexities of the school setting. Mentoring is *critical*. Mentors show the new teacher the ropes, help with lesson preparation, help find materials (sometimes even giving materials to the new teacher), share successful strategies, offer critiques, provide suggestions and hints for classroom management, and all sorts of other things that help the new teacher (Hanusain, 2010).

One way to help teachers learn the pedagogical applications of subject matter is through collaboration between colleges of education and the public schools they serve. In the last decade or two, schools and colleges have collaborated in teacher induction programs, acknowledging that new teachers need mentoring so they can apply their newly acquired content knowledge and teaching skills in the classroom. When you interview for a teaching position, you should feel free to ask whether the district (or school) has a new teacher mentoring program and, if so, what the program entails. Mentors are essential to the success of new teachers.

The most successful teacher mentoring programs have several features in common:

- They use experienced, well-trained teachers as mentors.
- They are based on well-articulated standards and goals.
- They are adequately funded.
- They include special and appropriate evaluation processes for new teachers.
- They extend beyond the new teacher's first year to include the second and sometimes the third years.
- They include a reduced teaching load for the new teacher.
- They provide appropriate class placements.
- They include opportunities to observe other teachers.
- They allow new teachers to participate in professional development opportunities.

View the TeachSource Video, "Mentoring First-Year Teachers: Keys to Professional Success." In this video, you will see new teacher, Dania Diaz, working with her mentor teacher, Abdi Ali. Throughout, Abdi observes Dania as she interacts with her students and colleagues and then reflects on her teaching practice. Be sure to watch the two bonus videos for more detail.

After you view the videos, answer the following questions:

1. What does a mentor teacher do?
2. Why is mentoring important for new teachers?

Education reform often results in innovative and improved learning space for students. Computers and Internet access are standard additions to school libraries and media centers across the nation.

© Catherine Ledner/Getty Images/The Image Bank

A s you saw in Chapter 9, one of the most sweeping changes occurring in education is computer-based technology. You have investigated some of the technological advances that are in our schools today. Now let us get a bit more specific about what technologies are being incorporated in the subject areas.

Social studies classes are making use of simulations. In these programs, students input data to solve realistic problems, and the program responds with graphic representations of the actions. For example, *SimCity*, a simulation that has been around since 1989, invites students to inquire into urban environments. A city plan is presented, and students are asked to respond to hypothetical changes in the community, such as sudden population changes, natural disasters, and rush-hour traffic fluctuations, by suggesting redesigns of the city. The results of their newly input suggestions are displayed so the students can see the results of their planning. Social studies classes are also making use of computer games that may or may not be competitive in nature. Tutorial games are available that ask students to answer questions after which pertinent information is provided. Many of these games are available online and can be found using an Internet search engine.

In science, teachers make use of *microcomputer-based laboratories* (MBLs), which are computerized ways of collecting and analyzing data from experimental procedures. The equipment for a lab typically includes a probe or sensor that gathers the data and a computer that analyzes the data and displays results either in graphic form or in numeric form. A few of these devices include temperature probes, light sensors, motion detectors, pH sensors, magnetic field sensors, salinity sensors, sound-level meters, and many more. Students (and others) can also participate in "citizen science" by accessing the Internet sites of research centers and submitting data they have collected on bird sightings, weather patterns, wildlife health (dead, sick, or injured wildlife sightings), butterfly populations, the weathering of historical gravestones, and much more.

Mathematics uses calculators, spreadsheets, computer problem-solving equipment, interactive geometry software, and more. Technology is used to help in rudimentary computation and algorithms to leave the students free to develop problem-solving and higher-order thinking skills, although teachers have to be careful not to replace numerical knowledge with technological assistance. There are graphing programs for use at all levels that construct graphs from the data students input.

In English and language arts, teachers have available thousands of computer-based technology applications that can help them enrich their teaching. There is a huge array of tutorial programs used to augment English language instruction for students for whom English is a second language. Some of the ways in which English/language arts teachers use technological advances to enhance their teaching include creating visual aids to help with the teaching, providing access to online literature libraries, integrating video clips into teaching, developing web-based alternative ways for students to demonstrate their learning, using online tutorials to augment grammar instruction, and many more. Students can use technology to prepare online school literacy magazines and a class web page.

Interdisciplinary work utilizes all of the technological advances mentioned previously plus other advances that are not subject-specific. For instance, students as young as kindergarteners can use digital cameras to develop brochures about their class and the work they have accomplished. Applications are available that enable students to use photographs they have taken by integrating them into slides and movies to develop stories. And computer applications companies are working with textbook publishers to develop e-textbook strategies for all grades, K–12 (Tomassini, 2012a).

There are so many technological applications available today for teachers to use as they augment their instruction and make it more meaningful to students. The number of applications is growing rapidly, and you need to keep up with what is going on so you will know what is available to you when you are a teacher. But always remember that technology is used to augment and enhance instruction, not to replace it. Please do yourself a favor. If you have not already done this, begin a notebook or electronic journal that is wholly dedicated to technology you can use in the classroom for instruction or management. You can do this online in a blog or wiki, or you might find it more convenient to use a spreadsheet or database program on your own computer. For each item, write its name, its URL (address) if it is a website, and a brief description of what it does. After you use it, write a very brief critique of it, including how you used it. Keep this for use during your teacher preparation program and during your first year or two of teaching.

■ SUMMARY

The reform of U.S. education is being undertaken in response to concerns voiced by business, government, and society at large. Education reform extends to all aspects of education, including curriculum, instruction, assessment, teacher preparation, and accountability.

- Many organizations are spearheading or assisting in reform efforts. The federal government collects data, provides funding, and acts in an advisory capacity. State governments establish policies for their state education programs. Nonprofit organizations offer various types of assistance in education reform efforts.

- The National Governors Association has developed Common Core State Standards in mathematics, English language arts, and literacy in history, social studies, science, and technology.

- Subject-specific professional education organizations have developed standards that have shaped curricular and instructional reform. States have adopted and implemented these standards to varying degrees. National and international tests reveal trends about student achievement and its relationship to curriculum.

- Reforms in standards and curriculum necessarily affect instruction and assessment. Effective instructional strategies include those that allow students to participate in hands-on and minds-on activities and strategies that allow instruction to be differentiated based on individual student need. Some schools and teachers are also reforming instruction by making it interdisciplinary.

- Efforts to reform assessment focus on gaining accurate information about students' achievement of knowledge and skills. Assessments must be designed so teachers know what the students *really* understand. This means using authentic assessment strategies such as portfolios, journal, interviews, and performance assessments.

- Teacher education reform aims to ensure that all teachers are experts in both pedagogy and subject matter, and that they possess professional dispositions necessary for success in the field.

- Reform efforts focus heavily on teacher accountability and ways to establish and evaluate the effectiveness of teachers and their impact on student learning. Much controversy exists regarding how teachers should be evaluated and to what extent students' test grades should factor into this measure.

■ Key Terms and Concepts

Authentic assessment, 387
Common Core State
 Standards, 370
Education reform, 366
Formative assessment, 387
Interview, 387

Journal, 387
New Math, 377
Pedagogical knowledge and
 skills, 389
Performance assessment, 387
Phonics, 380

Portfolio, 387
Standards movement, 369
Summative assessment, 387
Value-added analysis, 390
Whole language, 380

■ Construct and Apply

1. Name at least four areas of U.S. education being looked at from an education reform point of view. For each, summarize the reform efforts being undertaken.
2. List at least four thrusts that are common to the current curriculum standards that represent current directions in education.
3. Why is reforming assessment a high priority? What initiatives are today's schools undertaking to accomplish this reform?
4. What are some of the controversies regarding teacher accountability?
5. How is teacher education responding to reform movements?

▪ Deconstructing the Standards

1. Recall the InTASC Standards associated with the objectives for this chapter:

   InTASC Standard #4 reads, "The teacher understands the central concepts, tools of inquiry, and structures of the discipline(s) he or she teaches and creates learning experiences that make these aspects of the discipline accessible and meaningful for learners to assure mastery of the content."

   InTASC Standard #5 reads, "The teacher understands how to connect concepts and use differing perspectives to engage learners in critical thinking, creativity, and collaborative problem solving related to authentic local and global issues."

   InTASC #6 reads, "The teacher understands and uses multiple methods of assessment to engage learners in their own growth, to monitor learner progress, and to guide the teacher's and learner's decision making."

   InTASC Standard #9 reads, "The teacher engages in ongoing professional learning and uses evidence to continually evaluate his/her practice, particularly the effects of his/her choices and actions on others (learners, families, other professionals, and the community), and adapts practice to meet the needs of each learner."

   a. What part(s) of these standards does this chapter address?

   b. How will the concepts in this chapter help you apply these standards as a teacher?

2. Use your favorite search engine to find your state's standards for certification. When you find it, bookmark the site; you will refer to it often during this course.

   a. How are your conclusions about the topics of education reform that you read about in this chapter represented in your state standards?

   b. How do the InTASC Standards compare to your state's certification standards?

   c. Do you believe the degree of representation concerning education reform is adequate in your state certification standards? Why or why not?

▪ Your Portfolio

1. Obtain a copy of your state's standards for the subject(s) and level(s) you plan to teach. In your portfolio, reflect on how your cooperating teacher teaches the topics and skills in the curriculum. Comment on how this is like or is not like your experience learning the topics in school.

2. Find out how your state evaluates teacher effectiveness by visiting the Department of Education website. Include the relevant information and documents in your portfolio.

▣ Education CourseMate Resources

Check out this text's Education CourseMate website (at www.cengagebrain.com) for more information about school reform, standards, and the evolving curriculum in our schools. You will find the TeachSource videos, a guide for doing field experiences, glossary flash cards, activities, tutorial quizzes, direct links to the websites mentioned in the chapter, and more.

PART V Building a Teacher

NOW WE COME back to the *Self*. You have explored characteristics of excellent teachers, your philosophical ideas about education, and characteristics of students including their common needs and their unique perspectives and abilities. You have investigated characteristics of schools including their purposes, structures, and the interactions among students, teachers, and schools. You have explored the influences of society on education and schools, both past and present.

So, it is time to come back to *you*. Do you still want to become a teacher? Why? Or, why not?

Your Motives for Teaching

"Why do you want to be an elementary school teacher?"

  "Because I love kids!"

"Why do you want to be a high school teacher?"

  "Because I love my subject!"

"Why do you want to be a middle school teacher?"

  "I'm not sure..."

The conversation that begins this chapter represents the typical answers future teachers give when, on the first day of their introduction to education course, they are asked why they want to become teachers.

Everyone who wants to be a teacher has had powerful experiences in school, both positive and negative, that have informed their decision to pursue a career in education. As you now know, however, there is much to consider when thinking about teaching—a lot more than just the experiences you had in school. Most introductory education textbooks include a chapter on motives for teaching at the very beginning of the book. We suspect that it will not surprise you that this textbook, written in a constructivist voice, puts this chapter at the end. Certainly, your motives for teaching deserve exploration, especially in your first education class. Anyone considering teaching as a profession should carefully examine his or her motives before entering a teacher education program. But how well informed would your reasons have been in the beginning of this course—before your classes, before your investigations, and before your field experiences? Flip back to this textbook's table of contents and look at all you have explored. You knew a great deal about teaching, schools, and learning at the beginning of this course, but surely you know a lot more now than you did when you started. In this chapter, you will draw on the knowledge and experiences you have gained in this course to explore the question, "Why *do you* or *don't you* want to teach?"

Chapter Objectives

As a result of your explorations in this chapter, you will be able to:

1. Describe your motives for wanting—or not wanting—to teach, in terms of self, students, school, and society.

   InTASC Standard #9: Professional Learning and Ethical Practices

2. Discuss how you can promote the profession of teaching and how you can continue your professional development.

   InTASC Standard #9: Professional Learning and Ethical Practices

Identifying Your Reasons for Teaching

Review the organization of this book. You started out by exploring what *you* already know and believe about effective teachers and teaching. Then, you moved to an examination of *students*—how they are alike and how they are different—and what that means for teaching. Next, you investigated *schools*, where learning, the act of teaching, and the teacher–student relationship takes place. Finally, you saw that a school has general and specific purposes and structures that serve the community in which it is located. Such communities are a function of *society* and its beliefs.

Self, students, schools, and society. Where do your motives for teaching lie? Let us investigate all four areas.

Self

What is it you know about your *self* that makes you believe you would be a good teacher? If you review the qualities of effective teachers and teaching you investigated in Chapter 1, you probably identify with some of them.

Your *Self* as a Teacher

List the personal qualities and skills you have that you believe will help you to be an effective teacher. If you have decided not to teach, to what other professions might these qualities and skills be suited?

- How does this list compare with the characteristics of excellent teachers and effective teaching you listed in Chapter 1?
- How can you acquire these qualities and skills? Which ones are innate and which can you learn?

There is an age-old debate about whether teaching is an art or a science. If you believe it is an art, your motives for teaching might include your belief that you have an innate talent for it. You might think that some individuals are naturally talented teachers. Have you had a teacher who seemed naturally talented in this way? Such teachers seem to have a knack for getting people to learn. Perhaps someone has told you that you are a "natural" teacher.

Yet, as you have seen, there are certain teaching methods and strategies that research has shown to impact student achievement. These are skills that can be learned, sort of like science.

Whether teaching is more an art or a science is a classic debate. Psychologist B. F. Skinner (see Chapter 2) believed that teachers could be trained to use educational strategies and materials effectively. To Skinner, teaching is truly a science, with a methodology to be practiced and followed. On the other hand, Elliot Eisner, Stanford University professor emeritus of art and education, argues that teaching is more of an art. He notes that teachers must deal creatively with the unexpected in their students' learning and behavior. Rigid models, methods, and templates for instruction or management do not apply to every classroom situation. Teachers must possess the intuition of how, when, and where to use their skills effectively (Eisner, 1983). Gage (1978) combines the two views to assert that teaching is an art that is informed by science. He writes, "in medicine and engineering, where the scientific basis is unquestionable, the artistic elements also abound" and "in teaching, where the artistic elements are unquestionable, a scientific base can also be developed" (p. 18).

Some believe that certain people have a predisposition toward teaching, somewhat akin to the talents children inherit from their parents. A parent who possesses a talent for drawing, singing, or playing a musical instrument, for example, often has a child with similar artistic talent. Many teachers and future teachers will tell you that they come from a family of educators. As with doctors, police officers, and other professionals, several generations of a family may be involved in education. Perhaps you belong to such a family and count your family's teaching experience as one of your motives for teaching. Does this mean that you could have inherited a talent for teaching? Or does it mean that

Teaching is both an art and a science. Effective teachers know how to best assist students. To what extent are those skills based on knowledge and/or talent?

Courtesy of Bill Lisenby

teachers pattern themselves after other teachers in their families? We leave this for you to ponder.

Your attitude toward the content you teach, your colleagues, your students, your students' parents, and the community in which your school is located can be thought of as your disposition. Understanding, patience, acceptance, and kindness toward others can be learned from important and influential people in your life who demonstrate these qualities. These are certainly dispositions that will help you become an effective teacher. Your disposition also includes aspects of professional behavior such as accepting responsibility, being accountable, taking initiative, and even performing such seemingly simple behaviors as being where you are supposed to be, when you are supposed to be there. There too are qualities that you can learn by observing others, but you can develop these skills as you progress through your teacher education coursework and experience.

When considering your motives for teaching, did you think of emotions associated with a passion for teaching? One characteristic common among successful teachers is passion. These successful teachers are passionate about teaching their content and their students. These teachers may believe that teaching is a "calling."

Look around your education class. You might see students who are coming to teaching as a second career. What motives do you think would influence someone to leave an existing career and study to become a teacher? If you are choosing teaching as a second career, what influenced your decision? Have you heard someone in your class say, "I've always wanted to teach"? Maybe you have said these words yourself. What does this statement imply about the speaker's motives for teaching?

What do you know about your *self* that makes you think you would (or would not) be a good teacher? At the beginning of this course, you knew that you were interested in teaching. Now you know that effective educators need to have certain dispositions and skills. If you have chosen to continue in your teacher education program, you believe you have some innate talent for teaching or can learn the necessary skills. Your learning in this course and your field experiences may have helped you identify your passion for teaching, or you may have discovered that you are not passionate about education. Either way, we hope you have clarified your motives for teaching—or not teaching—in the context of your *self*.

The Student

The hypothetical conversation at the beginning of this chapter seems to indicate that a person's passion for teaching depends on his or her major. It seems to suggest that if you are studying to be an elementary teacher, you are passionate about children. If you are going to be a secondary teacher, you are passionate about content. And if you are pursuing a middle-grades certification, you are passionate about both.

Of course, this "conversation" was meant only to introduce the chapter and to provide a bit of a laugh. All successful teachers, regardless of major, are passionate about their students. In fact, when someone asks you what you want to teach, we hope that your first answer will be "students." If you are not fond of young people in the age group you want to teach, it will not matter how much you love your content. You have seen that teachers have a relationship with each and every student, whether or not they want one. Many teachers cite this relationship as the initial source of their motivation to teach.

In Chapter 1, you recalled your favorite teacher. Did this teacher seem to like the students in his or her class? Did this teacher seem passionate about the well-being and achievement of each and every student? Did this teacher inspire you to go into education? Many teachers saw how a certain teacher affected their lives and the lives of others—and were inspired to do the same.

We have heard teacher education students proclaim, "If I can help just one student learn, it will be reward enough." Actually, if you chose to pursue a career in education, you will help far more students than you realize. You will see evidence of this learning

disposition The qualities of one's character.

What are some of the ways passionate teachers inspire and motivate students?

on tests and through other measures of achievement, but every once in a while, a former student will contact you. You may be surprised that the student discusses not only the content from your class, but also the quality of your relationship with that student and how it affected his or her life. If you haven't already done so, find out how to contact your favorite teachers and let them know how they affected you and influenced what you are doing with your life. Do it now, before you forget. It will make their day!

Some individuals had a negative relationship with a teacher. Inspiration can come from bad experiences as well as good. Imagine a teacher telling a student: "You don't belong in this class. Don't count on getting into college." What choices does that student have? He could change his schedule and get out of that class. Or he could be inspired to prove the teacher wrong. He might even be inspired to become a teacher himself and make sure that other students do not have the same experience. Does this motivation apply to anyone you know?

The opportunity to work with students is a strong motive for many who desire to become a teacher. You may have thought that you want to teach because you love kids. Now you know that students are as different as they are alike. Recall from Chapters 3, 4, and 5 that the common needs, unique perspectives, and unique abilities students bring to your classroom have significant implications for teaching. In your field experience, you may have discovered that you do not love all of your students all of the time. You may have even been relieved when you saw that a particularly challenging student was not in class one day. However, you now know that you must have what classroom management expert Harry Wong calls "unconditional positive regard" for every student (Wong and Wong, 2009). What do you think unconditional positive regard for every student means?

The opportunity to work with students is a powerful motivation to teach. However, perhaps in your field experiences, you had quite enough of being with children or adolescents each day and you have decided you do not want to work with students full-time. Or perhaps your investigations and field experiences have caused you to change your mind about the age group you would like to teach. Regardless, you are now aware of the challenges and the rewards of working with students.

The School

Some of us enjoyed the whole experience of school. We earned good grades and thrived in the social and academic atmosphere. Some people choose to go into education because they had very positive experiences in school. (Some even stay in school so long that they become professors of education, teaching others how to teach.) One might think that anyone who wants to be a teacher must have liked school. This is not always the case. Some students had less-than-enjoyable experiences in school but are choosing education as a career to make others' school experiences more positive and enjoyable.

Those who really enjoyed school and who seemed to work well in a structured academic environment may be motivated to teach by the atmosphere of learning. They count among their skills the ability to organize and plan well. They enjoy the daily schedule, whether it is from class to class in a middle or high school or from day to day in an elementary classroom. They enjoy the intellectual stimulation that comes with being in a school environment.

Some individuals like the control that comes with teaching, not in the sense of controlling behavior, but in the sense of designing and conducting lessons. Some teachers like the attention they get from being at the front of the class. Indeed, it has been said that teachers must be good actors. But even though attention and effort in a school is focused on students most of the time, many people in a school must work together to make it all happen. You may be attracted by the apparent autonomy that you can have in your classroom, but you must collaborate and cooperate with myriad other individuals in the building to promote the purpose of the school.

All of these other people in the school—the students, the other teachers, the administrators, and other personnel—have expectations. Now you know that teaching is more than managing your classroom, implementing the curriculum, and instructing and assessing students. Among other duties, you are responsible for student safety. You are expected to participate in noninstructional and extracurricular activities. You are expected to be certified and highly qualified. You have to be current in educational research and theories, practices, and technologies through participation in professional development activities.

Would it surprise you to learn that some individuals are interested in teaching because they want weekends and summers off? This response may come from seeing teaching from a pupil's point of view. Now, however, you know that teaching requires a lot of time and effort, especially for new teachers. Maybe you are even shaking your head at the time it takes to prepare, teach, and evaluate a lesson. However, you know that with time, teachers gain experience and become more fluent in their practice, able to meet school and professional expectations while having the occasional weekend and a few weeks in the summer to rest and recuperate or participate in professional development opportunities. Besides, some school districts are changing the school year from the traditional, agriculture-based nine months with summers off to schedules with shorter summer vacations, and even the trimester system with three one-month vacations after each three months of school.

The opportunities for lifelong learning and for working with others to promote a school's purpose may be a strong motivation for you to teach. Or you may have decided that it's just too much. Regardless, you have learned more about the place called school, and you understand more about the teacher's place in it.

The Place Called School

Teachers work in the place called school. List some characteristics of the school that you find attractive as a teacher, and list some characteristics that you find unattractive. How does the possibility of working in a school factor into your motivation for becoming a teacher?

Society

Earlier we mentioned that some refer to teaching as a "calling." Is this true for you? A calling is that inner urge which, in part, reflects your desire to make a contribution to society.

The Big Picture

What do you hope to contribute to society by teaching? Do you believe that your day-to-day efforts in the classroom can produce a ripple outside the school? If so, how? Describe a chain of impact that your teaching could have on society.

How, what, when, and where teachers teach can be influenced by external factors, such as parents, the community, the government, and the law.

View the TeachSource Video, "Becoming a Teacher: Choices and Advice from the Field." In this video, you'll hear from new and experienced teachers as they reflect on the reasons they chose to enter the teaching profession.

After watching this video, answer the following questions:

1. Why did Tony Byers, Danielle Coucette, and Nathalie DeFusco want to become teachers? Was it related to self? Students? School? Society?

2. What do you need to do before you make the final decision to become a teacher? What can *you* do?

3. What traits do you need to be successful as a teacher?

In your study of the history of education in the United States, you learned that Americans in each generation have sought to educate the next generation to become conscientious citizens and to contribute positively to society. Teachers can contribute to society by guiding the development of future conscientious citizens. The draw to the classroom is the power to affect society through teaching. You now know, however, that the teacher alone does not hold this power. The many stakeholders in education also have a strong influence. You know that, beyond the people in the school building, members of society have a stake in education, with a huge investment in and influence on not only *what* is taught and *how* it is taught, but also on educational policy, procedures, ethics, and law. As a classroom teacher, you must respond to current social issues and the reforms they instigate. And don't forget that teachers are held accountable for their teaching.

The opportunity to work with and for these stakeholders may motivate you to continue your study of education. On the other hand, you may have decided that too many people are telling you what to do and you do not wish to be held accountable for factors beyond your control. Either way, you have learned a great deal about the place that teaching and schools occupy in society.

You now know that 21st-century teachers must be aware that the populations of society—and therefore of our classrooms—are diverse. Students represent many different ideas about what constitutes a positive contribution to society. As a teacher, your contribution is *not* to teach what you believe, but to guide students in acquiring the skills to make their own decisions about what *they* believe.

Are your reasons for becoming a teacher based on an adequate perception of what teaching is really like? We hope that the investigations you made using this textbook and through your class and field experiences have allowed you to construct a realistic understanding of students, teaching, and schools.

What Do Teachers Say?

How do your reasons for wanting to teach compare with the reasons given by practicing teachers? Every five years, the National Education Association (NEA) conducts a survey of teachers, entitled *The Status of the American Public School Teacher*. The most recent survey was given in 2006 for the 2005–2006 school year; results were published in 2010. The 2006 survey asked teachers why they originally chose teaching as a career and why they chose to stay in teaching. The desire to work with young people topped both lists. Table 15.1 summarizes the reasons cited in the survey (National Education Association, 2010).

The NEA survey also looked at why teachers stay in the profession. It showed that 66 percent of teachers would choose to teach again, and that 43 percent of teachers said they plan to stay in the classroom until they voluntarily retire. Twenty-six percent said they would stay until they are required to retire. Four percent said that they definitely plan to leave teaching as soon as possible, and 10 percent said they would probably stay until something better comes along (National Education Association, 2010).

Nieto (2003) surveyed several teachers in the Boston area, each highly respected and in the teaching profession for more than 25 years, to assess why these people stayed in teaching. The teachers gave the following basic reasons for staying in the profession:

■ Autobiography: The teachers are deeply involved in their teaching. Teaching has become their defining characteristic.

TABLE 15.1 Why Teachers Chose Teaching as a Career

Reason Cited for Becoming a Teacher	Percent of Respondents
Desire to work with young people	71%
Value or significance of education in society	42%
Interest in subject-matter field	39%
Influence of teacher in elementary or secondary school	31%
Never really considered anything else	14%
Influence of family	19%
Long summer vacation	19%
Job security	17%
Opportunity for a lifetime of self-growth	8%

Note: Respondents were asked to select the three main reasons they chose to teach.
Source: National Education Association, 2010. Courtesy National Education Association.

- Love: The teachers love their students and the subjects they teach.
- Hope and possibility: The teachers have hope and faith in their students, their abilities as teachers, and the profession of teaching.
- Intellectual work: The teachers constantly update their knowledge and teaching skills.
- Democratic practice: The teachers are committed to social justice and the ideals of democracy, fair play, and equality.
- Ability to shape the future: The teachers feel their work and actions are of greater consequence than those of almost any other profession.

How do the reasons for staying in teaching that the teachers in the NEA survey give and Nieto's sample compare with your own reasons for becoming a teacher?

As you consider your motives for teaching, you must also consider why teachers leave the profession. Some teachers believe that they made the wrong career choice. Those who took the 2006 NEA survey were asked to indicate whether they would choose teaching as a career again. Although 66 percent of respondents indicated that they would choose to be teachers again, 16 percent said that they might or might not choose teaching again, and 19 percent said that teaching would not be their choice (National Education Association, 2010). Table 15.2 shows the reasons teachers gave in the NEA survey for wanting to leave the profession before retirement.

The rate of attrition (the gradual decrease of staff due to resignation, retirement, and so on) of new teachers is of great concern. The National Commission on Teaching and America's Future (2005) found that nearly one out of every two teachers, or close to 50 percent, leave the classroom within five years, and this was reiterated by Diane Ravitch in 2012 (Ravitch, 2012). Furthermore, according to the 28th annual MetLife Survey of the American Teacher, teachers' satisfaction with their jobs has declined precipitously in recent years (Heitin, 2012). Table 15.3 shows the percent of teachers expressing job satisfaction on the survey between 1984 and 2011.

Responding to these alarming statistics, the commission (and many other scholars and teacher support groups) recommends strengthening teacher induction programs to

attrition The gradual decrease of staff due to resignation, retirement, and so on.

TABLE 15.2 Why Teachers Want to Leave Teaching before Retirement

Reason for Leaving Teaching	Percent of Respondents
Low salary	26%
Teaching/working conditions	13%
Too many nonteaching duties	8%
Lack of independence	5%
Family-related	8%
Health-related	5%
Student-related	5%
Administration-related	6%

Note: The percentages do not total 100 percent because only factors selected by 5 percent or more of the respondents are included.
Source: From National Education Association Survey, 2010. Courtesy National Education Association.

TABLE 15.3 Percent of Teachers Expressing Job Satisfaction, 1984–2011

Year	Percent of Teachers Expressing Job Satisfaction
1984	40%
1985	44%
1986	33%
1987	40%
1988	50%
1989	44%
1995	54%
2001	52%
2003	57%
2006	56%
2008	62%
2009	59%
2011	44%

© Cengage Learning 2014

help new teachers make a smooth and rewarding transition from the teacher preparation program to actual classroom situations (see also Chapters 9 and 14). The National Center for Education Statistics has instituted a survey to gain statistics on teacher attrition. They found that, of teachers who began in 2007 and were not assigned a mentor, 16 percent left after one year and 23 percent left after two years. However, of teachers who began in 2007 and were assigned a mentor, only 8 percent left the field after one year and 10 percent left after two years (Kaiser, 2011). These statistics certainly validate the essential nature of teacher induction and mentoring programs.

Is your passion for getting into education strong enough to sustain your motivation throughout your career, given what you now know about the challenges and complexities of being a teacher? Peske et al. (2001) suggest that, contrary to earlier times when people thought in terms of a single career and lifetime loyalty to a single organization, people today think in terms of several careers with several different organizations. In a large survey, these researchers found that "While there were respondents who planned to make teaching a lifetime career, they were surprisingly few in number" (p. 305). This finding suggests that some people may perceive teaching as one of several careers they will pursue. In fact, you may be one of those considering teaching as a new or different career path.

I'm Outta Here!

BUILDING BLOCK 15.4

Look at the reasons teachers cited for wanting to leave the profession in Table 15.2. Which are related to the skills and dispositions required for teaching? Which have to do with students? Which have to do with the context of the school? Which have to do with society?

We hope you have become better informed regarding the issues cited in Table 15.2 as you have explored the topics in this textbook, participated in class discussions, and completed your field experiences. If you have decided to continue in the teacher preparation program, you can do so better informed. For some, however, these issues may be significant enough for them to decide against teaching as a career. Regardless of your final decision, you now understand the teacher's role in society and the challenges that affect that role. How can you, as a member of your community, help teachers—and therefore the students who are the future citizens of your community—be successful?

© Blend Images/Alamy

Positively affecting the lives of young people is a reward of teaching that far outweighs minor challenges.

A Member of the Community
Elizabeth Day

Twenty-eight years ago, the phone rang at my house at eight in the evening. It was the superintendent of the school district in which I now teach, informing me that the Board of Education had decided to hire new teachers. If I accepted the sixth-grade position for which I applied, I would be teaching in the district that I had attended as a student. I was indeed excited to know that, when the new school year rolled around, not only would I have my first teaching job, but I would be able to return to my own community to be with the people I had been brought up with and had learned so much from. Along with the decision to teach in my community, I made the choice to live there, as well. I was returning to Mechanicville, New York, "The Friendly City," to see just what I might accomplish as a teacher and what I might be able to give back to my community. Because my two greatest role models, my mom and dad, gave so unselfishly to our city for so many years, I believed that this could be my chance to do the same.

As a teacher, I led by example. Nevell Bovee, an American author and lawyer, had stated, "Example has more followers than reason." Because I live in the same community in which I teach, the example I set—as my students see me both in and out of the classroom—gives them an opportunity to follow. I am a role model when I am a spectator at their sports events outside of school, an active participant in community bands and local theater, and a parent actively engaged in my own child's education. Through church activities, I joyously sing at former students' weddings, and I compassionately share the grief that accompanies the death of students or their family members. Whatever I'm doing, I work diligently with the members of my community in positive interpersonal relationships. My students and the community see me as a teacher-leader, a resource, an active community member, and a friend. I feel responsibilities to my students and to my community; perhaps through me, my students see that they have responsibilities to me and to their community, as well. Being a positive role model comes with great responsibility and is of utmost importance to me.

Teaching in my community and making a difference in the lives of the people with whom I work and live has held great reward for me. Reflecting back on my teaching experience, I realize that almost everyone under 40 in my town is someone who has sat in my classroom. I also know that I have influenced many people both inside and outside of my classroom. Teaching is my chance to make a positive difference in the lives of many. As my students make their journeys, I hold close to the idea that they, too, will continue to make a difference in the hearts and minds of those they encounter. If what they do can in any way be traced back to something I did, an example I set, or a role that I played, then my desire to reach out to others has come full circle, and I know that I have done my job well.

Elizabeth F. Day
2005 New York Teacher of the Year
Mechanicville Middle School
Mechanicville, New York

Courtesy of Elizabeth Day

BUILDING BLOCK 15.5

So You Want (Or Don't Want) To Be a Teacher?

Using the understandings you have constructed about teaching as a career, write a statement listing the reasons why you want to become a teacher. If you have decided *not* to continue in the field of education, or if you are undecided, write a statement listing your reasons for your current thinking.

Teaching as a Profession

You have reviewed the strong relationships among teaching, schools, and society. It is clear that teaching is a noble profession, but you probably have received mixed messages about how society regards teachers. Television shows, public service announcements, and awards (such as state or national teacher of the year awards) honor

Teaching requires significant preparation and training, self-governance, a code of ethics, and reliance on specific intellectual techniques and methods. In what other ways can teaching be considered a profession and not a trade or a job?

teachers and their contributions. Yet some portrayals of teachers are less than flattering. Perhaps friends and relatives wonder about your motives for wanting to teach. Consider the nontraditional students in your class. Many of them have chosen education as a *second* career. Why do you think nontraditional students did not go into teaching in the first place?

Professional Organizations

The education profession has a great number of professional organizations. You saw references to quite a few of these professional organizations earlier in this textbook. The most prominent are shown in Table 15.4. Remember that there are also regional and state organizations. One of the responsibilities of teachers is to keep up with the times regarding both subject matter and pedagogy. As you proceed through your teacher education program, keep these and other professional organizations in mind as reliable sources of current trends in the fields they represent. Some of what they have to offer is free on the Internet.

You have investigated teacher unions in this text; the two largest are the American Federation of Teachers (AFT) and the National Education Association (NEA). It is clear that there is no shortage of organizations for educators! However, these organizations do not govern the actual act of teaching. As you have seen, for most of the school day, teachers and students interact within the classroom walls, where most decisions are made by the authority in the room: the teacher. However, you have also learned that many individuals, committees, and professional organizations outside of the classroom and the school building exert great influence on teachers. The local school board is an example. Although doctors, lawyers, and even real estate agents are governed by boards of their colleagues and peers (other doctors, lawyers, and agents), school boards are usually not made up of teachers. What are the advantages and disadvantages of this arrangement?

Your Chosen Profession

So far in this chapter, you have considered your motives for teaching in the context of yourself, the students, the school, and society. You have seen that it is not completely clear whether teaching can be called a profession. Most individuals who choose or consider teaching as a career probably believe that teaching is a profession. But others in society may not be so sure. What can you do to raise the prestige of teachers and teaching?

TABLE 15.4 Prominent Professional Organizations for Educators

Discipline	Organization
Art education	National Art Education Association
Early childhood education	Association for Early Childhood Education International (ACEI) National Association for the Education of Young Children (NAEYC)
English, language arts, and reading education	International Reading Association (IRA) National Council of Teachers of English (NCTE)
Foreign language education and teaching English to speakers of other languages	American Council on the Teaching of Foreign Languages Teachers of English to Speakers of Other Languages, Inc. (TESOL)
Mathematics education	National Council of Teachers of Mathematics (NCTM) School Science and Mathematics Association
Music education	National Association for Music Education
Physical Education	National Association for Sport and Physical Education
Science Education	National Science Teachers Association National Association of Biology Teachers Chemistry Education Association American Association of Physics Teachers School Science and Mathematics Association
Social studies education	National Council for the Social Studies
Special needs and gifted education	Council for Exceptional Children (CEC) National Association for Gifted Children
Technology education	International Society for Technology in Education (ISTE)
Other organizations for teachers	American Counseling Association American Educational Research Association (AERA) American Federation of Teachers National Education Association Association for Supervision and Curriculum Development (ASCD) Association for Middle Level Education National School Boards Association

You can access these organizations through the direct links available on the Education CourseMate website.

One obvious answer is that if you want to be perceived as a professional, you must act like one. You looked at some elements of professionalism in Chapter 9. Your teacher education program has professionalism components on which you will be evaluated. What are these components?

Factors such as tardiness, poor communication or collaboration with the cooperating teacher or college supervisor, inappropriate attire, inappropriate interactions with students, lack of preparation, and breaches of confidentiality are behaviors that warrant remediation. From the moment you complete your introductory education course and move on to other education courses, your professionalism is being scrutinized. Is this appropriate and fair? How does knowing about this scrutiny influence your thoughts about whether or not teaching is a profession?

After you have obtained your first teaching position, you will of course continue to model professionalism. Not only will your behavior and professional dispositions be observed by your colleagues and administrators, but you will also be watched by your students, their parents, and the entire community. Being under the community's watchful eye also has implications for your behavior outside of school. As you have seen, teachers are held to higher standards than others in the community.

If you want to bolster others' perception of you as a professional, what can you do in your school? Your first two or three years of teaching will be spent polishing your skills, increasing your repertoire, and settling into the culture. Once you become fluent and established, you can consider taking on some leadership roles in your school and your community. As a teacher, you will have the opportunity to be involved in school committees that focus on issues such as textbook adoption, school policy and accreditation reviews, technology plans, and the like. You may also work with students who are involved with athletic teams, the yearbook, school newspaper, extracurricular clubs, or social functions. Choose to participate in these activities. Doing so not only demonstrates your commitment to your profession and to your students, it adds another level of reward to your professional life. (You may already sincerely like your students while they are in your class, but wait until you get to know them before and after school! You might discover facets of their personalities that are more interesting, creative, and humorous than the classroom allows.) What extracurricular activities might you be interested in sponsoring as a faculty member? Seek opportunities to volunteer in these activities as you progress in your teacher education program.

You may choose to take on some administrative responsibilities. After you have gained some experience, you may pursue the opportunity to become department chair or team leader. Or you may wish to become a learning support specialist or lead teacher, whose responsibilities extend beyond a department or grade level to the entire school. If you focus your required professional development activities on receiving additional endorsements and certifications in areas such as reading, English for speakers of other languages, gifted and talented education, and special education, not only will you broaden your professional knowledge and skills, you may also get a pay increase. National Board Certification and graduate degrees also carry benefits and prestige.

Beyond your school building, you can promote excellence in education by being a member of some professional organizations such as those listed in Table 15.4. Select your professional organizations carefully and focus on one or two. Attending the state, regional, or national conference of an organization is a wonderful way to interact with colleagues, exchange ideas, and reinvigorate your motivation. As you gain experience, you may decide to present papers at these conferences, reaching out to a larger audience of educators by sharing your knowledge and experience. You can become more active in your professional organization by volunteering or taking on a leadership role. You can help out at a conference and serve on (or eventually chair) the organization's governing body or service committee. Again, by getting involved, not only do you serve your professional development, you also help to bolster the prestige of the profession itself.

Finally, modeling professionalism in your classroom—by exhibiting professional behavior, taking on leadership roles in your school and professional organization, and participating in lifelong learning—lets you motivate *your* students to become teachers. They will see through you what a challenging, exciting, and rewarding career teaching can be. *You* will be the teacher they mention when they are asked about their motives for becoming teachers.

▶❚❚ TeachSource Video

View the TeachSource Video, "The First Year of Teaching: One Colleague's Story." In this video, fourth-grade teacher Will Starner speaks candidly about his first year teaching—what he has learned about himself, the best way to approach difficult situations, and the value he places on camaraderie with his fellow teachers.

After you view the videos, answer the following questions:

1. What are some of the challenges Mr. Starner encountered in his first year of teaching?

2. How did he respond to these challenges?

3. What advice does Mr. Starner give to new teachers?

Your Philosophy of Education ... Again

**BUILDING BLOCK
15.6**

Revise your philosophy of education statement to reflect your motives for teaching and the understanding about teaching and education that you have gained in this course.

Look again at the metaphor you chose for teaching. Do you still agree with it? Should you change it? Write down the metaphor you now believe describes you as a teacher, and refer to it throughout your teacher preparation program.

FROM THE FIELD

Courtesy of Bill Blythe

Getting Better Every Day
Bill Blythe

I am not where I should be, nowhere near where I want to be, but hopefully I am much better today than I was yesterday. I had this paraphrased quote laminated on one of my science cabinets near the classroom door and I thought I was the only one who ever looked at it. Occasionally, someone would ask me what this meant, and I would explain that it was important to me because I have committed myself to getting better every day and I consider it a wasted day if I am not, but I never really took it much deeper and explored exactly how I go about doing that and how that would look to my students and colleagues.

On the last day of the past school year, one of my students asked if she could have the laminated quote because she really believed in the thought. I was pleased to let her have it and more than happy to see that she had displayed it as her profile picture on Facebook. With this young lady asking for this quote, I began to think about my philosophy of education, which seems to closely resemble a deeper philosophy of life signified by constantly striving to become better at whatever your passion may be.

I believe we build ourselves every day and that this can be of either a positive or a negative nature, but even the things that may be wrong or seemingly counterproductive, can be the best teachers. I am a constructivist at heart but I understand that neither my students, colleagues, nor I can become better at anything if we don't make some mistakes along the way and, more importantly, admit when we don't know something. I have been a department chair at my school for the past few years, and it is absolutely amazing to me how teachers will insist that they do not have areas that are in need of improvement. Things began to change the moment that I admitted to the things that I don't know or where I have a weakness; fortunately, my colleagues then began to analyze where they are in terms of development. It is destructive to any development to ever think you don't have an area of improvement—whether a student, a teacher, or an administrator. One of the best examples that I can set for my students and peers is to admit where my deficiencies are and know that I can only get better when I truthfully know where I can start my construction.

I am far from the content expert in my school, and moving from the middle grades to high school this year is cause for a little anxiousness but I know I will work hard to increase my content knowledge every day. I will never be a complete content expert, in my eyes, because the content area that I teach deepens exponentially by the minute. I do know that if perfection becomes my focus, then I am doing my students a disservice. I am a teacher of lifelong learners and not of a specific content area. The best example that I can set for my students is for them to see me developing—making mistakes and getting better every day. Believe me, I would love for my students to become science content experts, but I really think I prefer they become excited enough about science that they would pursue it further and, more importantly, become excited about learning itself. I must remember not to get caught up in all the other stuff, and remember my mission for my students and peers—to strive to find a way to be better tomorrow than we were today.

Bill Blythe
Pope High School
Formerly McCleskey Middle School Teacher of the Year
Marietta, Georgia

Let us close with some "words to the wise" that are sure to keep you happy and fulfilled as a teacher. Teaching is one of the hardest and one of the best professions you can choose, but only if it is where your heart lies. You have to have a passion for it; the actual act of teaching has to feed this passion, because, as you have learned, there are a great many factors that may tax you. If you know that you will love helping *all* children learn (and if you love learning yourself) and if you know that you will step up to the challenge of working with others—parents, colleagues, administrators, politicians—to help your learners become the best people that they can be, then teaching is for you. The rewards will be more than you can measure.

■ SUMMARY

In this chapter, you recalled the motives for teaching you had when you began this course. You considered those motives in the context of the information you have read in this textbook, and you examined whether teaching is a profession—and what you can do to promote it as such.

- Your motives for teaching come from many places—your *self*, the *students*, the *school* itself, and *society*. Self-based motivations include your innate desire to engage in the art and science of teaching, your predispositions, and your emotional feelings for teaching. Student-based motivational factors are represented by your desire to help students. School-based factors include a comfort zone in this place called school, your love of your subject matter, and a schedule that is favorable for teachers with school-aged children. Societal reasons include your contributions to the community and society as a whole. Of these, the desire to work with young people heads the list of reasons why existing teachers first entered the profession. Attrition among teachers is high, with half leaving the profession during the first five years. It has been shown that mentors are effective in reducing this rate of attrition.

- Teaching is a profession that is accompanied with many opportunities for professional development. Active participation in one or more international education organizations helps teachers keep up with the times. As a professional, teachers are expected to exhibit appropriate professional behaviors.

We mentioned early in this chapter that most introductory education textbooks place the chapter on students' motives for teaching at the very beginning of the book. Considering that this textbook is constructivist-oriented, why do you think this chapter comes at the very end?

What have you concluded about your motives for teaching or not teaching? Can you state one prevailing reason? Should you be able to? Remember the educational philosophy of eclecticism (see Chapter 2). Does it apply to your motives for teaching?

You might think it unusual for the concluding paragraphs of a textbook's last chapter to be so full of questions. Realize that this book, and the class for which you have read it, is actually the very beginning of a complex learning experience: your teacher education program. Knowing what you now know about how a constructivist-oriented lesson begins, does it surprise you that we are asking you more questions?

■ Key Terms and Concepts

Attrition, 403
Disposition, 399

■ Construct and Apply

1. Young children often say they want to be teachers when they grow up. Why do you suppose this is? What might their motives be for saying this? In what ways could these motives change as they get older? How might they stay the same?
2. People admire and trust teachers and yet are quick to point the finger of blame at teachers first when test scores drop. How do you explain this seeming contradiction in the public perception of teachers?
3. What is meant by "professionalism" with regard to teachers and teaching?

■ Deconstructing the Standards

1. Recall the InTASC standard associated with the objectives for this chapter:

   InTASC Standard #9: Professional Learning and Ethical Practice reads, "The teacher engages in ongoing professional learning and uses evidence to continually evaluate his/her practice, particularly the effects of his/her choices and actions on others (learners, families, other professionals, and the community), and adapts practice to meet the needs of each learner."

   a. What part(s) of this standard does this chapter address?

   b. How will the concepts in this chapter help you apply theis standard as a teacher?

2. Use your favorite search engine to find your state's standards for certification. When you find it, bookmark the site. You will refer to it often as you progress through this book.

   a. How are your conclusions about motives for teaching represented in your state certification standards?

   b. How do the InTASC standards compare to your state's certification standards regarding motives for teaching?

   c. Do you believe the degree of representation concerning motives for teaching is adequate in your state certification standards? Why or why not?

■ Your Portfolio

Include your final philosophy of education and describe additional thoughts you might have as a result of completing this textbook, your course, and your field experience. Discuss how these activities have influenced your thinking, thereby demonstrating your ability to reflect.

■ Education CourseMate Resources

Check out this text's Education CourseMate website (at www.cengagebrain.com) for more information about the teaching profession. You will find the TeachSource Videos, a guide for doing field experiences, glossary flash cards, activities, tutorial quizzes, direct links to the websites mentioned in the chapter, and more.

Glossary

1.5 Generation students Refers to individuals who have graduated from a high school in the United States and who have entered higher education while still learning English.

accreditation The formal, official approval signifying that the requirements of excellence described in professional standards developed by professionals in a particular discipline have been met.

aesthetic Creatively, beautifully, or artistically pleasing.

alternative school A school with the primary purpose of educating students who, for various reasons, do not thrive in traditional schools.

anchor activities An ongoing assignment that is related to the curriculum on which students may work independently.

apps Abbreviation for "application"; a downloadable program that can be run on a computer or portable device.

assistive technology Technology that individuals with disabilities may use to perform tasks that would otherwise be difficult or impossible.

at-risk student A student considered at high risk of failing to complete school.

attention deficit disorder A disorder characterized by not being able to maintain attention or control impulses. Usually not accompanied by the hyperactivity component of ADHD.

attention deficit/hyperactivity disorder A disorder characterized by not being able to maintain attention or to control impulses. Often includes incidence of increased distraction and energy resulting in not being able to stay still.

attrition The gradual decrease of staff due to resignation, retirement, and so on.

authentic assessment Education tasks that resemble the real-world applications of the skills and knowledge being assessed.

autism A spectrum of disorders in which communication, social interactions, and the ability to participate in relationships is impaired.

autocratic teacher A teacher who controls every part of the classroom and student behavior, demonstrating no flexibility or receptiveness to student input.

axiology The branch of philosophy concerned with values.

basic needs Those needs that must be met for people to live satisfied lives.

behaviorism The psychological approach that explains behavior by examining external experiences.

bell-shaped curve The bell-shaped graph of a distribution that may and may not be symmetrical.

bilingual education Instruction provided in both a student's native language and in English.

block scheduling A scheduling system in which a school's daily schedule is organized into large blocks of time.

blog A blend of the terms *Web* and *log*. Individuals can develop blogs online that contain text, audio, photo, and video postings on a particular subject.

Board of Education The official policy-making authority for the school district.

Brown v. Board of Education of Topeka U.S. Supreme Court decision in 1954 that required schools in the United States to desegregate.

bullying The act of one or more people repeatedly exposing another person to negative actions to which the person has difficulty defending himself or herself.

Carnegie unit Unit of credit awarded to students for the completion of a full year's work in a subject taught four or five times a week.

case law A law that is the result of decisions made by the courts.

categorical grants Funding from the federal government to provide for elementary and secondary programs approved through federal legislation.

certification add-on An additional area of certification typically added onto an existing certification area by an individual completing the certification requirements for the area.

charter school A school that has been granted permission by state educational agencies to operate with freedom from one or more of the regulations that apply to traditional public schools.

chief state school officer The state superintendent of schools.

clickers *See* **classroom response system**.

childhood obesity A condition of children being overweight.

classical conditioning A form of learning in which an organism learns to associate a stimulus with a nonrelated response.

classroom response system (CRS) An electronic interactive assessment system in which students in a classroom use a handheld response system, similar in appearance to a remote control, on which they may press buttons to indicate their answers to multiple-choice questions. The input of the class is collected by a receiver, analyzed, and displayed almost immediately.

code of ethics A guide to acceptable professional behavior.

cognitive ability The ability to learn, know, and understand.

cognitive development The intellectual development of the mind.

cognitive needs Those needs associated with learning, knowing, and understanding.

cognitive psychology The psychological approach that explains behavior by examining mental processes.

collaborative teacher A teacher who solicits and uses student input in the creation of classroom rules and procedures, demonstrating respect for all.

Common Core State Standards Standards designed to be "robust and relevant to the real world, reflecting knowledge and skills that our young people need for success in college and careers" (Common Core State Standards Initiative, 2010).

common law Case law or precedent developed through decisions of courts.

common school Elementary school in the 19th century that was free and public.

competitive grants Grants awarded through a competitive process involving an evaluative review of proposals.

conservation With regard to cognitive development, the ability to recognize that the amount of material does not change when volume or shape changes.

constitutional law A law based on the U.S. Constitution or a state constitution.

constructivism A learning theory that proposes that students construct their own knowledge by combining information they already have with new information, so that new knowledge takes on personal meaning to the student.

contract An agreement with specific terms between two or more people or entities in which there is a promise to do something in return for a valuable benefit.

cooperative teaching A method of distributing teaching responsibilities in elementary schools such that teachers assume responsibility for their areas of expertise.

copyright The exclusive right of the author or creator of a literary or artistic property (such as a book, movie, or musical composition) to print, copy, sell, license, distribute, transform to another medium, translate, record, perform, or otherwise use (or not use) their work, and to give it to another by will.

corporal punishment The infliction of physical pain on someone as punishment for committing an offense.

cosmology The branch of metaphysics in philosophy concerned with the origin and structure of the universe.

cooperative teaching A method of distributing teaching responsibilities in elementary schools such that teachers assume responsibility for their areas of expertise.

co-teaching Two or more certified teachers (such as a general education teacher and a special education teacher) teaching a class together.

cultural deficit model A multicultural paradigm that assumes that nonmainstream students may fail to achieve due to deficits that are imposed on them by their culture.

cultural deprivation model A multicultural paradigm that assumes that nonmainstream students may fail to achieve because their culture deprives them of resources and experiences.

cultural difference model A multicultural paradigm that assumes that nonmainstream students may fail to achieve due to differences between their culture and the culture of the classroom.

cultural mismatch model A multicultural paradigm that assumes that nonmainstream students may fail to achieve due to a mismatch between the students' culture and the culture of the classroom.

culturally relevant pedagogy Teaching that acknowledges students' culture in the design of lessons.

culture The customary beliefs, social forms, and material traits of a racial, religious, or social group.

cyberbullying The act of bullying through email, text and picture messages, websites, posts on social networking sites and chat rooms, and cell phones.

dame schools Colonial school for girls.

deductive reasoning The type of reasoning that proceeds from the most general to the most specific.

defendant The person, people, or entity against whom a lawsuit is filed.

deficiency needs In Maslow's hierarchy of needs, those needs that are critical to a person's well-being and that must be satisfied first and foremost. These include physiological needs, safety and security, love and belonging, and self-worth and self-esteem.

Department of Education (DOE) The state-level governing body for education policies developed by the state board of education, including use of state and federal funds, teacher certification, curriculum, and testing.

differentiated instruction Instruction that is tailored to the different needs of individual students.

digital divide Disparity in access to computers and the Internet among different groups of people.

disposition The qualities of one's character.

diversity The condition of being different from one another.

due process A person's legal right to be adequately notified of charges or proceedings involving him or her and to be given the opportunity to be heard.

dyslexia A learning disability in which an individual has difficulty with reading comprehension and writing.

eclectic Selecting from a variety of sources.

education management organization A corporation that assumes responsibility for some or all facets of school management, including curriculum, instruction, building maintenance and operation, and administration.

education reform Changing and refining the education system to meet the needs of the students and the society to which they belong.

Elementary and Secondary Education Act (ESEA) Enacted in 1965, the ESEA provided federal guidance and funds to school districts with large numbers of disadvantages students; reauthorized in 2001 as the No Child Left Behind Act.

empathetic Having understanding of or participating in someone else's feelings or ideas.

English as a foreign language (EFL) Individuals who are learning English in a country where English is not the native language.

English as a second language (ESL) A support program of instruction for ELLs.

English language learner (ELL) A person learning to speak English whose primary language is other than English.

epistemology The study of knowledge.

ethnicity Affiliation with a group that has general customs, language, and social views and based on common racial, national, tribal, religious, linguistic, or cultural origin or background.

exceptional students Students who require some form of modification to the standard educational program.

fair use provision of the copyright act The use of copyrighted materials determined to be fair and not an infringement of the copyright act based on four factors: (1) whether the use is commercial in nature or for nonprofit educational purposes; (2) the nature of the copyrighted work; (3) the portion used in relation to the copyrighted work as a whole; and (4) the effect of the use on the potential market value of the copyrighted work.

Family Educational Rights and Privacy Act of 1974 (FERPA) Guarantees parents and students confidentiality and fundamental fairness concerning the maintenance and use of student records.

felony A serious crime, usually involving violence, that is punishable by imprisonment.

formative assessment An assessment that is implemented during the course of instruction so that teachers and students may be informed of the students' progress in achieving objectives.

formula funding Funding that is provided on the basis of the application of a formula that uses specified data to determine need.

freedom of expression The liberty to speak and otherwise express oneself and one's opinions, guaranteed by the First Amendment to the U.S. Constitution.

freedom of religion The right to choose a religion (or no religion) without interference by the government, guaranteed by the First Amendment to the U.S. Constitution.

full inclusion The strategy of including students who may have exceptionalities in with the population of all students in all classes and activities.

GI Bill A federal act that provides funds to returning war veterans to attend college.

gifted and talented student A student who has potentially outstanding abilities that allow him or her to excel in one or more areas of intellectual endeavor, creativity, leadership, and artistic pursuits.

governance How an organization is controlled, including who has the authority to exercise this control.

growth needs In Maslow's hierarchy of needs, the upper three levels of needs, which humans will try to satisfy after their **deficiency needs** have been met. These levels include the need to know and understand, aesthetic needs, and the need for self-actualization.

hidden curriculum What children learn in school that is not content related, but rather a part of being in a school. The hidden curriculum includes the procedures and routines of school functions.

hierarchy An order of rank.

Higher Education Act A federal program that provides grants and loans to students in college (often in the form of Pell grants).

home schooling An educational alternative in which children learn under the supervision of their parents at home rather than at a conventional school.

Hornbook A single-faced wooden paddle used to teach reading in colonial times.

humanism The psychological approach that stresses people's capacity and desire for personal growth.

in loco parentis "In place of parents."

inclusion The practice of assigning students with below-normal or above-normal IQs or disabling conditions to the same classrooms they would attend if they were not disabled.

individualized education program A plan for meeting the educational needs of an individual student who may have disabilities.

inductive reasoning The type of reasoning that proceeds from the most specific to the most general.

information processing theory A cognitive psychology that explains learning by manipulation of sensory register, short-term memory, and long-term memory.

instructional duties Teacher duties directly associated with planning, instruction, and evaluation.

insubordination An act of disobedience to proper authority (Garner, 2009).

interactive whiteboard A large touch-sensitive display surface that is connected to a computer. Whatever is on the computer is displayed on the surface and responds to touch much like a computer responds to the input from a mouse.

interview An assessment method that consists of a structured or open conversation between student and teacher in which the teacher asks questions relating to the objectives of a lesson.

journal Students' writings, including what they did, what they learned, and their reflections, often used as an element of authentic assessment.

latchkey kid A child who spends unsupervised or self-supervised time after school.

Latin grammar schools Schools in the New England colonies for upper-class males that taught the subjects necessary for admission to college.

lead teacher A teacher whose responsibilities include assisting teachers in developing and implementing strategies to reach all types of learners and whose focus is on aiding teachers.

learning disability A disorder that interferes with the learning process.

learning modality An individual's preference about how information is presented and taken in. Learning modalities include visual, auditory, and tactile/kinesthetic.

learning style An individual's preference about how information is presented and taken in. Learning styles include visual, auditory, and tactile/kinesthetic.

LGBTQ Lesbian, gay, bisexual, transgendered, and questioning.

learning support specialist (LSS) A teacher whose responsibilities include assisting teachers in developing and implementing strategies to reach all types of learners and whose focus is on aiding individual students.

library media specialist (LMS) Professional educator whose specialty includes library science and multimedia management.

limited English proficiency (LEP) Refers to individuals who lack the mastery of English to be successful in a mainstream classroom. This term is not a preferred term because it implies that these individuals are deficient. Instead, *ELL* is preferred because it acknowledges the individual as a learner.

lobbying The process of influencing local, state, or government policy.

liable (legal liability) A legal responsibility, duty, or obligation; the state of one who is legally bound to do something that may be enforced by legal action.

locus of control A characteristic that describes whether an individual attributes responsibility for failure or success to internal or external factors.

logic The branch of philosophy concerned with reasoning.

looping A system of assigning students in elementary schools to the same teacher for two or more consecutive years.

magnet school A school that focuses on specific curricular areas—such as the arts, math, or science—to attract students with special aptitudes and interests in those areas.

mainstreaming Placing a disabled student in regular school classes.

Massachusetts Act of 1647 The "Old Deluder Satan Act" that required towns with at least 50 households to hire a schoolmaster to teach children to read and write, and required towns of 100 households or more to have a school that would prepare children to attend Harvard College.

McGuffey Readers Primary reading texts in the 19th century.

mentor A trusted and experienced guide in the profession.

merit pay A teacher's salary that is based on the quality of the teacher's performance; *see also* **pay for performance**.

metaphor A figure of speech in which two seemingly unlike objects or ideas are compared based on something they have in common.

metaphysics The branch of philosophy concerned with questions of reality.

misdemeanor A less serious crime than a felony, punishable by a fine and a possible jail term.

mission statement A written public statement crafted by the stakeholders in an organization (such as a school) that identifies the organization's perceived purpose.

monitorial system Teacher preparation program wherein future teachers received training in the schools they, themselves, attended.

Morrill Act of 1862 Land Grant College Act that gave land to states to develop colleges.

multiage education A system of clustering students of different ages in elementary schools in the same class.

multiple intelligence theory A proposition by Howard Gardner asserting that traditional measures of intelligence are limited and that individuals possess different types of intelligences. These intelligences include spatial, bodily–

kinesthetic, musical, linguistic, logical–mathematical, interpersonal, intrapersonal, and naturalistic intelligences.

National Defense Education Act (NDEA) Enacted in 1958, the NDEA provided federal aid for education in the United States at all levels, for public and private schools.

New England Primer A small book used to teach reading in the New England colonies.

New Math A mathematics program in which students were taught the theoretical basis of mathematics through the use of actual mathematical language and notations.

noninstructional duties Teacher duties not directly associated with instruction of students.

normal curve The symmetrical, bell-shaped curve of a **normal distribution**.

normal schools Schools in the late 19th and early 20th century for the preparation of elementary school teachers.

Old Deluder Satan Act Nickname for the Massachusetts Act of 1647.

online learning Learning that takes place online using the Internet.

ontology The branch of metaphysics concerned with the nature of being and reality.

operant conditioning An approach to learning in which the consequences of a behavior produce changes in the likelihood that the behavior will occur again.

paraprofessional Teacher aide.

Parent–Teacher Association (PTA) A local school-based organization comprised of parents, teachers, and other school personnel who work for the improvement of the school.

Parent–Teacher–Student Association (PTSA) A school-based organization comprised of parents, teachers, students, and other school personnel who work for the improvement of the school.

pay for performance A teacher's salary that is based on the quality of the teacher's performance; *see also* **merit pay.**

pedagogical content knowledge The knowledge of how to teach the content to others and the ability to develop higher-order thinking skills in learners.

pedagogical knowledge and skills The knowledge and skills of how to teach content information to learners.

pedagogy The art and science of teaching.

Pell grant A federally sponsored grant system for postsecondary education.

perception A mental image of what one experiences.

performance assessment An assessment that requires the learner to actually demonstrate—or perform—the skill.

permissive teacher A teacher who lets students get away with anything in the way of classroom behaviors, causing a stressful and chaotic classroom environment.

phonics A method for teaching reading and spelling that is based on interpreting the sounds of the letters.

plagiarism Representing the writings, literary concepts (a plot, characters, words), or other original work of another as one's own product.

plaintiff The person, people, or entity who files the lawsuit.

podcast (pod = play on demand) An audio broadcast over the Internet that may be recorded for later access.

portfolio An authentic assessment method consisting of a container or folio of evidence that shows a student's progress toward achieving the knowledge and skills of a subject.

poverty level The minimum amount of income that is determined to be adequate.

private school A school that restricts its population of students to those who meet certain criteria established by the school.

professionalism The ethical behavior exhibited by teachers.

programmed instruction A teaching strategy in which students work their way through small chunks of information. At the end of each part, students are tested over the material. Correct answers earn praise as a reward and the student progresses on to additional information. Incorrect answers result in remediation.

Project Head Start A federal program that funds preschools for children from families of poverty.

psychosocial development Development of psychological and social factors within an individual.

psychosocial needs Those needs associated with getting along with one's self and others.

psychosocial theory Theory addressing the psychological and social aspects of identity development.

race A group of people that possesses traits that are inherited and sufficient to characterize the group as a distinct human type.

regulation A rule that is enacted by a state or local agency to ensure compliance with the law.

resource classroom A classroom staffed with a special education teacher or teachers, equipped and managed to meet the needs of students with exceptionalities according to their IEPs.

response to intervention A method used for the early identification of students who may have special needs that employs deliberate strategies to impact learning. If the student does not respond to the intervention, it may be determined that the student has a learning disability.

risky behavior Behavior that may result in adverse consequences.

schemata (sing. *schema***)** Cognitive structures.

school board (Board of Education) The official policy-making authority for the school district.

school choice The freedom to choose which school children will attend.

school improvement plan A plan that identifies a school's priorities for the coming years, methods to implement these priorities, and ways to assess the results.

search and seizure Examination of a person's premises by law enforcement officers looking for evidence of the commission of a crime, and taking articles of evidence (seizure and removal).

self-actualization The state of having become everything a person is capable of becoming, realizing one's full potential, capacities, and talents.

service learning A teaching strategy that engages students in meaningful service to their communities through integration of community issues and the school curriculum.

sexually transmitted disease A disease transmitted largely through sexual behavior.

site-based management A system of management in which plans and decisions involve all employees in a site.

socioeconomic Involving both social and economic factors.

socioeconomic status A position influenced by a combination of social and economic factors including income, education, occupation, and place in the community.

special education Instruction that is specifically designed to meet the unique needs of students who are recognized as exceptional.

stakeholder A person or institution with an interest in education.

standards movement An educational reform movement in which exemplary performances in specific areas of education are identified, especially in curriculum, instruction, and teacher preparation.

statute A law passed by the federal, state, or local legislature.

stereotype A standard image or idea that represents an uninformed opinion or biased attitude toward a group.

student–teacher ratio The average number of students assigned to one teacher.

summative assessment An assessment that is implemented at the end of an instructional unit to measure student achievement of objectives.

superintendent of schools The head of the school district.

tablet computer A small computer, contained in a single tablet-like panel that contains a touch screen for input.

teacher certification A state's official recognition that a person has met the requirements to be a professional teacher in that state.

tenure A teacher's status as a permanent member of the faculty in a school district.

theology The branch of metaphysics in philosophy concerned with God and the relations among God, mankind, and the universe.

theory of multiple intelligences A proposition by Howard Gardner asserting that traditional measures of intelligence are limited and that individuals possess different types of intelligences. These intelligences include spatial, bodily–kinesthetic, musical, linguistic, logical–mathematical, interpersonal, intrapersonal, existential, and naturalistic intelligences.

Title I A federal program that provides funds to meet the needs of students in high-poverty schools.

Title VII A federal program that provides financial aid for the education of students with limited English ability (also known as the Bilingual Education Act).

Title IX A federal act providing for equal athletic opportunities regardless of gender.

tort A wrongful act, other than a breach of contract, for which relief may be obtained in the form of damages.

value-added analysis A statistical method that uses standardized test scores and other data to inform the evaluation of teacher performance.

vernacular schools Schools in the New England colonies for lower-class males that taught reading, writing, arithmetic, and religion.

virtual school A school that offers most of or its entire curriculum online using the Internet.

vision A foresight into the possible future of a school.

vocational school A public high school that provides various types of vocational education programs in addition to an academic curriculum; also called career and technical schools.

vodcast (vod = video on demand) A video broadcast over the Internet that may be recorded for later access.

WebQuest A learning activity in which some or all of the information with which students interact comes from the Internet, similar to a scavenger hunt.

white privilege The idea that the white race is afforded unearned advantages and positive treatment due to race.

whole language A constructivist approach to teaching reading and writing in which students learn from first-hand experiences.

wiki A collaborative website on which content can be edited by anyone who has access to it.

zero-tolerance policies Policies that entail a strict and swift disciplinary response to students or school personnel who engage in violent activities, who bring to or use weapons in school, or who bring or use controlled substances.

References

ABC Nightline. (2010). The college cheating culture. *ABC News,* December 13. Retrieved from http://abcnews.go.com/Nightline/video/college-cheating-culture-12389056.

About.com Elementary Education. (2012). Pros and cons of merit pay for teachers. Retrieved from http://k6educators.about.com/od/assessmentandtesting/a/meritypay.htm.

Achieve, Inc. (2012). *The next generation science standards: Frequently asked questions.* Retrieved from www.nextgen-science.org/faq.

ACLU. (2011a). *ACLU demands Flour Bluff High School allow Gay-Straight Alliance Student Club to meet.* Retrieved from www.aclu.org/lgbt-rights/aclu-demands-flour-bluff-high-school-allow-gay-straight-alliance-student-club-meet-0.

ACLU, (2011b). *Flour Bluff High School acknowledges Gay-Straight Alliance Club has the right to meet.* Retrieved from www.aclu.org/lgbt-rights/flour-bluff-high-school-acknowledges-gay-straight-alliance-club-has-right-meet.

Adcock v. Board of Education of San Diego Unified School District. 10 Cal.3d 60, 109 Cal.Rptr. 676, 513 P.2d 900 (1973).

Adesman, A., and Ellison, A. T. *ADHD: Top 10 myths.* Webcast, September 5, 2007. Health Talk. Retrieved from www.everydayhealth.com/adhd/webcasts/adhd-top-10-myths-transcript-1.aspx.

Administration for Children and Families. (2010). *Head start impact study final report: Executive summary.* Retrieved from www.acf.hhs.gov/programs/opre/hs/impact_study/reports/impact_study/executive_summary_final.pdf.

Administrative Office of the U.S. Courts. (2011). *Statistical tables for the federal judiciary* and "Bankruptcy Statistics," www.uscourts.gov/bnkrpctystats/statistcs.htm. Retrieved from www.census.gov/compendia/statab/2011/tables/11s0771.pdf.

AFL-CIO. (n.d.). About the AFL-CIO. Retrieved from www.aflcio.org/About.

AFL-CIO. (n.d.). *AFL-CIO unions.* Retrieved from www.aflcio.org/About/AFL-CIO-Unions.

The African American Registry. (n.d.). *The African Free School opens.* Retrieved from www.aaregistry.org/historic_events/view/african-free-school-opens-new-york-city.

The Afterschool Investments Project. (2006). *Promoting physical activity and healthy nutrition in afterschool settings: Strategies for program leaders and policymakers.* U.S. Department of Health and Human Services. Retrieved from http://nccic.acf.hhs.gov/afterschool/fitness_nutrition.html.

AIDS Alert. (2005). Teen sexual risk behavior news is both good and bad: Experts promote comprehensive education. *AIDS Alert 20*(3), 32–34.

Aikens, N. L., and Barbarin, O. (2008). Socioeconomic differences in reading trajectories: The contribution of family, neighborhood, and school contexts. *Journal of Educational Psychology 100,* 235–51.

Albright, L. (2005, July 23). Jeb plays games with Florida class size. *People's Weekly World.*

Alderfer, C. (1972). *Existence, relatedness, & growth.* New York: Free Press.

Alelo. (2012). Therapy for autistic children. Alelo. Retrieved from www.alelo.com/autism.html.

Alexander, K., and Alexander, M. D. *American public school law.* Belmont, CA: Wadsworth Cengage Learning.

Alger, Christianna L. (July 2009). Secondary teachers' conceptual metaphors of teaching and learning: Changes over the career span. *Teaching and Teacher Education, 25*(5), 743–51. doi: 10.1016/j.tate.2008.10.004.

Alleghany Institute for Public Policy. (2011). *Teacher strikes in Pennsylvania.* Retrieved from http://alleghenyinstitute.org/education/teacherstrikes.html.

American Academy of Pediatrics. (2005). Policy statement: Condom use by adolescents. *PEDIATRICS (115)*5, 1438, doi:10.1542/peds.2005-0464.

American Federation of Teachers. (n.d.). About AFL: *American Federation of Teachers, AFL-CIO.* Retrieved from www.aft.org/about/.

American Psychological Association. (2004). *Council policy manual: Sexual orientation, parents, & children.* Retrieved from www.apa.org/about/governance/council/policy/.

American Psychological Association. (2010). *APA survey raises concern about health impact of stress on children and families.* Retrieved from www.apa.org/news/press/releases/stress/index.aspx.

American Psychological Association. (2011). *Education & socioeconomic status: Fact sheet.* Retrieved from www.apa.org/pi/ses/resources/publications/factsheet-education.aspx.

Anasari, Maryam. (2010). Teacher, school sued for bullying kid. *Boston Personal Injury News,* June 3. Retrieved from http://bostonpersonalinjurynews.com/2010/06/teacher-school-sued-for-bullying-kid.html.

Anderson, D. J. (2003, September 27). *The historical context for understanding the test score gap.* Paper presented at Race, Culture, Identity, and Achievement lecture series, Wheelock College, Boston, MA.

Anderson, N. (2011). Most schools could face "failing" label under No Child Left Behind, Duncan says. *The Washington Post,* March 10, 2011, p. A01.

Anderson, R. H. (1966). *Teaching in a world of change.* New York: Harcourt, Brace, & World.

Andren, Kari. (2011). Legislation would allow Pennsylvania teachers to wear religious insignias. *The Patriot-News,* June 12. Retrieved from www.pennlive.com/midstate/index.ssf/2011/06/post_208.html.

Arwood, E. (2011) *Language function: an introduction to pragmatic assessment and intervention for higher order thinking and better literacy.* London, UK: Jessica Kingsley Publishers.

ASCD.org. (n.d.) Common core standards adoption by state. *ASCD .org.* Retrieved from www.ascd.org/common-core/common-core-standards.aspx.

Ash, K. (2012). Rethinking testing in the age of the iPad. *Education Week,* February 8, 2012. Retrieved from www.edweek.org/dd/articles/2012/02/08/02mobile.h05.html.

Associated Press. (2012). Some states toughening standards to award teachers tenure. New Jersey Real-Time News, January 25. Retrieved from www.nj.com/news/index.ssf/2012/01/states_toughening_standards_to.html.

Association for Middle Level Education (formerly the National Middle School Association). (2010). *This we believe: Keys to educating young adolescents.* Columbus, OH: author.

Ausubel, D. P., Novak, J. D., and Hanesian, H. (1978). *Educational psychology: A cognitive view,* 2nd ed. New York: Holt, Rinehart and Winston.

Baer, J., Baldi, S., Ayotte, K., and Green, P. (2007). *The reading literacy of U.S. fourth-grade students in an international context: Results from the 2001 and 2006 Progress in International Reading Literacy Study (PIRLS) (NCES 2008–017).* National Center for Education Statistics, Institute of Education Sciences, U.S. Department of Education. Washington, DC.

Baker, D., and LeTendre, G. (2005). *National differences, global similarities: World culture and the future of schooling.* Stanford, CA: Stanford University Press.

Balfanz, R. (2009). Can the American high school become an avenue of advancement for all? *The Future of Children 19*(1), 17–36.

Bandler, R., and Grinder, J. (1979). *Frogs into princes: Neuro linguistic programming.* Moab, UT: Real People Press.

Banks, J. A. (2008). *An introduction to multicultural education,* 4th ed. Boston: Pearson Education, Inc.

Banks, James, A. (1988). *Multiethnic Education: Theory and practice,* 2nd ed. Boston: Allyn and Bacon.

Barlow, Sarah E., Bobra, Sonal R., Elliott, Michael B., Brownson, Ross C., and Haire-Joshu, Debra. (2007). Recognition of childhood overweight during health supervision visits: Does BMI help pediatricians? *Obesity.* Retrieved from www.nature.com/oby/journal/v15/n1/abs/oby2007535a.html.

Barrett, D. B., Kurian, G. T., and Johnson, T. M. (Eds.). (2001). *World Christian encyclopedia: A comparative survey of churches and religions in the modern world,* 2nd ed. Oxford, U.K.: Oxford University Press.

Baum, S. (2003). College financial aid. In J. W. Guthrie (Ed.), *Encyclopedia of education,* 2nd ed., pp. 376–78. New York: Macmillan Reference USA.

Bay v. State Board of Education. 378 P.2d 558 561.

Beare, Kenneth. (2012). ESL acronymns. About.com, English as a 2nd Language. Retrieved from http://esl.about.com/od/teachingenglish/a/esl_acronyms.htm.

Begley, Sharon. (2012). *New high in U.S. autism rates inspires new debates.* Reuters, March 29. Retrieved from www.reuters.com/article/2012/03/29/us-autism-idUSBRE82S0P320120329.

Beilock, S. L., Gunderson, E. A., Ramirez, G., and Levine, S.C. (2010). Female teachers' math anxiety affects girls' math achievement. *Proceedings of the National Academy of Sciences of the United States 107,* 1,860–63.

Benbenutty, H. (2011). The first word: Homework's theory, research, and practice. *Journal of Advanced Academics 22*(2), 185–92.

Berger, S. (1998). *College planning for gifted students,* 2nd ed. Arlington, VA: Council for Exceptional Children.

Berk, L. (2000). *Child development,* 5th ed. Boston: Allyn & Bacon.

Berliner, D. C. (1985). Effective classroom teaching: The necessary but not sufficient condition for developing exemplary schools. In G. R. Austin and H. Barber (Eds.), *Research on exemplary schools.* Orlando, FL: Academic Press.

Bethel School District No. 403 v. Fraser, 478 U.S. 675, 106 S.Ct. 3159, 92 L.Ed.2d 549 (1986). (Case No. 117).

Bill and Melinda Gates Foundation. (December, 2010). *Learning about teaching: Initial findings from the measures of effective teaching project.* Seattle, WA: Bill and Melinda Gates Foundation.

Binder, F. M. (1974). *The age of the common school, 1830–1865.* New York: John Wiley and Sons.

Blackwell v. Issaquena County Board of Education, 363 F.2d 749 (5th Cir. 1966).

Blum, D. (1999, July). What's the difference between boys and girls? A funny thing happened when we left "puppy dogs' tails" and "sugar and spice" behind. Scientists discovered that it's not just our culture that makes rules about gender-appropriate behavior—it's our own body chemistry. *Life,* 22(8), 44.

Board of Education v. Earls, 122 S. Ct. 2559 (2002).

Boehner, J. (Chairman). (2003). Press release: House approves bills to help states put a qualified teacher in every classroom. *News from the Committee on Education and the Workforce.*

Bohlin, Lisa, Durwin, Cheryl Cisero, and Reese-Weber, Marla. (2009). *Ed psych: Modules.* New York: McGraw-Hill.

Bomer, R., Dworin, J. E., May, L., and Semingson, P. (2008). Miseducating teachers about the poor: A critical analysis of Ruby Payne's claims about poverty. *Teachers College Record 110*(12), 2,497–2,531.

Boone, Christian, and Leslie, Katie. (April 21, 2009). *At vigil for Jaheem, mother weeps over his suicide.* Atlanta Journal-Constitution.

Borum, Randy, Cornell, Dewey G., Modzeleski, William, and Jimerson, Shane. (2010). What can be done about school shootings? A review of the evidence. *Educational Researcher 39*(1), 27–37.

Boudreaux, G. (1993). *Louis Sullivan: The growth of an idea.*

Brandt, R., and Voke, H. (2002). A lexicon of learning: What educators mean when they say . . . . Association for Supervision and Curriculum Development.

Brar, Sandeep Singh. (2003). Sikhism. Retrieved from www.sikhs.org/.

Brenner, Jason, Frost, Ashley, Haub, Carl, Mather, Mark, Ringheim, Karin, and Zuehlke, Eric. (2010). World population highlights: Key findings from PRB's 2010 world population data sheet. *Population* Bulletin 65(2).

Brewster, C., and Railsback, J. (2001). *Schoolwide prevention of bullying*. Washington, DC: Office of Educational Research and Improvement.

Brezicki, C. (2010/2011). Kindle: The Amazon e-reader as an educational tool. *Phi Delta Kappan 92*(4), 22–23.

Briggs, T. W. (2007). College students struggle on history test. *USA Today*, September 19, 2007. Retrieved from www.usatoday.com/news/education/2007-09-17-history-test_N.htm.

Brooks, D.M. (1985). The first day of school. *Educational Leadership, 42*(8), 76–79.

Brooks, J. G., and Brooks, M. G. (1999). *In search of understanding: The case for constructivist teaching*. Alexandria, VA: Association for Supervision and Curriculum Development.

Brown v. Board of Education, 347 U.S. § 483 (1954).

Bruner, J. S. (1965). *The process of education*. Cambridge, MA: Harvard University Press.

Buckley, J. (2011). NAEP High School Transcript Study, 2009. Washington, DC: National Center for Education Statistics. Retrieved from http://nces.ed.gov/whatsnew/commissioner/remarks2011/A_13_2011.asp.

Bully Police USA. (2011). *State anti-bullying laws*. Retrieved from www.bullypolice.org/.

Burke, L. M., and Sheffield, R. (2011). School choice in America 2011: Educational opportunity reaches new heights. Washington, DC: *Backgrounder, The Heritage Foundation*. Retrieved from http://thf_media.s3.amazonaws.com/2011/pdf/bg2597.pdf.

Burns, M. (2005/2006). Tools for the mind. *Educational leadership 63*(4), 48–53.

Callaghan, Alice. (2010). Quality counts. *The Los Angeles Times*, July 11.

Camarota, Steven A. (2010, November). *Immigration and economic stagnation: An examination of trends 2000 to 2010*. Center for Immigration Studies. Retrieved from www.cis.org/highest-decade.

Canady v. Bossier Parish School Board, 250 F.3d 437 (5th Cir. 2002).

Canter, L. (1985). *Assertive discipline*. Santa Monica, CA: Canter and Associates.

Carnegie Council on Adolescent Development. (1989). *Turning points: Preparing American youth for the 21st century: The report of the Task Force on Education of Young Adolescents*. New York: Author.

Carter, Kylie. (2010). New Buffalo teacher sentenced for exposing himself to young boy. WNDU.com, May 12. Retrieved from www.wndu.com/localnews/headlines/93644114.html.

Cartwright, Madeline, and D'Orso, Michael. (1999). *For the children: Lessons from a visionary principal*. Ardmore, PA: Berger-Cartwright.

Carver, P. R., and Lewis, L. (2010). Alternative schools and programs for public school students at risk of educational failures: 2007–2008. U.S. Department of Education, National Center for Education Statistics. Retrieved from http://nces.ed.gov/pubs2010/2010026.pdf.

Cavanagh, Sean. (2011a). Eighteen states changed tenure laws in 2011, report says. *State EdWatch*, August 23. Retrieved from http://blogs.edweek.org/edweek/state_edwatch/2011/08/post_8.html.

Cavanagh, S. (2011b). Online-learning mandate on the move in Idaho. *Education Week, 31*(4), 10.

Center for Education Reform. (2009). National Charter School Directory. Retrieved from www.charterschoolsearch.com/schoolsbyState.cfm.

Center for Effective Discipline. (2011). Discipline and the law. Retrieved from www.stophitting.com/index.php?page=laws-main.

Center for Responsive Politics. (2011). *Lobbying: Who's up? Who's down?* Retrieved from www.opensecrets.org/lobby/incdec.php.

Center for Safer Wireless. (n.d.). Cell phone towers and antennas on school property. Retrieved from http://centerforsaferwireless.org/Cell-Phone-Towers-and-Antennas-on-School-Property.php.

Centers for Disease Control. (2010). Increasing prevalence of parent-reported attention-deficit/hyperactivity disorder among children—United States, 2003 and 2007. *Morbidity and Mortality Weekly Report (MMWR) 59*(44): 1,439–43. Retrieved from www.cdc.gov/mmwr/preview/mmwrhtml/mm5944a3.htm.

Chambers, G. (2000, November 16). Distinguished Educator Series Lecture, Bagwell College of Education, Kennesaw State University, Kennesaw, GA.

Chan, S. (1991). *Asian Americans, an interpretive history*. Boston: Twayne.

Chapman, C., Laird, J., Ifill, N., and Kewal-Ramani, A. (2011). *Trends in high school dropout and completion rates in the United States: 1972–2009* (NCES 2011-012). National Center for Education Statistics, Institute of Education Sciences, U.S. Department of Education. Washington, DC. Retrieved from http://nces.ed.gov/pubs2012/2012006.pdf.

Charlesworth, R., and Lind, K. K. (2010). *Math and science for young children*. Belmont, CA: Wadsworth/Cengage Learning.

Chen, C-U. (2011). Numbers and types of public elementary and secondary schools from the Common Core of Data: School year 2009–2010 (NCES 2011-345). Washington, DC: U.S. Department of Education, National Center for Education Statistics. Retrieved from http://nces.ed.gov/pubs2011/2011345.pdf.

Christian, Vanessa L. (2008). Cognitive development and academic achievement: A study of African American, Caucasian, and Latino children. Retrieved from ProQuest Digital Dissertations. (Publication number 3350945).

Christie, K., and Zinth, D. (2011). Teacher tenure or continuing contract laws, updated. Denver, CO: Education Commission of the States. Retrieved from www.procon.org/sourcefiles/Teaching-Quality-ECS-2011.pdf.

CIA. (2009). *The World Factbook 2009*. Washington, DC.: Central Intelligence Agency. Retrieved from www.cia.gov/library/publications/the-world-factbook/index.html.

Clabough, Raven. (2011). Texas school board approves pro-evolution materials. *The New American*, July 23. Retrieved from www.thenewamerican.com/culture/education/item/324-texas-school-board-approves-pro-evolution-materials.

Cleaver, Samantha. (2011). Why are we still hitting? Scholastic. Retrieved from www.scholastic.com/browse/article.jsp?id=3751247.

Cloonan, Patrick. (2011). MASD teacher fired for immorality to get appeal hearing. *McKeesport Daily News*, April 14. Retrieved from http://pittsburghlive.com/x/dailynewsmckeesport/s_732249.html.

College Board. (2012). Take control of homework so it doesn't control you. Retrieved from https://bigfuture.collegeboard.org/get-started/inside-the-classroom/take-control-of-homework.

Collins, P. (n.d.). Incarcerated fathers involvement in children's lives and education: An overview of research, policy, and programs. (Special report.) Long Beach, CA: California State University (Graduate School of Education).

Combs, A. (1993, July 19). Effectiveness of the helping professional. From a lecture at Kennesaw State University, Kennesaw., GA.

Common Core State Standards for English Language Arts and Literacy in History, Social Studies, Science, and Technical Subjects. (2010). Retrieved from www.corestandards.org.

Common Core State Standards Initiative. (2011). *Mission statement.* Retrieved from www.corestandards.org/.

Cook, Joan Littlefield, and Cook, Greg. (2009). *Child development: Principles and perspectives.* New York: Pearson Education, Inc.

Cookson, P. W. (1994). *School choice: The struggle for the should of American education.* New Haven, CT: Yale University Press.

Cooper v. Eugene School District, No. 4J, 301, Or. 358 (1986), appeal dismissed, 480 U.S. 942 (1987).

Cooper, H., Robinson, J. C., and Patall, E. A. (2006). Does homework improve academic achievement? A synthesis of research, 1987–2003. *Review of Educational Research* 76(1), 1–62.

Cortiella, Candace. (2001). Response-to-intervention: *An emerging method for LD identification.* Retrieved from www.greatschools.org/special-education/LD-ADHD/883-emerging-method-for-ld-identification.gs?page=all.

Costa, A. L. (2007). *The school as a home for the mind: Creating mindful curriculum, instruction, and dialogue,* 2nd ed. Thousand Oaks, CA: Corwin Press.

Council for American Private Education. (n.d.). *Private education.* Germantown, MD: author.

Council of Chief State School Officers. (2010). *Model core teaching standards: A resource for dialogue.* Washington, DC: Council of Chief State School Officers. Retrieved from www.ccsso.org/Documents/2010/Model_Core_Teaching_Standards_DRAFT_FOR_PUBLIC_COMMENT_2010.pdf.

Crawford, J. (2002). Obituary: The Bilingual Education Act 1968–2002. *Rethinking Schools Online* 16(4).

Crosnoe, Robert, Johnson, Monica Kirkpatrick, and Elder, Jr., Glen H. (2004). "Intergenerational bonding in school: The behavioral and contextual correlates of student-teacher relationships." *Sociology of Education* 77(1), 60–81.

CSU Institute for Education Reform. (1996). Is less more? Exploring California's new class size reduction initiative. The California Education Policy Seminar and the California State University Institute for Education Reform. Retrieved from www.calstate.edu/ier/reports/reduction.pdf.

Culross, R. (n.d.). Gifted and talented: Question and answer, by Rita Culross, PhD. *Family Education.*

Cunha, Flavio, and Heckman, James J. (2006). *Investing in our young people.* University of Chicago. Retrieved from www.news.uchicago.edu/releases/06/061115.education.pdf.

Curtis, Lindsey. (2011, February 28). *FBISD pushes some clubs off campus following gay-straight alliance controversy.* KRISTV.COM. Retrieved from www.kristv.com/news/fbisd-pushes-some-clubs-off-campus-following-gay-straight-alliance-controversy/.

D.A.R.E. (2012). About D.A.R.E. *Drug Abuse Resistance Education.* Retrieved from www.dare.com/home/about_dare.asp.

D'Orso, M., and Cartwright, M. (1999). *For the children: Lessons from a visionary principal.* Ardmore, PA: Berger-Cartwright.

Damon, Tanjua. (2011). In-school suspension statistics presented. *Vernon Patch,* July 10. Retrieved from http://vernon.patch.com/articles/in-school-suspension-statistics-presented.

Darling-Hammond, L. (2000). Teacher quality and student achievement: A review of state policy evidence. *Education Policy Analysis Archives,* 8(1).

Darling-Hammond, Linda. (2009, December,). Recognizing and enhancing teacher effectiveness. *The International Journal of Educational and Psychological Assessment 3.* Time Taylor Academic Journals, pp. 1–24.

Day, J. C. (2001). *National population projections.* Washington, DC: U.S. Census Bureau.

DeLaire, T., and Kalil, A. (2001). *Good things come in 3's: Single-parent multigenerational family structure and adolescent adjustment.* Chicago: University of Chicago, Harris Graduate School of Public Studies.

Democrat Herald. (2010). Oregon House lifts ban on religious clothing in the classroom. *Democrat Herald,* February 10. Retrieved from http://democratherald.com/news/local/article_c9cf5562-1699-11df-8dc9-001cc4c002e0.html.

Devaney, L. (2011). More states look to online learning for students. *eSchoolNews.* Retrieved from www.eschoolnews.com/2011/11/02/more-states-look-to-online-learning-for-students/.

DeVine, Josh. (2012). Teacher disciplined after writing "stupid" on student's forehead. WSMV.com, January 10. Retrieved from www.wsmv.com/story/16317736/teacher-disciplined-after-writing-stupid-on-students-forehead.

DeYoung, A. J. (1995). Constructing and staffing the cultural bridge: The school as change agent in rural Appalachia. *Anthropology & Education Quarterly* 26(2), 168–92.

Dickard, N., and Schneider, D. (2011). The digital divide: Where we are. *Edutopia.* Retrieved from www.edutopia.org/digital-divide-where-we-are-today.

Dickenson, P. (2012). Reform for English language learners. *Education Week* blog. Retrieved from http://blogs.edweek.org/edweek/rick_hess_straight_yp/2012/01/reform_for_english_language_learners.htm.

Dickersen, D. (2011). Hitting the reset button: Using formative assessment to guide instruction. *Phi Delta Kappan,* 92(7), 26–31.

Dieker, Lisa A., and Murawski, Wendy W. (2003). Co-teaching at the secondary level: Unique issues, current trends, and suggestions for success. *The High School Journal* 86(4). Retrieved from www.jstor.org.proxy.kennesaw.edu/stable/40364319?seq=2.

Dillon, S. (2011a). Tight budgets mean squeeze in classroom. *The New York Times,* March 6. Retrieved from www.nytimes.com/2011/03/07/education/07classrooms.html.

Dillon, Sam. (2011b). Teacher grades: Pass or be fired. *The New York Times,* June 27. Retrieved from www.nytimes.com/2011/06/28/education/28evals.html?pagewanted=all.

Dillon, Sam. (2011c). U.S. students remain poor at history, tests show. *The New York Times,* June 14. Retrieved from www.nytimes.com/2011/06/15/education/15history.html.

Dirksen, Debra. (2011). Hitting the reset button: Using formative assessment to guide instruction. *Phi Delta Kappan 92*(7), 27–31.

Dodge, B. (1995). WebQuests: A technique for Internet-based learning. *Distance Educator 1,* 2, pp. 10–13.

Dodge, B. (1999). Original Webquest template. Retrieved from http://webquest.org/.

Doe v. Little Rock School District. (2004). US Eighth Circuit Court. (No. 03-3268).

Donaldson, M. J., and Johnson, S. M. (2011). Teach for America teachers: How long do they teach? Why do they leave? *Kappanmagazine.org 93*(2), 47–51. Retrieved from www.edweek.org/ew/articles/2011/10/04/kappan_donaldson.html.

Donovan, Lisa. (2010). CPS teacher negligent for leaving 7th graders unattended: Lawsuit. *Chicago Sun Times,* April 23. Retrieved from www.studentsfirst.us/news/contentview.asp?c=226796.

Dottin, E. S. (2001). *The development of a conceptual framework.* Lanham, MD: University Press of America.

DuFour, R., and Marzano, R. J. (2011). The most important factor in student achievement. http://pages.solution-tree.com/LOLQA.html?from=MRLtwitter.

Duke, Alan. (2012). California teacher pleads not guilty in student "bondage" case. CNN, February 21. Retrieved from http://articles.cnn.com/2012-02-21/justice/justice_california-school-case_1_guilty-plea-duke-lacrosse-lacrosse-players?_s=PM:JUSTICE.

Duncan, A., and Richardson, J. (2009). Quality education is our moon shot. *Phi Delta Kappan 91*(2), 24–25.

Dunifon, R., and Kowaleski-Jones, L. (2002). Who's in the house? Race differences in cohabitation, single parenthood, and child development. *Child Development 73*(4), 1249–64.

Dunn, R. (1988). Teaching students through their perceptual strengths or preferences. *Journal of Reading 31*(4), 304–08.

Dunne, Diane Weaver. (2005). *ADHD: What is it?* Education World. Retrieved from www.educationworld.com/a_issues/issues/issues148.shtml.

Eakin, S. (2000). Giants of American education. *Technos Quarterly 9*(2), 1–9.

Ebeling, D. G. (2000). Adapting your teaching to any learning style. *Phi Delta Kappan 28*(3), 247–48.

EdisonLearning. (2011a). Is online high school right for your student? Retrieved from http://edisonlearning.com/content/20110901/online-high-school-right-your-student.

EdisonLearning. (2011b). Press release. Retrieved from www.edisonlearning.com/press-releases.

Education Commission of the States. (2012). *Site-based management.* Retrieved from www.ecs.org/html/issue.asp?issueid=111.

Education Week. (2012). Class size. Retrieved from www.edweek.org/ew/issues/class-size/.

Educational Leadership. (2010/2011). What makes a great teacher? *Educational Leadership 68*(4), 74–75, 91.

Eggers, D., and Calegari, N. C. (2011). The high cost of low teacher salaries. *The New York Times,* April 30, 2011. Retrieved from www.nytimes.com/2011/05/01/opinion/01eggers.html?_r=1&pagewanted=print.

Egley, Jr., Arlen, and Howell, James C. (2011). *Highlights of the 2009 national youth gang survey.* U.S. Department of Justice, Office of Justice Programs, Office of Juvenile Justice and Delinquency Prevention.

Eisner, E. W. (1983). The art and craft of teaching. *Educational Leadership, 40*(4), 5–13.

Eisner, E. W. (2002). Questionable assumptions about schooling. *Phi Delta Kappan 84*(9), 648–57.

Ellison, Phyllis Anne Teeter. (2003). AD/HD myths: Science over cynicism. *Attention!* Retrieved at www.help4adhd.org/en/about/myths.

Erb v. Iowa State Board of Public Instruction, 216 N.W.2d 339 (Sup.Ct. Iowa 1974).

ERIC Clearinghouse on Disabilities and Gifted Education. (2006). Common myths about gifted students; Common truths about gifted students. Author. Retrieved from www.hoagiesgifted.org/eric/fact/myths.html.

Erikson, E. H. (1968). *Identity: Youth and crisis.* New York: Norton.

eSchoolNews. (2011a). Five things students say they want from education. www.eschoolnews.com/2011/07/28/five-things-students-say-they-want-from-education/.

eSchool News. (2011b). Teen "sexting": Less common than parents, educator might fear. *eSchool News,* December 6. Retrieved from www.eschoolnews.com/2011/12/06/teen-sexting-less-common-than-parents-educators-might-fear/.

Evans, Stephanie. (2006). Gay-straight alliance clubs: How homosexual student organizations harm our schools. *Findings.* North Carolina Family Policy Council. Retrieved from www.ncfpc.org/PolicyPapers/Findings%200611-GSA.pdf.

Family Center on Technology and Disability. (2010). *Assistive technology and the IEP.* WETA. Retrieved from LDOnline at www.ldonline.org/article/Assistive_Technology_and_the_IEP.

Federal Register, Department of Agriculture: Food and Nutrition Service. (2012). Nutrition standards in the national school lunch and school breakfast programs. *Federal Register, 77*(7). Retrieved from www.federalregister.gov/articles/2012/01/26/2012-1010/nutrition-standards-in-the-national-school-lunch-and-school-breakfast-programs.

Federal Register. (2011). Cited in Gafner Law Firm, P.C. (2011). *Poverty guidelines release: I864 Affidavit of support and I134 Affidavit of support.* www.gafnervisalaw.com/2011/01/24/2011-poverty-guidelines-released-i-864-affidavit-of-support-and-i-134-affidavit-of-support/.

Feistritzer, C. E., and Haar, C. K. (n.d.). Overview of research on alternate routes. Washington, DC: National Center for Alternative Certification. Retrieved from www.teach-now.org/research%20about%20alternate%20routes.pdf.

Feistritzer, C. Emily, and Haar, Charlene K. (2008). *Alternative routes to teaching.* Columbus, OH: Merrill.

Felder, Richard M. (2010). *Are learning styles invalid? (Hint: No!).* On-Course Newsletter, September 27. Retrieved from www4.ncsu.edu/unity/lockers/users/f/felder/public/Papers/LS_Validity(On-Course).pdf.

Flannery, Mary Ellen. (September 13, 2010). Top eight challenges teacher face this school year. *NEA Today.* National Education Association. Retrieved from http://neatoday.org/2010/09/13/top-eight-challenges-teachers-face-this-school-year/.

Fleischman, D., and Heppen, J. (2009). Improving low-performing high schools: Searching for evidence of promise. *America's High Schools 19*(1). Retrieved from www.princeton.edu/futureofchildren/publications/journals/article/index.xml?journalid=30&articleid=50&sectionid=189.

Fleischman, H. L., Hopstock, P. J., Pelczar, M. P., and Shelley, B. E. (2010). Highlights from PISA 2009: Performance of U.S. 15-year-old students in reading, mathematics, and science literacy in an international context (NCES 2011-004). U.S. Department of Education, National Center for Education Statistics. Washington, DC.: U.S. Government Printing Office.

Florida Department of Education. (n.d.). Class size reduction amendment. Retrieved from www.fldoe.org/classsize/?style=print.

Florida Department of Education. (n.d.). Public virtual schools: FAQs. Retrieved from www.fldoe.org/schools/virtual-schools/faqs.asp?style=print.

Food and Nutrition Service. (2010). *National School Lunch Program Fact Sheet*. United States Department of Agriculture. Retrieved from www.fns.usda.gov/cnd/lunch/AboutLunch/NSLP-FactSheet.pdf.

Fowler, D. (2011). School discipline feeds the "pipeline to prison." *Phi Delta Kappan 93*(2), 14–19.

Fox v. Board of Education of Doddridge County et al. No. 13920. 160 W. Va. 668, 236 (S.E.2d 243 1977). In Deschaine, M. C. (2002). Can a school district assign teachers duties set outside regular classroom instruction? Graduate Student Portfolio. Grand Rapids, MI: Central Michigan University.

FoxNews. (2010, December 29). *Small knife in lunchbox gets N.C. student suspended, charged with weapon possession.* Retrieved from www.foxnews.com/us/2010/12/29/nc-high-school-senior-suspended-charged-possesion-small-knife-lunchbox/.

Friedman, M. S., Marshal, M. P., Guadamuz, T. E., Wei, C., Wong, C. F., Saewyc, E. M., and Stall, R. (2011). A meta-analysis of disparities in childhood sexual abuse, parental physical abuse, and peer victimization among sexual minority and sexual non-minority individuals. *American Journal of Public Health*, doi: 10.2105/AJPH.2009.190009.

Friedman, T. L. (2005). *The world is flat. A brief history of the twenty-first century.* New York: Farrar, Strauss, and Giroux.

Fry, Richard. (2010). *Hispanics, high school dropouts and the GED.* Pew Hispanic Center. Retrieved from http://pewhispanic.org/reports/report.php?ReportID=122.

Fuller, Bruce. (2008). The bilingual debate: Transitional classrooms. *Education Watch*, September 28. Retrieved from http://campaignstops.blogs.nytimes.com/2008/09/28/the-bilingual-debate-transitional-classrooms/.

Furco, Andrew, and Root, Susan. (February 2010). Research demonstrates the value of service learning. *Phi Delta Kappan 91*(5), 16–20.

Gabriel, R., Day, J. P., and Arlington, R. (2011). Exemplary teacher voices on their own development. *Phi Delta Kappan 92*(8), 38–41.

Gabriel, Trip. (2010). Plagiarism lines blur for students in digital age. *The New York Times*, August 1. Retrieved from www.unc.edu/world/2010CCSymposium/Readings/NYT_plagarismdigitalage.pdf.

Gage, N. L. (1978). *The scientific basis of the art of teaching.* New York: Teachers College Press.

Garcia, D. R., Barber, R., and Molnar, A. (2009). Profiting from public education: Education management organizations and student achievement. *Teachers College Record 111*(5), 1352–1379. ERIC document no. EJ842200.

Gardner, H., and Hatch, T. (1989). Educational Implications of the Theory of Multiple Intelligences. *Educational Researcher, 18*(8) 4–10.

Gargiulo, M. M. (2006). *Special education in contemporary society,* 2nd ed. Belmont, CA: Wadsworth/Thomson Learning.

Gargiulo, Richard. M. (2011). *Special education in contemporary society: An introduction to exceptionality.* Thousand Oaks, CA: Sage Publications.

Garner, Bryan A. (2009). *Black's law dictionary,* 9th ed. Eagan, MN: West Law.

Gates, Gary, J. and Cooke, Abigail M. (2011). United States census snapshot: 2010. *The Williams Institute.* Retrieved from williamsinstitute.law.ucla.edu/wp-content/uploads/Census2010 Snapshot-US-v2.pdf.

Gault, 387, U.S. 1; 875 S. Ct. 1428; 18 L. Ed. 2d 527 (1967).

Geary, Jason. (2010). Former teacher David McCall found guilty of trespassing. *The Ledger,* June 16. Retrieved from www.theledger.com/article/20100616/news/6165047.

George, L. J. (2011). What's the purpose of high school? *The Citizen.* Retrieved from http://auburnpub.com/lifestyles/article_fd2a691c-58db-11e0-a412-001cc4c002e0.html.

Gersten, R., Marks, S. U., Keating, T., and Baker, S. (1998). Recent research on effective instructional practice for content-area ESOL. In R. M. Gersten and R. T. Jiménez (Eds.), *Promoting learning for culturally and linguistically diverse students.* Belmont, CA: Wadsworth Publishing Company.

Gibson, Elizabeth. (2011). West Perry teacher's state certificate revoked after theft conviction. The Patriot-News, November 15. Retrieved from www.pennlive.com/midstate/index.ssf/2011/11/west_perry_teachers_state_cert.html.

Glasser, W. (1993). *The quality school teacher.* New York: Harper Perennial.

Glasser, W. (1998). *Choice theory: A new psychology of personal freedom.* New York: Harper Perennial.

Glover v. Williamsburg Local School District Board of Education, 20F.Supp.2d 1160 (Ohio 1998).

GLSEN. (2006). *GLSEN deeply concerned after North Carolina school board bans GSAs.* Retrieved from www.glsen.org/cgi-bin/iowa/all/news/record/1956.html.

GLSEN. (2009). *11-year-old hangs himself after enduring daily anti-gay bullying.* GLSEN, April 9. Retrieved from www.glsen.org/walker.html.

GLSEN. (2011). *Background and information about gay-straight alliances.* Retrieved from www.glsen.org/cgi-bin/iowa/all/library/record/2336.html.

Gonzales Patrick, Guzmán Juan Carlos, Partelow Lisette, Pahlke Erin, Jocelyn Leslie, Kastberg David, and Williams Trevor. (2004). *Highlights from the Trends in International Mathematics and Science Study (TIMSS) 2003 (NCES 2005–005).*

U.S. Department of Education, National Center for Education Statistics. Washington, DC: U.S. Government Printing Office. Retrieved from http://nces.ed.gov/pubs2005/2005005.pdf.

Gonzales, P., Williams, T., Jocelyn, L., Roey, S., Kastberg, D., and Brenwald, S. (2008). *Highlights From TIMSS 2007: Mathematics and Science Achievement of U.S. Fourth- and Eighth-Grade Students in an International Context (NCES 2009–001 Revised)*. National Center for Education Statistics, Institute of Education Sciences, U.S. Department of Education. Washington, DC. Retrieved from http://nces.ed.gov/pubsearch/pubsinfo.asp?pubid=2009001.

Gonzalez, S. (2012). Inside the mathematical equation for teacher merit pay. *State/Impact Florida*. Retrieved http://stateimpact.npr.org/florida/2012/02/16/inside-the-mathematical-equation-for-teacher-merit-pay/.

Gordon, D. (2011). Off the beaten path. *The Journal, Rural Schools* (feature). Retrieved from http://thejournal.com/Articles/2011/10/04/Off-the-Beaten-Path.aspx?p=1.

Gorski, P. (2005). *Celebrating the joys of exclusion: The internal undermining of multicultural education*. [working paper.]. St. Paul, MN: EdChange.

Goss v. Lopez, 419 U. S. 565, 95 Ct. 729, 42 L.Ed.2d 725 (1975). (Case No. 127).

Graham, Deborah. (2012). Religious organizations can discriminate in hiring—They're above the law protecting workers. Lawyers.com, January 17. Retrieved from www.jdsupra.com/post/fileServer.aspx?fName=402dbf73-1516-40f6-b0e5-72248f798ac8.pdf.

Gratz, D. G. (2005). Lessons from Denver: The pay for performance pilot. *Phi Delta Kappan* 86(8), 568–81.

Gray, Lucinda, and Lewis, Laurie. (2009). Educational technology in public school districts: Fall 2008. *US Department of Education*. Retrieved from http://nces.ed.gov/pubs2010/2010003.pdf.

Gruber, J. E., and Fineran, S. (2008). Comparing the impact of bullying and sexual harassment victimization on the mental and physical health of adolescents. *Sex Roles*, doi: 10.1007/s11199-008-9431-5.

Gurian, Michael, Stevens, Kathy, and Daniels, Peggy. (2009) *Successful single-sex classrooms: A practical guide to teaching boys and girls separately*. San Francisco: Jossey-Bass.

Haar, C. K. (1999). *Teacher unions and parental involvement*. Washington, DC: Education Policy Institute.

Hakuta, K. (2011). Educating language minority students and affirming their equal rights: Research and practical perspectives. *Educational Researcher* 40(4), 163–74.

Hanes v. Board of Education of City of Bridgeport, 783 A.2d 1 (Conn. App. Ct. 2001).

Hanuscin, D. L. (2010). Everybody needs a Betsy. *Science and Children* 47(9), 41–43.

Hearn v. Board of Education, 191 F.3d 1329 (11th Cir. 1999).

Hein, S. (2003). Invalidation. *EQ Informational Site on Emotions, Emotional Intelligence, Teen Suicide, and More*.

Herbert, M. (2011). The school choice movement marches forward in 2011. *District Administration*. Retrieved from www.districtadministration.com/article/school-choice-movement-marches-forward-2011.

Heros. (2009). Project STAR fact sheet. Retrieved from http://dvn.iq.harvard.edu/dvn/dv/star/faces/study/StudyPage.xhtml;jsessionid=45ffe0745e1e2d87cbb306f014db?globalId=hdl:1902.1/10766&tab=files&studyListingIndex=0_45ffe0745e1e2d87cbb306f014db.

Hinduja, S., and Patchin, J. W. (2010a). *Cyberbullying: Identification, prevention, and response*. The Cyberbullying Research Center. Retrieved from www.cyberbullying.us/Cyberbullying_Identification_Prevention_Response_Fact_Sheet.pdf.

Hinduja, S. and Patchin, J. W. (2010b). Bullying, cyberbullying, and suicide. *Archives of Suicide Research* 14(3), 206–21.

Hirsch, Jr., E. D. (1987). *The new dictionary of cultural literacy: What every American needs to know*. New York: Houghton Mifflin.

Hirsch, Jr., E. D. (1988). *Cultural literacy: What every American needs to know*. Madison, WI: Turtleback Books.

Hirsch, Jr., E. D. (1994). *What your third grader needs to know: Fundamentals of a good third-grade education (the Core Knowledge series)*. New York: Dell.

Hirsch, Jr., E. D. (1995a). *What your fifth grader needs to know: Fundamentals of a good fifth-grade education (the Core Knowledge series)*. New York: Dell.

Hirsch, Jr., E. D. (1995b). *What your sixth grader needs to know: Fundamentals of a good sixth-grade education (the Core Knowledge series)*. New York: Dell.

Hirsch, Jr., E. D. (1997). *What your kindergartner needs to know: Preparing your child for a lifetime of learning (the Core Knowledge series)*. New York: Dell.

Hirsch, Jr., E. D. (1998). *What your first grader needs to know: Fundamentals of a good first-grade education (the Core Knowledge series)*. New York: Dell.

Hirsch, Jr., E. D. (1999). *What your second grader needs to know: Fundamentals of a good second-grade education (the Core Knowledge series)*. New York: Dell.

Hirsch, Jr., E. D. (2004). *The new first dictionary of cultural literacy: What your child needs to know*. Madison, WI: Turtleback Books.

Holland, Gale, (2008). "Model minority" myth hides reality: The achievement of some Asian American overshadows academic diversity of other students, report says. *Los Angeles Times*, June 10. Retrieved from http://articles.latimes.com/2008/jun/10/local/me-asian10.

Home School Legal Defense Association. (2011). *State laws concerning participation of homeschool students in public school activities*. Retrieved from www.hslda.org/docs/nche/Issues/E/Equal_Access.pdf.

Hopkins, M. (2008). Training the next teachers for America: A proposal for reconceptualizing Teach for America. *Phi Delta Kappan* 89(10), 721–33, 736.

Howell, James C. (2010). *Gang prevention: An overview of research and programs*. U.S. Department of Justice, Office of Justice Programs, Office of Juvenile Justice and Delinquency Prevention. Retrieved from www.ncjrs.gov/pdffiles1/ojjdp/231116.pdf.

Hu, W. (2011). New recruit in homework revolt: The principal. *The New York Times*. Retrieved from www.nytimes.com/2011/06/16/education/16homework.html.

Huang, D. Leon, S., La Torre, D., and Mostafavi, S. (2008). Examining the relationship between LA's best program attendance and academic achievement of LA's best students. Los Angeles, CA: National Center for Research on Evaluation, Standards, and Student Testing.

Huang, G. (1994). Beyond culture: Communicating with Asian American children and families. ERIC Digest 94 (ED366673).

Hubbard, Jeremy. (2010). *Fifth gay teen suicide in three weeks sparks debate.* ABC News, October 3. Retrieved from http://abcnews.go.com/US/gay-teen-suicide-sparks-debate/story?id=11788128.

Huffman, Sara. (2011). *Encouraging little girls to get dirty could protect their health later.* ConsumerAffairs.com, January 27. Retrieved from www.consumeraffairs.com/news04/2011/01/encouraging-little-girls-to-get-dirty-could-protect-their-health-later.html.

Humphrey, D. C., and Wechsler, M. E. (2005). Insights into alternative certification: Initial findings from a national study. *Teachers College Record*, September 2.

Hutchins, R. M. (1952). *Great books of the Western world. Encyclopaedia Britannica, Inc., in collaboration with the University of Chicago.* Chicago: W. Benton.

Imig, D. G. (2002, April 23). Lecture at Kennesaw State University, Kennesaw, GA.

Immigration Policy Center. (2012). Q & A guide to state immigration laws. Retrieved from http://immigrationpolicy.org/special-reports/qa-guide-state-immigration-laws.

Infoplease.com. (2007). Corporal punishment in public schools, by state. Retrieved from www.infoplease.com/ipa/A0934191.html.

Ingraham v. Wright, 430 U.S. 651, 97 S.Ct. 1401, 51 L.Ed.3d 711 (1977). (Case No.124).

InTASC (Interstate New Teacher Assessment and Support Consortium). (2011). InTASC model core teaching standards: A resource for state dialog. www.ccsso.org/Documents/2011/InTASC_Model_Core_Teaching_Standards_2011.pdf.

International Center for Education Statistics. (2010). Teachers' use of educational technology in U.S. Public Schools. Washington, DC: U.S. Department of Education. Retrieved from http://nces.ed.gov/pubs2010/2010040.pdf.

International Reading Association. (1996). *Standards for the English language arts.* Retrieved at www.reading.org/General/CurrentResearch/Standards/LanguageArtsStandards.aspx.

International Society for Technology in Education. (2007). NETS for students. Retrieved from www.iste.org/standards/nets-for-students.aspx.

Interstate New Teacher Assessment and Support Consortium (INTASC). (1992). Model standards for the beginning teacher licensing, assessment and development: A resource for state dialogue. Retrieved from http://thesciencenetwork.org/docs/BrainsRUs/Model%20Standards%20for%20Beg%20Teaching_Paliokas.pdf.

Jabali-Nash, Naimah. (2011). Mary Kay Letourneau, sex scandal teacher, now a grandmother. *CBS News*, January 28. Retrieved from www.cbsnews.com/8301-504083_162-20029908-504083.html.

James, S. (2011). Hispanics rank high on digital divide. *New York Times.* Retrieved from www.nytimes.com/2011/06/17/us/17bcjames.html.

James, W. (1892/1962). *Psychology: Briefer course.* New York: Collier.

Jay, J. and Jay, J. (2008). Autism and the science classroom. *NSTA Reports,* 19(9).

Jenkins v. Anderson. (2007). Supreme Court of New Jersey, 2007, 191 N.J. 285, 922 A.2d 1279. In Alexander & Alexander (2012), p. 648.

John C. Diehl Elementary School. (2012). *About our school.* Retrieved from www.eriesd.org/diehl/about.htm.

Johnson, B. (2011). How to creatively integrate science and math. *Edutopia.* Retrieved from www.edutopia.org/blog/integrating-math-science-creatively-ben-johnson.

Johnson, F., Zhou, L., and Nakamoto, N. (2009). Revenues and expenditures for public elementary and secondary education: School year 2008–2009. Washington, DC: National Center for Education Statistics. Retrieved from http://nces.ed.gov/pubs2011/2011347.pdf.

Johnson, Frank, Zhou, Lei, and Nakamoto, Nanae. (2011). Revenues and expenditures for public elementary and secondary education: School year 2008–09 (Fiscal year 2009). *National Center for Education Statistics, U.S. Department of Education.* Retrieved from http://nces.ed.gov/pubs2011/2011329.pdf.

Johnston, L. D., O'Malley, P. M., Bachman, J. G., and Schulenberg, J. E. (2004, December 21). *Overall teen drug use continues gradual decline; but use of inhalants rises.* Ann Arbor, MI: University of Michigan News and Information Services.

Johnston, L. D., O'Malley, P. M., Bachman, J. G., and Schulenberg, J. E. (2012). *Monitoring the future national results on adolescent drug use: Overview of key findings, 2011.* Ann Arbor: Institute for Social Research, The University of Michigan.

Jones, Michael. (2011, March 4). *Protesters call on Flour Bluff High School to recognize gay-straight alliance.* Retrieved from http://news.change.org/stories/protesters-call-on-flour-bluff-high-school-to-recognize-gay-straight-alliance.

Jones, R. (2005). Head Start study suggests minimal benefits. National Public Radio, June 10, 2005.

Jones, V., and Jones, L. (2013). *Comprehensive classroom management: Creating communities of support and solving problems,* 10th ed. Old Tappan, NJ: Pearson Education.

Josephson Institute of Ethics. (2011, February, 10). The ethics of American youth: 2010. What would honest Abe Lincoln say? Retrieved from http://charactercounts.org/programs/reportcard/2010/installment02_report-card_honesty-integrity.html.

Jurist. (2011). DOJ warns Alabama schools on state immigration law. Jurist paper chase newsburst. Retrieved from http://jurist.org/paperchase/2011/11/doj-warns-alabama-schools-on-state-immigration-law.php.

Kaiser, A. (2011). Beginning teacher attrition and mobility: Results from the first through third waves of the 2007–08 beginning teacher longitudinal study. Washington, DC: National Center for Education Statistics. Retrieved from http://nces.ed.gov/pubsearch/pubsinfo.asp?pubid=2011318.

Kalman, B. (1947). *Early schools.* (The Early Settler Life Series). New York: Crabtree.

Kang, C. (2011). Obama touts plan to get wireless Internet to 98 percent of U.S. Washington, DC: *The Washington Post*. Retrieved from www.washingtonpost.com/wp-dyn/content/article/2011/02/10/AR2011021005765.html.

Kang, Cecelia. (2011). Survey of online access finds digital divide. *The Washington Post*, February 17. Retrieved from www.washingtonpost.com/wp-dyn/content/article/2011/02/17/AR2011021707234.html.

Kellough, Richard D., and Carjuzaa, Jioanna. (2009) *Teaching in the middle and secondary schools*. Boston: Pearson Publishing.

Keyishian v. Board of Regents, 385 U.S. 589 (1967).

Kilpatrick v. Wright, 437 F. Supp. 397 (M.D. Ala. 1977).

Kim, Hyun Sik. (2011). Consequences of parental divorce for child development. *American Sociological Review* 76(3), 487–511.

King, Kelley, Gurian, Michael, and Stevens, Kathy. (2010). *Gender-friendly schools*. Educational Leadership. Retrieved from www.ascd.org/publications/educational_leadership/nov10/vol68/num03/Gender-Friendly_Schools.aspx.

Kirby, M., Maggi, S., and D'Angiulli, A. (2011). School start times and the sleep-wake cycle of adolescents: A review and critical evaluation of available evidence. *Educational Researcher, 40*(2), 56–61.

Kitagawa, M. M. (2000). Profile: The light in her eyes: An interview with Sonia Nieto. *Urbana, 78*(2), 158–64.

Knox County Education Association v. Knox County Board of Education, 158 F.3d 361 (6th Cir. 1998).

Koebler, J. (2012). Governors Association examines teacher merit pay. *U.S. News, Education, High School Notes*. Retrieved from www.usnews.com/education/blogs/high-school-notes/2012/01/09/governors-association-examines-teacher-merit-pay.

Kohn, A. (2001). Fighting the tests: A practical guide to rescuing our schools. *Phi Delta Kappan*, 82(5), 349–357.

Kohn A. (2006). Abusing research: The study of homework and other examples. *Phi Delta Kappan* 88(13), 8–22.

Kosciw, J. G., Greytak, E. A., Diaz, E. M., and Bartkiewicz, M. J. (2010). *The 2009 National School Climate Survey: The school-related experiences of our nation's lesbian, gay, bisexual and transgender youth*. New York: GLSEN.

Kowalski, Robin M. (2008). Cyber bullying: Recognizing and treating victim and aggressor. *The Psychiatric Times*. Retrieved from www.psychiatrictimes.com/display/article/10168/1336550?pageNumber=2.

Kozol, J. (1991). *Savage inequalities: Children in America's schools*. New York: Harper Perennial.

Kreeger, K. Y. (2002). Yes, biologically speaking, sex does matter: Researchers move beyond the basics to better understand the differences between men and women. *The Scientist*, 16(1), 35–37.

Kreis, S. (2000). John Locke, 1632–1704. *The history guide: Lectures on modern European intellectual history*. Retrieved at www.historyguide.org/intellect/locke.html.

Kunjufu, J. (2006). *An African centered response to Ruby Payne's poverty theory*. Chicago: African American Images.

Laborde, G. Z. (1984). *Influencing integrity: Management skills for communication and negotiation*. Palo Alto, CA: Syntony.

Ladson-Billings, G. (1994). *The dreamkeepers: Successful teaching for African-American students*. San Francisco: Jossey-Bass.

Ladson-Billings, G. (2009). *The dream-keepers*, 2nd ed. San Francisco: Wiley.

Lanier, J. (1987). From a tape recording of an address to the first Holmes Group conference.

Larrabee, T., and Kim, Y. (2010). Pre-service elementary teachers' perceptions of family: Considering future instruction on lesbian- and gay-headed families. *Journal of Research in Childhood Education* 24(4), 251–365.

Laughlin, Lynda. (2010). *Who's minding the kids? Child care arrangements: spring 2005 and summer 2006*. Current Population Reports, P70-121. U.S. Census Bureau, Washington, DC, 2005. Retrieved from www.census.gov/prod/2010pubs/p70-121.pdf.

Lawson, A. E. (1978). The development and validation of a classroom test of formal reasoning. *Journal of Research in Science Teaching*, 15(1), 11–24.

Lee, Danielle Moss. (2012). Creating an anti-racist classroom. Edutopia. Retrieved from www.edutopia.org/blog/anti-racist-classroom-danielle-moss-lee.

Lee, J., Lee, Y. A., and Amaro-Jiménez, C. (2011). Teaching English language learners (ELLs) mathematics in early childhood. *Childhood Education* 87(4), 253–60.

Lee, Okhee, and Buxton, Cory A. (2010). *Diversity and equity in science education*. New York: Teachers College Press.

Legal Information Institute (n.d.) Keyes v. School District No. 1, Denver, Colorado. Cornell University. Retrieved from www.law.cornell.edu/supct/html/historics/USSC_CR_0413_0189_ZS.html.

Lenhart, A., Madden, M., Smith, A., Purcell, K., Zickuhr, K., and Rainie, L. (2011, November 9). *Teens, kindness, and cruelty on social network sites: How American teens navigate the new world of "digital citizenship."* Pew Research Center's Internet and American Life Project. Retrieved from www.pewinternet.org/~/media/Files/Reports/2011/PIP_teens_Kindness_Cruelty_SNS_Report_Nov_2011_FINAL_110711.pdf.

Leon, Kim, and Spengler, Leanne. (2005). *Helping children adjust to divorce: A guide for teachers*. University of Missouri Extension. Retrieved from http://extension.missouri.edu/explorepdf/hesguide/humanrel/gh6611.pdf.

Levs, Jason. (2005). Georgia teacher fired for stand on sleeping student. NPR, May 16. Retrieved from www.npr.org/templates/story/story.php?storyId=4653085.

Lewis, R. (n.d.) Up from slavery: A documentary history of Negro education. *ChickenBones. A Journal for Literary & Artistic African-American Themes*.

Liptak, A. (2009). Supreme Court says child's rights violated by strip search. *New York Times*, June 26, 2009. Retrieved from www.nytimes.com/2009/06/26/us/politics/26scotus.html?_r=1&pagewanted=print.

Los Angeles Times. (2010). How teachers can comment. *Los Angeles Times*, August 15. Retrieved from www.latimes.com/news/local/la-me-teachers-value-invite-20100815,0,5886812.story.

Love, J. M., Kisker, E., Ross, C., Raikes, H., Constantine, J., Boller, K., Brooks-Gunn, J., Chazan-Cohen, R., Tarullo, L. B., Schochet, P. Z., Brady-Smith, C., Fuligni, A. S., Paulsell, D., and

Vogel, C. (2005). The effectiveness of Early Head Start for 3-year old children and their parents: Lesson for policy and programs. *Development Psychology* 41, 885–901.

Lucas, C. J. (1980). The more things change. *Phi Delta Kappan* 61(6), 414–16.

MacDonald, Mary. (2002a). 28 scholars back Cobb on evolution: Skeptical approach to Darwinism urged. *Atlanta Journal-Constitution*, September 21, 2002.

MacDonald, Mary. (2002b). Scientists jump into Cobb evolution debate. *Atlanta Journal-Constitution*, September 19, 2002.

MacDonald, Mary. (2004a). Cox: "Evolution" a negative buzz-word: Word purge defended. *Atlanta Journal-Constitution*, January 30, 2004.

MacDonald, Mary. (2004b). "Evolution" back in teaching plan: Superintendent say her "effort to avoid controversy" backfired. *Atlanta Journal-Constitution*, February 6, 2004.

Macedo, D. (2010). Advocates debate using advertising in schools to raise funds in budget crisis. *FoxNews.com*. Retrieved from www.foxnews.com/story/0,2933,601524,00.html.

Mahlios, M., Massengill-Shaw, D., and Taylor, A. (2010). Making sense of teaching through metaphors: A review across three studies. *Teachers and Teaching: Theory and Practice*, 16(1), 49–71, doi: 10.1080/13540600903475645.

Mahoney, J. L., Lord, H., and Carryl, E. (2005). Afterschool program participation and the development of child obesity and peer acceptance. *Applied Developmental Science* 9, 202–215.

Manning, M. L., and Baruth, L. G. (2009). *Multicultural education of children and adolescents*, 5th ed. Boston, MA: Pearson.

Marchiechay. (2010). Texas might abandon the 22-to-1 student-teacher cap. *Austin Post*, August 25, 2010. Retrieved from www.austinpost.org/content/22-1-student-teacher-cap-may-be-increased.

Martin, D. J. (2012). *Elementary science: A constructive approach*. Belmont, CA: Wadsworth/Cengage Learning.

Maslow, A. (1968). *Toward a psychology of being*, 2nd ed. New York: Van Nostrand Reinhold.

Mathes, E. (1981). Maslow's hierarchy of needs as a guide for living. *Journal of Humanistic Psychology*, 21, 69–72.

McCambridge, T. R. (1997). *Liberal education and American schooling*. Doctoral dissertation, University of California at Los Angeles.

McCleskey, James, and Waldron, Nancy L. (2011). Educational programs for elementary students with learning disabilities: Can they be both effective and inclusive? *Learning Disabilities Research & Practice* 26: 48–57, doi: 10.1111/j.1540-5826.2010.00324.x.

McDermott, P., and Rothenberg, J. (2000, April). *The characteristics of effective teachers in high poverty schools: Triangulating the data*. Paper for roundtable discussion at the annual meeting of the American Educational Research Association, New Orleans, LA. ERIC Document Reproduction Service No. ED450353.

McIntosh, Peggy. (1989, July/August). White privilege: Unpacking the invisible knapsack. *Peace and Freedom*. Retrieved from www.library.wisc.edu/EDVRC/docs/public/pdfs/LIReadings/InvisibleKnapsack.pdf.

Meador, D. (n.d.). Homework policy. *About.com: Teaching*. Retrieved from http://teaching.about.com/od/SchoolPolicy/a/Homework-Policy.htm.

Medeiros v. Sitrin. (2009). Supreme Court of Rhode Island, 2009, 984 A.2nd 620 in Alexander & Alexander (2012), p. 643.

MedicineNet.com. (2012) Learning disabilities. Retrieved from www.medicinenet.com/learning_disability/article/htm.

Medina, J. (2010). Teachers set deal with city on discipline process. *New York Times*, April 15, 2010. Retrieved from www.nytimes.com/2010/04/16/nyregion/16rubber.html.

Medina, Jennifer. (2010). Last day of "rubber rooms" for teachers. *The New York Times*, June 28. Retrieved from www.nytimes.com/2010/06/29/education/29rubber.html.

Mendicino, M., Razzaq, L., and Heffernan, N. T. (2009). A comparison of traditional homework to computer-supported homework. *Journal of Research in Technology* 14(2), 331–59.

Menendez, R. (Director). (1988). *Stand and deliver*. [Motion picture]. United States: Warner Studios.

Merriam-Webster. (2012). *Merriam-Webster's collegiate dictionary*, 11th ed. Springfield, MA: Author.

Mertens, Steven B., Flowers, Nancy, and Mulhall, Peter F. (May 2003). Should middle grades students be left alone after school? *Middle School Journal*, 34(5), p. 57–61.

Milanowski, A. (2012). Assessing teaching practice. Wisconsin Center for Education Research. Retrieved from www.wcer.wisc.edu/news/coverStories/2012/assessing_teaching_practice.php.

Miller, P. M. (2011). A critical analysis of the research on student homelessness. *Review of Educational Research*, 81(3), 308–37.

Miller, R. (1999). *District 1 Old Center School House*. Burlington, CT. Retrieved from http://burlingtonct.us/wp-content/uploads/2011/03/District1School.pdf.

The Miniature Earth Project. (2010). The Miniature Earth Project. Retrieved from www.miniature-earth.com/docs/ME_2010_text.pdf.

Minnesota Department of Education. (2011). Magnet schools. Retrieved from http://education.state.mn.us/MDE/Academic_Excellence/School_Choice/Public_School_Choice/Magnet_Schools/index.htm.

Minor, L. C., Onwuegbuzie, A. J., and Witcher, A. E. (2000, November). *Preservice teachers' perceptions of characteristics of effective teachers: A multi-stage mixed methods analysis*. Paper presented at the annual meeting of the Mid-South Educational Research Association, Lexington, KY. ERIC Document Reproduction Service No. ED454500.

Miron, G., and Urschel, J. L. (2011). Profiles of nonprofit education management organizations: 2009-2010. Boulder, CO: National Education Policy Center. Retrieved from http://nepc.colorado.edu/publication/EMO-NP-09-10.

Molnar, A., Miron, G., and Urschel, J. L. (2010). Profiles of for-profit education management organizations, 2009–2010. Boulder, CO: National Education Policy Center. Retrieved from http://nepc.colorado.edu/files/EMO-FP-09-10.pdf.

Moreno, G., and Wong-Lo, M. (2011). Considerations and practices in working with students and families from Latino and Asian-American backgrounds. *Multicultural Learning & Teaching* 6(1).

Morgan, P. L., Farkas, G., Hillemeier, M. M., and Maczuga, S. (2009). Risk factors for learning-related behavior problems at 24 months of age: Population-based estimates. *Journal of Abnormal Child Psychology 37*, 401–13.

Morse v. Frederick (No. 06-278). 439 F. 3d 1114 (2007).

Mortgage Bankers Association of America. (2011). MBA mortgage originations estimates. *National Deliquency Survey, quarterly.* Retrieved from www.mortgagebankers.org.

Moskowitz, Clara. (2010). *When teachers highlight gender, kids pick up stereotypes.* LiveScience, November 16. Retrieved from www.livescience.com/8966-teachers-highlight-gender-kids-pick-stereotypes.html.

MSNBC News. (2005). Utah snubs federal No Child Left Behind act. Retrieved from www.msnbc.msn.com/id/7713931/ns/us_news-education/t/utah-snubs-federal-no-child-left-behind-act/.

Murphy, J. F., and Tobin, K. J. (2011). Homelessness comes to school. *Kappan 93*(3), 32–37.

Naftzger, N., et. al. (2007). 21st century community learning centers (21st CCLC) analytic support for evaluation and program monitoring: An overview of the 21st CCLC performance data: 2005–06. Washington, DC: U.S. Department of Education.

Nagel, D. (2009). 10.5 million PreK–12 students will attend classes online by 2014. *The Journal.* Retrieved from http://thejournal.com/articles/2009/10/28/10.5-million-prek-12-students-will-attend-classes-online-by-2014.aspx.

Nagel, David. (2010). Teachers spend $1.3 billion out of pocket on classroom materials. *THE Journal.* Retrieved from http://the-journal.com/articles/2010/07/08/teachers-spend-1.3-billion-out-of-pocket-on-classroom-materials.aspx.

National Association for Bilingual Education. (2009). *Does bilingual education really work?* Retrieved from www.nabe.org/b_ed_effective.html.

National Association for Gifted Children. (2008). *What is giftedness?* Retrieved from www.nagc.org/index.aspx?id=574&ir.

National Association for Single Sex Public Education. (2011). *Single-sex schools/schools with single-sex classrooms/what's the difference?* Retrieved from www.singlesexschools.org/schools-classrooms.htm.

National Association for the Education of Homeless Children and Youth. (n.d.). Facts about homeless Education. Retrieved from www.naehcy.org/facts.html.

National Association of Colleges and Employers. (2012). NACE salary survey: Starting salaries for new college graduates. Executive Summary, April 2012. Retrieved from www.naceweb.org.

National Board for Professional Teaching Standards. (1999) *What teachers should know and be able to do.* Southfield, MI, and Arlington, VA: National Board for Professional Teaching Standards.

National Campaign to Prevent Teen and Unplanned Pregnancy. (2004a). *Fact sheet: Recent trends in teen pregnancy, sexual activity, and contraceptive use.* Washington DC: Author.

National Campaign to Prevent Teen and Unplanned Pregnancy. (2004b). *Fact sheet: Why the education community cares about preventing teen pregnancy.* Washington, DC: Author.

National Campaign to Prevent Teen and Unplanned Pregnancy. (2004c). *With one voice 2004: America's adults and teens sound off about teen pregnancy.* Washington, DC: Author.

National Campaign to Prevent Teen and Unplanned Pregnancy. (2010). Why it matters: Teen pregnancy and education. Retrieved from www.thenationalcampaign.org/why-it-matters/pdf/education.pdf.

National Campaign to Prevent Teen and Unplanned Pregnancy. (2012). Teen birth rates: How does the United States compare? Retrieved from www.thenationalcampaign.org/resources/pdf/FastFacts_InternationalComparisons.pdf.

National Center for Alternative Certification. (2010). Teacher certification: A state by state analysis. Retrieved from www.teach-now.org/overview.cfm.

National Center for Education Statistics. (2001). *Digest of education statistics, 2001, Chapter 1. All levels of education.* And Table 69. Highest degree earned, number of years teaching experience, and average class size for teachers in public elementary and secondary schools, by state: 1993–94.

National Center for Education Statistics. (2004). Fourth-graders' average scores for the combined literacy scale, literacy subscale, and informational subscale by country (PIRLS). Retrieved from http://nces.ed.gov/pubs2004/pirlspub/figures/fig3.asp?popup=true.

National Center for Education Statistics. (2007). Progress in International Reading Literacy Study (PIRLS), Table 1: 2006. Retrieved from http://nces.ed.gov/surveys/pirls/table_1.asp.

National Center for Education Statistics. (2008a). *Education Longitudinal Study of 2002 (ELS:2002), "School Administrator Questionnaire Base Year."* Retrieved from http://nces.ed.gov/pubs2008/2008035.pdf#page=37. Institute of Education Sciences, U.S. Department of Education, Washington, DC.

National Center for Education Statistics. (2008b). Fast facts. Washington, DC: Author. Retrieved from http://nces.ed.gov/fastfacts/display.asp?id=46.

National Center for Education Statistics. (2009a). *The nation's report card: Mathematics 2009* (NCES 2010–451). Institute of Education Sciences, U.S. Department of Education, Washington, DC.

National Center for Education Statistics. (2009b). *The nation's report card: Reading 2009* (NCES 2010–458). Institute of Education Sciences, U.S. Department of Education, Washington, DC.

National Center for Education Statistics. (2009c). Highlights from TIMSS 2007: Mathematics and science achievement of U.S. fourth- and eighth-grade students in an international context. Washington, DC: Author. Retrieved from http://nces.ed.gov/pubsearch/pubsinfo.asp?pubid=2009001.

National Center for Education Statistics. (2010a). *State nonfiscal survey of public elementary/secondary education, 1994–95 through 2007–08; and National public elementary and secondary enrollment by race/ethnicity model, 1994–2007.* Common Core of Data (CCD), Institute of Education Sciences, U.S. Department of Education, Washington, DC. Retrieved from http://nces.ed.gov/programs/projections/projections2019/figures/figure_03.asp?referrer=report.

National Center for Education Statistics. (2010b). Digest of education statistics, 2010. Figure 1, The structure of education in the United States. Washington, DC: Author. Retrieved from http://nces.ed.gov/programs/digest/d10/figures/fig_01.asp?referrer=figures.

National Center for Education Statistics. (2010c). Digest of Education Statistics, Table 82. Estimated average annual salary of teachers in public elementary and secondary schools: Selected years, 1959–60 through 2009–10. Retrieved from http://nces.ed.gov/programs/digest/d10/tables/dt10_082.asp.

National Center for Education Statistics. (2010d). *Digest of Education Statistics, Fast Facts, Table 68*. Washington, DC: Author. Retrieved from http://nces.ed.gov/fastfacts/display.asp?id=28.

National Center for Education Statistics. (2010e). Estimated average annual salary of teachers in public elementary and secondary schools: Selected years, 1959–60 through 2009–10. Digest of education statistics: 2010. Retrieved from http://nces.ed.gov/programs/digest/d10/tables/dt10_082.asp?referrer=report.

National Center for Education Statistics. (2011a). Characteristics of public schools (Indicator 27-2011). Washington, DC: U.S. Department of Education, Author. http://nces.ed.gov/programs/coe/indicator_cps.asp.

National Center for Education Statistics. (2011b). The condition of education, Indicator 3-2011: Charter School Enrollment. http://www.hoagiesgifted.org/eric/fact/myths.html.

National Center for Education Statistics. (2011c). The condition of education, indicator 6: Home schooled students. Retrieved from http://nces.ed.gov/programs/coe/indicator_hsc.asp.

National Center for Education Statistics. (2011d). The condition of education, private school enrollment. Washington, DC: U.S. Department of Education, Author. Retrieved from http://nces.ed.gov/programs/coe/indicator_pri.asp.

National Center for Education Statistics (2011e). *The nation's report card: Geography 2010*. Institute of Education Sciences, U.S. Department of Education, Washington, DC. Retrieved from http://nces.ed.gov/nationsreportcard/pdf/main2010/2011467.pdf.

National Center for Education Statistics (2011f). *The nation's report card: U.S. History 2010*. Institute of Education Sciences, U.S. Department of Education, Washington, DC. Retrieved from http://nces.ed.gov/nationsreportcard/pdf/main2010/2011468.pdf.

National Center for Education Statistics. (2011g). Numbers and types of public elementary and secondary schools from the common core of data: School year 2009-2010, Table 2. Washington, DC: U.S. Department of Education, Author. Http://nces.ed.gov/pubs2011/pesschools09/tables/table_02.asp.

National Center for Education Statistics. (2011h). Public elementary and secondary school student enrollment and staff count s from the common core of data: School year 2009–2010, Table A. Retrieved from http://nces.ed.gov/pubs2011/snf200910/tables/table_04.asp.

National Center for Education Statistics. (2012). *Private School Universe Survey (PSS)*. Retrieved from http://nces.ed.gov/surveys/pss/xls/table_whs_02.xls.

National Center for Health Statistics. (2005). *Health, United States, 2005: With chartbook on trends in the health of Americans*. Hyattsville, MD: Author.

National Center for Learning Disabilities. (2011). *Learning disability fast facts*. Retrieved from www.ncld.org/ld-basics/ld-explained/basic-facts/ld-fast-facts.

National Center on Accessible Information Technology. (2011). *What is assistive technology?* University of Washington. Retrieved from www.washington.edu/accessit/articles?109.

National Clearinghouse for Educational Facilities. (2011). Data and statistics: School building statistics. Washington, DC: Author. Retrieved from www.ncef.org/ds/statistics.cfm#.

National Clearinghouse for English Language Acquisition. (2011). *Frequently asked questions*. Retrieved from www.ncela.gwu.edu/faqs/.

National Commission on Excellence in Education. (1983). *A nation at risk: The imperative for educational reform*. Washington, DC: Author.

National Commission on Teaching and America's Future. (2005). *Induction into learning communities*. Washington, DC: Author.

National Council for the Accreditation of Teacher Education. (2002). *Professional standards for the accreditation of schools, colleges, and departments of education*, 2002 edition. Washington, DC: National Council for the Accreditation of Teacher Education.

National Council for the Accreditation of Teacher Education (NCATE). (2010). Unit standards in effect 2008. Retrieved from www.ncate.org/Standards/NCATEUnitStandards/UnitStandardsinEffect2008/tabid/476/Default.aspx.

National Council for the Social Studies. (2008). *A vision of powerful teaching and learning in the social studies: Building social understanding and civic efficacy*. Retrieved from www.socialstudies.org/positions/powerful.

National Council for the Social Studies. (n.d.) *National curriculum standards for the social studies: Executive summary*. Retrieved from www.socialstudies.org/standards/execsummary.

National Council of Teachers of English. (2008). *English language learners: A policy research brief*. Retrieved from www.ncte.org/library/NCTEFiles/Resources/PolicyResearch/ELLResearchBrief.pdf.

National Education Association. (1975). *Code of ethics for the education profession*. Washington, DC: Author.

National Education Association. (2003a). *School safety*. Retrieved from www.nea.org/home/16364.htm.

National Education Association. (2003b). *Status of the American public school teacher 2000–2001*. Washington, DC: Author.

National Education Association. (2009). Rankings of the states in 2009 and estimates of school statistics 2010. Retrieved from www.nea.org/assets/docs/010rankings.pdf.

National Education Association. (2010). *The status of the American public school teacher: 2006–2006*. Retrieved from http://www.nea.org/assets/docs/HE/2005-06StatusTextandAppendixA.pdf.

National Education Association. (2011a). About NEA: Our history. Retrieved from www.nea.org/home/1704.htm.

National Education Association. (2011b). Rankings & Estimates: Rankings of the states 2010 and estimates of school statistics, 2011. Retrieved from http://www.nea.org/assets/docs/HE/NEA_Rankings_and_Estimates010711.pdf.

National Education Association. (2012). *Code of ethics*. Retrieved from www.nea.org/home/30442.htm.

National Gang Intelligence Center. (2011). *2011: National gang threat assessment: Emerging trends*. Retrieved from www.fbi.gov/stats-services/publications/2011-national-gang-threat-assessment/2011%20National%20Gang%20Threat%20Assessment%20%20Emerging%20Trends.pdf.

National Paideia Center. (2011). The three columns of teaching practices. Retrieved from www.paideia.org/about-paideia/teaching-practices/.

National Research Council. (1996). *National science education standards*. Washington, DC: National Academy Press.

National Resource Center for the First-Year Experience and Students in Transition. (2009). National survey of first/year seminars. [Data file]. Retrieved from http://sc.edu/fye/research/surveyfindings/pdf/Executivesumm73008.pdf.

National School Safety Center. (2010). *National School Safety Center's report on school associated violent deaths*. Retrieved from www.schoolsafety.us/media-resources/school-associated-violent-deaths.

National Science Teachers Association. (2011). Next generation of science standards. Retrieved from www.nsta.org/about/standardsupdate.aspx?print=true.

National Science Teachers Association. (2012). Science fairs go online. *NSTA Reports, 22*(6), 1–2.

National Service Learning Clearinghouse. (2011). What is service learning? Retrieved from www.servicelearning.org/what-service-learning.

Nationwide Children's Hospital. (2010). Sexual minority youth bullied more than heterosexual youth. *ScienceDaily*. Retrieved from www.sciencedaily.com/releases/2010/01/100127182503.htm.

NCATE News and Press Releases. (2010). NCATE and TEAC form new accrediting body: The Council for the Accreditation of Educator Preparation (CAEP). Retrieved from www.ncate.org/Public/Newsroom/NCATENewsPressReleases/tabid/669/EntryId/121/NCATE-and-TEAC-Form-New-Accrediting-Body-The-Council-for-the-Accreditation-of-Educator-Preparation-CAEP.aspx.

NCATE News and Press Releases. (2012). *Q&A on CAEP as NCATE and TEAC transition to a unified accrediting body*. CAEP. Retrieved fromfrom www.ncate.org/Public/Newsroom/NCATENewsPressReleases/tabid/669/EntryId/166/Q-A-on-CAEP-as-NCATE-and-TEAC-Transition-to-a-Unified-Accrediting-Body.aspx.

NCTM (National Council of Teachers of Mathematics). (1989). *Curriculum and evaluation standards for school mathematics*. Reston, VA: NCTM.

NCTM (National Council of Teachers of Mathematics). (2000). *Principles and standards for school mathematics*. Reston, VA: Author.

Neal, A. D., Martin, J. L., and Moses, M. (2000). *Losing America's memory: Historical illiteracy in the 21st century*. Washington, DC: American Council of Trustees and Alumni.

Nelson, L. L., Arthur, E. J., Jensen, W. R., and VanHorn, G. (2011). Trading textbooks for technology: New opportunities for learning. *Kappanmagazine.org 92*(7), 46–50. Retrieved from www.kappanmagazine.org/content/92/7/46.abstract.

New Hanover County, North Carolina, Schools. (2011). School building administration. *Board of Education Policy Manual*. Retrieved from www.nhcs.net/policies/series2000/2080.pdf.

New Haven County, North Carolina, Schools. (2011). Policy 6412: Extracurricular and non-instructional study assignments. Retrieved from www.nhcs.k12.nc.us/policies/series6000/6412.pdf.

New Jersey v. T.L.O., 469 U.S. 325, 105 S.Ct. 733, 83 L.Ed.2d 720 (1985). (Case No.123).

New2Teaching. (2011). *Dealing with divorce*. ATL: The Education Union. Retrieved from www.new2teaching.org.uk/tzone/education/skills/divorce.asp.

Nieto, S. M. (2003). What keeps teachers going? *Educational Leadership, 60*(8), 14–18.

Nieto, Sonia. (2009) From Surviving to Thriving. *Educational Leadership, 66*(5), 8–13.

No Child Left Behind Executive Summary. (2001). Retrieved from www2.ed.gov/offices/OIIA/pfie/whoweare/nochild2.html.

Norton, J. L. (1997, November 13). *Learning from first-year teachers: Characteristics of the effective practitioner*. Paper presented at the Annual Meeting of the Mid-South Educational Research Association, Memphis, TN. ERIC Document Reproduction Service No. ED418050.

NTSA. (2012). Science fairs go online. *NSTA Reports 22*(6), 1–2.

O'Brien, Joseph. (2011). Negligence lawsuit against Tolland High gym teacher advances in superior court. *The Tolland Patch*, February 15. Retrieved from http://tolland.patch.com/articles/negligence-lawsuit-against-tolland-high-gym-teacher-advances-in-superior-court.

Office of Educational Research and Improvement. (1999). *Highlights from TIMSS, the Third International Mathematics and Science Study: Overview and key findings across grade levels*.

Office of Educational Research and Improvement. (2001). *Highlights from the Third International Mathematics and Science Study–Repeat (TIMSS–R)* national Center for Education Statistics.

Office of Educational Technology. (2010). Transforming American education: Learning powered by technology. Retrieved from www.ed.gov/sites/default/files/netp2010-execsumm.pdf.

Office of Indian Education Programs. (n.d.). *About us*. Retrieved from www2.ed.gov/about/offices/list/oese/oie/programs.html.

Office of the Press Secretary. (2010, March 1). *President Obama announces steps to reduce dropout rate and prepare students for college and careers*. The White House. Retrieved from www.whitehouse.gov/the-press-office/president-obama-announces-steps-reduce-dropout-rate-and-prepare-students-college-an.

Ogden Cynthia, and Carroll, Margaret. (2010). *Prevalence of obesity among children and adolescents: United States, trends 1963–1965 through 2007–2008*. National Center for Health Statistics.

Ogle, L., Sen, A., Pahlke, E., Jocelyn, L., Kastberg, D., Roey, S., and Williams, T. (2003). *International comparisons in fourth-grade reading literacy: Findings from the Progress in International Reading Literacy Study (PIRLS) of 2001 NCES 2003–073)*. U.S. Department of Education, NCES. Washington, DC: U.S. Government Printing Office.

Olsen, Laurie, and Spiefel-Coleman, Shelly. (2010). A skill, not a weakness. *The Los Angeles Times,* July 11.

Olweus, Dan. (2011). What is Bullying? Retrieved from http://olweus.org/public/bullying.page.

Oppenheimer, T. (2003). *The flickering mind: The false promise of technology in the classroom and how learning can be saved.* New York: Ransom House.

Orr, A. J. (2003). Black-white differences in achievement: The importance of wealth. *Sociology of Education 76*, 281–304.

Otterman, S. (2011). New York City abandons teacher bonus program. *The New York Times,* July 17. Retrieved from www.nytimes.com/2011/07/18/education/18rand.html?r=1& pagewanted=print.

Otuya, W. (1992). *Alternative teacher certification: An update.* ERIC Document Reproduction Service No. ED351312.

Owings. W. A., and Kaplan, L. S. (2006). *American public school finance.* Belmont, CA: Thomson/Wadsworth.

Padolsky, D. (2002). NCELA FAQ No. 5: What are the most common language groups for ELL students? *National Clearinghouse for English Language Acquisition & Language Instruction Educational Programs.*

Palmer v. Board of Education of the City of Chicago, 603 F.2d 1271 (7th Cir. 1979), cert.den., 444 U.S. 1026 (1980).

Palmer, P. (1998). *The courage to teach: Exploring the inner landscape of a teacher's life.* San Francisco: Jossey-Bass.

Pang, V. O., Han, P. P., and Pang, J. M. (2011). Asian American and Pacific Islander students: Equity and the achievement gap. *Educational Researcher, 40*(8), 378–89.

Parke, Ross D., and Gauvain, Mary. (2008). *Child psychology: A contemporary viewpoint.* New York: McGraw-Hill.

Parrish v. Moss, 200 Misc. 375, 106 N.Y.S.2d 577 (1951), aff. 279 App.Div. 608, 107 N.Y.S.2d 580 (1951).

Passell, J. S. (2005). Estimates of the size and characteristics of the undocumented population. Washington, DC: *Pew Hispanic Center.* Retrieved from http://pewhispanic.org/files/reports/44.pdf.

Passow, A. Harry, and Rudnitski, Rose A. (n.d.). *State policies regarding education of the gifted as reflected in legislation and regulation.* Neag Center for Gifted Education and Talent Development. Retrieved from www.gifted.uconn.edu/nrcgt/passrudn.html.

Pastor, P. N., and Reuben, C. A. (2008). Diagnosed attention deficit hyperactivity disorder and learning disability: United States, 2004–2006. National Center for Health Statistics. *Vital Health Stat 10*(237).

Patchen, Terri, and Crawford, Teresa. (May/June 2011). From gardeners to tour guides: The epistemological struggle revealed in teacher-generated metaphors of teaching. *Journal of Teacher Education, 62*(3), 286–98.

Patrnogich-Arieli, Ana. (2009). *Academic success: Helping students with low socioeconomic status achieve academically.* Retrieved from www.sierranevada.edu/UserFiles/file/TED/THESES_SU_09/Ana%20Patrnogich-Arieli%20Thesis.pdf.

Payne, R. K. (1998). *A framework for understanding poverty,* rev. ed. Highlands, TX: RFT Publishing.

Perry, Kimball. (2011). Baby worth legal fight with church. *Cincinnati Enquirer.* December 27. Retrieved from http://news.cincinnati.com/article/AB/20111226/NEWS010702/312270011/Baby-worth-legal-fight-church.

Peske, H. G., Liu, E., Johnson, S. M., Kauffman, D., and Kardos, S. M. (2001). The next generation of teachers: Changing conceptions of a career in teaching. *Phi Delta Kappan, 83*(4), 304–311.

Phi Delta Kappan. (2011). Dropouts by the numbers. *Phi Delta Kappan, 92*(5), 14–15.

Piaget, J. (1972). *The psychology of the child.* New York: Basic Books.

Pickering v. Board of Education, 391 U.S. 563, 88 S. Ct. 1731 (1968).

Plante, Isabelle, Protzko, John, and Aronson, Joshua. (2010). Girls' internalization of their female teacher's anxiety: A "real-world: stereotype threat effect? *Proceedings of the National Academy of Sciences of the United States 107*(20), E79.

Polhamus B., Dalenius K., Mackintosh H., Smith B., and Grummer-Strawn L. *Pediatric nutrition surveillance 2009 report.* (2011). Atlanta: U.S. Department of Health and Human Services, Centers for Disease Control and Prevention. Retrieved from www.cdc.gov/pednss/pdfs/PedNSS_2009.pdf.

Porter, A., McMaken, J., Hwang, J., and Yang, R. (2011). Common core standards: The new U.S. intended curriculum. *Educational Researcher, 40*(3), 103–16.

PRNewswire. (2012). NSSEA releases study on teacher spending on classroom materials. Author. Retrieved from http://www.prnewswire.com/news-releases/nssea-releases-study-on-teacher-spending-on-classroom-materials-98015529.html.

Public Agenda Online. (2003). *Now that I'm here: What America's immigrants have to say about life in the U.S. today.* Retrieved from www.publicagenda.org/files/pdf/now_that_im_here.pdf.

Public Employment Law Press. (2010). Teacher's license revoked after hearing officer finds that the educator engaged in inappropriate sexual conduct in the presence of a student. New York Public Personnel Law, March 1. Retrieved from http://publicpersonnellaw.blogspot.com/2010/03/teachers-license-revoked-after-hearing.html.

Quillen, I. (2012a). Ed-tech credential effort to start with online teachers. *Education Week, 312*(18), 11.

Quillen, I. (2012b). Variety of models fuel hybrid charter growth. *Education Week, 31*(23), S–10.

Quiroz, Hilda Clarice. (2006). *Talking with Hilda Clarice Quiroz about bullying.* National School Safety Center. Retrieved from www.schoolsafety.us/free-resources/bullying-in-schools-talking-with-hilda-about-bullying/talking_with_hilda_about_bullying.pdf?attredirects=0&d=1.

Quiroz, Hilda Clarice, Arnette, June Lane, and Stephens, Ronald D. (2006). *Bullying in schools: Fighting the bully battle. Bullying Fact Sheet Series.* National School Safety Center. Retrieved from www.schoolsafety.us/free-resources/bullying-in-schools-fact-sheet-series/bullying_fact_sheets.pdf?attredirects=0&d=1.

Rapp, K. (2011). School's out for the summer, but online learning is in. *Education Update.* Alexandria, VA: Association for Supervision and Curriculum Development.

Ravitch, Diane. (2012). How, and how not, to improve the schools. *The New York Review,* March 22. Retrieved from www.nybooks.com/articles/archives/2012/mar/22/how-and-how-not-improve-schools/?page=1.

Richardson, Joan. (2009). "Quality education is our moon shot": An interview with Secretary of Education Arne Duncan. *Phi Delta Kappan 9*(1), 24–25.

Robers, S., Zhang, J., and Truman, J. (2010). *Indicators of school crime and safety: 2010* (NCES 2011-002/ NCJ 230812). National Center for Education Statistics, U.S. Department of Education, and Bureau of Justice Statistics, Office of Justice Programs, U.S. Department of Justice. Washington, DC.

Robinson, J. P., and Espelage, D. L. (2011). *Inequities in education and psychological outcomes between LGBTQ and straight students in middle and high school. Educational Researcher 40*(7), 315, doi: 10.3102/0013189X11422112.

Robinson, Joseph P., and Lubienski, Sarah T. (2010). The development of gender achievement gaps in mathematics and reading during elementary and middle school: Examining direct cognitive assessments and teacher ratings." *American Educational Research Journal.* Published online before print June 7, 2010, doi: 10.3102/0002831210372249.

Roorda, D. L., Koomen, H. M. Y., Spilt, J. L., and Oort, F. J. (2011). The influence of effective teacher-student relationships on students' school engagement and achievement: A meta-analysis approach. *Review of Educational Research 81*(4), 493–529.

Rose, M. (2009/2010). Standards, teaching, and learning. *Phi Delta Kappan, 91*(4), 21–27.

Rotherham, D. J. (2011). When it comes to class size, smaller isn't always better. *TIME*, March 3. Retrieved from www.time.com/printout/0,8816,2056571,00.html.

Rowan, J. (2001). A guide to humanistic psychology: The person-centered approach. Alameda, CA: Association for Humanistic Psychology.

Rubenstein, G. (2011). Panel with Ravitch and Rhee, Part II. Retrieved from http://garyrubinstein.teachforus.org/2011/10/01/panel-with-ravitch-and-rhee-part-ii/.

Rust, Susan. (2011). Plastic bag lobby wins favorable revision for school textbooks. *The Sacramento Bee*, August 19, 2011. Retrieved from www.sacbee.com/2011/08/19/3847824/plastic-bag-lobby-wins-favorable.html.

Rutherford, F. J., and Ahlgren, A. (1990). *Science for all Americans.* New York: Oxford University Press.

Ryan, Kevin. (1986). *The induction of new teachers.* Fastback No. 237. Phi Delta Kappa Educational Foundation.

The Sacramento Bee. (2011). Plastic bag lobby wins favorable revision for school textbooks. Author. Retrieved from www.sacbee.com/2011/08/19/3847824/plastic-bag-lobby-wins-favorable.html.

Sadker, David. (2002). A special section on gender equity: An educator's primer on the gender war. *Phi Delta Kappa 84* (3): 235–44.

Salem Witch Museum. (2005). *The Salem Witch Trials of 1692.* Salem, MA: Author.

San Diego Unified School District v. Commission on Professional Competence, 2011. (Super. Ct. No. 37-2009-00093780- CU-WM-CTL). Retrieved from http://slotelaw.com/sites/default/files/San%20Diego%20USD%20v.%20Commn%20on%20Prof%20Competence%20(teacher%20dismissal).pdf.

Sanders, W. L., and Rivers, J. C. (1996). Cumulative and residual effects of teachers on future academic achievement. Knoxville, TN: University of Tennessee Value-Added Research and Assessment Center.

Schneider, T., Walker, H., and Sprague, J. (2000). *Safe school design: A handbook for educational leaders.* Eugene, OR: ERIC Clearinghouse on Educational Management. (ERIC Document Reproduction Service No. EA 030 490).

Schroeder, Betsy A., Messina, Allison, Schroeder, Diana, Good, Karla, Barto, Shiryl, Saylor, Jennifer, and Masiello, Matthew. (2011). The implementation of a statewide bullying prevention program: Preliminary findings from the field and the importance of coalitions. *Health Promotion and Practice,* doi: 10.1177/1524839910386887. Retrieved from http://www.allentownsd.org/cms/lib01/PA01001524/Centricity/Domain/1155/The_Implementationof_a_Statewide_Bullying_Prevention_Program.pdf.

Seal, K. R., and Harmon, H. L. (1995). Realities of rural school reform. *Phi Delta Kappan 77*(2), 119–25.

The Search Institute. (2011). What kids need: Developmental assets. Retrieved from www.search-institute.org/developmental-assets.

Search Institute. (n.d.). Discovering what kids need to succeed. Retrieved from www.search-institute.org/.

Severson, Kim. (2011). Systematic cheating is found in Atlanta's school system. *New York Times,* July 5. Retrieved from www.nytimes.com/2011/07/06/education/06atlanta.html.

Shah, N. (2011). Academic gains vary widely for charter networks. *Education Week.* Retrieved from www.edweek.org/ew/articles/2011/11/04/11charter.h31.html?r=1799563615&print=1.

Shah, N. (2012a). Gay slurs found to be common talk in schools. *Education Week, 31*(18), p. 5.

Shah, N. (2012b). New standards aim to guide sex education. *Education Week, 31*(17), 1, 12–13.

Sherman, Aliza. (2011). How cities are closing the digital divide. *Mashable Tech,* April 20. Retrieved from http://mashable.com/2011/04/20/close-digital-divide/.

Simon, Mallory. (2009). *My bullied son's last day on earth.* CNN, April 23. Retrieved from http://articles.cnn.com/2009-04-23/us/bullying.suicide_1_bullies-gay-tired?_s=PM:US.

Smith, J. N. (Director). (1995). *Dangerous minds.* [Motion picture]. United States: Hollywood Pictures.

Smith, Mark K. (2002) *Howard Gardner and multiple intelligences,* The Encyclopedia of Informal Education. Retrieved from www.infed.org/thinkers/gardner.htm.

Society for Research in Child Development. (2010). Highlighting gender promotes stereotyped views in preschoolers. *Science Daily,* November 16. Retrieved from www.sciencedaily.com-/releases/2010/11/101116081430.htm.

Sousa, D. A., and Tomlinson, C. A. (2011). *Differentiation and the brain.* Bloomington, IL: Solution Tree Press.

Sparks, S. (2005). Study: Small classes early on can keep students in school: Sustained small-group K–3 structure has lasting effects on graduation, academics. *Education Daily 38*(89), 3.

Sparks, S. D. (2010). Class size shows signs of growing. *Education Week Online.* Retrieved from http://edweek.org/ew/articles/2010/11/24/13size_ep.h30.html?r=2108906112.

Spring, K., Grimm, R., and Dietz, N. (2009). *Community service and service-learning in America's schools, 2008.* Washington, DC: Corporation for National and Community Service, Office of Research and Policy Development. Retrieved from www .nationalservice.gov/pdf/08_1112_lsa_prevalence.pdf.

St. George, Donna. (2011). Suicide turns attention to Fairfax discipline procedures. *The Washington Post*, February 20. Retrieved from www.washingtonpost.com/wp-dyn/content/article/2011/02/19/AR2011021904528.html?sid=ST2011021904571.

Stansbury, M. (2011). Ten ways schools are using social media effectively. *eSchool News*, October 21. Retrieved from www .eschoolnews.com/2011.20/21/ten-ways-schools-are-using-social-media-effectively/.

Stecher, Brian, Vernez, Georges, and Steinberg, Paul. (2010). *Accountability for NCLB: A report card for the No Child Left Behind Act*. Rand Corporation. Retrieved from www.rand.org/ publications/randreview/issues/summer2010/nclb.html.

Stephens, K. R., and Karnes, F. A. (2000). State definitions for the gifted and talented revisited. *Exceptional Children*, 66(2).

Studios, J., and Dove, S. (2011). School reform math in Baltimore: Fewer suspensions equal better results. *The Washington Post*, January 2, 2011, p. CO5. Retrieved from www.washingtonpost .com/wp-dyn/content/article/2011/01/01/AR2011010102317.html.

Substance Abuse and Mental Health Services Administration. (2011). *Results from the 2010 National Survey on Drug Use and Health: Summary of national findings*. NSDUH Series H-41, HHS Publication No. (SMA) 11-4658. Rockville, MD: Substance Abuse and Mental Health Services Administration.

Suellentrop, K. (2011). *What works 2011–2012: Curriculum-based programs that help prevent teen pregnancy*. The National Campaign to Prevent Teen and Unplanned Pregnancy: Washington, DC. Retrieved from www.thenationalcampaign. org/resources/pdf/pubs/WhatWorks.pdf.

Sundius, Jane, and Shawn Dove. (2011). School reform math in Baltimore: Fewer suspensions equal better results. *The Washington Post*, January 2. Retrieved from www.washingtonpost.com/wp-dyn/ content/article/2011/01/01/AR2011010102317.html.

Swan, W. W. (2004). *Impact of Ruby Payne's Instructional Framework on student achievement in East Allen County Schools, Indiana, 2001–03*.

Swanson, Christopher B. (June 2, 2010). Diplomas count: Graduation by the numbers. Putting data to work for student success. *Education Week* 29(34), 22–23, 30. Retrieved from www.edweek .org/ew/toc/2010/06/10/index.html.

Tamura, E. H. (2003). Introduction: Asian Americans and educational history. *History of Education Quarterly* 43(1), 1–9.

Taylor, B. (2010). Campion Seventh-day Adventist Church: Powerful metaphors by Barry Taylor Retrieved from www.campion-church.org/article/134/video-content/powerful-metaphors-by-barry-taylor-08-07-2010.

Teacher strikes in Pennsylvania. (2011). Pittsburgh, PA: Allegheny Institute for Public Policy. Retrieved from http://alleghenyinsti-tute.org/education/teacherstrikes.html?tmpl=component& print=1.

Terbush, S. (2012). Survey: Cheating, lying widespread among high school students. *USA Today*, March 9, 2012. Retrieved from http://yourlife.usatoday.com/parenting-family/teen-ya/ story/2011/02/survey-cheating-lying-widespread-among-high-school-students/43627926/1.

Thomas B. Fordham Institute. (2004). *The mad mad world of textbook adoption*. Washington, DC: Author.

Tienken, C. H. (2011a). Common core standards: The emperor has no clothes or evidence. *Kappa Delta Pi Record*, 47(2), 58–62.

Tienken, C. H. (2011b). Pay for performance: Whose performance? *Kappa Delta Pi Record* 47(4), 152–54.

Tinker v. Des Moines Independent Community School District, 393 U.S. 503, 89S.Ct.733 21 L.Ed.2d 731 (1969).

Todorov, Kerana. (2011). Former teacher to stand trial on sex charges. *Napa Valley Register*, November 30. Retrieved from http://napavalleyregister.com/news/local/former-teacher-to-stand-trial-on-sex-charges/article_8976a95e-1bb3-11e1-b0bd-001cc4c03286.html.

Tomassini, J. (2012a). Apple unveils e-textbook strategy for K-12. *Education Week* 31(18), 8.

Tomassini, J. (2012b). Educators weigh E-Textbook cost comparison-ns. *Education Week*, May 9, 2012. Retrieved from www .edweek.org/ew/articles/2012/05/09/30etextbooks_ep.h31 .html?print=1.

Tomlinson, C. H. (2008). The goals of differentiation. *Educational Leadership* 66(3), 26–30.

Tomlinson, Carol Ann, and Imbeau, Marcia B. (2010). *Leading and managing a differentiated classroom*. ASCD. Retrieved from www.scribd.com/doc/44415762/Leading-and-Managing-a-Differentiated-Classroom.

Tomlinson, Carol Ann. (2008). *The goals of differentiation*. Educational Leadership, November. Retrieved from http://jo-online.vsb. bc.ca/bondi/wp-content/uploads/2009/02/educational-leader-ship_giving-students-ownership-of-learning_the-goals-of-di.pdf.

Torres, K., and Rankin, B. (January 15, 2005.) Disclaimers on evolution killed: Cobb schools' warning stickers in science books unconstitutional. *The Atlanta Journal-Constitution*, p. A1.

Tosolt, B. (2008a). "Middle school students' perceptions of caring teacher behaviors: Differences by minority status." Paper presented at the annual meeting of the MWERA Annual Meeting, Westin Great Southern Hotel, Columbus, Ohio Online. Retrieved from www.allacademic.com/meta/p275281_index.html.

Tosolt, B. (2008b). "Measuring middle school students' perceptions of caring teacher behaviors." Paper presented at the annual meeting of the MWERA Annual Meeting, Westin Great Southern Hotel, Columbus, Ohio Online. Retrieved from www .allacademic.com/meta/p275283_index.html.

Tyack, D. B. (Ed.). (1967). *Turning points in American educational history*. Waltham, MA: Blaisdell.

Tyre, P. (2011). Does class size really matter? *Salon.com*. Retrieved from www.salon.com/2011/08/06/good_school_excerpt/.

U.S. Bureau of Labor Statistics. (2011a). *Employment characteristics of families—2010*. Retrieved from http://www.bls.gov/news .release/archives/famee_03242011.pdf.

U.S. Bureau of Labor Statistics. (2011b). *The employment situation—September 2011*. U.S. Department of Labor. Retrieved from www.census.gov/compendia/statab/2012/tables/12s0592. pdfhttp://www.bls.gov/news.release/pdf/empsit.pdf.

U.S. Bureau of Labor Statistics. (2011c). *Employment and earnings online, January 2011; March 2011*. Retrieved from www.bls .gov/opub/ee/home.htm; www.bls.gov/cps/home.htm.

U.S. Census Bureau. (2010a). Race data. The Asian alone population in the United States: 2010: Detailed tables. U.S. Department of Labor. Retrieved from www.census.gov/population/www/socdemo/race/ppl-aa10.html.

U.S. Census Bureau. (2010b). *Census Bureau releases estimates of same-sex married couples.* Retrieved from http://2010.census.gov/news/releases/operations/cb11-cn181.html.

U.S. Census Bureau. (2011a). Families and living arrangements. Retrieved from www.census.gov/population/www/socdemo/hh-fam.html.

U.S. Census Bureau. (2011b). Statistical abstract of the United States: 2011. Retrieved from www.census.gov/compendia/statab/2011/tables/11s0075.pdf.

U.S. Census Bureau. (2011c). Table 4. People and families in poverty by selected characteristics: 2009 and 2010. www.census.gov/hhes/www/poverty/data/incpovhlth/2010/table4.pdf.

U.S. Copyright Office. (2009). *Fair Use.* Retrieved from www.copyright.gov/fls/fl102.html.

U.S. Department of Commerce. (2002). *A nation online: How Americans are expanding their use of the internet.* Retrieved from www.esa.doc.gov/sites/default/files/reports/documents/anationonline2.pdf.

U.S. Department of Education (2002a). Executive summary: The No Child Left Behind Act of 2001.

U.S. Department of Education (2002b). *No child left behind.*

U.S. Department of Education, Office for Civil Rights. (2008a). Civil Rights Data Collection: 2004 and 2006. Retrieved from http://nces.ed.gov/programs/digest/d08/tables/dt08_053.asp.

U.S. Department of Education, Office for Civil Rights. (2008b). *Sexual harassment: It's not academic.* Retrieved from www2.ed.gov/policy/eseaflex/status-state-requests.pdfhttp://www2.ed.gov/about/offices/list/ocr/docs/ocrshpam.html.

U.S. Department of Education, Office of Special Education and Rehabilitative Services, Office of Special Education Programs. (2004). *Teaching children with attention deficit hyperactivity disorder: Instructional strategies and practices,* Washington, DC. Retrieved at www2.ed.gov/rschstat/research/pubs/adhd/adhd-teaching-2006.pdf.

U.S. Department of Education. (2009a). About ED: What we do. Retrieved from www2.ed.gov/about/what-we-do.html.

U.S. Department of Education. (2009b). *Race to the Top Program executive summary.* Retrieved from www2.ed.gov/programs/racetothetop/executive-summary.pdf.

U.S. Department of Education. (2010a). Priorities in A Blueprint for Reform. www2.ed.gov/policy/elsec/leg/blueprint/publication_pg3.html.

U.S. Department of Education. (2010b). Evaluation of evidence-based practices in online learning: A meta-analysis and review of online learning studies, Washington, DC: U.S. Department of Education, Office of Planning, Evaluation, and Policy Development, Policy and Program Studies Service. Retrieved from www2.ed.gov/rschstat/eval/tech/evidence-based-practices/final-report.pdf.

U.S. Department of Education. (2010c). *A blueprint for reform: A reauthorization of the elementary and secondary education act.* Retrieved from http://www2.ed.gov/policy/elsec/leg/blueprint/blueprint.pdf.

U.S. Department of Education. (*2011a*). ESEA Flexibility. Retrieved from www.ed.gov/esea/flexibility.

U.S. Department of Education. (*2011b*). 21st Century Community Learning Centers. Retrieved from www2.ed.gov/programs/21stcclc/index.html.

U.S. Department of Education. (*2011c*). Federal partners celebrate anti-bullying efforts and pledge to continue work at7 second annual bullying summit. Retrieved from www.ed.gov/news/press-releases/federal-partners-celebrate-anti-bullying-efforts-and-pledge-continue-work-second.

U.S. Department of Education. (2011d). Our future, our teachers: The Obama administration plan for education reform and improvement. Washington, DC: Author.

U.S. Department of Education. (2011e). Fast facts: What is Title IX? Retrieved from http://nces.ed.gov/fastfacts/display.asp?id=93.

U.S. Department of Education. (2012a). 26 more states and D.C. seek flexibility from NCLB to drive education reforms in second round of requests. Retrieved from www.ed.gov/news/press-releases/26-more-states-and-dc-seek-flexibility-nclb-drive-education-reforms-second-round.

U.S. Department of Education. (2012b). William Mendoza appointed director of White House Initiative on American Indian and Alaska Native Education. Retrieved from www.ed.gov/news/press-releases/william-mendoza-appointed-director-white-house-initiative-american-indian-and-al.

U.S. Department of Education. (2012c, February 28). *Status of state requests.* Retrieved from www2.ed.gov/policy/eseaflex/status-state-requests.pdf.

U.S. Department of Homeland Security. (2011). *Table 1: Persons obtaining legal permanent resident status: Fiscal years 1820 to 2010.* Yearbook of Immigration Status: 2010. Retrieved from www.dhs.gov/files/statistics/publications/LPR10.shtm.

U.S. Department of Labor. (2011). Occupational outlook handbook, 2010–2011 edition. Washington, DC: Author. Retrieved from www.bls.gov/oco/ocos007.htm.

U.S. Department of Labor. (n.d.). Title IX, Education amendments of 1972. Washington, DC: US Department of Labor. Retrieved from www.dol.gov/oasam/regs/statutes/titleix.htm.

U.S. Department of Transportation, Federal Highway Administration, Office of Planning, Environment, & Realty. (2003). Census issues: Frequently asked questions. Retrieved from www.fhwa.dot.gov/planning/census_issues/metropolitan_planning/faqa2cdt.cfm.

U.S. Environmental Protection Agency. (2009). IAQTFS Action kit: Portable classrooms. Washington, DC: Author. Retrieved from www.epa.gov/iaq/schools/tfs/guidej.html.

U.S. National Center for Health Statistics. (2010). *National vital statistics reports (NVSR), births, marriages, divorces, and deaths: Provisional data for 2009.* Vol. 58(25). Retrieved from www.census.gov/compendia/statab/2012/tables/12s0133.pdf.

United States v. Board of Education for the School District of Philadelphia, 911 F.2d 882 (3rd Cir. 1990).

United States v. South Carolina, 445 F. Supp. 1094 (D.S.C. 1977).

USA Today. (2011). Ex-Ohio teacher convicted in student sex case. *USA Today,* October 27. Retrieved from www.usatoday.com/news/nation/story/2011-10-27/gym-teacher-sex-students/50963106/1.

Vang, Christopher Thao. (2010). *An educational psychology of multicultural methods in education.* New York: Peter Lang Publishing, Inc.

Vatterott, C. (2011). Making homework central to learning. *Educational Leadership* 69(3), 60–64.

Veronia School District 47J v. Acton, 515 U.S. 646 (1995).

Visconti, L. (2011). Can a white man speak with authority on diversity? *DiversityIn c.com.* http://diversityinc.com/ask-the-white -guy/can-a-white-man-speak-with-authority-on-diversity/.

Vossekuil, B., Fein, R. A., Reddy, M., Borum, R., and Modzeleski, W. (2002, May). *The final report and findings of the Safe School Initiative: Implications for the prevention of school attacks in the United States.* Washington, DC: U.S. Secret Service and U.S. Department of Education.

Walker, T. (2011). Van Roekel announces plan to strengthen teaching profession. *NEA Today.* Retrieved from http://neatoday. org/2011/12/08/van-roekel-announces-plan-to-strengthen-teaching-profession.

Walsh, M. (1999). Harassment ruling poses challenge. *Education Week on the Web.*

Walt, Carmen DeNavas, Proctor, Bernadette D., and Smith, Jessica C. (2011). *Income, poverty, and health insurance coverage in the United States: 2010.* U. S. Census Bureau. Retrieved from www. census.gov/prod/2011pubs/p60-239.pdf.

Wang, F. K. (2005). *Education culture gap: Tugging at a few threads of truth behind the model minority myth.* New Orleans, IMDiversity.

Washington, J. (2011). New digital divide seen for blacks, Hispanics. *The Washington Times.* Retrieved from www.washingtontimes. com/news/2011/jan/9/new-digital-divide-seen-for-blacks-hispanics/?page=all.

Watkins, S. C. (2011). Digital divides & digital literacies: An ongoing report. National Public Radio. Retrieved from www.they-oungandthedigital.com/mobile/digital-divides-digital-literacies-an-ongoing-report/.

Webb, L., D., Metha, A., and Jordan, K. F. (2000). *Foundations of American Education.* Columbus, OH: Merrill.

Wenglinsky, H. (2000). *How teaching matters: Bringing the classroom back into discussions of teacher quality.* Princeton, NJ: Educational Testing Service.

Westera, Wim. (2010). Technology-enhanced learning: Review and prospects. *Serdica Journal of Computing 4,* 159–82.

The White House. (2009). Fact sheet: Race to the top. Retrieved from http://whitehouse.gov/the-press-office/fact-sheet-race-top.

The White House. (2011, December 2). Executive Order 13592— Improving American Indian and Alaska Native educational opportunities and strengthening tribal colleges and universities. Retrieved from www.whitehouse.gov/the-press-office/2011/12/02/ executive-order-improving-american-indian-and-alaska-native-educational.

Whitehurst, G. J., and Chingos, M. M. (2012). Class size: What research says and what it means for state policy. *Brookings Institute.* Retrieved from www.brookings.edu/papers/2011/0511_ class_size_whitehurst_chingos.aspx?p=1.

Whittaker, Bill. (2010). *High school dropouts costly for American economy.* CBS News, March 28. Retrieved from www.cbsnews. com/stories/2010/05/28/eveningnews/main6528227.shtml.

Wolfgang, C. H., and Glickman, C. D. (1986). *Solving discipline problems: Strategies for teachers.* Boston: Allyn & Bacon.

Wong, H. K., and Wong, R. T. (2001). *The first days of school.* Mountain View, CA: Harry K. Wong Publications.

Wong, H., and Wong, R. T. (2009). *The first days of school: How to be an effective teacher,* 4th ed. Mountain View, CA: Harry K. Wong Publications.

Woolfolk, A. (2010). *Educational psychology,* 8th ed. Boston: Allyn & Bacon.

World Almanac Books. (2011). *World Almanac and Book of Facts.* New York:

Yellowitz, I. (n.d.). Child labor. *History.com.* Retrieved at http:// www.history.com/topics/child-labor.

Yohalem, N., Pittman, K., and Edwards, S. (2010) Strengthening the youth development/after-school workforce: Lessons learned and implications for funders. Washington, DC: The Forum for Youth Investment and Cornerstones for Kids.

Young, B. N., Whitley, M. E., and Helton, C. (1998, November). *Students' perceptions of characteristics of effective teachers.* Paper presented at the annual meeting of the Mid-South Educational Research Association, New Orleans, LA. ERIC Document Reproduction Service No. ED426962.

Zittleman, Karen, and Sadker, David. (2009). *Still failing at fairness: How gender bias cheats girls and boys in schools and what we can do about it.* New York: Scribner.

Index

Society

School

Student

Self

To conceptualize the content, context, and organization of this book, think of a series of concentric circles that looks like a target. Who is at the center of this target? YOU are. This book starts with YOU. The "bull's-eye" of the target symbolizes your *self*—what you, the reader, already know and believe about teaching, learning, and schools. The circles represent the *student*, the *school*, and *society* respectively. Why do you suppose we have chosen this conceptualization? Consider how the circles are organized. What might this diagram indicate about *your* place in the scheme of beginning to study teacher education? Consider the sizes of the circles. What might they indicate about the breadth and complexity of topics addressed in this book? Would you think that the lines between the circles should be solid? Why or why not? Keep this conceptualization in mind as you progress through this book and your program of teacher education.

Interstate Teacher Assessment and Support Consortium (InTASC) Standards: A Correlation Chart

The Interstate Teacher Assessment and Support Consortium (InTASC) is dedicated to the improvement of education by raising the quality of teaching. InTASC has established 10 standards describing the knowledge, skills, and dispositions that teachers should possess. The following chart indicates which chapters and activities in this text address each of the standards.

INTASC STANDARD	CHAPTERS	RELATED FEATURES, ACTIVITIES, AND TEACHSOURCE VIDEOS
THE LEARNER AND LEARNING		
Standard 1: Learner Development—The teacher understands how learners grow and develop, recognizing that patterns of learning and development vary individually within and across the cognitive, linguistic, social, emotional, and physical areas, and designs and implements developmentally appropriate and challenging learning experiences.	Chapter 3 "The Student: Common Needs" Chapter 4 "The Student and the Teacher: Acknowledging Unique Perspectives" Chapter 12 "Social Issues and the School's Response"	**Chapter 3** • Building Blocks 3.2, 3.3, 3.4, 3.5, 3.6, 3.7, 3.8, 3.9, and 3.10 • TeachSource Video, "Social and Emotional Development: The Influence of Peer Groups" • Controversies in Education, "Criticism of Piaget's Theory" • Technology and Education, "Getting Technical on the First Day of School" **Chapter 4** • Building Blocks 4.3, 4.4, 4.5, 4.6, 4.8, 4.9, 4.10, and 4.11 • TeachSource Video, "Culturally Responsive Teaching: A Multicultural Lesson for Elementary Students" **Chapter 12** • Building Blocks 12.2, 12.4, and 12.6 Controversies in Education, "Teen Pregnancy"
Standard 2: Learning Differences—The teacher uses understanding of individual differences and diverse cultures and communities to ensure inclusive learning environments that enable each learner to meet high standards.	Chapter 2 "Your Philosophy of Education" Chapter 4 "The Student and the Teacher: Acknowledging Unique Perspectives" Chapter 5 "The Student and the Teacher: Acknowledging Unique Abilities" Chapter 12 "Social Issues and the School's Response"	**Chapter 2** • Building Blocks 2.9 and 2.10 • TeachSource Video, "Using Information Processing Strategies: A Middle School Science Lesson" • TeachSource Video, "Vygotsky's Zone of Proximal Development: Increasing Cognition in an Elementary Literacy Lesson" • Technology and Education. "Programmed Instruction and Video Games" **Chapter 4** • Building Blocks 4.1, 4.2, and 4.7 • TeachSource Video, "The Debate over Bilingual Education" • TeachSource Video, "Gender Equity in the Classroom: Girls and Science" • Controversies in Education, "Bilingual Education" • Technology and Education, "Different Strokes for Different Folks" **Chapter 5** • Building Blocks 5.1, 5.3, 5.8, and 5.9 • Controversies in Education, "Issues in Special Education" • Technology and Education, "Assistive Technology" • TeachSource Video, "Inclusion: Classroom Implications for the General and Special Educator" **Chapter 12** • Building Blocks 12.2, 12.3, 12.4, 12.5, and 12.6
Standard 3: Learning Environments—The teacher works with others to create environments that support individual and collaborative learning, and that encourage positive social interaction, active engagement in learning, and self motivation.	Chapter 3 "The Student: Common Needs" Chapter 6 "Purposes of School" Chapter 7 "Structure of Schools" Chapter 8 "The School and the Student: Expectations and Responsibilities" Chapter 11 "School Governance and Finance" Chapter 12 "Social Issues and the School's Response"	**Chapter 3** • Building Blocks 3.8, 3.9, and 3.11 • Technology and Education, "Getting Technical on the First Day of School" **Chapter 6** • Building Blocks 6.1, 6.2, 6.3, 6.5, 6.6, 6.7, 6.8, and 6.11 • TeachSource Video, "Rethinking How Kids Learn: KIPP" • TeachSource Video, "A Positive School Climate Reduces the Achievement Gap" • Controversies in Education, "Education Management Organizations" • Technology and Education, "Virtual Teaching and Learning" **Chapter 7** • Building Block 7.1, 7.2, 7.3, 7.7, and 7.8 • TeachSource Video, "Collaborating with School Specialists: An Elementary Literacy Lesson" • Controversies in Education, "Does Class Size Matter?" **Chapter 8** • Building Blocks 8.1, 8.3, and 8.4 • TeachSource Video, "Cyberbullying" • Controversies in Education, "GSA or No GSA?" **Chapter 11** • Building Block 11.1 **Chapter 12** • Building Block 12.1 • Technology and Education, "Sexting"
CONTENT KNOWLEDGE		
Standard 4: Content Knowledge—The teacher understands the central concepts, tools of inquiry, and structures of the discipline(s) he or she "teaches and creates learning experiences that make the discipline accessible and meaningful for learners to assure mastery of the content.	Chapter 14 "Education Reform: Standards and Accountability"	**Chapter 14** • TeachSource Video, "Common Core Standards: A New Lesson Plan for America" • Controversies in Education, "The Common Core State Standards"
Standard 5: Application of Content—The teacher understands how to connect concepts and use differing perspectives to engage learners in critical thinking, creativity, and collaborative problem solving related to authentic local and global issues.	Chapter 12 "Social Issues and the School's Response" Chapter 14 "Education Reform: Standards and Accountability"	**Chapter 12** • Building Block 12.3, 12.5, 12.7, and 12.8 • TeachSource Video, "Divorce and Children" **Chapter 14** • TeachSource Video, "School Reform: One High School Literacy Initiative" • TeachSource Video, "Reading in the Content Areas: An Interdisciplinary Unit on the 1920s"

INTASC STANDARD	CHAPTERS	RELATED FEATURES, ACTIVITIES, AND TEACHSOURCE VIDEOS
INSTRUCTIONAL PRACTICE		
Standard 6: Assessment—The teacher understands and uses multiple methods of assessment to engage learners in their own growth, to monitor learner progress, and to guide the teacher's and learner's decision making.	Chapter 14 "Education Reform: Standards and Accountability"	Chapter 14 • Building Blocks 14.13 and 14.14
Standard 7: Planning for Instruction—The teacher plans instruction that supports every student in meeting rigorous learning goals by drawing upon knowledge of content areas, curriculum, cross-disciplinary skills, and pedagogy, as well as knowledge of learners and the community context.	Chapter 8 "The School and the Student: Expectations and Responsibilities" Chapter 9 "The School and the Teacher: Expectations and Responsibilities"	Chapter 8 • Building Blocks 8.2, 8.5, and 8.6 • Technology and Education, "Electronic Gadgets and Students" Chapter 9 • Building Blocks 9.1, 9.2, and 9.7 • Technology and Education, "Technology for Teachers"
Standard 8: Instructional Strategies—The teacher understands and uses a variety of instructional strategies to encourage learners to develop deep understanding of content areas and their connections and to build skills to apply knowledge in meaningful ways.	Chapter 1 "Teaching Excellence and You" Chapter 4 "The Student and the Teacher: Acknowledging Unique Perspectives" Chapter 5 "The Student and the Teacher: Acknowledging Unique Abilities"	Chapter 1 • Building Blocks 1.1, 1.4, 1.5, and 1.7 • TeachSource Video, "Teaching as a Profession: What Defines Effective Teaching?" • TeachSource Video, "Freedom Writers: Teachers Can Inspire Students to Learn and Achieve" • Technology and Education, "Does Technology Make a Teacher Effective?" Chapter 4 • Building Block 4.7 • TeachSource Video, "Bilingual Education: An Elementary Two-Way Immersion Program" Chapter 5 • Building Blocks 5.1, 5.3, 5.5, 5.8, and 5.9 • TeachSource Video, "Assistive Technology in the Inclusive Classroom: Best Practices"
PROFESSIONAL RESPONSIBILITY		
Standard 9: Professional Learning and Ethical Practice—The teacher engages in ongoing professional learning and uses evidence to continually evaluate his/her practice, particularly the effects of his/her choices and actions on others (learners, families, other professionals, and the community), and adapts practice to meet the needs of each learner.	Chapter 1 "Teaching Excellence and You" Chapter 2 "Your Philosophy of Education" Chapter 9 "The School and the Teacher: Expectations and Responsibilities" Chapter 10 "Historical Perspectives" Chapter 13 "Teachers, Students, and the Law" Chapter 14 "Education Reform: Standards and Accountability" Chapter 15 "Your Motives for Teaching"	Chapter 1 • Building Blocks 1.2, 1.3, and 1.6 • Controversies in Education, "Test Scores and Measures of Teacher Excellence" Chapter 2 • Building Blocks 2.1, 2.2, 2.8, and 2.11 • TeachSource Video, "Philosophical Foundations of American Education: Four Philosophies in Action" • Controversies in Education, "The Power of Beliefs in Education: Homework" Chapter 9 • Building Blocks 9.3, and 9.5 • TeachSource Video, "Mentoring First-Year Teachers: Keys to Professional Success" • TeachSource Video, "Teacher Incentive Pay: Pay for Performance" • Controversies in Education, "Merit Pay" Chapter 10 • Building Blocks 10.1, 10.2, 10.3, 10.4, 10.5, 10.6, 10.7, 10.8, 10.9, 10.10, and 10.11 • TeachSource Video, "Foundations: Aligning Instruction with Federal Legislation" • Technology and Education, "The Evolution of Instructional Technology" Chapter 13 • Building Block 13.2, 13.3, 13.5, 13.6, and 13.7 • Technology and Education, "I Found It on the Internet!" Chapter 14 • Building Block 14.3, 14.4, 14.5, 14.6, 14.7, 14,.8, 14.9, 14.10, 14.11, 14.12, and 14.13 • Technology and Education, "Technology in the Subject Areas" Chapter 15 • Building Block 15.3 and 15.5 • TeachSource Video, "Becoming a Teacher: Choices and Advice from the Field" • TeachSource Video, "The First Year of Teaching: One Colleague's Story"
Standard 10: Leadership and Collaboration—The teacher seeks appropriate leadership roles and opportunities to take responsibility for student learning, to collaborate with learners, families, colleagues, other school professionals, and community members to ensure learner growth, and to advance the profession.	Chapter 11 "School Governance and Finance"	Chapter 11 • Building Blocks 11.1, 11.2, 11.3, 11.4, 11.6, 11.8, and 11.11 • TeachSource Video, "Education and Equity" • TeachSource Video, "High Schools in Low-Income Communities Receive a Failing Grade" • Controversies in Education, "Textbooks and Evolution"

SOURCE: Interstate Teacher Assessment and Support Consortium: http://www.ccsso.org